MIDDLE EG LITERATURE

EIGHT LITERARY WORKS OF THE MIDDLE KINGDOM

JAMES P. ALLEN

CAMBRIDGE
UNIVERSITY PRESS

CAMBRIDGE
UNIVERSITY PRESS

University Printing House, Cambridge CB2 8BS, United Kingdom

Cambridge University Press is part of the University of Cambridge.

It furthers the University's mission by disseminating knowledge in the pursuit of education, learning and research at the highest international levels of excellence.

www.cambridge.org
Information on this title: www.cambridge.org/9781107456075

First published 2015

A catalogue record for this publication is available from the British Library

ISBN 978-1-107-08743-9 Hardback
ISBN 978-1-107-45607-5 Paperback

CONTENTS

ILLUSTRATIONS

INTRODUCTION

THIS BOOK WAS WRITTEN to serve as a companion volume to the third edition of my Middle Egyptian grammar.[1] It provides editions of both well-known and lesser-known texts for students to apply their knowledge of the language to the exercise of working with real Middle Egyptian compositions.

Besides that pedagogic purpose, the book has two other goals: to make the texts more readily available than is currently the case, and to present them in a fashion as close to the original as possible. All but one of the originals are written in hieratic on papyrus. Unlike other editions, this book presents hieroglyphic transcriptions in the same orientation as the originals: right to left, and in columns as well as lines.[2]

Each text is presented in hieroglyphs, transliteration, translation, and textual notes. The notes deal with matters of both grammar and interpretation; the former are keyed to the relevant sections of my grammar, and the latter sometimes cross-reference the essays in that book. Grammatical notes are extensive for the first text, for which every form and construction is discussed. They diminish in frequency in subsequent texts, as students (ideally) become more proficient in working with the language.

Five of the texts are those that any student of Middle Egyptian should read: the stories of the Shipwrecked Sailor and Sinuhe, the instructions of Kagemni's father and Ptahhotep, the discourses of the Eloquent Peasant, and the Debate between a Man and His Soul. The other three were chosen to complement these: the Loyalist Instruction, to illustrate the attitude toward the king that underlies the story of Sinuhe; the tale of the Herdsman, because it is on the same papyrus as the Debate; and the Hymns to Senwosret III, to exemplify the genre of hymns.

The great anthologies of Egyptian literature in translation contain many more works than these, but the compositions here have been singled out for two more reasons. First is the question of genre. Egyptian literature can be divided into two categories. Many texts that are literary in quality were composed not as literature but for an external purpose: for example, hymns, for use in temple or royal ceremonies; and biographical inscriptions, designed to record the deeds of their subjects as evidence of their worthiness to receive offerings after their deaths. In a narrower sense, "true" Egyptian literature consists of works that were composed for no purpose other than their own existence: primarily instructions, discourses, and stories. While Text 8 exemplifies the first category, the rest belong to the second.

1 James P. Allen, *Middle Egyptian: an Introduction to the Language and Culture of Hieroglyphs*, 3rd ed.; Cambridge, 2014.

2 Hieratic signs originally in red are filled in black in the hieroglyphic transcription, and the corresponding transliteration and translation are presented in **bold** type.

Second is the question of date. Recent research has demonstrated that the corpus of Middle Kingdom literature is both broader and narrower than was previously thought to be the case (Stauder 2014). It is broader because it contains two works that have been traditionally identified as compositions of the Old Kingdom, the instructions of Kagemni's father and Ptahhotep. While the texts themselves place their authors in the Old Kingdom, the language in which they are written is Middle Egyptian, and the document on which they are preserved is of Middle Kingdom date. In fact, there is no evidence whatsoever for the second, "true" genre of Egyptian literature prior to the Middle Kingdom. The corpus is also narrower because a number of works once thought to have been written in the Middle Kingdom have features of the language that do not appear until the Second Intermediate Period or later, and survive only in copies later than the Middle Kingdom. With the exception of a few texts, mostly fragmentary, the works in this book are the only examples of "true" literature that are undoubtedly of Middle Kingdom origin, since they all are preserved on sources of Middle Kingdom date. As such, they represent the golden age of Middle Egyptian.

STYLE

All of the works in this book are written in verse. As far as we can tell, ancient Egyptian verse was similar to the "free verse" form of modern poetry. Its lines did not have a regular pattern of stresses, and they did not (normally) rhyme with one another. Nonetheless, it did obey certain rules of composition.

The basic unit of composition was what has been called the "thought couplet" (Foster 1975). This is two lines of verse that form a coherent thought, in which the second line mirrors, complements, contrasts with, or expands on the first: for example,

nn wn rwj ꜥḥꜣw.f *nn jtḥ pḏt.f* (Sin. B 62–63)	There is none who can escape his arrow, none who can draw his bow.
nb jm(ꜣ)t pw ꜥꜣ bnjt *jṯ.n.f (m) mrwt* (Sin. B 65–66)	He is a master of kindness, great of sweetness: he has taken possession through love.
jnk pw mdw n.k *(j)m(j)-r pr wr pw sḫꜣy.k* (Peas. B1 51–52)	The one who speaks to you is I, but the one you mention is the chief steward.
sꜥnd.k ḏd bjn *m tm ḫsf sw m ꜣt.f* (Ptahhotep 65)	You belittle one who speaks badly by not opposing him in his moment.

As these couplets illustrate, each line is normally a self-contained unit. Things that belong closely together, such as a verb and its subject or a preposition and its object, are not broken between lines. The second line does not have to be a complete sentence, and can therefore consist of an adjunct, as in the last example; in some cases, this can even extend to pseudo-verbal predicates that have a long subject in the first line.

The identification of a couplet is based primarily on meaning. By that criterion, Middle Kingdom literature also uses single lines, mainly as headings; groups of three lines, known as tercets; and occasionally a group of four, called a quatrain. There are few rules that can help identify when these other groups are used, and the division is partly a matter of interpretation. For example, the following text can be parsed either as a couplet or a tercet:

mj.k jrrt.sn pw r sḫtjw.sn
  jww n ktḫt r gs.sn mj.k jrrt.sn pw (Peas. B1 76–77)
Look, that is what they do to their peasants
  who come to others besides them; look, that is what they do.

mj.k jrrt.sn pw r sḫtjw.sn
  jww n ktḫt r gs.sn
  mj.k jrrt.sn pw (Peas. B1 76–77)
Look, that is what they do to their peasants
  who come to others besides them;
  Look, that is what they do.

One criterion that can help in parsing lines of verse is that of meter. Meter is simply the pattern of stresses in a line of verse: for example, the pattern of 4–3–4–3 in the opening lines of Lewis Carroll's poem, "The Walrus and the Carpenter":

The **sun** was **shi**ning **on** the **sea**,
Shining with **all** his **might**:
He **did** his **ve**ry **best** to **make**
The **bil**lows **smooth** and **bright**—
And **this** was **odd**, be**cause** it **was**
The **mid**dle **of** the **night**.

While Egyptian verse does not seem to use a regular, repeating meter such as this, studies have determined that its lines do conform to a general pattern of stresses. Most lines have two or three stresses. Lines can have as few as one or as many as five, but apparently never more than five.

Hieroglyphic writing, of course, does not reveal how words were stressed, but we can make educated guesses based partly on common sense, partly on syntax, and partly on Coptic, which does reflect stress. Small words such as prepositions, particles, and dependent pronouns were probably not stressed, but independent pronouns can be stressed or not, depending on their meaning (see § 13.6 and p. 94 n. 5). Prepositional phrases and adverbs are stressed, with the exception of the dative with a suffix pronoun (§ 13.6). Indirect genitives have two stresses but direct genitives have only one (which is why nothing can normally come between the two elements): ***hrw n mst*** (Coptic ϩⲟⲟⲩ ⲛⲙⲓⲥⲉ = **how** 'n**mee**suh) but *hrw-**mst*** "birthday" (Coptic ϩⲟⲩⲙⲓⲥⲉ = hoo**mee**suh). The direct genitive rule also applies to an infinitive followed by a noun as its subject or object, which is a genitival construction (§§ 13.4.2, 13.5.1). There is some ambiguity about adjectives that modify nouns, including demonstrative pronouns and the quantifier *nb*, since Coptic shows two patterns: *sṯj **nfr*** "good smell" (Coptic **ⲥϯⲛⲟⲩϥⲉ** = stee**noo**fuh "perfume") and ***sṯj nfr*** (Coptic **ⲥⲑⲟⲓ ⲛⲟⲩϥⲓ** = **stoy noo**fee). Verbs and nominal subjects and objects are generally stressed. Using these guidelines, we can reconstruct the stress patterns of the opening lines of the Shipwrecked Sailor as follows (the – dash links words with a single stress):

3	*ḏd jn–šmsw jqr*	Recitation by an able follower.
3	*wḏꜣ jb.k ḥꜣt(j)-ꜥ*	Be informed, high official:
2	*mj.k–pḥ.n.n ḫnw*	look, we have reached home.
4	*šzp ḫrpw ḥw mjnt*	The mallet has been taken, the mooring-post has been hit,
3	*ḥꜣtt rdj.t(j) ḥr–tꜣ*	and the prow-rope is set on land.
4	*rdj ḥknw dwꜣ nṯr*	Praise has been given, and thanks,
2	*z(j)–nb ḥr–ḥpt–snnw.f*	and every man is embracing the other.
3	*jzwt.ṯn jj.t(j) ꜥd.t(j)*	Our crew has returned safe,
2	*nn–nhw n–mšꜥ.n*	with no loss of our expedition.
2	*pḥ.n.n pḥwj–wꜣwꜣt*	We have reached the end of Wawat,
2	*zn.n.n znmwt*	we have passed Bigga.
2	*mj.k–r.f–n–jj.n m–ḥtp*	So, look, we have returned in peace;
2	*tꜣ.n pḥ.n–sw*	our land, we have reached it.

Although parsing the verse structure of a work of Middle Kingdom literature is sometimes a matter of interpretation, there is good evidence that the structure itself was a deliberate creation of the ancient author and not an accidental feature of the text. In the Debate (Text 6), for example, the man's second speech divides thematically into two parts, the first of which records the soul's arguments for death (cols. 5–29) and the second, his argument against life and the man's response to it (cols. 29–55): the fact that the two sections each contain thirty-six lines is undoubtedly not mere coincidence. Moreover, this verse structure is a clue to meaning as well. Among other things, it shows that the line *ḏdt.n n.j bꜣ.j* "what my ba said to me" (cols. 30–31) is not the heading of a new section in which the soul responds to the man but the second line of a couplet and a phrase in apposition to *štꜣw ẖt.j* "the secrets of my belly" in the first line.

The ancient writers used tercets both for variety, to break up what might otherwise be a monotonous string of couplet after couplet, and for thematic effect. A good example of the latter is the first half of the speech discussed in the last paragraph. It contains two tercets (cols. 8–10 and 15–17), each of which marks the end of a sub-section in the text. Tercets are also used in litanies, a verse form in which a common first line is followed by different couplets; examples can be found in the Debate and in the Hymns to Senwosret III (Texts 6 and 8).

Versification can also be an aid to understanding grammar. The story of Sinuhe's battle against the champion from Retjenu, for example, contains the following lines:

The beginning (B 132–34) is easily analyzed as a couplet:

3 *jb–nb mr.(w)–n.j ḏd.sn*
4 *jn–jw–wn ky–nḫt ꜥḥꜣ r.f*
Every mind was sick for me, saying,
"Is there another strongman who can fight against him?"

The text that follows has been universally understood as a SUBJECT–stative construction introduced by *ꜥḥꜥ.n* (B 134–35), followed by a *sḏm.n.f* clause as object of the compound preposition *m ḫt* (B 135–36), and a second *sḏm.n.f* clause followed by an adverbial phrase and an adverb clause (B 136–37). Since the SUBJECT–stative construction has six units of stress (*ꜥḥꜥ.n jkm.f mjnb.f ḥpt.f nt–nsjwt ḫr.(w)*), it has been divided into two lines; for example,

Then his shield, his axe,
his armful of javelins fell (Parkinson 1997, 33)

And then his shield, his dagger,
his armour, his holder of spears fell (Quirke 2004, 63).[3]

This analysis separates the SUBJECT–stative construction into two lines, which is not a feature elsewhere in Middle Kingdom verse. Moreover, it requires the next sentence to begin with a preposition, which is something that Middle Egyptian regularly limits to the preposition *jr*:

3 These two examples are chosen because they translate the story as verse. Other translations are mostly presented as prose.

after I had escaped his weapons and made them pass by me (Parkinson 1997, 33)[4]

As I approached his weapons
I made my face dodge (Quirke 2004, 63).

These difficulties prompt a different analysis. The anomalies of both versification and grammar can be avoided by understanding  as a second participle followed by the preposition *n*, despite the spelling without the usual determinative , and *ḫr* as the particle that allows a prepositional phrase to stand at the beginning of the sentence (§ 15.6.13), yielding two tercets with the same pattern of stresses:

3 *jb–nb mr.(w)–n.j ḏd.sn*
4   *jn–jw–wn ky–nẖt ꜥḥꜣ r.f*
5   *ꜥḥꜥ n–jkm.f mjnb.f ḥpt.f nt–nsjwt*
3 *ḫr–m–ḫt spr.n.j ḫꜥw.f*
4   *rdj.n.j swꜣ ḥr.j ꜥḥꜣw.f*
5   *zp n–jwtt wꜥ ḥr–ẖn m–wꜥ*

Every mind was sick for me, saying,
   "Is there another strongman who can fight against him,
   who can stand up to his shield, his axe, his clutch of spears?"
Afterward, I made his weapons come out.
   I made his arrows pass by me
   to no avail, one chasing the other.

Versification is therefore not just an incidental feature of Middle Kingdom literature: it is integral to the compositions and essential for understanding the texts as their authors intended—insofar as that is still possible. This book is also meant to provide material for the study of that aspect of Middle Kingdom literature.

BIBLIOGRAPHY

Foster, John L. "Thought Couplets in Khety's 'Hymn to the Inundation'." *Journal of Near Eastern Studies* 34 (1975), 1–29.

Parkinson, Richard B. *The Tale of Sinuhe and Other Ancient Egyptian Poems 1940–1640 BC*. Oxford, 1997.

Quirke, Stephen. *Egyptian Literature 1800 BC, Questions and Readings*. Egyptology 2. London, 2004.

Stauder, Andréas. *Linguistic Dating of Middle Egyptian Literary Texts*. Lingua Aegyptia Studia Monographica 12. Hamburg, 2014.

4 In this translation, this is the first clause of a complex sentence that extends beyond B 137.

TEXT 1
THE STORY OF THE SHIPWRECKED SAILOR

THIS TEXT is the oldest surviving ancient Egyptian story. It is preserved in a single manuscript, a papyrus now in the Hermitage Museum, St. Petersburg, Russia (pHermitage 1115).[1] The text is written in hieratic, the handwritten form of hieroglyphic (§ 1.9), mostly in vertical columns but at one point in horizontal lines.[2] With some exceptions, red ink is used to mark the beginning of a new section in the narration. The grammar of the text and the paleography of the hieratic date the composition to the early Middle Kingdom (ca. 2000–1900 BC).

The story is unusual in several respects: its rather abrupt beginning, its anonymous characters, its literary device of a story within a story within a story, and its downbeat ending. The moral of the tale is perseverance through travails. At the beginning of the story, an expedition up the Nile to Africa has returned apparently without success. The expedition leader has to report to the king, and to encourage him, one of the crew members tells the leader how he survived a worse situation, being shipwrecked alone on a previous mission. In the course of his story, the sailor meets a god in the form of a giant snake, who encourages the sailor by telling him how he persevered through an even worse disaster, the loss of his entire family.

Like all early Middle Kingdom literature, the Story of the Shipwrecked Sailor is composed in narrative verse (Foster 1988). Besides the basic unit of the couplet, this text also makes liberal use of tercets, the occasional single line, and one possible sestet (group of six lines). Like all literary compositions, it also uses devices such as metaphor and alliteration.

The original papyrus has yet to be properly published. The text here is transcribed, and the hieratic signs used in the notes are drawn, after Golenischev 1913; the use of red ink is from Golenischev 1912. For this first text, the columns and lines of the papyrus have been separated into discrete columns or lines corresponding to the verse lines of the composition; the hieroglyphic transcription of Texts 2–8 will be presented consecutively, according to the columns or lines of the original. The numbers to the right of the transliteration indicate the probable units of stress in each line (see pp. 3–4, above).

1 Two probable citations from the story are attested in later texts: Allen 2008, 32–33; Simpson 1958, 50.

2 Cols. 1–123 are vertical; lines 124–76, horizontal in six pages (124–32, 133–42, 143–51, 152–60, 161–69, 170–76); and the rest of the papyrus, vertical (cols. 177–89).

Episode 1 — Setting the Scene (cols. 1–21)

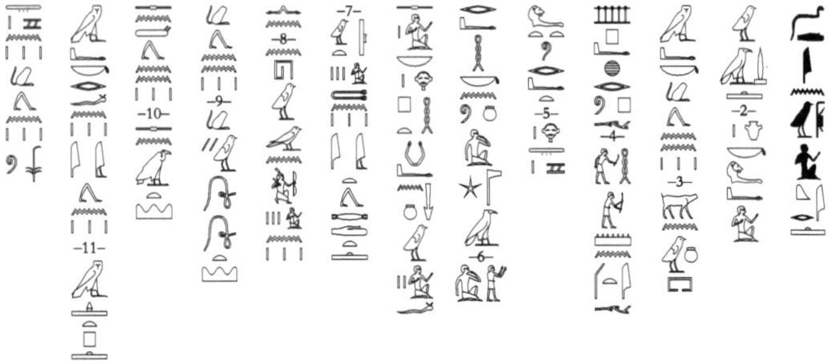

1	***ḏd jn šmsw*** *jqr*	(heading)
1–3	*wḏꜣ jb.k ḥꜣt(j)-ꜥ*	3
	mj.k pḥ.n.n ẖnw	2
3–5	*šzp ḫrpw ḥw mjnt*	4
	ḥꜣtt rdj.t(j) ḥr tꜣ	3
5–6	*rdj ḥknw dwꜣ nṯr*	4
	z(j) nb ḥr ḥpt snnw.f	2
7–8	*jzwt.ṯn jj.t(j) ꜥd.t(j)*	3
	nn nhw n mšꜥ.n	2
8–10	*pḥ.n.n pḥwj wꜣwꜣt*	2
	zn.n.n znmwt	2
10–11	*mj.k r.f n jj.n m ḥtp*	2
	tꜣ.n pḥ.n sw	2

1 **Recitation by an** able **follower**.

1–3 Be informed, high official:
look, we have reached home.

3–5 The mallet has been taken, the mooring-post has been hit,
and the prow-rope is set on land.

5–6 Praise has been given, and thanks,
and every man is embracing the other.

7–8 Our crew has returned safe,
with no loss of our expedition.

8–10 We have reached Wawat's wake,
we have gone by Bigga.

10–11 So, look, we have returned in peace;
our land, we have reached it.

The numbers in the hieroglyphic text refer to the columns or lines of the original manuscript. The opening section of the story sets the scene: an expedition up the Nile from Egypt into Africa has returned home.

1 *ḏd jn* — infinitive with *jn* marking the agent (§ 13.4.1). A *sḏm.jn.f* is unlikely, since that form regularly expresses the consequence of some previous action or statement (§ 19.10). It has been argued, however, that the beginning of the story has been lost (Bolshakov 1993). The fact that the adjective *jqr* is in black suggests that it has a separate stress of its own.

šmsw — basic title for a low-ranking royal attendant (Berlev 1978, 206–29).

1–3 *wḏꜣ jb.k* — literally, "may your mind become sound" (Essay 25).

ḥꜣtj-ꜥ — literally, "one who is front of arm." *ḥꜣtj* is a nisbe (§ 6.1) from *ḥꜣt* "front," and the whole phrase is a *nfr ḥr* construction (§ 6.5). *ḥꜣtj-ꜥ* is a title indicating a high-ranking official; in this case, the expedition leader. In keeping with the anonymity of the story's characters, the official's functional title is not mentioned.

ẖnw — literally, "the inside": in this case, "inside" Egypt. The term is also used to refer to the capital, Memphis, but the locale mentioned in col. 10 sets the scene in Aswan, first home port for a river expedition returning from the south.

3–5 A couplet referring to the docking of the expedition boat. The *mjnt* "mooring-post" (hieroglyphic : see P 11 in the Sign List) was a wood stake, driven into the ground with a mallet, to which the *ḥꜣtt* "prow-rope" was tied.

šzp ... ḥw — passive *sḏm.f* (§ 19.5).

ḥꜣtt rdj.t(j) — SUBJECT–stative (§ 16.8). *ḥꜣtt* is a feminine nisbe (§ 6.1) from *ḥꜣt* "front." The stative is 3fs, literally "given, put." Note the contrast between the first line of the couplet, referring to two past actions, and the second, referring to the state resulting from a past action.

5–6 This couplet reflects the structure of the preceding one: two past actions in the first line followed by a description of the present situation in the second.

rdj ... dwꜣ — passive *sḏm.f* (§ 19.5). In the phrase *dwꜣ-nṯr*, the *nṯr* sign is put first, in honorific transposition (§ 4.15). To "worship god" is an Egyptian idiom for giving thanks, so the second clause means that the god has been thanked for a safe return.

z(j) nb ḥr ḥpt snnw.f — pseudo-verbal construction with *ḥr* plus the infinitive, denoting action in progress at the moment of speaking (§ 14.2). *snnw* literally means "second" (§ 9.3): in other words, "every man is embracing the other."

7–8 *jzwt.ṯn jj.t(j) ꜥd.t(j)* — SUBJECT–stative (§ 16.8), with a second stative used as an unmarked adverb clause (§ 20.8). The suffix *ṯn* is for 1s *n*: is a way of indicating that the feminine ending of *jzwt* was pronounced before a suffix pronoun (Essay 17).

nn nhw n mšꜥ.n — a negated adverbial sentence (§ 11.4) used as an unmarked adverb clause (§ 20.15). It can also be interpreted as an independent statement, "Our expeditionary force has no loss(es)." *mšꜥ* was an armed force sent on expeditions; the term later came to mean "army."

8–10 Note the alliteration in the two lines of this couplet: ***pḥ**.n.n **pḥ**wj wꜣwꜣt* and ***zn**.n.n **zn**mwt*.

pḥwj wꜣwꜣt — Wawat was the name of northern Nubia, bordering Egypt. Since the Egyptians oriented themselves to the south (Essay 2), the "end of Wawat" means the northern border of Wawat.

znmwt — Bigga is an island south of Aswan, one of the first two places in Egypt proper that would be encountered by an expedition sailing north from Wawat.

10–11 This is the final couplet of the opening description of the expedition's homecoming.

mj.k r.f n jj.n — SUBJECT–stative (§ 16.8), with the older form of the 1pl stative pronoun (§ 16.2). *r.f* is literally, "with respect to it," where the pronoun refers to what has been said previously (§ 15.7.2).

tꜣ.n pḥ.n sw — the object of the verb is topicalized by preposing it (§ 17.4). Various interpretations are possible for *pḥ.n*, none of which is completely satisfactory. Normally, a *sḏm.n.f* would be expected, as in cols. 2 and 8, so perhaps *pḥ.n* is an error for *pḥ.n.n*. This text does use the *sḏm.f* as a past tense elsewhere (cols. 76–77: see § 18.4), so perhaps also here, but with transitive verbs the meaning is usually past ("we reached") rather than perfect ("we have reached"); a gnomic or present-tense meaning ("we reach": see § 18.5) is ruled out by the context, since the previous couplets describe the expedition as already at home. An archaic use of the transitive stative as an active perfect is also possible (§ 16.5).

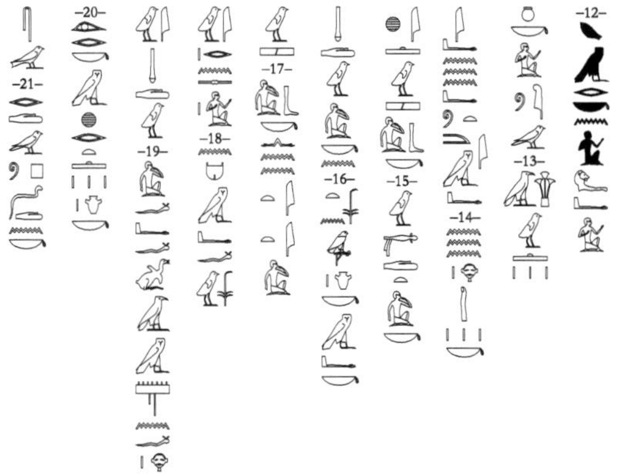

12–13 ***sḏm r.k n.j*** *ḥꜣt(j)-ꜥ* 3
jnk šw ḥꜣw 2
13–15 *jꜥ tw jmj mw ḥr ḏbꜥw.k* 4
jḫ wšb.k wšd.t(w).k 2
15–17 *mdw.k n nswt jb.k m ꜥ.k* 4
wšb.k nn njtjt 2
17–19 *jw r n z(j) nḥm.f sw* 3
jw mdw.f dj.f ṯꜣm n.f ḥr 4

20–21 *jr r.k* (or *jrr.k*) *m ḫrt jb.k* 2
swrd pw ḏd n.k 2

12–13 **So, listen to me**, high official:
I am free of excess.
13–15 Wash yourself, put water on your fingers:
then you can answer when you are addressed.
15–17 You can speak to the king with your wits about you;
you can answer without stuttering.
17–19 For the mouth of a man saves him;
for his speech makes leniency for him.
20–21 But you act as you have in mind;
speaking to you is wearisome.

Although it has returned safely, with no loss of life, the expedition has apparently been unsuccessful in its mission. The leader has to report to the king, and the sailor tries to encourage him.

12–13 *sḏm r.k* — imperative: literally, "listen, with respect to yourself" (§ 15.7.2).

jnk šw ḥꜣw — an A B nominal sentence (§ 7.14): literally, "I am one free of excess." *šw ḥꜣw* is a *nfr ḥr* construction (§ 6.5). Normally, however, the expression is *šw m* "free from" (§ 8.2.3), with the preposition *m*; the preposition may have been overlooked here when the scribe moved from the bottom of col. 12 to the top of col. 13. *ḥꜣw* refers to "excess" of words: i.e., exaggeration.

13–15 This couplet refers to the Egyptian practice of washing before any formal occasion: in this case, the official's forthcoming audience with the king.

jꜥ ... jmj — imperatives (§ 15.3, 15.2.3).

jḫ wšb.k — a construction indicating result (§ 18.11).

wšd.t(w).k — the *sḏm.f* with passive suffix *tw* (§ 18.3), used in an unmarked adverb clause of concomitant circumstance (§ 20.11). The suffix *tw* is written here before the determinative, as if it was part of the verb stem or an ending.

15–17 *mdw.k ... wšb.k* — the two *sḏm.f* forms here have future sense (§ 18.7).

jb.k m ꜥ.k — an adverbial sentence used as an unmarked adverb clause (§ 20.7). It means literally, "your mind in your hand" (§ 8.3.1).

nn njtjt — a negative adverb clause with the infinitive (§§ 13.15, 20.15). *njtjt* "stutter" is clearly onomatopoeic (probably *ni'ít'it).

17–19 The use of the particle *jw* in both lines of this couplet relates the two statements to the preceding couplet (§§ 10.3, 15.6.1). The sense can be conveyed in English by the initial "for." In both lines, *jw* is followed by the SUBJECT–*sḏm.f* construction, expressing a gnomic generalization (§ 18.6).

dj.f ṯȝm n.f ḥr — literally, "gives veiling of the face for him" (*ṯȝm* is infinitive). The idiom refers to the idea of a listener concealing his emotions: in other words, if the official is persuasive in his report, he can make the king ignore his anger at the failure of the expedition.

20–21 In this couplet, the last of the opening section of the story, the sailor tells the official to do whatever he wants, since he is apparently not responding to the sailor's advice.

jr r.k (or *jrr.k*) *m ḫrt jb.k* — two interpretations are possible for the first three signs: either an imperative with self-referential *r.k* (§ 15.7.2) or the geminated *sḏm.f* as the predicate of an emphatic sentence (§§ 25.4, 25.6). The first option makes sense stylistically, since *r.k* would be used here as a bridge from the previous statements, as it was in col. 12 *sḏm r.k n.j*. An emphatic sentence also makes sense, however, since the sailor is not just telling the official to act but to act as he wants: *m ḫrt jb.k* is the rheme (§ 25.2). The last phrase means literally, "as that which is with your mind"; *ḫrt* is a nisbe from the preposition *ḫr* (§ 8.6.10), a means of indicating possession: i.e, "what your mind has."

swrd pw ḏd n.k — an A *pw* B nominal sentence with two infinitives (§§ 7.10, 13.13). *swrd* is the causative of *wrd* "become weary." The sentence does not mean "Speaking is wearisome for you," since *n.k* in that case would follow *swrd*, not *ḏd*.

Episode 2 — The Sailor's Story Begins (cols. 21–32)

21–24 ***sḏd.j r.f*** *n.k mjtt jrj* 3
ḫpr.(w) m ʿ.j ḏs.j 3
šm.kw r bjȝ n jtj 3
24–27 *hȝ.kw r wȝḏ-wr m dpt* 3
nt mḥ 120 m ȝw.s 2
mḥ 40 m sḫw.s 2
27–28 *sqdw 120 jm.s* 2
m stp n kmt 2

28–30 *mꜣ.sn pt mꜣ.sn tꜣ* 4
mjkꜣ jb.sn r mꜣw 3
30–32 ***sr.sn*** *ḏꜥ nj jjt* 3
nšnj nj ḫprt.f 2

21–24 **Nonetheless, let me relate** to you something similar
that happened to me myself,
when I went to the mining country for the sire.
24–27 I went down to the sea in a boat
of a hundred twenty cubits in length
and forty cubits in width,
27–28 a hundred twenty sailors in it
of the choice of Egypt.
28–30 Whether they saw sky or saw land,
their mind was more observant than lions.
30–32 **They could predict** a gale before it came,
a thunderstorm before it happened.

The beginning of the story within a story is the sailor's description of the boat and its crew. This part is repeated almost verbatim in cols. 89–101, when the sailor tells the serpent how he came to be shipwrecked.

21–23 *sḏd.j r.f* — *sḏd* is the causative of *ḏd*, but it means "report, relate" rather than "cause to speak." *r.f* is relational, with the pronoun referring back to what was said previously (§ 15.7.2). Since the sailor has just told the official that "speaking to you is wearisome," a translation such as "nonetheless" makes better sense here than "so."

mjtt jrj — *mjtt* is a feminine nisbe made from a feminine nisbe of the preposition *mj* "like" (§ 8.6.2). The feminine is used to refer to an unspecified antecedent (§ 22.15). *jrj* is the adverbial form of the preposition *jr* (§§ 8.2.7, 8.15). The phrase as a whole means literally, "a likeness thereunto."

ḫpr.(w) m ꜥ.j — in Egyptian, things happen "with" (*m ꜥ*, literally "in the hand of") someone rather than "to" them. Since *mjtt*, the antecedent of *ḫpr*, is feminine, *ḫpr* should be feminine as well. The use of the masculine form here is probably related to a similar phenomenon noted for *ḫt nbt* "any thing," which is often *ḫt nb* when *ḫt* doesn't refer to any "thing" in particular (i.e., "anything" as opposed to "any thing"). The similar line in Episode 10 (line 125) shows that *ḫpr.(w)* is the 3ms stative used in an unmarked relative clause (§ 22.11); *mjtt* is therefore undefined ("a likeness").

23–28 *šm.kw ... hꜣ.kw* — the stative used as a past tense (§ 16.5). The *šm.kw* clause could be an independent statement as well as an umarked adverb clause (§ 20.8).

bjꜣ — the word *bjꜣ* means "metal"; with the determinative it refers to the (desert) place where metal was mined (probably a nisbe, *bjꜣj*). In most cases, the Sinai is meant, the source of much of ancient Egypt's copper. The main deposit was at Serabit el-Khadim, located halfway down the Sinai peninsula and 16 miles (26 km) inland from its east coast. A nautical expedition to there (as described in the following columns) would have set sail from a port on the Egyptian coast of the Red Sea.

n jtj — in the repetition of this line in cols. 90–91, the sailor's voyage is described as *wpwt jtj* "the sire's mission," so the preposition *n* "for" is more likely here than an indirect genitive "of the sire." For the spelling of *jtj*, see Essay 6.

wꜣḏ-wr — literally, "great blue-green": see Essay 2. The term was used for the Red Sea as well as the Mediterranean.

mḥ 120 m ꜣw.s mḥ 40 m sḫw.s — literally, "cubit 120 in its length, cubit 40 in its width." The measurements are equivalent to 206.7 feet (63 m) and 68.9 feet (21 m) (§ 9.7.1). *ꜣw* and *sḫw* are verbal nouns (§ 13.1) from *ꜣwj* "extend" and *wsḫ* "become broad"; 3-lit. verbs with initial *w* often lose that radical in verbal nouns.

sqdw 120 jm.s — an adverbial sentence used either independently or as an unmarked adverb clause (§ 20.7).

m stp n kmt — *stp* is a verbal noun from *stp* "choose." For *kmt*, literally "Blackland," see Essay 2.

28–30 The opening line of this couplet reflects the ancient practice of sailing whenever possible within sight of land; when land is out of sight, only the sky is visible on the horizon. There is a deliberate word-play between the verb *mꜣꜣ* "see" in the first line and the noun *mꜣw* "lions" in the second.

mꜣ.sn pt mꜣ.sn tꜣ — the *sḏm.f* used to express an initial condition (§§ 18.12, 25.8.1). The literal meaning is close to that of the more archaic English translation "Saw they sky, saw they land."

mjkꜣ jb.sn r mꜣw — the meaning of *mjkꜣ* has been discussed recently in Graefe 2013. Egyptian usually prefers the singular when referring a body part belonging to multiple owners: thus *jb.sn* "their mind" rather than *jbw.sn* "their minds." The clause is an adjectival sentence of comparison (§ 7.4.2). In such sentences, Egyptian also prefers to compare body parts to owners: thus, *r mꜣw* "than lions" rather than *r jbw mꜣw* "than lions' minds." The language has no construction analogous to English "than those of lions."

30–32 Despite the use of red ink here, repeated in col. 97, this line belongs with this episode rather than the next. The scribe's choice of marking it as a new section was evidently influenced by the mention of *ḏꜥ* "gale," the theme of Episode 3.

sr.sn — in hieroglyphic, the verb *sr* is often determined with the sign of a giraffe (E 27), whose long neck allows it to see farther into the distance than animals closer to the ground. In hieratic, the giraffe is usually replaced by the Seth animal (E 20).

nj jjt ... nj ḫprt.f — negated *sḏmt.f* (§ 19.14), in the first case with unexpressed subject; the repetition in col. 98 has *nj jjt.f*.

nšnj — thunderstorms were seen as a manifestation of Seth; hence the determinative.

Episode 3 — The Shipwreck (cols. 32–46)

32–34	*ḏꜥ pr.(w) jw.n m wꜣḏ-wr*	3
	dp ꜥ sꜣḥ.n tꜣ	2
34–37	*fꜣ.t(w) ṯꜣw jr.f wḥmyt*	4
	nwyt jm.f nt mḥ 8	3
	jn ḫt ḥ(w)ḥ(w) n.j s(j)	2
37–39	*ꜥḥꜥ.n dpt m(w)t.(tj)*	3
	ntjw jm.s nj zp wꜥ jm	4
39–41	*ꜥḥꜥ.n.j rdj.kw r jw*	3
	jn wꜣw n wꜣḏ-wr	2
41–42	*jr.n.j hrw 3 wꜥ.kw*	3
	jb.j m snnw.j	2
42–45	*sḏr.kw m ẖnw n kꜣp n ḫt*	4
	qnj.n.j šwyt	2
45–46	*ꜥḥꜥ.n dwn.n.j rdwj.j*	3
	r rḫ djt.j m r.j	2

32–34 A gale came up while we were at sea,
before we could touch land,
34–37 the wind lifted repeatedly,
with a swell of eight cubits from it.
The mast was what broke it for me.
37–39 Then the boat died,
and of those who were in it, not one survived.

39–41 Then I was put on an island
by a wave of the sea.
41–42 I spent three days alone,
my mind as my only companion,
42–45 lying inside a thicket,
having embraced the shade.
45–46 Then I stretched my legs
to learn what I might put in my mouth.

This section has two parts. The first describes the shipwreck; the second, the sailor's first days as a castaway. Like Episode 2, the first part is repeated almost verbatim when the sailor tells the serpent how he came to be shipwrecked (cols. 101–10).

32–34 The second line of this couplet explains why the boat was caught in a gale, even though the sailors could predict one.

ḏꜥ pr.(w) — SUBJECT–stative used as a past tense for an intransitive verb (§ 16.8).

jw.n m wꜣḏ-wr — an adverbial sentence used as an unmarked adverb clause (§ 20.7). Egyptian is more specific than English in using the preposition *m*, literally "in" the sea.

dp ꜥ sꜣḥ.n tꜣ — the *sḏm.f* used in unmarked noun clause as object of the compound preposition *dp ꜥ* (literally, "atop the arm of") (§ 21.9). The verb *sꜣḥ* means literally "toe" (the hieroglyph with which it is written here: Sign List D 63): the image is of setting foot on land.

34–37 *fꜣ.t(w) ṯꜣw* — the *sḏm.f* with passive suffix, which can be interpreted as either an independent past tense (§ 18.4) or an unmarked adverb clause of concomitant circumstance ("the wind being lifted"), dependent on the preceding sentence (§ 20.11). For the writing of the verb, see the note to col. 15 *wšd.t(w).k*, above; the arm sign is a second determinative (for D 40: see D 36 in the Sign List).

jr.f wḥmyt — literally, "it making repetition," an unmarked adverb clause of concomitant circumstance with the *sḏm.f* (§ 20.11). *wḥmyt* is a verbal noun of *wḥm* "repeat."

nwyt jm.f nt mḥ 8 — an adverbial sentence, either independent or an unmarked adverb clause (§ 20.7). *nwyt* "swell" is derived from *nwy* "waters" (of the sea, as opposed to *mw* "water" as a substance). It evidently refers to a rogue wave caused by the storm; the height is 13.8 feet (4.2 m).

jn ẖt ḥ(w)ḥ(w) n.j s(j) — participial statement (§ 23.10). The noun *ẖt* "wood, stick, tree" probably refers to the ship's mast, which English-speaking sailors still call the "stick." The verb is otherwise unattested (except for the repetition in col. 105), but its first determinative indicates that it is related to the verb *ḥwj* "hit," and the reduplication indicates multiple action: rather than "pummel" (since the wave hit the mast only once), the sense is probably "break into pieces." The line apparently refers to the sailor taking cover behind, or tied to, the mast when the wave swept over the boat.

37–39 *ꜥḥꜥ.n dpt m(w)t.(tj)* — SUBJECT–stative as a past tense after *ꜥḥꜥ.n* (§ 16.8). The 3fs stative suffix is not written because the verb ends in *t* (§ 16.2); the repetition in col. 106 has *m(w)t.t(j)*.

ntjw jm.s nj zp wꜥ jm — literally, "those in it, one thereof did not survive." The marked relative clause *ntjw jm.s* (§ 22.4) is logically the object of the final preposition *jm*, topicalized by putting it in front; the preposition is then in the adverbial form (§§ 8.2.3, 8.15, 9.4).

39–41 *ꜥḥꜥ.n.j rdj.kw r jw* — SUBJECT–stative as a past tense after *ꜥḥꜥ.n* (§ 16.8); literally, "then I was given to an island." The stative is used to express the passive with a pronominal subject (§ 19.3).

41–45 This sentence consists of a main clause and four unmarked adverb clauses.

wꜥ.kw ... sḏr.kw — 1s stative describing concomitant state (§ 20.8), literally "I being single" and "I having lain down."

jb.j m snnw.j — an adverb clause with adverbial predicate (§ 20.7), literally "my mind as my second."

kꜣp n ḫt — literally, "private place of wood."

qnj.n.j šwyt — adverb clause of prior circumstance with the *sḏm.n.f* (§ 20.10).

45–46 *ꜥḥꜥ.n dwn.n.j rdwj.j* — *sḏm.n.f* as a past tense after *ꜥḥꜥ.n* (§ 17.9).

r rḫ — infinitive after the preposition *r*, expressing purpose (§ 13.11.3). For the meaning of *rḫ*, see § 16.5.

djt.j — relative *sḏm.f* as a noun, object of *rḫ* (§ 22.14).

Episode 4 — Exploring the Island (cols. 47–56)

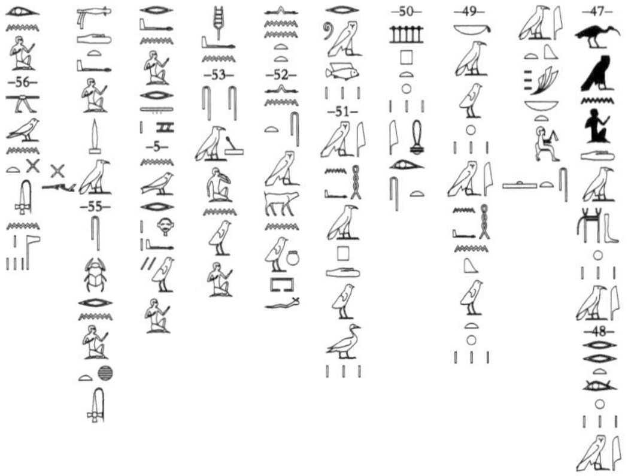

47–48 ***gm.n.j*** *dꜣbw jꜣrrt jm* 4
jꜣqt nbt špst 2
49–50 *kꜣw jm ḥnꜥ nq(ꜥ)wt* 3
šzpt mj jr.t(w).s 2
50–52 *rmw jm ḥnꜥ ꜣpdw* 3
nn ntt nn st m ẖnw.s 2
52–54 *ꜥḥꜥ.n ssꜣ.n.(j) wj* 2
rdj.n.j r tꜣ n wr ḥr ꜥwj.j 4
54–56 *šdt.j ḏꜣ sẖpr.n.j sḏt* 4
jr.n.j zj n sḏt n nṯrw 3

47–48 **I found** figs and grapes there,
and all (kinds of) fine vegetables.
49–50 Green and ripe sycamore figs were there,
and melons as if cultivated.
50–52 Fish were there, and birds:
there was nothing that was not inside it.
52–54 Then I sated myself,
and put some down because of how much was on my arms.
54–56 I took a fire-stick, created a fire,
and made a burnt offering to the gods.

This section describes the natural riches that the sailor found on the island.

47–48 *špst* — the bookroll determinative is written next to the final *t* at the end of the column, so as not to break the word between columns.

49–50 *kꜣw ... nq(ꜥ)wt* — both terms refer to figs of the sycamore tree: *kꜣw* is the unripe fruit and *nq(ꜥ)wt* (usually spelled with an ayin), the ripe fruit (Manniche 1989, 103).

šzpt mj jr.t(w).s — literally, "melons like it was made." The suffix pronoun of *jr.t(w).s* shows that *šzpt* is a collective, treated as a feminine singular (§ 4.6). The verb *jrj* "make" is used of cultivating plants: *jr.t(w).s* is the *sḏm.f* with passive suffix, used as object of the preposition *mj* (§ 21.9).

50–52 *nn ntt nn st m ẖnw.s* — a negated adverbial sentence, *nn st m ẖnw.s* "it (was) not inside it" (§ 11.4), made into a marked indirect relative clause by means of *ntt* "that which" (§§ 22.4, 22.6), negated in turn by *nn* (§ 11.4): literally, "that which (was) not inside it (was) not."

52–54 *ꜥḥꜥ.n ssꜣ.n.(j) wj* — *sḏm.n.f* as a past tense after *ꜥḥꜥ.n* (§ 17.9), with unwritten 1s subject before the 1s dependent pronoun *wj* (§ 17.5). *ssꜣj* is the causative of 3ae-inf. *sꜣj* "become sated."

rdj.n.j r tꜣ — the object of *rdj.n.j* is unexpressed.

n wr ḥr ꜥwj.j — literally, "for much on my arms": the sailor found so much to eat that there was too much for him to carry.

54–56 The final couplet describes the sailor's act of thanksgiving to the gods for his being spared and provided with food.

šdt.j ḏꜣ — *ḏꜣ* "fire-stick" is the object depicted by the hieroglyph , a piece of wood rubbed briskly between the two hands against another piece of wood; the friction ignites a flame. The two determinatives are written to the left of the word to keep them in the same column as the phonograms. The verb form *šdt.j* is troublesome. It is usually interpreted as the "narrative infinitive" (from 3ae-inf. *šdj* "take": see Berg 1990), but the context does not suit the usual use of that form (§ 13.14.2). Nor is it the *sḏmt.f*, since it is not preceded by *nj* or the prepositions *r* or *ḏr* (§ 19.14). The relative *sḏm.f* is possible as the first element of an A B nominal sentence — "what I took (was) a fire-stick" — but that pattern of the nominal sentence is normally reserved for inalienable subjects in Middle Egyptian (§ 7.7). Since the *sḏm.n.f* would be normal here (*šd.n.j*), perhaps the  (hieratic ) has been misread by the scribe from an original  (hieratic ) in which  is the determinative.

zj n sḏt — literally, "go-away of fire." The phrase is a single term, therefore probably with a single stress instead of two.

Episode 5 — Encountering the Snake (cols. 56–66)

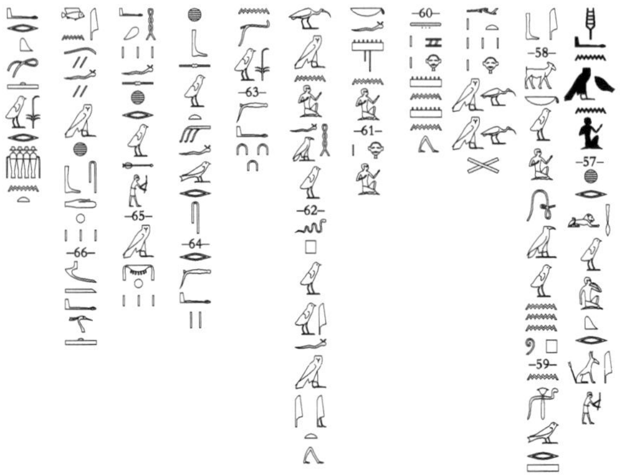

56–59 ***ꜥḥꜥ.n sḏm.n.j*** *ḫrw qrj* 3
jb.kw wꜣw pw n wꜣḏ-wr 3
59–60 *ḫtw ḥr gmgm* 2
tꜣ ḥr mnmn 2
60–62 *kf.n.j ḥr.j* 2
gm.n.j ḥfꜣw pw jw.f m jjt 3
62–64 *n(j)-sw mḥ 30* 2
ḫbswt.f wr s(j) r mḥ 2 3
64–66 *ḥꜥw.f sḫr.w m nbw* 3
jnḥwj.fj m ḫsbd mꜣꜥ 3
ꜥrq sw r ḫnt 2

56–59 **Then I heard** a sound of thunder;
I thought it was a wave of the sea.
59–60 Trees were cracking,
the ground was quaking.
60–62 When I uncovered my face,
I found it was a snake, and he was coming.
62–64 He was thirty cubits long,
and his beard, it was greater than two cubits.
64–66 His body was plated with gold,
his eyebrows were real lapis-lazuli,
and he was bent forward.

56–59 *qrj* — the basic form of this word is *qrr*, usually describing a storm-cloud (for the Seth-animal determinative, see the note to col. 32 *nšnj*, above). The form here probably represents the loss of the second *r* (§ 2.4, Essay 17).

jb.kw wꜣw pw n wꜣḏ-wr — the 1s stative used as a past tense (§ 16.5). The rest of the sentence is an A *pw* nominal sentence used as an unmarked noun clause, object of *jb.kw* (§ 21.7).

59–60 *ḫtw ḥr gmgm tꜣ ḥr mnmn* — two pseudo-verbal constructions describing action in progress (§ 14.2).

60–62 This couplet is a good example of narrative style. It is not necessary for the author to first tell us that he covered his face (in fear), since that action is implied by the words "I uncovered my face."

kf.n.j ... gm.n.j — the initial verb is 3-lit. *kfꜣ*; the final consonant has been lost in pronunciation and is therefore not written. These two *sḏm.n.f* forms describe two consecutive actions. They can be interpreted as two independent statements ("I uncovered … and I found") or as an emphatic sentence in which the first clause is logically subordinate to the second (§ 25.8.3).

ḥfꜣw pw — An A *pw* nominal sentence serving as an unmarked noun clause, object of *gm.n.j* (§ 21.7).

jw.f m jjt — a pseudo-verbal construction with *m* plus the infinitive, implying that the snake's arrival was imminent (§ 14.2). It can be understood as an unmarked relative clause modifying the undefined antecedent *ḥfꜣw* "a snake" (§ 22.10) as well as an independent statement ("and he was about to come").

62–64 *n(j)-sw mḥ 30* — literally, "he belonged to thirty cubits," an A B nominal sentence of adherence (§ 7.8). The measurement is equivalent to 51.7 feet (15.75 m) (§ 9.7.1).

ḫbswt.f wr s(j) r mḥ 2 — an adjectival sentence with the subject topicalized and resumed by the dependent pronoun *s(j)* (§§ 7.3, 7.4.2). The beard identifies the snake as a god; its length exceeded 3.4 feet (1.05 m) (§ 9.7.1).

64–66 *ḥꜥw.f sḫr.w m nbw* — SUBJECT–stative. *ḥꜥw* is the plural of *ḥꜥ* "limb" but is regularly used as a kind of collective for "body" — in this case, aptly, since snakes don't have limbs. The skin of gods was thought to be gold, since it, like the gods, is immutable. The verb is originally *sẖr*; the *ẖ* has become *ḫ* in this scribe's dialect.

jnḥwj.fj m ḫsbd mꜣꜥ — the word for "eyebrow" normally has a , omitted here. The dual strokes are commonly found after the 3ms suffix pronoun of dual nouns (§ 5.7). The hair of gods was regularly described as blue in color (lapis-lazuli) rather than black; in this case, the hair is genuine lapis-lazuli.

ꜥrq sw r ḫnt — an adjectival sentence with a passive participle as the adjectival predicate (§ 24.5). *r ḫnt* means literally "to the fore": the image is that of a cobra, rearing with its head bent to strike.

Episode 6 — The Snake Captures the Sailor (cols. 67–80)

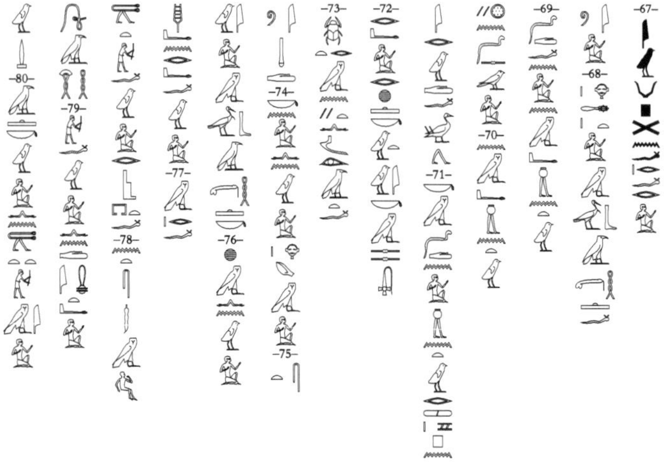

67–68 ***jw wp.n.f*** *r.f r.j* 3
jw.j ḥr ẖt.j m bꜣḥ.f 2
69–70 *ḏd.f n.j n-mj jn tw* 3
zp 2 nḏs n-mj jn tw 5
70–73 *jr wdf.k m ḏd n.j jn tw r jw pn* 4
rdj.j rḫ.k tw jw.k m zz 3
ḫpr.t(j) m ntj nj mꜣ.t(w).f 3
73–76 *jw mdw.⸢n.f⸣ n.j nn wj ḥr sḏm.{j} st* 2
jw.j m bꜣḥ.⸢f⸣ ḫm.n.(j) wj 2
76–78 *ꜥḥꜥ.n rdj.f wj m r.f* 3
jt.f wj r jst.f nt snḏm 3
78–80 *wꜣḥ.f wj nn dmjt.j* 2
wḏꜣ.kw nn jtt jm.j 3

67–68 **He opened** his mouth at me,
as I was on my belly in his presence,
69–70 saying to me, "Who fetched you?
Who fetched you, mister? Who fetched you?
70–73 If you delay telling me who fetched you to this island,
I will make you find yourself as ash,
having become one who is not seen."

73–76 But he spoke to me without my hearing it,
 though I was in his presence, because I had fainted.
76–78 Then he put me in his mouth,
 took me away to his place of residence,
78–80 and set me down without my being touched,
 sound, with nothing taken from me.

67–68 *jw wp.n.f r.f* — the use of *jw* here relates the snake's act of opening his mouth directly to the preceding context, as opposed to a simple past act (§§ 10.3, 17.7).

jw.j ḥr ẖt.j m bꜣḥ.f — adverbial sentence used as an unmarked adverb clause (§ 20.7).

69–70 *ḏd.f* — *sḏm.f* in an unmarked adverb clause of concomitant circumstance (§ 20.11).

n-mj jn tw — participial statement (§ 23.10). *n-mj* is a "phonetic" spelling of *jn mj* as a single word (*iníma).

zp 2 — repeats the preceding question (§ 9.5).

nḏs — this term was used during the Middle Kingdom to refer to a person of modest means who did not hold a specific office (Franke 1998). Its literal meaning is "little," which also has an ironic sense here, given the snake's size.

70–73 *jr wdf.k m ḏd n.j jn tw r jw pn* — protasis of a conditional sentence with the *sḏm.f* (§ 18.12): literally, "if you delay in saying to me." *jn* is an active participle.

rdj.j rḫ.k tw — the *rdj sḏm.f* construction (§ 21.8), in which *rdj.j* has future sense (§ 18.7): literally, "I will give that you learn yourself."

jw.k m zz — adverbial sentence used as an unmarked adverb clause (§ 20.7): literally, "you being as ash." The clause implies that the snake will incinerate the sailor with his fiery breath.

ḫpr.t(j) m ntj nj mꜣ.t(w).f — *ḫpr.t(j)* is the 2s stative used in an unmarked adverb clause (§ 20.8); *ḫpr m* means "evolve into." The relative clause marked by *ntj* is direct (the unexpressed antecedent is identical with the subject of the relative clause), but the suffix pronoun is required because it is the subject of the negated *sḏm.f*. The clause means literally, "one who he is not seen" (§§ 18.3, 18.13).

73–76 *jw mdw.⸢n.f⸣ n.j* — the text has *jw mdw.k* "you speak," which could be interpreted as part of the snake's speech, as a virtual question ("Do you speak to me?"), but the second line of the couplet (see next) indicates that the snake is not the speaker. The scribe has evidently misread an original ligatured hieratic  as . For the use of half-brackets, see § 3.7. As in col. 67 *jw wp.n.f*, the use of *jw* relates this statement directly to the preceding context.

nn wj ḥr sḏm.{j} st — the usual negative counterpart of the pseudo-verbal construction with *ḥr* plus infinitive is *nj sḏm.n.f* (§§ 14.8, 17.11). The unique construction here may have been prompted by the need to express action in progress ("I was not hearing it"), which *nj sḏm.n.f* does not specifically connote. Alternatively, the superfluous suffix of *sḏm* suggests that the scribe was thinking of *nn* plus the infinitive (*nn sḏm.j st* "without my hearing it": § 13.15), which he converted to *nn wj ḥr sḏm st* "without me (upon) hearing it" in order to avoid the usual future meaning of *nn sḏm.j st* ("I would not hear it": § 18.14), but without omitting the (original?) 1s suffix of the infinitive. In any case, this clause is an umarked adverb clause (§ 20.7).

jw.j m bꜣḥ.⸢f⸣ — an unmarked adverb clause with adverbial predicate (§ 20.7). The text has *jw.j m bꜣḥ.k*, which, like *jw mdw.k* in the first line, could be taken as part of the snake's speech: "Do you speak to me? I am not hearing it, though I am in your presence." Against such an interpretation, however, is the fact that *ḫm.n.(j) wj* can only refer to the sailor (see next). Moreover, the object of *m bꜣḥ* "in the presence of" is regularly a superior, so the snake would not likely describe himself as being in the sailor's presence.

ḫm.n.(j) wj — a *sḏm.n.f* with unwritten 1s suffix before *wj* (§ 17.5), used in an unmarked adverb clause of prior circumstance (§ 20.10). The verb *ḫm* means "not know, be ignorant, be unaware": the clause means literally, "I was unaware of myself," the usual Egyptian idiom for losing consciousness.

76–78 *ꜥḥꜥ.n rdj.f wj m r.f* — an unusual use of the *sḏm.f* for past action instead of the *sḏm.n.f* (§ 18.4).

jt.f wj — the verb *jṯj* has become *jtj* in this text's dialect. The verb means basically "take possession of" and not "take" someone somewhere; its use here implies the snake's taking control of the sailor. In the *sḏm.f* here, it could be an unmarked adverb clause ("taking me away": § 20.11) but more likely continues the past sense of *rdj.f* in the preceding line.

snḏm — an infinitive (§ 13.10). It is the causative of *nḏm* "become sweet, easy" but is regularly used with reference to a person's residence: this use of *snḏm* is similar to the English idiom "taking it easy."

78–80 *wꜣḥ.f wj* — like *jt.f wj* in the preceding stanza, the sense is probably past rather than circumstantial.

nn dmjt.j — an unmarked adverb clause with *nn* plus the infinitive (§ 13.15), with the pronominal suffix as object rather than subject of the infinitive (§ 13.5.1). *dmj* is a 3-lit. verb (originally, and still in some Middle Kingdom texts, *dmr*), and should therefore have an infinitive without *t* (§ 13.3); it is possible that the scribe has misread an original 𓂋 as 𓏏. The only other possible interpretations of the form do not make sense in this context: passive *nn dmj.t(w).j* should mean "I would not be touched" (§ 18.14), and *nn* with a relative *sḏm.f* would mean "without that which I might touch" (§ 22.14). Since the snake has in fact "touched" the sailor, the sense is one of harm, as in "the storm never touched us."

wḏꜣ.kw — 1s stative in an unmarked adverb clause (§ 20.8).

nn jtt jm.j — *jtt* is a feminine passive participle used as a noun: literally, "without that which was taken from me" (cf. § 11.4). In other words, the snake did not bite off any of the sailor's limbs.

Episode 7 — The Sailor Repeats His Story (cols. 81–110)

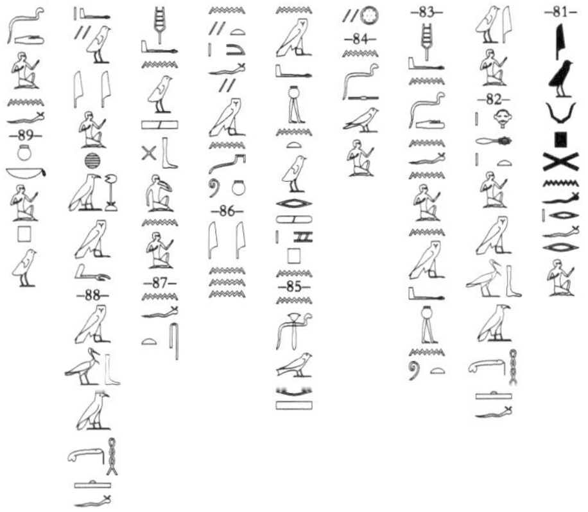

81–82 ***jw wp.n.f*** *r.f r.j* 3
jw.j ḥr ẖt.j m bꜣḥ.f 2
83–84 *ꜥḥꜥ.n ḏd.n.f n.j n-mj jn tw* 4
zp 2 nḏs 3
84–86 *n-mj jn tw r jw pn n wꜣḏ-wr* 4
ntj gs(wj).fj m nwy 3
86–89 *ꜥḥꜥ.n wšb.n.j n.f st* 2
ꜥwj.j ḫꜣm.(w) m bꜣḥ.f 3
ḏd.j n.f jnk pw 2

81–82 **He opened** his mouth at me,
as I was on my belly in his presence.
83–84 Then he said to me, "Who fetched you?
Who fetched you, mister?
84–86 Who fetched you to this island of the sea,
whose two sides are in the waters?"
86–89 Then I answered him,
my arms bent in his presence,
saying to him, "It was I.

This section is basically a repetition of Episodes 2 and 3, with the same marking of *sr.sn ḏꜥ* as the beginning of a new section. The notes below address points supplemental to those for Episodes 2–3 (cols. 21–46).

81–82 A repetition of the opening couplet of Episode 6 (cols. 67–68).

83–84 Essentially the same as cols. 69–70, except for the opening clause *ꜥḥꜥ.n ḏd.n.f n.j*.

84–86 *ntj gs(wj).fj m nwy* — a marked indirect relative clause with adverbial predicate (§ 22.6). The dual strokes after the suffix pronoun indicate that the noun is in the dual (§ 5.7), even though it is written as a singular. The dual suggests that the author was thinking of north–south or east–west, although islands are by definition surrounded on all sides by water. For *nwy*, see the note to col. 35 *nwyt*, above.

86–89 *wšb.n.j n.f st* — the verb *wšb* "answer" requires a direct object in Egyptian, here the neutral pronoun *st* (§ 5.4), referring to the snake's questions.

ꜥwj.j ḫꜣm.(w) m bꜣḥ.f — SUBJECT–stative in an unmarked adverb clause (§ 20.8). "Arms bent" refers to the Egyptian posture of worship or respect: . The double reed-leaf in *ꜥwj.j* is phonetic (*ꜥúwai > *ꜥúway).

ḏd.j n.f — the *sḏm.f* in an unmarked adverb clause of concomitant circumstance (§ 20.11), literally, "I saying to him."

jnk pw — an A *pw* nominal sentence (§ 7.9), answering the snake's question.

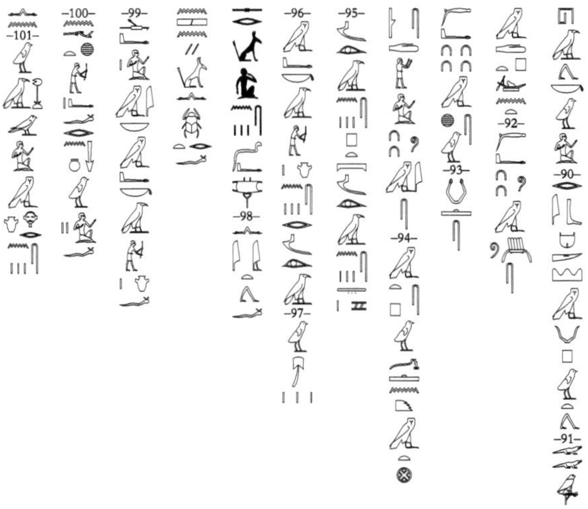

89–93 *hꜣ.kw r bjꜣ m wpwt jtj* 3
m dpt nt mḥ 120 m ꜣw.s 3
mḥ 40 m sḫw.s 2
93–94 *sqdw 120 jm.s* 2
m stpw n kmt 2
95–97 *mꜣ.sn pt mꜣ.sn tꜣ* 4
mjkꜣ jb.sn r mꜣw 3
97–98 ***sr.sn** ḏꜥ nj jjt.f* 3
nšnj nj ḫprt.f 2

99–101 *wꜥ jm nb mjkꜣ jb.f* 3
nḫt ꜥ.f r snnw.f 2
nn wḫꜣ m ḥr(j) jb.sn 2

89–93 I went down to the mining country on the sire's mission
in a boat of a hundred twenty cubits in length
and forty cubits in width,
93–94 a hundred twenty sailors in it
of the choice of Egypt.
95–97 Whether they saw sky or saw land,
their mind was more observant than lions.
97–98 **They could predict** a gale before it came,
a thunderstorm before it happened.
99–101 Each one of them, his mind was more observant
and his arm more forceful than his companion;
there was no fool in their midst.

89–94 This tercet and couplet repeat the opening of the sailor's story, with a slightly different phrasing in the tercet.

97–98 This differs from the couplet in Episode 2 (cols. 30–32) in using a suffix pronoun with the *sḏmt.f* in the first line (*nj jjt.f*).

99–101 This tercet, expanding on the description of the crew, is additional, not in the initial version of the sailor's story.

wꜥ jm nb — adverbial *jm* (§ 8.2.3) is one of the few elements that can come between the adjective *nb* and the noun it modifies, indicating that this phrase has a single stress. For *wꜥ jm*, see § 9.4.

mjkꜣ jb.f nḫt ꜥ.f r snnw.f — a sentence with two adjectival predicates, both with comparative sense (§ 7.4.2).

nn wḫꜣ m ḥr(j) jb.sn — a non-verbal statement of negative existence (§ 11.4). *ḥrj jb* is a nisbe from *ḥr jb* "on the heart," an expression for "middle" or "midst."

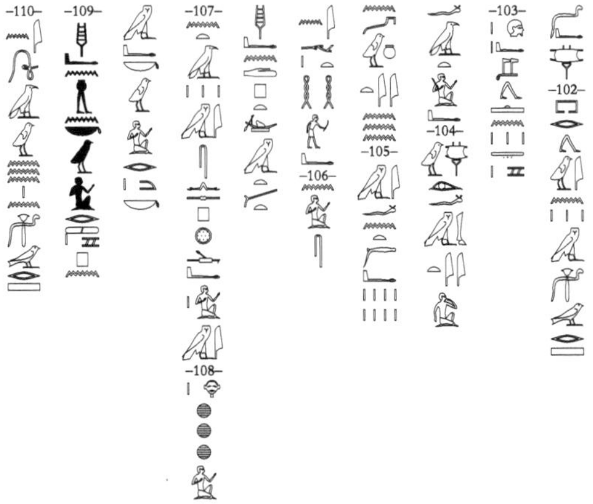

101–103	*ḏꜥ pr.(w) jw.n m wꜣḏ-wr*	3	
	dp ꜥ sꜣḥ.n tꜣ		2
103–106	*fꜣ.t(w) ṯꜣw jr.f wḥmyt*	4	
	nwyt jm.f nt mḥ 8		3
	jn ḫt ḥ(w)ḥ(w) n.j s(j)		2
106–108	*ꜥḥꜥ.n dpt m(w)t.t(j)*	3	
	ntjw jm.s nj zp wꜥ jm ḥr ḫw.j		5
	mj.k wj r gs.k		1
109–10	***ꜥḥꜥ.n.(j) jn.kw** r jw pn*	3	
	jn wꜣw n wꜣḏ-wr		2

101–103 A gale came up while we were at sea,
before we could touch land,
103–106 the wind lifted repeatedly,
with a swell of eight cubits from it.
The mast was what broke it for me.
106–108 Then the boat died,
and of those who were in it, not one survived except me,
and here I am beside you.
109–10 **Then I was fetched** to this island
by a wave of the sea."

106–108 A slightly different version of the couplet in Episode 3 (cols. 37–39), expanded to a tercet by the final line.

ꜥḥꜥ.n dpt m(w)t.t(j) — the stative suffix is written here, as opposed to col. 38.

ḥr ḫw.j — a compound preposition meaning literally, "upon my exemption." *ḫw* is a verbal noun from *ḫwj* "exempt, defend."

mj.k wj r gs.k — an adverbial sentence introduced by *m.k* (§ 10.4.1): literally, "Look, I am at your side."

109–110 Although marked in red, this final couplet is part of the sailor's account and belongs with this episode rather than the next. This is a slightly different version of the corresponding couplet in Episode 3 (cols. 39–41), with *jn.kw* substituted for *rdj.kw* in response to the snake's question.

ꜥḥꜥ.n.(j) jn.kw — with the 1s stative, *ꜥḥꜥ.n* regularly has a 1s suffix pronoun: in this manuscript, cols. 39 (the parallel to this line), 131, and 155. In cases such as this, therefore, the 1s suffix is probably unwritten rather than omitted (so also in lines 157, 169, 174, and col. 177).

Episode 8 — The Snake's Prediction (cols. 111–123)

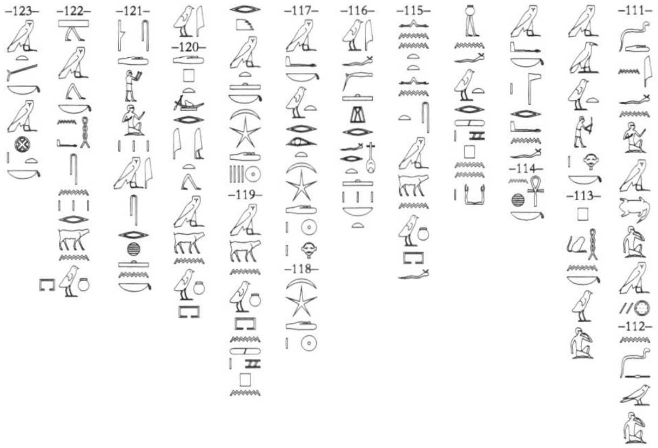

111–13	*ḏd.jn.f n.j m snḏ zp 2 nḏs*	4
	m ꜣtw ḥr.k pḥ.n.k wj	3
113–14	*mj.k nṯr rdj.n.f ꜥnḫ.k*	3
	jn.f tw r jw pn n kꜣ	4
115–16	*nn ntt nn st m ẖnw.f*	2
	jw.f mḥ.(w) ḫr nfrwt nbt	2
117–19	*mj.k tw r jrt jbd ḥr jbd*	3
	r kmt.k jbd 4 m ẖnw n jw pn	4
119–21	*jw dpt r jjt m ẖnw*	3
	sqdw jm.s rḫ.n.k	3
122–23	*šm.k ḥnꜥ.sn r ẖnw*	3
	m(w)t.k m njwt.k	2

111–13 So, he said to me, "Don't fear, don't fear, mister.
Don't blanch because you have reached me.
113–14 Look, the god, he has let you live
by fetching you to this island of ka.
115–16 There is nothing that is not inside it,
for it is full of all good things.
117–19 Look, you are to spend month upon month,
until you have completed four months inside this island.
119–21 A boat is to come from home,
with sailors you know in it.
122–23 You will go home with them,
and die in your town.

111–13 *ḏd.jn.f* — the *sḏm.jn.f*, indicating that the snake's speech follows as a consequence of the sailor's tale (§ 19.10).

m snḏ m zp 2 — negative imperative (§ 15.4), with *zp 2* for the repeated *snḏ* (§ 9.5).

m ꜣtw ḥr.k — negative imperative with third-person subject of the negatival complement (§ 15.4): literally, "Don't (let) your face get white." Blanching (*ꜣt*) was a stereotypical reaction to seeing a snake.

pḥ.n.k wj — unmarked adverb clause of prior circumstance with the *sḏm.n.f*, here expressing causality (§ 20.10).

113–14 This is an emphatic sentence with a rhematic adverb clause (§ 25.7), the latter unmarked with the *sḏm.f* (§ 20.11). The first clause (*mj.k nṯr rdj.n.f ꜥnḫ.k*) is given information (since the sailor has in fact been spared the fate of his shipmates) and the new information, or rheme, is the adverb clause that explains how "he has let you live."

rdj.n.f ꜥnḫ.k — the *rdj sḏm.f* construction (§ 21.8). The subject of the *sḏm.n.f*, *nṯr* "the god," is topicalized (§ 17.4).

jw pn n kꜣ — Gardiner (1908, 65) interpreted the reference to the ka here as a statement that the island was not real but "phantom." The phrase *rdj.n.f ꜥnḫ.k* as well as the couplet following, however, point to the primary sense of "life force" (Essay 7): the island contains everything needed to sustain life (Vandersleyen 1990, 1022).

115–16 The first sentence of this couplet is a repetition of the sailor's comment on the island in Episode 4 (cols. 51–52).

jw.f mḥ.(w) ẖr nfrwt nbt — the SUBJECT–stative construction expressing a state (§ 16.10). Egyptian uses the preposition *ẖr* "under" here rather than *m* "with" because the island is in fact "under" the things it is full of.

117–19 This couplet is the first part of the snake's prophecy. It and the next couplet use the pseudo-verbal SUBJECT *r sḏm* construction to express an involuntary future (§ 18.7).

r kmt.k jbd 4 — the *r sḏmt.f* construction (§ 19.14).

119–21 *sqdw jm.s rḫ.n.k* — *sqdw jm.s* is an adverbial sentence used as an unmarked adverb clause (§ 20.7). *rḫ.n.k* is the *sḏm.n.f* used as an unmarked relative clause after an undefined antecedent (§ 22.12); for the meaning of *rḫ.n.k*, see § 17.10.

122–23 In this couplet, the future is expressed by the *sḏm.f*, because it is voluntary (*šm.k*) and subjective (*m(w)t.k*).

m(w)t.k m njwt.k — Because of the necessity of mummification and a proper tomb for the afterlife (Essay 8), Egyptians were concerned not to die away from home.

Episode 9 — The Snake's Story (lines 124–136)

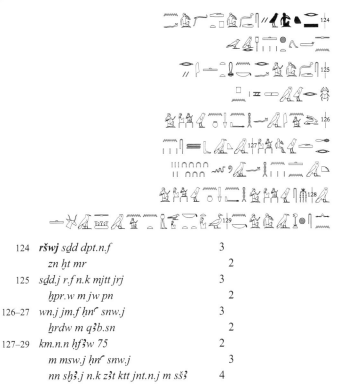

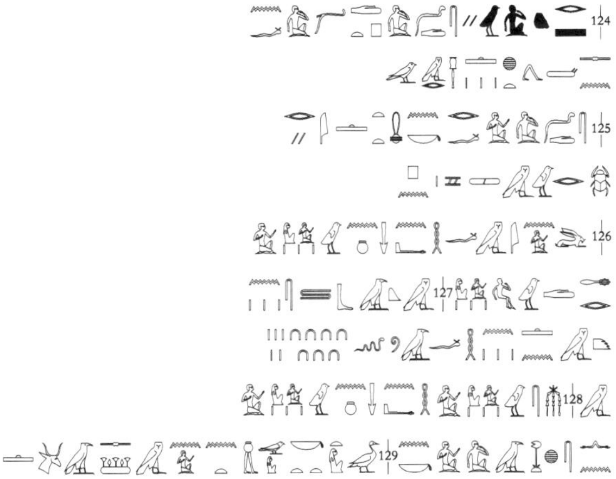

124	***ršwj*** *sḏd dpt.n.f*	3	
	zn ḫt mr		2
125	*sḏd.j r.f n.k mjtt jrj*	3	
	ḫpr.w m jw pn		2
126–27	*wn.j jm.f ḥnꜥ snw.j*	3	
	ẖrdw m qꜣb.sn		2
127–29	*km.n.n ḥfꜣw 75*	2	
	m msw.j ḥnꜥ snw.j		3
	nn sḫꜣ.j n.k zꜣt ktt jnt.n.j m sšꜣ	4	

124 **How happy** is he who relates what he has tasted
when something painful passes.

125 So, let me relate to you something similar
that happened in this island.

126–27 I was in it with my siblings
and children amid them.
127–29 We totaled seventy-five snakes,
consisting of my offspring and my siblings,
without me mentioning to you, from experience, the little daughter I got.

Episode 9 is the story within a story within a story. At this point in the papyrus, the scribe switched from columns of text to horizontal lines. The reason for the change is unknown.

124 *ršwj sḏd dpt.n.f* — an exclamatory adjectival sentence (§ 7.2). The subject is a participial phrase with an active participle governing a relative *sḏm.n.f* (§ 22.12) as object (§ 22.15). *dpt.n.f* "what he has tasted" means "what he has experienced."

zn ẖt mr — an unmarked adverb clause with the *sḏm.f* (§ 20.11). For masculine *mr* modifying feminine *ẖt*, see the note to col. 22 *ḫpr.(w) m ꜥ.j*, above.

125 This couplet is similar to the one with which the sailor began his tale (Episode 2, cols. 21–23).

ḫpr.w — the 3ms suffix is written here.

126–27 *wn.j jm.f* — the *sḏm.f* of *wnn* here serves to cast what is essentially an adverbial sentence into the past (§ 18.9). Since the verb is ungeminated, probably a single point in time is meant, rather than extended existence.

ẖrdw m qꜣb.sn — an adverb sentence used as an unmarked adverb clause (§ 20.7). *m qꜣb* is a compound preposition (§ 8.3): literally, "in the innards."

127–29 *m msw.j ḥnꜥ snw.j* — for this meaning of the preposition *m*, see §§ 8.2.3 and 9.4.

nn sḫꜣ.j n.k — an adverb clause with *nn* plus the infinitive (§ 13.15). It is also possible to understand this as the *nn sḏm.f* construction (§ 18.14) "I will not mention to you." The verb *sḫꜣ* means "bring to mind."

jnt.n.j — relative *sḏm.n.f*; the gender ending shows that *zꜣt ktt* is defined (§ 22.12).

m sšꜣ — following Gardiner 1927, § 457, this prepositional phrase has been understood with *jnt.n.j*, usually as Gardiner's "through prayer" but also as "through knowledge, skill, foresight" (Derchain-Urtel 1974, 97–99). These interpretations involve two separate words: *sšꜣ* "entreat" and *šsꜣ* "experience" (often written *sšꜣ*). The bookroll determinative here, as in line 139, is better suited to the latter; the former is regularly determined with . Although the phrase follows *jnt.n.j*, it can be understood to modify *nn sḫꜣ.j n.k*, since the object phrase *zꜣt ktt jnt.n.j* belongs grammatically together after *nn sḫꜣ.j n.k*. The sense of the passage is evidently that the snake knows, from experience, that bringing to mind "the little daughter I got" is painful.

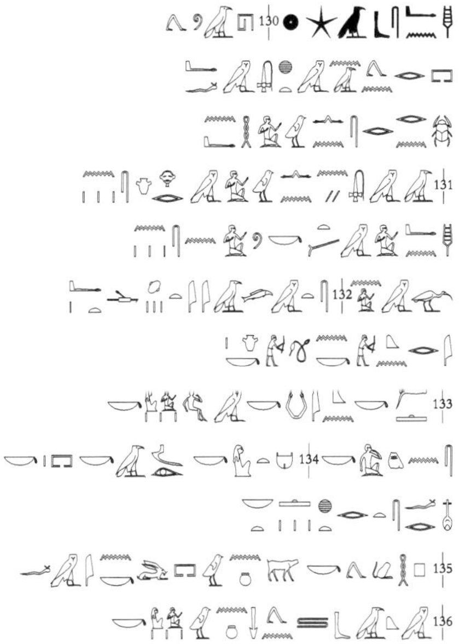

129–30 ***ꜥḥꜥ.n sbꜣ*** *hꜣ.w* 3
pr.n nꜣ m ḫt m ꜥ.f 3
130–31 *ḫpr.n r.s nn wj ḥnꜥ* 3
ꜣm.nj nn wj m ḥr(j) jb.sn 3
131–32 *ꜥḥꜥn.j m(w)t.kw n.sn* 3
gm.n.j st m ẖꜣyt wꜥt 2
132–33 *jr qn.n.k rwḏ jb.k* 3
mḥ.k qnj.k m ẖrdw.k 3
133–34 *sn.k ḥjmt.k mꜣ.k pr.k* 4
nfr st r ḫt nbt 2
135–36 *pḥ.k ẖnw wn.k jm.f* 4
m qꜣb n snw.k 2

129–30 **Then a star** came down,
and those went up in fire from it.
130–31 But it happened while I was not along:
they burned up when I was not in their midst.
131–32 Then I died for them,
after I found them as one pile of corpses.

132–33 If you have persevered, with your mind firm,
you will fill your embrace with your children;
133–34 you will kiss your wife and see your home:
it is better than anything;
135–36 you will reach home and be in it
amid your siblings."

129–30 *ꜥḥꜥ.n sbꜣ hꜣ.w* — SUBJECT–stative as a past tense after *ꜥḥꜥ.n* (§ 16.8).

130–31 This passage is discussed in § 17.5. The negated adverbial sentences in both lines are unmarked adverb clauses. *ḥnꜥ* is the adverbial form of the preposition (§ 8.2.9).

131–32 This passage is discussed in § 20.10. The story within a story within a story ends here.

132–33 *jr qn.n.k* — this is a conditional apodosis with the *sḏm.n.f*. The verb *qnj* means essentially "persevere, not give up." The common connotation of bravery derives from the context of battle: one who perseveres in battle is "brave." Egyptian soldiers who displayed this trait were rewarded by the king with a gold fly, because flies "persevere" in annoying people even when swatted at.

rwḏ jb.k — *sḏm.f* used in an adverb clause of concomitant circumstance (§ 20.11).

mḥ.k qnj.k m ẖrdw.k — this is the first of five apodoses of the conditional sentence (§ 18.12); the other four follow in the next two couplets. The snake's mention of this outcome is touching, given the loss of his own children. Note also the use of the words in the last couplet in comparison with the snake's words in line 126.

133–34 *sn.k ḥjmt.k* — the verb *sn* means basically "smell" (hence the first determinative) but also "kiss": Egyptians apparently "kissed" with the nose rather than the lips.

nfr st r ḫt nbt — an adjectival sentence with comparative meaning (§ 7.4.2).

135–36 *wn.k jm.f* — the *sḏm.f* of *wnn* is used to cast what is essentially an adverbial sentence into the future (§ 18.9).

Episode 10 — The Sailor's Response (lines 136–148)

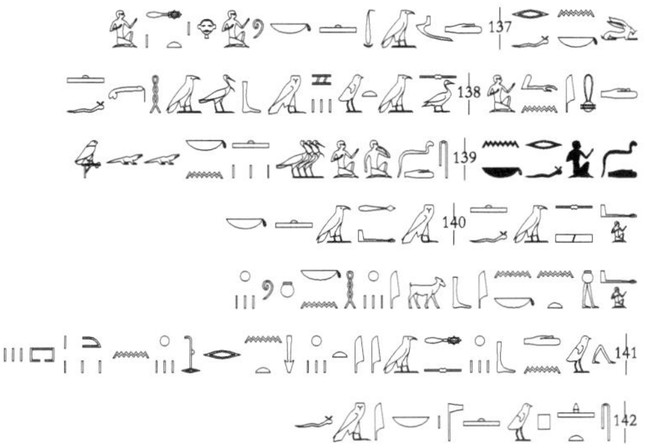

136–38 *wn.k(w) r.f dmꜣ.kw ḥr ẖt.j* 3
dmj.n.j zꜣtw m bꜣḥ.f 3
138–40 ***ḏd.j r.f n.⸢f⸣*** *sḏd.j bꜣw.k n jtj* 4
dj.j sšꜣ.f m ꜥꜣ.k 3
140–42 *dj.j jn.t(w) n.k jbj ḥknw* 4
jwdnb ḫzꜣyt sntr n gsw prw 4
sḥtpw nṯr nb jm.f 3

136–38 At that, I wound up prostrate on my belly,
having touched the ground in his presence,
138–40 **and saying to him**, "I will relate your impressiveness to the sire
and make him aware of your greatness.
140–42 I will have fetched to you *jbj*-oil and *ḥknw*-oil,
jwdnb-resin and *ḫzꜣyt*-resin, the incense of temple stores,
with which every god is contented.

136–38 *wn.k(w) r.f dmꜣ.kw* — two 1s statives. The first is an archaic use of the form as a narrative past tense (§ 16.5), in place of the more contemporary *sḏm.f* (cf. col. 126). The construction serves as a way of situating the state described by *dmꜣ.kw* "stretched out" over a period of time in the past (cf. § 18.9). *r.f* links this sentence with the preceding episode (§ 15.7.2).

dmj.n.j — the *sḏm.n.f* expressing prior circumstance in an unmarked adverb clause (§ 20.10).

138–40 *ḏd.j r.f n.⸢f⸣* — red ink marks the beginning of the sailor's speech. The 2ms suffix can be interpreted as written ("So, let me tell you that I will relate"), but that would leave the sailor's speech without an introduction; a circumstantial use of the *sḏm.f* in an unmarked adverb clause (§ 20.11) makes better sense in the context.

bꜣw.k — an abstract written as a "false plural" (Essay 7, § 4.6).

dj.j sšꜣ.f — the *rdj sḏm.f* construction (§ 21.8).

140–42 *dj.j jn.t(w)* — a second instance of the *rdj sḏm.f* construction, with the passive suffix on the second *sḏm.f* (§ 18.3).

jbj ḥknw jwdnb ḫzꜣyt — two kinds of oil and two kinds of resin or bark, the last perhaps cassia, a type of cinnamon from Arabia. *jbj* is a form of *jbr* (§ 2.8.4); it has been identified as laudanum, but the evidence is slight. *ḥknw* was used in funerary rituals, and cassia was used in oils for anointing.

gsw prw — literally, "sides of the houses." A *gs pr* was a room on either side (*gs*) of the main axis of a temple (*pr*), in which supplies for temple rituals were kept.

sḥtpw nṯr nb jm.f — literally, "which every god is contented with it." *sḥtpw* is either a masculine singular relative *sḏm.f* (§ 22.13) with passive sense, or the passive participle in the special use discussed in § 24.6.

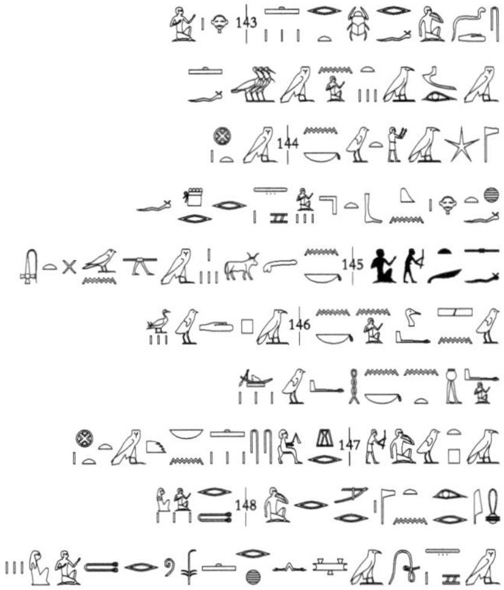

142–43	*sḏd.j r.f ḫprt ḥr.j*	3
	m mꜣt.n.j m bꜣw.⸢k⸣	2
143–44	*dwꜣ.tw n.k nṯr m njwt*	3
	ḫft ḥr qnbt tꜣ r ḏr.f	3
144–46	***zft.j** n.k kꜣw m zj n sḏt*	3
	wšn.n.j n.k ꜣpdw	2
146–47	*dj.j jn.t(w) n.k ḥꜥw*	3
	ꜣtp.w ḫr špss nb n kmt	3
147–48	*mj jrrt n nṯr mrr rmṯ*	4
	m tꜣ wꜣ nj rḫ sw rmṯ	4

142–43 And when I relate what happened to me,
what I have seen of your impressiveness,
143–44 you will be thanked in the town
in front of the council and the whole land.
144–46 **I will slaughter** for you bulls as a burnt offering,
having wrung the necks of birds for you.
146–47 I will have fetched to you ships
loaded with every specialty of Egypt,
147–48 like that which is done for a god people love,
in a far-off land that people don't know."

142–43 This can be taken as an emphatic sentence with an initial circumstantial clause (§ 25.8.3), as translated here, or as two independent statements ("I will relate … You will be thanked").

143–44 *dwꜣ.tw n.k nṯr* — see the note to *dwꜣ-nṯr* in Episode 1 (col. 5–6), above.

ḫft ḥr qnbt tꜣ r ḏr.f — *ḫft ḥr* is a compound preposition: literally, "opposite the face of." The *qnbt* was the local body of officials and elders who adjudicated disputes. For *tꜣ r ḏr.f*, see § 6.7; the phrase is hyperbole for "everyone."

144–46 *zfṯ.j* — The reason for the use of red ink is unclear; perhaps it is related to the meaning of the verb.

zj n sḏt — see the note to this phrase in Episode 5 (col. 56).

wšn.n.j — the form can be understood as written, as a circumstantial use of the *sḏm.n.f* (§ 20.10). A *sḏm.f*, however, would make better sense in the context (*wšn.j* "I will wring the neck"); it is possible that the second *n* is superfluous, influenced by the final radical of *wšn*. The verb refers to killing birds (here, for sacrifice) by wringing the neck; English has no one-word equivalent for this action.

146–47 *dj.j jn.t(w)* — see the note to this phrase in line 140, above.

ꜣtp.w ẖr špss nb n kmt — *ꜣtp.w* is a 3pl stative serving as an unmarked relative clause after an undefined antecedent (§ 22.11); the determinative is the same one used for *fꜣj* "lift" in cols. 34 and 103 ( = ) but without the "stick," making it equivalent to  (). Egyptian is more literal than English in using the preposition *ẖr* "under" rather than *m* "with" with the verb *ꜣtp* "load." *špss* is an abstract from the adjective *špsj* "fine, special." The group  is the determinative of *kmt*;  is superfluous, influenced by the writing of *njwt* "town" (cf. line 144).

147–48 *mj jrrt n nṯr* — *jrrt* is a geminated passive participle, expressing customary action (§ 24.4), serving as object of the preposition *mj*.

mrr rmṯ — *mrr* is also geminated. It could be either a relative *sḏm.f* (§ 22.13) or an active participle ("who loves people": § 23.7); the previous two lines, describing actions done for a god, indicate the former.

m tꜣ wꜣ — *wꜣ* is a participle from the verb *wꜣj*, "go far away." This line goes with *nṯr* ("a god in a far-off land") rather than *jrrt* ("that which is done in a far-off land"). The snake lives "in a far-off land that people don't know."

nj rḫ sw rmṯ — a clause with the negated *sḏm.f* (§ 18.3), serving as an unmarked relative clause after an undefined antecedent (§ 22.13).

Episode 11 — The Snake's Reaction (lines 149–154)

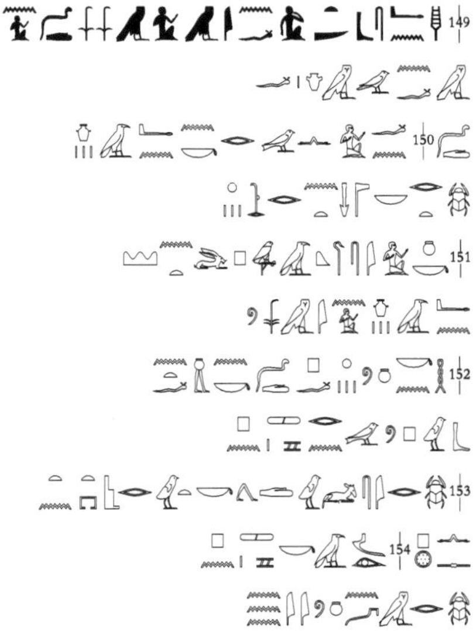

149	***ꜥḥꜥ.n sbt.n.f jm.j m nn ḏd.n.j***	5	
	m nf m jb.f		2
149–50	*ḏd.f n.j nj wr n.k ꜥntjw*	3	
	ḫpr.t(j) nb sntr		2
151	*jnk js nb pwnt*	2	
	ꜥntjw n.j jm sw		2
152	*ḥknw pf ḏd.n.k jn.t(w).f*	3	
	bw pw wr n jw pn		3
153–54	*ḫpr js jwd.k tw r jst tn*	3	
	nj zp mꜣ.k jw pn		3
	ḫpr.(w) m nwy		2

149 **Then he laughed at me, at what I said to him**,
in error in his opinion,

149–50 saying to me, "Do you have so much myrrh,
and have you become owner of incense?
151 For I am lord of Punt
and myrrh, it is mine.
152 That *ḥknw*-oil you said would be fetched,
it is the chief thing of this island.
153–54 And when you come to separate yourself from this place,
you will never see this island,
once it has become waters."

149 *ꜥḥꜥ.n sbt.n.f jm.j* — the *sḏm.n.f* as a past tense after *ꜥḥꜥ.n* (§ 17.9). *sbt* (originally *zbṯ*) means both "grin" and "laugh"; the determinative  represents a tooth, exposed in both actions. The preposition *m* here (*jm* with pronominal suffix: § 8.2.3) and in the next phrase indicates the reason for the snake's laughter.

m nn ḏd.n.j — a second prepositional adjunct of *sbt.n.f. nn* is the neutral demonstrative pronoun (§§ 5.8–9). *ḏd.n.j* is a (masculine singular) relative *sḏm.n.f* used after a defined antecedent (§ 22.12).

m nf m jb.f — the snake found the sailor's promises of gifts outlandish enough to be amusing. The phrase *m jb.f* "in his mind" often means "in his opinion."

149–50 *ḏd.f* — circumstantial use of the *sḏm.f* (§ 20.11).

nj wr n.k ꜥntjw — the words after *nj* are an adjectival sentence, literally "myrrh is much for you." Since such sentences are regularly negated by *nn* (§ 11.6), is most likely a writing of the particle *jn* introducing questions (§ 15.6.2). The term *ꜥntjw* "myrrh" here and in the next couplet has the generic sense of "aromatic resin," covering the more specific terms *jwdnb*, *ẖzꜣyt*, and *sntr* promised by the sailor.

ḫpr.t(j) nb sntr — the verb *ḫpr* is regularly used with the preposition *m* before a person or thing that the subject "becomes" (*ḫpr m* X "evolve into X") but is occasionally used with a direct object, as here. The verb form is the 2s stative, used in an unmarked adverb clause (§ 20.8): literally, "you having become." *nb* implies ownership (§ 11.9.1), but here it probably also implies mastery ("lord of incense").

151 This couplet and the next tell why the snake found the sailor's promises of resin (used for incense) and oil funny.

jnk js nb pwnt — a nominal sentence subordinated by *js* (§ 20.5). The particle here ties the statement *jnk nb pwnt* to the preceding sentence (i.e., "You have become lord of incense even though I am lord of Punt?"). Punt, usually identified as either Somalia or Yemen, was known for its incense trees, and was a regular goal of Egyptian expeditions.

ꜥntjw n.j jm sw — for this construction, see § 11.9.2. *ꜥntjw* is topicalized and resumed by the dependent pronoun *sw*.

152 Having established that he has no need for aromatic resins, the snake now does the same for the oil promised by the sailor.

ḏd.n.k jn.t(w).f — an indirect relative clause in which the relative *sḏm.n.f* governs a noun clause with the *sḏm.f* (§ 22.17.4): literally, "you said it would be fetched."

bw wr pw n jw pn — An A *pw* nominal sentence (§ 7.9). *bw* is a term used for any non-specific "thing." The snake means that *ḥknw* is the island's chief product.

153–54 *ḫpr js jwd.k tw r jst tn* — *js* here marks the sentence as a second subordinate statement ("even though I am lord of Punt … and even though … you will never see this island again"). This is a complex emphatic sentence in which the first line is logically subordinate to the second (§ 25.8.3). In this line, *jwd.k tw r jst tn* is an unmarked noun clause with the *sḏm.f*, serving as subject of the verb *ḫpr* (§ 21.11): literally, "(that) you separate yourself from this place happens." The verb *jwd* means basically "push off from land" and is used with a direct object and the preposition *r* indicating what is being pushed off from: literally, "you push yourself off with respect to this place."

nj zp mꜣ.k jw pn — *nj zp sḏm.f* usually has past sense (§ 18.13) but here is clearly future.

ḫpr.(w) m nwy — *ḫpr.(w)* is the 3ms stative (referring to the island) used as an unmarked adverb clause (§ 20.8). "Becoming waters" could mean that the island will sink into the sea but probably just refers to it sinking below the horizon as the sailor sails away.

Episode 12 — Rescue (lines 155–160)

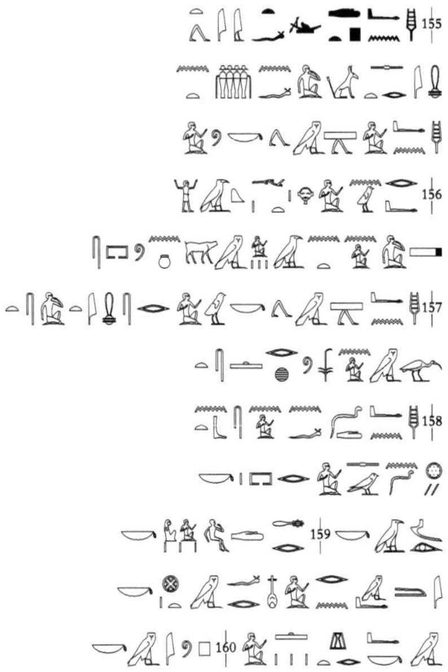

155 ***ꜥḥꜥ.n dpt tf*** *jj.t(j)* 3
mj srt.n.f ḫnt 2
155–56 *ꜥḥꜥ.n.j šm.kw* 2
rdj.n.(j) wj ḥr ẖt qꜣ 3
sjꜣ.n.j ntjw m ẖnw.s 3
157 *ꜥḥꜥ.n.(j) šm.kw r smjt st* 3
gm.n.j sw rḫ.(w) st 2
158–59 *ꜥḥꜥ.n ḏd.n.f n.j snb.t(j)* 3
zp 2 nḏs r pr.k 3
mꜣ.k ẖrdw.k 2
159–60 *jmj rn.j nfr m njwt.k* 3
mj.k ẖrt.j pw jm.k 2

155 **Then that boat** came
as he had predicted before.
155–56 Then I went
and put myself on a high tree,
and I recognized those who were inside it.
157 Then I went to report it
and I found him aware of it.
158–59 Then he said to me, "Farewell,
farewell, mister, to your house.
You will see your children.
159–60 Put my good name in your town.
Look, that is what I need from you."

The sailor's story now jumps ahead four months, to the arrival of the ship that the snake had predicted in Episode 8.

155 *ꜥḥꜥ.n dpt tf jj.t(j)* — SUBJECT–stative as a past tense after *ꜥḥꜥ.n* (§ 16.8).

mj srt.n.f ḫnt — *srt.n.f* is a feminine relative *sḏm.n.f* serving as a noun, object of the preposition *mj*: literally, "like that which he had predicted." *ḫnt* is the adverbial form of the preposition *ḫnt* (§ 8.2.12).

155–56 *sjꜣ.n.j ntjw m ẖnw.s* — this fulfills the second part of the snake's predication: "with sailors you know in it" (col. 121). *ntjw m ẖnw.s* is a direct relative clause (§ 22.3).

157 This passage is discussed in § 20.10.

gm.n.j sw rḫ.(w) st — this passage involves the 3ms stative used as an unmarked adverb clause after *gmj* (§ 20.8). For the syntax of *rḫ.(w) st*, see § 16.5: literally, "I found him having learned it." This may be a sign of the snake's prescience, or maybe simply his height.

158–59 *snb.t(j)* — the 2s stative used as a command (§ 16.6): literally, "be well" (which is also the original meaning of English *farewell*). *zp 2* is used for the repetition of this command in the second line (§ 9.5).

159–60 *ẖrt.j pw jm.k* — *ẖrt* is a nisbe from the preposition *ẖr* "under" and is used to express both possession (§ 8.8: what one is "under" = what one has) and need (the requirement that one is "under"). The second sense is relevant here: the snake is telling the sailor that he only needs the sailor to speak well of him, and not all the material goods the sailor had promised to send.

Episode 13 — The Snake's Gifts (lines 161–166)

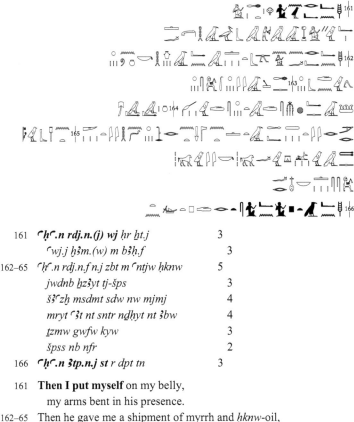

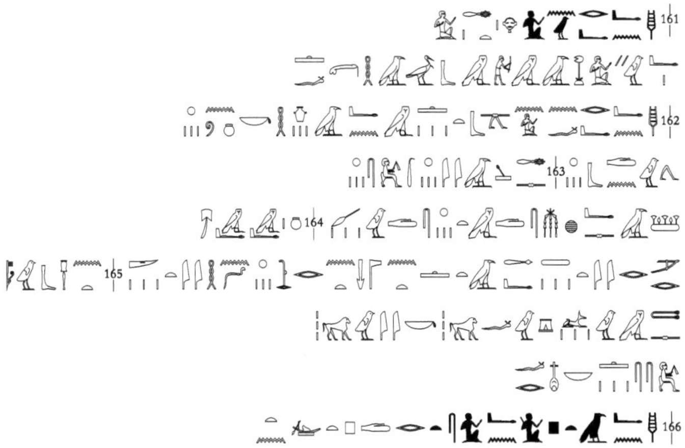

161 ***ꜥḥꜥ.n rdj.n.(j) wj*** *ḥr ẖt.j* 3
ꜥwj.j ẖꜣm.(w) m bꜣḥ.f 3
162–65 *ꜥḥꜥ.n rdj.n.f n.j zbt m ꜥntjw ḥknw* 5
jwdnb ẖzꜣyt tj-šps 3
šꜣꜥzẖ msdmt sdw nw mjmj 4
mryt ꜥꜣt nt sntr nḏḥyt nt ꜣbw 4
ṯzmw gwfw kyw 3
špss nb nfr 2
166 ***ꜥḥꜥ.n ꜣtp.n.j st*** *r dpt tn* 3

161 **Then I put myself** on my belly,
my arms bent in his presence.
162–65 Then he gave me a shipment of myrrh and *ḥknw*-oil,
jwdnb-resin, *ẖzꜣyt*-resin, *tj-šps* wood,
šꜣꜥzẖ plants, galena, tails of giraffe,

big lumps of incense, teeth of elephant,
hounds, monkeys, apes:
every good specialty.

166 **Then I loaded it** onto that boat.

This section consists of an opening couplet followed by a list of thirteen kinds of goods given to the sailor by the snake. It is not certain that the list adheres to the verse form of the story or is a prose insert, but if it is in verse, it is an unusual stanza of six lines (a sestet). The section ends with a single line.

161 For the second line, see the note to the same clause in Episode 8 (cols. 87–88).

162–65 *zbt* — a verbal noun from *zbj* "send": i.e., something to be "sent" with the sailor.

ʿntjw ḥknw jwdnb ḫzꜣyt — these first four items are the ones the sailor promised to send to the snake in Episode 12.

tj-šps — an aromatic kind of wood.

šꜣʿzḫ — an unknown kind of plant. The word is apparently not Egyptian.

msdmt — a lead mineral, used by the Egyptians for black eye-paint.

sdw nw mjmj — giraffe tails were prized by the Egyptians as fly-whisks.

mryt ʿꜣt nt snṯr — *mryt* is a collective (§ 4.6).

nḏḥyt nt ꜣbw — i.e., elephant-tusk ivory. *nḏḥyt* is also a collective.

ṯzmw gwfw kyw — hounds were desirable for hunting; monkeys and apes were kept as pets.

166 Despite the red ink, this line belongs with this section; the scribe apparently used it here at the top of a new column.

Episode 14 — Departure (lines 166–172)

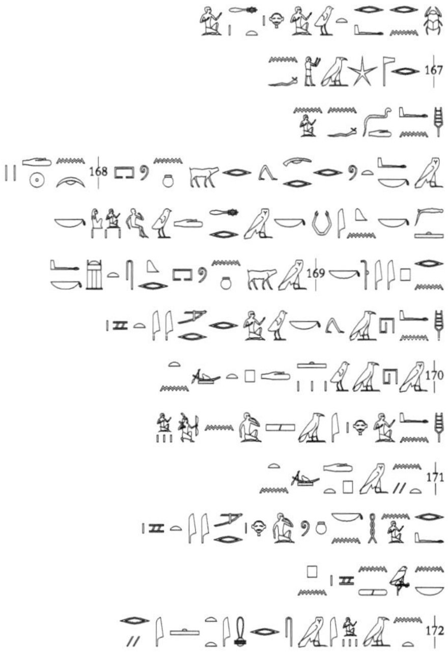

166–67	*ḫpr.n rdjt.(j) wj ḥr ẖt.j*	3
	r dwꜣ n.f nṯr	2
167–68	*ꜥḥꜥ.n ḏd.n.f n.j*	2
	mj.k tw r spr r ḫnw n jbd 2	3
168–69	*mḥ.k qnj.k m ẖrdw.k*	3
	rnpy.k m ḫnw qrst.k	3
169–70	*ꜥḥꜥ.n.(j) hꜣ.kw r mryt*	3
	m hꜣw dpt tn	1
170–71	*ꜥḥꜥ.n.j ḥr jꜣš n mšꜥ*	3
	ntj m dpt tn	2
171–72	*rdj.n.j ḥknw ḥr mryt*	3
	n nb n jw pn	2
	ntjw jm.s r mjtt jrj	4

166–67 Once I had put myself on my belly
to thank him,

167–68 then he said to me,
“Look, you are to arrive home in two months.
168–69 You will fill your embrace with your children
and be rejuvenated inside your entombment.”
169–70 Then I went down to the shore
in that boat’s vicinity.
170–71 Then I was calling to the expedition
that was in that boat.
171–72 I gave praise on the shore
to the lord of that island,
and those who were in it did likewise.

166–67 *ḫpr.n rdjt.(j) wj ḥr ẖt.j* — *rdjt.(j)* is the infinitive with an unwritten 1s suffix (cf. § 17.5) serving as subject of *ḫpr.n*: literally, “my putting myself on my belly happened.” This is the first half of a balanced sentence (§ 25.9), the second half of which is in the next couplet.

167–68 *mj.k tw r spr r ẖnw* — the pseudo-verbal construction connotes an involuntary future (§ 18.7). The verb *spr* “arrive” uses the preposition *r* to denote the goal of the action: literally, “arrive to the inside” (for *ẖnw*, see the note to col. 3 in Episode 1).

n jbd 2 — literally, “for two months”: see §§ 8.2.6 and 9.4.

168–69 *mḥ.k ... rnpy.k* — the *sḏm.f* connotes a voluntary future (§ 18.7). The second line refers to the rebirth of the spirit inside the tomb (Essay 8); it is an alternative way of expressing the same promise made by the snake in Episode 9 (col. 123), *m(w)t.k m njwt.k* “you will die in your town.”

169–71 *ꜥḥꜥ.n.j ḥr jꜣš* — the pseudo-verbal construction after *ꜥḥꜥ.n* (§ 14.6). *jꜣš* is a common Middle Kingdom spelling of the verb *ꜥš*, reflecting the change of the initial ayin to a glottal stop (*ꜥiš > ’iš).

mšꜥ ntj m dpt tn — a marked direct relative clause (§ 22.3). For *mšꜥ*, see the note in Episode 1 (col. 8).

171–72 *ntjw jm.s r mjtt jrj* — a direct marked relative clause used as a noun (§ 22.4). The suffix of *jm.s* refers to feminine *dpt* “boat.” *r mjtt jrj* means literally, “with respect to the likeness thereunto,” with the adverbial form of the preposition *r* (§ 8.2.7).

Episode 15 — The Sailor's Return Home (lines 172–176 and cols. 177–79)

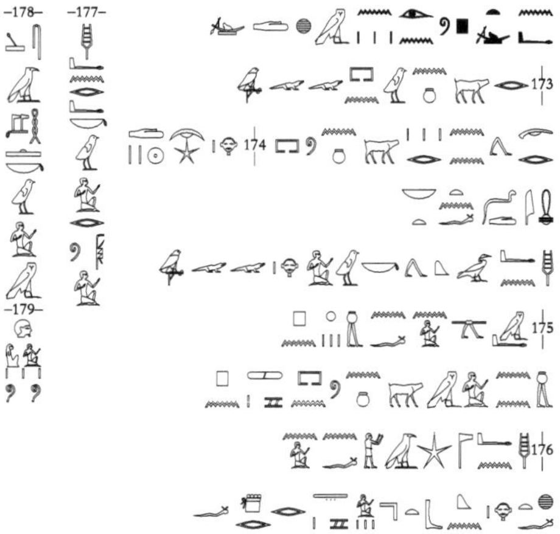

172–73	***nꜥt pw jr.n.n*** *m ḫd*	3
	r ẖnw n jtj	2
173–74	*spr.n.n r ẖnw ḥr jbd 2*	3
	mj ḏdt.n.f nbt	1
174–75	*ꜥḥꜥ.n.(j) ꜥq.kw ḥr jtj*	3
	mjz.n.j n.f jnw pn	2
	jn.n.j m ẖnw n jw pn	3
176	*ꜥḥꜥ.n dwꜣ.n.f n.j nṯr*	3
	ḫft ḥr qnbt tꜣ r ḏr.f	3
177–79	*ꜥḥꜥ.n.(j) rdj.kw r šmsw*	3
	sꜣḥ.kw m dp 200	2

172–73	**What we did was to sail** downstream
	to home and the sire.
173–74	We arrived home in month two,
	like all that he had said.
174–75	Then I entered to the sire
	and presented him with the cargo
	that I had gotten inside that island.
176	Then he thanked me
	in front of the council and the whole land.
177–79	Then I was appointed follower
	and endowed with two hundred servants.

This section ends the sailor's story. The scribe reverted to columns at the end of the papyrus, again for unknown reasons.

172–74 *nꜥt pw jr.n.n* — a *sḏm pw jr.n.f* construction (§§ 13.14.3, 22.24).

m ḫd — literally, "in going downstream"; *ḫd* is a verbal noun (§ 13.11.2). The phrase here refers to sailing north, since the island was in the Red Sea (see the note to *bjꜣ* in Episode 2).

r ẖnw n jtj — this can also be read "to the home of the sire," as a reference to the capital (Memphis or Lisht), but the interpretation of *n* as the preposition rather than the indirect genitive makes somewhat better sense; see § 8.2.6.

spr.n.n ... ḥr jbd 2 — an emphatic sentence with rhematic prepositional phrase (§§ 25.6; 25.13.2). Note the use of the preposition *ḥr* "upon" here as opposed to *n* "in" in Episode 14 (line 168): the latter implies that the voyage would take at least two months, and the former indicates that that was in fact the case.

mj ḏdt.n.f nbt — see the note to col. 155 *mj srt.n.f ḫnt* in Episode 14.

174–75 *ꜥḥꜥ.n.(j) ꜥq.kw ḥr jtj* — SUBJECT–stative as a past tense after *ꜥḥꜥ.n* (§ 16.8). In Egyptian, one enters (*ꜥq*) *r* "to" a place but *ḥr* "upon" a person.

mjz.n.j — the verb is *mzj*; the biliteral *mj* (Sign List D 38, here written as D 36) is often used after *m* in words beginning with that consonant, probably representing a syllable *ma.

jnw pn jn.n.j — *jnw* means basically things that have been "gotten" (*jnj*) from somewhere. It is often used to refer to goods brought back from an expedition or presented to the king as tribute. *jn.n.j* is the masculine singular relative *sḏm.n.f* used after a defined antecedent (§ 22.12).

176 *ḫft ḥr qnbt tꜣ r ḏr.f* — note that this is the same phrase that the sailor used in promising that the snake would be thanked (Episode 10, line 144).

177–79 *ꜥḥꜥ.n.(j) rdj.kw r šmsw* — literally, "then I was given to (be) follower." The stative is used here to express the passive with a pronominal subject (§ 19.3). For the sense of the preposition *r*, see the first example in § 25.7. *šmsw* here refers to the rank of "follower" (see the note to col. 1, above) rather than to a person.

sꜣḥ.kw — a second stative dependent on *ꜥḥꜣ.n*. The verb *sꜣḥ* "toe" (see Episode 3, col. 34) is, for some reason, also used of endowing someone with property.

dp 200 — literally, "two hundred head": *dp* "head" is sometimes used when speaking of servants, similar to the English idiom *head of cattle*. The number is absurdly large, in keeping with the fantastic nature of the story.

Episode 16 — The End of the Story (cols. 179–86)

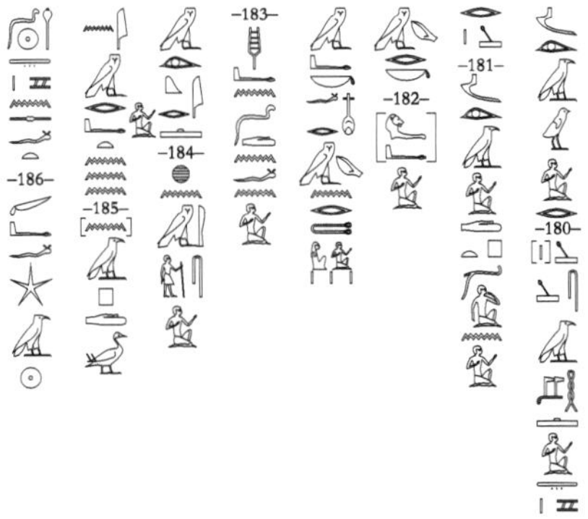

179–81 *mꜣ wj r sꜣ sꜣḥ.j tꜣ* 3
r sꜣ mꜣ.j dpt.n.j 2
181–82 *sḏm r.k [ḥꜣt(j)-ꜥ]* 2
mj.k nfr sḏm n rmṯ 3
183–84 *ꜥḥꜥ.n ḏd.n.f n.j* 2
m jr jqr ḫnms 3
184–86 *jn mj rdjt mw [n] ꜣpd* 4
ḥḏ tꜣ n zft.f dwꜣ 4

179–81 See me, after my touching land,
after my seeing what I have tasted.
181–82 So, listen, high official:
look, it is good for people to listen.
183–84 Then he said to me,
"Don't act so accomplished, friend.
184–86 What is the point of giving water to a bird
at the dawn of its slaughter in the morning?"

After the end of the sailor's narrative, the story itself ends with a final exchange between the sailor and the official. The tops of cols. 177–89 are damaged, with some signs lost (restored here in brackets). This part of the papyrus was on the tightly rolled inside when the papyrus was rolled up.

179–81 *mꜣ wj* — imperative (§ 15.1). The sense is "see how I have turned out."

r sꜣ sꜣḥ.j tꜣ — *r sꜣ* is a compound preposition (§ 8.3): literally, "with respect to the back." For *sꜣḥ.j tꜣ*, see the note to col. 34 in Episode 3. *sꜣḥ.j* could be the *sḏm.f*, as in col. 34 (and col. 103) but is more probably the infinitive here (§ 13.4.2). The phrase here means "after returning from my ordeal."

r sꜣ mꜣ.j dpt.n.j — *mꜣ.j* is the same form as *sꜣḫ.j*; for the infinitive, see § 13.3.2c. This phrase echoes the snake's observation at the beginning of Episode 9. For *dpt.n.j*, see the note to line 124 there.

181–82 *sḏm* — the sense of the verb here is not merely "listen" but "heed": *mrr sḏm pw jrr ḏdt* "One who does what is said is one who loves hearing" (Ptahhotep 554: Exercise 24, no. 8).

nfr sḏm n rmṯ — an adjectival sentence with the infinitive as subject. The sentence could mean "listening to people is good," but wisdom texts such as the Instruction of Ptahhotep (Essay 19) use the term in the sense of a pupil listening to a teacher.

183–84 *m jr jqr* — literally, "don't act the accomplished one."

184–86 *jn mj rdjt mw n ꜣpd* — an A B nominal sentence with interrogative *jn mj* as A and the infinitive *rdjt* as B (§ 7.13.1): literally, "what is giving water to a bird?"

ḥḏ tꜣ n zft.f dwꜣ — literally, "when the land becomes bright for his slaughter in the morning." *ḥḏ tꜣ* is a *sḏm.f* used as an unmarked adverb clause (§ 20.11); the "land brightening" is an idiom for "dawn" (§ 25.8.3). *zft.f* is an infinitive with suffix pronoun as object (§ 13.5.1). *dwꜣ* "morning" is a noun used adverbially (§ 8.14). The sentence as a whole means "What is the point of giving water to a bird at dawn when it's going to be slaughtered that morning?" The metaphor indicates that the official expects the king to punish him for the failure of his expedition — though not necessarily by death — and therefore considers the sailor's advice, to persevere in the face of hardship, useless to him. This pessimistic reaction to an "instruction" is unusual, but it may have been intended as a second moral to the story, pointing out the fate of one who does not "listen."

The Colophon (cols. 186–89)

jw.f pw ḥ3t.f r pḥ(wj).fj mj gmyt m zẖ3
[m] zẖ3 zẖ3w jqr n ḏbꜥw.f
z3-jmny jmn-ꜥ3.(w) ꜥnḫ-wḏ3-snb

That is how it goes, beginning to end, like what has been found in writing, in the writing of the scribe of accomplished fingers,
Ameny's son Amenaa, lph.

As is common in literary papyri, the colophon gives the name of the scribe who penned the papyrus rather than that of the text's author. This part of the text is in prose rather than verse.

jw.f pw — an A *pw* nominal sentence with the *sḏm.f* in an umarked noun clause as A (§ 21.12): literally, "it is (that) it comes."

ḥ3t.f r pḥ(wj).fj — literally, "its front to its end." The dual strokes after the second suffix pronoun indicate that the noun is in the dual: see the comment to col. 85 *gs(wj).fj* in Episode 7. The noun *pḥ* "end" is often used in the dual even when only one "end" is meant.

mj gmyt m zẖ3 — *gmyt* is a passive participle (§ 24.1). This phrase indicates that the papyrus was copied from another manuscript.

jqr n ḏbꜥw.f — the *nfr ḥr* construction with an indirect genitive (§ 6.5): literally, "one accomplished of his fingers."

z3-jmny jmn-ꜥ3.(w) ꜥnḫ-wḏ3-snb — as usual in Middle Kingdom texts, the father's name is put first, in honorific transposition (§ 4.15). The son's name is a SUBJECT–stative construction, meaning "Amun is great" (§ 16.10). For *ꜥnḫ-wḏ3-snb* "lph," see § 20.9.2. While this phrase is used mostly for royalty and superiors, it can also be applied to ordinary people: see the letter quoted in Lesson 25.

BIBLIOGRAPHY

Allen, James P. "The Historical Inscription of Khnumhotep at Dahshur: Preliminary Report." *Bulletin of the American Schools of Oriental Research* 352 (November, 2008), 29–39.

Berg, David. "Syntax, Semantics and Physics: the Shipwrecked Sailor's Fire." *Journal of Egyptian Archaeology* 76 (1990), 168–70.

Berlev, Oleg. *Общественные отношения в Египте эпохи Среднего царства.* Moscow, 1978.

Bolshakov, Andrey O. "Some *de visu* Observations on P. Hermitage 1115." *Journal of Egyptian Archaeology* 79 (1993), 254–59.

Derchain-Urtel, Maria T. "Die Schlange des 'Schiffbrüchigen'." *Studien zur Altägyptischen Kultur* 1 (1974), 83–104.

Foster, John L. "'The Shipwrecked Sailor': Prose or Verse? (Postponing Clauses and Tense-neutral Clauses)." *Studien zur Altägyptischen Kultur* 15 (1988), 69–109.

Franke, Detlef. "Kleiner Mann (*nḏs*) — was bist Du?" *Göttinger Miszellen* 167 (1998), 33–48.

Gardiner, Alan H. "Notes on the Tale of the Shipwrecked Sailor." *Zeitschrift für ägyptische Sprache und Altertumskunde* 45 (1908), 60–66.

————. *Egyptian Grammar*. Oxford, 1927.

Golenishchev, Vladimir. *Le conte du naufragé*. Bibliothèque d'Étude 2. Cairo, 1912.

————. *Les papyrus hiératiques no. 1115, 1116 A et 1116 B de l'Ermitage Impérial à St.-Pétersbourg*. St Petersburg, 1913.

Graefe, Erhart. "*mkꜣ*  'aufmerksam sein', 'erkennen' und der ramessidische Gebetsanruf *mkꜣ.tw ḫft sḏm.tw*." In *Decorum and Experience: Essays in Ancient Culture for John Baines*, ed. by E. Frood and A. McDonald (Oxford, 2013), 43–46.

Manniche, Lise. *An Ancient Egyptian Herbal*. London and Austin, 1989.

Simpson, William K. "Allusions to *The Shipwrecked Sailor* and *The Eloquent Peasant* in a Ramesside Text." *Journal of the American Oriental Society* 78 (1958), 50–51.

Vandersleyen, Claude. "En relisant le Naufragé." In Sarah Israelit-Groll, ed., *Studies in Egyptology presented to Miriam Lichtheim* (Jerusalem, 1990), 1019–24.

Text 2
The Story of Sinuhe

THIS TEXT is widely considered the greatest of all Middle Kingdom literary compositions. It was also revered by the ancient Egyptians themselves, surviving in five Middle Kingdom papyri, two New Kingdom papyri, and twenty-five New Kingdom ostraca, all in hieratic. None of these preserves the full story, and many are only fragments. The texts presented here are the five Middle Kingdom copies:

B — pBerlin 3022 and pAmherst n–q

The beginning of the story is lost (to R 5), but the papyrus otherwise preserves the full text, including a colophon at the end (without the scribe's name).[1] It has the best Middle Kingdom version of the tale but is not always the most reliable of the copies. Parkinson 2012, CD folder "Pap. Berlin P. 3022 The Tale of Sinuhe B."

La — pUCL 32106C

A fragment of six columns (R 24–32 = B 1–8): Collier and Quirke 2004, 35 and CD file "UC32106B-b."

H — pUCL 32773

A fragment of four columns (B 103–10). Gardiner 1916, 177–78, and Koch 1990, 45–46 (vertical arragement reconstructed).

BA — papyrus in the Museum of Natural History, Buenos Aires

A fragment of eleven columns (B 251–57). Rosenvasser 1934.

R — pRamesseum A (Berlin 10499), verso

This is the only copy written completely in horizontal lines,[2] and the only one that preserves the beginning of the story; the end is lost. It has a number of additions not found in earlier manuscripts, which were also reproduced in some New Kingdom copies. The recto is inscribed with a copy of the Eloquent Peasant (Text 5). Gardiner 1909, with addition in Koch 1990, 39–41.

1 Some 20 columns of the beginning are lost except for pAmherst n–q (Parkinson 2009, 92 n. 45). These and lines B 1–177 are vertical. B 178–276 are horizontal, in seven pages (178–92, 193–206, 207–19, 220–34, 235–48, 249–62, 263–76). Vertical columns resume to the end of the papyrus (B 277–311).

2 R 1–78 is in thirteen pages of six lines each; R 79–85, one page of seven lines; R 86–97, two pages of six lines each; R 98–139, seven pages of six lines each; and R 140–203, eight pages of eight lines each.

B can be dated to the period of the coregency between Senwosret III and Amenemhat III (ca. 1859–1840 BC: see pp. 115, 229, and 238); La, H, and BA are roughly contemporary with one another, and with B; and R dates to the first part of Dyn. XIII or slightly earlier. The story is set in the reign of Senwosret I (ca. 1961–1917 BC), beginning with the death of his father and coregent, Amenemhat I (ca. 1952 BC), and is at least as old as the early reign of Amenemhat III.[3]

With the exception of its opening section, the story is composed in verse. It follows the model of older and contemporary tomb biographies (Essay 21) but is purely a work of literature; there is no evidence for an historical individual corresponding to the story's hero, nor for his tomb described at the end of the tale. Other genres reflected in the composition are travel journals (Essay 21), hymns (Essay 23), and letters (Essay 25).

The historical background to the story is the death of Amenemhat I in his thirtieth regnal year and the tenth of his coregency with his son, Senwosret I. Amenemhat was the first king of Dyn. XII, possibly vizier under the last king of Dyn. XI, Mentuhotep IV. Historical records reflect significant opposition to his rule, and a New Kingdom literary text, the Instruction of Amenemhat, indicates that he was the target of an attempted assassination. Whether or not that was the cause of the death recorded in the story, his demise would have been an occasion for the opposition to coalesce against his successor, Senwosret I.

In the story, Sinuhe is a servant of Queen Neferu, daughter of Amenemhat I and sister and wife of Senwosret I (for such relationships, see Essay 3). When Sinuhe hears of Amenemhat's death, he fears that he will be targeted by the opposition along with the royal family, and flees Egypt. Eventually, he settles in Syria, where he becomes a successful tribal leader. After a climactic battle against a more powerful opponent (reminiscent of the story of David and Goliath in the Bible), however, he begins to long for home, concerned about a proper burial for his afterlife. Senwosret I hears of Sinuhe's exploits and sends him a letter urging him to return. Though Sinuhe fears the king's retribution because he doubted Senwosret's ability to prevail against any opposition, he does return to Egypt. Instead of being punished, he is rewarded with riches and a tomb in the royal cemetery.

As a literary composition, the Story of Sinuhe falls into the Middle Kingdom genre of works extolling the king and urging loyalty to him. Its moral, trust in the king, is similar to that of another Middle Kingdom composition, the Loyalist Instruction (Text 3).

3 A citation from the text appears in an inscription dating to the end of the reign of Senwosret III or the beginning of the reign of Amenemhat III: Allen 2008, 36. For later citations, see Parkinson 2009, 176–80.

Prologue — Sinuhe's Titles (B Am1, R 1–5)

B Am1

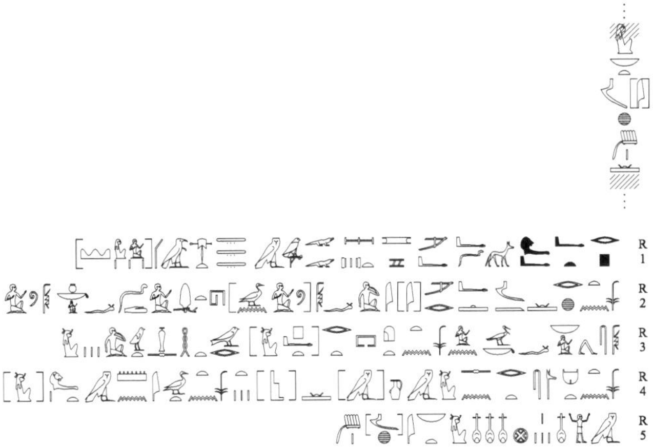

R 1 ***(j)rj-pꜥt ḥꜣt(j)-ꜥ*** *zꜣb*
ꜥḏ-mr spꜣ[w]t jtj m tꜣw sttjw
R 2 *rḫ-nswt mꜣꜥ mry.f šms[w zꜣ-n]ht ḏd.f*
R 2–3 *jnk šmsw šms nb.f*
bꜣk n jpꜣt-nswt (j)rt-[pꜥt] wrt ḥzwt
R 4 *ḥjmt-nswt-z-n-wsrt m ẖnm-[js]wt*
R 5 *zꜣt-nswt-jmn-m-ḥꜣt m qꜣ-nfrw*
nfrw nbt jmꜣḫ

R 1 **Member of the elite, high official**, dignitary,
administrator of the sire's estates in the Asiatics' land,
R 2 true king's acquaintance, whom he desired, follower Sinuhe, who says:
R 2–3 I am a follower who follows his lord,
king's-apartment servant of the member of the elite, great of blessing,
R 4 king's wife of Senwosret in United of Places,
R 5 king's daughter of Amenemhat in High of Perfection,
Neferu, possessor of honor.

Following the model of tomb biographies, the story's prologue lists the titles of Sinuhe, followed by *ḏd.f* "who says" (§ 22.16) and a short exposition of his responsibilities. This part of the tale is in prose.

R 1 *(j)r(j) pꜥt* — literally, "one who pertains to the elite." The first word is the nisbe of the preposition *r* (§ 8.6.4). *pꜥt* is a collective referring to the ruling elite; see Essay 3.

zꜣb — a ranking title of uncertain meaning; "dignitary" is a conventional translation.

ꜥḏ-mr — literally, "canal hacker," usually written . The title originally identified the man entitled to breach the side of a canal during the inundation season to let the water flood the field. Eventually it designated the administrator in charge of royal domains in the Delta or (as in this case) the desert (*ḫꜣst*, including foreign lands: see Essay 2).

sttjw — literally, "shooters," a masculine plural nisbe of a feminine noun "bow," from the verb *sṯj* "shoot." The term identified settled peoples in/from the lands east of Egypt, as opposed to the nomadic *nmjw-šꜥ* "sand-trekkers" (see the note to B 73, below).

R 2 *rḫ-nswt mꜣꜥ mry.f* — title identifying Sinuhe as someone with access to the king. *rḫ-nswt* and *mry.f* are both relative *sḏm.f*s, and *mꜣꜥ* is an adjective modifying the first.

zꜣ-nht — the name means "The Sycamore's Son" and is an alternative form of the more common Middle Kingdom name *zꜣ-ḥwt-ḥrw* "Hathor's Son"; the sycamore was associated with Hathor.

R 3 *jpꜣt* — term denoting the private quarters of a home (or palace). Sinuhe was an attendant of the queen and her children.

R 3–5 *(j)rt-pꜥt ... nbt jmꜣḫ* — This is a second object of the indirect genitive following *bꜣk*.

ḥjmt-nswt-z-n-wsrt ... zꜣt-nswt-jmn-m-ḥꜣt — the addition of the royal names (without cartouche) was necessary because, at the time of the story, there were two *nswt*'s, Amenemhat I and his coregent, Senwosret I.

ẖnm-jswt ... qꜣ-nfrw — the names of the two kings' palaces.

nfrw — as the story indicates, she was the daughter of Amenemhat I and wife of Senwosret I. She was also the mother of the next king, Amenemhat II.

nbt jmꜣḫ — see Essay 21.

Episode 1 — The Death of Amenemhat I (B Am 2–An1, R 5–11)

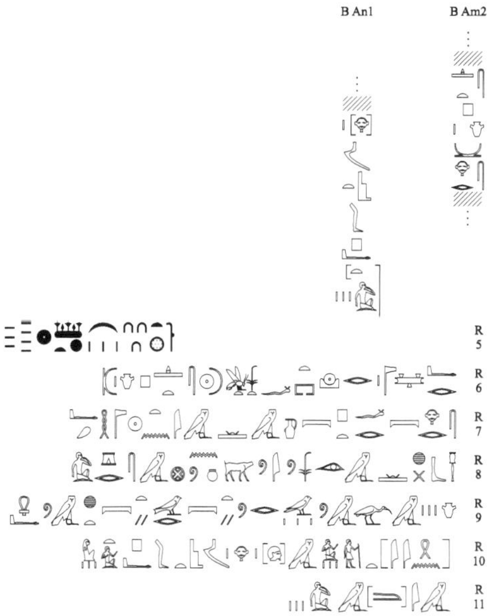

R 5	***rnpt-ḥsb 30 3 ꜣḫt 7***	(heading)
R 6–7	*ꜥr nṯr r ꜣḫt.f nswt-bjt SḤTP-JB-Rꜥ*	4
	sḥr.f r pt ẖnm.(w) m jtn	4
	ḥꜥ-nṯr ꜣbḫ.(w) m jr sw	3
R 8–9	*jw ẖnw m sgr*	2
	jbw m gmw	2
	rwtj wrtj ḫtm.w	2
R 10–11	*[šny]t m [dp] ḥr mꜣst*	3
	pꜥt m jmw	2

R 5 **Regnal year 30, 3 Inundation 7**.

R 6–7 The god's ascent to his Akhet, Dual King Sehetepibre,
going off to the sky, united with the sun-disk,
the god's body mingled with the one who made it.

R 8–9 The residence was in stillness,
minds in grief,
the great double gate shut,

R 10–11 the circle with head on lap,
the elite in mourning.

The story proper begins with an historical event, described in the style of ancient Egyptian annals (Essay 21), with a date in the civil calendar followed by an infinitive.

R 5 See §§ 9.8–9. The date is approximately Feb. 12, 1952 BC.

R 6–7 *ꜥr nṯr* — infinitive with nominal subject (§ 13.4.1). This passage was copied in the Dyn. XVIII tomb biography of Amenemhab, to describe the death of Thutmose III (approximately Feb. 27, 1425 BC).

rnpt-ḥsb 54 3 prt ꜥrqy ḫr [ḥm] n nswt-bjt MN-ḪPR-Rꜥ mꜣꜥ ḫrw
sḥr.f r pt ẖnm.(w) m jtn
ḥꜥw-nṯr ꜣbḫ m jr sw (Urk. IV, 895, 16 – 896, 3)
Regnal Year 54, 3 Growing last, during the Incarnation of the Dual King Menkheperre, justified,
he going off to the sky, united with the sun-disk,
the god's body mingled with the one who made it.

SḤTP-JB-Rꜥ — the throne name of Amenemhat I, meaning "he who content's the Sun's mind." In hieratic, usually only the beginning and end of the cartouche sign are drawn.

R 8–9 *ẖnw* — the residence was at the new capital of Lisht, founded by Amenemhat I. See the map on p. 67, below.

rwtj wrtj — the two leaves of the gate at the entrance of the palace.

R 10–11 *šnyt m dp ḥr mꜣst* — the *šnyt* was the circle of family and officials with immediate access to the king. "Head on lap" was a traditional posture of mourning.

Episode 2 — Senwosret Receives the News (B An2–Ap3, R 11–22)

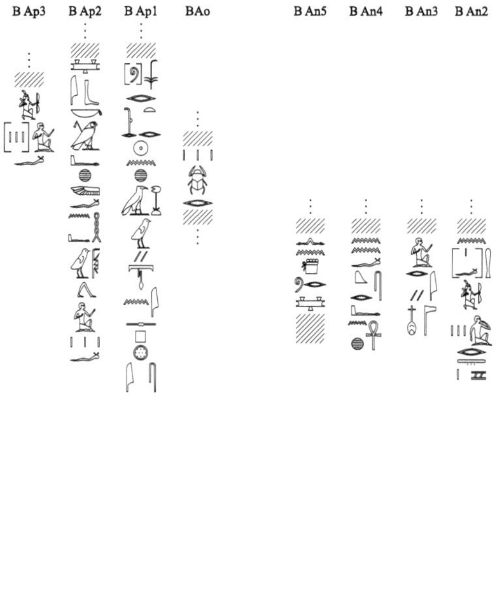

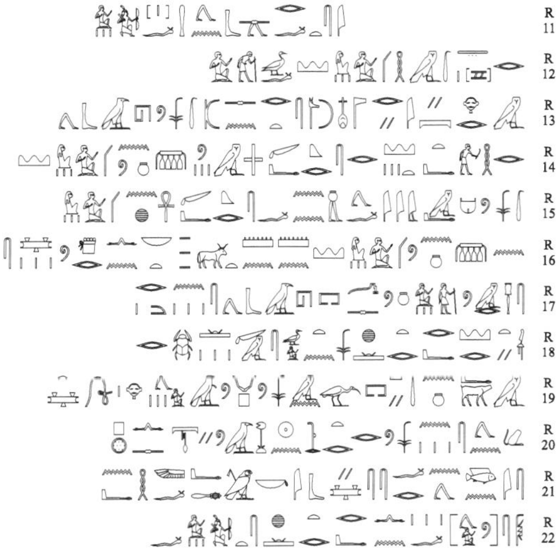

R 11–13 *jst r.f zb.n ḥm.f mšꜥ r tꜣ tjmḥw* 4
zꜣ.f smsw m ḥrj jrj 4
nṯr nfr Z(J)-N-WSRT 2
R 13–14 *tj sw hꜣb.(w) r ḥwt ḫꜣswt* 2
r sqr jmjw ṯḥnw 1
R 15–16 *tj sw ḥm jy.f* 1
jn.n.f sqrw-ꜥnḫ n ṯḥnw 3
mnmnt nbt nn ḏrw.s 2
R 17–19 *smrw nw stp-z(ꜣ) hꜣb.sn r gs jmntj* 5
r rdjt rḫ zꜣ-nswt 2
sšmw ḫpr.(w) m ꜥḫnwtj 3
R 19–20 *gm.n sw wpwtjw ḥr wꜣt* 3
pḥ.n.sn sw r tr n ḫꜣwj 3
R 20–22 *nj zp sjnn.f rssj* 3
bjk ꜥḫ.f ḥnꜥ šmsw.f 3
nn rdjt rḫ st mšꜥ.f 3

R 11–13 Now, His Incarnation had sent an expedition to the land of the Tamahu,
his eldest son in charge of it,
the young god Senwosret,
R 13–14 he having been sent to hit the deserts
and to smash those in Tjehenu.

R 15–16 And as he was returning,
having gotten captives of the Tjehenu
and every kind of herd without limit,
R 17–19 the courtiers of the escort were sending word to the western side
to let the king's son know
events had happened in the audience-hall.
R 19–20 The messengers found him on the way;
they reached him at the time of dusk.
R 20–22 He did not dally at all:
the falcon flew off with his followers
without letting his expeditionary force know it.

R 11–13 *jst r.f* — see §§ 20.3.

tjmḥw — term denoting the Libyan desert from the region of the Fayum south into Nubia.

nṯr nfr — a term applied to the king in contrast to his father, the *nṯr ꜥꜣ* "great god." In most cases, the latter is the previous, deceased king, but during coregencies it denoted the senior king and *nṯr nfr*, his junior partner. The text uses Senwosret's nomen rather than his throne name (*ḫpr-kꜣ-rꜥ*), presumably because of his junior status.

R 13–14 *tj* — see § 20.4.

ṯḥnw — literally, "Glittering." The term refers to the white sands of northern Libya, and denotes the area from the region of the Fayum north to the Mediterranean coast. The initial description of Sinuhe's flight in R 29 / B 6 places the campaign in the desert west of the Delta.

R 15–16 *tj sw ḥm jy.f* — although it is the latest Middle Kingdom copy, R represents a dialect in which the SUBJECT–*sḏm.f* construction has its original connotation of a progressive rather than its later gnomic sense (§ 18.6).

sqrw-ꜥnḫ — literally, "those smashed alive" (passive participle with qualifying stative). The term refers to enemy survivors of a battle who were taken captive.

R 17–19 *stp-z(ꜣ)* — the term is usually written  and means, literally, "choosing protection." It is used to refer to escort duty around the king. With the "house" determinative, as here, it refers to the area of the royal residence within which the king was protected by guards.

sšmw ḫpr.(w) m ꜥḫnwtj —a SUBJECT–stative construction used as an unmarked noun clause (§ 21.7); *ḫpr* is written without plural strokes in all copies and is therefore the stative rather than an active participle. *ꜥḫnwtj* denotes the area of the palace in which the king appeared on his throne to receive officials, foreign delegates, and other visitors. This line seems to indicate that Amenemhat I died at such an occasion.

R 20–22 *nj zp sjnn.f* — the verb is written similarly, with two s before the determinative, in all copies. Since the construction uses the *sḏm.f* (§ 18.13), and not the *sḏm.n.f*, the verb is apparently a geminated form of *sjnj* "delay"; the stem suggests a meaning of extended or multiple "delay." B Ap1 has interpreted  as a writing of the particle *jn* (§ 15.6.2); this is the case later in the story, but at this point only the negation makes sense.

bjk ꜥẖ.f — both B and R have the same wording, although B Ap2 has *ꜥḫ.f*, either a dialectal variant or a later form of *ꜥẖ.f* (B's form is also present in New Kingdom copies). In R, SUBJECT–*sḏm.f* (§ 18.6) has the older progressive value (see the note to B 1–2, below): "the falcon was flying off." In B, however, it is usually gnomic but also expresses the simple past, as here.

Episode 3 — Sinuhe Hears the News (B Ap2–5, La 1–4, R 22–29)

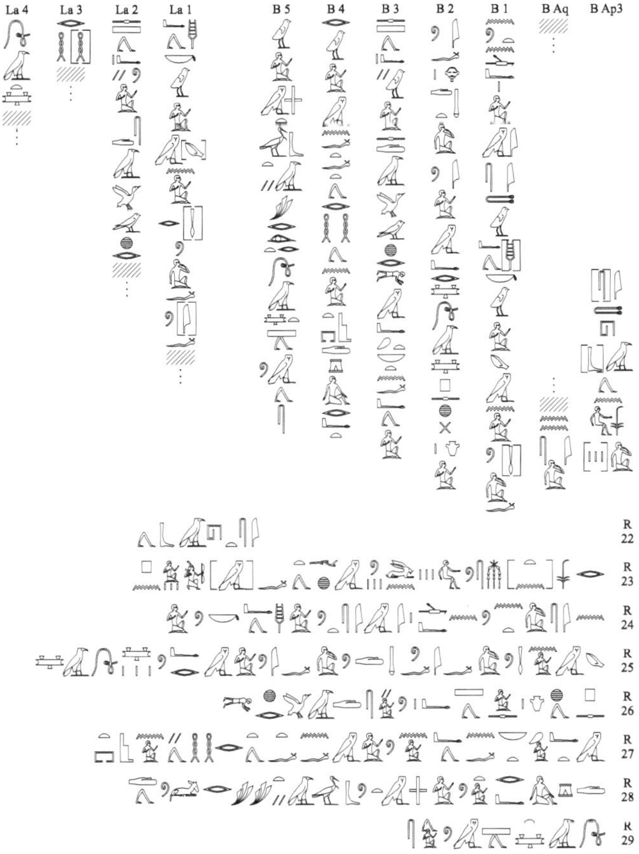

B Ap3– *j[s]ṯ hꜣ[b] n ms[w]-nswt* 2
B1 *[wnw m ḫt.f m mšꜥ p]n* 3
njs.n.tw n wꜥ jm jsṯ wj [ꜥḥ]ꜥ.kw 3

B 1–2	*sḏm.n.j [ḫr]w.f jw.f ḥr mdt*	3	
	jw.j m ꜥr wꜣ		2
B 2–3	*pzḫ jb.j zn ꜥwj.j*	4	
	sdꜣ ḫr.(w) m ꜥt nbt		3
B 3–4	*nfꜥ.j {r} wj m nftft*	2	
	r ḥ(j)ḥ(j) n.j jst dg		2
B 4–5	*r djt.(j) wj jmt bꜣtj*	2	
	r jrt wꜣt šmw.s		3

B Ap3– B 1 But word was sent to the king's children
who were in his following in this expedition,
and one of them was summoned while I was in attendance.

B 1–2 I heard his voice as he was speaking,
while I was on a rise some distance away,

B 2–3 and my mind became confused, my arms spread out,
with trembling fallen on my every limb,

B 3–4 and I took myself off by leaps and bounds
to look for a place to hide

B 4–5 until I put myself between two bushes,
until the path made its going.

B Ap3– B 1 *hꜣ[b] ... njs.n.tw* — the two different forms focus attention on the verb itself (*hꜣb*) and on the adverb clause *jsṯ wj [ꜥḥ]ꜥ.kw* "while I was standing" (emphatic *njs.n.tw*).

B 1–2 *jw.f ḥr mdt* — R 25 has the more older form *jw.f mdw.f*: see § 20.11. The 3ms subjects refer to *wꜥ jm* "one of them" in the previous line.

jw.j m ꜥr wꜣ — literally, "I (was) on a distant rise." The noun *ꜥrw* is derived from the verb *ꜥr* "ascend." Sinuhe evidently means that he was within earshot but not party to the conversation.

B 2–3 *pzḫ jb.j zn ꜥwj.j* — two unmarked adverb clauses with the *sḏm.f*, expressing result (§ 20.13).

B 3–5 *nfꜥ.j wj* — the 𓂋 in B 3–4 is probably an error; it cannot be the self-referential phrase *r.(j)* "with respect to myself" (§ 15.7.2), since the word order in that case would be *nfꜥ.j wj r.(j)*. The *sḏm.f* in B, if legitimate (all other copies have the *sḏm.n.f*), continues the adverbial clauses of the preceding couplet.

r djt.(j) wj — the *sḏmt.f* after *r* (§ 19.14). A narrative infinitive *rdjt.j wj* (§ 13.14.2) is possible but unlikely: in this text, that use of the form marks the beginning of episodes, as in the first line of the next episode.

r jrt wꜣt šmw.s — probably also the *sḏmt.f*; the scribe of B often writes a complementary 𓂋 after 𓁹 in forms of the verb *jrj* with the ending *t*. R has a more comprehensible *r jwd wꜣt šmw.s* "separate from the path and its traveler." The absence of a seated-man determinative in B 5 suggests a verbal noun *šmw* "going." The clause probably refers to the departure of the rest of the expedition.

Episode 4 — Sinuhe's Flight: Stage One (B 5–10, La 4–6, R 29–34)

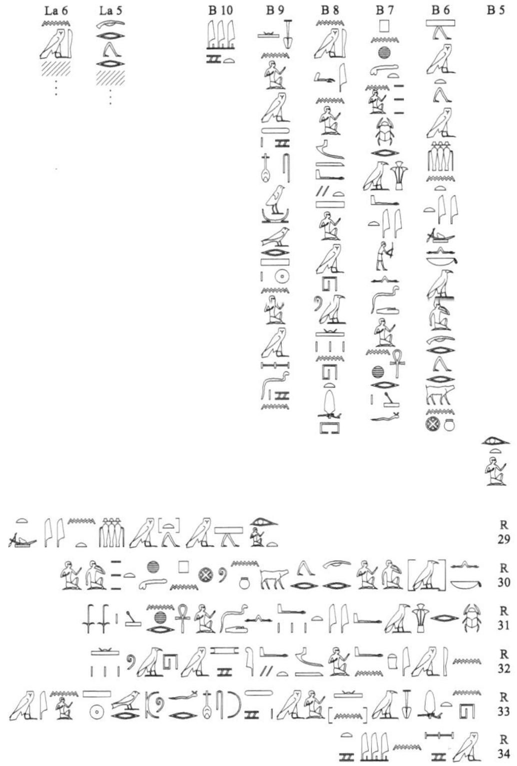

B 5–6	*jrt.j šmt m ḫntyt*	(heading)
B 6–7	*nj kꜣ.j spr r ẖnw pn*	3
	ḫmt.n.j ḫpr ḥꜣꜥyt	3
	nj ḏd.j ꜥnḫ r sꜣ.f	3
B 8–10	*nmj.n.j mꜣꜥtj{.j} m hꜣw nht*	3
	zmꜣ.n.j m jw SNFRW	2
	wrš.n.j m ꜥḏ n sḫt	3

B 5–6 My making off upstream.

B 6–7 I did not intend to arrive at that residence,
having anticipated that unrest would develop,
and I did not think to live after him.

B 8–10 I traversed Two-Maats Canal in the area of Sycamore,
landed at Snefru's Island,
and spent the day on the edge of the cultivation.

Sinuhe's flight begins with a journey southeast, from the Libyan desert to the edge of the cultivation near Dahshur.

B 5–6 Sinuhe's flight from Egypt is presented in journal form (Essay 21), with each major stage marked by an initial narrative infinitive (§ 13.14.2). For the places mentioned in the story, see the map on the next page.

jrt.j šmt — literally, "my making a going"; both forms are infinitives.

m ḫntyt — "upstream," meaning south. With the initial terminus of this first leg of the flight, this places the starting point in the Libyan desert west of the Delta.

B 6–7 *ḫmt.n.j* — the plural strokes are borrowed from the word *ḫmtw* "three" (§ 9.2). R 30 has *ḫmt.j* "anticipating."

nj ḏd.j — literally, "I did not say."

r sꜣ.f — the pronoun evidently refers to Amenemhat I. The demonstrative *nn* "that" in R 31 refers to *ḥꜣꜥyt* "unrest."

B 8–10 *mꜣꜥtj* — the name of a major canal between Memphis and Dahshur. The seated man is probably a misreading of the second determinative 𓈘 as in R 32.

nht — R 33 and all later texts write this word as if it refers to a tree, but the determinative in B 8 points to a structure. Evidently some kind of landmark is meant.

zmꜣ.n.j — the normal idiom is *zmꜣ tꜣ* "join land," a term for landing from a voyage on water; the object is omitted here. The use of the term refers to the eastern end of Sinuhe's crossing of the Two Maats canal.

jw SNFRW — the term *jw* "island" was used not only of land surrounded by water but also of an area of cultivation; the latter is meant here. The mention of Snefru probably indicates the region of Dahshur, where two of that king's three pyramids are located. "Snefru's Island" was probably a name for one of the agricultural estates supporting the pyramid cult.

wrš.n.j — R 33 adds *jm* "there."

m ꜥḏ n sḫt — the term *ꜥḏ* refers to the area where the agricultural land along the Nile met the desert; *sḫt* is a general term for agricultural land.

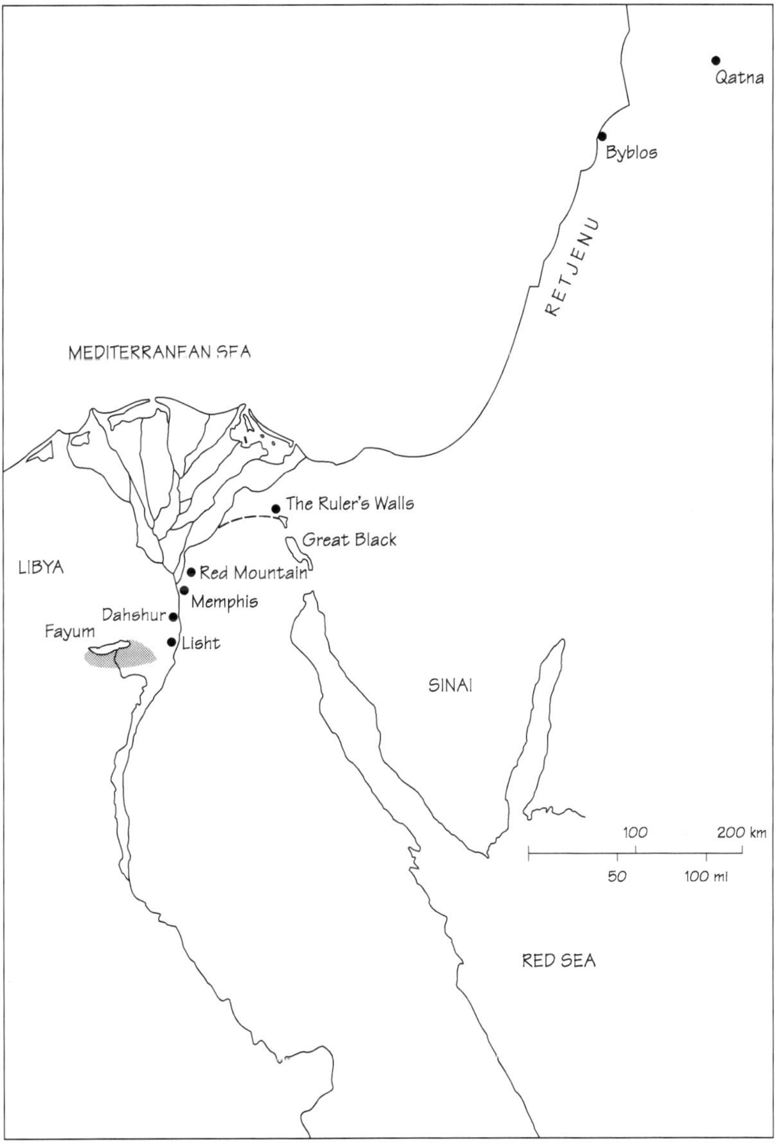

Map showing the major sites mentioned in the story of Sinuhe

Episode 5 — Sinuhe's Flight: Stage Two (B 10–15, R 34–41)

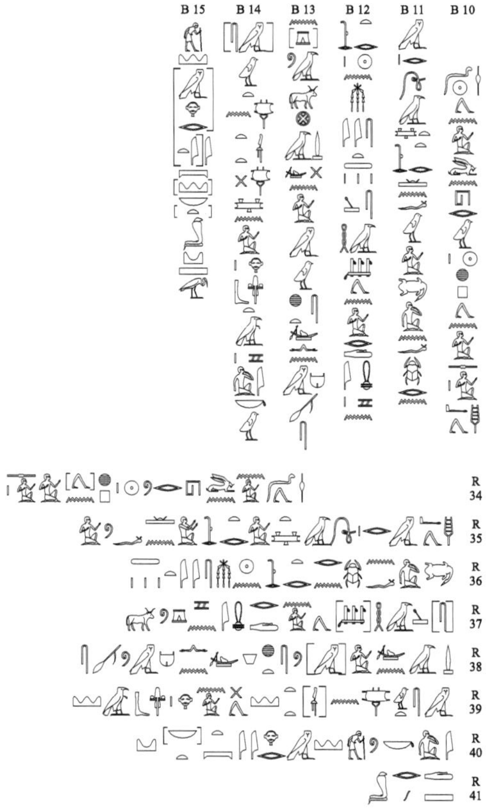

B 10–11	*wḏ.n.j wn hrw*	3
	ḫp.n.j zj ꜥḥꜥ.(w) m r wꜣt	4
	tr.n.f wj snḏ.(w) n.f	2
B 11–13	*ḫpr.n tr n msyt*	3
	sꜣḥ.n.j r dmj n n[g]ꜣw	3
B 13–14	*ḏꜣ.n.j m wsḫt nn ḥm.s*	3
	[m s]wt(j) n jmntt	2
B 14–15	*swꜣ.n.j ḥr jꜣbtjw jkw*	2
	[m ḥryt] nb[t] ḏw (d)š(r)	1

B 10–11 I set out when it was daytime
and met a man standing in the mouth of my path.
He avoided me, being afraid for himself.
B 11–13 When the time of supper came,
I set foot at Steer Harbor.
B 13–14 I crossed in a barge with no rudder,
by means of a gust of the west wind.
B 14–15 I passed by the eastern side of the quarry
on the upland of Red Mountain's Lady.

The second stage of Sinuhe's journey takes him across the Nile and into the desert east of modern Cairo.

B 10–11 *wḏ.n.j* — R 34 represents what is probably the original verb here, 3ae-inf. *wḏj*. B 10 adds the sun-disk determinative, probably from the similarity between and in hieratic, indicating that the scribe was thinking of 2-lit. *ḥḏ* "grow light." New Kingdom copies have followed B, without the walking legs, reinterpreting the passage as *ḥḏ n.j* "when it grew light for me."

tr.n.f wj — the verb is 3-lit. *twr* "show respect, keep away from," often written without the medial radical, like *mwt* "die."

snḏ.(w) n.f — The encounter points to a general atmosphere of apprehension and mistrust in the region following the death of Amenemhat I.

B 11–13 A good example of an emphatic sentence, in which the interest is not on the main clause (*ḫpr.n tr n msyt*) but on an adverbial adjunct (*sꜣḥ.n.j r dmj n ngꜣw*): literally, "the time of supper happened when I had set foot at Steer Harbor" (§ 25.8.3).

dmj n n[g]ꜣw — a site on the riverbank in the region of modern Giza, a day's walk (20 miles, 33 km) from the area of Dahshur.

B 13–14 *ḏꜣ.n.j m wsḫt nn ḥm.s* — that is, crossed from the west bank of the Nile to the east bank. A *wsḫt* is literally a "broad" boat. The fact that its wood rudder was missing suggests that Sinuhe appropriated an unattended boat after dark.

m swt(j) n jmntt — B 14 adds the sail determinative to the last word as well, indicating "west wind." The noun *swt(j)* is attested only here; the indirect genitive *n* indicates that it is masculine.

B 14–15 *jkw* — the limestone quarry of Tura, west of modern Cairo, source of the fine white limestone used in buildings and for the outer layer of pyramids.

nb[t] ḏw (d)š(r) — probably the name of the peak now known as Muqattam. The ancient name of the mountain range has survived in the Arabic name al-Gabal al-Aḥmar "the Red Mountain." The spelling of *dšr* "red" in B 15 is defective.

Episode 6 — Sinuhe's Flight: Stage Three (B 15–19, R 41–45)

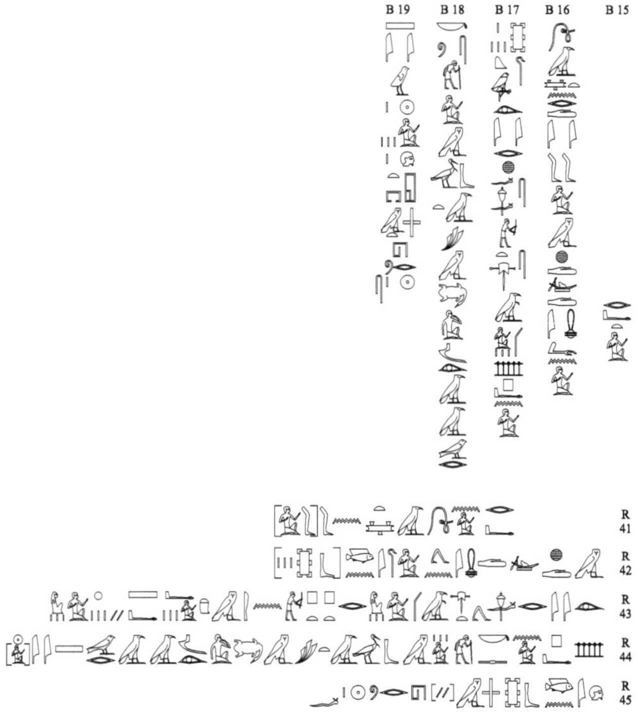

B 15–16 *rdjt.j wꜣt n rdwy.j m ḫd* (heading)
B 16–17 *dmj.n.j jnbw ḥqꜣ* 2
jry r ḫsf sttjw 3
B 17–19 *šzp.n.j ksw.j m bꜣt* 3
m snḏ mꜣꜣ wršyw dp ḥwt jmt hrw.s 5

B 15–16 My giving a path to my feet downstream.
B 16–17 I touched the Ruler's Walls,
made to bar the Asiatics.
B 17–19 I took up my crouch in a bush,
in fear that the watchmen on duty on the enclosure might see.

Leaving the Nile Valley, Sinuhe travels east to the Sinai, probably by means of the Wadi Tumilat (dashed line on the map on p. 67), the regular "highway" between the Sinai and the Delta.

B 15–16 *rdjt.j* — the narrative infinitive here marks a new "journal entry." B is followed by all other copies except R 41, which substitutes *rdj.n.j* "I gave."

rdwy.j — the double reed-leaf is phonetic: *ridwá'i > *ridwáy.

B 16–17 *jnbw ḥq3* — a fort built by Amenemhat I at the eastern end of the Wadi Tumilat, to control traffic into Egypt from the east.

r ptpt nmjw-šꜥj — "and to trample the sand-trekkers." This phrase is added to the second line of the couplet in R 43 and all later copies.

B 17–19 *m snḏ m33 wršyw* — *wršyw*, a noun from *wrš* "spend the day," is the subject of the *sḏm.f*. The unexpressed object is the 1s dependent pronoun *wj* "me," added in some New Kingdom copies.

dp ḥwt jmt hrw.s — literally, "atop the wall, which was in its day." R 45 has *dp jnb jm[j] hrw.f* "the watchmen atop the wall, who was in his day." Though feminine, *jmt hrw.s* cannot refer to *ḥwt*; the scribe of B was evidently thinking of *wršyw* as a collective. The was added as an afterthought, after the scribe had begun the next sentence.

Episode 7 — Sinuhe's Flight: Stage Four (B 19–23, R 45–48)

B 23 B 22 B 21 B 20 B 19

R 45
R 46
R 47
R 48

B 19–20	*jr(t).j šmt tr n ḫ3w(j)*	(heading)
B 20–21	*ḥḏ.n t3 pḥ.n.j ptn*	4
	ḫn.kw r jw n km-wr	3
B 21–23	*ḫr.n jbt 3s.n.f w(j)*	3
	ntb.kw ḫḫ.j ḫm.w	3
	ḏd.n.j dpt m(w)t nn	3

B 19–20 My making off at the time of dusk.
B 20–21 At dawn I reached Peten,
and landed at an island of the Great Black.
B 21–23 Thirst fell and surprised me,
so that I was seared, my throat dusty.
I said, "This is the taste of death."

Once it is dark enough to avoid detection from the fort, Sinuhe sets off into the Sinai. Traveling by night, he reaches at dawn the area of the saltwater lakes known today as the Bitter Lakes (through which the Suez Canal now passes).

B 19–20 *jr(t).j* — most likely an error for R 45 *jrt.j* rather than the *sḏm.f* used as a past tense (§ 18.4). which is not typical for this text.

tr n ḫ3w(j) — this noun phrase is used adverbially (§ 8.14).

B 20–21 *ḥd.n t3 pḥ.n.j ptn* — the location of Peten is unknown, though a night's walk places it no more than some 20 miles (33 km) east of the fort. For the construction, literally "the land became bright and I reached Peten," see § 25.8.3.

r jw — R 46 and later copies have *ḥr jw* "on an island."

B 21–23 *ḫr.n jbt 3s.n.f w(j)* — the use of the *sḏm.n.f* for the first verb indicates that this is an emphatic sentence rather than a simple statement of fact (§ 25.13.2). The verb *3s* means "hurry" (intransitive and transitive): the sense here is that thirst came upon Sinuhe quickly. The 3ms suffix pronoun referring to *jbt* in B 22 indicates that the scribe interpreted *jbt* as an infinitive (§ 13.8); the 3fs suffix pronoun in R 47, as a verbal noun.

ntb.kw —The stative here, from the verb *nṯb* "sear," expresses a resulting state; compare English *The hunters shot the lion dead.* R 47 substitutes *nḏ3.kw* "I was parched."

ḫḫ.j ḫm.w — *ḫm* "become dusty" is a denominal verb, from the noun *ḫmw* "dust." The three *ḫ*'s make a nice sound-play on the notion of a dusty throat.

ḏd.n.j — or "I thought": cf. R 31 / B 7 in Episode 4, above.

Episode 8 — Rescued by Asiatics (B 23–28, R 48–52)

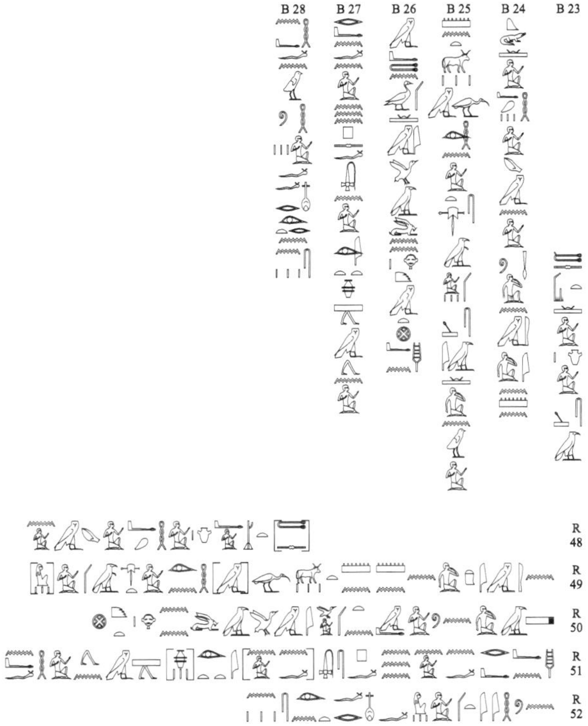

B 23–24	*ṯzt.j jb.j sꜣq.j ḥꜥw.j*	(heading)
B 24–25	*sḏm.n.j ḫrw nmj mnmnt*	2
	gmḥ.n.j sttjw	2
B 25–26	*sꜣj.n wj mjtn(j) jm*	3
	pꜣ wnn ḥr kmt	2
B 26–27	*ꜥḥꜥ.n rdj.n.f n.j mw*	3
	psf n.j jrtt	2
B 27–28	*šm.n.j ḥnꜥ.f n wḥw.f*	3
	nfr jrt.n.sn	2

B 23–24 My lifting up my mind and collecting my limbs.

B 24–25 I heard the sound of a herd's lowing,
and spotted Asiatics.

B 25–26 Their pathfinder recognized me,
who had once been in Blackland.
B 26–27 Then he gave me water
and cooked milk for me.
B 27–28 I went with him to his tribesmen.
What they did was good.

Although *sttjw* normally refers to settled Asiatics, the reference to their pathfinder indicates that these were at least semi-nomadic, as would be expected in the desert of the Sinai.

B 23–24 R 48 omits the infinitive *sꜣq.j* "my collecting" and has the singular *ḥꜥ.j* "my body."

B 24–25 *sḏm.n.j ḫrw n nmj* — R 48–49 omits *ḫrw n* "the sound of." The verb *nmj* means "moan"; its use here indicates that the herd consisted of cattle.

B 25–26 *sꜣj.n wj* — i.e., recognized me as an Egyptian. Although the scout "had once been in Egypt," it is improbable that he would have encountered a palace servant in the capital. *sꜣj* is a spelling of 3-lit. *sjꜣ* "recognize."

mjṯn(j) jm — literally, "the pathfinder therefrom." *mjṯnj* is a nisbe from *mjṯn* "path." The  sign in B 26 is an error for R 50 ; in B, the two signs are distinguished only by two strokes representing the wings of the latter, which the scribe has omitted here.

pꜣ wnn ḥr kmt — *pꜣ* is a participle from the verb meaning "do once, in the past," followed by the infinitive: cf. § 18.13. *ḥr kmt* means literally, "on the Blackland" (see Essay 2).

B 26–27 *psf n.j jrtt* — R 51 has *pfs.[n.f n.j] jrtt* (resoration based on a New Kingdom copy). The verb is originally 3ae-inf. *psj* and survives as such in Coptic ⲡⲓⲥⲉ/ⲡⲓⲥⲓ. In the dialect of R 51, however, the initial consonant became affricated as p^f (*písi > p^{f}ísi: cf. German *Pfad* vs. English *path*) and is therefore written as *pf*; in other dialects, it became *f* (*físi), and the verb is accordingly spelled *fsj*. The same form *pfs* is found in B 88 and B 92. B 27 *psf* is therefore most likely for *pfs* with the suffixes *n.f* omitted (cf. § 17.5); a similar case occurs in B 104. Cooking milk, now known as pasteurization, retards spoilage from harmful microbes. Although the ancients did not know about microbes, they would have learned from experience that cooking milk allows it to be consumed without harmful effects.

B 27–28 *n wḥw.f* — R 52 has the collective *wḥyt.f* "his tribe."

Episode 9 — Sinuhe Meets Ammunanši (B 28–47, R 52–71)

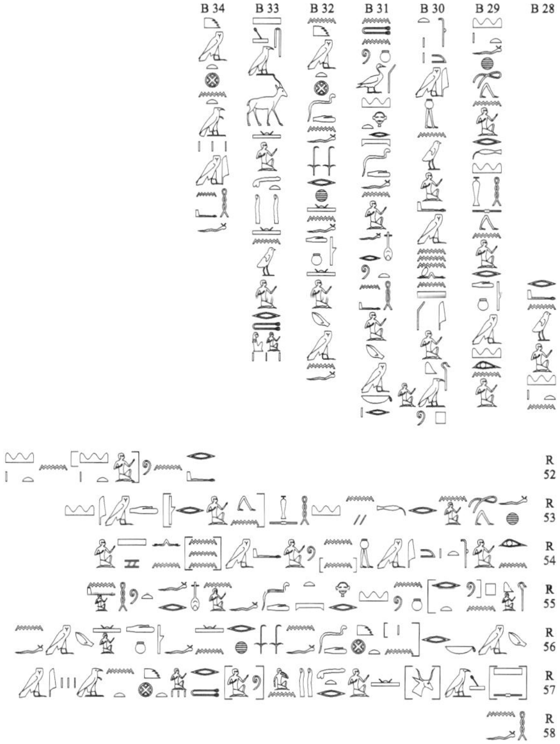

B 28–29 *rdj.n wj ḫꜣst n ḫꜣst* 3
fḫ.n.j r kp(nj) ḥz.n.j r qdm 4
B 29–31 *jr.n.j rnpt ½ jm* 3
jn wj {zꜣ} ꜥmmw-nnš 2
ḥqꜣ pw n ṯnw ḥrt 2
B 31–32 *ḏd.f n.j nfr tw ḥnꜥ.j* 3
sḏm.k r n kmt 3
B 32–34 *ḏd.n.f nn rḫ.n.f qd.j* 4
sḏm.n.f šsꜣ.j 2
mt.n wj rmṯ kmt ntjw jm ḥnꜥ.f 4

B 28–29 Country gave me to country.
I left Byblos and went on to Qatna.

B 29–31 When I had spent half a year there,
Ammunanši fetched me —
he was a ruler of Upper Retjenu —
B 31–32 saying to me, "It is good you are with me.
You will hear the speech of Blackland."
B 32–34 He said this because he had learned of my character
and had heard of my experience,
Egyptians who were there with him having witnessed to me.

From the Sinai, Sinuhe travels north to Byblos in Lebanon and then to the area of Qatna in Syria, where he meets a local ruler.

B 28–29 *rdj.n wj* — two New Kingdom copies have *rdjt wj*, with the infinitive, as a final single "journal entry" heading in this part of the story. In that case, the line following is a couplet ("I left Byblos / and went on to Qatna").

fḫ.n.j r — literally, "I left with respect to" (§ 8.2.7).

kp(nj) ... qdm — Egyptian renderings of the local names Gubla (Greek Byblos) and Qatanu. Byblos, on the Mediterranean coast north of modern Beirut, was the major trading partner of Egypt (for cedar) in Lebanon. Qatna was a link between Mesopotamia and the Mediterranean coast. The  jar in B 29, as in the word *qd* "character" in B 32 and R 56, comes from an original determinative ○ and is not phonetic.

B 29–31 *jr.n.j ... jn wj* — an emphatic construction rather than a simple statement, with the *jr.n.j* clause second in importance to the *jn* clause (§ 25.8.3). R 54 has *jn.n wj*.

{zꜣ} ꜥmmw nnš — Middle Egyptian group writing (Essay 17) representing *ꜥam-mu-nan-š(i), an Amorite name meaning "Ammu (a god) is exalted" (Morenz 1997, 4–5). The scribe of B has secondarily inserted a  sign between the two elements of the name, evidently inderstanding it as *zꜣ-ꜥmmw nnšj* "Ammu's son Nanši" (§ 4.15).

ḥqꜣ pw n ṯnw ḥrt — this is a parenthetic statement, because it intervenes between the clause *jn wj {zꜣ} ꜥmmw-nnš* and the adverb clause *ḏd.f n.j* dependent on it. Retjenu was the name for the Mediterranean coast of what is now Lebanon and Syria. Lower Retjenu was the coast itself, and Upper Retjenu, the highlands to the east; For unknown reasons, the B text always omits the initial *r*; for the  sign in B 31 *ṯnw*, see the note to *mjṯn(j)* in B 26, above.

B 31–32 *nfr tw ḥnꜥ.j* — an adjectival sentence, literally "You are good with me."

B 32–34 *šsꜣ.j* — the scribe of B has drawn a large hieroglyphic sign as the first determinative.

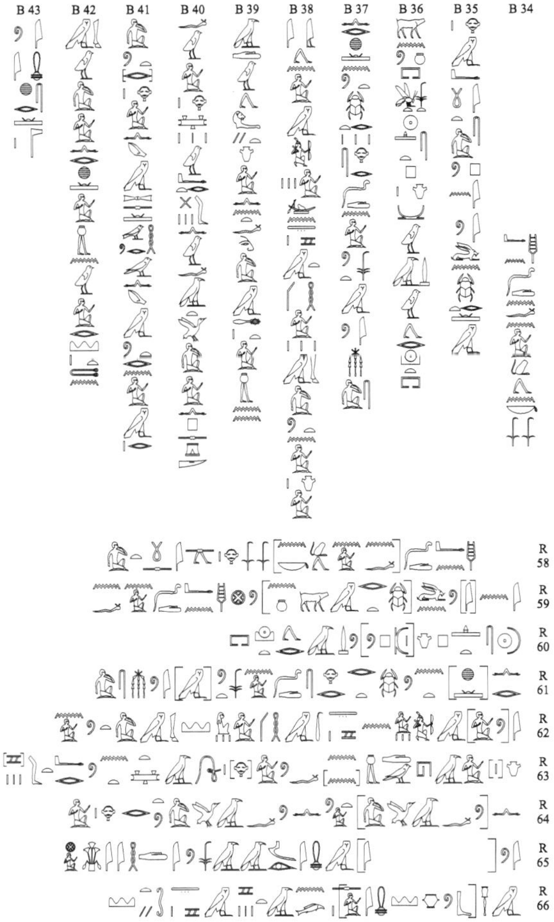

B 34–36 *ꜥḥꜥ.n ḏd.n.f n.j* 2
pḥ.n.k nn ḥr mj jšst pw 4
jn jw wn ḫprt m ẖnw 3
B 36–37 *(ꜥḥꜥ.n ḏd.n.j n.f)* 2
nswt-bjt SḤTP-JB-Rꜥ *wḏꜣ.w r ꜣḫt* 4
nj rḫ.n.tw ḫprt ḥr.s 3
B 37–39 *ḏd.n.j swt m jwms* 2
jj.n.j m mšꜥ n tꜣ tmḥw 3
wḥm.tw n.j jb.j ꜣd.w 3

B 39–40 *ḥꜣtj.j nj ntf m ẖt.j* 3
jn.n.f wj ḥr wꜣwt wꜥrt 2
B 40–41 *nj wfꜣ.t(w).j nj psg.tw [r] ḥr.j* 3
nj sḏm.(j) ṯꜣz ḥwrw 3
nj sḏm.tw rn.j m r wḥmw 3
B 42–43 *nj rḫ.j jn wj r ḫꜣst ṯn* 3
jw mj sḫr nṯr 1

B 34–36 Then he said to me,
“Why have you reached here? What is it?
Is there something that has happened at home?”
B 36–37 Then I said to him,
“Dual King Sehetepibre has proceeded to the Akhet,
and what will happen because of it is unknown.”
B 37–39 I also said, by way of persuasion,
“When I came back from an expedition to Tamahu-land,
it was recounted to me and my mind became feeble.
B 39–40 My heart—that’s not what was in my body,
and it brought me away on the ways of flight.
B 40–41 I was not reproached, no one spat at my face,
I did not hear a wretched phrase,
my name was not heard in the herald’s mouth.
B 42–43 I do not know who brought me to this country:
it is like a god’s plan.”

B and R have somewhat divergent versions of this episode, and B’s earlier version is expanded in R and later copies by a final couplet, which B has in lines 225–26.

B 34–36 *ḥr mj jšst pw* — R 58 and later copies have *ḥr zj jšst*, “on (account of) which or what?”

B 36–37 *ꜥḥꜥ.n ḏd.n.j n.f* — this introduction to Sinuhe’s answer, omitted in B, is present in R 59 and later copies.

nswt-bjt *SḤTP-JB-Rꜥ* *wḏꜣ.w* — B is the only copy to use the title *nswt-bjt*. The size of the lacuna in R 60 indicates that that text had *SḤTP-JB-Rꜥ [pw] wḏꜣ.(w)* “It is that Sehetepibre has proceeded” (§ 21.12), as in most later copies.

B 37–39 *ḏd.n.j swt m jwms* — see § 15.7.7. The term *jwms* implies a statement that is not completely accurate, as is true of the second line of the couplet. Sinuhe is trying to persuade Ammunanši that he is not a criminal fugitive.

jb.j ꜣd.w — the verb *ꜣd*, also in B 255, also occurs in a medical papyrus as a disorder of the heart (*ḥꜣtj*) leading to poor circulation. R 63 has *ꜣhd.(w)* “exhausted.”

B 39–40 *ḥ3tj.j nj ntf m ẖt.j* — this line, only in B, is repeated in col. 255. Despite the spelling here, *ntf* is the 3ms independent pronoun (spelled correctly in col. 255); the scribe apparently read his original as *nn tf* "without spitting," in anticipation of the tercet following. The construction is an affirmative adverbial sentence with a negated subject (for which, see § 11.7): the sentence means that something other than Sinuhe's (normal) heart was in his body.

B 40–41 *nj psg.tw [r] ḥr.j* — R 64 erroneously repeats the verb *wf3.tw* "discussed."

nj sḏm.(j) ṯ3z ḥwrw — this line is repeated in col. 227, where the 1s suffix pronoun is written. A "wretched phrase" means that no one cursed at Sinuhe.

nj sḏm.tw rn.j m r wḥmw — the *wḥmw* "herald" (literally, "repeater") was charged with conveying an official message. The sentence means that there was no order for Sinuhe's arrest.

B 42–43 *nj rḫ.j jn wj r ḫ3st ṯn* — the masculine participle *jn* indicates that Sinuhe is thinking of a person rather than a situation. This is an answer to Ammunanši's initial question *ḥr mj* "on account of what?" It is also possible to read *jnw.j* "how I was brought."

jw mj sḫr nṯr — the subject is omitted (§ 10.9). R 65 has a line that begins with *jw* and ends with *[j]m* — perhaps *jw [sḫr nṯr j]m* "a god's plan was in it."

R 65–66 *mj m33 sw jdḥy m 3b[w*
mj] zj n ḫ3t m t3-stj
like a Deltan seeing himself in Elephantine,
like a man of the marshland in Bowland."

This couplet, omitted in B, is present in all later copies. The notion of a man from the Delta finding himself in Elephantine or Nubia ("Bowland") reflects the rarity of long-distance travel for most Egyptians. The sentence means that Sinuhe finds himself out of place in Ammunanši's country.

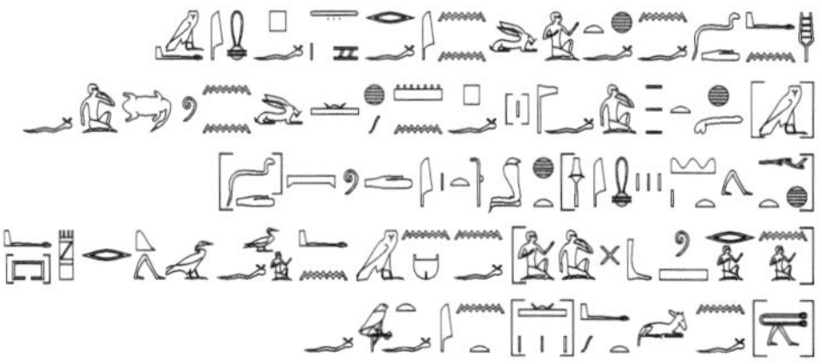

R 67
R 68
R 69
R 70
R 71

B 43–44 *(ꜥḥꜥ.n ḏd.n.f ḫft.j)* 3
wnn jr.f tꜣ pn mj mj m ḫmt.f 4
B 44–45 *nṯr pf mnḫ wnnw snḏ.f ḫt ḫꜣswt* 5
mj sḫmt rnpt jdw 2
B 45–47 *ḏd.k(w) r.j n.f wšb.j n.f* 2
nḥmn zꜣ.f ꜥq.(w) r ꜥḥ 3
jt.n.f jwꜥꜥt nt jt.f 3

B 43–44 Then he said in response to me,
"What will that land be like without him,
B 44–45 that effective god, terror of whom used to be throughout the countries
like Sekhmet in a year of plague?"
B 45–47 So, I said to him, answering him,
"Surely his son has entered the palace
and taken the inheritance of his father.

This short section introduces the hymn of praise to Senwosret I that follows.

B 43–45 *ꜥḥꜥ.n ḏd.n.f ḫft.j* — R 67 and later copies have the expected introductory clause to Ammunanši's question, omitted in B. The preposition *ḫft* "opposite" is used instead of *n* "to" or *ḫr* "in the presence of" (§ 8.2.13) when someone speaks in response to someone else's statement or question.

m ḫmt.f — a compound preposition; *ḫmt* is a verbal noun from *ḫm* "not know, be ignorant of": thus literally, "in ignorance of him." The determinative in B is unusual.

wnnw snḏ.f ḫt ḫꜣswt — an indirect relative clause with the relative *sḏm.f* of *wnn* (geminated stem): literally, "who his fear used to be throughout the countries" (§ 22.13).

mj sḫmt rnpt jdw — Sekhmet (the goddess of violence) was associated with the desert, and plagues were thought to come from the desert and the sky (hence the determinative of *jdw*). *rnpt jdw* is a noun phrase used adverbially (§ 8.14).

B 45–47 *ḏd.k(w) r.j* — an archaic use of the stative as a past tense (§ 16.5); the suffix is written without *w*, as in Old Egyptian. *r.j* is self-referential: literally, "I said, for my part."

jwꜥꜥt — the second *ꜥ* in B 47 is evidently superfluous; the word is *jwꜥwt*, a nisbe from *jwꜥw* "heir" (i.e., "that of the heir"), itself a noun from *jwꜥ* "inherit."

Episode 10 — Sinuhe's Hymn (B 47–70, R 71–94)

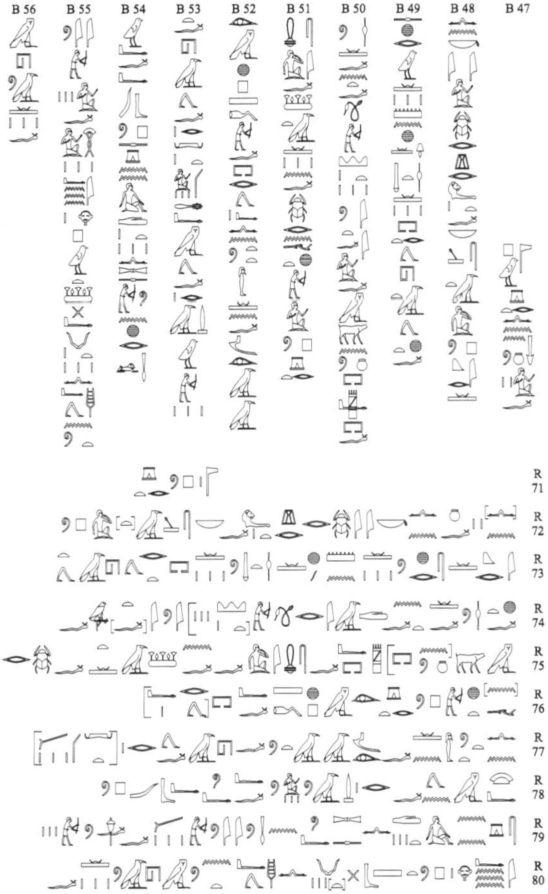

B 47–48 *nṯr pw grt nn snnw.f* 2
nn ky ḫpr.(w) ḫr ḥꜣt.f 3
B 48–50 *nb sꜣt pw jqr sḫrw mnḫ wḏt-mdw* 3
prt hꜣt ḫft wḏ.f 3
B 50–51 *ntf dꜣr ḫꜣswt jw jt.f m ẖnw ʿḥ.f* 4
smj.f šꜣt.n.f ḫpr 3
B 51–52 *nḫt pw grt jr m ḫpš.f* 3
pr ʿ nn twt n.f 2

B 52–53	*m33.t(w).f h3.f r-pḏwt*	3	
	ḫꜥm.f r-ḏ3w		2
B 54–55	*wꜥf ꜥb pw sgnn ḏrwt*	3	
	nj ṯ3z.n ḫrwyw.f skw		3
B 55–56	*jꜥ ḥr pw tš3 wpwt*	3	
	nj ꜥḥꜥ.n.tw m h3w.f		2

B 47–48 "Moreover, he is a god without equal,
with none in existence preceding him.
B 48–50 He is a master of wisdom, accomplished of plans, effective of governance:
going up and going down are in accordance with his command.
B 50–51 He is the one who suppressed countries when his father was in his palace,
reporting what he had decided should happen.
B 51–52 He is also a forceful one who acts with his forearm,
an active one with equal to him
B 52–53 when he is seen descending on archery
and charging opposition.
B 54–55 He is a horn-deflecter who softens hands:
his enemies cannot muster troops.
B 55–56 He is one who takes vengeance, who splits open foreheads:
none can stand in his vicinity.

Sinuhe continues his reply to Ammunanši's question with a hymn of praise of Senwosret I. The first part of the hymn extols the king's wisdom and his prowess in battle.

B 47–48 *nn ky ḫpr.(w) ḫr ḥ3t.f* — *ḫpr.(w)* is a 3ms stative modifying undefined *ky* as an unmarked relative (§ 22.11). *ḫr ḥ3t.f*, literally "under his front," connotes precedence; like the first line, this statement expresses Senwosret's superiority.

B 48–50 *jqr sḫrw mnḫ wḏt-mdw* — two *nfr ḥr* constructions (§ 6.5). *wḏ mdw*, literally "command speech," is an idiom for "govern"; *wḏt* is a verbal noun.

prt h3t — two infinitives. Together, they mean "movement of any sort."

B 50–51 *ntf d3r ḫ3swt* — a participial statement (§§ 23.10–11, 25.3). The spelling *d3jr* in R 74 reflects the change from original (3-lit.) *d3j* to Middle Egyptian *d3r*.

smj.f š3t.n.f ḫpr — *š3t.n.f* is a relative *sḏm.n.f* (*sḏm.f* in R 75) governing the infinitive *ḫpr*: literally, "what he determined to happen." R 75 has *smj.f n.f* "reporting to him": the *f* of *smj.f* refers to Senwosret, and those of *n.f* and *š3t.n.f* / *š3t.f*, to his father. The line means that Senwosret successfully carried out his father's commands.

B 51–52 *grt* — the particle here marks the transition from Senwosret's role as junior king to that of a king in his own right.

ḫpš.f — as the determinative indicates, the term refers to the leg of a bull: the image is that of the king as a bull.

pr ꜥ — *pr* is an active participle with the transitive meaning of *prj*, "send forth" (cf. *prt-ḫrw* § 22.25.3): thus, "one who sends forth the arm." This is an idiom for forceful activity.

B 52–53 This couplet consists of two adverb clauses dependent on *nn twt n.f* "none like him" in the last line of the preceding couplet.

hꜣ.f — a transitive use of the verb *hꜣj* "go down, descend."

r-pḏwt ... r-ḏꜣw — two compound nouns formed with the initial element *r*, literally "mouth." *pḏwt* is a collective for the archers of an army (like English *cavalry* for the mounted contingent); *r-pḏwt* thus means something like "the situation of archers." *ḏꜣw* is an abstract from *ḏꜣj* "cross": thus, "the situation when an enemy crosses one."

ẖꜥm.f — R 78 has *ḫꜥm.n.f* "when he has charged." The two different initial consonants are dialectal variants: see the note to R 21 *bjk ꜥẖ.f*, above. Interestingly, that case is the reverse of this one (R *ẖ* = B *ḫ*).

B 54–55 *wꜥfꜥb* — the image is of the king deflecting a charging bull.

sgnn ḏrwt — see § 23.7.

nj ṯꜣz.n ḫrwyw.f skw — *ṯꜣz* means literally "to together." In place of *skw*, R 79 has *ḫsfw* "confronters," from a misreading of the hieratic sign used in B.

B 55–56 *jꜥ ḥr* — literally, "one who washes the face," an idiom for taking vengeance.

tšꜣ wpwt — this refers to the common Egyptian battle weapon, the mace. R 80, which spells the word with uniliteral signs, has misread a hieratic  as .

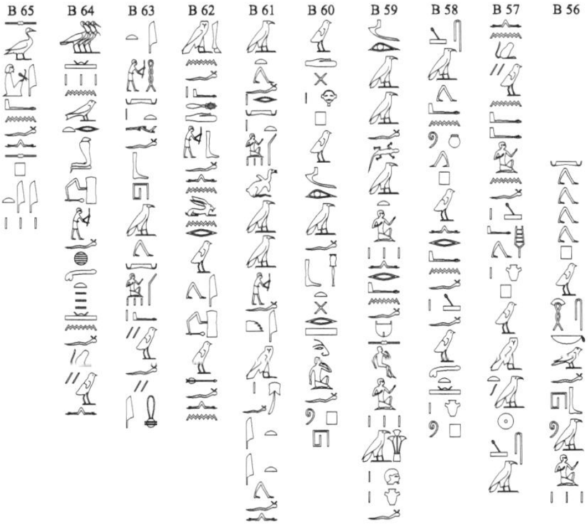

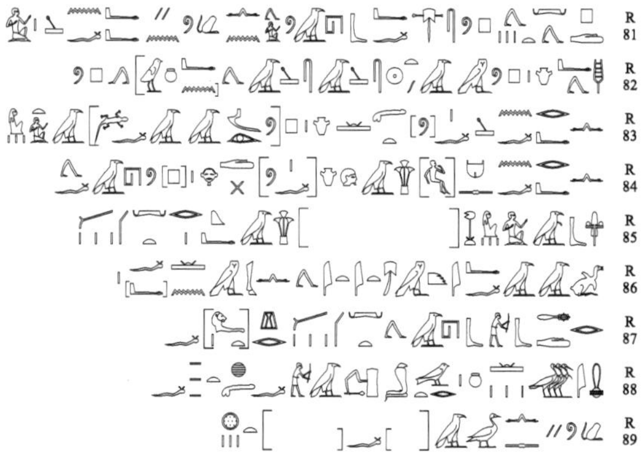

B 56–57	*pḏ nmtwt pw sk.f bhꜣw*	3
	nn pḥwj n dd n.f sꜣ	3
B 57–58	*ꜥḥꜥ jb pw m ꜣt sꜣsꜣ*	2
	ꜥnw pw nj rdj.n.f sꜣ.f	3
B 58–59	*wmt jb pw mꜣꜣ.f ꜥšꜣt*	3
	nj rdj.n.f ḥmsw ḥꜣ jb.f	3
B 60–61	*wd ḥr pw mꜣ.f ꜣbt*	3
	rš.f pw hꜣt.f r-pḏwt	3
B 61–62	*tꜣꜣ.f jkm.f tjtj.f*	3
	nj wḥm.n.f ꜥ ẖdb.f	2
B 62–63	*nn wn rwj ꜥḥꜣw.f*	3
	nn jtḥ pḏt.f	2
B 63–64	*bhꜣ pḏwt ꜥwj.fj*	3
	mj bꜣw n wrt	2
B 64–65	*ꜥḥꜣ.f ẖmt.n.f pḥwj*	3
	nj zꜣj.n.f nj zpyt	2

B 56–57 "He is stretched of strides when he wipes out the fugitive:
there is no recourse for the one who shows him the back.

B 57–58 He is steady-minded in the moment of backing,
he is a returner who does not show his back.

B 58–59 He is stout-minded when he sees a multitude:
he allows no inactivity in his mind.

B 60–61 He is aggressive when he sees a halt:
his descending on archery is his joy.

B 61–62 When he takes up the shield, he pounds;
he does not have to repeat an act of his killing.

B 62–63 There is none who can escape his arrow,
  none who can draw his bow.
B 63–64 Archers flee his arms
  like the impressiveness of the Great Goddess.
B 64–65 He fights having anticipated the outcome,
  he takes no heed of the aftermath.

B 56–57 *sk.f bhꜣw* — R 81 has again misread the *sk* sign, this time as an ideogram for *stj* "shoot."

pḥwj — literally, "end," referring to the end of battle: no one can escape him by running away.

B 57–58 This couplet continues the metaphor of *sꜣ* "back," with which the last couplet ended: both lines here end with the same syllable.

ꜥḥꜥ jb pw m ꜣt sꜣsꜣ — the first phrase means literally, "standing of mind": cf. English *steadfast*. The verb *sꜣsꜣ* connotes the repetitive action of "backing": i.e., retreat. The next line shows that this refers to an Egyptian retreat rather than that of the enemy.

B 58–59 *wmt jb* — literally, "thick of mind": cf. English *stout-hearted.*

ḥmsw — B 59 writes this word as if it were a plural participle, "sitters"; R 84 has room for only one determinative, probably the same as that in all later copies. The word is a verbal noun from *ḥmsj* "sit down," here a metaphor for inactivity.

B 60–61 *wd ḥr* — literally, "one who pushes the face."

mꜣ.f ꜣbt — the determinative in B 60 is not that of either 3-lit. *ꜣb* "stop" () or 3ae-inf. *ꜣbj* "desire" (), but *ḥmsw* "sitting still" in the previous couplet suggests the former: the king keeps pushing forward when his army stops advancing. Note the use of the base stem of *mꜣꜣ* here with a singular object versus the geminated stem in B 59 *mꜣꜣ.f ꜥšꜣt*, where the object is plural in sense: cf. § 23.7. R 84–85 has reinterpreted this clause as *hꜣ.f jꜣbtjw* "when he descends on easterners."

rš.f pw hꜣt.f r-pḏwt — the *f* of *hꜣt.f* was added secondarily. For this line, R 85 has *ḫꜣ[...] ḥꜣq r-pḏwt* "[...] plunder archery."

B 61–62 *tꜣꜣ.f jkm.f tjtj.f* — a balanced sentence (§ 25.9). The *f* of *ṯꜣꜣ.f* was added secondarily.

nj wḥm.n.f ꜥ ḫdb.f — i.e., his first blow kills. R 86–87 has *[ꜥ] r ḫdb* "an action in order to kill."

B 62–63 R omits the second line of this couplet.

B 63–64 *bhꜣ pḏwt ꜥwj.fj* — in place of *ꜥwj.fj* "his arms," R 87 and later copies have *ḫr [ḥꜣt].f* "before him."

bꜣw n wrt — for *bꜣw*, see Essay 7. *wrt* "Great" (feminine) is an epithet for the uraeus.

B 64–65 *nj zꜣ.n.f nj zpyt* — *zꜣj* "guard" can also mean "watch out for." The second  is an occasional writing of the preposition *n* before a noun (§ 8.2.6). *zpyt* is a verbal noun from *zpj* "remain, be left over."

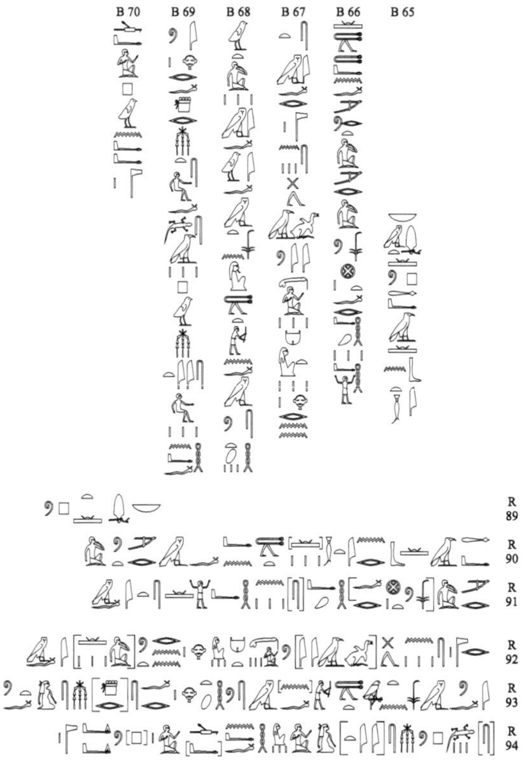

B 65–66 *nb jm(ꜣ)t pw ꜥꜣ bnjt* 2
jṯ.n.f (m) mrwt 2
B 66–67 *mr sw njwt.f r ḥꜥw* 3
ḥꜥ st jm.f r nṯr.sn 3
B 67–68 *swꜣ ṯꜣyw ḥjmwt* 3
ḥr rnnwt jm.f jw.f m nswt 3
B 68–69 *jt.n.f m swḥt* 2
jw ḥr.(f) r.f ḏr mst.f 3
B 69–70 *sꜥšꜣ pw msyt ḥnꜥ.f* 3
wꜥ pw n dd nṯr 3

B 65–66 "He is a master of kindness, great of sweetness:
he has taken possession through love.
B 66–67 His town loves him more than itself,
they are more excited about him than their god.

B 67–68 Men and women surpass
exultation in him, now that he is king.
B 68–69 He took possession in the egg;
his face was toward it from before he was born.
B 69–70 Those born with him are multiple,
but he is a unique one of the god's giving.

The end of Sinuhe's hymn emphasizes that Senwosret has become king not merely through the prowess detailed in the first part but through kindness and his unique nature.

B 65–66 *nb jm(ꜣ)t pw ꜥꜣ bnjt* — the first phrase connotes possession (§ 6.9). *bnjt/bnrjt* is an abstract from *bnr* "sweet" (originally *bnj*: Schenkel 1965).

jt.n.f (m) mrwt B 66 has omitted the preposition, present in R 90.

B 66–67 *mr sw njwt.f r ḥꜥw* — see § 18.5. R 91 has *ḥꜥw.[s]n* "their body," where the plural suffix pronoun refers to the inhabitants of *njwt.f* rather than to the (feminine singular) noun itself, as in the next line.

ḥꜥ st jm.f r nṯr.sn — see § 23.8. Here, *st* refers to *njwt.f* as a collective.

B 68–69 *jw ḥr.(f) r.f* — B 69 has probably overlooked a second  after that which denotes the complementary and suffix pronoun of *ḥr.f*; R 93 has *ḥr.f r.s* (without the particle *jw*).

ḏr mst.f — the preposition *ḏr* plus the *sḏmt.f* with passive meaning (§ 19.14). R 93 has reinterpreted the clause as *ḏr ms.tw.f* "since he was born."

B 69–70 *sꜥšꜣ pw msyt ḥnꜥ.f* — an A *pw* B sentence in which A is a passive participle ("made many"); B has the collective *msyt* "offspring." An A *pw* sentence referring to the king ("He is a multiplier of those born with him") makes no sense in the context, and *pw* would not separate the participle and its object.

n dd nṯr — see § 21.10. R 94 omits the indirect genitive, making *dd nṯr* a relative *sḏm.f* ("he is the unique one the god gives").

Episode 11 — Sinuhe's Advice (B 70–77, R 95–104)

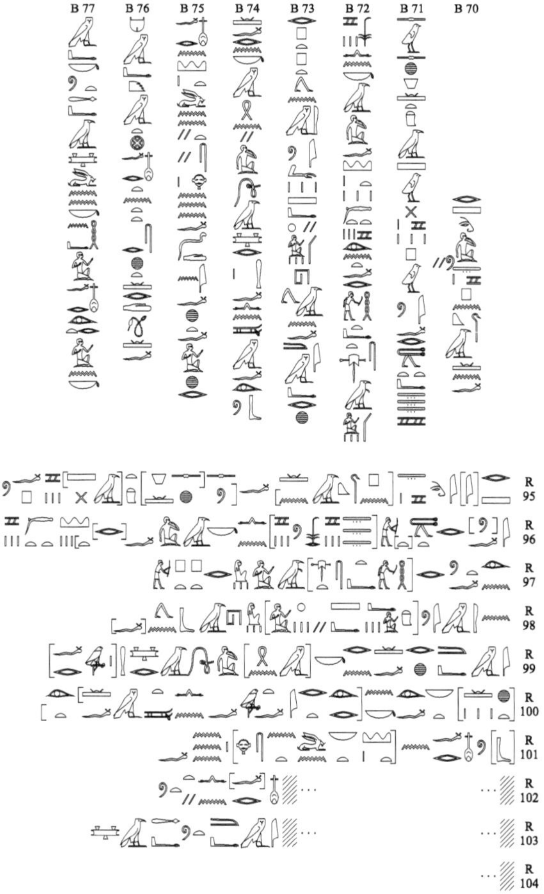

B 70–71	*ršwj tꜣ pn ḥqꜣ.n.f*	3	
	swsḫ tꜣšw pw		1
B 71–72	*jw.f r jtt tꜣw rsw*	3	
	nn kꜣ.f ḫꜣswt mḥtt		3
B 72–73	*jr.n.tw.f r ḥwt sttjw*	2	
	r ptpt nmjw-šꜥj		1
B 73–74	*hꜣ(b) n.f jmj rḫ.f rn.k*	4	
	m šnj wꜣ.(w) r ḥm.f		3

B 74–75 *nn tm.f jr bw nfr* 3
n ḫ3st wnntj.sj ḥr mw.f 3
B 75–76 *ḏd.jn.f ḫft.j ḫr ḥm kmt nfr.t(j)* 4
(n) ntt.s rḫ.t(j) r(w)d.f 3
B 77 *mj.k tw ʿ3 wnn.k ḥnʿ.j* 3
nfr jrt.j n.k 2

B 70–71 "How joyful the land he has begun to rule!
He is one who broadens borders.
B 71–72 He is to take possession of the southern lands,
he will not consider the northern countries.
B 72–73 He has been made to hit the Asiatics,
to trample the sand-trekkers.
B 73–74 Send word to him, let him know your identity
as one who inquires about His Incarnation from afar.
B 74–75 He will not fail to do good
to the country that will be loyal to him."
B 75–76 So, he said in response to me, "And so, Blackland must be happy,
because it knows he will be firm.
B 77 But you are here and will stay with me;
what I will do for you is good."

Sinuhe ends his speech by discussing relations between Egypt and Asia and urging Ammunanši to establish ties with Senwosret. Ammunanši replies by welcoming Sinuhe to his land.

B 70–71 *ršwj* — the scribe of B added the *wj* secondarily.

t3 pn ḥq3.n.f — the completed action expressed by the *sḏm.n.f* here applies to the onset of "ruling," since Senwosret is still ruling at the time of speaking. The *sḏm.n.f* could be circumstantial "now that he has begun to rule," but the use of *pn* signals a relative clause (cf. ShS. 175 *jnw pn jn.n.j* "the cargo that I had gotten").

t3šw — R 95 has *t3[š]w.f* "its borders."

B 71–72 *nn k3.f ḫ3swt mḥtt* — later texts, including probably R 96, add the preposition *r* before *ḫ3swt mḥtt*. Sinuhe here is assuring Ammunanši that Senwosret has no plans to acquire (*jṯj* "take possession of") Asiatic territories.

B 72–73 This is an emphatic sentence: *jr.n.tw.f* is a given; the rheme is the two clauses with *r* plus infinitive. The fact that Senwosret has no territorial ambitions in Asia does not rule out military expeditions against some of its settled peoples (*sttjw*) and nomads (*nmjw-šʿj*).

B 73–75 In light of the preceding couplet, Sinuhe advises Ammunanši to initiate friendly relations with Egypt.

hꜣ(b) n.f — the sentence could be advising Ammunanši to go to Egypt ("go down to him"), but more likely the scribe of B has omitted the 𓃀 of *hꜣb*, which is present in R 98 and the one later copy surviving at this point.

m šnj wꜣ.(w) r ḥm.f — the prepositional phrase probably belongs with *šnj* rather than *wꜣ.(w)* ("who is far from His Incarnation"). R, however, probably has understood the latter and added a second phrase, *[r ḫt] nbt*: "as one who, far from His Incarnation, inquires about anything."

jr.f n.k [jrrt jt.f] — "he will do for you what his father used to do." This line is added in R 100 and the one later copy surviving at this point, before the final line of B's closing tercet.

wnntj.sj ḥr mw.f — literally, "who will exist (*sḏmtj.fj*) upon his water," an idiom for loyalty.

B 75–76 *ḫr ḥm kmt nfr.t(j)* — a SUBJECT–stative construction introduced by the particle *ḫr*, expressing necessity (§ 15.6.13).

(n) ntt.s rḫ.t(j) r(w)d.f — the scribe of B has omitted the initial preposition (§ 21.4). The text in R 102 has 𓈖 for the preposition (§ 8.2.6) and *ntj* for *ntt* (cf. § 22.2); it may have read *nj ntj tw [rḫ.(w) r(w)d.f]* "because one knows he will be firm" (for *tw*, see § 16.7). *r(w)d.f* is a *sḏm.f* used as an unmarked noun clause, object of *rḫ* (§ 21.7). B and R are the only texts to survive at this point.

B 77 *mj.k tw ꜥꜣ wnn.k ḥnꜥ.j* — literally, "Look, you are here, and you will exist with me." R 103 has *jmj tw ꜥꜣ* "Put yourself here."

jrt.j — it is possible to read *jrrt.j*, with the geminated stem, but see the note to B 3–5 *r jrt wꜣt šmw.s*, above.

Episode 12 — Sinuhe Settles in Retjenu (B 78–97, R 104–118)

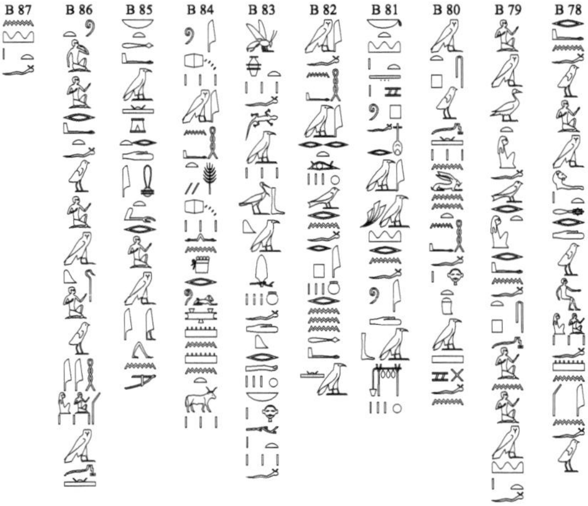

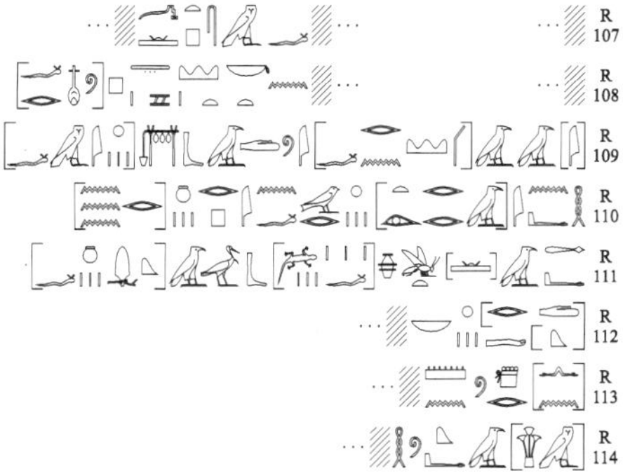

B 78–79 *rdj.n.f wj m ḥꜣt(j) ẖrdw.f* 2
mjn.n.f wj m zꜣt.f wrt 3
B 79–81 *rdj.n.f stp.j n.j m ḫꜣst.f* 3
m stpw n wnnt ḥnꜥ.f 3
ḥr tꜣš.f n kt ḫꜣst 2
B 81 *tꜣ pw nfr* 2
jꜣꜣ rn.f 2
B 81–82 *jw dꜣbw jm.f ḥnꜥ jꜣrrt* 3
wr n.f jrp r mw 3
B 82–83 *ꜥꜣ bjt.f ꜥšꜣ bꜣqw.f* 4
dqr nb ḥr ḫtw.f 2
B 84–85 *jw jtj jm ḥnꜥ btj* 3
nn ḏrw mnmnt nbt 2
B 85–87 *ꜥꜣ grt dmjt r.j m jj-n-mrwt* 4
rdjt.f wj m ḥqꜣ wḥy 2
m stp n ḫꜣst.f 2

B 78–79 He put me as leader of his children
and married me to his eldest daughter.
B 79–81 He had me choose from his country,
from the choice of what he had,
on his border with another country.
B 81 It was a good land,
called Rush.
B 81–82 There were figs in it, and grapes:
it had more wine than water.
B 82–83 Much was its honey and many its olive-trees,
with every kind of fruit on its trees.

B 84–85 There was barley there, and emmer,
with no limit of all kinds of herds.

B 85–87 Great indeed was what accrued to me as an adoptee:
his putting me as a tribe's ruler
in the choice of his country.

Sinuhe is adopted by Ammunanši, given land and a family, and becomes a successful tribal leader. This section is badly damaged in R, with lines 104–106 completely lost.

B 78–79 *m ḥ3t(j) ẖrdw.f* — the reading is indicated by use of the same phrase in B 108, where *ḥ3t* has a seated-man determinative; *rdj m* "put (someone) as" a position is also used in B 86.

mjn.n.f wj m z3t.f wrt — literally, "he moored me with his eldest daughter." Despite the *mn* sign, the reed-leaf represents the second radical of the verb (*mjnj*) rather than the fourth.

B 81 *j33 rn.f* — the plant determinative in B 81 indicates that the author or scribe was thinking of *j33*, a variant of *j3r* "rush." The one later copy surviving at this point has the determinative instead of , however, so the spelling in B 81 may be a false etymology for a Semitic name.

B 81–82 *wr n.f jrp r mw* — an adjectival sentence with comparative prepositional phrase (§ 7.4.2): literally, "wine was greater for it than water."

B 85–87 *jj-n-mrwt* — literally, "one who came because of love."

rdjt.f wj m ḥq3 wḥy m stp n ḫ3st.f — this clause summarizes the preceding stanzas and explains what is meant by *ꜥ3 grt dmjt r.j* "Great indeed was what accrued to me." *rdjt.f* is an infinitive; because it occurs in the second line of a couplet and in the middle of an episode, it is not a narrative use of the form. For *ḥq3*, R 114 has *[ḥ]3q* "plunderer," probably an error. With the exception of a fragment in R 118, R is lost from here until R 133, at the end of Episode 13.

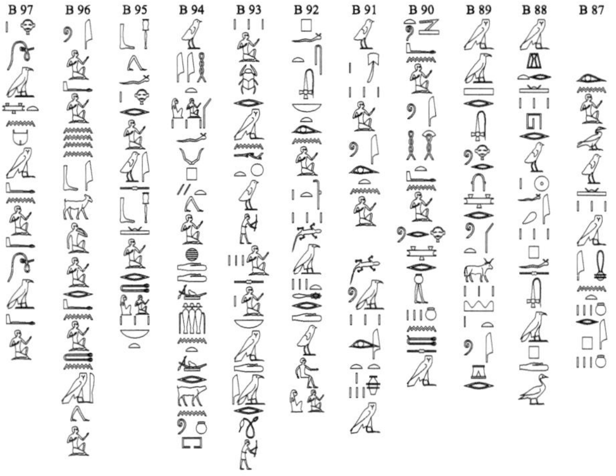

R 118

B 87–88	*jr n.j ꜥqw m mjnt*	3
	jrp m ẖrt hrw	2
B 88–89	*jf pfs.(w) ꜣpd m ꜣšr*	4
	ḥrw r ꜥwt ḫꜣst	2
B 89–91	*jw grg.t(w) n.j jw wꜣḥ.t(w) n.j*	2
	ḥrw r jnw n ṯzmw.j	3
B 91–92	*jw jr.t(w) n.j (bnrj) ꜥšꜣw*	3
	jrtt m pfst nbt	2
B 92–94	*jr.n.j rnpwt ꜥšꜣt*	3
	ẖrdw.j ḫpr.(w) m nḫtw	3
	zj nb m dꜣjr wḥyt.f	2
B 94–95	*wptj ḫdd ḫnt r ẖnw*	4
	ꜣb.f ḥr.j jw sꜣb.j rmṯ nbt	4
B 96–97	*jw.j dj.j mw n jb*	3
	rdj.n.j ṯnm ḥr wꜣt	3
	nḥm.n.j ꜥwꜣ	2

B 87–88 Rations were made for me in daily amounts,
and wine as daily fare,
B 88–89 meat cooked and fowl in roasts,
apart from the country's flocks:
B 89–91 for game would be hunted for me and presented to me,
apart from the catch of my hounds,
B 91–92 and many sweets would be made for me,
and milk into everything cooked.
B 92–94 When I had spent many years,
my boys grew into strongmen,
each man his tribe's suppresser.
B 94–95 The messenger who would come north or go south to home
used to stop by me, for I made every person stop.
B 96–97 I used to give water to the thirsty,
I put the lost on the path,
I rescued the robbed.

B 87–89 *mjnt … ẖrt hrw* — two nisbes, the first from *mjn* "now" ("that of now"), and the second from the preposition *ẖr* "under" ("that which the daytime has": § 8.8).

ḥrw r ꜥwt ḫꜣst — this phrase indicates that the meat and poultry came from wild game rather than domesticated animals, as the next couplet indicates.

B 89–91 *jw grg.t(w) n.j jw wꜣḥ.t(w) n.j* — *jw* here and in the next couplet marks the clauses as explanations of the preceding couplet. Both verbs have omitted subjects; *wꜣḥ.t(w)* means literally, "set down" (i.e., before Sinuhe).

jnw n ṯzmw.j — this refers to the game Sinuhe caught himself, with his hunting dogs. For *jnw*, see the note to ShS. 175 *jnw jn.n.j*.

B 91–92 *(bnrj)* — the gap in B 91 reflects either damage in the original from which this papyrus was copied or a hieratic group that the scribe could not read. The missing word, , is supplied by a later copy.

jrtt m pfst nbt — this refers to desserts made with cooked milk, still common in the Middle East today.

B 92–94 *jr.n.j rnpwt ⸢ꜥšꜣt ẖrdw.j ḫpr.(w) m nḫtw* — translated here as an emphatic sentence (§ 25.8.3), but a straightforward statement is also possible: "I spent many years, and my boys grew into strongmen."

dꜣjr wḥyt.f — the sense is "suppresser of (aggression for) his tribe."

B 94–95 *wptj ḥdd ḫnt r ḫnw ꜣb.f ḥr.j* — see §§ 18.6 and 23.3.

B 96–97 *jw.j dj.j mw n jb* — a SUBJECT–*sḏm.f* construction expressing customary action (§ 18.6); *jw* links this statement to the preceding one.

Episode 13 — Sinuhe as a Warrior (B 97–109, H 1–3, R 133–135)

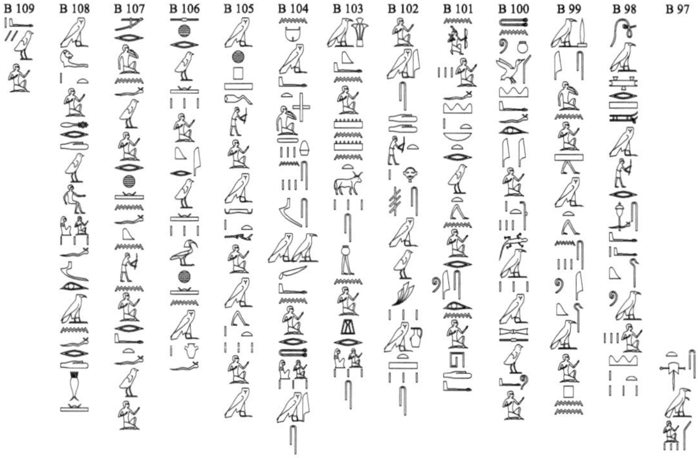

R 133

R 134

B 97–99 *sttjw wꜣ.(w) r štm* 3
r sḫsfꜥ ḥqꜣw ḫꜣswt 1
ḏꜣsj.n.j šmt.sn 2
B 99–101 *jw ḥqꜣ pn n ṯnw dj.f jry.j rnpwt ꜥšꜣ* 5
m ṯꜣzw n mšꜥ.f 2
B 101–102 *ḫꜣst nbt rwt.n.j r.s* 3
jw jr.n.j hd.j jm.s 3
d⸢r⸣.t(j) ḥr smw ḫnmwt.s 2
B 103–104 *ḥꜣq.n.j mnmnwt.s jn.n.j ḫrw.s* 4
nḥm wnmt.sn 2
B 104–106 *smꜣ.n.j rmṯ jm.s m ḫpš.j* 4
m pḏt.j m nmtwt.j m sḫrw.j jqrw 3
B 106–107 *ꜣḫ.n m jb.f mr.n.f wj* 3
rḫ.n.f qn.n.j 2
B 107–109 *rdj.⸢n⸣.f wj m ḥꜣt(j) ẖrdw.f* 2
mꜣ.n.f r(w)dꜥwj.j 3

B 97–99 Asiatics started to defy
and cause opposition to the hand of the countries' rulers,
and I discussed their movement,
B 99–101 for that ruler of Retjenu had me spend many years
as marshaler of his army.
B 101–102 Every country I went away from,
once I had made my attack in it,
was driven from pasture and its wells.

B 103–104 I plundered its herds and got its underlings,
their food having been taken away.
B 104–106 I killed some of its people by my strong arm,
by my bow, by my strides, by my accomplished plans.
B 106–107 It became useful in his mind and he desired me,
when he learned how I had persevered.
B 107–109 He put me as leader of his children,
when he saw my arms being firm.

This episode continues Sinuhe's description of his life in Retjenu, recounting his exploits as a military commander on behalf of Ammunanši and his allies.

B 97–99 *sttjw wꜣ.(w) r štm r sḫsf* — *wꜣj* "go away" has the meaning "start" when used with the preposition *r* plus an infinitive. Two infinitives are involved here, both with *ꜥ ḥqꜣw ḫꜣswt* as object. Since it is the rulers that are being defied and opposed, this line evidently refers to the opposition of polities against control by another polity, as a bid either for independence or for alliance with a different overlord.

ḏꜣjs.n.j šmt.sn — The verb is 4-lit. *ḏꜣjs*, written here with the last two radicals reversed. The suffix of *šmt.sn* probably refers to its nearest antecedent, *ḥqꜣw ḫꜣswt*. The sense is that Sinuhe advised Ammunanši and his allies how to proceed.

B 99–101 *jw ḥqꜣ pn n ṯnw dj.f jry.j rnpwt ꜥšꜣ* — a SUBJECT–*sḏm.f* construction expressing customary action (§ 18.6), introduced by *jw*, which links it to the preceding statement.

B 101–102 *rwt.n.j r.s* — *rwj r* can mean "leave to" or "leave from" a place. The latter sense is suggested here by the New Kingdom version *ḫꜣst nb jy.n.j jm.s[n]* "every country I came back from."

jw jr.n.j hd.j jm.s — the particle *jw* was inserted secondarily by the scribe. Its purpose here seems to be to prevent the following *sḏm.n.f* clause from being interpreted as a main clause ("Every country …, I made my attack in it").

d⸢r⸣.t(j) ḥr smw ẖnmwt.s — this is the main clause of the sentence. The scribe has made the second sign like rather than . The preposition *ḥr* here expresses the origin of the action (§ 8.2.10). The second sign of *smw* is a variant form of M 21 by way of F 37 (see the Sign List).

B 103–106 *jn.n.j* — B 103 has only one , but H 1 indicates that the *sḏm.n.f* is meant.

rmṯ jm.s — the preposition here probably has partitive sense (§§ 8.2.3, 9.4).

B 107–107 *ꜣḫ.n m jb.f* — both B and R have no subject for the initial verb, indicating that it is used impersonally.

rḫ.n.f qn.n.j — H 3 has the geminated *sḏm.f*: "when he learned how I used to persevere." Both forms are unmarked noun clauses, used as the object of *rḫ* (§ 21.7).

B 107–109 *rdj.⌜n⌝.f* — as written, the form in B 107 appears to be the infinitive, but a narrative use of the form is out of place here. H 3 has the expected *sḏm.n.f*. B's version was probably influenced by the similar line in B 86.

mꜣ.n.f r(w)d ꜥwj.j — despite its determinative, the second verb is *rwd* "become firm" and not *rd* "grow." A New Kingdom copy has the correct determinative, as in B 76. The *sḏm.f* is an unmarked noun clause as object of *mꜣꜣ*.

Episode 14 — Sinuhe's Challenge (B 109–127, H 4, R 135–146)

B 109–10	*jwt nḫt n ṯnw*	3	
	mṯꜣ.f wj m jmꜣm.j		2
B 110–11	*pry pw nn snnw.f*	2	
	dr.n.f s(j) r ḏr.s		2
B 111–12	*ḏd.n.f ꜥḥꜣ.f ḥnꜥ.j*	3	
	ḫmt.n.f ḥwt(f).f wj		2
B 112–13	*kꜣ.n.f ḥꜣq mnmnw(t).j*	3	
	ḫr zḥ n wḥyt.f		2

B 109–10 Coming of a strongman of Retjenu,
challenging me in my tent.
B 110–11 He was a champion without peer,
for he had subdued it entirely.
B 111–12 He said he would fight with me,
he anticipated that he would rob me:
B 112–13 he intended to plunder my herds
with the counsel of his tribe.

In this episode, reminiscent of the story of David and Goliath in the Bible, Sinuhe is challenged by a strongman from another tribe. The first part of the episode describes the challenge and the second part, Sinuhe's response.

B 109–10 *jwt* — narrative infinitive signaling the start of a new episode.

mṯꜣ.f wj m jmꜣm.j — H 4 has *mṯꜣ.n.f wj m ꜥf[ꜣy.j]* "he challenged me in my camp." The word for "tent" is *jmꜣ*; the spelling *jmꜣm* shows loss of the final consonant.

B 109–10 *pry pw* — literally, "he was an emerger." The word refers to someone who "emerges" in front of the rest of the army in battle (Donner 1956).

dr.n.f s(j) — the feminine pronominal object refers to Retjenu (§ 4.4 end). The sentence means that Sinuhe's challenger had bested every other fighter in the land.

B 111–12 R 137 does not have enough space in the lacuna for both lines of this couplet; one or the other was omitted

ḥwt(f).f wj — the verb is *ḥwtf* "rob," confirmed by New Kingdom copies; the verb *ḥwj* "hit" is normally written without . The scribe of B 112 has omitted the final radical of the verb.

B 112–13 *ẖr zḥ n wḥyt.f* — the phrase indicates that Sinuhe's challenger was acting with the consent of his tribe.

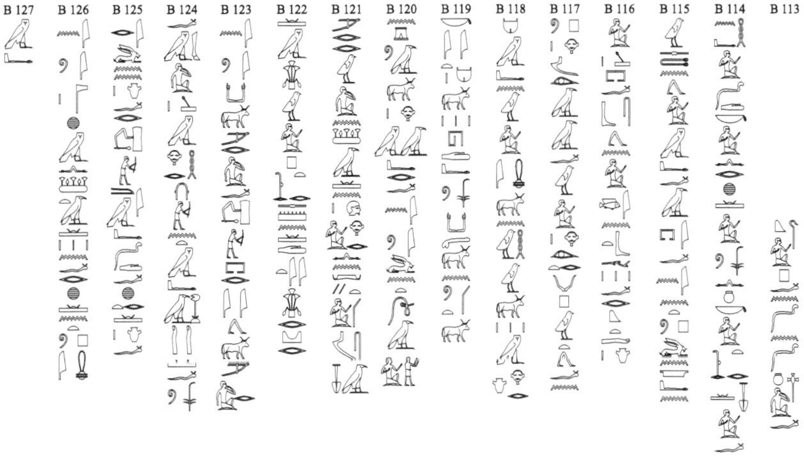

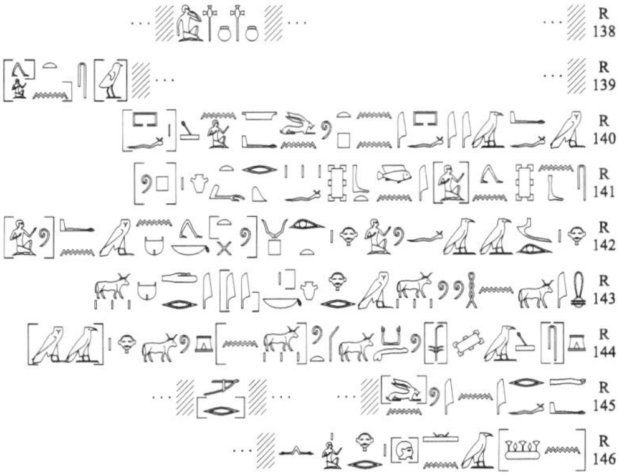

B 113–14	*ḥqꜣ pf ndnd.f ḥnʿ.j*	3
	dd.k(w) nj rḫ.j sw	2
B 114–15	*nj jnk tr zmꜣ.f*	2
	wstn.j m ʿfꜣj.f	2
B 115–16	*jn nt pw wn.n.j sꜣ.f*	3
	s(n)b.n.j jnbwt.f	2
B 116–17	*rqt jb pw*	1
	ḥr mꜣꜣ.f wj ḥr jrt wpwt.f	2
B 117–20	*nḥmn wj mj kꜣ n ḥww m ḥr(j) jb ky jd⌜r⌝*	3
	hd sw kꜣ n ʿwt	3
	ngꜣw ḥr ꜣm r.f	3

B 120–22 *jn jw wn twꜣ mrrw n šꜣ n dp-ḥr(j)* 5
nn pḏtj smꜣ.(w) m jdḥw(j) 3
ptr smn dyt r ḏw 4
B 123–24 *jn jw kꜣ mr.f ꜥḥꜣ* 3
pry mr.f wḥm sꜣ 4
m ḥr nt(j) mḫꜣ.f sw 2
B 125 *jr wnn jb.f r ꜥḥꜣ* 3
jmj ḏd.f ḫrt jb.f 3
B 126–27 *jn jw nṯr ḫm.(w) šꜣt.n.f* 3
rḫ.(w) nt pw mj mj 3

B 113–14 That ruler consulted with me.
I said, "I do not know him.
B 114–15 Am I his ally,
striding about in his camp?
B 115–16 Is it a fact that I have opened his tent-flap
or scaled his walls?
B 116–17 It is contrary-mindedness,
because he sees me doing his job.
B 117–20 I am surely like a bull of the wild in the midst of another herd,
whom the alpha-bull attacks
while the steer fastens on to him.
B 120–22 Is there a dependant loved to the same degree as the chief servant?
No bowman is allied with a reed-man.
Who can fasten papyrus to a mountain?
B 123–24 Does a bull want to fight
and a champion bull want to back off
in terror of one whom he matches?
B 125 If his mind is set on fighting,
let him say what he has in mind.
B 126–27 Is the god unaware of what he has fated
or aware what the situation is like?"

B 113–14 *ḥqꜣ pf nḏnḏ.(n).f ḥnꜥ.j* — this is an example of the SUBJECT–*sḏm.f* construction used in B to express a simple past act rather than generalizations or normative actions (§ 18.6).

ḏd.k(w) — see the note to B 45 *ḏd.k(w) r.j*, above.

B 114–15 *nj jnk tr zmꜣ.f* — the enclitic particle *tr* marks this as a question (§ 15.7.11). [hieroglyph] is a spelling of the proclitic particle *jn* (§ 15.6.2), confirmed by New Kingdom copies.

B 115–16 *jn nt pw wn.n.j sꜣ.f* — an A *pw* B sentence in which B is an unmarked noun clause, with the particle *jn* marking it as a question. *nt* is the feminine nisbe of the preposition *n* (§ 22.2), occasionally used as a noun meaning "fact, case, situation." The sense of *sꜣ.f* is uncertain. It may refer to the "lid" (Sign List Aa 17), or entry-flap, of a tent, for which the normal words for "door" are unsuited; alternatively, it may mean "the back of his house," referring to the private quarters.

s(n)b.n.j jnbwt.f — the verb is *znb*, as in R 141. The meaning is suggested by this passage, where the object refers to the wood palisade erected around a camp.

B 116–17 *rqt jb* — the verb *rqj* means "oppose, rebel against."

wpwt.f — R 142 has *wp[wt].k* "your mission." The 3ms pronoun, however, also makes sense, implying jealousy on the part of the challenger because of Sinuhe's success as a military commander, described in the preceding episode.

B 117–20 The first of three tercets in which Sinuhe contrasts himself with his adopted country. This one and the third use the metaphor of animal husbandry.

mj kꜣ n ḥww m ḥr(j) jb ky jd⌜r⌝ — the image here is of a rogue bull infiltrating a herd, just as Sinuhe has inserted himself into the midst of the Asiatics. The meaning of *ḥww* is uncertain, but the use here suggests animals that do not belong to a herd. B's scribe has misunderstood the word *jdr*, preserved in R 143, as *jdwt* "cows."

hd sw kꜣ n ꜥwt — an unmarked relative clause with the *sḏm.f* (§ 22.13). *kꜣ n ꜥwt*, literally "bull of the animals," refers to the alpha bull of the herd, protecting his herd from the intruder — a metaphor for Sinuhe's challenger. R 144, damaged at the beginning, has subsituted the verb *gsꜣ* "topple" for *hd* "attack."

ngꜣw ḥr ꜣm r.f — an unmarked adverb clause with pseudo-verbal predicate (§ 20.7). The term *ngꜣw* refers to a longhorn bull raised for slaughter. Such animals are normally castrated before sexual maturity both to control reproduction in the herd and because steers produce more and higher-quality beef than uncastrated bulls. The image here is of a steer depending on the alpha bull for protection, and is therefore a rather derogatory reference to the people supporting Sinuhe's challenger.

B 120–22 *twꜣ ... dp ḥr(j)* — the first noun, from the verb *twꜣ* "respect," denotes a person of inferior rank, someone who shows respect for a superior. The normal idiom for "superior" is *ḥrj dp* "one who is over the head," but the two components are reversed in both B and R (the only two surviving texts at this point). *dp* here probably has the sense of "servant" (see the note to ShS. 179 *dp 200*), with *ḥr(j)* "chief" modifying it. The two terms *twꜣ* and *dp ḥr(j)* are meant as contrastive, as in the next two lines of the tercet, rather than as references to specific characters in the story.

n šꜣ n — literally, "for the worth of."

nn pḏtj smꜣ.(w) m jdḥw(j) — *pḏtj* "bowman" refers to a desert-dweller (where wild game was abundant in ancient times); *jdḥw(j)* is a nisbe from *jdḥw* "reeds" and refers to the marshes of the Delta. *smꜣ.(w)* is a 3ms stative modifying an undefined antecedent. The sentence is a non-verbal negation of existence (§ 11.4).

ptr smn dyt r ḏw — This sentence, a non-verbal question (§ 7.13.2) with participial subject, reverses the imagery of the preceding line. *dyt* is a variant of *ḏwwt* "papyrus." The 𓂋 at the end of col. 122 is most likely an error for the "stone" determinative 𓊌 (Sign List O 39).

B 123–24 *kꜣ mr.f ... pry mr.f* — SUBJECT–*sḏm.f* expressing normative action (§ 18.6). The sentence is marked as a question by *jn* and as referring to the current situation by *jw*. In the metaphor, *kꜣ* refers to the challenger and *pry*, in a deliberate reversal of the description in the second couplet, to Sinuhe himself.

wḥm sꜣ.f — literally, "to repeat his back," evidently referring to repeatedly backing off.

nt(j) mḫꜣ.f sw — literally, "one who he balances him," a marked indirect relative clause: *ntj* and *sw* refer to the *kꜣ* of the first line, and the suffix *f* to the *pry* of the second line; *mḫꜣ* refers to the action of weighing something in a scale (*mḫꜣt*) by balancing it against an object of known weight. The sense is that no "champion bull" will turn away "in terror" from a challenger he feels equal to. *ntj* here is the relative counterpart of *jw* and denotes the statement of the relative clause as limited in applicability to the situation described (§ 22.5).

B 125 *jr wnn jb.f r ꜥḥꜣ* — literally, "if his mind is (continually) toward fighting."

jmj ḏd.f ḫrt jb.f — see the note to ShS. 20 *jr r.k* (or *jrr.k*) *m ḫrt jb.k*. This line reflects the ancient Near Eastern custom, and requisite, of a formal announcement of hostilities before a battle. The Instruction for King Merikare (Essay 19) decries the Asiatic as one who "does not report the day of battle, like a thief that society has banished."

B 126–27 *šꜣt.n.f* — given the second line of the couplet, this probably does not reflect a fatalistic view of the battle's outcome but is instead a reference to the battle as part of the god's plan for Sinuhe (cf. B 156–57 in the next episode).

nt pw mj mj — literally, "it is the situation like what," an A *pw* sentence serving as an unmarked noun clause, object of *rḫ*. The question in each line is rhetorical, since the god is surely aware of what he has planned for Sinuhe. The couplet as a whole echoes the sentiment of the tercet preceding, as a statement that Sinuhe has no choice but to fight.

Episode 15 — Sinuhe's Battle (B 127–146, R 154–171)

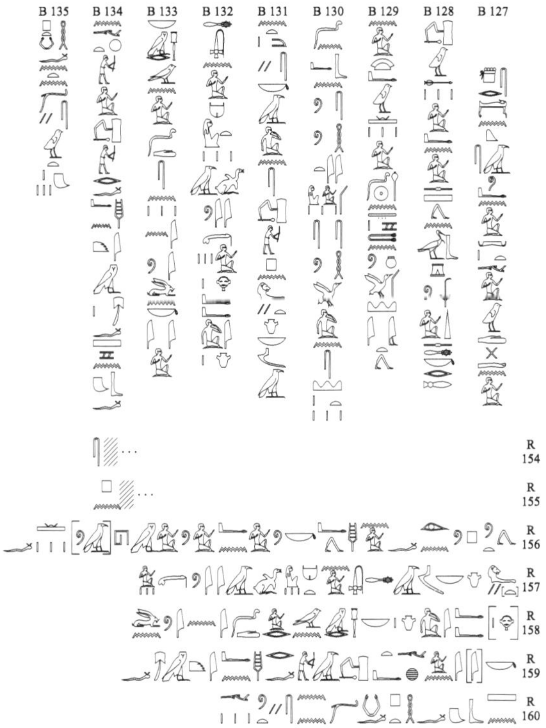

B 127–28	*sḏr.n qꜣs.n.j pḏt.j*	3
	wd.n.j ꜥḥꜣw.j	2
B 128–29	*dj.n.j zn n bꜣgsw.j*	3
	sḫkr.n.j ḫꜥw.j	2
B 129–30	*ḥḏ.n tꜣ ṯnw jj.t(j)*	4
	ḏnb.n.s wḥwyt.s	2
B 130–31	*sḥw.n.s ḫꜣswt nt gs(wj).sj*	3
	kꜣ.n.s ꜥḥꜣ pn	3
B 131–32	*ḥꜣtj nb mꜣḫ.(w) n.j*	2
	ḥjmwt ṯꜣyw ḥr ꜥ(j)ꜥj	3
B 132–35	*jb nb mr.(w) n.j ḏd.sn*	3
	jn jw wn ky nḫt ꜥḥꜣ r.f	4
	ꜥḥꜥ n jkm.f mjnb.f ḥpt.f nt nsjwt	5

B 127–28 During the night, I strung my bow
and shot my arrows,
B 128–29 gave play to my dagger
and embellished my weapons.
B 129–30 At dawn, Retjenu came,
having incited its tribes
B 130–31 and collected the countries around it,
having intended this fight.
B 132–35 Every heart smoldered for me,
women and men were wailing.
B 132–35 Every mind was sick for me, saying,
"Is there another strongman who can fight against him,
who can stand up to his shield, his axe, his clutch of spears?"

B 127–29 *sḏr.n* — an impersonal use of the verb *sḏr* "lie down, spend the night." The construction is the same as that of the more common *ꜥḥꜥ.n sḏm.n.f* and is actually emphatic, with the first verb expressing an action logically subordinate to that of the second: *sḏr.n qꜣs.n.j pḏt.j* "as night was spent, I strung my bow"; *ꜥḥꜥ.n sḏm.n.f* "as it arose, he heard."

dj.n.j zn n bꜣgsw.j — literally, "I gave passage to my dagger."

B 129–30 *ḥḏ.n tꜣ ṯnw jj.t(j)* — see § 25.8.3; literally, "the land became bright with Retjenu come." Retjenu here refers to the supporters of Sinuhe's challenger, since "he had subdued it entirely" (B 110–11). The challenger and his allies evidently arrived during the night and, as the final tercet of this episode implies, set up camp next to Sinuhe's camp.

nt gs(wj).sj — literally, "of its (two) sides." See the note to ShS. 85 *ntj gs(wj).fj m nwy*.

R 156 adds a couplet here: *jwt pw jr.n.f n.j ꜥḥꜥ.kw / dj.n.j wj m h[ꜣ]w.f* "What he did was come to me as I stood (waiting), and I put myself in his vicinity."

B 132–35 *ḏd.sn* — the suffix pronoun expresses the plural implicit in *jb nb*. R 158 has *r ḏd* "saying" (§ 13.11.3).

ꜥḥꜥ n jkm.f — see the Introduction, pp. 5–6, above. The first three signs are written in both B and R as if the scribes understood the introductory word meaning "then." If so, however, a verb form must follow, which here can only be *ḫr* as a stative *ḫr.(w)* "fell." Such an interpretation is unlikely, however, because Egyptian does not like overly long subjects before the stative, preferring a construction such as *ꜥḥꜥ.n jkm.f ḫr.(w) ḥnꜥ mjnb.f ḥpt.f nt nsjwt*. Despite the missing determinative, the line makes much more sense if *ꜥḥꜥ* is a second participle modifying *ky nḫt*.

mjnb.f — the 𓈙 is for N 36 𓈘, used in writing the word *mr* "canal" (hence the following 𓈗 in B 134). Because that word became *mj* (§ 2.8.4), the sign was used as a biliteral *mj* at the beginning of some words.

B 146 B 145 B 144 B 143 B 142 B 141 B 140 B 139 B 138 B 137 B 136 B 135

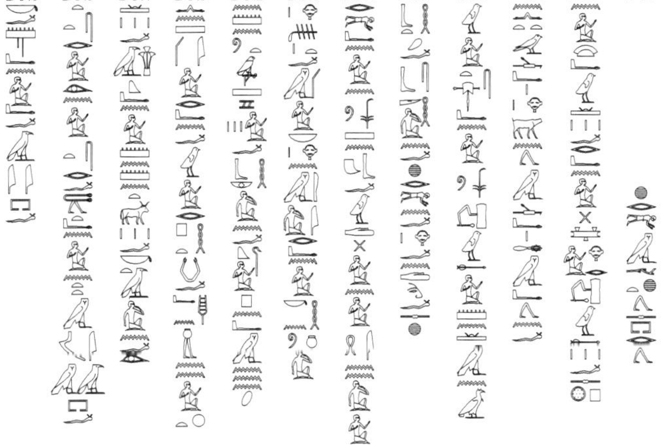

R 160 R 161 R 162 R 163 R 164 R 165 R 166 R 167 R 168 R 169 R 170 R 171

B 135–37 *ḫr m ḫt spr.n.j ḫꜥw.f* 3
rdj.n.j swꜣ ḥr.j ꜥḥꜣw.f 4
zp n jwtt wꜥ ḥr ẖn m wꜥ 5

B 137–39 *ẖmꜥ.n.f wj st.n.j sw* 2
ꜥḥꜣw.j mn.(w) m nḥbt.f 3

B 139–40 *sbḥ.n.f ḫr.n.f ḥr fnd.f* 3
sḫr.n.j sw (m) mjnb.f 2

B 140–41 *wd.n.j jšnn.j ḥr jꜣt.f* 3
ꜥꜣm nb ḥr nmj 2

B 141–42 *rdj.n.j ḥknw n mntw* 3
mrw.f ḥ(ꜣ)b.(w) n.f 2

B 142–43 *ḥqꜣ pn {zꜣ} ꜥmmw-nnšj* 2
rdj.n.f wj r ḥpt.f 2

B 143–45 *ꜥḥꜥ.n jn.n.j ḫwt.f ḥꜣq.n.j mnmnwt.f* 4
kꜣt.n.f jrt st r.j jr.n.j st r.f 5

B 145–46 *jt.n.j ntt m jmꜣm.f* 3
kf.n.j ꜥfꜣy.f 2

B 135–37 Afterward, I made his weapons come out.
I made his arrows pass by me
to no avail, one chasing the other.

B 137–39 He charged me and I shot him,
and my arrow stuck in his neck.

B 139–40 He cried out and fell on his nose,
and I felled him with his axe.

B 140–41 I emitted my cry of victory over his back,
while every Asiatic was moaning;

B 141–42 I gave praise to Montu,
while his dependants mourned for him.

B 142–43 That ruler, Ammunanši,
put me in his embrace.

B 143–45 Then I got his things and plundered his herds:
what he intended to do to me, I did it to him;

B 145–46 I took possession of what was in his tent,
and stripped his camp.

B 135–37 *ḫr m ḫt spr.n.j ḫꜥw.f* — *ḫr* is a particle used to allow a prepositional phrase to stand at the beginning of a sentence (§ 15.6.13); *sprj* is a rare causative of *prj* "emerge." The clause means that Sinuhe invited or incited his opponent to shoot first. R 160–61 has emended this line to *ḫr.n m ḫt pr.n.(j) m ḫꜥw.f* "Afterward, it fell that I escaped from his weapons."

zp n jwtt — a phrase used adverbially: literally, "(being) a case of nothing."

B 137–39 R 163 inserts a couplet at this point: *ꜥḥꜥ.n jr.n.f pḥ.f r.j / ḫmt.n.f ḥwtf.j* "Then he made his approach to me, / having anticipated robbing me."

ẖꜥm.n.f wj — see § 25.9. R 164 has *ḫꜥm.n.f w[j]*: see the note to B 53 *ẖꜥm.f*, above.

ꜥḥꜣw.j mn.(w) m nḥbt.f — R 165 has *ḫr.[n ꜥḥꜣw.j m n]ḥbt.f* "my arrow fell into his neck." The New Kingdom version follows B.

B 139–40 *sḫr.n.j sw (m) mjnb.f* — B has omitted the preposition, present in R 166. Although the challenger had already "fallen," the causative *sḫr* "fell (cause to fall)" is used because the weapon is an axe: the image is that of chopping down a tree.

B 140–42 These two couplets contrast Sinuhe's celebration with the mourning of the challenger's followers: *wdj jšnn* "emit a cry of victory" versus *nmj* "moan" (the same word used for the sound of cattle in B 24–25), and *rdj ḥknw* "give praise" versus *ḥꜣbj* "mourn." *ꜥꜣm* "Asian" is an ethnic term.

wd.n .j jšnn.j — the verb *wdj* means "push"; it is also used of shooting arrows in B 127. R 167 substitutes *dj.n.j* "I gave." The word *jšnn* is attested only in B 140; its meaning is deduced from the context.

rdj.n.j ḥknw n mntw — Montu (originally *mnṯw*) was the god of war.

B 142–43 *{zꜣ} ꜥmmw-nnšj* — see the note to this name in B 30, above.

B 143–46 Sinuhe's actions imply that the challenger's camp and tent were not far from his own encampment.

Episode 16 — Sinuhe Longs for Home (B 146–156)

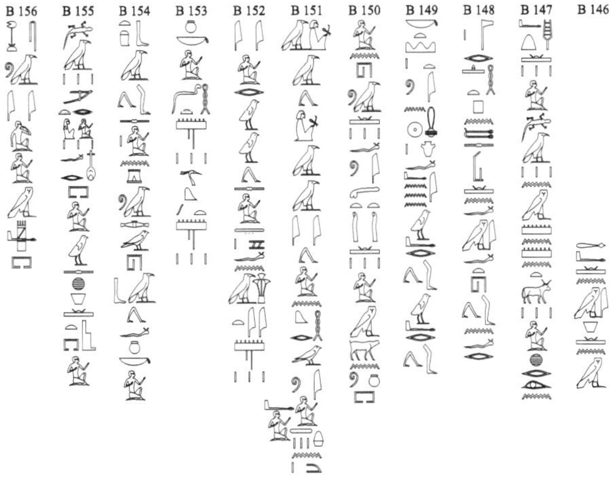

B 146–47 *ꜥꜣ.n jm wsḫ.n m ꜥḥꜥw.j* 4
ꜥšꜣ.n m mnmnwt.j 2

B 147–49 *ḫr jr.n nṯr r ḥtp* 3
n ṯz.n.f jm.f th.n.f r kt ḫꜣst 4
jw mjn jb.f jꜥ.(w) 3

B 149–50 *wꜥr wꜥr n hꜣw.f* 3
jw mtt.j m ẖnw 2

B 151–52	*zꜣꜣ zꜣꜣy n ḥqr*	3
	jw.j dj.j t n gsy.j	3
B 152–53	*rww zj tꜣ.f n ḥꜣyt*	4
	jnk ḥḏt pꜣqt	3
B 154–55	*btꜣ zj n gꜣw hꜣb.f*	3
	jnk ʿšꜣ mrt	2
B 155–56	*nfr pr.j wsḫ jst.j*	4
	sḫꜣwy.j m ʿḥ	2

B 146–47 Since enlargement has come from it, broadening in my riches,
and increase in my herds,
B 147–49 the god has to have acted in contentment
to one whom he reproached and led astray to another country:
now his mind is washed.
B 149–50 Though a fugitive flees for his circumstances,
my core is at home.
B 151–52 Though a crawler crawls for hunger,
I give bread to my neighbor.
B 152–53 Though a man leaves his land for nakedness,
mine are white clothes and fine linen.
B 154–55 Though a man runs for lack of one he can send,
I have many dependants.
B 155–56 My house is good, my place is broad,
but my thought is in the palace.

The battle, with its possibility of death for Sinuhe, is a turning point in the story. Despite his welcome in Retjenu, and his success as a tribal and military leader, he now begins to think of home, a longing he expresses eloquently in a short poem. This section is lost in R.

B 146–47 *ʿꜣ.n ... wsḫ.n ... ʿšꜣ.n* — three *sḏm.n.f*'s with omitted subject (the seated man after the first verb in the transcriptions of Blackman and Koch does not exist): literally, "it has become big … it has become broad … it has become many." In the first clause, *jm* evidently refers to Sinuhe's appropriation of his opponent's property, described in the preceding tercet. As all three verbs are intransitive, the use of the *sḏm.n.f* probably signals an emphatic sentence rather than three simple statements of fact (§ 25.13.2): the three clauses of this couplet are background to the clause that follows in the first line of the next tercet.

B 147–49 *ḫr jr.n nṯr* — the particle *ḫr* signals necessity (§ 15.6.13), here with the *sḏm.n.f* rather than the *sḏm.f* (§ 18.11).

r ḥtp — literally, "with respect to contentment."

ṯz.n.f jm.f ... th.n.f — the subject of both relative *sḏm.n.f* forms refers to *nṯr* of the first line. *ṯzj m*, literally, "lift in/from," is an idiom for "rebuke, reproach"; the suffix pronoun of *jm.f* refers to the unexpressed antecedent of the relative form.

jw mjn jb.f jꜥ.(w) — *jꜥj jb* "wash the mind" refers to the removal of anger. Like English, Egyptian often puts the adverb *mjn* "now" first in the sentence.

B 149–50 The first four couplets of the poem have the same structure, an emphatic sentence in which a generalization in the first line serves as background to the contrasting situation of Sinuhe in the second. Though each initial line is a generalization, each also applies to Sinuhe himself before he became successfully settled in Retjenu. In each, a prepositional phrase with *n* "for, because of" expresses the reason for the action (§ 8.2.6).

wꜥr wꜥr n hꜣw.f — a construction in which the subject of a *sḏm.f* is the participle of the same verb. *hꜣw* can mean either spatial or temporal "vicinity"; the former is indicated here by *m ẖnw* in the second line.

mtt.j — this word is normally found in the expression *mtt nt jb* or *mtt jb*, denoting innermost thoughts or feelings.

B 151–52 *gsy.j* — a nisbe from *gs* "side"; the double reed-leaf reflects the combination of the nisbe ending with the 1s suffix pronoun (*gási+i > *gasíyi).

B 152–53 *jnk ḥḏt pꜣqt* — a statement of adherence, with *nj* omitted before the pronoun (§ 7.8). The feminine ending of *ḥḏt* rules out a *nfr ḥr* construction ("I am white of fine linen").

B 154–55 *btꜣ zj n gꜣw hꜣb.f* — the reference is to a messenger running with a message. *hꜣb.f* is a relative *sḏm.f.*

jnk ꜥšꜣ mrt — an A B nominal sentence with a *nfr ḥr* construction as B (§ 6.5).

B 155–56 *sḫꜣwy.j* — the verb *sḫꜣ* means basically "bring to mind," either to oneself ("remember") or to another ("remind"); *sḫꜣw* is a verbal noun expressing the act of doing so; the double reed-leaf reflects the combination of the vocalic ending represented by *w* with the 1s suffix pronoun. The sentence means that Sinuhe keeps thinking of the palace.

Episode 17 — Sinuhe's Prayer (B 156–173, R 188–201)

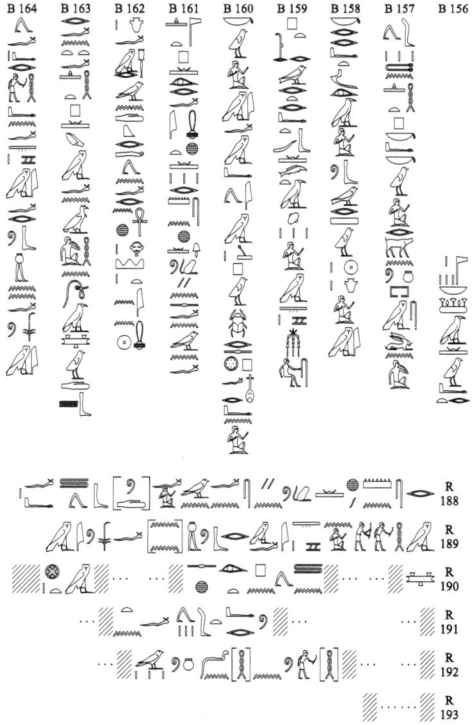

B 156–57	*nṯr{w} nb šꜣ wꜥrt ṯn*	3
	ḥtp.k dj.k wj r ẖnw	3
B 157–58	*smwn.k r rdjt mꜣ.j bw*	4
	wršw jb.j jm	3
B 159–60	*ptr wrt r ꜥbt ẖꜣt.j*	3
	m tꜣ ms.k wj jm.f	3
B 160–61	*mj m sꜣ pw ḫpr zp nfr*	3
	dj n.j nṯr ḥtp	3
B 161–62	*jrr.f mj ḫt r smnḫ pḥwj*	3
	n sfn.n.f jb.f mr.(w)	3
	n dqr.n.f r ꜥnḫ ḥr ḫꜣst	3
B 162–63	*jn mjn r.f ntt.f ḥtp.(w)*	3
	sḏm.f nḥ n wꜣ	3

B 163–64 *wdb.f ꜥ r ḫw.n.f tꜣ jm.f* 5
r bw jn.n.f sw jm 3

B 156–57 Whichever god fated this flight,
may you become content and put me home.
B 157–58 Perhaps you are to let me see the place
my mind spends the day in.
B 159–60 What is more important than interring my corpse
in the land you gave me birth in?
B 160–61 It means, come after, so that a good deed may happen
and the god give me contentment.
B 161–62 May he act in such a way as to improve the end
for one he has afflicted, whose mind is pained;
for one he has pressed into life on the desert.
B 162–63 So, if now it is that he has become content,
may he hear the prayer of one far away,
B 163–64 and turn the arm from where he has landed
to the place he got him from.

Sinuhe's thoughts of home prompt a prayer to "whichever god fated this flight," one of the few witnesses to a direct relationship between non-royal Egyptians and their gods prior to the New Kingdom. The prayer is in two parts. The first, in fifteen lines, asks the god to bring Sinuhe back to Egypt; the second, also in fifteen lines, asks for Sinuhe's return to the royal household.

B 156–57 *nṯr{w} nb* — literally, "any god" (vocative). The plural strokes are an error, since the address to the god continues in the singular.

B 159–60 *ptr wrt r ꜥbt ḫꜣt.j m tꜣ* — literally, "what is something great with respect to uniting my corpse with the land."

ms.k wj jm.f — it is possible to read *ms.kw jm.f* "I was born in," with the 1s stative in an unmarked relative clause, but that would require an undefined antecedent ("a land": § 22.11), which does not suit this context, since Sinuhe is speaking of Egypt. *ms.k wj* is the (masculine singular) relative *sḏm.f* (§ 22.13).

B 160–61 *mj m sꜣ pw* — this is an A *pw* sentence in which A is the imperative *mj m sꜣ* "come after (me)" (§ 21.12), an Egyptian idiom for "help."

ḫpr zp nfr — literally, "a good occasion happens," with the *sḏm.f* used as an unmarked adverb clause of purpose (§ 20.13).

B 161–62 *jrr.f mj ḫt r smnḫ pḥwj* — literally, "he acts like a thing to make effective the end." This is an emphatic sentence, with everything following the verb as the rheme: Sinuhe is asking the god not merely to act, but to act in a particular way.

B 162–63 *jn mjn r.f ntt.f ḥtp.(w)* — this sentence is based on the statement in the preceding episode, *jw mjn jb.f jʿ.(w)* (B 149). The particle *jn* (§ 15.6.2) has a specifying function, often translatable by English "it is the fact (that)." The first line of the couplet provides the grounds for the request in the second line; English requires a conjunction such as "if" or "since." The construction is an adverbial sentence with the predicate *mjn* "now" first (§ 10.2); the subject is *ntt.f ḥpt.(w)*, a marked noun clause "that he is content" (§ 21.4).

B 163–64 *wdb.f ʿ r ḥw.n.f tꜣ jm.f* — literally, "he turns the arm with respect to the one he hit land in it"; the first suffix pronoun refers to the god, and the second, to Sinuhe. *ḥwj tꜣ* "hit land" is an idiom used several times in this text to denote traveling to places; compare English *We started out at noon and hit our first destination at six. ḥw.n.f* is a relative *sḏm.n.f*, with an unexpressed antecedent, referring to Retjenu, where Sinuhe ended his flight. The preposition *r* in this line has the meaning "from" rather than "to." R 189 has emended the relative clause to *m ḥw.n.j tꜣ jm.f* "from where I landed in."

r bw jn.n.f sw jm — i.e., Egypt. The pronouns refer to the god and Sinuhe, respectively.

R 190–92 adds a number of lines here not present in other copies and only partially preserved: *wꜣ[…] dbn pn jr.t(w) sḫ[…] m njwt […] wʿrt.f tn […] ḥw.w n [ḥ]ḏnw […]* "[…] far […] this reversal; may […] be made […] in the town […] this flight of his […] struck because of annoyance […]."

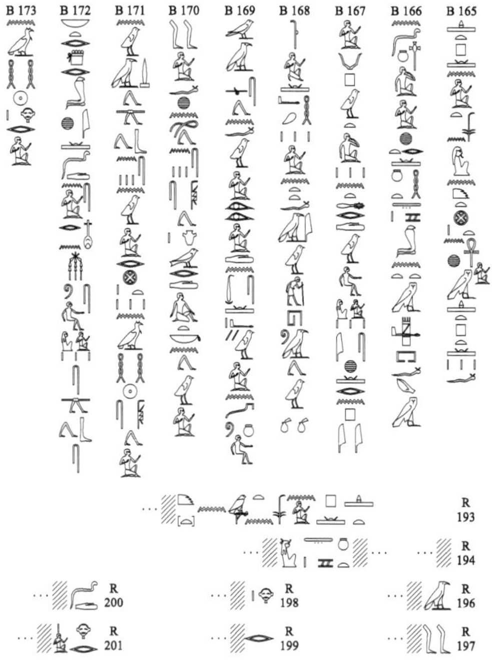

B 165–66	*ḥtp n.j nswt n kmt*	3
	ꜥnḫ.j m ḥtpwt.f	2
B 166–67	*nḏ.j ḫrt ḥnwt-tꜣ ntt m ꜥḥ.f*	4
	sḏm.j wpwt nt ẖrdw.s	3
B 167–68	*jḫ rnpy ḥꜥw.j*	2
	(n) ntt (r).f jꜣw hꜣ.w	3
	wgg ꜣs.n.f wj	2
B 169–70	*jrtj.j dns.(w)*	2
	ꜥwj.j nw.(w)	2
B 170	*rdwj.j fḫ.n.sn šms jb*	3
	wrd tknw n wḏꜣ	3
B 170–72	*zb.sn-n-wj r njwwt nḥḥ*	2
	šms.j nbt-r-ḏr	2
B 172–73	*jḫ ḏd.s n.j nfr n msw.s*	3
	zb.s nḥḥ ḥr.j	3

B 165–66 May the king of Blackland be gracious to me,
for I live by his grace.
B 166–67 May I greet the land's mistress who is in his palace
and hear the messages of her children;
then my body will rejuvenate.
B 167–68 For old age has descended,
and fatigue, it has come suddenly upon me.
B 169–70 My eyes have become heavy,
my arms inert.
B 170 My legs, they have lost how to follow the mind;
one close to the funeral procession is weary:
B 170–72 they send me to the towns of continuity,
and I will follow the Lady to the Limit.
B 172–73 Then she will speak well for me to her children,
and send continuity over me.

B 165–66 See § 25.6. This is the beginning of the second part of Sinuhe's prayer.

B 166–67 *nḏ.j ḫrt* — literally, "may I inquire the condition" (compare English *How are you?*).

ḥnwt-tꜣ ntt m ꜥḥ.f — i.e., the queen. The use of *ntt* carries the connotation "who is currently in his palace": § 22.5.

B 167–68 This couplet may be a loose citation from the Instruction of Ptahhotep 8–9 (see Text 4).

(n) ntt (r).f — the scribe has omitted the two prepositions; a New Kingdom copy has *ḥr ntt r.f* (see § 21.4). The enclitic *r.f* is used here to link the statement to the last line of the preceding tercet (§ 15.7.2).

B 170 *wrd tknw n wḏꜣ* — *tknw* is a noun from the verb *tkn* "come near," which is used with the preposition *n* "to" as well as *ḥr* "upon" (R 198). The phrase *tknw n wḏꜣ* is a euphemism for one who is close to dying; a reasonable English substitute is "one in his twilight years."

B 170–72 *zb.sn-n-wj* — the suffix pronoun refers to *rdwj* "legs" in the preceding couplet. The extra *n* before the dependent pronoun is phonetic, reflecting the pronunciation of the verb and its object as a single word (*sabiásunwi).

njwwt nḥḥ — a metaphor for the cemetery.

nbt-r-ḏr — an epithet of Hathor, appropriate because of Sinuhe's name (see the note to R 2, above) but also because of her role as mother, which identifies her as Nut, mother of Osiris and therefore of the deceased.

B 172–73 *msw.s* — the stars, with whom the deceased wished to travel at night.

zb.s nḥḥ ḥr.j — meant both literally and as a reference to Nut as the lid of the coffin, within which the deceased lies as in a womb, awaiting rebirth.

Episode 18 — Word from Home (B 173–177, R 202)

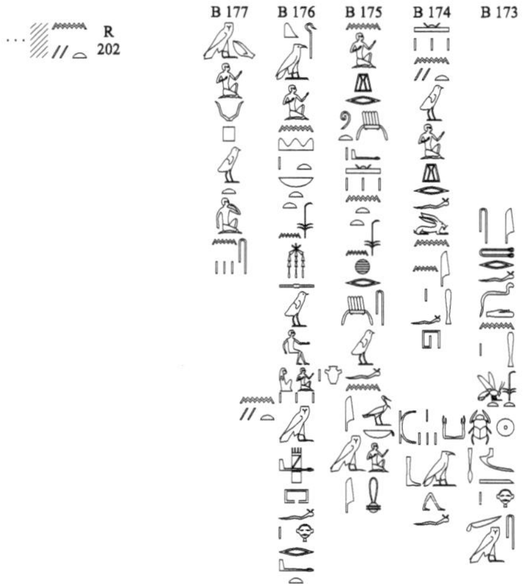

B 173–74 *jsṯ r.f ḏd n ḥm n nswt-bjt ḪPR-Kꜣ{W}-Rꜥ mꜣꜥ ḫrw* 5
ḥr sšm pn ntj wj ḫr.f 3
B 174–75 *wn.jn ḥm.f hꜣb.f n.j* 3
ḫr ꜣwt-ꜥ nt ḫr-nswt 2

B 175–76 *sȝw.f jb n bȝk jm* 3
mj ḥqȝ n ḫȝst nbt 2
B 176–77 *msw-nswt ntj m ʿḥ.f* 3
ḥr rdjt sḏm.j wpwt.sn 3

B 173–74 Now, the Incarnation of Dual King Kheperkaure, justified, was told
about the situation that I was in.
B 174–75 As a result, His Incarnation sent word to me,
with gifts of the king's own,
B 175–76 delighting a humble servant
like a ruler of any country,
B 176–77 and the king's children who were in his palace
were letting me hear their messages.

This episode opens the second half of Sinuhe's story, in which he recounts his return to Egypt and the court. The remainder of R is lost after a fragment of the first line.

B 173–74 *ḏd* — passive *sḏm.f* with unexpressed subject (§ 19.3).

ḪPR-KȝW}-Rʿ — the scribe has written the name horizontally. This is an erroneous form of the throne name of Senwosret I, *ḫpr-kȝ-rʿ*, influenced by that of Senwosret III, *ḫʿ-kȝw-rʿ*. Coupled with the error in the beginning of the king's decree (B 180), this indicates that the scribe was writing during the nineteen-year period of coregency between Senwosret III and Amenemhat III (ca. 1859–1840 BC), when he was most familiar with their names.

mȝʿ-ḫrw — this epithet, deriving from the final judgment (Essay 8), was routinely appended to the name of a deceased king. If original, it indicates that the story was composed after the death of Senwosret I, but it could also have been added by the scribe of the B papyrus.

B 174–75 *wn.jn ḥm.f hȝb.f* — for *wn.jn*, see § 19.10. This is not an instance of the usual SUBJECT–*sḏm.f* construction, which is used in B for generalizations (see the note to B 113–14 *ḥqȝ pf nḏnḏ.(n).f ḥnʿ.j*, above). The regular constructions with *wn.jn* are SUBJECT *ḥr sḏm* and SUBJECT–stative (§§ 14.6, 16.8). Since the language apparently prefers not to use the *sḏm.n.f* after *wn.jn* (§ 17.9), and neither the pseudo-verbal construction nor SUBJECT–stative is suitable for the description of a single past act of a transitive verb, the *sḏm.f* is substituted as a past tense (§ 18.4). As examples of that construction are attested with the *sḏm.f* following *wn.jn* directly, *ḥm.f* here is simply preposed rather than part of a dedicated construction with the *sḏm.f*.

ȝwt-ʿ nt ḫr-nswt — the first noun phrase involves a verbal noun of *ȝwj* "extend," literally, "extending of the arm." *ḫr-nswt* is a prepositional phrase used as a noun, with *nswt* in honorific transposition: literally, "of near the king." It connotes a personal gift from the king's own property.

B 175–76 *sȝw.f jb* — literally, "lengthening the mind," causative of the idiom for happiness (§ 20.8).

bȝk jm — see Essay 25.

mj ḥqȝ n ḫȝst nbt — gifts were exchanged between rulers to cement friendly relations.

Episode 19 — The King's Decree (B 178–199)

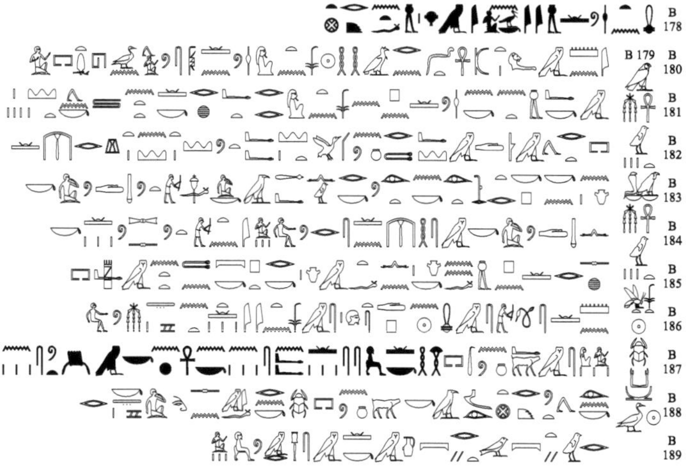

B 178	***mjt n wḏ jny n bꜣk jm ḥr jnt.f r kmt*** (heading)	
B 179–80	*ḥrw ꜥnḫ mswt nbtj ꜥnḫ mswt*	4
	nswt-bjt ḪPR-KꜢ-Rꜥ	2
	zꜣ-rꜥ JMN-M-ḤꜢT ꜥnḫ.(w) ḏt r nḥḥ	5
	wḏ-nswt n šmsw zꜣ-nht	3
B 181–82	*mj.k jn.t(w) n.k wḏ pn n nswt*	3
	r rdjt rḫ.k ntt dbn.n.k ḫꜣswt	4
	pr.t(j) m qdm r ṯnw	3
B 182–83	*dd tw ḫꜣst n ḫꜣst*	3
	ḫr zḥ n jb.k n.k	3
B 183	*ptr jrt.n.k*	2
	jr.t(w) r.k	2
B 183–84	*nj wꜥꜣ.k ḫsf.tw mdw.k*	3
	nj mdw.k m sḥ n sr(j)w	2
	jtn.tw ṯꜣzw.k	2
B 185	*sḫr pn jn n.f jb.k*	3
	nj ntf m jb r.k	3
B 185–86	*pt.k ṯn ntt m ꜥḥ*	3
	mn s(j) rwḏ s(j) m mjn	3
B 186–87	*dpts.s m nsyt nt tꜣ*	3
	ḫrdw.s m ꜥḫnwtj	2

B 187 ***wꜣḥ.k špss n dd.sn n.k*** 3
ʿnḫ.k m ꜣwt.sn 2
B 188 *jr n.k jwt r kmt* 3
mꜣ.k ẖnw ḫpr.n.k jm.f 4
B 188–89 *sn.k tꜣ r rwtj wrtj* 4
ẖnm.k m smrw 2

B 178 **Copy of the decree brought to your servant, about fetching him to Egypt.**
B 179–80 Horus Living One of Birth, Two Ladies Living One of Birth,
Dual King Kheperkare,
Sun's Son Amenemhat, alive forever continually:
king's decree to follower Sinuhe.
B 181–82 Look, this decree of the king is brought to you
to let you know that although you have gone around countries,
having gone up from Qatna to Retjenu,
B 182–83 country gave you to country
only under the counsel of your mind for you.
B 183 What did you do,
that one should act against you?
B 183–84 You did not blaspheme, that your speech should be barred;
you did not argue with the counsel of officials,
that your phrases should be contradicted.
B 185 That plan that got your mind,
not *that* was in mind for you.
B 185–86 That sky of yours who is in the palace,
she is set, she is firm now,
B 186–87 her headgear from the kingship of the land,
her children in the audience-hall.
B 187 **You shall keep the finery of their giving to you,**
and live on their generosity.
B 188 Make a return to Egypt,
that you may see the home you gew up in,
B 188–89 kiss the earth at the great double gate,
and join with the courtiers.

After the introductory line (B 178), the decree is laid out to reproduce an official royal missive, with the beginning of the king's titulary in a column before the horizontal lines of the decree proper.

B 179–80 The titulary is correct for Senwosret I, but the scribe has written *JMN-M-ḪꜢT* instead of *ZJ-N-WSRT* as the king's own name, probably an unconscious reference to the personal name he was most familiar with, that of Amenemhat III.

šmsw zꜣ-nht — Sinuhe is given only a generic court title (see the note to the beginning of the Shipwrecked Sailor), which may have been his title when he fled Egypt. The second part of his name has the "house" determinative also used by this scribe in B 8 *nht*, the name of a place in the region of Dahshur.

B 181–83 This tercet and couplet are an emphatic sentence in which the verb of the rheme governs a noun clause that is itself an emphatic sentence, the rheme of which is also an emphatic sentence. The point of the initial clause is not the fact that the decree has been issued (*jn.t(w) n.k wḏ pn n nswt*), which is evident from the decree itself, but the reason for it (*r rdjt rḫ.k*). In the noun clause, the initial verb phrase and its adverbial complement (*dbn.n.k ḫꜣswt pr.t(j) m qdm r ṯnw*) state something that Sinuhe already knows, so they are background information rather than rhematic; the rheme is the final clause, itself an emphatic sentence whose first clause also states a known fact (*dd tw ḫꜣst n ḫꜣst*): its rheme, and that of the entire sentence, is the final line (*ẖr zḥ n jb.k n.k*). The sentence as a whole is a finely crafted construction, building by stages to the denouement of the final line.

pr.t(j) m qdm r ṯnw — this statement indicates that Sinuhe did not stay in the area of Qatna but moved toward the mountain highlands of the coast (see the note to R55 *ḥqꜣ pw n ṯnw ḥrt* in Episode 9a, above).

B 183–84 *nj mdw.k m sḥ n sr(j)w* — *mdwj m* "speak" can have the same sense as the English idiom *have words with.*

B 185 *nj ntf m jb r.k* — the same construction as in B 39 *ḥꜣtj.j nj ntf m ḫt.j* (see above), in which *ntf* is the negated and emphasized subject of the adverbial sentence. The king means, "That's not what anyone had in mind for you."

B 186–87 *dpts.s m nsyt nt tꜣ* — the initial noun is formed from a feminine nisbe of *dp* "head"; the final *s* is an element added to items of regalia (for example, *mks* "scepter," formed from the verb *mkj*, "protect"); *nsyt* is an abstract formed from *nswt* "king," originally *nswwt* > *nswyt.* Although the queen participates in the "kingship of the land," she does not exercise the office of *nswt*, so the statement means that her headgear derives from her relationship to the king. The headgear in question is the uraeus, originally an attribute of the king but adopted by queens in the Middle Kingdom.

B 187 The reason for the use of red ink is unclear; it is repeated in the only surviving New Kingdom copy at this point. It may have been intended to mark the transition to the subject of the end of the letter (B 188–99).

n dd.sn n.k — see § 21.10.

B 188 *ḫpr.n.k jm.f* — literally, "you developed in it." The verb *ḫpr* is used to express passage through the various stages of development from infancy to adulthood.

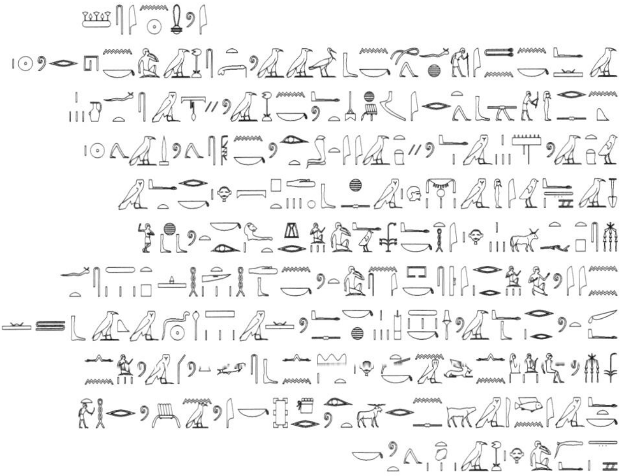

B 189
B 190
B 191
B 192
B 193
B 194
B 195
B 196
B 197
B 198
B 199

B 189–90 *jw mjn js šꜣꜥ.n.k ṯnj* 3
fḫ.n.k bꜣꜣt 2
B 190–91 *sẖꜣ n.k hrw n qrs* 3
zb.t(j) r jmꜣḫ 2
B 191–92 *wḏꜥ.tw n.k ḫꜣwj m sft* 3
wtꜣw m ꜥwj tꜣyt 2
B 192–93 *jr.tw n.k šms wḏꜣ hrw zmꜣ tꜣ* 3
wj m nbw dp m ḫsbd 4
B 193–94 *pt ḥr.k dj.t(j) m mstpt* 4
jḥw ḥr jtḥ.k šmꜥw ḫr ḥꜣt.k 4
B 194–96 *jr.tw ḫbb nnyw r r js.k* 3
njs.tw n.k dbḥt ḥtp 2
sft.tw r r ꜥbꜣw.k 2
B 196–97 *jwnw.k ḫws.w m jnrw ḥḏ* 3
m qꜣb msw-nswt 1
B 197 *nn wn m(w)t.k ḥr ḫꜣst* 3
nn bs tw ꜥꜣmw 2
B 197–98 *nn dj.t(w).k m jnm n zr* 3
jr.tw ḏr.k 2
B 198–99 *jw nꜣ ꜣw.(w) r ḥwt tꜣ* 3
mḥ ḥr ḫꜣt jwt.k 3

B 189–90 For since it is now that you have started to age
and have lost potency,

B 190–91 think of the day of entombment,
when you are sent to the state of honor.
B 191–92 The evening is separated for you with cedar oil
and bandaging in Tayet's arms.
B 192–93 The procession's following is made for you on the day of interment,
the mummy-case of gold, with head of lapis-lazuli,
B 193–94 the sky above as you lie on the bier,
oxen drawing you, chanters in front of you.
B 194–96 Funerary dances are done for you at your tomb's mouth,
the offering-list is recited for you,
and slaughter is done at the mouth of your offering-slabs,
B 196–97 your columns constructed of limestone
amid the king's children.
B 197 Your death will not be on the desert,
Asians will not bury you,
B 197–98 you will not be put in the skin of a ram
when your grave is made.
B 198–99 This has become too long now to wander:
be concerned about illness, and come back.

B 189–90 *jw mjn js šꜣʿ.n.k ṯnj* — As in B 162–63 *jn mjn r.f ntt.f ḥtp.(w)*, this is an adverbial sentence with the predicate first and the unmarked noun clause *šꜣʿ.n.k ṯnj* as subject. The initial *jw* specifies the statement as limited in validity (§ 10.3). Additionally, the clause is subordinated by *js* (§ 20.5), probably not to the preceding sentence but to the imperative that follows in the next couplet. The verb *ṯnj* means "become distinguished"; it is used to imply the distinction that came with old age in Egypt.

B 190–91 *zb.t(j) r jmꜣḫ* — see Essay 21.

B 191–92 The three couplets and tercet in B 191–96 constitute one of the most precise descriptions of ancient Egyptian funerary rites, from the night before the burial (B 191 *ḫꜣwj*) to the funerary procession and the rites at the tomb itself.

wḏʿ.tw n.k ḫꜣwj — the verb *wḏʿ* "separate" here refers to the division of the night before the funeral into hourly "watches," each devoted to a stage in the wrapping of the body.

m sft wtꜣw m ʿwj tꜣyt — wrapping in linen bandages, anointed with cedar oil, was the final stage in mummification. Tayet was the goddess of linen.

B 192–94 These two couplets describe the procession from the embalming house to the tomb.

wj m nbw dp m ḫsbd — the term *wj* refers to a coffin in the shape of a mummy (see Fig. 1, below). First introduced in Dyn. XI, it served as the immediate container for the mummy, which was then placed inside a wood coffin. For *ḫsbd*, see the note to ShS.65–66 *jnḥwj.fj m ḫsbd mꜣʿ*.

Fig. 1. The Mummy on the Bier
(Tomb of Tutankhamun, KV 62, Dyn. XVIII; author's photo)

pt ḥr.k dj.t(j) m mstpt — literally, "the sky above you, you having been placed in the bier." The image is illustrated by Fig. 1; note the "sky" sign at the top of the scene. The *mstpt* (originally, *msṯpt*) was a platform covered by a canopy, used to transport the mummy to the tomb. It was usually covered (Fig. 2); the illustration in Fig. 1 dispenses with the cover so as to show the mummy inside.

jḥw ḥr jtḥ.k — the bier was placed on a sled, pulled by oxen. The illustration in Fig. 1 shows the sled symbolically pulled by Tutankhamun's high officials.

šmʿw ḫr ḥȝt.k — the verb *šmʿj*, from *šmʿ* "thin," refers to a keening sound. Though the term *šmʿw* here is masculine, "chanters" were also women, both from the deceased's family and hired professionals, who wailed during the funeral procession (Fig. 2).

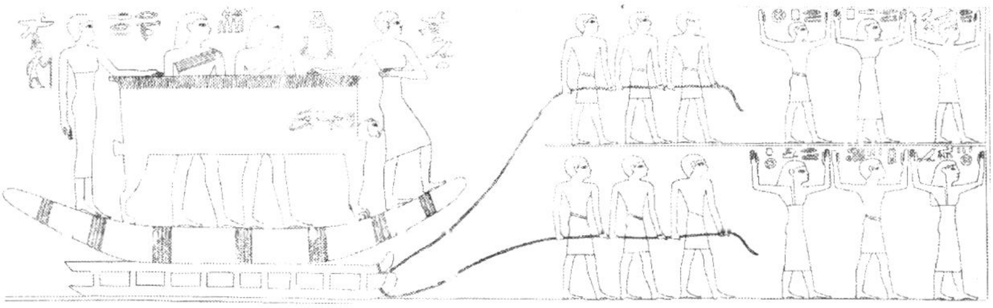

Fig. 2. Chanters Preceding the Bier
(Tomb of Intefiqer and Senet, TT 60, Dyn. XII; after Davies 1920, pl. 19)

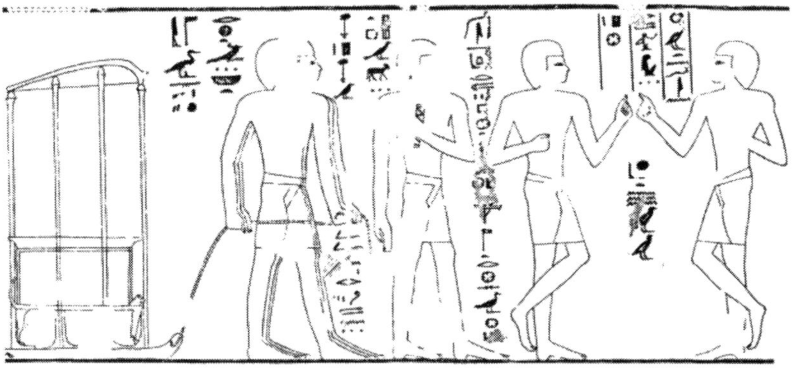

Fig. 3. Dancers Welcoming the Funeral Procession at the Tomb
(Tomb of Amenemhat, TT 82, Dyn. XVIII; after Davies 1915, pl. 11)

B 194–96 This tercet describes the rites at the tomb itself.

ḫbb nnyw — literally, "dance of the inert ones." This refers to a ritual in which performers representing the ancestors of the deceased welcomed the arrival of the procession at the tomb (Fig. 3). The term *nnyw* is a reinterpretation of the original designation of the dancers, *mww* (see the label between the two dancers in Fig. 3), of unknown meaning, perhaps a plural nisbe of *mw* "water," *mwjw* "watery ones" (Altenmüller 1975).

njs.tw n.k dbḥt ḥtp — literally, "the requisition of offering is called for you." The *dbḥt-ḥtp* was a list of offerings, mostly food, often represented in tabular form.

ꜥbꜣw.k — the *ꜥbꜣ* is a stone slab, usually carved with images of food and vessels, on which offerings were laid in front of the false door (see Essay 8 and Fig. 7 there).

B 196–97 This couplet describes a tomb constructed in the royal cemetery, and serves as a bridge between the funeral rites described in the preceding stanzas and the kind of burial Sinuhe can expect if he stays in Retjenu, the subject of the two stanzas that follow. Limestone (*jnr ḥḏ* "white stone") was the preferred building material for elite tombs.

B 197–98 This couplet refers to Asiatic burial practices, in which the body was wrapped in wool and buried in a grave. The Egyptians used wool, but for unknown reasons, it was taboo in temples and tombs. Herodotus reports that "nothing of wool is brought into temples or buried with them; that is forbidden" (*Histories* II, 81).

nn bs tw ꜥꜣmw — the verb *bzj* means "introduce": here, into the grave.

B 198–99 *ḥwt tꜣ* — literally, "hit land." See the note to B 163–64 *wdb.f ꜥ r ḥw.n.f tꜣ jm.f*, above.

Episode 20 — Sinuhe's Response (B 199–241)

B 199–200	***spr.n wḏ pn r.j***	3
	ꜥḥꜥ.kw m ḥr(j) jb wḥwt.j	2
B 200–201	*šd.n.t(w).f n.j dj.n.(j) wj ḥr ẖt.j*	3
	dmj.n.j zꜣtw	2
B 201–202	*dj.n.j sw zn.(w) ḥr šnbyt.j*	3
	dbn.n.j ꜥfꜣy.j ḥr nhm r ḏd	4
B 202	*jr.tw nn mj mj n bꜣk*	4
	th.n jb.f r ḫꜣswt ḏrḏryt	4
B 202–204	*ḫr ḥm nfr wꜣḥ jb nḥm wj m ꜥ m(w)t*	4
	jw kꜣ.k r rdjt jry.j pḥwj ḥꜥw.j m ẖnw	5

B 199–200	**This decree reached me**
	as I was standing in the midst of my tribe.
B 200–201	When it was read to me, I put myself on my belly
	and touched the ground.
B 201–202	I put it opened on my breast
	and went around my camp, yelling,
B 202	"How was this done for a servant
	whose mind went astray to strange countries?
B 202–204	And the determination that saved me from death has to be good,
	for your ka is to let me make my body's end at home."

Sinuhe replies to the pharaoh's decree with a letter (B 204–41), to which this section serves as a short prologue. The scribe continues his use of horizontal lines in anticipation of the letter that follows, also presented in epistolary form.

B 199–200 An emphatic sentence (§ 25.7).

B 200–201 Also emphatic (§ 25.8.3). Both B and the single surviving later copy write the initial verb as *šdj* "take" rather than *šdj* "read" (determinative ), but the latter makes more sense in the context. An Egyptian of Sinuhe's background would have been able to read and write, but as a successful tribal leader Sinuhe would have employed a scribe to handle his correspondence.

B 202 *jr.tw nn mj mj* — see § 25.5.

b3k th.n jb.f — *thj* must be intransitive, since its transitive sense would require an object (*th.n sw jb.f*).

B 202–204 In this couplet, Sinuhe is addressing the king. The first line is an adjectival sentence, with the particle *ḫr* denoting necessity (§ 15.6.13).

w3ḥ jb — literally, "setting of the mind." The idiom implies both determination and patience; its use here probably refers to the king's forbearance toward Sinuhe's transgression.

Episode 21 — Sinuhe's Letter (B 204–238)

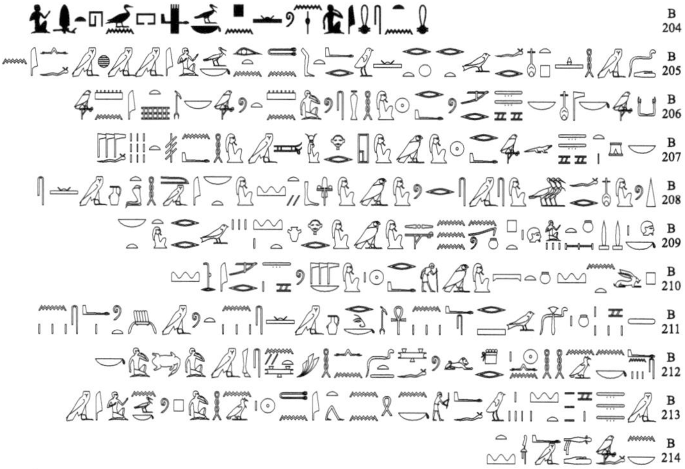

B 204	***mjt n smj n wḏ pn***	(heading)
B 204–205	***b3k ˁḥ z3-nht ḏd***	3
	m ḥtp nfr wrt	3
B 205–206	*rḫ.t(w) wˁrt ṯn jrt.n b3k jm m ḥm.f*	5
	jn k3.k nṯr nfr nb t3wj	3
	mrw rˁ ḥsw mntw nb w3st	5
B 206–208	*jmn nb nst t3wj sbkw rˁ*	4
	ḥrw ḥwt-ḥr tm ḥnˁ psḏt.f	3
	spdw nfr-b3w smsrw ḥrw j3btj	5

B 208–209	*nbt-jmḥt ḫnm.s dp.k*	3
	ḏꜣḏꜣt dpt n nw	3
	mnw ḥrw ḥr(j) jb ḫꜣswt	3
B 209–11	*wrrt nbt pwnt nwt*	3
	ḥrw smsw rꜥ	2
	nṯrw nbw tꜣ-mrj jww nw wꜣḏ-wr	3
B 211	*dj.sn ꜥnḫ wꜣs r fnḏ.k*	4
	ḫnm.sn tw m ꜣwt-ꜥ.sn	2
B 212	*dj.sn n.k nḥḥ nn ḏrw.f*	3
	ḏt nn ḥntj.s	2
B 212–13	*wḥm snḏ.k m tꜣw ḫꜣswt*	4
	wꜥf n.k šnnt jtn	3
B 213–14	*nḥ pw n bꜣk jm n nb.f*	3
	šd.(w) m jmnt	2

B 204 **Copy of the response to this decree.**
B 204–205 **Palace-servant Sinuhe**, who says:
In very good peace!
B 205–206 The flight your servant did, in his ignorance, has been learned
by your ka, young god, lord of the Two Lands,
whom the Sun desires and Montu, lord of Thebes, blesses.
B 206–208 Amun, lord of the Two Lands' throne, Sobek and the Sun,
Horus, Hathor, Atum and his Ennead,
Sopdu, Young of Impressiveness, Semseru, Eastern Horus;
B 208–209 Lady of the Cavern, uniting with your head;
the first conclave of Nu,
Min, Horus in the midst of the countries;
B 209–11 the Uraeus, Lady of Punt, Nut,
Horus the Elder and Sun,
and all the gods of Canal-land and the islands of the sea—
B 211 may they give life and dominion to your nose
and unite you with their generosity;
B 212 may they give you continuity without limits
and eternity without end;
B 212–13 may fear of you be repeated in the flatlands and deserts,
may what the sun disk encircles be subdued to you.
B 213–14 This is the prayer of your servant for his lord,
now that he has been saved from the West.

Sinuhe's reply to the king's decree, in the form of a letter, has five parts. Egyptian letters commonly begin by invoking the blessings of gods on the recipient. In this case, the gods are those of Thebes and those associated with royalty and with the East, from where Sinuhe is writing (Yoyotte 1964).

B 204 *smj* — literally, "report": the response required by a royal decree.

B 205–206 *rḫ.t(w) wꜥrt* — the *sḏm.f* used to express a past action (§ 18.4: "has been learned" = "is known"). It is possible to read *r ḫt wꜥrt* "with respect to the matter of the flight," and the single New Kingdom copy at this point has *ḥr ḫt* "about the matter." This would require the second and third lines of the tercet to be a participial statement with *jn* plus the relative *sḏm.f* rather than a participle: "Your ka ... is what the Sun desires and Montu ... blesses." *ḫt* "thing, matter," however, is regularly written with plural strokes (e.g., B 215). A statement with *rḫ* "learn" at the beginning of this section is better suited to the parallel with *sjꜣ* "perceive" at the beginning of the next. The second and third lines of this tercet, together with the first two lines of the tercet in B 214–15, were paraphrased in an inscription from the reigns of Senwosret III–Amenemhat III (Allen 2008, 36).

B 206–211 The names in these three tercets are all topicalized subjects of B 211 *dj.sn*.

B 206–208 *jmn nb nst tꜣwj* — Amun was chief god of Thebes, hometown of Dyn. XII, and was regarded as the source of the pharaoh's legitimacy.

sbkw rꜥ — Sobek, identified as a form of the sun, was chief god of the region of Lisht, capital of Dyn. XII.

ḥrw ḥwt-ḥr tm ḥnꜥ psḏt.f — the first two gods are associated with kingship. Atum and his Ennead are representative both of the creation and of all the gods.

spdw nfr-bꜣw smsrw ḥrw jꜣbtj — all four names are associated with Sopdu, god of the eastern desert and countries to the east.

B 208–209 This tercet repeats the pattern of the previous one. The first line invokes the uraeus, sign of the pharaoh's authority; the second, the gods of creation; and the third, two gods associated with the deserts.

B 209–11 The third tercet follows a similar pattern, with the first line invoking the uraeus, as well as Hathor ("Lady of Punt") and Nut. Horus the Elder is a reference to the god's role as the kingship inherent in the sun. The final line brings in the entire pantheon, both native and foreign.

B 213–14 *šd.(w) m jmnt* — the verb form is the 3ms stative, referring to *bꜣk jm* in the preceding line. The New Kingdom copy has *šd sw m jmntt* "who saved him from the West," where *šd* is a participle referring to *nb.f* and the dependent pronoun refers to *bꜣk jm*.

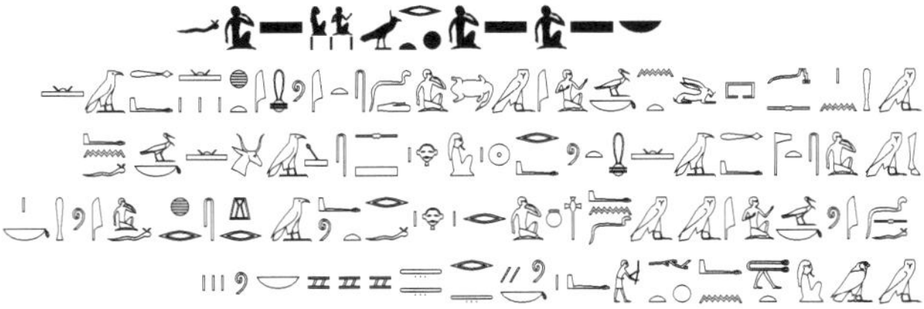

B 214 / B 215 / B 216 / B 217 / B 218

B 214–215 ***nb sjꜣ sjꜣ rḫwt*** 3
sjꜣ.f *m ḥm n stp-z(ꜣ)* 3
wnt bꜣk jm snḏ.(w) ḏd st 4
B 215–17 *jw mj ḫt ꜥꜣ wḥm st* 2
nṯr ꜥꜣ mjtw rꜥ ḥr sšsꜣ bꜣk n.f ḏs.f 5
B 217 *jw bꜣk jm m ꜥ nḏ r ḥr.f* 3
dj.tw ꜣ ẖr sḫr.f 2
B 217–18 *jw ḥm.k m ḥrw jt* 3
nḫt ꜥwj.k r tꜣw nbw 3

B 214–215 **The lord of perception, who perceives the subjects**
perceives in the incarnation of the escort
what your servant has been afraid to say,
B 215–17 for it is like something big to repeat it:
the great god, the Sun's likeness, himself informing one who works for him.
B 217 For your servant is in the hand of one who consults about him
and should just be put under his counsel.
B 217–18 For Your Incarnation is Horus who takes possession:
your arms are forceful against all lands.

The red ink here evidently marks the change from the introductory wishes to the subject of the letter proper (Assmann 1983, 30).

B 214–15 *nb sjꜣ* — see Essay 13.

stp-z(ꜣ) — see the note to R 17 *stp-z(ꜣ)*, above. The *ḥm n stp-z(ꜣ)* "incarnation of the escort" is the king himself.

wnt bꜣk jm snḏ.(w) ḏd st — *wnt* here is probably not a marker of a noun clause (§ 21.4), since B uses *ntt* for that purpose (B 181), but a relative form of the verb *wnn* (§ 22.21). The verb is used as a means of casting the SUBJECT–stative construction *bꜣk jm snḏ.(w)* into the past (§ 18.9).

B 215–17 *ḏs.f* in the second line modifies *nṯr ꜥꜣ mjtw rꜥ* rather than *bꜣk n.f*: the "big thing" is the fact that the king himself is writing to Sinuhe.

B 217 *nḏ r ḥr.f* — *nḏ* is an active participle referring to the king. *nḏ r* "inquire the mouth" is an idiom for seeking advice. The suffix pronoun of *ḥr.f* refers to *bꜣk jm*.

dj.tw ꜣ — the particle emphasizes the verb (§§ 15.7.1). At the time of writing, Sinuhe is not in fact "under the counsel" of the king.

B 217–18 This couplet advances the theme of *m ꜥ* "in the hand" of the preceding couplet. It also serves as a bridge to the next part of the letter.

B 219	***wḏ grt ḥm.k jn.t(w) (n).f***	3
	mjkj m qdmj ḫntjwdjwš m ḫnt kṯw	4
	mnnws m tꜣwj fnḫw	2
B 221–22	*ḥqꜣw pw mtrw rnw*	2
	ḫpr.w m mrwt.k	2
B 222–23	*nn sḫꜣ ṯnw*	1
	n.k jm s(j) mjtt ṯzmw.k js	2

B 219 **Moreover, Your Incarnation should command to have fetched to him**
the *maki* from Qatna, the *khantudawiš* from the south of Kizzu,
or the *munines* from the two lands of the woodworks:
B 221–22 they are rulers renowned of names,
who grew up in love of you,
B 222–23 without thinking of Retjenu:
it is yours, as something like your hounds.

Following on the statement in the preceding couplet, Sinuhe now mentions three Asiatic rulers, both as illustration of the king's dominance over "all lands" and as an example of the proper kind of recipient of a king's letter as opposed to Sinuhe, who considers himself like the king's hunting dogs.

B 219–21 *jn.t(w) (n).f* — the nearest antecedent of the suffix pronoun is *ḥm.k*, which is not a proper object of the king's command. Most likely, the scribe has omitted an *n* before the suffix pronoun. The New Kingdom copy has *jn.tw n.k* "that there be fetched to you."

mjkj m qdmj — the first word can be explained as the Egyptian rendering of a Semitic word for "king" (Schneider 2002, 261–63).

ḫntjwdjwš m ḫnt kṯw — the first word is probably a rendering of Luvian *ḫantawattiš* "ruler," with for (suggestion of Christian Casey). The place name is then most likely Kizzu, the area of Luvian supremacy, in the southeastern part of Turkey; *ḫnt* "front" can be understood as a reference to the southern part of this region (Schneider 2002, 263–66).

mnnws m tꜣwj fnḫw — the first word has been explained as a rendering of Hurrian *ammummines* "sovereign" (Schneider 2002, 266–68). The reference of *tꜣwj fnḫw* is uncertain. The second word has been explained as a form of Egyptian *fnḫ* "do carpentry," but it could also be a rendering of a foreign ethnic name. If *mnnws* is in fact Hurrian, the "two lands" were probably located in the region of Hurrian dominance, today at the confluence of eastern Turkey, northern Syria and Iraq, and northwestern Iran.

B 221–22 *ḥqꜣw* — the scribe has written instead of .

ḫpr.w — 3pl stative, since *ḥqꜣw* is most likely undefined.

B 222–23 *nn sḫꜣ ṯnw* — Retjenu is closer to Egypt than the three locales mentioned in the preceding tercet and was a loose confederation of tribes and towns rather than an established state — both, reasons why it could be considered as part of Egypt's sphere of influence.

n.k jm s(j) — for the construction, see § 11.9.2.

mjtt ṯzmw.k js — see § 15.7.3.

B 223–24 *wꜥrt ṯn jrt.n bꜣk (jm) nj ḥmt.(tw).s* 4
nn s(j) m jb.j nj qmd.j s(j) 3

B 224–25 *nj rḫ.j jwdw.j r jst* 3
jw mj sšm rswt 1
B 225–26 *mj mꜣꜣ sw* ***jdḥy m ꜣbw*** 3
zj n ḫꜣt m tꜣ-stj 3
B 226–28 *nj snḏ.j nj zḫz.t(w) m sꜣ.j* 3
nj sḏm.j ṯꜣz ḥwrw 3
nj sḏm.tw rn.j m r wḥmw 3
B 228–30 *wpw ḥr nf n ḏdf ḥꜥw.j* 3
rdwj.j ḥr hwhw jb.j ḥr ḫrp.j 4
nṯr šꜣ wꜥrt tn ḥr stꜣs.j 4
B 230–31 *nj jnk js qꜣ sꜣ ḫnt snḏ* 4
zj rḫ tꜣ.f 3
B 231–32 *dj.n rꜥ snḏ.k ḫt tꜣ* 4
ḥr.k m ḫꜣst nb 3
B 232–33 *mj wj m ẖnw mj wj m jst ṯn* 2
ntk js ḥbs ꜣḫt tn 3
B 233–34 *wbn jtn n mrt.k* 3
mw m jtrw swrj.t(w).f mr.k 4
ṯꜣw m pt ḫnm.t(w).f ḏd.k 4

B 223–24 The flight that your servant did, it was not anticipated,
it was not in my mind, I did not contrive it.
B 224–25 I do not know how I was separated to the place:
it is like the guidance of a dream,
B 225–26 like **a Deltan** seeing himself **in Elephantine**,
a man of the marshland in Bowland.
B 226–28 I did not fear, no one ran after me,
I did not hear a hue and cry,
my name was not heard in the herald's mouth —
B 228–30 nothing but my goose bumps,
my feet scurrying, my mind managing me,
the god who fated that flight pulling me.
B 230–31 For I am not an arrogant person, prominent, feared,
a man his land knows,
B 231–32 whereas the Sun has put fear of you throughout the land,
terror of you in every country.
B 232–33 It does not matter whether I am at home or whether I am in this place,
for you are one who covers this Akhet.

B 233–34 The sun disk rises for love of you;
water in the river, it is drunk when you like;
air in the sky, it is breathed when you say.

The letter switches abruptly to Sinuhe's apology for his flight. This section repeats in part Sinuhe's explanation to Ammunanši in B 38–43 and R 65–66.

B 223–24 *bꜣk (jm)* — the scribe has omitted the adverb.

nj ẖmt.(tw).s — the passive suffix has been omitted because the verb ends in *t*: cf. § 16.2. It is also possible to read *nj ẖmt.(j) s(j)* "I did not anticipate it," with unwritten 1s suffix.

B 224–26 *jwdw.j r jst* — passive *sḏm.f* used as an unmarked noun clause. The New Kingdom copy has *nj rḫ.tw jnw.j r ḫꜣst tn* "It is not known how I was fetched to this country," with a participle. The order of signs in B 224 makes participial *jwd wj* "who separated me" unlikely. *jwd r* normally means "separate from," but the New Kingdom version suggests the opposite sense. The scribe of B may have omitted the demonstrative *tn* "this" after *jst*.

In the second line, the motive for the use of red ink is unclear, perhaps merely for emphasis. "Bowland" is the first nome of Upper Egypt, with its capital at Aswan.

B 226–28 *nj snḏ.j* — the 1s suffix pronoun was added secondarily. Sinuhe here is technically telling the truth, since his statements in B 2–3 and 38–40 do not mention fear.

B 228–30 *wpw ḥr nf n ḏdf ḥꜥw.j* — literally, "apart from that crawling of my limbs." For *nf n*, see § 5.9.

stꜣs.j — the verb is usually *sṯꜣ* "pull"; *sṯꜣs/stꜣs* may be a variant form, but the final *s* could also derive from a misreading (as 𓊃) of the determinative 𓍣 with which the verb is regularly written.

B 230–31 In this couplet, Sinuhe claims that his status was not prominent enough to warrant the god's attention. The first clause is a nominal-predicate construction negated by *nj* ... *js* (§ 11.5). *qꜣ sꜣ* means literally "high of back" and describes the demeanor of someone who is, or considers himself to be, above others.

B 231–32 This couplet contrasts the universal respect due the king with the more limited kind theoretically available to an ordinary Egyptian, as described in the preceding couplet. In turn, it sets the stage for the next couplet.

B 232–33 In this couplet, Sinuhe concedes that his flight was pointless, since the pharaoh's authority extends as far as the ends of the earth (the Akhet: see Essay 2), where Sinuhe has fled to (*ꜣḫt tn* "this Akhet"). For *mj* ... *mj*, see § 15.6.7.

B 233–34 Three emphatic sentences, the first with a rhematic prepositional phrase (*n mrt.k*); the others, with rhematic adverb clauses (*mr.k* ... *ḏd.k*). See §§ 25.6, 25.7.

B 234–36 *jw bꜣk jm r swḏt* 2
(n) ***ṯꜣt.j jr.n bꜣk jm m jst ṯn*** 4
jwt pw jry r bꜣk jm 3
B 236 *jrr ḥm.k m mrr.f* 3
ꜥnḫ.tw m ṯꜣw n dd.k 3
B 237–38 *mr rꜥ ḥrw ḥwt-ḥrw fnd.k pw špss* 5
mrrw mntw nb wꜣst ꜥnḫ.f ḏt 5

B 234–36 Your servant is to hand over
to **my brood your servant made in this place**,
now that what has been done is to come for your servant.
B 236 Let Your Incarnation do as he likes:
one lives from the air of your giving.
B 237–38 May the Sun, Horus, and Hathor desire that fine nose of yours
that Montu, lord of Thebes, desires to live forever.

Sinuhe's letter ends with a statement indicating his agreement to return, and with wishes that echo those with which the letter began.

B 234–36 *jw bꜣk jm r swḏt* — the pseudo-verbal construction implies a compulsory future act: § 18.7. In the change from the end of the line containing *swḏt* and the beginning of the next line, at the top of a new page, the scribe has omitted the preposition *n*, present in the New Kingdom copy. The red ink, more appropriate to the beginning of the sentence, marks both a new topic and the top of the page. The suffix pronoun of the collective *ṯꜣt.j* "my brood" was added secondarily. Although *ṯꜣt* is feminine, the relative *jr.n* shows that the writer is thinking of male children.

jwt pw jry — this is the passive counterpart of the *sḏm pw jr.n.f* construction, usually found in narrative (§§ 13.14.3, 22.24), with a passive participle. Here it is used as an unmarked adverb clause, supplying the reason for the action in the first two lines.

B 236 Two emphatic sentences, each of which also has an unmarked noun clause with the geminated *sḏm.f* (§§ 21.9–10). With this statement, Sinuhe places himself at the mercy of the king after his return to Egypt.

B 237–38 *mrrw mntw ... ꜥnḫ.f* — an indirect relative clause with the relative *sḏm.f* governing a verb whose subject is the coreferent of the antecedent *fnd.k* (§ 22.17.4).

Episode 22 — Sinuhe's Return (B 238–247)

B 238
B 239
B 240
B 241
B 242
B 243

B 238–39	*rdjt jry.j hrw m jȝȝ*	4	
	ḥr swḏt ḫwt.j n msw.j		2
B 239–40	*zȝ.j smsw.j m sȝ wḥyt.j*	3	
	wḥyt.j ḫwt.j nbt m ʿ.f		3
B 240–41	*ḏt.j mnmnt.j nbt*	2	
	dqrw.j ḫt.j nb bnrj		3
B 241–42	*jwt pw jr.n bȝk jm m ḫntyt*	4	
	ḥdb.n.j ḥr wȝwt-ḥrw		2
B 242–43	*ṯȝzw jm ntj m sȝ pḥrt*	3	
	hȝb.f wpwt r ẖnw		3
	r rdjt rḫ.tw		2

B 238–39 My being allowed to spend a day in Rush
  handing over my things to my children:
B 239–40 my eldest son in charge of my tribe,
  my tribe and all my things in his hand,
B 240–41 my personnel, my every herd,
  my fruit trees, and my every date tree.
B 241–42 What your servant did was to come upstream.
  When I set down on Horus's Ways,
B 242–43 the marshaler there who was in charge of the patrol
  sent a message to the interior
  to let it be known.

The story resumes after the exchange of letters. The scribe continued writing in horizontal lines for the rest of the page (B 238–48) and for two more pages (B 249–62 and 263–76) before returning to vertical columns for the rest of the text.

B 238–39 *rdjt* — probably the narrative infinitive, marking the beginning of a new episode in the story, rather than passive *rdj.t(w)*.

B 239–41 The 1s suffixes of *zꜣ.j smsw.j* were added secondarily. The phrase means literally, "my son, my eldest."

m sꜣ — literally, "in back of." This is an idiom for "in charge of," deriving from herding, where the herders who drive the animals are "in back of" them.

B 241–42 *bꜣk jm* — this substitute for the first-person singular is out of place here, in the narrative, perhaps carried over unconsciously from the preceding letter. It is, however, also present in the New Kingdom copy.

ḥdb.n.j — this is the predicate of an emphatic sentence, the rheme of which is *hꜣb.f* in the next couplet (§ 25.8.3). This is a good example of the difference between the meaning of an emphatic sentence and its grammar. In terms of meaning, this line belongs with the next couplet. Grammatically, however, it is a main clause ("I set down on Horus's Ways") and the following couplet is an adverb clause ("with the marshaler … sending a message").

wꜣwt-ḥrw — the name of the main route across the north of the Sinai peninsula from Asia to Egypt, ending at the "Ruler's Walls": see the note to B 17 *jnbw ḥqꜣ* in Episode 6, above.

B 242–43 *ṯꜣzw* ... *hꜣb.f* — this is a *sḏm.f* with its nominal subject preposed because of its length, rather than a SUBJECT–*sḏm.f* construction.

pẖrt — a collective from the verb *pẖr* "go around."

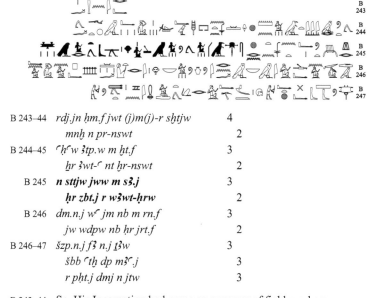

B 243
B 244
B 245
B 246
B 247

B 243–44	*rdj.jn ḥm.f jwt (j)m(j)-r sẖtjw*	4	
	mnḫ n pr-nswt		2
B 244–45	*ꜥḥꜥw ꜣtp.w m ḫt.f*	3	
	ḫr ꜣwt-ꜥ nt ḫr-nswt		2
B 245	***n sttjw jww m sꜣ.j***	3	
	ḥr zbt.j r wꜣwt-ḥrw		2
B 246	*dm.n.j wꜥ jm nb m rn.f*	3	
	jw wdpw nb ḥr jrt.f		2
B 246–47	*šzp.n.j fꜣ n.j ṯꜣw*	3	
	šbb ꜥtḫ dp mꜣꜥ.j		3
	r pḥt.j dmj n jtw		3

B 243–44 So, His Incarnation had come an overseer of field-workers,
an efficient one of the king's house,

B 244–45 with masted ships in his wake
loaded with the generosity of the king's own

B 245 **for the Asiatics who had come in charge of me,**
sending me to Horus's Ways.

B 246 I called each one of them by name,
while every attendant was at his duty.

B 246–47 I set off after the wind was raised for me,
with kneading and brewing beside me
until I reached the harbor of Lisht.

B 243–45 *ˁḥˁw* — term for a ship with a mast (𓊢), suitable for sailing upstream on the Nile using the prevailing north wind.

ꜣwt-ˁ nt ḫr-nswt — see the note to this phrase in Episode 18, above.

n sttjw jww m sꜣ.j ḥr zbt.j r wꜣwt-ḥrw — the initial preposition was added secondarily. The scribe used red ink here probably because he initially thought this line was the beginning of a new section, with the first verb form a 3pl stative *jw.w* rather than a plural participle ("Asiatics came in charge of me"). The line refers to the Asiatics who accompanied Sinuhe from Retjenu to Egypt.

B 246 This couplet describes how the "generosity of the king's presence" was distributed to the Asiatics: Sinuhe called each one forward by name, and an attendant (*wdpw*, literally "cup-bearer") handed out the gifts. The suffix of *jrt.f*, a nisbe meaning "what pertains to him," can refer to *wdpw nb*, as translated above, or to *wˁ jm nb* "each one of them," which case *jrt.f* refers to the gifts each Asiatic was to receive: "while every attendant was seeing to (*ḥr* "upon") his share."

B 246–47 *šzp.n.j fꜣ n.j ṯꜣw* — the verb *šzp* "receive" is also used to refer to the initiation of an action, probably from the idiom *šzp wꜣt* "set off, start out" (literally, "receive the way"). The second verb is a passive *sḏm.f*: see the note to ShS. 34 *fꜣ.t(w) ṯꜣw*. This part of Sinuhe's return voyage takes place by ship on the easternmost branch of the Nile in the Delta, south to the mainstream and then to the capital at Lisht.

šbb ˁṯḫ dp mꜣˁ.j — a clause with adverbial predicate and two infinitives as subject. The verb *šbb* refers to the action of preparing bread for baking; *ˁṯḫ*, literally "straining," is part of the process of brewing beer, in which the barley seeds are separated from the liquid after it has fermented. The passage as a whole means that Sinuhe received food and drink during the trip.

jtw — a phonological rendering of the name of the capital at Lisht, *jṯ-tꜣwj* "the one who takes possession of the Two Lands": *aṯi-táʼwa > *attáwa.

Episode 23 — Sinuhe Before the King (B 248–263, BA 1–11)

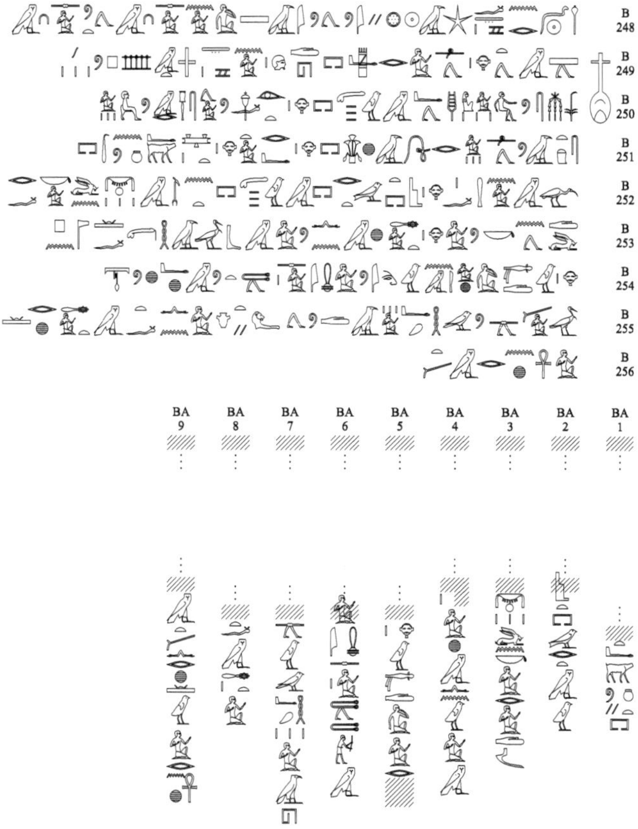

B 248 *ḥḏ.n r.f tꜣ dwꜣ zp 2* 4
jw jw jꜣš n.j 2
B 248–49 *zj 10 m jwt zj 10 m šmt* 4
ḥr stꜣ.j r ꜥḥ 2
B 249–50 *dh(n).n.j tꜣ jmjtw šzpw* 3
msw-nswt ꜥḥꜥ.(w) m wmtw ḥr jrt ẖsfw.j 4
B 250–51 *smrw stꜣw r wꜣḫ* 3
ḥr rdjt.j ḥr wꜣt ꜥḫnwtj 2
B 252 *gm.n.j ḥm.f ḥr jst wrt* 3
m wmtw nt ḏꜥm 2

B 252–53 *wn.k(w) r.f dwn.kw ḥr ẖt.j* 3
ḫm.n.(j) wj m bꜣḥ.f 2
B 253–55 *nṯr pn ḥr wšd.j ḫnm.w* 3
jw.j mj zj jt.w m ꜥḫḫw 3
B 255 *bꜣ.j zj.w* 2
ḥꜥw.j ꜣd.w 2
B 255–56 *ḥꜣtj.j nj ntf m ẖt.j* 3
rḫ.j ꜥnḫ r m(w)t 3

B 248 So, it was dawn, very early,
when a summons came for me,
B 248–49 ten men coming, ten men going,
conducting me to the palace.
B 249–50 I touched forehead to ground between the sphinxes,
while the king's children stood in the thickness making my reception,
B 250–51 and the courtiers who conduct to the Marsh
were putting me on the way to the audience hall.
B 252 I found His Incarnation on the great seat
in a thickness of electrum.
B 252–53 At that I wound up stretched out on my belly,
and I lost consciousness in his presence.
B 253–55 That god was addressing me in delight,
but I was like a man possessed by darkness,
B 255 my ba gone,
my limbs feeble.
B 255–56 My heart — not *it* was in my body,
that I might know life from death.

After reaching Lisht, Sinuhe is summoned to court the next morning to appear before the king.

B 248 *ḥḏ.n r.f tꜣ dwꜣ zp 2* — for the construction, see § 25.8.3. *dwꜣ zp 2* means literally, "in the morning, in the morning," with the noun used adverbially. Egyptian uses repetition for emphasis, as English does in expressions such as *a big, big mistake.*

jw jw jꜣš n.j — a *sḏm.f* with past reference (§ 18.4); the geminated stem (§ 12.6.2) is used probably because the "summons" involved "ten men." The particle *jw* marks the action as specific to the preceding clause.

B 248–49 The size of the contingent reflects the importance accorded Sinuhe. The escort could have involved four of the men as bearers of a carrying chair and an escort of two on each side and one each in the front and rear. The scribe began to write  at the end of B 248 but stopped before completing the sign. The large 𓄤 to the right of B 249–50 may be related, perhaps signaling the end of the scribe's original at that point.

B 249–51 *dh(n).n.j* — the verb *dhn* denotes an action involving the head, both intransitive ("nod") and transitive ("touch with the forehead"); the final radical is omitted, perhaps because it was in contact with the suffix *n* (*dahanni). Touching the forehead to the ground is an act of homage.

jmjtw šzpw — the image is of sphinxes—the plural indicates at least four—flanking the path to the palace's gate.

wmtw — the word refers to an entranceway that is several feet deep, as in the pylons at the entrance to a temple.

B 251–52 *wꜣḫ* — the word refers to a columned hall in which the columns represent papyrus plants, as in a marsh; it is derived from the verb *wꜣḫj* "flood."

jst wrt — a common designation of the throne.

m wmtw nt ḏʿm — the throne was set on a raised platform at the end of the columned hall, within a booth or naos plated with electrum.

B 252–53 *wn.k(w) r.f dwn.kw* — the initial stative, used as a past tense (§ 16.5), situates at a point in time the state described by the second stative. BA 3–4 has *wn.k(w) r.j dmꜣ.[kw]* "for my part, I was prostrate" (see ShS. 136–37).

B 253–55 *ḫnm.w* — a 3ms stative describing the king's state ("delighted"). The verb *ḫnm* is used both intransitively ("become delighted") and transitively ("delight"). BA 5–6 has *ḥr wšd.j r[…]*, probably either *r[š.w]* "joyful" or *r [ḫnmw]* "delightedly" (Rosenvasser 1934, 49; cf. § 8.14).

ʿḫḫw — this is a variant, probably the original form, of the word normally written *jḫḫw*. In Middle Egyptian, the initial *ʿ* of words with *ḥ* or *ḫ* as a second radical is sometimes weakened or disappears: for example, *ʿḥꜣ* "fight" (*ʿáḥa'), sometimes written *jḥꜣ* (*'áḥa').

bꜣ.j zj.w — i.e, Sinuhe was like someone who had died: see Essays 7 and 8.

ḥʿw.j ꜣd.w — BA 7–8 has *ḥʿw.j ꜣh[d.w]* "my limbs exhausted": see the note to B 38–39 *jb.j ꜣd.w*, above.

B 255–56 *ḥꜣtj.j nj ntf m ẖt.j* — see the note to this sentence in B 39, above.

rḫ.j ʿnḫ r m(w)t — BA 9 has *[nj rḫ.(j) wj r] m(w)t nj rḫ.(j) wj r ʿnḫ* "I did not know myself with respect to death, I did not know myself with respect to life" — i.e., "whether I was dead or alive" (Rosenvasser 1934, 49).

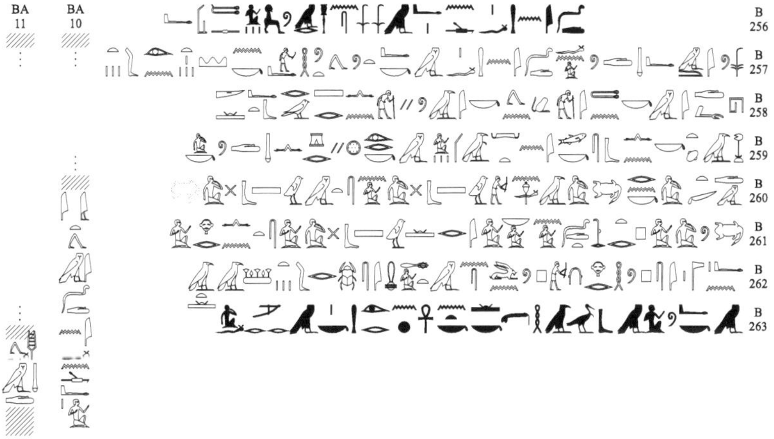

B 256–57 ***ḏd.jn ḥm.f n wꜥ m nn n smrw*** 5
ṯz sw jmj mdw.f n.j 4
B 257 *ḏd.jn ḥm.f mj.k tw jw.t(j)* 3
ḥw.n.k ḫꜣswt 2
B 257–58 *jr.n wꜥrt hd jm.k ṯnj* 5
pḥ.n.k jꜣwj 2
B 258–59 *nn šrr ꜥbt ḫꜣt.k* 2
nn bs.k jn pḏtjw 2
m jr r.k zp 2 gr 3
B 259–60 *nj mdw.k dm.t(w) rn.k* 3
snḏ ꜣ n ḫsf 2
B 260–61 *wšb.n.j st m wšb snḏw* 2
ptr ḏdt n.j nb.j jr(j) 4
B 261–62 *wšb.j st nn ḥr.j ꜥ* 3
n nṯr js pw 1
B 262 *ḥr(t) pw wnn.s m ẖt.j* 3
mj sḫpr wꜥrt šꜣꜣt 3
B 263 ***mj.k wj m bꜣḥ.k ntk ꜥnḫ*** 3
jrr ḥm.k m mrr.f 3

B 256–57 **So, His Incarnation said to one of those courtiers,**
“Lift him up; have him speak to me.”
B 257 So, His Incarnation said, “Look, you have returned
after roaming countries.

B 257–58 The flight has taken a toll on you, old man:
you have reached old age.
B 258–59 Not insignificant is your corpse's interment:
nor will you be buried by bowmen.
Don't act against yourself any more.
B 259–60 You did not answer when your name was pronounced:
be not afraid of punishment."
B 260–61 I answered with the answer of one afraid,
"What will my lord say to me about it?
B 261–62 I should answer with no haste on my part,
for he is a god:
B 262 it is that terror exists in my belly,
like the cause of the fated flight.
B 263 **Look, I am in your presence, and life is yours:**
let Your Incarnation do as he likes."

B 256–57 The red ink signals the beginning of a new topic, the king's address to Sinuhe. BA 10–11 has a different version, partly repeated in New Kingdom copies: *[ḏd.jn ḥm.f mj.k tw] jj.t(j) ḏd.jn.f n wꜤ [m nn n smrw jmj] Ꜥḥ Ꜥ.f mdw.[f n.j]* "So, His Incarnation said, "Look, you have returned." So, he said to one of those courtiers, "Have him stand up and speak to me." B's version is superior, since the first sentence seems out of order.

B 257–58 *jr.n wꜤrt hd jm.k* — literally, "the flight has made an attack on you."

B 258–59 *nn šrr Ꜥbt ẖꜣt.k* — a negated adjectival sentence (§ 11.6).

m jr r.k zp 2 — the *zp 2* indicates repetition of *r.k*. The first *r.k* is referential (§ 15.7.2), the second is the prepositional phrase "against you(rself)."

B 259–60 *snḏ ꜣ n ḫsf* — the particle *ꜣ* here is probably an archaic variant of the negative particle *w* (§ 26.26.4). The author has the king speak in very refined speech to reflect his wisdom and command of the language.

B 260–61 *wšb.n.j st* — for the pronominal object, referring to the king's speech, see the note to ShS. 86–87 *wšb.n.j n.f st*. At the end of B 260, the scribe wrote , then erased it and wrote the word at the beginning of B 261.

ptr ḏdt n.j nb.j — literally, "what is that which my lord will say to me": for the sense of the *sḏm.f* relative, see § 22.14.

jr(j) — the couplet that follows indicates that adverbial *jr(j)* refers to the king's statement "you did not answer": in other words, Sinuhe is asking the king, "What would you have me say?"

B 261–62 *wšb.j st nn ḥr.j Ꜥ* — an emphatic sentence, with *nn ḥr.j Ꜥ* the rheme. The latter means literally, "without a hand upon me." The word order (cf. § 10.7) is influenced by the prepositional phrase from which this clause is derived, *ḥr ʿ* "immediately" (literally, "upon the hand"). Sinuhe is excusing his not responding by claiming that he should weigh his answer carefully, since the king "is a god."

n nṯr js pw — a nominal sentence subordinated (to the preposition *n*) in a noun clause by *js* (§ 21.3). The third person refers to *nb.j* "my lord" in the preceding couplet.

B 262 This couplet finally provides the answer that the king requested, the reason why Sinuhe "did not answer when your name was pronounced."

ḥr(t) pw wnn.s m ḫt.j — the suffix of *wnn.s* shows that *ḥr(t)* is feminine, even though the feminine *t* is omitted. The sentence is a nominal A *pw* construction, with A either a SUBJECT–*sḏm.f* construction ("terror exists in my belly"), as translated, or undefined *ḥr(t)* followed by an unmarked relative clause ("it is a terror that exists in my belly").

mj sḫpr wʿrt šꜣꜣt — since *ḥr(t)* is feminine and has been resumed by a feminine pronoun (*wnn.s*), *sḫpr* is probably not an active participle referring to it ("the one that created"). It can be analyzed as an infinitive: literally, "like causing to happen the fated flight." The geminated stem of *šꜣꜣt* indicates that Sinuhe was thinking of his flight as an extended episode rather than a single event. The final two signs of *šꜣꜣt* were written below the line at the end of the page.

B 263 Having answered, Sinuhe now places himself at the king's mercy. Even though Senwosret was "delighted" to see him and said "be not afraid of punishment," the possibility of retribution still exists in Sinuhe's mind until the king has pronounced his final decision. The red ink properly belongs with the start of a new section, which begins at the end of B 263, but the scribe has used it for the entire line, probably because it is at the top of the page.

Episode 24 — The King's Family Intervenes (B 263–283)

B 263
B 264
B 265
B 266
B 267
B 268

B 263–64 **rdj.jn.(tw)** *sṯꜣ.tw msw nswt* 3
ḏd.jn ḥm.f n ḥjmt-nswt 3
B 264–65 *mj.t zꜣ-nht j.w* 2
m ʿꜣm qmꜣm.n sttjw 3
B 265–66 *wd.s sbḥ ʿꜣ wrt* 4
msw-nswt m dnyt wʿt 3

B 266–68 *ḏd.jn.sn ḫft ḥm.f* 2
nj ntf pw m mꜣꜥt jtj nb.j 4
ḏd.jn ḥm.f ntf pw m mꜣꜥt 4

B 263–64 **So, one had** the king's children conducted in,
and His Incarnation said to the king's wife,
B 264–65 "Look, Sinuhe has returned
as an Asian that the Asiatics have created."
B 265–66 She emitted a very great cry,
with the king's children in one shriek,
B 266–68 and they said in response to His Incarnation,
"Is it really he, sire my lord?"
and His Incarnation said, "It is really he."

The king's children and the queen are now brought into the audience hall to meet Sinuhe.

B 263–65 *rdj.jn.(tw)* — judging from the position of the 𓈖, the scribe intended to add the required suffix *tw* but neglected to do so.

j.w —the 3ms stative of *jjj* "come" is usually written as if formed from the geminated stem *jw*.

B 265–66 *wd.s* — the *sḏm.f* used to express a past event (§ 18.4).

B 266–68 *nj ntf pw* — 𓂜 here is a writing of the particle *jn*, as indicated both by the syntax (§ 11.5) and by the New Kingdom copy, which has *jn jw*. Grammatically, it is possible that *nj* negates of *ntf* ("it is someone else"), but culturally it is unlikely that the queen would directly contradict the king's statement.

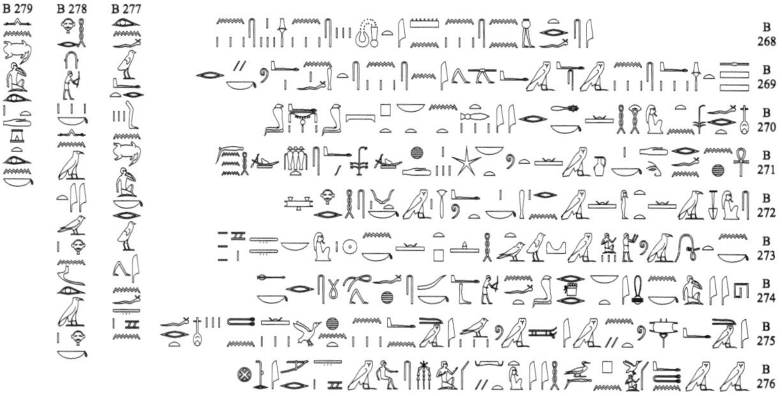

B 268–69 *jst r.f jn.n.sn mnjwt.sn ꜥbꜣw.sn* 3
zššwt.sn m ꜥ.s(n) 2
B 269 *mz.jn.sn st n ḥm.f* 2
(ḏd.jn.sn n ḥm.f) 2
B 269–70 *ꜥwj.k r nfrt nswt wꜣḥ* 4
ẖkryt nt nbt-pt 2
B 270–71 *dj nbw ꜥnḫ r fnd.k* 4
ẖnm tw nbt sbꜣw 2
B 271–72 *ḫd šmꜥs ḫnt mḥs* 4
zmꜣ.(w) t(w)t.w m r n ḥm.k 4
B 272–73 *dj.tw wꜣḏ m wpt.k* 3
sḥr n.k twꜣw m ḏwt 3
B 273–74 *ḥtp n.k rꜥ nb tꜣwj* 3
hy n.k mj nbt-r-ḏr 2
B 274–75 *nft ꜥb.k sfḫ ššr.k* 4
jmj ṯꜣw (n) ntj m jtmw 4
B 275–76 *jmj n.n ḫnt.ṯn nfrt* 3
m mjṯn(j) pn zꜣ mḥyt 2
pḏtj ms.(w) m tꜣ-mrj 3
B 277–78 *jr.n.f wꜥrt n snḏ.k* 3
rwj.n.f tꜣ n ḥr.k 3
B 278–79 *nn ꜣyt ḥr n mꜣ ḥr.k* 4
nn snḏ jrt dgt n.k 4

B 268–69 Now, they had brought their menits and their scepters,
and their sistra were in their hand.
B 269 So, they presented them to His Incarnation
and they said to His Incarnation,
B 269–70 "May your hands be toward something good, lasting king,
the ornaments of the sky-lady.
B 270–71 May the Gold give life to your nose
and the stars' lady unite with you.
B 271–72 Let the Nile-Valley crown go downstream and the Delta Crown upstream,
joined and reconciled through the mouth of Your Incarnation.
B 272–73 Now that the Green has been put on your brow,
distance for yourself dependants from evil,
B 273–74 so that the Sun, the Two Lands' lord, will be content for you,
and acclaim will be yours like the Lady to the Limit.

B 274–75 Lower your horn, loosen your arrow,
give air to the one who is in suffocation.
B 275–76 Give us our good outlay
in this pathfinder, the Northwind's son,
a bowman born in Canal-land.
B 277–78 He made a flight for fear of you,
he left the land for terror of you.
B 278–79 No face of one who will see your face should blanch,
no eye that will look at you should fear."

B 268–69 *jst r.f* — see § 20.3.

mnjwt.sn ꜥbꜣw.sn zššwt.sn — the *mnjt* is a counterweight worn between the shoulder-blades and used to counterbalance the weight of a necklace; the straps attaching it to the necklace were often beaded (Fig. 4). The reading of [hieroglyphs] is uncertain; it could also be *sḫmw*. The sistrum is an instrument with disks on cords or wires (Fig. 4), used to make a rattling sound.

Fig. 4. Menit (left) and Woman with Sistrum (right)

B 269 *mz.jn.sn st n ḥm.f* — the rustling noise made by menits and sistra was used in temple rituals to placate the gods. The queen and king's children here are attempting to ward off the king's possible wrath against Sinuhe.

ḏd.jn.sn n ḥm.f — the expected introductory clause to the speech that follows, preserved in the New Kingdom copy, is omitted in B, probably through homoioteleuton (the identical endings of both lines of the couplet).

B 269–70 *ꜥwj.k r nfrt ... ẖkryt nt nbt-pt* — the king is urged to turn his attention away from Sinuhe. Menits and sistra were both associated especially with Hathor, goddess of love (as opposed to wrath), who is often called *nbt-pt* "sky-lady."

B 270–71 *nbw ... nbt sbꜣw* — "Gold" is a name commonly applied to Hathor; the second epithet is otherwise unknown until the Ptolemaic Period but probably also refers to Hathor.

B 271–72 The image in this couplet is of the unification of opposites under the king. The reference also serves as a subtle reminder to Senwosret that he is meant to be a force for good rather than for wrath or revenge.

šmꜥs ... mḥs — see the note to B 186 *dpts.s m nsyt nt tꜣ*, above. The nouns here are formed from *šmꜥw* "Nile Valley" (literally, "Thin") and *mḥw* "Delta" (literally, "Immersed").

B 272–73 *wꜣḏ* — perhaps an error for *wꜣḏt* "Wadjet," but in any case a reference to the uraeus. The point of this couplet is to encourage the king to use the striking power of the uraeus to protect his subjects, not to harm them.

B 274–75 *nft ꜥb.k sfḫ ššr.k* — images of the king as a bull ready to charge and an archer ready to shoot, the latter reflecting the line in Sinuhe's hymn, "There is none who can escape his arrow" (Episode 10).

B 275–76 *jmj n.n ḫnt.ṯn nfrt* — the 𓍿 in the second suffix represents the pronounced *t* of the noun: see the note to ShS. 7 *jzwt.ṯn jj.t(j) ꜥḏ.t(j)*. The noun *ḫnt* refers to offerings made as supplies for a festival.

mjṯn(j) pn zꜣ mḥyt — the reference to Sinuhe as a "pathfinder" reflects both his adopted identity as an Asiatic and the fact that he has found his way from Asia into Egypt. The eipthet "Northwind's son" is both a play on Sinuhe's name and a reflection of the fact that he has been deposited in Lisht by the north wind.

pḏtj ms.(w) m tꜣ-mrj — for *pḏtj* see the note to B 121–22 *nn pḏtj smꜣ.(w) m jdḥw(j)*, above. Since *pḏtj* is undefined, *ms* is a 3ms stative rather than a passive participle.

B 278–79 *nn ꜣyt ḥr n mꜣ ḥr.k* — see the note to ShS. 112 *m ꜣtw ḥr.k*.

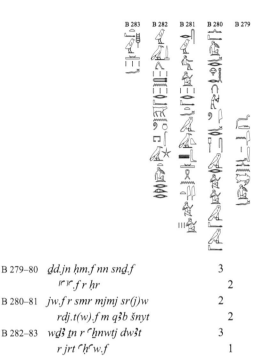

B 279–80	*ḏd.jn ḥm.f nn snḏ.f*	3
	⸢ꜥ⸣⸢ꜥ⸣.f r ḥr	2
B 280–81	*jw.f r smr mjmj sr(j)w*	2
	rdj.t(w).f m qꜣb šnyt	2
B 282–83	*wḏꜣ ṯn r ꜥḫnwtj dwꜣt*	3
	r jrt ꜥḥꜥw.f	1

B 279–80 So, His Incarnation said, "He should not fear
or babble for terror.

B 280–81 He is to be a courtier among the officials
and will be put amid the circle.

B 282–83 You proceed to the morning audience-hall
to make his attendance."

B 279–80 *⸢ꜥ⸣⸢ꜥ⸣.f r ḥr* — the verb is *ꜥjꜥj*; the scribe has written [hieroglyph] in error for the first 𓂝. The *sḏm.f* serves either as a second predicate negated by *nn* or as an unmarked adverb clause ("babbling in terror").

B 282–83 *wḏꜣ ṯn r ꜥḫnwtj dwꜣt* — the verb is written with plural strokes, so is therefore probably a plural imperative followed by a dependent pronoun (§§ 15.1, 15.3) rather than the *sḏm.f*. The *ꜥḫnwtj dwꜣt* is probably related to the term *pr dwꜣt*, where bathing is done (in the *dwꜣw* "morning") (Gardiner 1916, 109–10); the determinative of *dwꜣt* derives from the verb *dwꜣ* "worship (in the morning)." The king is instructing his family to get Sinuhe cleaned up, as detailed in the next episode.

r jrt ꜥḥꜥw.f — for the spelling of *jrt* (infinitive), see the note to B 5 *r jrt wꜣt šmw.s*, above. For the sense of *ꜥḥꜥw.f*, literally "his standing," see B 1 *jsṯ wj [ꜥḥ]ꜥ.kw*.

Episode 24 — Sinuhe Restored (B 283–295)

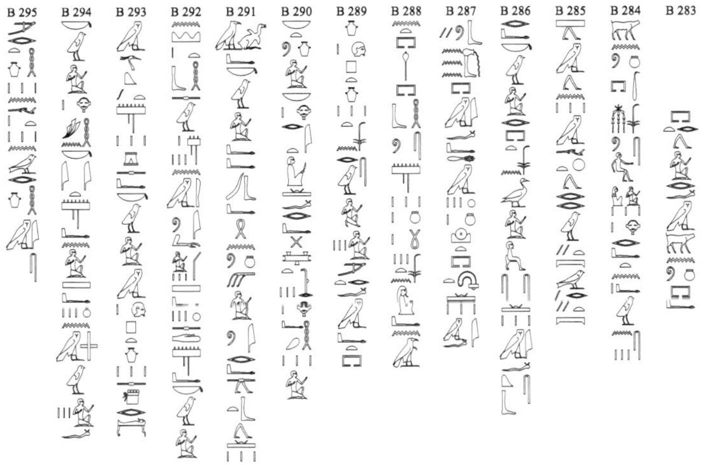

B 283–85 *prt.j r.f m ẖnw ˁẖnwtj* 2
msw-nswt ḥr rdjt n.(j) ˁw.sn 3
šm.n m ḫt r rwtj wrtj 3
B 286–87 *rdj.kw r pr z3-nswt špssw jm.f* 4
sqbbwj jm.f ˁẖmw nw 3ḫt 4
B 287–89 *ḫtmwt jm.f nt pr-ḥḏ* 3
ḥbsw nw sšr nswt 2
ˁntjw dpwt nswt sr(j)w 3
B 289–90 *mrt.f m ˁt nbt* 2
wdpw nb ḥr jrt.f 2
B 290–91 *rdj sw3 rnpwt ḥr ḥˁw.j* 4
ṯ3.kw ˁˁb šnw.j 3
B 291–92 *jw rdj zbt n ḫ3st* 3
ḥbsw n nmjw šˁ 2
B 292–94 *sd.kw m p3qt gs.kw m dpwt* 4
sḏr.kw ḥr ḥnkyt 2
B 294–95 *dj.n.j šˁ n jmjw.f* 3
mrḥt n ḫt n wrḥ jm.s 4

B 283–85 At that, my emergence from inside the audience hall,
the king's children giving me their arms
as we went thereafter to the great double gate.

B 286–87 I was taken to a king's son's house with finery in it,
    a bathroom in it, and icons of the Akhet,
B 287–89 sealed things from the treasury in it,
    clothes of king's linen,
    myrrh and king's first-class oil of officials:
B 289–90 whatever he might want in every room,
    every attendant at his duty.
B 290–91 Years were made to pass from my limbs;
    I was depilated and my hair was combed,
B 291–92 while a cargo was given to the desert
    and clothes to the sand-trekkers.
B 292–94 I was dressed in fine linen and anointed with first-class oil,
    as I lay on a bed.
B 294–95 I gave over the sand to those in it,
    and oil of a tree to the one anointed with it.

Following the king's directive, Sinuhe is escorted from the audience hall and transformed from an Asiatic to a proper Egyptian.

B 283–85 *prt.j* — the infinitive here marks the beginning of the final section of the story.

B 286–87 *rdj.kw r pr zꜣ-nswt* — literally, "I was given to a king's son's house." This is the place where Sinuhe is taken to be cleaned up.

ʿḫmw nw ꜣḫt — it is not evident what these images are. Since the king ordered Sinuhe taken to a "morning audience hall," however, they are probably paintings of animals and plants reacting to the rising of the sun from the Akhet.

B 287–89 *ḫtmwt ... nt pr-ḥḏ* — this refers to the kinds of precious items kept under seal in the treasury and allocated to qualified officials for their personal use.

B 289–90 *dpwt nswt sr(j)w mrt.f m ʿt nbt* — it is possible to read *dpwt* with the preceding line and this line as *sr(j)w-nswt mrr.f m ʿt nbt* "king's officials whom he loves in every room." *sr(j)w-nswt* "king's officials," however, is not otherwise known as a designation of titularies, and it is unlikely that such individuals would be assigned to every room of the prince's house; if *mrr.f* modifies *sr(j)w-nswt*, moreover, it should be plural. The two hieratic signs after  are identical in shape to those in the word *prt.j* in B 283, indicating *mrt.f*, a relative *sḏm.f* whose subject refers to *zꜣ-nswt* in the second couplet. This in turn indicates that the first three words are a direct genitive whose first term is itself a direct genitive: "king's first-class oil of officials."

B 290–91 *ṯꜣ.kw ʿʿb šnw.j* — see § 19.3. The verb *ṯꜣj* means "pluck"; here it refers to the removal of excess body hair by plucking rather than shaving.

B 291–92 The initial *jw* relates the statement of this couplet to the preceding one and continues the image of the preceding line: Sinuhe's Asiatic clothes as well his plucked hairs are discarded in the desert, where they came from.

B 292–94 Since Sinuhe's cleansing in the prince's house is a temporary event, *sḏr.kw* here probably refers to his posture while being attended to rather than to sleeping. The reference to a bed, in a house, implies a contrast with the situation of an Asiatic, lying on a mat on the ground, in a tent.

B 294–95 *dj.n.j* here probably does not refer to the "giving" of actual items but the act of leaving sand and tree-oil to the Asiatics whose life-style they characterize.

mrḥt n ḫt — probably a reference to cedar oil. In Egypt, this oil was used for anointing mummies rather than the living.

Episode 25 — Sinuhe's New Life (B 295–310)

B 295–96	*jw rdj n.j pr n nb-š(j)*	3
	m wn m ꜥ smr	2
B 296–97	*jw ḥmw ꜥšꜣ ḥr qd.f*	3
	ḫt.f nb srd.(w) m mꜣwt	3
B 297–98	*jw jn.⸢t⸣(w) n.j šꜣbw m ꜥḥ*	3
	zp 3 zp 4 n hrw	3
B 299–300	*ḥrw r ddt msw-nswt*	3
	nn ꜣt nt jrt ꜣbw	2

B 295–96 I have been given the house of a basin-owner,
the kind that a courtier should have.
B 296–97 Many craftsmen are building it,
its every tree has been planted anew.
B 297–98 Food is fetched for me from the palace
three or four times a day,
B 299–300 apart from what the king's children give,
without a moment of stopping.

Restored to a position at court, Sinuhe is given a house and lands, and a proper tomb is built for his burial. The story changes, for this final episode, from historical narrative to the viewpoint of the present. The final episode has four sections, each introduced by *jw*, describing Sinuhe's accommodations, tomb, tomb statue, and relationship with the king.

B 295–96 *pr n nb š(j)* — the word *šj* denotes a depression in the landscape, which can be filled with water ("lake") or agricultural land ("plot"). In agricultural terms, it refers to a depression that retains water after the annual inundation recedes, making it ideal for growing crops. The owner of such a plot was a man of some means, and his house therefore appropriately grand.

m wn m ʿ smr — literally, "as one that should be in the hand of a courtier." The participle *wn* could have either subjunctive sense, as translated here, or past reference, meaning that it had previously belonged to a court official. The reference to its construction, in the next couplet, indicates the former.

B 296–97 *srd.(w)* — literally, "made to grow." The scribe inserted two signs of this word secondarily.

B 297–98 *jn.⸢t⸣(w)* — the second of the three 𓈖 signs is probably an error for the 𓏏 of the passive suffix.

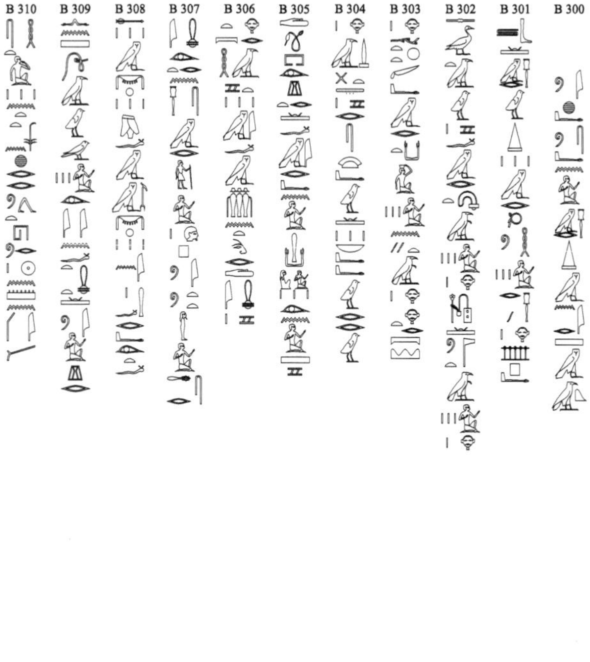

B 300–301	*jw ḫwsw n.j mr*	2
	m jnr m qꜣb mrw	2
B 301–303	*(j)m(j) r mḏḥw ḥr šzp zꜣtw.f*	2
	(j)m(j) r ḫtmtjw ḥr zẖꜣ	2
	gnwtjw ḥr {ḥr} ḫtt	2
B 303–304	*(j)m(j) r kꜣwt ntjw ḥr ḥrt*	3
	ḥr ḏꜣt tꜣ r.s	2
B 304–305	*ḫʿw nb ddw r rwd*	3
	jr ẖrt.f jm	3
B 305–307	*rdj n.j ḥmw-kꜣ jr n.j š(j) ḥrt*	4
	ꜣḥwt jm.f m ḫnt r dmj	4
	mj jrrt n smr dp(j)	3
B 307–308	*jw twt.j sẖr.(w) m nbw*	3
	šnḏyt.f m ḏʿm	2
B 308–309	*jn ḥm.f rdj jr.t(w).f*	3
	nn šwꜣw jry n.f mjtt	3
B 309–310	*jw.j ẖr ḥswt nt ḫr-nswt*	2
	r jwt hrw n mjn	3

B 300–301 A pyramid has been built for me
of stone amid the pyramids,
B 301–303 the overseer of stone-masons receiving its ground,
the overseer of seal-bearers writing,
the sculptors carving,
B 303–304 the overseer of works on the plateau
crossing the land for it;
B 304–305 every kind of paraphernalia put in a strong-room,
its possessions have been made therefrom;
B 305–307 I have been given ka-servants, and a plateau plot has been made for me,
with fields in it, in front of the harbor,
like what is done for a top courtier.
B 307–308 My statue has been plated with gold,
its kilt with electrum:
B 308–309 His Incarnation is the one who had it made;
there is none lowly for whom the like has been done.
B 309–310 I have the blessings of the king's presence
until the day of mooring has come.

B 300–301 *jw ḫwsw n.j mr* — the completion described by the passive *sḏm.f* applies here to the onset of work, since the next three lines describe the work as being in process. Compare the sense of *ḥqꜣ.n.f* "he has begun to rule" in B 70.

B 301–303 *mḏḥw* — the verb *mḏḥ* means basically "carve" and is used of working both wood and stone, the latter both statues and buildings, whose walls were "carved" into final shape once the rough stone blocks composing them had been set in place.

ḥr šzp zꜣtw.f — this refers to both the site and the ground-plan of the structure being assigned to the head stone-mason.

(j)m(j) r ḫtmtjw ḥr zḫꜣ gnwtjw ḥr {ḥr} ḫtt —these lines describe the decoration of the chapel attached to the pyramid: *zḫꜣ* "write" refers to the drawing of the images and texts on its walls and *ḫtj* "carve," to the sculpting of these into raised or sunk relief. The "writing" was done by a  *zḫꜣw-qdwt* "scribe of shapes." It is likely that *ḫtmtjw* "seal-bearers" in B 302 is a miscopy of the second word; a New Kingdom copy has the proper term. The scribe has erroneously repeated the preposition *ḥr* at the top of column 303.

B 301–303 *ḥrt* is the desert plateau on which cemeteries were located. The overseer's activity of "crossing the land" is the recruitment of workers for the project. The suffix pronoun of *r.s* refers to the project as a single *kꜣt* "work (project)."

B 304–305 *ḫꜥw nb ddw r rwd jr ḫrt.f jm* — the first five words are the object of the preposition *m*, topicalized by preposing them; the preposition is in the adverbial form. This line and the next two are not introduced by *jw* because they serve as unmarked adverb clauses to the initial statement *jw ḫwsw n.j mr*, like the four SUBJECT–*ḥr*–*sḏm* clauses preceding. The phrase *ddw r rwd* characterizes the burial equipment (*ḫꜥw*) as costly enough to be put under seal in a room whose walls are firm (*rwd*) enough to deter robbery.

B 305–307 *ḥmw-kꜣ* — this term refers to people hired to care for the tomb and to present offerings in its chapel after the burial.

š(j) ḥrt ꜣḥwt jm.f m ḫnt r dmj — this refers to the agricultural land that was part of every funerary estate, whose fields provided both the grain used in offerings in the tomb chapel and the crops needed for the income of the ka-servants. In this case, *ḥrt* describes land near, rather than on, the desert plateau, which is higher (*ḥrt*) than that nearer the Nile. Despite its elevation, the land can be watered because of its proximity to the harbor; the latter term refers to the terminus of a canal leading from the Nile to the foot of the desert plateau.

B 307–309 These two couplets describe the statue meant to be installed in the tomb chapel, commissioned (and paid for) by the king himself.

jry n.f mjtt — literally, "done for him the like": see § 24.6. The singular suffix pronoun indicates that the plural strokes of *šwꜣw* are erroneous. The word *šwꜣw* refers to the lowest elements of society; although it is not an appropriate characterization of Sinuhe at this point, it was often applied to Asiatic immigrants and is therefore an indirect reference to Sinuhe's past.

B 309–310 *hrw n mjn* — the verb *mjnj* "moor" was a euphemism for death and burial, based on the metaphor of life as a voyage.

The Colophon (B 311)

B 311

jw.f pw ḥꜣt.f r pḥ(wj).fj mj gmyt m zẖꜣ

That is how it goes, beginning to end, like what has been found in writing.

This colophon is identical to the first line of that of the Shipwrecked Sailor; see the notes to that line. Unlike the scribe of the Shipwrecked Sailor, the copyist of Sinuhe B did not add his name, and so remains anonymous, like the tale's author.

BIBLIOGRAPHY

Allen, James P. "The Historical Inscription of Khnumhotep at Dahshur: Preliminary Report." *Bulletin of the American Schools of Oriental Research* 352 (November, 2008), 29–39.

Altenmüller, Hartwig. "Zur Frage der *mww*." *Studien zur Altägyptischen Kultur* 2 (1975), 1–37.

Assmann, Jan. "Die Rubren in der Überlieferung der Sinuhe-Erzählung." In M. Görg, ed., *Fontes atque Pontes: eine Festgabe für Hellmut Brunner* (Ägypten und Altes Testament 5; Wiesbaden 1983), 18–41.

Blackman, Aylward M. *Middle Egyptian Stories*. Bibliotheca Aegyptiaca 2. Brussels, 1932.

Collier, Mark, and Stephen Quirke. *The UCL Lahun Papyri: Religious, Literary, Legal, Mathematical and Medical*. BAR International Series 1209. Oxford, 2004.

Davies, Norman de G. *The Tomb of Amenemhēt (No. 82)*. Theban Tombs Series 1. London, 1920.

————. *The Tomb of Antefoḳer, Vizier of Sesostris I, and of His Wife, Senet (No. 60)*. Theban Tombs Series 2. London, 1920.

Donner, Herbert. "Zum 'Streitlustigen' () in Sinuhe B 110." *Zeitschrift für Ägyptische Sprache und Altertumskunde* 81 (1956), 61–62.

Gardiner, Alan H. *Die Erzählung des Sinuhe und die Hirtengeschichte.* Literarische Texte des Mittleren Reiches 2. Leipzig, 1909.

————. *Notes on the Story of Sinuhe.* Paris, 1916.

Koch, Roland. *Die Erzählung des Sinuhe.* Bibliotheca Aegyptiaca 17. Brussels 1990.

Morenz, Ludwig D. "Kanaanäisches Lokalkolorit in der Sinuhe-Erzählung und die Vereinfachung des Urtextes." *Zeitschrift des Deutschen Palästina-Vereins* 113 (1997), 1–18.

Parkinson, Richard B. *Reading Ancient Egyptian Poetry, Among Other Histories.* Oxford, 2009.

————. *Four 12th Dynasty Literary Papyri (Pap. Berlin P. 3022–5): a Photographic Record.* London and Berlin, 2012.

Posener, Georges. *L'enseignement loyaliste, sagesse égyptienne du Moyen Empire.* Centre de Recherches d'Histoire et de Philologie de la IVe Section de l'École Pratique des Hautes Études, II: Hautes Études Orientales. Geneva, 1976.

Rosenvasser, Abraham. "A New Duplicate Text of the Story of Sinuhe." *Journal of Egyptian Archaeology* 20 (1934), 47–50.

Schenkel, Wolfgang. "Die Wurzel *bnj* 'süß'." *Mitteilungen des deutschen archäologischen Instituts, Abteilung Kairo* 20 (1965), 115.

Schneider, Thomas. "Sinuhes Notiz über die Könige: syrisch-anatolische Herrschertitel in ägyptischer Überlieferung." *Ägypten und Levante* 12 (2002), 257–72.

Yoyotte, Jean. "A propos du panthéon de Sinouhé (B 205–212)." *Kêmi* 17 (1964), 69–73.

TEXT 3
THE LOYALIST INSTRUCTION

THIS TEXT is one of the few literary creations of ancient Egypt for which we know the author, or at least the supposed author—in this case, thanks to a graffito discovered in 2005 in a tomb at Assiut (Verhoeven 2009). The earliest preserved copy of the text is on the back side of the stela of Sehetepibre (named after Amenemhat I), who was deputy of the treasurer during the reign of Amenemhat III (ca. 1859–1813 BC) (Fig. 5). This is also the shortest version of the instruction: in addition to the graffito mentioned above, 69 more copies survive, on three papyri, a wood tablet, and 65 ostraca, all of New Kingdom date or later (Posener 1976). The Middle Kingdom version may have been abridged, but it is more likely that the later versions are expanded from this shorter original. The text on the stela begins in the middle of a longer inscription detailing the titles and some of the accomplishments of Sehetepibre (lines 8–20 of 26 lines).

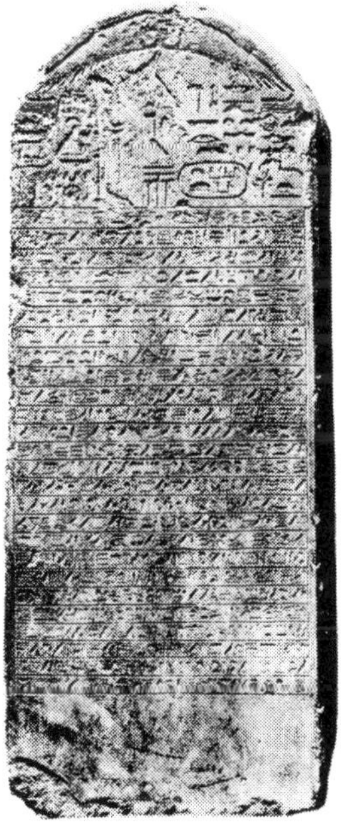

Fig. 5. Stela of Sehetepibre, verso (Cairo 20538: Lange and Schaefer 1902–1925, IV, pl. 40)

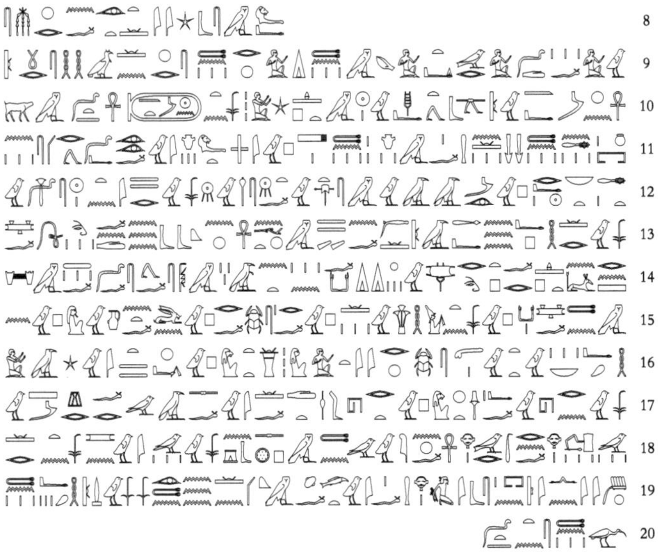

8–9	*ḥ3t ͑ m sb3yt jrt.n.f ẖr msw.f*	(heading)
9–10	*ḏd.j wrt dj.j sḏm.ṯn*	4
	dj.j rḫ.ṯn sḫr n nḥḥ	4
	sšr ͑nḫ n m3͑w zbt ͑ḥ͑w m ḥtp	4
10–11	*dw3 nswt* NJ-M3͑T-R͑ *͑nḫ.(w) ḏt*	5
	m ẖnw n ẖwt.ṯn	2
	snsn ḥm.f m jbw.ṯn	3
11–12	*sj3 pw jmj ḥ3t(j)w*	2
	jw jrtj.f ḏ͑r.sn ẖt nbt	3
12	*r͑ pw m33w m stwt.f*	3
	sḥḏw(j) sw t3wj r jtn	3
12–13	*sw3ḏw(j) sw r ḥ͑p ͑3*	2
	mḥ.n.f t3wj m nḫt ͑nḫ	3
13–14	*qbb fndw w3.f r nšn*	4
	ḥtp.f r tpr ṯ3w	2
14–15	*ḏd.f k3w n ntjw m šms.f*	4
	sḏf(3).f mḏd mṯn.f	3
15	*k3 pw nswt ḥ3w pw r.f*	4
	sḫpr.f pw wnnt(j).f	2

15–16 *ḫnmw pw n ḥꜥw nb* 2
wttw sḫpr rḫyt 3
16–17 *bꜣstt pw ḫwt tꜣwj* 3
jw dwꜣ sw r nhw ꜥ.f 2
17–18 *sḫmt pw r th wdt.f* 3
jw sfꜣ.f r ḫr(j) šmꜣw 2
18 *ꜥḥꜣ ḥr rn.f tjwr ḥr ꜥnḫ.f* 4
šw.ṯn m zp n b(ꜣ)gsw 3
18–19 *jw mr.n nswt r jmꜣḫy* 3
nn jz n sbj ḥr ḥm.f 3
jw ḫꜣt.f m q̣m(ꜣ) n mw 3
19–20 *jr.ṯn nn wḏꜣ ḥꜥw.ṯn* 4
gm.ṯn st n ḏt 2

8–9 Beginning of the teaching that he made to his children.
9–10 I will say something important and have you hear;
I will let you know the method of continuity,
the system of living correctly, of conducting a lifetime in peace.
10–11 Worship the king—Nimaatre, alive forever—
in your innermost beings,
associate his incarnation with your minds.
11–12 He is Perception, which is in hearts,
for his eyes probe every torso.
12 He is the Sun, by whose rays one sees;
how much more illuminating of the Two Lands is he than the sundisk!
12–13 How much more freshening is he than a high inundation,
for he has filled the Two Lands with the force of life.
13–14 Noses are refreshed when he is distant from storming,
his contentment is necessary for inhaling air.
14–15 He gives sustenance only to those in his following,
he feeds the one who adheres to his path.
15 The king is ka, his mouth is excess;
the one who will exist is the one he fosters.
15–16 He is Khnum for every body,
the begetter who creates the subjects.
16–17 He is Bastet, who defends the Two Lands,
for the one who worships him will be one whom his arm shelters.
17–18 He is Sekhmet against the one who transgresses his command,
for the one he detests will be one who has rejection.

18 Fight for his name, be respectful of his oath,
and be free of any laxity.
18–19 For the one the king has loved will be worthy:
there is no tomb for the one who rebels against His Incarnation,
and his body is something thrown into the water.
19–20 If you do this, your body will be sound,
and you will find it so for eternity.

8–9 The title indicates that the text is Sehetepibre's own composition. That may have been the case, but the grafitto in the Assiut tomb supplies the name of a different author:

1–2 *ḥꜣt ꜥ m sbꜣyt jrt.n (j)r(j) pꜥt ḥꜣt(j)-ꜥ*
2 *jt-nṯr mryw-nṯr*
3–4 *ḥrj sštꜣ n pr-nswt ꜥnḫ-wḏꜣ-snb*
4–5 *ḥrj dp n tꜣ r ḏr.f*
5–6 *sm ḫrp šndyt nb*
6–7 *(j)m(j) r njwt ṯꜣt(j) kꜣ-jr-s(w)*
7–8 *ḏd.f m sbꜣyt ḫr msw.f*
8 *ḏd.j wrt dj.j sḏm […*

Beginning of the teaching made by the member of the elite, high official,
god's father, god's beloved,
secretary of the king's house lph,
chief of the entire land,
sem-priest, manager of every kilt,
city-overseer, vizier Kairsu,
when he spoke in instruction to his children.
[I will say something] important and have [you] hear […

This, however, is no more reliable an indication of the author's identity than the stela. Kairsu, "the (king's) ka is the one who made him," is an Old Kingdom name, but no historical vizier with that name is known. Most likely, the text has been attributed to him to give it the authority of age, as is the case with the instructions of Kagemni and Ptahhotep (Text 4).

ẖr msw.f — the preposition *ẖr* is used instead of *n* "to" because of the plurality of its object: see § 8.2.13.

9–10 *sḫr n nḥḥ* — that is, a manner of living that is continually applicable: see Essay 9.

n mꜣꜥw — literally, "for Maat-ness": see Essay 10.

10–11 The king's name (of Amenemhat III) and *ꜥnḫ.(w)-ḏt* are probably added here—one indication that the composition is earlier in date than the stela. The title *nswt* alone is not normally used in place of *nswt-bjt* before the throne name. The original was probably therefore a couplet:, with the first line *dwꜣ nswt m ẖnw n ḥwt.ṯn*.

12 *mꜣꜣw m stwt.f* — see § 24.7.

sḥḏw(j) sw tꜣwj r jtn — see § 23.8.

12–13 *swꜣḏw(j) sw r ḥꜥp ꜥꜣ* — see § 23.8. The term *ḥꜥp ꜥꜣ* "big inundation" refers to a flood that was sufficient to water every field. The second line of the couplet continues the image: the inundation carried not only water but silt, depositing fertile soil—the "force of life"—throughout Egypt.

13–14 *qbb fndw wꜣ.f r nšn* — literally, "noses become cool when he is distant with respect to storming." The verb *qbb* implies not only the lowering of temperature but also becoming refreshed: when the king rages, his subjects cannot breathe because of fear. New Kingdom copies have replaced the first verb with *ḏbb*, interpreting the line as "noses become stopped up when he starts to rage" (see the note to Sin. B 97–98 *sttjw wꜣ.(w) r štm*).

ḥtp.f r tpr ṯꜣw — a SUBJECT–*r-sḏm* construction that is difficult to render in English. The subject is the unmarked noun clause *ḥtp.f* and the infinitive has passive sense: literally, "(that) he is content is with respect to air being breathed." The second verb is *tpj*; the form *tpr* is a false etymology (i.e., *tpj* < **tpr*).

15–16 *ẖnmw pw n ḥꜥw nb* — Khnum was the god who formed bodies on a potter's wheel and united (*ẖnm*) them with their ka.

16–17 *jw dwꜣ sw r nhw ꜥ.f* — an adverbial sentence in which the subject is the participial phrase *dwꜣ sw* and the prepositional phrase has a relative *sḏm.f*.

18 *tjwr ḥr ꜥnḫ.f* — *tjwr* is a spelling of the verb *twr* "respect." *ꜥnḫ.f* could mean "his life," but the first clause indicates that the word is *ꜥnḫ* "oath" (§ 3.4), which was taken on the name of the king in the Middle Kingdom (§ 25.8.2).

zp n b(ꜣ)gsw — literally, "an occasion of laxity."

18–19 The instruction began with a reference to "living correctly" and "conducting a lifetime in peace" and ends, appropriately, with a tercet on death.

jmꜣḫy — see Essay 21.

jw ẖꜣt.f m qm(ꜣ) n mw — the passive participle *qm(ꜣ)* is masculine and therefore probably refers to the corpse's owner rather than to the corpse, which is feminine: literally, "his corpse is (that of) one thrown to the water."

19–20 *jr.ṯn nn wḏꜣ ḥꜥw.ṯn* — an emphatic sentence: see § 25.8.1.

gm.ṯn st n ḏt — where the instruction began as the *sḫr n nḥḥ* "method of continuity," it ends as something *n ḏt* "eternally valid" (see Essay 9). The New Kingdom version continues for many more lines, but the character of the final tercet and couplet of the Middle Kingdom version suggests that it was a complete composition, later expanded.

BIBLIOGRAPHY

Lange, Hans O., and H. Schäfer, *Grab- und Denksteine des Mittleren Reichs*. Cairo Catalogue Générale 20001–20780. 4 vols. Berlin, 1902–1925.

Verhoeven, Ursula. "Von der 'Loyalistischen Lehre' zur 'Lehre des Kairsu'." *Zeitschrift für ägyptische Sprache und Altertumskunde* 136 (2009), 87–98.

Posener, Georges. *L'enseignement loyaliste: sagesse égyptienne du Moyen Empire*. Centre de Recherches d'Histoire et de Philologie de la IVe Section de l'École pratique des Hautes Études, II: Hautes Études Orientales, 5. Geneva, 1976.

TEXT 4
THE INSTRUCTIONS OF KAGEMNI'S FATHER AND PTAHHOTEP

THESE TWO TEXTS are preserved on a single Middle Kingdom papyrus, known as Papyrus Prisse, now in the Bibliothèque Nationale in Paris. It is written in hieratic in horizontal lines; that feature and the style of its handwriting suggest a date in the second half of the Middle Kingdom, probably the reign of Amenemhat III, although the text itself may have been composed as early as the beginning of Dyn. XII.

The 214 lines of the papyrus are divided into 18 pages. The first two of these contain the end of the instruction of an anonymous vizier to his children; the end of the instruction mentions a man named Kagemni, apparently one of the children, who becomes vizier under the first king of Dyn. IV, Seneferu (ca. 2575 BC). A blank page follows, and the rest of the papyrus is devoted to the instruction of a vizier named Ptahhotep, who is said to have served under King Izezi of Dyn. V (ca. 2375 BC).[1]

Despite these ascriptions, both texts are creations of the Middle Kingdom, written in Middle Egyptian, with no evidence of translation from an Old Egyptian original. Like the New Kingdom version of the Loyalist Instruction (Text 3), the two compositions are back-dated to give them thc authority of age.

The Instruction of Kagemni survives only in the Middle Kingdom copy. That of Ptahhotep, however, was copied several times in the New Kingdom, on four papyri, a wood tablet, and three ostraca. These later copies contain a revised version of the text, the most important of which is represented by a fragmentary papyrus in the British Museum (BM 10409, usually referred to as L_2).[2]

Both instructions are important sources for the moral and ethical standards of ancient Egypt—in other words, the practical application of Maat to daily life. Both are unfortunately also quite difficult to understand in places, and perhaps not always correctly copied from their original. The end of the first instruction preserves four maxims, a short conclusion, and a rudimentary colophon. After a lengthy introduction, the instruction of Ptahhotep contains thirty-six maxims of varying length, most of which have an introductory line or two in red ink; it ends with a lengthy conclusion and a colophon, anonymous like that of the B manuscript of the story of Sinuhe.

1 The lines of the first instruction are cited by page and line number. Those of Ptahhotep's instruction are generally cited by the sequential line numbers assigned by Žába 1956. The beginning of the papyrus seems not to have disappeared (Jéquier 1911, 7); the text of the first instruction may therefore have been continued from another scroll.

2 Žába's sequential numbers include some assigned to the text of L_2, not in pPrisse.

The Instruction of Kagemni's Father: Maxims

MAXIM X+1 — MODERATION IN BEHAVIOR (1,1–3)

1,1
1,2
1,3

1,1 *wḏꜣ snḏw ḥs mt* 4
wn ẖn n grw 3
1,2–3 *wsḫ jst nt hr m mdww* 4
spd dsw r th mjtn 4
nn ḥn nj js ḥr zp.f 2

1,1 Sound is the cautious, blessed is the moderate,
open is the tent to the quiet man.
1,2–3 Broad is the place of the one calm in speech,
sharp are knives against him who oversteps the path.
There should be no haste except at its proper time.

1,1–3 This is probably the end of a maxim rather than one complete in itself. The first four lines contain five adjectival predicates, including two passive participles (*ḥs* and *wn*; see § 24.5).

snḏw — literally, "fearful." The verb *snḏ* implies not only fear but also caution and respect.

grw — the verb *gr* in the Middle Kingdom denotes stillness or quietness rather than silence. The "quiet man" is one who acts with calm and consideration rather than passion or rashness. The line means that the quiet man is always welcome.

wsḫ jst — cf. Sin. B 155. The idiom apparently refers to extensive resources.

nj js ḥr zp.f — literally, "not on its occasion": see § 11.7.

MAXIM X+2 — ADVICE AGAINST OVEREATING (1,3–7)

1,3
1,4
1,5
1,6
1,7

1,3–4 *jr ḥms.k ḥnꜥ ꜥšꜣt* 2
msd t mrr.k 3
1,4–5 *ꜣt pw ktt dꜣjr jb* 3
ḫw pw ꜣfꜥ jw ḏbꜥ.t(w) jm 4

1,5–6 *jw jkn n mw ꜥḫm.f jbt* 4
mḥt r n šww smn.f jb 4
1,6 *jw nfrt jdn bw nfr* 3
jw nh n ktt jdn wr 4
1,6–7 *ẖz pw ḥnt n ẖt.f swꜣ tr* 5
smḫ nf wstn ẖt m pr.sn 4

1,3–4 If you sit down with a multitude,
hate the bread you love.
1,4–5 Suppressing the appetite is a little moment;
gluttony is a taboo, for it is pointed at.
1,5–6 For a cup of water quenches thirst,
a mouthful of herbs settles the appetite.
1,6 For a good thing substitutes for goodness,
for a little bit substitutes for much.
1,6–7 He who is untimely voracious for his belly is a wretch:
those forget one whose belly made free in their house.

1,3–7 *jb* — the word here and in the next maxim connotes desire, as in the English idiom *have a mind* to do something.

ḥw pw ꜣfꜥ — the first word is an abstract from the verb *ḥwj* "defend, exempt"; the context indicates something defended against rather than defended or exempted.

jw ḏbꜥ.t(w) jm — the verb comes from the noun *ḏbꜥ* "finger." The particle *jw* here and in the next two couplets relates the clause to the initial statement "gluttony is a taboo."

jw nfrt jdn bw nfr — the meaning is that a representative sample is more than adequate. In both lines of the couplet, *jdn* is probably a *sḏm.f* with unexpressed subject.

swꜣ tr — literally, "when the (appropriate) time passes" — i.e., who keeps eating after he should have had enough.

nf — demonstrative pronoun (§ 5.8), referring to *ꜥšꜣt* "multitude" in the first couplet.

wstn ẖt — a *nfr ḥr* construction (§ 6.5) with the participle of *wstn* "stride freely."

MAXIM X+3 — HOW TO BEHAVE WHEN OTHERS OVERINDULGE (1,7–12)

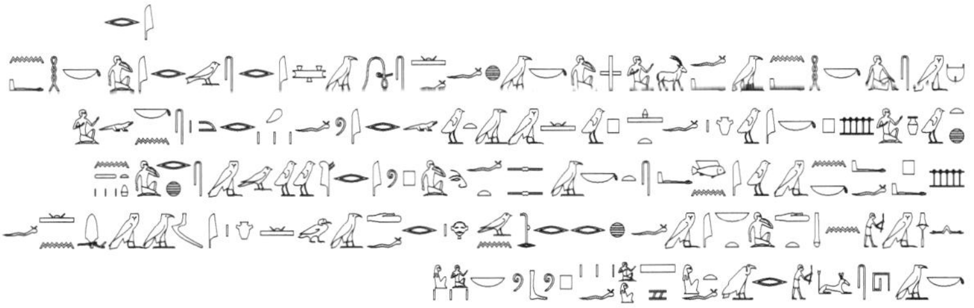

1,7
1,8
1,9
1,10
1,11
1,12

1,7–8	*jr ḥms.k ḥnꜥ ꜣfꜥ*	2	
	wnm.k ꜣḫf.f swꜣ.(w)		3
1,8–9	*jr swrj.k ḥnꜥ tḫw*	2	
	šzp.k jw jb.f ḥtp.w		3
1,9–10	*m ꜣtw r jwf r gs skn*	3	
	šzp.k dj.f n.k		2
	m wjn st kꜣ ssft pw		2
1,10–11	*jr šww m srḫ n t*	3	
	nj sḫm.n mdt nbt jm.f		3
1,11–12	*ḫr (t)r n ḥr r dfꜣ jb*	3	
	jmꜣm n.f kꜣhs r mjwt.f		3
	mrw.f pw bw-nb		2

1,7–8 If you sit down with a glutton,
you should eat only when his lust has passed.
1,8–9 If you drink with a drunkard,
you should accept once his appetite is satisfied.
1,9–10 Don't rage for meat beside one who is ravenous:
you should accept only when he gives to you.
Don't reject it, then it will be something soothing.
1,10–11 As for him who is free of an accusation of bread,
no word can take control of him.
1,11–12 He whose face is averted from feeding the appetite,
the harsh man has to be kinder to him than his mother,
and everyone is his dependant.

1,7–12 *wnm.k* ... *šzp.k* ... *šzp.k* — three emphatic sentences with rhematic adverb clauses (§ 25.7). It is unclear why *jw* introduces the adverb clause in the second sentence but not in the first and third.

m ꜣtw r jwf — the verb is *ꜣd* "rage." The noun is *jf*; the spelling *jwf* derives from the fact that the particle *jw* with 3ms suffix pronoun (*jw.f*) and the word *jf* "meat" were both pronounced the same: *'uf.

kꜣ ssft pw — the particle *kꜣ* (§ 15.6.15) here introduces an A *pw* nominal sentence. *ssft* is the feminine active participle of the causative of *sf* "be mild."

srḫ n t — the verb *srḫ* "cause to know" is used of bringing someone to the attention of authorities. An "accusation of bread" means a reproach for gluttony.

nj sḫm.n mdt nbt jm.f — this line continues the judicial metaphor, where *mdt* refers to a guilty verdict. The line means that one who cannot be reproached for gluttony cannot be adversely judged for that failing.

ḥr (t)r n ḥr r df3 jb jm3m n.f k3hs r mjwt.f — the clause *(t)r n ḥr r df3 jb* is topicalized and resumed by the suffix pronoun of *n.f* and *mjwt.f*. The biliteral  and the determinative  point to the verb *twr* "avoid, avert, shun" which can be spelled without the radical *w*; the scribe has evidently forgotten the initial *t* (cf. Barns 1972, though with a different interpretation of the verb). *tr n ḥr* is a *nfr ḥr* construction (§ 6.5) "averted of face." *df3* is otherwise unknown, but the determinative suggests it is a form of *ḏf3* "feed (someone)." The sentence as a whole is a *ḥr sḏm.f* construction, expressing necessity (§ 18.11), and means that someone who avoids gluttony is treated more kindly, even by the harshest of judges, than by his own mother.

MAXIM X+4 — ADVICE AGAINST HUBRIS (1,12 – 2,2)

1,12 / 2,1 / 2,2

1,12–2,1	*jmj pr rn.k*	3
	jw gr.k m r.k njs.t(w).k	3
2,1–2	*m ˁ3 jb.k ḥr ḫpš m ḥr(j) jb ḏ3mw.k*	4
	z3w jtn.k	2
2,2	*nj rḫ.n.tw ḫprt*	2
	jrrt nṯr ḫft ḥsf.f	3

1,12–2,1 Let your name emerge,
but be quiet with your mouth when you are summoned.

2,1–2 Don't get big-headed about power in the midst of your cohort,
lest you create opposition.

2,2 One cannot know what might happen,
or what the god might do when he punishes.

1,12–2,2 The first couplet means, "Make a name for youself, but don't brag when you are noticed."

m ˁ3 jb.k — literally, "don't (let) your mind get big": § 15.4.

ḏ3mw — the word refers to people of one's own generation and social status (Stefanović 2007).

z3w jtn.k — literally, "beware that you create opposition"; the imperative *z3w* can often be translated by the English conjunction *lest*.

For the final couplet, see § Exercise 22, no. 23.

The Instruction of Kagemni's Father: Conclusion (2,3–9)

2,3–4 *rdj.jn ṯꜣt(j) njs.t(w) nꜣy.f n ẖrdw* 5
m ḫt ꜥrq.f sḫr rmṯ 2
bjt.sn m jjt ḥr.f 3
2,4–5 *ḏr.n ḏd.n.f n.sn* 3
jr ntt nbt m zẖꜣ ḥr pꜣ šfdw 3
sḏm st mj ḏd.j st m zn ḥꜣw ḥr šꜣꜣt 5
2,5–6 *wn.jn.sn ḥr rdjt st ḥr ẖwt.sn* 3
wn.jn.sn ḥr šdt st mj ntt m zẖꜣ 4
2,6–7 *wn.jn nfr st ḥr jb.sn* 3
r ḫt nbt ntj m tꜣ pn r ḏr.f 3
wn.jn ꜥḥꜥ.sn ḥms.sn ḫft 4

2,3–4 So, the vizier had his boys summoned
after he came to understand the manner of people,
their nature being what had come upon him.
2,4–5 In the end, he said to them,
"As for everything in writing on this scroll,
hear it as I say it; don't exceed what is decided."
2,5–6 So, they were putting it on their bellies,
and they were reading it like what is in writing.
2,6–7 So, it was better in their mind
than anything that is in this entire land,
so they conducted themselves accordingly.

ḏr.n — the *sḏm.n.f* of an intransitive verb serving as an introductory particle, like *ꜥḥꜥ.n*: see the note to Sin. B 127 *sḏr.n*.

wn.jn.sn ḥr rdjt st ḥr ẖwt.sn — the line following indicates that this refers to the typical posture of an Egyptian scribe, sitting legs crossed and a scroll opened for reading on his stretched kilt.

ꜥḥꜥ.sn ḥms.sn — literally, "they stood and sat," an idiom for customary behavior. The two *sḏm.f* forms have gnomic sense, set into the past by *wn.jn*: see § 18.4.

2,7
2,8
2,9

2,7–9 *ꜥḥꜥ.n ḥm n nswt-bjt ḤWNJ mjn.(w) n.f*
ꜥḥꜥ.n sꜥḥꜥ ḥm n nswt-bjt SNFRW m nswt mnḫ m tꜣ pn r ḏr.f
ꜥḥꜥ.n rdj kꜣ-gm-n.j m (j)m(j)-r njwt ṯꜣt(j)
jw.f pw

2,7–9 Then the Incarnation of Dual King Huni moored for him.
Then the Incarnation of Dual King Snefru was installed as effective king in this entire land.
Then Kagemni was made city-overseer and vizier.
That is how it goes.

mjn.(w) n.f — This sentence and the next two are in prose. Since *mjnj* is an intransitive verb, the stative with following dative is likelier than a *sḏm.n.f* (§ 16.5). For the idiom, see the note to Sin. B 310 *hrw n mjn*. Huni was the last king of Dyn. III (ca. 2575 BC). The death of Huni's incarnation means the death of his body.

The Instruction of Ptahhotep: Introduction (1–41: 4,1–5,6)

1/4
5
6

1/4 ***sbꜣyt nt (j)m(j)-r njwt ṯꜣt(j) ptḥ-ḥtp***
5 *ḥr ḥm n nswt-bjt JSSJ ꜥnḫ.(w) ḏt r nḥḥ*
6 *(j)m(j)-r njwt ṯꜣt(j) ptḥ-ḥtp ḏd.f*

1/4 **Teaching of city-overseer and vizier Ptahhotep**
5 during the Incarnation of Dual King Izezi, alive forever continually.
6 City-overseer and vizier Ptahhotep says:

The introduction consists of three parts, a title in prose (1/4–6), a speech by Ptahhotep to the king (7–23), and the king's response (28–41). The title sets the fictional era in the reign of Izezi of Dyn. V (ca. 2381–2353 BC); several historical viziers named Ptahhotep are known from this period.

1/4–5 *(j)m(j)-r njwt* — the "city" overseen by the vizier in the Old and Middle Kingdoms was the complex of officials' tombs surrounding the royal pyramid; in the New Kingdom, it came to refer to Thebes and the royal necropolis there.

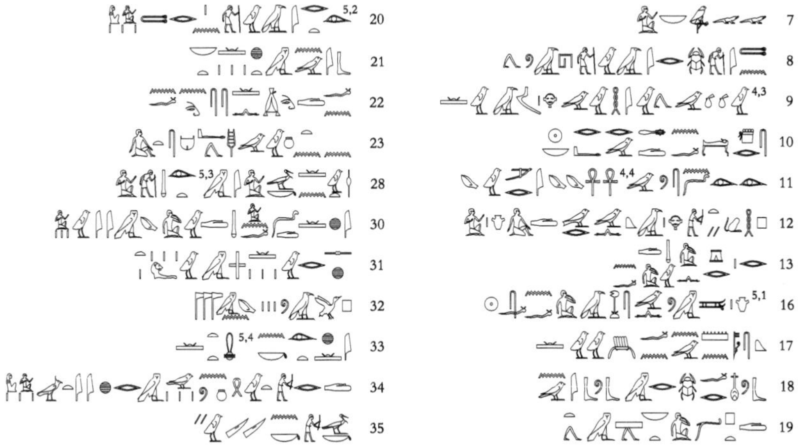

7	*jtj nb.j*	2
8	*ṯnj ḫpr.(w) jꜣw hꜣ.w*	4
9	*wgg j.w jḥw ḥr mꜣw*	4
10	*sḏr.(w) n.f ẖdr.(w) rꜥ nb*	3
11	*jrtj nḏs.w ꜥnḫwj jmr.w*	4
12	*pḥtj ḥr ꜣq nj wrd-jb*	3
13	*r gr.(w) nj mdw.n.f*	3
16	*jb tm.w nj sḫꜣ.n.f sf*	4
17	*qs mn.(w) n.f n ꜣww*	3
18	*bw nfr ḫpr.(w) m bw bjn*	3
19	*dpt nbt šm.t(j)*	2
20–21	*jrrt jꜣw n rmṯ bjn.(w) m ḫt nbt*	5
22	*fnd ḏbꜣ.(w) nj ssn.n.f*	3
22–23	*n tnw ꜥḥꜥ ḥmst*	2
28	*wḏ.t(w) n bꜣk jm jrt mdw-jꜣw*	3
30	*jḫ ḏd.j n.f mdw sḏmyw*	2
31–32	*sḫrw jmjw-ḥꜣt pꜣw sḏm n nṯrw*	3
33	*jḫ jr.t(w) n.k mjtt*	2
34	*dr.tw šnw m rḫyt*	3
35	*bꜣk n.k jdbwj*	2

7 "Sire, my lord,
8 distinction has happened, old age has descended.
9 Distress has come, helplessness is renewing,
10 one lies from it anguished every day.

11 The eyes have shrunk, the ears have grown deaf,
12   strength is collapsing for the weary-minded.
13 The mouth has grown quiet, without being able to speak,
16   the mind is closed, without being able to remember yesterday,
17   the bone is in pain at length.
18 Goodness has become badness,
19   every sense is gone.
20–21 What old age does to people is bad in every respect;
22   the nose is stopped up and cannot breathe
22–23   for the effort of standing and sitting.
28 Let your servant be ordered to make a staff of old age,
30   and I will tell him the speech of listeners,
31–32   the ways of forebears who once listened to the gods.
33 Then the same will be done for you,
34   troubles will be driven from the subjects,
35   and the Two Banks will work for you."

Ptahhotep's speech requests that the king appoint Ptahhotep's son as a "staff of old age" for his father: this was a custom that began in the First Intermediate Period, allowing an aging official to remain in office while his son or other representative assumed the duties of the position (Blumenthal 1987). Ptahhotep argues that this will ensure a smooth continuation of the bureaucracy. In reply, the king accepts the logic of Ptahhotep's argument and agrees to his request.

6–23 *ṯnj* — see the note to Sin. B 189–90.

jḥw — the word is attested only here; its meaning is derived from the context. New Kingdom copies substitute *jswt* "antiquity."

sḏr.(w) n.f ḫdr.(w) — the stative is used for the first verb to express a state ("lie"); the *sḏm.f* would imply an action ("lie down"). The suffix of *n.f* refers to *jḥw* of the previous line. The identity and meaning of the second stative are conjectural; New Kingdom copies have *sḏr.(w) jb rmw/wrd* "lying with weeping/weary mind" (Ptahhotep 15).

nj wrd-jb — for 𓂜 see § 8.2.6. The determinative after *wrd-jb* indicates a person rather than an abstract ("because of weariness of mind").

r gr.(w) nj mdw.n.f — the last signs of this line were compressed in order to finish the sentence on the page.

qs mn.(w) n.f — the order of the determinative and preposition is inverted. The suffix of the dative refers to *qs* ("is in pain for itself").

bjn.(w) m ḫt nbt — literally, "has become bad in everything."

28–41 *jmjw-ḥꜣt* — literally, "those in front."

pꜣw sḏm — "who once listened": § 23.12. This line means that Ptahhotep will pass down the wisdom first imparted by the gods.

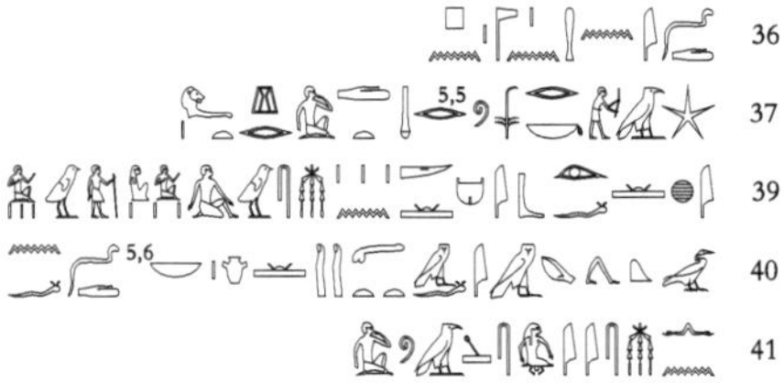

36 *ḏd.jn ḥm n nṯr pn* 3
37 *sbꜣ r.k sw r mdt ẖr ḥꜣt* 3
39 *jḫ jr.f bj(ꜣ) n msw srjw* 3
40 *ꜥq sḏm jm.f* 3
mtt jb nb ḏd n.f 2
41 *nn msy sꜣ.w* 2

36 So, the Incarnation of that god said,
37 "So, teach him to speak from the start,
39 and he will be a model for officials' children.
40 Let hearing enter him,
and exactness of every thought said to him.
41 There is none born experienced."

The Instruction of Ptahhotep: Prologue (42–59: 5,6–10)

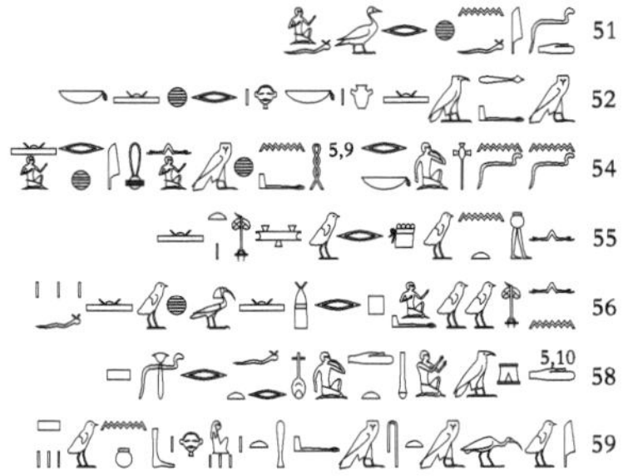

42 ***ḥꜣt ꜥ m tꜣzw n mdt nfrt*** 3
43 *ḏdt.n (j)r(j) pꜥt ḥꜣt(j) ꜥ* 3
jt-nṯr mry-nṯr 2
44 *zꜣ-nswt smsw n ẖt.f* 3
46 *(j)m(j)-r njwt ṯꜣt(j) ptḥ-ḥtp* 3

47 *m sbꜣ ẖmw r rḫ* 2
48 *r dp ḥsb n mdt nfrt* 2
49 *m ꜣḫt n sḏmt(j).fj* 2
50 *m (w)ggt n ntj r tht st* 3
51 *ḏd.jn.f ḫr zꜣ.f* 2
52 *m ꜥꜣ jb.k ḥr rḫ.k* 3
54 *nḏnḏ r.k ḥnꜥ ẖm mj rḫ* 3
55 *nj jn.tw ḏrw ḥmt* 2
56 *nn ḥmww ꜥpr ꜣḫw.f* 2
58 *dgꜣ mdt nfrt r wꜣḏ* 3
59 *jw gm.t(w).s m ꜥ ḥmwt r bnw* 3

42 **Beginning of the phrases of good speech**
43 **said by** member of the elite, high official,
god's father, god's beloved,
44 king's son, eldest of his body,
46 city-overseer and vizier Ptahhotep,
47 in teaching the ignorant to learn
48 according to the standard of good speech,
49 as what is useful for him who will listen,
50 as what is distressful for him who will overstep it.
51 So, he said to his son:
52 Don't get big-headed over your knowledge,
54 but consult with the ignorant like the knowledgeable.
55 The limit of craft is not attained:
56 there is no craftsman complete in his mastery.
58 Good speech is more hidden than malachite,
59 yet it is found with maidservants at the millstones.

The instruction proper begins with a prologue in two parts, a descriptive title (42–50) and a preliminary admonition (51–59). The latter is identified as part of the prologue both by the absence of red ink and by the theme of *mdt nfrt* "good speech" introduced in the first part. This phrase refers to speech that is edifying rather than finely crafted. Ptahhotep describes it as both a "standard" (*dp-ḥsb*) and "hidden" (*dgꜣ*), and Maat is described in similar terms in the Instruction of the Eloquent Peasant (Text 5: B1 213 and 342): "good speech" is therefore speech in accord with Maat.

jt-nṯr mry-nṯr — two priestly titles.

zꜣ-nswt smsw n ẖt.f — this phrase is undoubtedly fictitious, since the king's eldest son would have succeeded him as the next king.

dp-ḥsb — literally, "head of counting." The term denotes a means of reckoning and is applied mostly to quantifiable referents, such as mathematical formulas, weighing, and architecture. In this context, it indicates that Ptahhotep's "good speech" is a yardstick by which proper conduct can be measured.

(w)ggt — the scribe has overlooked the initial radical (cf. the writing in 9, above), probably because of its similarity in hieratic to the *m* that precedes.

ḏd.jn.f ḫr zꜣ.f — the use of *ḫr* instead of *n* is interesting, since it does not conform to the usual motives for the preposition (§ 8.2.13). Its use here may reflect the fact that Ptahhotep is speaking to his son indirectly, through the text.

ꜥpr ꜣḫw.f — literally, "equipped of his effectiveness," a *nfr ḥr* construction with a passive participle. For *ꜣḫw*, see Essay 13.

dgꜣ mdt nfrt r wꜣḏ — An adjectival sentence with passive participle (§ 24.5). Malachite is a green crystalline mineral, used by the Egyptians for eyepaint.

The Instruction of Ptahhotep: Maxims

MAXIM 1 — AN ARGUMENTATIVE SUPERIOR (60–67: 5,10–13)

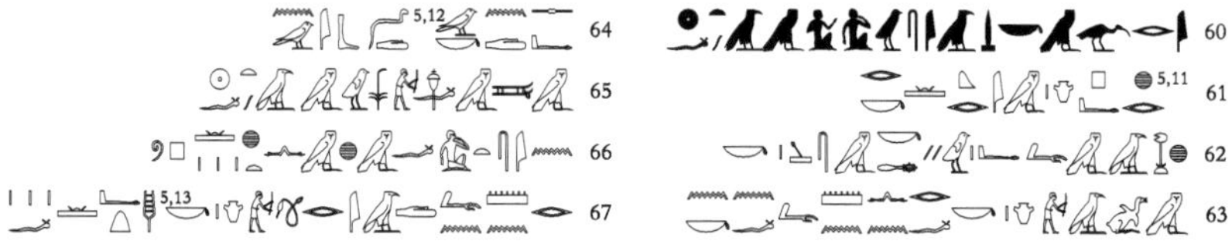

60 ***jr gm.k ḏꜣjsw m ꜣt.f*** 3
61 *ḫrp jb m jqr r.k* 3
62 *ḫꜣm ꜥwj.k* 2
ẖms sꜣ.k 2
63 *mṯꜣ jb.k r.f* 2
nn (r)mn.n.f n.k 2
64 *sꜥnd.k ḏd bjn* 3
65 *m tm ḫsf sw m ꜣt.f* 3
66 *njs.t(w).f m ḫm ḫt pw* 2
67 *rmn.n dꜣjr jb.k ꜥḥꜥw.f* 3

60 **If you find a conversant in his moment**
61 and determined, one more accomplished than you,
62 bend your arms,
bow your back,
63 challenge your mind with respect to him
and he won't be able to match you.

64 You belittle one who speaks badly
65 by not opposing him in his moment.
66 He will be called, "He is an ignoramus,"
67 when the suppression of your mind has matched his resources.

The first three maxims offer advice on how to behave toward someone who is argumentative — in this case, a superior.

ḏ3jsw — a noun from *ḏ3js* "discuss": i.e., someone with whom one is speaking.

3t — the sense is "moment of anger."

ḫrp jb — literally, "who manages/directs the mind."

ḫ3m ʿwj.k — see the note to ShS. 87 *ʿwj.j ḫ3m.(w) m b3ḥ.f.*

nn (r)mn.n.f n.k — see § 17.11. The scribe has omitted the initial consonant of *rmn*. The verb means literally "shoulder." It is used to refer to association (compare English *rub shoulders with*), but here it has the sense of coming up to the same height as.

ḫm ḫt — literally, "one who does not know things."

MAXIM 2 — AN ARGUMENTATIVE EQUAL (68–73: 5,13–14)

68 *jr gm.k ḏ3jsw m 3t.f* 3
69 *mjtw.k ntj m rmnwt.k* 3
70 *dd.k ḫpr jqr.k r.f* 4
70–71 *m gr jw.f ḥr mdt bjnt* 3
72 *wr wf3 jn sḏmyw* 3
73 *rn.k nfr.(w) m rḫ n srjw* 4

68 If you find a conversant in his moment,
69 your equal, who is on your level,
70 you make your accomplishment become more than his
70–71 by being quiet while he is speaking badly.
72 Great will be the reproach by the hearers,
73 while your name is good in the knowledge of officials.

In this case, the disputant is an equal. The maxim is not marked by red ink, but it has the same initial line as the first and third maxims.

rmnwt.k — a verbal noun of the verb *rmnj* (see Maxim 1), which is written as a false plural (i.e., of **rmnt*: see § 4.6).

dd.k — the sentence is emphatic: the rheme is *m gr*.

jn sḏmyw — i.e., by those who hear the argument.

MAXIM 3 — AN ARGUMENTATIVE SUBORDINATE (74–83: 6,1–3)

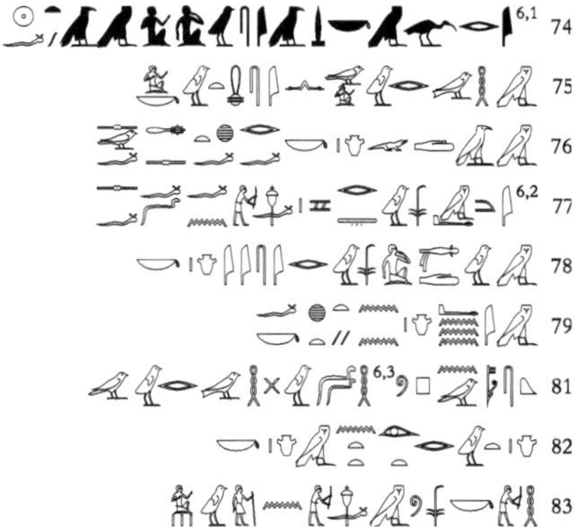

74 ***jr gm.k ḏꜣjsw m ꜣt.f*** 3
75 *m ḥwrw nj js mjtw.k* 2
76 *m ꜣd jb.k r.f ḫft ẖzz.f* 4
77 *jmj sw r tꜣ ḫsf.f n.f ḏs.f* 4
78 *m wšd sw r jsy jb.k* 3
79 *m jʿ jb n ntj ḫft.k* 4
81 *qsn pw ḥḏḏw ḥwrw* 3
82 *jb.tw r jrt ntt m jb.k* 4
83 *ḫsf.k sw m ḫsf n srjw* 3

74 **If you find a conversant in** his **moment**
75 who is an inferior and not your equal,
76 don't let your mind rage at him because he is wretched:
77 put him aside and he will punish himself by himself.
78 Don't address him to ease your mind,
79 don't wash the mind to one who is opposed to you:
81 he is one in difficulty, damaged, inferior.

82 One will have a mind to do what you have in mind
83 when you oppose him by the opposition of officials.

The third maxim deals with an argumentative inferior.

ḫft ẖzz.f — literally, "in accordance with (the fact) that he is wretched" (§ 21.9).

jmj sw r tꜣ — literally, "put him to the earth," an idiom for putting something down or aside.

r jsy jb.k — the verb *jzj* means "become light": literally, "with respect to your mind becoming light."

jꜥ jb — an idiom for the removal of anger: see Sin. B 149.

ḥḏḏw — a geminated 2-lit. passive participle (§ 24.2).

ḫsf.k sw m ḫsf n srjw — the sense of *ḫsf* here is "oppose, bar" rather than "punish," since the latter takes an indirect object, as in line 77. The prepositional phrase probably means "by the kind of opposition appropriate to officials."

MAXIM 4 — MAAT (84–98: 6,3–7)

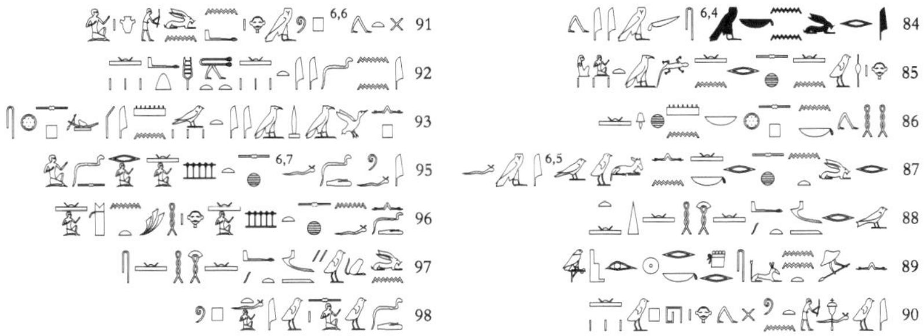

84	***jr wnn.k m*** *sšmy*	2
85	*ḥr wḏ n sḫr n ꜥšꜣt*	3
86	*ḥḥ n.k zp nb mnḫ*	3
87	*r wnt sḫr.k nn jw jm.f*	4
88	*wr mꜣꜥt wꜣḥ spdt.(s)*	4
89	*nj ẖn.n.t(w).s ḏr rk jsjr*	2
90	*jw ḫsf.tw n swꜣ ḥr hpw*	3
91	*swꜣt pw m ḥr n ꜥwn-jb*	3
92	*jn nḏyt jtt ꜥḥꜥw*	3
93	*nj pꜣ ḏꜣyt mjn zp.s*	4
95	*jw.f ḏd.f sḫt.j r.j ḏs.j*	3
96	*nj ḏd.n.f sḫt.j ḥr ḥnt.j*	3
97	*wn pḥwj mꜣꜥt wꜣḥ.s*	3
98	*ḏd w z(j) w jt.j pw*	3

84 **If you are** a leader,
85 giving commands for the conduct of many,
86 seek out for yourself every kind of effective deed,
87 until your conduct is without error in it.
88 Maat is great, its sharpness lasting:
89 it has not been able to be disturbed since Osiris's time.
90 Bypassing customs is punished;
91 it is what is bypassed in the intent of the greedy man.
92 Arrogance is what takes away riches;
93 transgression has not once moored its case.
95 For he says, "As for me, I net by myself";
96 he does not say, "I net by my service."
97 In the end, Maat lasts:
98 a man should not say, "It is my father's area."

r wnt sḫr.k nn jw jm.f — literally, "until your conduct is: there is no error in it." *wnt* is a *sdmt.f* (§ 19.14).

wȝḥ spdt.(s) — an adjectival sentence rather than a *nfr ḥr* construction, since *wȝḥ* is masculine. The scribe probably omitted the suffix pronoun (present in the New Kingdom copy).

hpw — ancient Egypt had no codified laws. In their place, society operated on the basis of customary behavior, ways of acting that time had proved to be beneficial to society as a whole. These customs were the practical manifestations of Maat.

swȝt pw — the feminine refers to *mȝʿt*.

m ḥr n ʿwn-jb — literally, "in the face of the robbery-minded." *ḥr* "face" is used to express the notions of intention or attention.

nj pȝ ḏȝyt mjn zp.s — i.e., transgression (*ḏȝyt*, literally "crossing") has never succeeded.

jw.f ḏd.f sḫt.j r.j ḏs.j — the suffix pronoun refers to *ʿwn-jb* "the greedy man." The verb *sḫt* "weave, net" is used of trapping game in a net. The sentence is an expression of independence and self-sufficiency, contrasted in the next line with making a living by honest labor.

wn pḥwj mȝʿt wȝḥ.s — two interpretations of this sentence are possible, both with similar meanings: two clauses (literally "the end exists and Maat lasts") or one (literally "the end of Maat is that it lasts"). The former is likelier, since it is doubtful that an Egyptian would have spoken of "the end of Maat."

ḏd w z(j) w jt.j pw — the first *w* is the archaic enclitic negation (§§ 15.7.4, 26.26.4). The second is the word meaning "district, area," regularly written with the determinative 𓈇, omitted here; the New Kingdom version has *ḫt jt.j* "my father's property." The sentence ilustrates what is meant by "Maat lasts": it is applicable to every generation, and never out of date.

MAXIM 5 — TRUST IN GOD (99–118: 6,8–10)

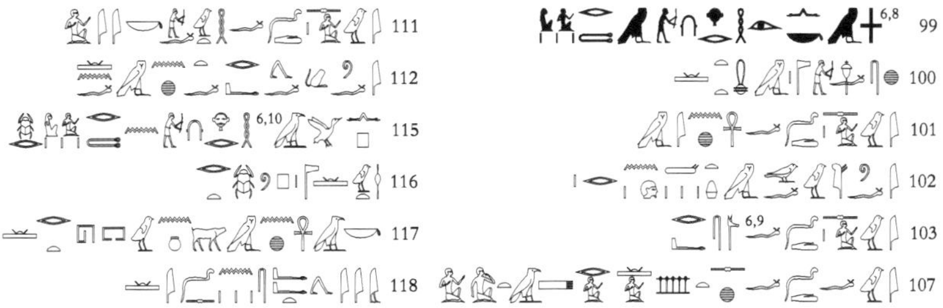

99 ***jm.k jr ḥr m rmṯ*** 4
100 *ḥsf nṯr m mjtt* 3
101 *jw z(j) ḏd.f ʿnḫ jm* 4
102 *jw.f šw.f m t n dp-r* 3
103 *jw z(j) ḏd.f wsr* 3
107 *jw.f ḏd.f sḫt.j r.j sꜣt.j* 3
111 *jw z(j) ḏd.f ḥwtf ky* 4
112 *jw.f pḥ.f rdjt.f n ḫm.n.f* 3
115 *nj pꜣ ḥr n rmṯ ḫpr* 4
116 *wḏt nṯr pw ḫprt* 2
117 *kꜣ ʿnḫ m ḫnw hrt* 3
118 *jy ddt.sn ḏsj* 3

99 **You should not make plans by people:**
100 the god makes opposition in like fashion.
101 For a man thinks to live thereby,
102 and he is devoid of the bread of the mouth.
103 For a man thinks to become powerful,
107 and he says, "I ensnare my own cleverness."
111 For a man thinks to rob another,
112 and he ends up giving to one he did not know.
115 No plans of people have ever come about:
116 what happens is what the god decrees.
117 Therefore, live inside calmness,
118 and what they give will come of its own accord.

In this maxim, Ptahhotep advises against trusting in people rather than the gods when making plans.

ḥr — the rest of the maxim indicates that this is a verbal noun of *ḥr* "prepare" rather than a form of *ḥryt* "terror."

ḫsf — the sense is probably "bar" rather than "punish": the sentence means that the god can oppose such plans by means of the unreliability of the human condition.

jw z(j) ḏd.f — the first of six *jw* sentences exemplifying the statement of the preceding couplet. For *ḏd* "think," see Sin. B 7.

t n dp-r — literally, "bread of atop-the-mouth."

sḫt.j r.j sꜣt.j — i.e., "I have used my understanding to my own disadvantage" (Burkard 1991, 201). Despite the spelling,  is a verbal noun of *sꜣꜣ* "gain understanding, experience" rather *sjꜣ* "perceive." The prepositional phrase *r.j* "with respect to me" is self-referential.

ḥwtf — see the note to Sin. B 112 *ḥwt(f).f wj*.

jw.f pḥ.f rdjt.f — literally, "he reaches his giving"; *rdjt* is an infinitive.

jy ddt.sn ḏsj — the suffix pronoun resumes the plurality inherent in the Egyptian notion of *nṯr* "god." *ḏsj* is an adverb from *ḏs* "self" (§ 8.14).

MAXIM 6 — TABLE MANNERS (119–44: 6,9–7,3)

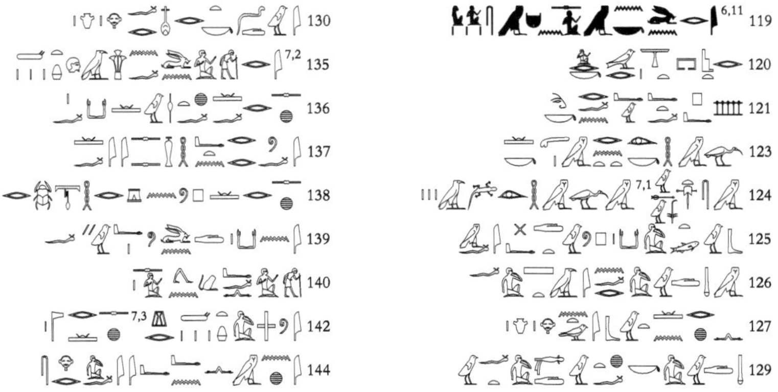

119–20 ***jr wnn.k m z n ḥms*** *r jst ṯt wr r.k* 5
121 *šzp.k djt.f djw r fnd.k* 4
123 *gmḥ.k r ntt m bꜣḥ.k* 3
124 *m stw sw m gmḥ ꜥšꜣ* 3
125 *bwt kꜣ pw wdt jm.f* 3
126 *m mdw n.f r jꜣšt.f* 3
127 *nj rḫ.n.tw bjnt ḥr jb* 3
129 *mdw.k ḫft wšd.f tw* 3
130 *jw ḏdt.k r nfr ḥr jb* 3
135 *jr wr wnn.f ḫꜣ t* 3
136 *sḫr.f ḫft wḏ kꜣ.f* 4

137 *jw.f r rdjt n ḥzy.f* 2
138 *sḫr pw n grḥ ḫpr* 3
139 *jn kꜣ dwn ꜥwj.f* 3
140 *wr dj.f nj pḥ.n z(j)* 4
142 *jw wnm t ẖr sḫr nṯr* 2
143 *jn ḫm ꜥnꜥy.f ḥr.s* 3

119–20 **If you are a guest** at the table of one greater than you,
121 you should accept what is given when it is given to you.
123 You should stare at what is in your presence;
124 don't shoot him with much staring:
125 pestering him is the ka's abomination.
126 Don't talk to him until he calls:
127 one cannot know what might be bad in the mind.
129 If you speak when he addresses you,
130 what you say will be good in the mind.
135 As for a great man who is at bread,
136 his custom is according as his ka dictates:
137 he will give to the one he favors,
138 and the outcome is a matter of obscurity.
139 The ka is what stretches out his arms;
140 the great man gives, and a man cannot attain it.
142 For the eating of bread is under the god's system:
143 only the ignorant will complain about it.

This maxim concerns table manners at a dinner with a superior. The host here is designated *kꜣ* "ka," because he is the source of the sustenance.

z(j) n ḥms — literally, "a man of a sitting," where *ḥms* refers to a group of people.

djw r fnd.k — literally, "when it has been given to your nose": *djw* is a passive *sḏm.f* with omitted subject, expressing prior circumstance in an unmarked adverb clause (§ 20.14).

m stw sw — The scribe has compressed the signs of *stw sw* at the end of the page.

wdt jm.f — literally, "pushing in him."

mdw.k ḫft wšd.f tw — probably an initial conditional clause (§ 25.8.1); literally, "you speak according as he addresses you."

sḫr pw n grḥ ḫpr — literally, "the happening (infinitive) is the system of night": i.e., no one can see what will happen.

nj pḥ.n z(j) — i.e., no one can force a great man to act.

jn ḫm ꜥnꜥy.f ḥr.s — a participial statement (§ 23.10): "the ignorant is the one who will complain about it."

MAXIM 7 — SLANDER (145–60: 7,3–5)

145 ***jr wnn.k m z n ꜥq*** 3
146 *hꜣbw wr n wr* 3
147 *mt ḥr qd hꜣb.f tw* 3
148 *jr n.f wpwt mj ḏd.f* 3
149 *ꜥḥꜣ.t(j) m sḏw* 2
149–50 *m mdt skntj wr n wr* 4
151 *ndr mꜣꜥt m zn.s* 3
152 *nj wḥm.t(w) js jꜥ n jb* 3
159–60 *m mdyw rmṯ nbt wr ktt* 3
160 *bwt kꜣ pw* 1

145 **If you are a man of entrée,**
146 whom one great man sends to another,
147 be completely exact when he sends you;
148 do for him the mission as he says.
149 Be mindful of denigrating
149–50 by speech that will debase one official to another;
151 hold Maat in its true form.
152 Washing of the heart should not be repeated
159–60 in the speech of any people, whether of great or small:
160 it is the ka's abomination.

This maxim deals with proper behavior as a messenger and warns in particular about transmitting malicious speech.

z(j) n ꜥq — the idiom refers to someone who has access to a superior, and implies a measure of trust.

ꜥḥꜣ.t(j) m sḏw — literally, "be combative about making bad."

skntj — as such only here. The verb *skn* means "be voracious" (see Kagemni 1,9), which does not suit this context. It may be instead a metathesized form of *snk* "sink," used transitively; the determinative reflects the oral nature of the action. The verb form is a *sḏmtj.fj* without suffix (§ 23.13).

nj wḥm.t(w) js jꜥ n jb m mdyw rmṯ nbt — a negated emphatic sentence (§ 25.11). The rheme is *m mdyw rmṯ nbt*: "it is not in the speech of any group that washing of the heart should be repeated," meaning that conversation about such matters should be private. The feminine ending of *nbt* shows that *rmṯ* is understood here as a collective.

wr ktt — the terms refer to the composition of *rmṯ nbt* rather than to the size of the group: i.e., a group of great men or people of no consequence.

MAXIM 8 — BEHAVIOR WHEN SUCCESSFUL (161–74: 7,5–7)

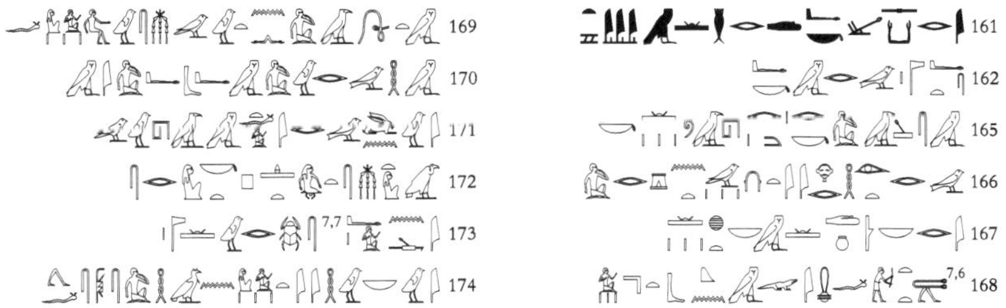

161 ***jr skꜣ.k ⸢rd⸣ m sḫt*** 3
162 *dj st nṯr wr m ꜥ.k* 4
165 *m sꜣ r.k r gs hꜣw.k* 3
166 *wr jrt ḥryt nt gr* 3
167 *jr nb qd m nb ḫwt* 2
168 *jtt.f mj mzḥ m qnbt* 3
169 *m twꜣ n jwt(j) msw.f* 2
170 *m ḥwrw m ꜥbꜥ jm* 3
171 *jw wn wr jt m ꜣhw* 4
172 *mjwt mst ḥtp kt r.s* 5
173 *jn wꜥ sḫprw nṯr* 3
174 *jw nb wḥyt nḥ.s šms.f* 3

161 **If you farm and there is growth in the field,**
162 and the god puts it greatly in your hand,
165 don't let your mouth get sated beside your neighborhood:
166 quiet makes for great respect.
167 As for the man of character who owns things,
168 he gains like a crocodile in the council.
169 Don't brag to one who is childless,
170 don't become inferior by boasting of it.
171 For there is many a father in distress,
172 and the mother who has given birth, another is more content than she.

173 The single man is the one whom the god fosters,
174 while the one with a tribe, it asks for his service.

The theme of this maxim is modest behavior in a situation of prosperity. The first three couplets deal with material prosperity and the second three, with success in raising a family.

⸢rd⸣ m sḫt — the scribe has written *dr*. The verb is a *sḏm.f* with omitted subject: literally, "(it) grows in the field."

m sꜣ r.k — the notion of satiety here probably has to do with words rather than food: i.e., don't brag about it to your neighbors.

wr jrt ḥryt nt gr — literally, "great is the making respect of quiet." For the notion of *gr* "quiet," see the note to Kagemni 1,1, above.

jr nb qd m nb ḫwt — literally, "as for the owner of character as owner of things."

jtt.f mj mzḥ m qnbt — probably emphatic, with *mj mzḥ* the rheme. The *qnbt* is the local conclave of officials and elders that settled disputes. The sense of the sentence is that a property-owner who has character will generally triumph in any dispute.

m twꜣ — the verb means "hold up for admiration"; the implied object here is reflexive ("yourself"). The sense of the couplet is not to vaunt one's success in raising a family to the man who has none.

m ꜥbꜥ jm — the implied object of *jm* is "your own family."

The last couplet means that the god will take care of the single man, while the head of a tribe has to take care of it himself.

MAXIM 9 — BEHAVIOR TOWARD SOMEONE SUCCESSFUL (175–85: 7,7–9)

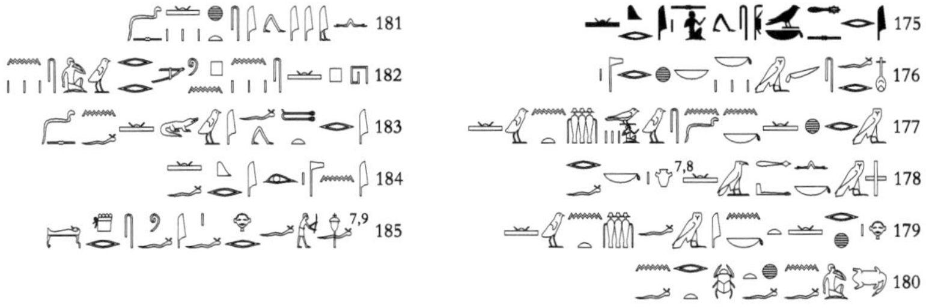

175	***jr ḫz.k šms z(j) jqr***	3
176	*nfr sšm.k ḫr nṯr*	3
177	*m rḫ.n.k nḏs.w ḫntw*	3
178	*jm.k ꜥꜣ jb.k r.f*	4
179	*ḥr rḫt.n.k jm.f ḫntw*	3
180	*snḏ n.f ḫft ḫprt n.f*	2
181	*nj jy js ḫwt ḏs*	3
182	*hp.sn pw n mrrw.sn*	2
183	*jr ṯtf jw sꜣq n.f ḏs*	3

184 *jn nṯr jr jqr.f* 3
185 *ḫsf.f ḥr.f jw.f sḏr.(w)* 3

175 **If you are lowly, serve an accomplished man.**
176 Let all your conduct be good before the god
177 with regard to one you know who was little before.
178 Don't get big-headed regarding him
179 because of what you know about him before:
180 respect him for what has happened to him.
181 Things do not come of themselves:
182 it is their custom for one they love;
183 as for overflow, it collects for him itself.
184 The god is the one who made his accomplishment,
185 intervening on his behalf while he was asleep.

This maxim offers advice on the proper attitude toward someone who has risen from humble beginnings: his success is a sign of the god's favor.

m rḫ.n.k nḏs.w ḫntw — the first verb form is a relative *sḏm.n.f* serving as an undefined noun (§ 22.15); the second is a 3ms stative modifying this noun as an unmarked relative clause (§ 22.11).

nj jy js ḫwt ḏs — an emphatic sentence (§ 25.11); adverbial *ḏs* is the rheme.

hp.sn pw n mrrw.sn — i.e., they amass for whomever they choose.

jw s3q n.f ḏs — the verb is a passive *sḏm.f* with omitted subject: literally, "(it) is collected." The suffix pronoun refers to *mrrw.sn* "one they love" in the preceding line.

ḫsf.f ḥr.f — literally, "he bars over him."

MAXIM 10 — PERSEVERANCE TOWARD GOALS (186–93: 7,9–10)

186 ***šms jb.k tr n wnn.k*** 4
187 *m jr ḥ3w ḥr mddwt* 3
188 *m ḫb tr n šms jb* 3
189 *bwt k3 pw ḥḏt 3t.f* 2
190 *m ngb zp ḫrt hrw* 2
191 *m ḥ3w n grg pr.k* 2

192 *ḫpr ḫwt šms jb* 1
193 *nn km.n ḫwt jw sfꜣ.f* 3

186 **Follow your mind as long as you exist.**
187 Don't add to what is said.
188 Don't lessen the time of following the mind:
189 wasting its moment is the ka's abomination.
190 Don't divert the task of daily requirements
191 in excess of founding your house.
192 The things of one who follows the mind come about;
193 things will not be able to accumulate when he is sluggish.

This maxim advises diligence in pursuing one's goals.

šms jb.k — the phrase refers to the pursuit of an idea or plan—in this case, the plan for one's life: cf. Lorton 1968.

tr n wnn.k — literally, "the time of your existing," used adverbially (§ 8.14).

mddwt — a feminine plural passive participle (§ 24.2), here probably referring to the advice in the preceding line.

ḥḏt ꜣt.f — literally, "damaging its moment." The suffix pronoun refers either to *tr* or *šms jb* in the preceding line.

m ngb zp — literally, "don't divert the occasion." The couplet means, don't do anything other than what you have to do every day to establish your estate.

šms jb — the suffix pronoun of *jw sfꜣ.f* indicates that *šms* here is an active participle.

MAXIM 11 — TREATMENT OF A SON (197–219: 7,10–8,2)

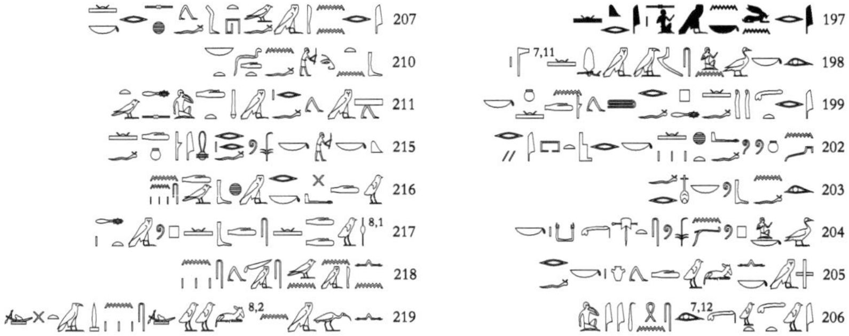

197 ***jr wnn.k m z(j) jqr*** 2
198 *jr.k zꜣ m smꜣm nṯr* 3

199 *jr mt.f pẖr.f n qd.k* 3
202 *nw.f ḫwt.k r jst jrj* 4
203 *jr n.f bw nb nfr* 2
204 *zꜣ.k pw nsw st kꜣ.k* 2
205 *jm.k jwd jb.k r.f* 4
206 *jw mtwt jr.s šnty* 3
207 *jr nnm.f th.f sẖr.k* 3
210 *btn.n.f ḏdt nbt* 2
211 *šm r.f m mdt ẖzt* 4
215 *⌈bꜣ⌉k.k sw r r.f mj qd.f* 3
216 *wd.(w) r.k m ḫbd n.sn* 4
217 *wdd sdb pw m ẖt* 3
218 *nj nnm.n sšm.sn* 2
219 *nj gm.n jww.sn ḏꜣt* 3

197 **If you are an accomplished man,**
198 you should make a son, the god willing.
199 If he is exact, serves your character,
202 and tends your things properly,
203 do for him all goodness:
204 he is your son; he belongs to your ka's ejaculation.
205 You should not separate your mind from him.
206 But seed can make strife.
207 If he errs and violates your way,
210 having disobeyed all that is said,
211 his mouth going with wretched speech,
215 you should task him completely according to his mouth,
216 pushed from you as hateful to them:
217 he is one decreed obstructive in the womb.
218 Their guidance cannot err;
219 the one they strand cannot find a way across.

This maxim offers advice on managing a son.

m smꜣm nṯr — literally, "by the god's beneficence." The verb is the causative stem of *jmꜣ* "be kind, gracious": see § 12.5.9.

pẖr.f n qd.k — literally, "he goes around for your character." The idiom refers to a servant circulating among guests.

r jst jrj — literally, "with respect to the place thereunto."

nsw st kꜣ.k — the ka, or life-force, was thought to be passed to children through the father's role in procreation.

jw mtwt jr.s šnty — this line belongs with neither the preceding nor the following line and is therefore single. It serves as a bridge to the second half of the maxim.

⸢bꜣ⸣k.k sw — for some reason, the scribe has written  instead of ; the New Kingdom version has the correct spelling.

m ḫdb n.sn — there is no obvious referent for the 3pl suffix pronoun here and in the next couplet, but the gods are certainly meant.

wdd sdb — a *nfr ḥr* construction (§ 6.5) with a passive participle: literally, "decreed of obstruction."

nj gm.n jww.sn ḏꜣt — the metaphor is derived from daily life, where a willing ferryman was necessary in order to cross the river. The line means that there is no hope for one whom the gods have abandoned.

MAXIM 12 — BEHAVIOR IN COURT (220–31: 8,2–6)

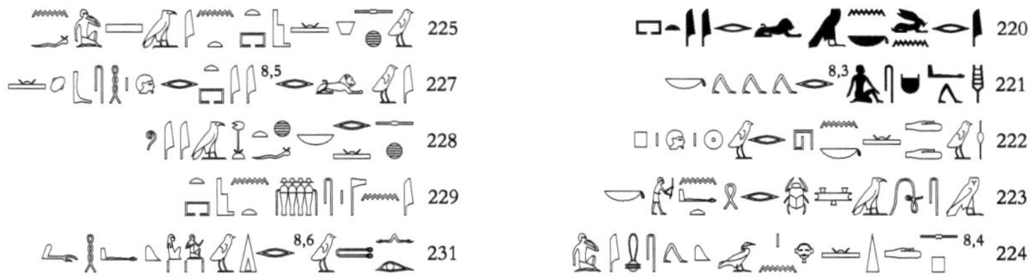

220–21 ***jr wnn.k m ryt ꜥḥꜥ ḥms*** 4
221–22 *r nmtw.k wdd n.k hrw dp(j)* 4
223 *m swꜣ ḫpr šnꜥ.t(w).k* 3
224 *spd ḥr n ꜥq smj.(w)* 3
225 *wsḫ jst nt jꜣš n.f* 3
227 *jw ryt r dp ḥsb* 2
228 *sḫr nb ḫft ḫꜣy* 2
229 *jn nṯr sḫnt jst* 3
231 *nj jr.ṯw rdjw qꜥḥ* 3

220–21 **Whenever you are in court, stand and sit**
221–22 according to your steps decreed for you the first day:
223 don't bypass, or you will turn out to be banned.
224 Sharp is the face of the one who enters reported,
225 wide the place of the one summoned.
227 Court operates to a standard;
228 every procedure is according to measure.

229 The god is the one who advances a place;
231 those who give the shoulder are not appointed.

How to behave in court. The *rwt* (> *ryt*) is the "portal" of a temple, where public hearings were held.

ꜥḥꜥ ḥms — i.e., behave: see the note to Kagemni 2,7, above.

wdd n.k hrw dpj — i.e., the order of speaking that was laid out on the first day of court.

ḫpr šnꜥ.t(w).k — a clause of result (§ 20.13): literally, "that you are banned happens."

spd ḥr — an idiom for "wise, clever." The couplet advises against speaking out of turn.

wsḫ jst — see the note to Kagemni 1,2, above.

jw ryt r dp ḥsb — literally, "the portal is with respect to a standard." For *dp ḥsb*, see the note to Ptahhotep 48, above.

nj jr.ṯw rdjw qꜥḥ — the verb *jrj* "make" is used of appointing someone to an office or function. *rdjw qꜥḥ* refers to people who force their way into a situation out of turn.

MAXIM 13 — CONCERN FOR NEIGHBORS (232–48: 8,6–11)

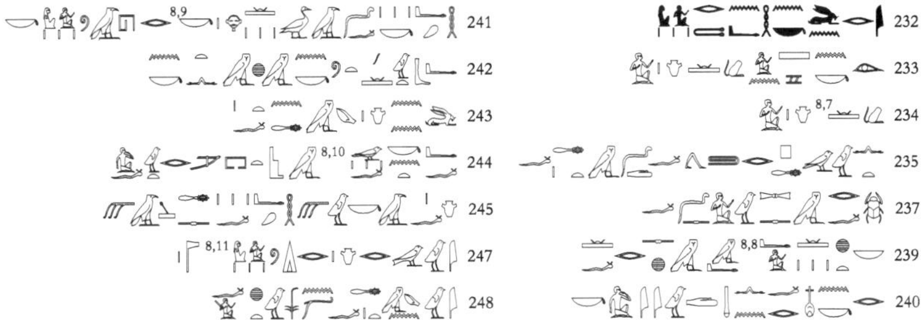

232	***jr wnn.k ḥnꜥ rmṯ***	2
233	*jr n.k mr n kfꜣ-jb*	3
234–35	*kfꜣ-jb jwt(j) pẖr.f ḏd m ẖt.f*	4
237	*ḫpr.f m ṯꜣzw ḏs.f*	3
239	*nb ḫwt dj.j mj m sḫr.f*	4
240	*rn.k nfr.(w) nn mdwy.k*	3
241	*ḥꜥw.k ḏfꜣ.(w)*	2
	ḥr.k r hꜣw.k	2
242	*ꜥb{wt}.tw n.k m ḫmt.n.k*	2
243	*wnn jb sḏm n ẖt.f*	3
244	*dj.f knwt.f m jst mrwt.f*	3
245	*jb fꜣk.w ḥꜥw.f ḥzꜣ.(w)*	4
247	*jw wr jb rdjw nṯr*	4
248	*jw sḏm n ẖt.f n-sw ẖft(j)*	3

232 **If you are with people,**
233 make a dependant a confidant for yourself.
234–35 A confidant who does not circulate the saying in his belly
237 becomes a commander himself,
239 a property-owner whose way is "What can I give?"
240 your name good without your speaking,
241 your body nourished.
241 Pay attention to your neighbors,
242 and one will gather for you as what you have not known.
243 The mind of one who listens to his belly is such
244 that it puts disdain of him place of love of him,
245 his mind bare, his limbs unanointed.
247 For the mind of those the god gives is great,
248 but he who listens to his belly belongs to an enemy.

In this maxim, Ptahhotep advises paying attention to dependants and neighbors rather than to one's own desires.

mr n kfꜣ-jb — literally, "a dependant for one discrete of mind."

jwt(j) pḫr.f ḏd m ẖt.f — i.e., who does not reveal confidences.

nb ḫwt dj.j mj m sḫr.f — literally, "an owner of things (who) 'What can I give?' is his manner"—i.e., one who is generous with his property; *dj.j mj m sḫr.f* is an unmarked relative clause. This line could also belong with the line following rather than the one preceding, as anticipatory to the suffix pronoun of *rn.k*.

rn.k nfr.(w) nn mdwy.k — i.e., your actions have established your reputation.

ḥr.k r ḥꜣw.k — literally, "your face toward your neighbors": see § 10.2.

ʿb{wt}.tw — the verb is *ʿb* "gather"; the scribe has perhaps misread the common determinative  (a pitchfork) as .

m ḫmt.n.k — i.e., from unexpected sources.

wnn jb ... dj.f — literally, "the mind exists ... putting."

jb fꜣk.w — the scribe has probably omitted the suffix pronoun *f* after *jb*.

MAXIM 14 — CONDUCT AS A MESSENGER (249–56: 8,11–14)

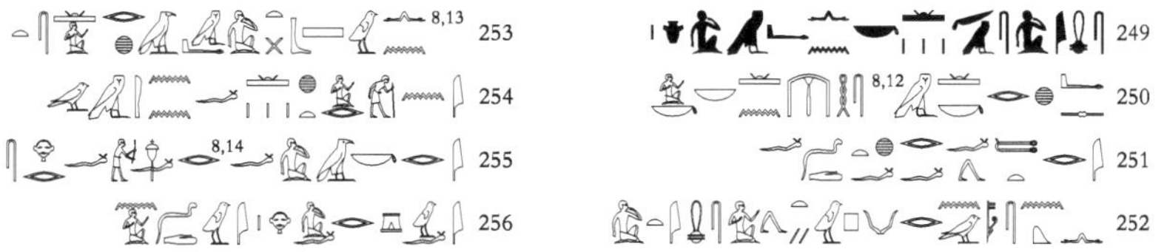

249 ***smj sšmw.k nn ꜥm jb*** 3
250 *dj sḫr.k m sḥ n nb.k* 4
251 *jr ṯṯf r.f ḫft ḏd.f* 2
252 *nn qsn r wpwtj smjt* 2
253 *nn wšb.t(w) mj ꜣ rḫ.j st* 3
254 *jn wr r ḫt.f nnm* 3
255 *jr kꜣ.f r ḫsf.f ḥr.s* 3
256 *jw.f gr.f ḥr jw ḏd.n.j* 2

249 **Report your assignment without negligence,**
250 for your manner is put in the counsel of your lord.
251 As for him who is fluent when he speaks,
252 it will not go hard for the report's messenger;
253 no one will reply, "Just what am I supposed to learn?"
254 He who is more important than his charge is the one who errs:
255 if he thinks of opposition to him because of it,
256 he is quiet, saying, "I have spoken."

This is one of the more difficult maxims, about conduct as a messenger.

ꜥm jb — literally, "swallowing the mind," a metaphor for forgetting to do something.

dj sḫr.k m sḥ n nb.k — i.e., your behavior will reflect on the message of the one who sent you.

ṯṯf r.f — "fluent with respect to himself."

mj ꜣ rḫ.j st — *st* resumes the interrogative: literally, "just what (is) that which I should learn it"—i.e., if a messenger is halting in speech or omits part of his message, the hearer is not sure what the message is about.

wr r ḫt.f — literally, "important with respect to his thing," meaning a messenger who is more concerned for himself than for his message.

ḫsf.f — infinitive with pronominal object as a suffix pronoun (§ 13.5.1): literally, "barring of him." This continues the thought of the preceding line, referring to a messenger who anticipates that an adverse reaction to his message will make problems for him.

jw.f gr.f — i.e., he does not respond to questioning after delivering the message.

ḥr — for *ḥr ḏd*: § 14.7.

MAXIM 15 — LEADERSHIP (257–62: 8,14–9,3)

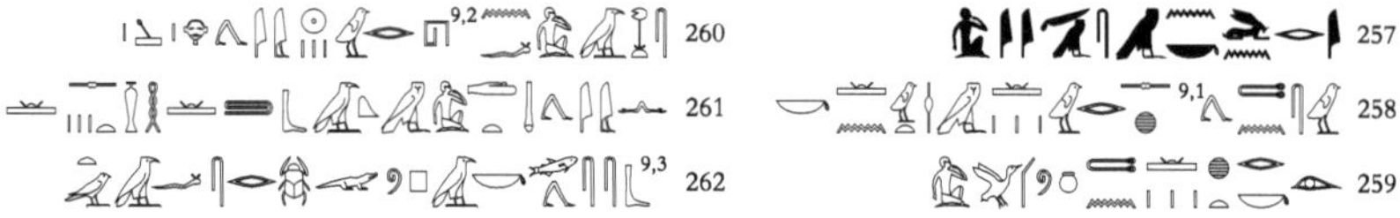

257 ***jr wnn.k m sšmy*** 2
258 *wstn sḫrw m wḏt.n.k* 2
259 *jr r.k ḫwt ṯnw* 2
260 *sḫꜣ nf hrww jj ḥr sꜣ* 5
261 *nj jj mdt m qꜣb ḥzwt* 3
262 *bss kꜣpw ḫpr sfꜣt* 4

257 **If you are a leader,**
258 wide-ranging of methods in what you have decreed,
259 do things of distinction:
260 those will be remembered in days that come after.
261 Contention does not come amid blessings;
262 the concealed crocodile gets in when disregard happens.

mdt — literally, "speaking": see the note to Sin. B 183–84

MAXIM 16 — DEALING WITH A PETITIONER (264–76: 9,3–7)

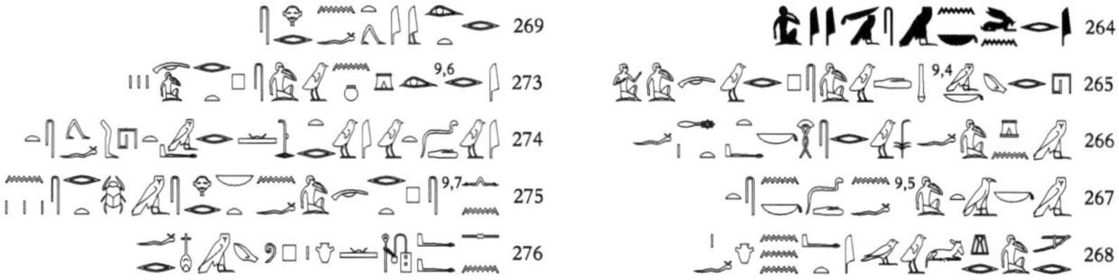

264 ***jr wnn.k m sšmy*** 2
265 *hr sḏm.k mdw sprw* 3
266 *m gnf sw r skt ḫt.f* 2
267 *m kꜣt.n.f ḏd n.k st* 2
268 *mr ḫr(j) jw jꜥt jb.f* 3
269 *r jrt jjt.n.f ḥr.s* 3
273 *jr jr gn(f)w sprwt* 2
274 *jw ḏd.tw jw tr r mj th.f st* 3
275 *nn sprt.n.f nbt ḥr.s m ḫprt(j).sn* 3
276 *snꜥꜥ jb pw sḏm nfr* 3

264 **If you are a leader,**
265 let your hearing a petitioner's speaking be calm.
266 Don't rebuff him from wiping his belly
267 of what he had planned to say to you.
268 One who has a wrong loves washing his mind
269 more than the doing of what he has come about.
273 As for one who makes rebuffing of petitions,
274 it is said, "To what end is he contravening them?"
275 Not all that he has petitioned about is what will come about,
276 so a good hearing means smoothing the mind.

gnf — the scribe has interpreted the final radical as the 3ms suffix pronoun; the New Kingdom version has the correct spelling.

r skt ẖt.f — or "until his belly is wiped" (*sḏmt.f*: § 19.14). The idiom refers to getting rid of a complaint.

gn(f)w — the scribe has omitted the final radical, perhaps because the spelling in the second couplet suggested a verb **gn*; the New Kingdom version has the correct spelling.

jw tr r mj th.f st — literally, "with respect to what does he contravene them"; *jw* marks the statement *th.f st* as true in the situation in which it is uttered (i.e., "now") instead of true in general (i.e., "always"): § 10.3.

MAXIM 17 — LUST (277–97: 9,7–13)

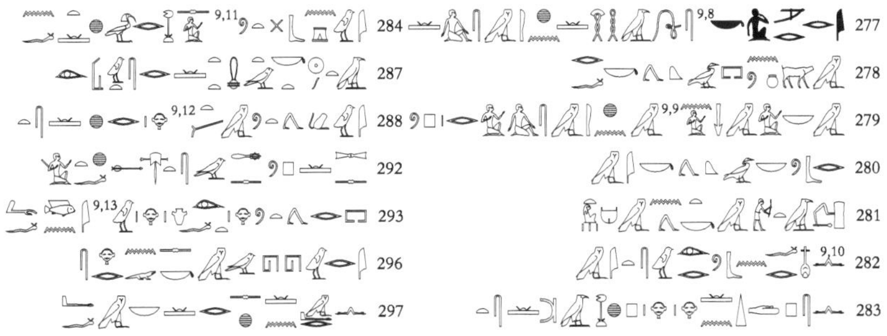

277 ***jr mr.k*** *swꜣḥ ẖnms* 2
278 *m ẖnw ꜥq.k r.f* 3
279 *m nb m sn m ẖnms r pw* 4
280 *r bw nb ꜥq.k jm* 3
281 *ꜥḥꜣ.t(j) m tkn m ḥjmwt* 3
282 *nj nfr.n bw jrrw st jm* 4
283 *nj spd.n ḥr ḥr pḫꜣ st* 3
284 *jw ngb.tw z(j) 1000 r ꜣḫt n.f* 3

287 *ꜣt ktt mjtt rswt* 3
288 *jw pḥ.tw m(w)t ḥr rḫ st* 3
292 *ṯꜣz pw ẖz st ḫft(j)* 3
293 *pr.tw ḥr jrt.f jb ḥr wjn.f* 4
296 *jr whh m skn ḥr.s* 3
297 *nj mꜥr.n sḫr nb m ꜥ.f* 3

277 **If you want** to make friendship last
278 in a home to which you enter,
279 as lord, as brother, or as friend
280 to any place in which you have entrée,
281 be mindful of getting near the women:
282 no place in which it is done can be good.
283 No face can be sharp while splitting it open,
284 for a thousand men are diverted from what is best for them:
287 a short moment, the likeness of a dream;
288 one attains death by experiencing it.
292 It is a wretched liaison, an inimical shooting,
293 one emerges from doing it with the mind rejecting it.
296 As for him who fails by lusting for it,
297 no plan can succeed with him.

This maxim warns against illicit sex with the women of a household. In several of its couplets, the author has used vocabulary with a double entendre reflecting the theme: *pḫꜣ* "split open" (283), *rḫ* "gain knowledge of" (288), *ṯꜣz* "knot" and *stj* "shoot" (292).

m nb — the reference is probably to a superior of some man in the household, rather than to the master of the house.

r bw nb — this phrase qualifies the three nouns of the preceding line: i.e., "as lord, brother, or friend with respect to any place."

ꜥq.k jm — the verb is normally used with the preposition *r* denoting the goal of the action, as in the preceding couplet; the preposition *m* denotes presence inside.

nj nfr.n bw ... nj spd.n ḥr — the construction is *nj sḏm.n.f* with a nominal subject rather than a negated adjectival sentence with unexpressed subject "it" followed by the preposition *n* "for" plus a noun, since the latter would employ *nn* (§ 11.6). For the idiom *spd ḥr*, see the note to Maxim 12, above.

ḥr pḫꜣ st — the double entendre refers to the private quarters of the house and the female sexual organ.

ꜣḫt n.f — the suffix pronoun refers to the numeral (§ 9.4).

ḥr rḫ st — the verb can be used with reference to sexual relations, as in the Bible.

ṯꜣz ... st — the double entendres involve social vs. sexual relations (*ṯꜣz* "knot") and a treacherous action (cf. English *stab in the back*) vs. ejaculation (*stj* "shoot": see the note to Maxim 11).

MAXIM 18 — GREED (298–315: 9,13–10,5)

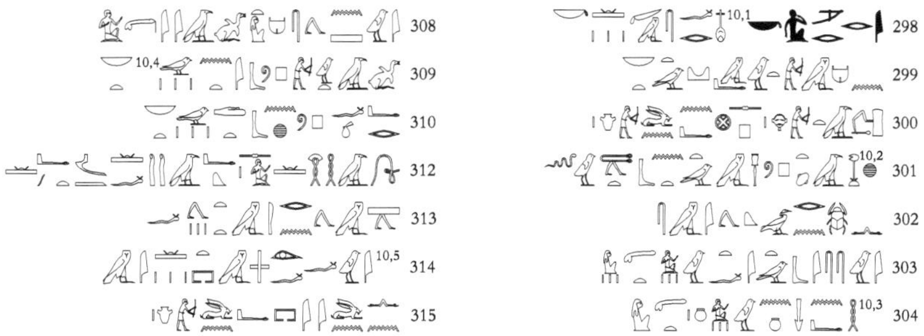

298 ***jr mr.k*** *nfr sšmw.k* 3
299 *nḥm tw m ꜥ ḏwt nbt* 2
300 *ꜥḥꜣ.t(j) ḥr zp n ꜥwn jb* 3
301 *ḫꜣt pw mrt nt btw* 3
302 *nj ḫpr.n ꜥq jm.s* 3
303 *jw.s sjbt.(s) jtw m(jw)wt* 3
304 *ḥnꜥ snw nw m(jw)t* 2
308 *jw nš.s ḥjmt ṯꜣy* 3
309 *ṯꜣwt pw bjnt nbt* 2
310 *ꜥrf pw n ḫbdt nbt* 2
312 *wꜣḥ z(j) ꜥqꜣ.f mꜣꜥt* 3
313 *šm.(w) r nmtwt.f* 2
314 *jw.f jr.f jmt-pr jm* 3
315 *nn wn j⸢z⸣ ꜥwn jb* 1

298 **If you want** your conduct to be good,
299 take yourself away from everything evil.
300 Be mindful about an instance of greed:
301 it is a painful disease of the shunned serpent.
302 no entrée can develop from it.
303 For it entangles fathers and mothers
304 and maternal siblings
308 and it alienates wife and husband.
309 It is robbery, everything bad;
310 it is a sack of everything despised.
312 A man lasts who is truly straight
313 and has walked according to his steps.

314 He makes a will thereby,
315 but greed has no tomb.

btw — the word is a passive participle from *bṯj* "avoid" and refers to the giant serpent Apophis, who tries to swallow the Sun's boat as it passes through the netherworld.

sjbt.(tj) — the verb is the causative of *jbṯ* "trap" (with a net). Because a stative used transitively is unusual (§ 16.5, with the 3fs suffix unwritten because it coincides with the final radical: § 16.2), and because of the parallel *jw.s nš.s* in the last line, it is probably a *sḏm.f* with the suffix pronoun *s* omitted by the scribe.

ḥnꜥ snw nw m(jw)t — it is unclear whether the preposition implies coordination ("as well as") or opposition (as in "fight with"). The noun phrase refers to siblings from the same mother.

r nmtwt.f — i.e., as he should.

jmt-pr jm — for the noun phrase, see § 8.9. The referent of *jm* is the actions described in the preceding couplet.

nn wn j⌜z⌝ ꜥwn jb — the scribe has written  instead of . For the construction, see § 11.4.

MAXIM 19 — GREED (316–323: 10,5–8)

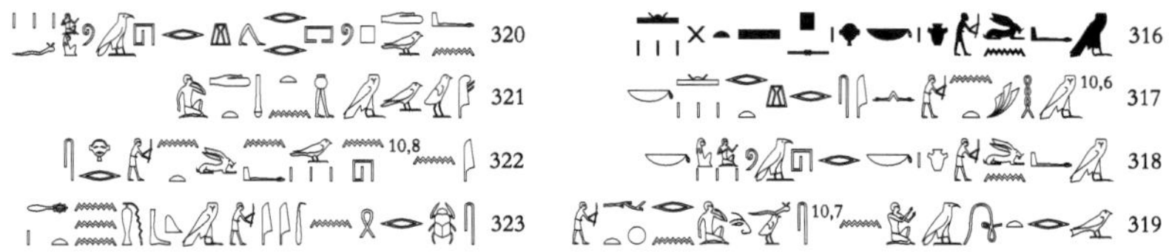

316 ***m ꜥwn jb.k ḥr pzšt*** 3
317 *m ḥnt nj js r ẖrwt.k* 2
318 *m ꜥwn jb.k r hꜣw.k* 3
319 *wr twꜣ n sfw r nḫt* 4
320 *ꜥnd pw prr ẖr hꜣw.f* 3
321 *šw m jnt mdt* 3
322 *jn nh n ꜥwnt ḥr.s* 3
323 *sḫpr šntyt m qb ẖt* 3

316 **Don't become greedy about a division;**
317 don't become covetous except for what you have.
318 Don't become greedy about your neighbors:
319 respect is greater for kindness than force.
320 He who undercuts his neighbors is small
321 and devoid of what contention might get.

322 A little of what one is grasping about
323 is what creates strife out of placidity.

prr ẖr ḥ3w.f — literally, "who goes out under his neighbors."

mdt — see the note to Maxim 15, above.

ʿwnt ḥr.s — a passive participle: literally, "what is grasped about" (§ 24.6).

qb ẖt — literally, "coolness of belly."

MAXIM 20 — TREATMENT OF A WIFE (325–338: 10,8–12)

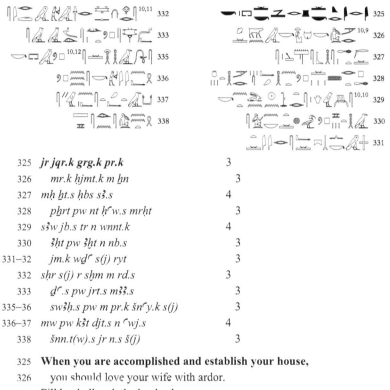

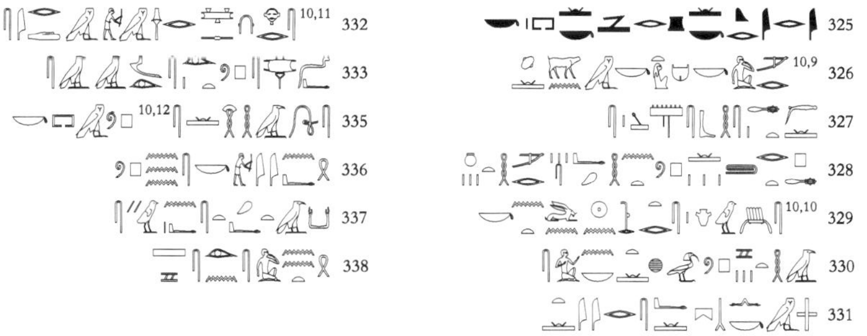

325 ***jr jqr.k grg.k pr.k*** 3
326 *mr.k ḥjmt.k m ẖn* 3
327 *mḥ ẖt.s ḥbs s3.s* 4
328 *pẖrt pw nt ḥʿw.s mrḥt* 3
329 *s3w jb.s tr n wnnt.k* 4
330 *3ḫt pw 3ḫt n nb.s* 3
331–32 *jm.k wḏʿ s(j) ryt* 3
332 *sḥr s(j) r sẖm m rd.s* 3
333 *dʿ.s pw jrt.s m33.s* 3
335–36 *sw3ḥ.s pw m pr.k šnʿy.k s(j)* 3
336–37 *mw pw k3t djt.s n ʿwj.s* 4
338 *šnn.t(w).s jr n.s š(j)* 3

325 **When you are accomplished and establish your house,**
326 you should love your wife with ardor.
327 Fill her belly, clothe her back;
328 ointment is the prescription for her limbs.
329 Make her happy as long as you exist:
330 she is a useful field for her lord,
331–32 and you should not adjudicate her.

332 Keep her away from control of her foot:
333 her eye when it looks is her gale;
335–36 your restricting her is the way to keep her in your house.
336–37 The vulva she gives at her disposal is water:
338 since it is requested, make for it a basin.

Much of the second half of this maxim (331–38) is not always completely clear as to syntax and meaning.

tr n wnnt.k — literally, "for the time of your existence"; *wnnt* is a verbal noun.

ꜣḥt pw ꜣḫt n nb.s — a reference to her potential for childbearing.

wḏꜥ s(j) ryt — *wḏꜥ ryt* "separate at the gate" is a term for judicial proceedings (van den Boorn 1985)—in this case, probably divorce is meant. The scribe has separated the top and bottom of the  sign, perhaps because he did not recognize it in his original.

sḥr s(j) r sḫm m rd.s — this tercet evidently advises restricting a wife's ability to circulate outside the household. In this line, the reed-leaf after *rd* is an error for .

ḏꜥ.s pw jrt.s mꜣꜣ.s — the meaning of the line as a whole is unclear; the gale's unpredictability and swift movement may be a metaphor for wanderlust.

swꜣḥ.s pw m pr.k šnꜥy.k s(j) — an A *pw* B sentence, in which A is the infinitive phrase *swꜣḥ.s m pr.k* "making her stay in your house" and B is the *sḏm.f* phrase *šnꜥy.k s(j)* "you restrict her" used as a noun clause (§ 21.11). Žába's division of lines 335–37 is based on a faulty understanding of the text.

mw pw kꜣt — this final couplet continues the "field" metaphor of line 330: in this case, the vulva not only is the receptacle of the seed but also nourishes it (*mw* "water").

djt.s n ꜥwj.s — literally, "which she gives to her arms"

šnn.t(w).s jr n.s mr — this line is the most problematic. The first word is a form of the verb *šnj*, which can mean "question, examine, recite, beseech, request, discuss, curse" and could be a relative *sḏm.f* "which she/it …" as well as a *sḏm.f* with passive suffix. The words following can be a passive *sḏm.f* ("made for her/it") or a *sḏm.n.f* ("she/it has made") as well as an imperative. Finally, the last word can be *mr* "canal" as well as *šj* "basin" (see the note to Sin. B 295–96 *pr n nb š(j)*). As translated here, the sentence is emphatic, with an initial adverb clause (§ 25.8.3) and an imperative as rheme. The line seems to be a metaphor for "make a home for her": just as the water of the inundation requires a *šj* in which to settle in order to nourish a field, so too does the wife's "water" require a home in order to nourish her offspring.

MAXIM 21 — CLOSE FRIENDS (339–349: 11,1–4)

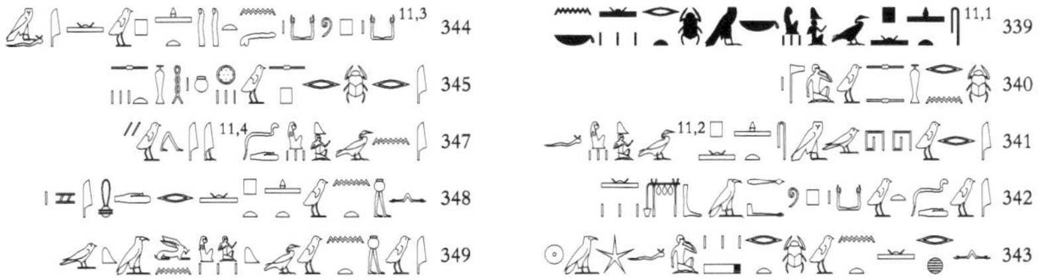

339 ***sḥtp ꜥqw.k m ḫprt n.k*** 3
340 *ḫpr.(w) n ḥzzw nṯr* 3
341 *jr whh m sḥtp ꜥqw.f* 3
342 *jw ḏd.tw kꜣ pw ꜥꜣb* 3
343 *nj rḫ.n.tw ḫprt* 2
sjꜣ.f dwꜣ 2
344 *kꜣ pw kꜣ n mt* 3
ḥtpw jm.f 2
345 *jr ḫpr zpw nw ḥzwt* 3
347 *jn ꜥqw ḏd jjwj* 3
348 *nj jn.tw ḥtpt r dmj* 3
349 *jw jn.tw ꜥqw wn ꜣq* 4

339 **Content your intimates with what has come to you,**
340 for it has come to one whom the god blesses.
341 As for him who fails to content his intimates,
342 one says, "He is a stingy ka."
343 What might happen cannot be known:
he should think of tomorrow.
344 The proper ka is the ka
that one can become content by.
345 When occasions of blessings happen,
347 intimates are the ones who say, "Welcome!"
348 Contentment is not fetched to harbor,
349 but intimates are fetched when there is ruin.

This maxim concerns relations with intimate friends. The key term is *ꜥqw*, literally "enterers," meaning those who have access to someone.

ḫpr.(w) — 3ms stative, or perhaps a *sḏm.f* with unexpressed subject: "for it comes."

kꜣ pw ꜥꜣb — as in Maxim 6, the term "ka" is used to refer to someone who is the source of sustenance—here probably in a broader sense than just food.

kꜣ n mt — literally, "the ka of exactness."

ḥtpw jm.f — a passive participle (§ 24.7): literally, "contented by it."

nj jn.tw ḥtpt r dmj — i.e., contentment is never fully achieved.

MAXIM 22 — GOSSIP (350–360: 11,5–8)

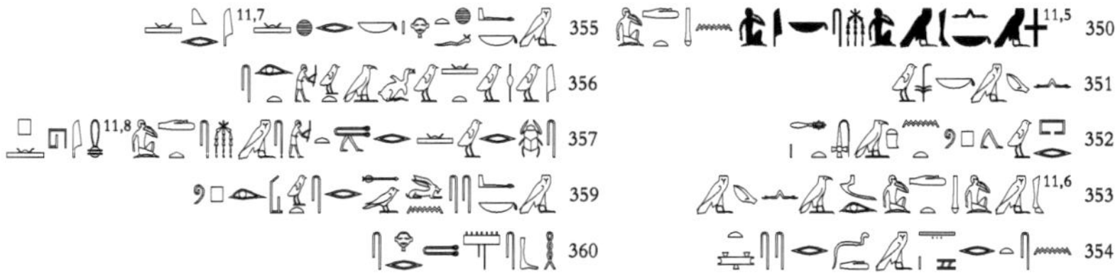

350	***jm.k wḥm mskj***	3
350–51	*n mdt nj sḏm.k sw*	2
352	*prw pw n tꜣ ẖt*	2
353	*wḥm mdt mꜣ nj sḏm*	4
354	*n(j) st r tꜣ m ḏd rsst*	4
355	*mj.k ḫft(j) ḥr.k rḫ.(w) jqr*	4
356	*jw wḏ.tw ṯꜣwt jr.t(w).s*	3
357	*sḫprw r jtt.s m msdt mj hp*	4
359–60	*mj.k sswn rswt pw ḥbs.ṯ(w) ḥr.s*	3

350 **You should not repeat gossip**
350–51 about a speech you have not heard:
352 it is the mark of belly-heat.
353 Repeat a speech that is seen, not heard,
354 when the one it belongs to is entirely out of the discussion.
355 Look, your interlocutor knows all too well,
356 for robbery is decreed when it is done.
357 The instigator will customarily do it out of hate:
359–60 look, it is a nightmare that ought to be covered over.

n mdt nj sḏm.k sw — the gossip in this cause concerns hearsay. *nj sḏm.k sw* is an unmarked relative clause (§ 22.13); *mdt* is an infinitive, therefore resumed by masculine *sw* (§ 13.8).

prw pw n tꜣ ẖt — the term *tꜣ ẖt* refers to ill-considered action, the opposite of *gr* "quiet" (see the note to Kagemni 1,1, above); *prw* is literally, "emergence," meaning something that is produced by rashness.

mdt mꜣ nj sḏm — i.e., a speech observed first-hand. *nj sḏm* is a passive participle negated as a word (§ 11.7): "not one that is heard."

n(j) st r tꜣ m ḏd rsst — literally, "the one it belongs to is aside from speaking entirely," referring to the person who originally made the statement in question. *n(j) st* is a nisbe phrase (§ 7.8) in which *st* refers to the original statement. For *r tꜣ*, see the note to Maxim 3, above; for *rsst*, a variant of *rssj*, see § 8.12.

ḫft(j) ḥr.k — literally, "the one opposite your face."

jqr — the adjective meaning "accomplished" used here as an adverb.

jw wḏ.tw ṯꜣwt jr.t(w).s — repeating someone's statement as gossip amounts to stealing the original speech. The feminine suffix pronoun here evidently reflects an unexpressed *mdt* "speech" as a verbal noun (feminine) rather than infinitive (masculine).

shprw r jtt.s m msdt mj hp — literally, "the creator is to take possession of it from hate like custom." The verb *jtj* "take possession" continues the metaphor of robbery.

sswn rswt — literally, "a dream's causing pain" (infinitive with a genitival noun subject: § 13.4.2).

ḥbs.ṯ(w) ḥr.s — "one should cover over it"; ⟹ is used for *t(w)*: § 2.8.4.

MAXIM 23 — SPEAKING (362–369: 11,8–11)

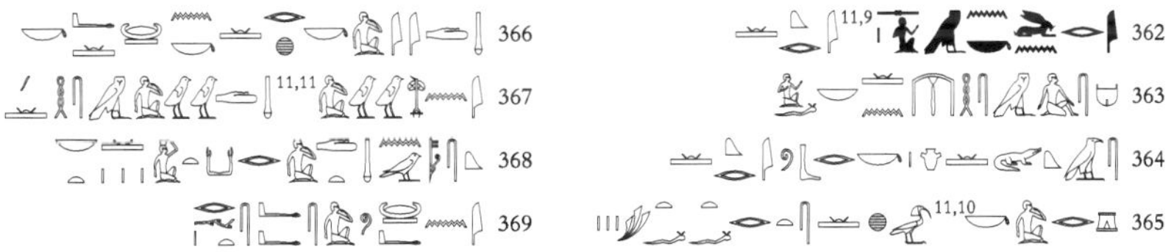

362 ***jr wnn.k m z(j)*** *jqr* 3
363 *ḥms.(w) m sḥ n nb.f* 3
364 *sꜣq jb.k r bw jqr* 3
365 *gr.k ꜣḫ st r tftf* 3
366 *mdy.k rḫ.n.k wḥꜥ.k* 3
367 *jn ḥmww mdww m sḥ* 3
368 *qsn mdt r kꜣt nbt* 2
369 *jn wḥꜥ s(j) dd s(j) r ḫt* 3

362 **If you are an** accomplished **man**
363 who sits in consultation with his lord,
364 collect your mind with respect to accomplishment:
365 your quiet, it is more effective than valerian.
366 You should speak only when you know your solution:
367 it is the craftsman who speaks in counsel.

368 Speaking is harder than any work:
369 the one who solves it is the one who subordinates it.

ḥms.(w) m sḥ n nb.f — literally, "sitting (3ms stative: § 22.11) in the counsel of his lord": the writing of *sḥ* indicates the abstract "counsel" rather than the substantive "council."

tftf — valerian is a perennial plant with pink or white flowers, whose root has a sedative effect. The sentence means that keeping quiet can have a soothing effect.

mdy.k rḫ.n.k wḥꜥ.k — an emphatic sentence: the rheme is the adverb clause (§ 25.7).

dd s(j) r ḫt — literally, "who puts it to the stick": the phrase *r ḫt* is an idiom for subordination.

MAXIM 24 — EMOTIONS AND TIME (370–387: 11,12–12,6)

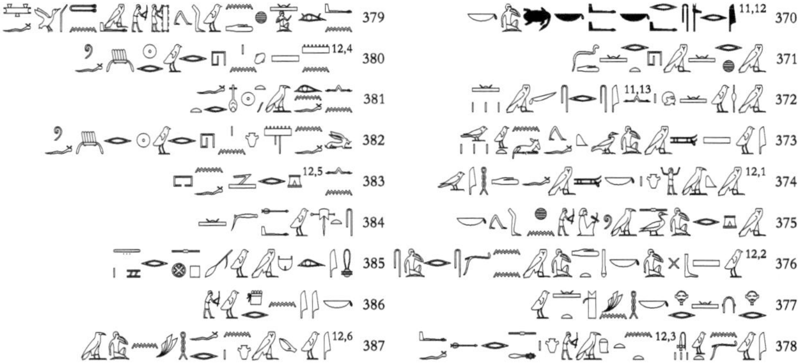

370 ***jr wsr.k dd.k snḏ**.k* 3
371 *m rḫ m hrt ḏd* 2
372 *m wḏ dp nj js r sšmw* 3
373 *jw štm ꜥq.f n jwt* 3
374 *m qꜣ jb.k tm.f dḥj* 4
375 *m gr zꜣw ḫnd.k* 3
376 *wšb.k mdt m {n}nsr.s* 3
377 *ḥr ḥr.k ḥn tw* 3
378 *jw nswt nt tꜣ jb sḫr.f* 3
379 *ꜥn ḫndw qd mjṯn.f* 4
380 *mnš n hrw r ꜣw.f* 3
381 *nn jr.n.f ꜣt nfrt* 2
382 *wnf jb n hrw r ꜣw.f* 3
383 *nn grg.n.f pr* 2

384 *st.w mḥ.(w)* 3
385 *mj jr ḥmw zp r tꜣ* 4
386 *ky nḏr.w* 2
387 *jw sḏm.n jb.f r ḥn ꜣ* 3

370 **If you are powerful, you should make respect** of you
371 through knowledge and calmness of speaking.
372 Don't give commands except for guidance,
373 for defiance leads to error.
374 Don't let your mind get big, and it won't be humbled;
375 don't be inactive, but beware when you tread.
376 When you answer a speech in its flaming,
377 prepare yourself, control yourself,
378 for flames and hotheadedness dissipate,
379 but the seemly of tread, his path has been built.
380 The one who worries for the whole day,
381 he will not be able to spend a good moment;
382 the one who is frivolous for the whole day,
383 he will not be able to establish a house—
384 the one fully shot,
385 like one who plies the rudder after docking;
386 the other preoccupied,
387 for his mind has listened to "If only …"

This maxim has two themes: management of emotions (370–79) and management of time (380–87).

wḏ dp — literally, "command the head."

jw štm ʿq.f n jwt — literally, "for defiance enters to error." The defiance is that of one who rebels against inappropriate commands.

wšb.k mdt m {n}nsr.s — an emphatic sentence; the rheme is the imperatives in the second line. The scribe apparently miscopied an original  and then added an ; "in its flaming" refers to a diatribe.

ḥr ḥr.k — the spelling of *ḥr.k* indicates a prepositional phrase rather than "your face": thus, literally "make preparations about yourself."

sḫr.f — the suffix pronoun refers to the second of the two coordinates (*tꜣ jb* "heat of mind") instead of both.

wnf jb — this passage is discussed at the end of § 17.11; see the note there.

st.w mḥ.(w) — two 3ms statives: "shot and filled," apparently referring to the pangs and engrossing nature of worry.

zp r tꜣ — literally, "when the cause is at land." The metaphor reflects the uselessness of worry.

nḏr.w — 3ms stative, literally "seized."

ḥn ꜣ — this is a variant of the particles *ḥꜣ ꜣ* (§ 15.6.12).

MAXIM 25 — AN ANGRY SUPERIOR (388–398: 12,6–9)

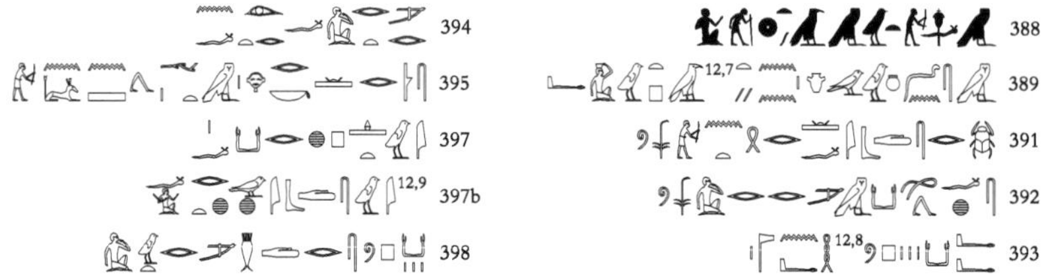

388	***m ḫsf tw m ꜣt wr***	2
389	*m sḥḏnw jb n ntj ꜣtp.w*	3
391	*ḫpr sdb.f r šnt sw*	3
392	*sfḫ kꜣ m mrr sw*	3
393	*dd kꜣw pw ḥnꜥ nṯr*	2
394	*mrrt.f jrrt n.f*	3
395	*sq⌜d⌝ r.k ḥr m ḫt nšn*	3
397	*jw ḥtp ḫr kꜣ.f jw sdb ḫr ḫft(j)*	4
398	*kꜣw pw srd mrwt*	3

388 **Don't insert yourself in the moment of a great one,**
389 don't vex the mind of one who is burdened.
391 His obstruction happens against one who contradicts him,
392 and the ka is released from the one who loves him.
393 He is one who gives sustenance along with the god;
394 what he loves is what is done for him.
395 So, turn the face back after a storm,
397 for peace is with his ka, and obstruction is with the enemy.
398 He is sustenance, which makes love grow.

m ḫsf tw — literally, "don't bar yourself," meaning "don't make an obstruction of yourself." For *ꜣt* "moment (of anger)," see the note to Maxim 1.

sdb — the reed-leaf is a misreading of the determinative , and the bookroll, of  (as in line 397).

sfḫ kꜣ m mrr sw — the meaning is that support is withdrawn from one who loves but contradicts him.

sq⌜d⌝ — the verb is the causative stem of *qdj* "go around." The scribe has written in place of .

MAXIM 26 — PATRONAGE (399–414: 12,9–13)

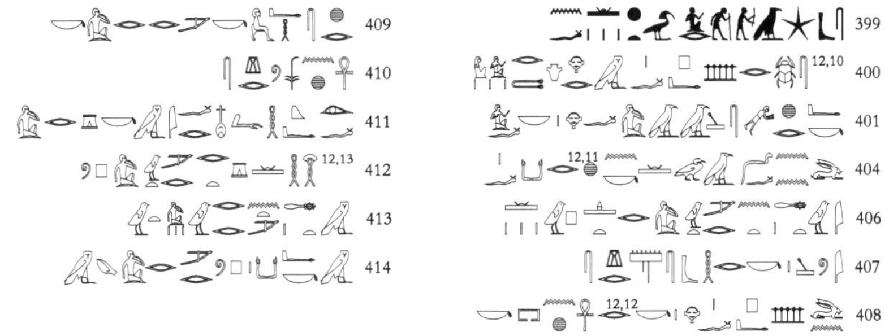

399	***sbꜣ wr r ꜣḫt n.f***	3
400	*sḫpr šzp.f m ḥr(j) jb rmṯ*	3
401	*dj.k ḫr sꜣꜣ.f ḫr nb.f*	4
404	*wnn ḏfꜣ⸢w⸣.k ḫr kꜣ.f*	3
406	*jw ẖt nt mrwt r ḥtpw*	3
407	*jw sꜣ.k r ḥbs ẖr.s*	3
408	*wn šzp.f ḥr.k r ʿnḫ*	4
408–409	*pr.k ḫr sʿḥ.k mrr.k*	3
410	*ʿnḫ sw ẖr.s*	2
411	*jr.f qʿḥ nfr jm.k gr*	3
412–13	*wꜣḥ grt mrwt pw m ẖt nt mrrw tw*	3
414	*mj.k kꜣ pw mrr sḏm*	3

399 **Teach a great man what is useful for him,**
400 create his acceptance in people's midst.
401 When you make his wisdom come to his lord's attention,
404 your nourishment will be from his ka;
406 for the belly of love is focused on contenting
407 and your back will be clothed from it:
408 when his acceptance exists, your face will live.
408–409 Your house is with your titulary whom you love:
410 it is alive because of that,
411 and makes a good support of you as well.
412–13 It also means setting love in the belly of those who love you;
414 look, he is a ka who loves hearing.

This maxim advises how to secure well-being and advancement through the patronage of a great man.

sb3 wr r 3ḫt n.f — literally, "teach a great man with respect to what is useful for him": English uses two direct objects, but Egyptian can use only one.

dj.k ḫr s33.f ḫr nb.f — literally, "you make his wisdom fall on his lord." This is an emphatic sentence; the rheme is the second line of the couplet (§ 25.8.3).

ḏf3⸢w⸣.k — the scribe has written 𓈖 instead of 𓏥.

jw ẖt nt mrwt r ḥtpw — literally, "the belly of love is toward contenting." The meaning is that one who loves looks to make happy the one he loves.

ẖr.s — literally, "under it," referring to *mrwt* "love."

pr.k ẖr sʿḥ.k — i.e., "your house is dependent on your patron."

ʿnḫ sw ẖr.s — an adjectival sentence, literally "it is alive (active participle) under it." The referent of *sw*, and of the 3ms suffix pronoun in the next line, is *pr.k* "your house." The referent of the suffix pronoun of *ẖr.s* is the fact stated in the first line: i.e., "your household is alive because it is dependent on your patron." The third line means "the house is also dependent on you"; *qʿḥ* "support" is literally "shoulder."

w3ḥ grt mrwt pw — an A *pw* nominal sentence; A is the infinitival phrase *w3ḥ mrwt* "the setting of love." The sentence means "your household will love you because your actions ensure its well-being."

mj.k k3 pw mrr sḏm — several interpretations of this line are possible. As translated here, it is an A *pw* sentence with the participial phrase *mrr sḏm* modifying *k3*. It can also be an A *pw* B sentence, "the one who loves hearing is a ka," but this makes somewhat less sense in the context. The referent of *pw* can be either the patron, meaning that he is one who rewards obedience, or, less likely, the son addressed in the maxim, in which case it is a statement of admiration made by the household.

MAXIM 27 — LEGAL SITUATIONS (415–421: 13,1–4)

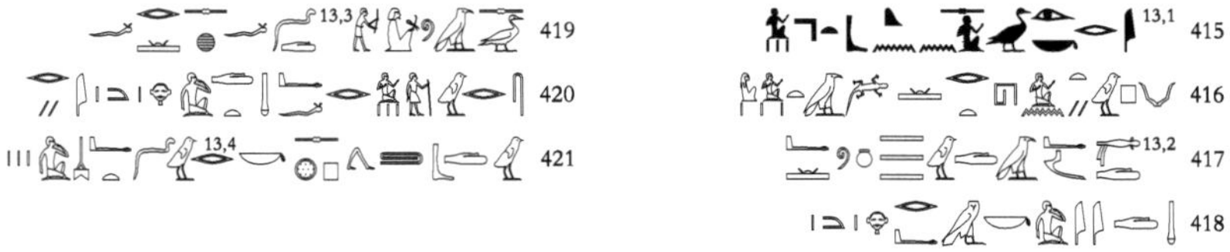

415 ***jr jr.k z3 z(j) n qnbt*** 3
416 *wpwtj n hrt ʿš3t* 2
417 *šd m3dw nwʿ* 3
418 *mdy.k m rdj ḥr gs* 3
419–20 *z3w ḏd.f sḫr.f (n) sr(j)w* 4
420 *rdj.f mdt ḥr gs jrj* 4
421 *wdb zp.k r wḏʿt* 3

415 **If you act as advocate for a court,**
416 a representative of the peace of many,
417 remove the yokes of an action.

418 When you contest with someone who is biased,
419–20 keep him from stating his opinion to officials
420 and making the matter biased to them:
421 turn your case over to judgment.

This maxim offers guidance on behavior in legal situations: in the opening tercet, how to act as a "friend of the court"; and in the final two couplets, how to deal with a biased opponent.

jr.k zꜣ z(j) — literally, "you make a man's son." The noun phrase is a term for a person of significant social standing.

wpwtj n hrt ⸢šꜣt — this line evidently refers to responsibility for public calm.

šd mꜣdw nw ⸢ — the meaning and significance of this line are obscure. The verb *šdj* with arm determinative means "take away" or "rescue." The plural *mꜣdw* (originally *mꜣd̲w*) seems to means "arches" or "yokes" (the determinative is uncertain). An ⸢ (with bookroll determinative) is a legal document ("action") containing the record of a judgment. Whether the line refers to removing the "yokes" imposed by such a document or those hindering it is unclear. It has also been interpreted as "safeguard the balance of justice" (Vernus 1997), with *mꜣdw* understood as referring to balancing poles.

mdy.k — the predicate of an emphatic sentence; the rheme is the second line. For the meaning, see the note to Maxim 15, above. The double reed-leaf is the result of a sound-change, from *mdw.k* (*maduwák > *maduyák).

rdj ḥr gs — literally, "one who puts on a side."

zꜣw d̲d.f ... rdj.f mdt — in other words, do not let him plead his case to officials unchallenged; instead, take the matter to court. The scribe has evidently omitted the preposition *n* before *sr(j)w*.

MAXIM 28 — PAST OFFENSES (422–425: 13,4–6)

422
423

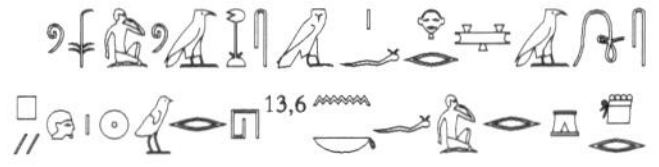
424
425

422 ***jr sf.k ḥr zp ḫpr.w*** 3
423 *gsꜣ.k n z(j) ḥr ⸢qꜣ.f* 3
424 *swꜣ ḥr.f m sḫꜣw sw* 3
425 *d̲r gr.f n.k hrw dpj* 3

422 **If you are lenient about a matter that has happened,**
423 and incline toward a man because of his rectitude,
424 pass over it, do not think of it,
425 since he will be quiet for you from the first day.

swꜣ ḥr.f m sḫꜣ sw — the pronouns refer to *zp* "a matter": Ptahhotep advises letting bygones be bygones.

d̲r gr.f n.k hrw dpj — i.e., because of his rectitude, he will behave properly from the outset.

MAXIM 29 — RICHES (428–436: 13,6–9)

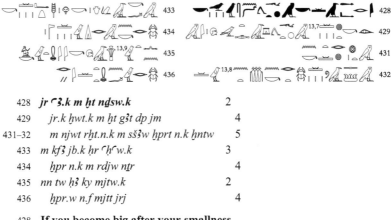

428 ***jr ꜥꜣ.k m ḫt nḏsw.k*** 2
429 *jr.k ḫwt.k m ḫt gꜣt dp jm* 4
431–32 *m njwt rḫt.n.k m sšꜣw ḫprt n.k ḫntw* 5
433 *m kfꜣ jb.k ḥr ꜥḥꜥw.k* 3
434 *ḫpr n.k m rdjw nṯr* 4
435 *nn tw ḥꜣ ky mjtw.k* 2
436 *ḫpr.w n.f mjtt jrj* 4

428 **If you become big after your smallness,**
429 acquiring property after lack in the past,
431–32 in a town you know, through experience of what happened to you before,
433 don't rely on your riches:
434 they happened to you from the god's giving.
435 You are no better than another like you
436 to whom the same has happened.

nḏsw.k — an abstract from *nḏs* "small": the qualification refers to social status: see the note to ShS. 69 *nḏs*.

jr.k ḫwt — literally, "you make things," an adverbial use of the *sḏm.f* (§ 20.11).

dp jm — literally, "head therein," an adverbial use of the prepositional phrase *dp m* "starting from."

m sšꜣw ḫprt n.k ḫntw — this prepositional phrase qualifies *jr.k ḫwt m ḫt gꜣt*: i.e., the memory of past want has prompted the acquisition of property.

m kfꜣ jb.k — this is an extended use of the phrase *kfꜣ jb* (Maxim 13): a "confidant" is one who can be relied on.

nn tw ḥꜣ ky mjtw.k — literally, "you are not behind," perhaps referring to the order of precedence in a procession, where the most important participants walk behind those of lesser significance.

ḫpr.w — 3ms stative as an unmarked relative (§ 22.11).

mjtt jrj — literally, "the like thereunto" (§ 8.15).

MAXIM 30 — OPPOSITION (441–456: 13,9–14,4)

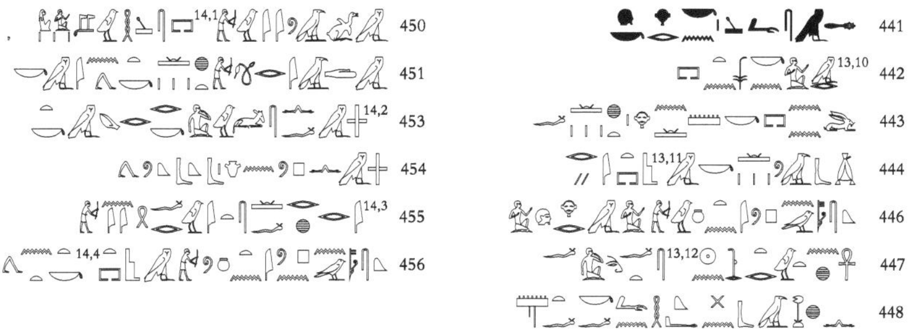

441	***ḫms sꜣ.k n ḥr(j) dp.k***	3
442	*(j)m(j)-r.k n pr-nswt*	2
443	*wnn pr.k mn.(w) ḥr ḫwt.f*	4
444	*ḏbꜣw.k m jst jrj*	3
446	*qsn pw jtnw m ḥr(j)-dp*	3
447	*ʿnḫ.tw tr n sft.f*	3
448	*nj ḫꜣb.n qʿḥ n kft.f*	3
450	*m ṯꜣwyw pr sꜣḥw*	2
451	*m dꜣjr ḫwt tkn jm.k*	3
452	*jm.f sjw r.k r sḏmt.k*	4
453	*jm pw n jb bqbqw*	3
454	*jr rḫ.f st jw.f r šny*	2
455	*qsn pw n jtnw m jst tknt*	3

441 **Bow your back to your boss,**
442 your overseer from the king's house,
443 and your house will be set from his property,
444 and your recompense as it should be.
446 An opponent as boss is a difficulty:
447 one lives only while he is lenient;
448 the shoulder cannot bend because of its stripping.
450 Don't seize neighbors' houses;
451 don't appropriate the property of one near you,
452 lest he complain about you until you are tried.
453 Resentment is grief for the mind:
454 if he experiences it, he will be a litigant;
455 it is a difficulty of opposition in a nearby place.

After an initial two couplets on behavior toward an influential boss (441–44), this maxim turns to the theme of opposition, both from a superior (446–48) and that created by one's own misdeeds (450–56).

ḥr(j) dp.k — literally, "one who is over your head."

wnn pr.k mn.(w) ḥr ḫwt.f — the *sḏm.f* of *wnn* allows the SUBJECT–stative construction *pr.k mn.(w)* "your house is set" to function as a result clause (§§ 20.13, 20.17). The meaning is that the boss will use his property (*ḥr ḫwt.f* "upon his things") to establish his subordinate's house.

jst jrj — see the note to Maxim 11.

qsn pw jtnw — an A *pw* B nominal sentence: see § 7.15.

ꜥnḫ.tw tr n sft.f — an emphatic sentence; the rheme is the noun phrase *tr n sft.f* "time of his leniency" used adverbially.

nj ḫꜣb.n qꜥḥ n kft.f — the final prepositional phrase of this line is problematic. The suffix pronoun can refer either to the boss, as in line two, or to the shoulder. The form is most likely an infinitive, deliberately parellel in phonology to *sft.f* "his leniency" in the preceding line; but it could also be a *sḏmtj.fj* "one who will strip." In any case, the line seems to mean "it is impossible to show respect when one's privileges are removed."

pr sꜣḥw — literally, "the house of those who abut."

m dꜣjr — literally, "don't subdue."

r sḏmt.k — a *sḏmt.f* with passive sense, literally "until you are heard." The verb *sḏm* is used of "hearing" a case.

jm pw n jb bqbqw — an A *pw* B sentence in which the meaning of both A and B is uncertain. Despite its spelling, *jm* is not a form of the verb *jmj*, because it is neither the *sḏm.f* nor an imperative (§ 12.7); most likely, it is the noun *jmw* "grief" (Sin. R 11). *bqbqw* is found only here; the meaning is a guess from the context.

šny — probably an active participle from *šnj* "curse, revile, quarrel" (§ 10.8). This continues the theme sounded in the last line of the peceding tercet.

qsn pw n jtnw — in this case, *jtnw* is written without the seated-man determinative and therefore is probably a verbal noun of action rather than agent. The sentence means that litigation can result from creating enmity with close neighbors.

MAXIM 31 — HOMOSEXUAL BEHAVIOR (457–462: 14,4–6)

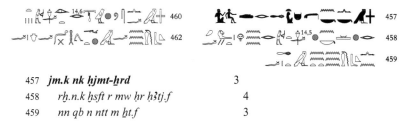

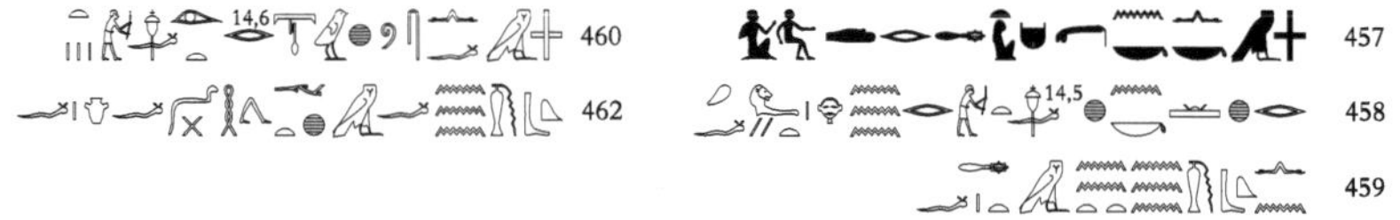

457	***jm.k nk ḥjmt-ẖrd***	3
458	*rḫ.n.k ḥsft r mw ḥr ḥꜣtj.f*	4
459	*nn qb n ntt m ẖt.f*	3

460 *jm.f swḫw r jrt ḫsft* 3
462 *qb.f m ḫt ḥḏ.f jb.f* 3

457 **You should not have sex with a woman-boy,**
458 though you know what is barred would be water on his heart,
459 for there is no cooling for what is in his belly.
460 He should not spend the night to do what is barred:
462 he will cool down only after he breaks his desire.

This maxim advises against homosexual behavior for both participants, identifying it as *ḫsft* "what is barred."

ḥjmt-ḫrd — evidently a compound noun; the masculine singular pronouns that follow make clear that a single male individual is meant, rather than a single female ("the wife of a boy") or two individuals ("a woman and a boy").

ḫsft r mw ḥr ḥꜣtj.f — i.e., would slake his emotional thirst. This is an adverbial sentence (§ 10.8) serving as an unmarked noun clause, object of *rḫ.n.k* (§ 21.7).

swḫw — this is a causative verb stem made from the noun *wḫ* "nighttime."

qb.f m ḫt ḥḏ.f jb.f — an emphatic sentence; the rheme is the prepositional phrase (§ 25.6).

MAXIM 32 — AN OFFENSE FROM A FRIEND (463–480: 14,6–12)

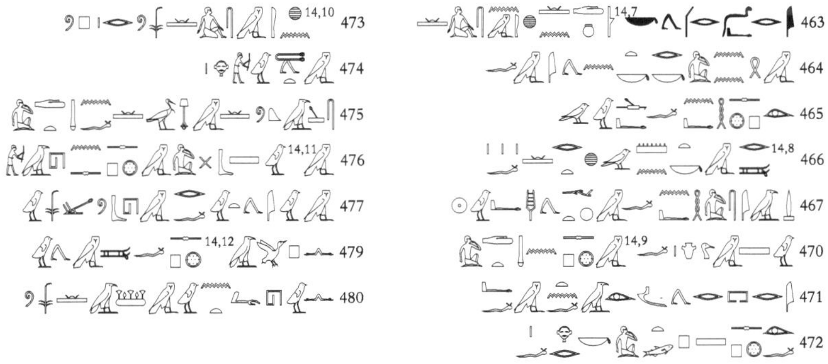

463 ***jr ḏʿr.k*** *qd n ḫnms* 3
464 *m šnn r.k* 2
tkn jm.f 2
465 *jr zp ḥnʿ.f wʿ.w* 3
466 *r tmt.k mn ḫrt.f* 3
467 *ḏꜣjs ḥnʿ.f m ḫt ʿḥʿw* 3
470 *wšm jb.f m zp n mdt* 4

471 *jr pr mꜣt.n.f m ʿ.f* 3
472 *jr.f zp špt.k ḥr.f* 4
473 *ḫnms sw r pw* 2
474–75 *m jtw ḥr sꜣq.w m wbꜣ n.f mdt* 5
476 *m wšb m zp n shꜣ* 3
477 *m wj(ꜣ) tw r.f m hbw sw* 3
479 *nj pꜣ zp.f tm jw* 4
480 *nj wh.n.tw m šꜣ sw* 2

463 **If you investigate** the character of a friend,
464 one who has been cursing about you,
approach him,
465 make a case with him alone,
466 until you are no longer troubled by his condition.
467 Discuss with him after a time,
470 test his mind with a case of dispute.
471 When what he has seen comes out of him,
472 he will make a case that you can get angry about,
473 or he is friendly.
474–75 Don't grimace in explaining the dispute to him;
476 don't respond with a case of denigration;
477 don't sever yourself from him; don't trample him.
479 His case has not once failed to come up;
480 no one can escape from the one who has fated him.

m šnn r.k — literally, "as one who curses with respect to you." *šnn* is a geminated active participle. Its sense here is not certain; besides "curse," the verb can mean "inquire": i.e., the friend has been asking questions about you.

wʿ.w — 3ms stative referring to the friend: i.e., don't involve anyone but him.

mn ḫrt.f — literally, "suffering (from) what he has."

ḫnms sw — an adjectival sentence. The phrase can also be an imperative, "befriend him," but the New Kingdom version has understood it adjectivally: *mj.k ḫ[nms] sw gr* "Look, he is still friendly."

m jtw ḥr sꜣq.w — literally, "don't take a face that is gathered" (3ms stative: § 22.11).

zp n shꜣ — literally, "a case of causing to go down."

nj pꜣ zp.f tm jw — the sense here is "come up for judgment": in a Middle Kingdom stela, a man says *nj jw zp.j nj ḫpr sk.j* "my case did not come up, a complaint against me did not happen" (Königliche Museen zu Berlin 1913, I, 261).

MAXIM 33 — GENEROSITY (481–488: 14,12–15,2)

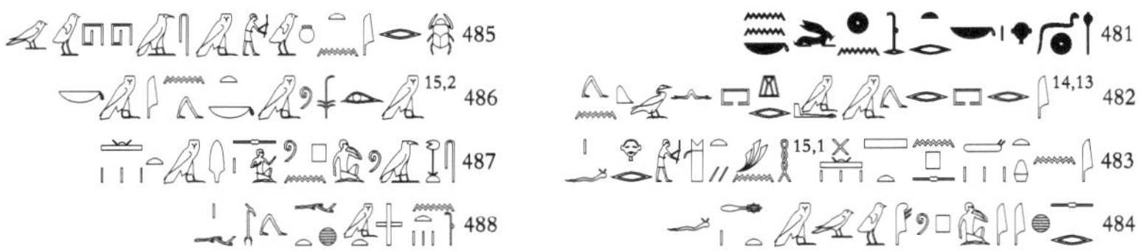

481 ***ḥḏ ḥr.k tr n wnn.k*** 4
482 *jr pr m mjḫr nj ʿq.n* 3
483 *jn t n pzšt ḥntj ḥr.f* 4
484 *srḫy pw šw m ẖt.f* 3
485 *ḫpr jtnw m sꜣhhw* 3
486 *m jr sw m tkn jm.k* 3
487 *sḫꜣ pw n z(j) jm(ꜣ)t* 3
488 *n rnpwt jmt ḫt wꜣs* 2

481 **Let your face be bright in the time of your existing;**
482 if something goes out of the storehouse, it does not reenter.
483 The bread of sharing is what is coveted;
484 the one empty in his belly is an accuser.
485 Opposition becomes sorrow-causing:
486 don't make it something near you.
487 Kindness is a man's memorial
488 for the years after the staff of authority.

ḥḏ ḥr.k — an idiom for "be generous."

jr pr ... nj ʿq.n — two verb phrases with unexpressed subject (for the *sḏm.n.f*, see § 17.5).

jn t n pzšt ḥntj ḥr.f — a participial statement with the passive participle: literally, "it is the bread of sharing that is coveted about it."

n rnpwt jmt ḫt wꜣs — i.e., after someone has retired from a position of authority. *jmt* is a prepositional nisbe modifying *rnpwt* (§ 8.6.1): literally, "that are in the wake."

MAXIM 34 — GENEROSITY (489–494: 15,2–5)

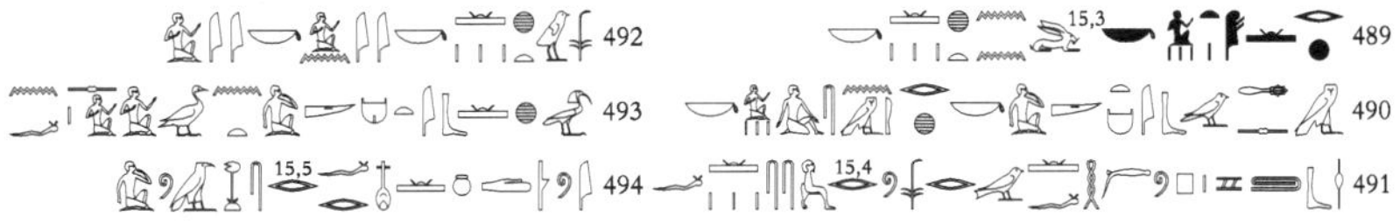

489 ***rḫ šwt.k*** *wnn ḫwt.k* 4
490 *m ẖz bj(ꜣ)t.k r ḫnmsw.k* 3
491 *wḏb pw mḥ.f* 2
wr sw r špssw.f 2
492 *ꜥjꜥw ḫwt ky n ky* 2
493 *ꜣḫ bj(ꜣ)t nt zꜣ-z(j) n.f* 4
494 *jw qd nfr r sḫꜣw* 3

489 **Be aware of your juniors** while your things exist;
490 don't let your nature be wretched to your friends.
491 It is a shore that fills,
which is greater than its finery,
492 for one man's things are for another.
493 The nature of a man of standing is useful for him,
494 for a good character will be a memorial.

rḫ šwt.k wnn ḫwt.k — possibly "your juniors know your things exist," but the New Kingdom version has *t(w)r šwt.k* "respect your juniors," indicating an imperative. *šwt*, literally "empties," is a collective denoting adolescents who have not yet begun a career (Berlev 1973, 71–72).

wḏb pw mḥ.f — *pw* refers to *bj(ꜣ)t* "nature," *mḥ.f* is an unmarked relative clause (§ 22.13); the suffix pronoun refers to *wḏb*. The image is of land lying along the Nile, which produces the largest crops because it is most thoroughly fertilized by the inundation.

wr sw r špssw.f — a second unmarked relative clause, this time with adjectival predicate (§ 22.10). *špssw* presumably refers to the lush growth of the "shore."

ꜥjꜥw ḫwt ky n ky — literally, "another man's things are for another man," meaning that wealth should be shared. The scribe has written  (hieratic ) instead of  (hieratic ).

MAXIM 35 — DISCIPLINE (495–498: 15,5–6)

495 ***ḫsf ḥr dp sbꜣ ḥr qd*** 4
496 *jw nḏrt ḫw r mn bj(ꜣ)* 2
497 *jr zp nj js ḥr jyt* 2
498 *rdj ḫpr ꜥnꜥy pw m jtnw* 2

495 **Punish in kind, teach in measure,**
496 for the treatment of misdeeds sets a kind of example.
497 As for a case other than about wrongdoing,
498 it is one that makes a complainer become an opponent.

ḥr dp ... ḥr qd — literally, "upon the head ... upon the character"; *dp* "head" can be used to refer to the way of doing something. The sentence means "make the punishment fit the crime."

jw nḏrt ḫw r mn bj(ꜣ) — literally, "the seizing of misdeeds is to (be) a kind of model."

jr zp nj js ḥr jyt — *zp* here refers to a case of punishment; in other words, don't punish someone for anything except a misdeed. *nj js ḥr jyt* is an unmarked relative clause modifying undefined *zp*: §§ 11.7, 15.7.3.

rdj ḫprꜥ nꜥy pw m jtnw — an A *pw* nominal sentence; *rdj* is an active participle referring to *zp* in the preceding line. The sentence means that punishing someone just for complaining will turn him into an opponent.

MAXIM 36 — A FAT WIFE (499–506: 15,6–8)

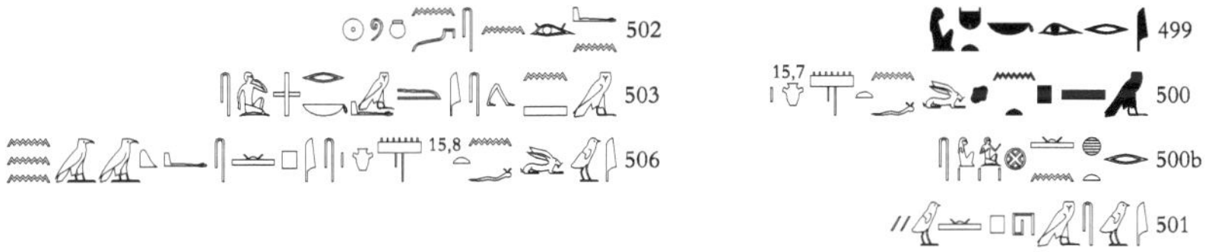

499–500	***jr jr.k ḥjmt m špnt***	3
500	*wnft jb rḫt.n njwt(j)w.s*	3
501–502	*jw.s m hpwj ꜥn n.s nw*	3
503	*m nš s(j) jmj wnm.s*	3
506	*jw wnft jb.s jp.s ꜥqꜣꜣ*	3

499–500 **If you marry a wife who is fat**
500 and frivolous, whom her townsfolk know,
501–502 who is twice the norm and to whom spending time is precious,
503 don't divorce her; let her eat,
506 for her frivolity assesses the proper dose.

jr jr.k ḥjmt — literally, "if you make a wife."

m špnt — literally, "as one who is fat."

wnft jb — see the note to Maxim 24.

rḫt.n njwt(j)w.s — this qualification apparently refers to the woman's reputation.

jw.s m hpwj — literally, "she is double custom," an adverbial sentence used as an unmarked relative clause (§ 21.10). This reflects the initial qualification *špnt*: i.e., she consumes twice the usual fare.

ʿn n.s nw — an adjectival sentence used as an unmarked relative clause: literally, "spending time is attractive to her." This evidently reflects the qualification *wnft jb*.

jw wnft jb.s jp.s ʿqꜣꜣ — a SUBJECT–*sḏm.f* construction, the meaning of which is uncertain. The verb may be either *jp* "assess" or *sjp* "account"; *wnft jb* can be a verbal noun phrase, "frivolity" or "her frivolity," or a participial phrase, "one who is frivolous" (in which case the verb must be *sjp*). The noun *ʿqꜣꜣ* is known only here; it may be derived from *ʿqꜣ* "exact," despite the lack of the usual determinatives (unless the second, hieratic, is miscopied from hieratic) or, in which case the determinative suggests an "exact amount of liquid." If so, the sentence apparently means that her frivolity somehow makes up for what she consumes.

Conclusion, Part 1 (507–532: 15,8–16,2)

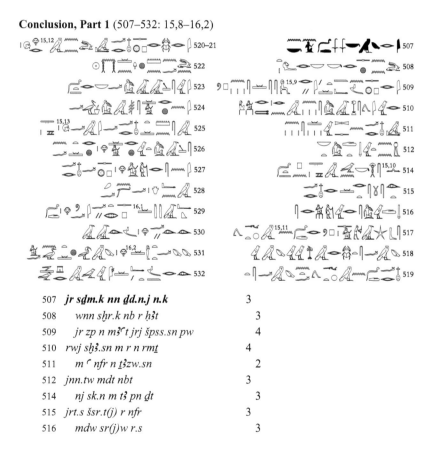

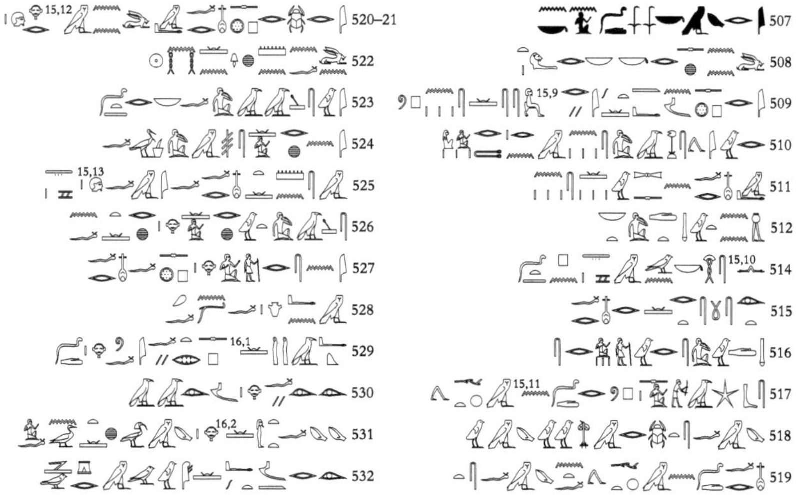

507 ***jr sḏm.k nn ḏd.n.j n.k*** 3
508 *wnn sḫr.k nb r ḥꜣt* 3
509 *jr zp n mꜣʿt jrj špss.sn pw* 4
510 *rwj sḫꜣ.sn m r n rmṯ* 4
511 *m ʿ nfr n ṯꜣzw.sn* 2
512 *jnn.tw mdt nbt* 3
514 *nj sk.n m tꜣ pn ḏt* 3
515 *jrt.s šsr.t(j) r nfr* 3
516 *mdw sr(j)w r.s* 3

517	*sbꜣ z(j) pw r ḏd n m ḫt*	3
518	*sḏm.f st ḫpr m ḥmww sḏm.w*	3
519	*nfr ḏd n m ḫt*	3
	ntf sḏm.f st	2
520–21	*jr ḫpr zp nfr m ꜥ wnn m ḥr(j) dp*	4
522	*wnn.f mnḫ.(w) n nḥḥ*	3
523	*jw sꜣꜣ.f nb r ḏt*	3
524	*jn rḫ sm bꜣ.f*	3
525	*m smnt nfr.f jm.f dp tꜣ*	4
526	*sꜣ.tw rḫ ḥr rḫt.n.f*	3
527	*jn sr(j) ḥr zp.f nfr*	3
528	*m ꜥ n jb.f ns.f*	3
529	*ꜥqꜣ zptj.fj jw.f ḥr ḏd*	3
530	*jrtj.fj ḥr mꜣꜣ*	2
531	*ꜥnḫwj.f t(w)t.(w) ḥr sḏm ꜣḫt n zꜣ.f*	5
532	*jr r mꜣꜥt*	2
	šw.(w) m grg	2

507 **If you hear these things I have said to you,**
508 your every method will be to the fore;
509 as for any pertinent instance of Maat, that is their worth.
510 Their memory will dance in the mouth of people
511 because of the perfection of their phrases.
512 When any maxim is used,
514 it cannot perish in this land forever,
515 the doing of it expressed to perfection,
516 and officials speak in accord with it.
517 It is teaching a man to speak to the future:
518 he hears it and becomes a craftsman who is heard.
519 It is good to speak to the future:
that is what will hear it.
520–21 When a good thing comes from one who is boss,
522 it is continually valid,
523 and all his wisdom will be eternal.
524 It is the knowledgeable who helps his ba,
525 by setting his goodness on earth through it.
526 The knowledgeable is sated, because of what he knows,
527 by an official, because of his good deed
528 through the action of his mind and his tongue.

529 His lips are accurate when he is speaking,
530 his eyes when seeing,
531 and both his ears hearing what is useful for his son;
532 one who acts in accord with Maat,
being free of lying.

The conclusion of Ptahhotep's instruction has seven discourses on the usefulness of his teaching, each marked by an introductory line in red ink.

jr zp n mꜣꜥt jrj špss.sn pw — literally, "as for a case of Maat thereto, it is their finery." The sentence means that their value will emerge when they are applied to any instance that requires correct behavior.

m ꜥ n jb.f ns.f — see Essay 14.

ꜥnḫwj.f t(w)t.(w) — literally, "his ears reconciled": § 20.9.1.

ꜣḫt n zꜣ.f — this is the object of each of the three *ḥr sḏm* phrases preceding. The tercet as a whole means that what Ptahhotep has told his son will make his son's teaching effective for his own son.

Conclusion, Part 2 (534–563: 16,3–13)

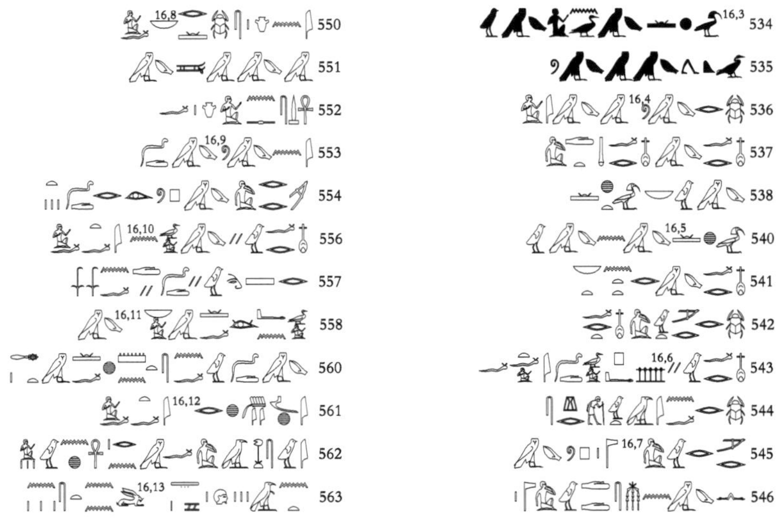

534 ***ꜣḫ sḏm*** 2
n zꜣ sḏm.w 2
535 ***ꜥq sḏm m sḏmw*** 3
536 *ḫpr sḏmw m sḏmj* 3
537 *nfr sḏm nfr mdt* 2
538 *sḏmw nb ꜣḫt* 2

540 *ꜣḫ sḏm n sḏmw* 3
541 *nfr sḏm r ntt nbt* 3
542 *ḫpr mrwt nfrt* 2
543 *nfrwj šzp zꜣ ḏd jt.f* 5
544 *ḫpr n.f jꜣwt ḫr.s* 3
545 *mrrw nṯr pw sḏm* 2
546 *nj sḏm.n msddw nṯr* 3
550 *jn jb sḫpr nb.f* 3
551 *m sḏm m tm sḏm* 3
552 *ʿnḫ-wḏꜣ-snb n z(j) jb.f* 3
553 *jn sḏmw sḏm ḏd* 3
554 *mrr sḏm pw jrr ḏdt* 3
556 *nfrwj sḏm zꜣ n jt.f* 4
557 *ršwj ḏddj n.f nn* 3
558 *zꜣ ʿn.f m nb sḏm* 3
560 *sḏm ḏdw n.f st mnḫ.f m ḫt* 4
561 *jmꜣḫy ḫr jt.f* 2
562 *jw sḫꜣ.f m r n ʿnḫw* 3
563 *ntjw dp tꜣ wnnt(j).sn* 3

534 **Hearing is useful**
for a son who is a hearer.
535 **When hearing enters in a hearer,**
536 the hearer becomes the heard,
537 good of hearing, good of speaking:
538 a hearer, master of what is useful.
540 Hearing is useful for the hearer:
541 hearing is better than anything that is,
542 for love of what is good ensues.
543 How good it is for a son to receive when his father speaks,
544 old age happens to him from it.
545 One who hears is one whom the god loves;
546 one whom the god hates cannot hear.
550 The mind is what makes its owner
551 into one who hears or one who does not hear;
552 a man's mind is lph for him.
553 The hearer is the one who hears speaking,
554 but he who does what is said is the one who loves hearing.

556 How good it is when a son listens to his father;
557 how joyful is he to whom this is said,
558 a son who is pleasing for having hearing.
560 The hearer to whom it is said becomes effective in the womb
561 and worthy with his father,
562 for his memory is in the mouth of the living
563 who are on earth or who will exist.

Parts 2–4 of the conclusion are an extended discourse on obedience ("hearing" the father's teaching).

sḏm.w — a 3ms stative as an unmarked relative clause after an undefined antecedent (§ 22.11).

šzp zꜣ ḏd jt.f — the verbs are either infinitives ("a son's receiving his father's speaking") or *sḏm.f*'s, as translated above. In the latter case, *šzp zꜣ* is a noun clause (subject of *nfrwj*) and *ḏd jt.f*, an adverb clause. The 3fs pronoun of *ḫr.s* in the next line suggests the second interpretation, since the infinitive is regularly masculine (§ 13.8).

ḫpr n.f jꜣwt ḫr.s — i.e., acceptance of the father's advice makes it possible for a son to reach old age.

ꜥnḫ-wḏꜣ-snb n z(j) jb.f — literally, "the lph (§ 20.9.2) of a man is his mind." This is an A B nominal sentence (§ 7.7.1), which is apparently possible because *jb*, like *rn* or a kinship term, is an inalienable feature.

ḏddj n.f nn — literally, "said to him this," with the passive participle (§§ 24.2, 24.6).

zꜣ ꜥn.f m nb sḏm — literally, "a son who is pleasing (§ 22.13) as an owner of hearing."

sḏm ḏdw n.f st mnḫ.f — a SUBJECT–*sḏm.f* construction in which the subject is the active participle *sḏm* modified by the relative clause *ḏdw n.f st*. The dependent pronoun *st* indicates that the latter involves a passive participle (literally, "said to him it": § 24.6) rather than a passive *sḏm.f* used as an unmarked relative clause (§ 22.13).

Conclusion, Part 3 (564–574: 16,13–17,4)

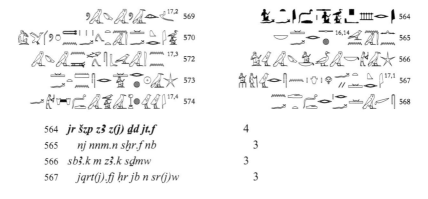

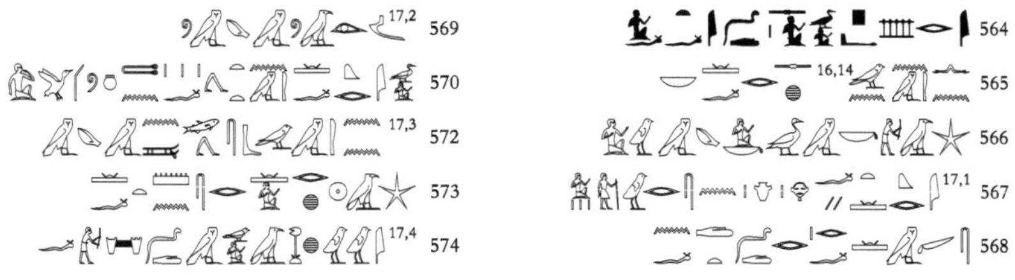

564 ***jr šzp zꜣ z(j) ḏd jt.f*** 4
565 *nj nnm.n sḫr.f nb* 3
566 *sbꜣ.k m zꜣ.k sḏmw* 3
567 *jqrt(j).fj ḥr jb n sr(j)w* 3

568 *sšm r.f r ḏddt n.f* 3
569 *mꜢw m sḏmw* 2
570 *zꜢ jqr.f nmtwt.f ṯn.w* 4
572 *nnm bs n tm sḏm* 4
573 *dwꜢ rḫ r smnt.f* 3
574 *jw wḫꜢ mḏd.f* 2

564 **When a man of standing accepts his father's speaking,**
565 no plan of his can err.
566 You will make of your son a hearer,
567 who will be accomplished in the opinion of officials,
568 who guides his mouth according to what has been said to him,
569 who is seen as a hearer.
570 A son who is accomplished, his steps are distinguished,
572 while the interference of him who does not hear errs.
573 The knowledgeable rises early to establish himself,
574 while the fool struggles.

The third part of the conclusion continues the discourse on obedience by describing its benefits.

sbꜢ.k m zꜢ.k sḏmw — literally, "you teach from your son a hearer."

bs — literally, "entrance," referring entrance into a situation.

dwꜢ — a verb meaning "do at dawn."

mḏd.f — literally, "he presses."

Conclusion, Part 4 (575–587: 17,4–9)

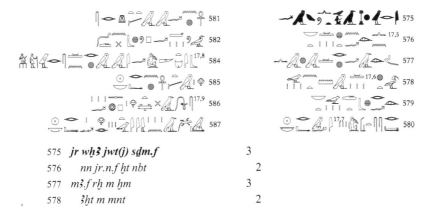

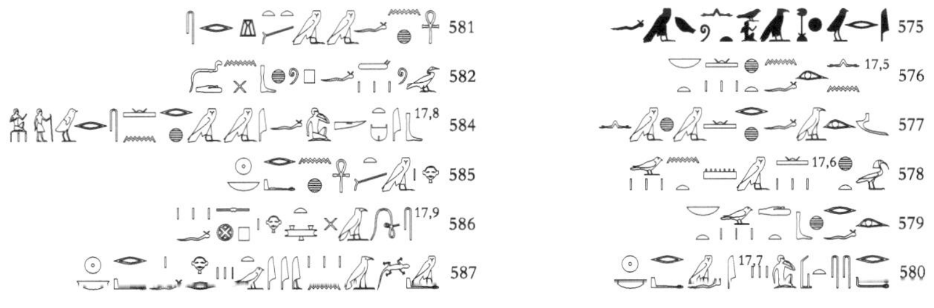

575 ***jr wḫꜢ jwt(j) sḏm.f*** 3
576 *nn jr.n.f ḫt nbt* 2
577 *mꜢ.f rḫ m ḫm* 3
578 *Ꜣḫt m mnt* 2

579 *jrr.f ḫbdt nbt* 3
580 *r ṯss.t(w) jm.f rꜥ nb* 3
581 *ꜥnḫ.f m m(w)tt ẖr.s* 3
582 *ꜥqw.f pw ḫbn ḏd* 2
584 *bjt.f jm m rḫ n sr(j)w* 4
585 *ḥr m(w)t ꜥnḫ.(w) rꜥ nb* 3
586 *swꜣ.t(w) ḥr zpw.f* 2
587 *m ꜥꜥšꜣ n jyt ḥr.f rꜥ nb* 4

575 **As for the fool who does not hear,**
576 he will not be able to do anything.
577 He sees knowledge as ignorance,
578 what is useful as what is painful.
579 He does everything hateful
580 to the point that he is reprimanded every day.
581 He lives on that which one dies from,
582 condemnation is his income.
584 His character from it is in the knowledge of officials,
585 because of dying alive every day.
586 His deeds are passed over
587 from the multitude of wrongs on him every day.

The fourth part of the conclusion contrasts the character of the son who is disobedient.

jwt(j) sḏm.f — a marked negative relative clause (§ 22.8).

r ṯss.t(w) jm.f — the preposition *r* governing a noun clause (§ 21.9). *ṯzj m* "raise from" is an idiom for accusation or indictment, referring to bringing something done by someone to official attention.

m(w)tt ẖr.s — a passive participle construction (§ 24.7).

ꜥqw — wages paid in the form of grain.

ḫbn ḏd — literally, "being found guilty of speaking," referring to a judicial verdict of wrongdoing. The line means that what he receives as daily recompense for his deeds are condemnations instead of a proper salary that he can eat or barter for food. It is for that reason that he "lives on that which one dies from" and "dies alive every day."

Conclusion, Part 5 (588–617: 17,10–18,12)

588	***zꜣ sḏm.w šms*** *ḥrw*	3
589	*nfr n.f m ḫt sḏm.f*	2
590	*jꜣww.f pḥ.f jmꜣḫ*	3
591	*sḏd.f m mjtt n ẖrdw.f*	3
592	*m smꜣw sbꜣw jt.f*	2
593	*z(j) nb sbꜣ.(w) mj jr.f*	3
594	*sḏd.f ḫr msw.f*	2
595	*jḫ ḏd.⸢sn n⸣ ẖrdw.sn*	2
596	*jr bj(ꜣ) m rdj⸢t ꜥ⸣dt.k*	3
597	*srwd mꜣꜥt ꜥnḫ msw.k*	4
598	*jr dpj jy ḫr jsft*	3
600–601	*jḫ ḏd rmṯ mꜣꜣt(j).sn mjtt js pfꜣ pw*	5
602–603	*ḏd.(j)n sḏmṯ(j).sn mjtt js pfꜣ pw gr*	5
604	*mꜣꜣ bw-nb.sn sgrḥ ꜥšꜣt*	4
607	*nn km.n špssw m ḥmt.sn*	3
608	*m jt mdt m jn s(j)*	3
609	*m rdj kt m jst kt*	3
611	*ꜥḥꜣ tw m wn jnjw jm.k*	4
612–13	*zꜣw tw r ḏd rḫ-ḫt sḏm r.k*	4
613–14	*mr.k smnt.k m r n sḏmyw*	4
615	*mdwy.k ꜥq.n.k m zp n ḥmww*	4
616	*mdw.k r zp n qn*	3
617	*wnn sḫr.k nb r jst.f*	3

588 **A son who has heard, who follows** Horus,
589 it goes well for him after he hears.
590 He grows old and reaches honor,
591 and relates likewise to his children,
592 in renewing his father's teaching,
593 each man taught as he did.
594 When he relates to his offspring,
595 then they will tell their children.
596 Set an example in giving your observation:
597 make Maat firm and your offspring will live.
598 As for a standard that has come under disorder,
600–601 then people who will see the like say, "Look, that's it";
602–603 and those who will hear the like also say, "Look, that's it."
604 See to all of them; soothe the multitude:
607 no finery will be able to be complete without them.
608 Don't take away a word, don't add it;
609 don't put one in place of another.
611 Be careful about opening the restraints on you,
612–13 guard against speaking like a pundit: listen to yourself.
613–14 If you want to fix yourself in the mouth of hearers,
615 speak only when you have mastered the craft.
616 When you speak from a state of completeness,
617 all your advice will be as it should.

ḥrw — though part of the first line, the god's name is written in black ink because red was associated with Seth, the enemy of Horus.

mj jr.f — i.e., like the father did.

jḫ ḏd.⸢sn n⸣ ẖrdw.sn — the scribe has written *jḫ ḏd n.sn ẖrdw.sn* "then their children will speak to them," which makes less sense in the context.

m rdj⸢t ⸢⸣ḏt.k — the scribe has written  instead of , probably from misreading a hieratic original.

js pf3 pw — this is an A *pw* sentence (*pf3 pw*) introduced by the exclamatory particle *js(w)* (§ 15.6.4). The particle cannot be the enclitic one (§ 15.7.3) subordinating *mjtt pf3 pw* "it is that one's likeness" (§ 21.3) because the word order would then have to be *mjtt pf3 js pw*. The demonstrative *pf3* refers to *jsft*, and *pw* refers to *dpj*. In other words, when people see a standard that has been corrupted, they identify it with the corrupting agent.

ḏd.(j)n — this line seems to follow on the preceding one, meaning that people who will hear (*sḏmtj.sn*) the observation of the first group (*m33tj.sn* "those who will see") will repeat the observation. In that case, the *sḏm.n.f* written by the scribe is inappropriate; most likely, he has omitted the reed-leaf of the *sḏm.jn.f* (§ 19.10).

gr — this adverb qualifies the verb rather than the quotation; its deferral to the end of the sentence reflects the normal Egyptian preference for the position of adverbs.

mꜢꜢ bw-nb.sn — literally, "see their everyone"; the verb *mꜢꜢ* can be used with the meaning "see to, take care of." This couplet refers to the "multitude" of offspring that the son is being advised to counsel.

m jtw mdt — this couplet refers to the father's instruction: in other words, pass it on word for word.

ꜥḥꜢ tw m wn jnjw jm.k — literally, "fight yourself in opening the restraints from you." This line follows on the previous one, advising the son not to pontificate when counseling his children.

zꜢw tw r ḏd rḫ-ḫt — literally, "guard yourself with respect to a knowledgeable one's speaking."

sḏm r.k — normally, this would mean "So, listen," with *r.k* referential (§ 15.7.2). In this context, however, *r.k* probably has full prepositional force: "listen with respect to yourself."

mr.k — the predicate of the initial clause of an emphatic sentence (§ 25.8.1). The rheme, in the second line of the couplet, is also emphatic, with its rheme the clause *ꜥq.n.k m zp n ḥmww*, literally, "you have entered into the case of a craftsman."

mdw.k r zp n qn — another emphatic sentence: literally, "you speak with respect to a case of completion." Despite the difference in spelling, the two verb forms *mdwy.k* and *mdw.k* must be the same; for the double reed-leaf, see the note to *mdy.k* in Maxim 27.

Conclusion, Part 6 (618–627: 18,12–19,3)

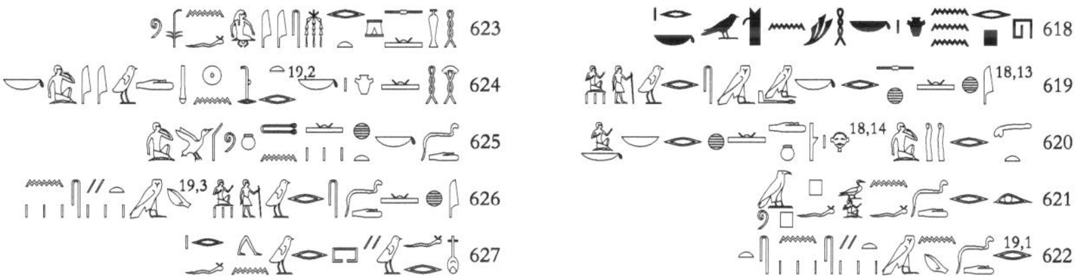

618 ***hrp jb.k ḥn r.k*** 4
619 *jḫ sḫr.k mjm sr(j)w* 2
620 *mtr ḥr qd ḫr nb.k* 3
621 *jr r ḏd n.f zꜢ pfꜢ pw* 3
622 *r ḏd n sḏmtj.sn st* 2
623 *ḥz grt msy n.f sw* 2
624 *wꜢḥ jb.k tr n mdwy.k* 4
625 *ḏd.k ḫwt ṯnw* 2
626 *jḫ ḏd sr(j)w sḏmtj.sn* 3
627 *nfrwj prw n r.f* 3

618 **Submerge your mind, order your mouth,**
619 then your advice will be among the officials.

620 Be completely exact with your master,
621 act so that he is told, "He is that one's son,"
622 and so that those who will hear it are told,
623 "Moreover, blessed is he to whom he was born."
624 Set your mind during the time of your speaking
625 and say things of distinction:
626 then the officials who hear will say,
627 "How good is the issue of his mouth."

jḫ sḫr.k mjm sr(j)w — a rare example of the particle *jḫ* followed by a non-verbal sentence rather than the *sḏm.f* (§ 18.11).

jr r ḏd n.f — *ḏd* is probably the infinitive: "act with respect to the saying to him." The sentence means "Act so that you will be identified as your father's son."

msy n.f sw — see § 24.6.

Conclusion, Part 7 (628–644: 19,3–8)

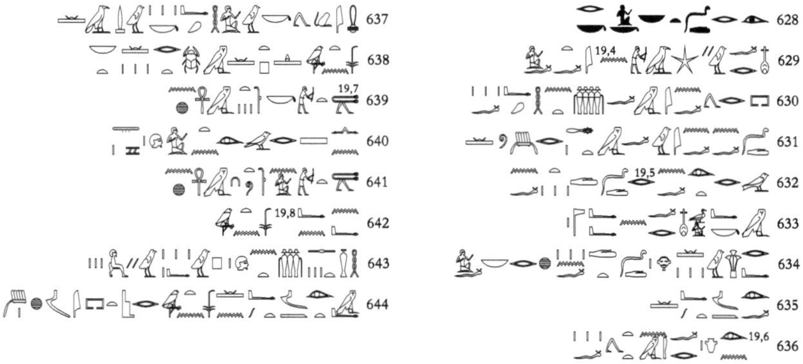

628 ***jr r ḏdt nb.k r.k*** 4
629 *nfrwj sbꜣ.n jt.f* 3
630 *pr.n.f jm.f ḫnt ḥꜥw.f* 3
631 *ḏd.n.f n.f jw.f m ẖt r ꜣw* 3
632 *wr jrt.n.f r ḏddt n.f* 3
633 *mj.k zꜣ nfr n dd nṯr* 2
634 *rdj ḥꜣw ḥr ḏddt n.f* 3
634–35 *ḥr nb.f jr.f mꜣꜥt* 3
636–37 *jr.n jb.f r nmtwt.f mj* 4

pḥ.k wj ḥꜥw.k wḏꜣ.(w) 3
638 *nswt ḥtp.(w) m ḫprt nbt* 3
639 *jt.k rnpwt m ꜥnḫ* 3
640 *nn šr jrt.n.j dp tꜣ* 3
641 *jt.n.j rnpt 110 m ꜥnḫ* 3
642–43 *n dd n.(j) nswt ḥzwt ḫnt dp(j)w-ꜥwj* 4
644 *m ꜥ jrt mꜣꜥt n nswt r jst jmꜣḫ* 3

628 **Act until your master says about you,**
629 "How good is he whom his father has taught!
630 When he emerged from him, foremost of his body,
631 he had told him completely while he was in the womb;
632 what he has done is greater than what was said to him.
633 Look, a good son of the god's giving,
634 who has added to what he was told.
634–35 His master has to have been doing Maat,
636–37 for his mind has acted similarly according to his steps."
You will reach me with your limbs sound,
638 the king content with all that happens,
639 and you will achieve years of life.
640 What I have done on earth is not small:
641 I have achieved one hundred and ten years of life
642–43 of the king's giving to me blessings beyond those before,
644 from doing Maat for the king to the state of honor.

Ptahhotep's concluding words encourage his son to act on the model that he has established, and thus reflect well on him.

r ḏdt nb.k — here the *sḏmt.f* is used rather than the infinitive of lines 621–22.

pr.n.f jm.f ḫnt ḥꜥw.f — the first suffix pronoun refers to the son, the second and third, to the father. *pr.n.f* is the predicate of an emphatic sentence (§§ 25.8.3, 25.13.2).

ḏd.n.f n.f jw.f m ẖt r ꜣw — the first suffix pronoun refers to the father, the second and third, to the son.

rdj ḥꜣw ḥr — literally, "who has given excess over."

ḫr nb.f jr.f mꜣꜥt — a gnomic SUBJECT–*sḏm.f* introduced by the particle *ḫr*, indicating necessity: see §§ 15.6.13 and 18.11.

jr.n jb.f r nmtwt.f mj — the referents of the suffix pronouns are not certain, but the first probably refers to the son and the second, to *nb.f* "his master." For adverbial *mj* "similarly," see §§ 8.2.4 and 8.15.

pḥ.k wj — i.e., you will attain the status that I have.

ḥzwt ḫnt dp(j)w-ꜥwj — literally, "blessings forward of those before." This phrase can also be a second object of 641 *jt.n.j*, in which case, it is the first line of a final couplet.

Colophon (645–646: 19,9)

645
646

jw.f pw ḥꜣt.f r pḥ(wj).fj mj gmyt m zẖꜣ

That is how it goes, beginning to end, like what has been found in writing.

BIBLIOGRAPHY

Barns, John W.B. "Some Readings and Interpretations in Sundry Egyptian Texts." *Journal of Egyptian Archaeology* 58 (1972), 159–66.

Berlev, Oleg. *Общественные Отношения в Египте Эпохи Среднего Царство: Социальный Слой "Царских ḥmww"*. Moscow, 1973.

Blumenthal, Elke. "Ptahhotep und der 'Stab des Alters'." In J.Osing and G. Dreyer, ed., *Form und Mass: Beiträge zur Literatur, Sprache und Kunst des alten Ägypten, Festschrift für Gerhard Fecht zum 65. Geburtstag am 6. Februar 1987* (Wiesbaden, 1987), 84–97.

van den Boorn, Guido P.F. "*Wḏꜥ-ryt* and Justice at the Gate." *Journal of Near Eastern Studies* 44 (1985), 1–25.

Burkard, Günter. "Die Lehre des Ptahhotep." In O. Kaiser, ed., *Weisheitstexte, Mythen und Epen: Weisheitstexte* II. Texte aus der Umwelt des Alten Testaments, 3. (Gütersloh, 1991), 195–221.

Fecht, Gerhard. "Cruces Interpretum in der Lehre des Ptahhotep (Maximen 7, 9, 13, 14) und das Alter der Lehre." In Université Paul Valéry, Institut d'égyptologie, ed., *Hommages à François Daumas* (Montpellier, 1986) I, 227–51.

Gardiner, Alan H. "The Instruction Addressed to Kagemni and His Brethren." *Journal of Egyptian Archaeology* 32 (1946), 71–74.

Jéquier, Gustave. *Le Papyrus Prisse et ses variantes: papyrus de la Bibliothèque Nationale (Nos. 183 à 194), Papyrus 10371 et 10435 du British Museum, tablette Carnarvon au Musée du Caire, publiées en fac-similé*. Paris, 1911.

Junge, Friedrich. *Die Lehre Ptahhoteps und die Tugenden der ägyptischen Welt*. Orbis Biblicus et Orientalis 193. Freiburg and Göttingen, 2003.

Königliche Museen zu Berlin. *Aegyptische Inschriften aus den königlichen Museen zu Berlin*, 2 vols. (Leipzig, 1913–24).

Lorton, David. "The Expression *Šms-ib*. *Journal of the American Research Center in Egypt* 7 (1968), 41–54.

Stefanović, Danijela. "*ḏ3mw* in the Middle Kingdom." *Lingua Aegyptia* 15 (2007), 217–29.

Vernus, Pascal. "Le vizir et le balancier: à propos de l'Enseignement de Ptahhotep." In C. Berger und B. Mathieu, ed., *Études sur l'Ancien Empire et la nécropole de Saqqâra dédiées à Jean-Philippe Lauer* (Orientalia Monspeliensia 9; Montpellier, 1997), 437–43.

Žába, Zbyněk. *Les maximes de Ptaḥḥotep*. Prague, 1956.

TEXT 5
THE DISCOURSES OF THE ELOQUENT PEASANT

AS A WORK OF LITERATURE, this composition is second in importance only to the Story of Sinuhe. It is attested in several Middle Kingdom copies, all in hieratic on papyri:

B1 — pAmherst 1 and pBerlin 3023
: The beginning of the composition is lost (to R 2,3) and the text breaks off before the end (B2 91–142).[1] This papyrus was written by the same scribe who wrote the B manuscript of Sinuhe. Parkinson 1991; Parkinson 2012a, CD folder "Pap. Berlin P. 3023 The Tale of the Eloquent Peasant B1."

B2 —pAmherst 2 and pBerlin 3025
: The papyrus as preserved contains the end of the composition (from B1 263) and is the only copy to preserve the final lines (after B1 357). It is written exclusively in vertical columns on the recto. Parkinson 1991; Parkinson 2012a, CD folder "Pap. Berlin P. 3025 The Tale of the Eloquent Peasant B2."

Bt — pButler (BM 10274)
: This copy preserves the beginning of the composition except for the opening lines (R 2,1–8,6). It is written in vertical columns except for the list of goods (Bt 1–14). Griffith 1892; Parkinson 1991.

R — pRamesseum A (Berlin 10499), recto
: This copy preserves the beginning of the text; the end is lost. Written horizontally except for three columns. Vogelsang and Gardiner 1908; Parkinson 1991.

B1 can be dated to the coregency of Senwosret III and Amenemhat III (p. 56, above), B2 and Bt are contemporary or slightly later (Parkinson 1991, xxvi), and R dates to the first part of Dyn. XIII or slightly earlier (p. 56, above).

The original was composed in the first half of Dyn. XII. An unusual blend of two genres, stories and wisdom texts, it begins and ends as a story but its bulk is devoted to nine lengthy discourses on the nature of Maat, which are the reason for its existence. The text is also the most consciously "literary" of Middle Egyptian compositions, replete with metaphors and carefully crafted sentences.

1 Some 12 columns of the beginning are lost (Parkinson 1991, xiv). The text is written on both the recto and verso: on the recto, in vertical columns to 108, then horizontal in three pages (109–21, 122–33, 134–45), vertical from 146–52, five pages of horizontals (153–66, 167–79, 180–92, 193–205, 206–18), and vertical from 219–87; on the verso, horizontal in five pages (288–96, 297–304, 305–15, 316–26, 327–35), and vertical to the end (336–57).

Episode 1 — The Departure (R 1, 1–6)

R 1,1
R 1,2
R 1,3
R 1,4
R 1,5
R 1,6

R 1,1–2	***z(j) pw wn.(w)*** *ḫw.n-jnpw rn.f*	4
	sḫtj pw n sḫt ḥmꜣ[t]	2
	jst wn ḥjmt.f mrt rn.s	4
R 1,2–3	***ḏd.jn sḫtj pn n ḥjmt.f tn***	3
	mj.t wj m hꜣt r kmt	2
	r jnt ꜥqw jm n ẖrdw.j	3
R 1,3–4	*šm swt ḫꜣ n.j nꜣ n jtj*	3
	ntj m pꜣ mjẖr m ḏꜣt n sf	4
	ꜥḥꜥ.n ḫꜣ.n.f n.s jtj ḥqꜣt 6	3
R 1,5	***ḏd.jn sḫtj pn n ḥjmt.f tn***	3
	mj.t dj.j n.t jtj ḥqꜣt 20	2
	r ꜥqw ḥnꜥ ẖrdw.t	2
R 1,6	*jrr.t n.j swt tꜣ jtj ḥqꜣt 6*	2
	m t ḥnqt n hrw nb	3
	kꜣ ꜥnḫ.j jm.f	2

R 1,1–2 **There once was a man** named Khueninpu.
He was a peasant of Salt Field,
and he had a wife named Meret.
R 1,2–3 **So, that peasant said to that wife of his,**
"Look, I am going down to Blackland
to get provisions there for my children.
R 1,3–4 Now, go measure for me the barley
that is in the storehouse as the balance as of yesterday."
Then he measured for her six heqat of barley.
R 1,5 **So, that peasant said to that wife of his,**
"Look, I will give you twenty heqat of barley
for income with your children.

R 1,6 And you make me those six heqat of barley
into bread and beer for every day,
and I will live on it."

The peasant prepares to set out from his home in the Wadi Natrun on a trading expedition to the Nile Valley. Although a "peasant" (*sḫtj* "field-man"), he is actually a fairly prosperous farmer, as indicated by the grain he has available and the goods listed in Episode 2. In addition to the notes for this text, the reader is advised to consult the much more extensive notes to be found in Parkinson 2012b.

R 1,1 *z(j) pw wn.(w)* —an A *pw* nominal sentence, with A *z(j) wn.(w)* "a man existed" used as a noun clause—i.e., "it is (that) a man existed" (§ 21.12). The peasant's name means "He Whom Anubis Has Protected" (§ 22.24).

sḫt ḥmꜣt — the oasis now known as the Wadi Natrun, characterized by its deposits of salt (natron). It lies some sixty miles northwest of modern Cairo, in the western desert, and some fifty miles southeast of Alexandria. The location lay outside Egypt ("Blackland") proper, and its inhabitants were therefore seen by the majority of Egyptians as provincial in both customs and language.

R 1,2 *jst wn ḥjmt.f* — a marked adverb clause (§ 20.3), literally "while there was his wife."

R 1,2–3 *ḏd.jn* — R routinely marks the introduction to speeches in red.

mj.t wj m hꜣt r kmt — see § 14.2. The peasant's destination, Herakleopolis (B1, 16–17), lay a hundred miles southeast of the Wadi Natrun.

ʿqw — from *ʿq* "enter," the term for monthly supplies in the form of food, given both as rations and salary.

R 1,3–4 *ḫꜣ* — literally, "weigh." Grain was tallied by weight rather than volume.

m ḏꜣt n sf — literally, "as the balance for yesterday." *ḏꜣt*, a verbal noun from *wḏꜣ* "become sound," is a mathematical term for the remainder of an operation of subtraction. The peasant wants to find out how much grain they have left in the storehouse.

jtj ḥqꜣt 6 — The amount is equivalent to 0.95 bushels (28.8 liters). The reading could be  "60 heqat" (§ 9.7.4), but the lesser value is likely from R 1,6 (see below).

jtj ḥqꜣt 20 — R uses the "dot" notation for single heqats (see R 19,3), so this is clearly 20 heqat rather than 2 (§ 9.7.4). In the early Middle Kingdom, Heqanakht allotted a total of some three heqat of barley as a monthly salary for his wife and six minor dependants (Allen 2002, 147). Since the peasant probably planned to be away for no more than a month (see next), this amount is probably intended to show that he had substantial resources.

R 1,6 *tꜣ jtj ḥqꜣt 6* — the demonstrative points to the amount given in 1,4. Six heqat of barley in the form of bread and beer would supply about a month's worth of food for a man not engaged in physical labor and consuming about 3,000 calories a day (Allen 2002, 146 n. 31). The journey to Herakleopolis and back would have taken perhaps 25 days, with a few more needed for bartering while there (Parkinson 2012b, 28–29). This is a likelier span of time than the ten months that would be implied by a reading of  "60 heqat."

Episode 2 — Setting Out (R 1,7–6,1; Bt 1–15, B1 1–15)

R 1,7

R 1,7 *h3t pw jr.n sḫtj pn r kmt* 4
3tp.n.f ⌜3[w].f 2

R 1,7 What that peasant did was to go down to Blackland,
having loaded his donkeys

This is essentially a couplet (a tercet in R), interrupted by a list of goods in account form.

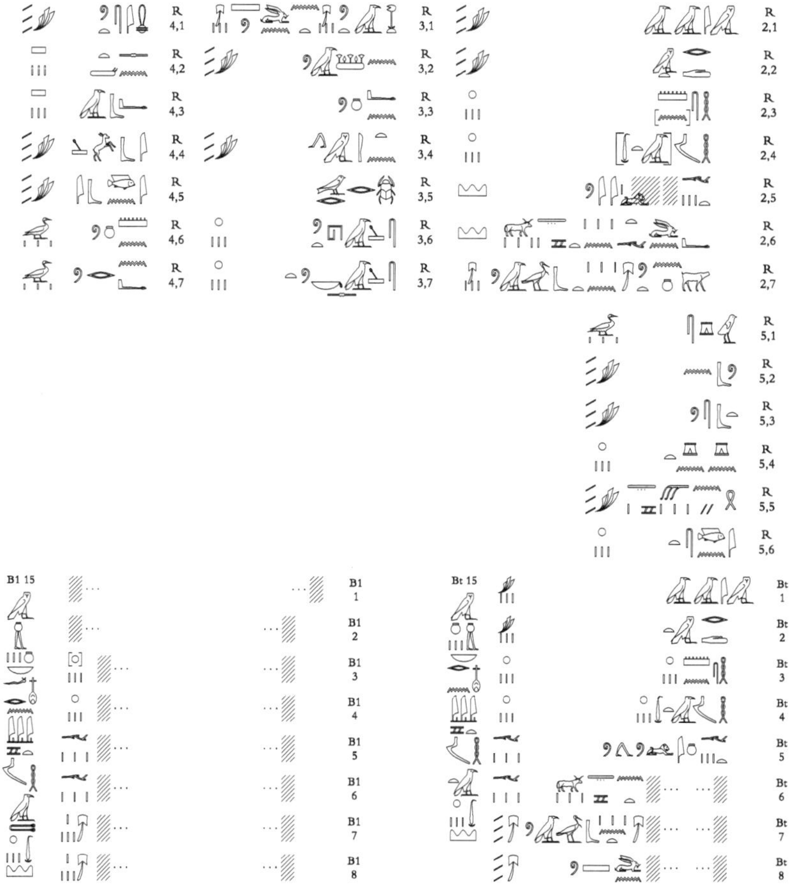

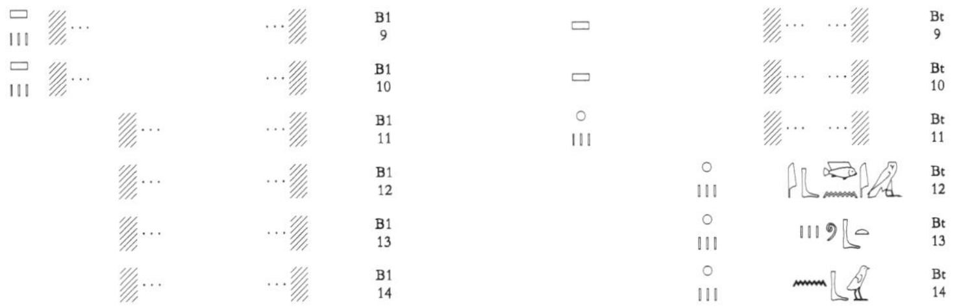

Bt	B1	R				
1	[1]	2,1	*m*	*jꜣꜣ*	with	reeds
2	[2]	2,2		*rdmt*		palm fronds
3	[3]	2,3		*ḥsmn*		natron
4	[4]	2,4		*ḥmꜣt*		salt
5	[5]	2,5		*ẖtw nw jrwjw*		sticks of *jrwjw*-wood
6	[6]	2,6		*ꜥwnwt nt tꜣ-jḥw*		staves of Farafra
7	[7]	2,7		*ẖnwt nt bꜣw*		leopard skins
8	[8]	3,1		*ẖꜣwt nt wnšw*		wolf pelts
—	—	3,2		*nšꜣw*		pondweed
9	[9]	3,3		*ꜥnw*		pebbles
—	—	3,4		*tnm*		"wander" plants
—	—	3,5		*ẖpr-wr*		"big-beetle" plants
—	—	3,6		*sꜣhwt*		resin
—	—	3,7		*sꜣkzwt*		*sꜣkzwt*
—	—	4,1		*mjswt*		*mjswt* plants
[10]	[10]	4,2		*znt*		ochre
[11]	[11]	4,3		*ꜥbꜣw*		*ꜥbꜣw* stones
—	—	4,4		*jbsꜣ*		mint
12	[12]	4,5		*jnbj*		*jnbj* plants
—	—	4,6		*mnw*		pigeons
—	—	4,7		*nꜥrw*		"catfish" birds
—	—	5,1		*wgs*		gutted birds
13	[13]	—		*tbw*		*tbw* plants
14	[14]	5,2		*wbn*		*wbn* plants
—	—	5,3		*tbsw*		*tbsw* plants
—	—	5,4		*gngnt*		arugula
—	—	5,5		*šnj-tꜣ*		fenugreek
—	—	5,6		*jnst*		*jnst* seeds

Bt 15 *m jnw nb nfr n sḫt-ḥmꜣt* 2
with every good product of Salt Field.

Bt and B1 have what was probably the same list, of 14 items. Both are arranged in one page of horizontal lines, 11 in Bt and 12 in B1, with the rest of the list atop the vertical columns 15–16. R has expanded the list considerably, to a total of 27 items. The identity of many of the items in the lists is unknown. See the notes in Parkinson 2012b, 30–35.

tꜣ-jḥw — literally, "Oxen-Land," an oasis 280 miles southwest of Wadi Natrun and 200 miles west of the Nile Valley.

ḥsmn — in Bt 3 the scribe began to write the next entry, *ḥmꜣt*, and corrected it to *ḥsmn*.

ꜥnw — probably smooth, round stones for use in slingshots (Parkinson 2012b, 32).

sꜣhwt — an amber-like resin (Parkinson 2012b, 34).

sꜣkzwt — the —— was added secondarily.

ꜥbꜣw — possibly related to *ꜥbꜣ* "glitter" and therefore a sparkling mineral (Harris 1961: 84–85).

wbn — the red sign in Bt 14 was added secondarily over an erasure.

šnj-tꜣ — literally, "earth hair," also used as a term for grass.

Bt 15 — This is the end of the second line of the couplet:

hꜣt pw jr.n sḫtj pn r kmt
ꜣtp.n.f ꜥꜣw.f ... m jnw nb nfr n sḫt-ḥmꜣt
What that peasant did was to go down to Blackland,
having loaded his donkeys ... with every good product of Salt Field.

R 6,1 adds *mḥ.(w)* "filled" at the beginning. This is probably to be read with the second line, with the remainder the third line of a tercet:

hꜣt pw jr.n sḫtj pn r kmt
ꜣtp.n.f ꜥꜣw.f ... mḥ.(w)
m jnw nb nfr n sḫt-ḥmꜣt
What that peasant did was to go down to Blackland,
having loaded his donkeys ... full
with every good product of Salt Field.

Episode 3 — The Encounter (Bt 16–63, B1 16–40; R 6,2–12,4)

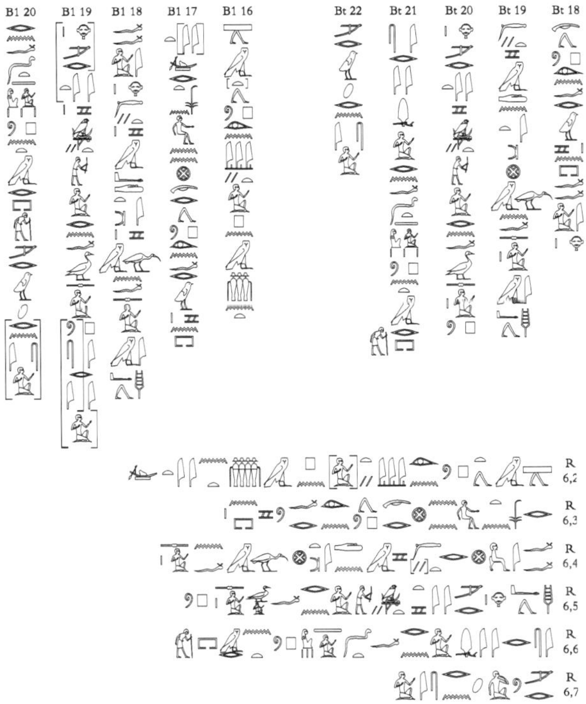

Bt 16–17 *šmt pw jr.n sḫtj pn* 3
m ḫntyt r nn-nswt 2
Bt 18–19 *spr pw jr.n.f* 2
r w n pr-ffj ḥr mḥtj mdnjt 3
Bt 19–20 *gm.n.f z(j) jm ˁḥˁ.(w) ḥr mryt* 5
nmtj-nḫt.(w) rn.f 2
Bt 20–22 *zꜣ z(j) pw jsry rn.f* 3
ḏt pw nt (j)m(j)-r pr wr zꜣ-mrw rnsj 4

Bt 16–17 What the peasant did was to go
upstream to Herakleopolis.
Bt 18–19 What he did was to arrive
at the district of Fefi's House, on the north of Madaniat,
Bt 19–20 and he found a man there, standing on the riverbank,
whose name was Nemtinakht;

Bt 20–22 he was a man of standing, son of a man named Isery,
they were personnel of the chief steward Meru's son Rensi.

On his way south, the peasant's caravan is spotted by a man who decides to confiscate it.

Bt 16–20 *nn-nswt* — literally, "King's Child," modern Ihnasya el-Medina, located 100 miles directly southeast of the Wadi Natrun. It was the capital during Dyn. IX–X, the time in which the story is set. The modern name Ihnasya comes from *ḥwt-nn-nswt* "Enclosure of the King's Child."

pr-ffj — probably near Dahshur, some fifty miles north of Herakleopolis (Parkinson 2012b, 37).

mdnjt — the name of the northernmost (twenty-second) Upper Egyptian nome, centered at Atfih on the east bank.

mryt — this indicates that the peasant was traveling south beside the river.

Bt 19–20 *nmtj-nḫt.(w)* — "Nemti is forceful." Nemti is the celestial ferryman, and was particularly honored in Middle Egypt.

Bt 20–22 *zꜣ z(j)* — the phrase does dual service here, identifying Nemtinakht's father and characterizing Nemtinakht himself as a man of standing in the community (see the note to Ptahhotep Maxim 27). Bt 31–32 shows that he had servants.

jsry — a nickname based on the word *jzr* "tamarisk."

ḏt — a collective from the word *ḏt* "person." The fact that it is followed by the feminine direct genitive *nt* indicates that it is meant here as a collective and therefore refers to both Nemtinakht and his father.

(j)m(j)-r pr wr zꜣ-mrw rnsj — this line provides two benchmarks for the date of the composition. The title, one of the three highest in the national administration, is first attested under Amenemhat I, and is therefore an anachronism in the story; honorific transposition of the father's name (§ 4.15) is last attested under Senwosret III (Parkinson 2012b, 40).

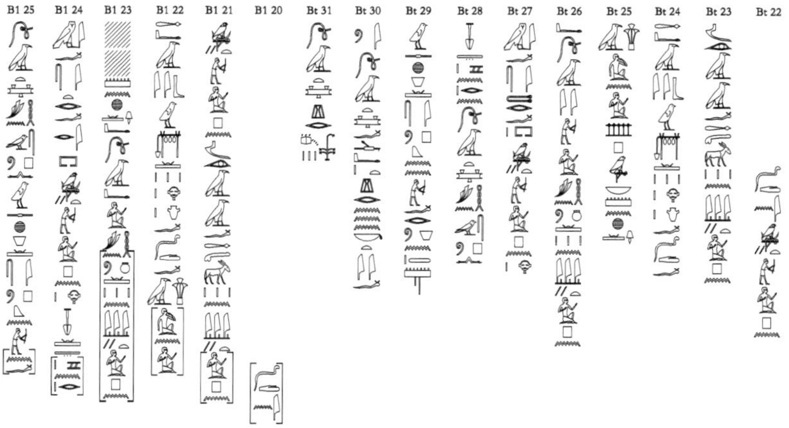

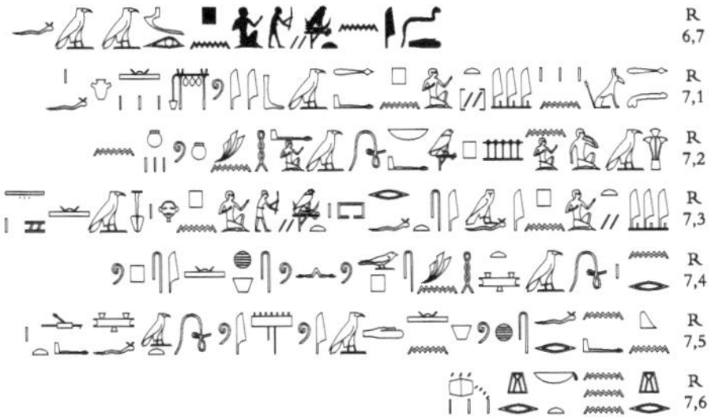

B1 27 B1 26

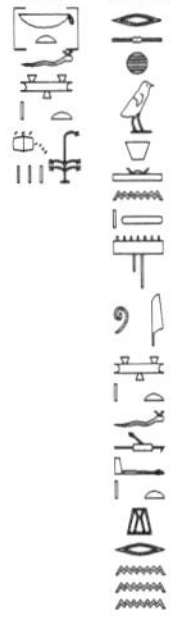

Bt 22–24 *ḏd.jn nmtj-nḫt.(w) pn mꜣꜣ.f ꜥꜣw n sḫtj pn* 5
ꜥꜣbyw ḥr jb.f 2
Bt 24–27 *ḏd.f ḥꜣ n.j šzp nb mnḫ* 3
ꜥwꜣy.j ḫnw n sḫtj pn jm.f 4
Bt 27–28 *jsṯ r.f pr nmtj-nḫt.(w) pn ḥr zmꜣ-tꜣ* 2
n r n wꜣt 2
Bt 28–29 *ḫns pw nj wsḫ js pw* 2
qn.n.f r sḫw n dꜣjw 3
Bt 30–31 *jw wꜣt.f wꜥt ḫr mw* 3
kty.f wꜣt ḫr šmꜥ 2

Bt 22–24 So, that Nemtinakht said, when he saw the donkeys of the peasant,
which were pleasing in his mind,
Bt 24–27 saying, "Would that I had any effective amulet,
so that I could steal the property of that peasant from him!"
Bt 27–28 Now, that Nemtinakht's house was on the landing
of the mouth of the path.
Bt 28–29 It was a narrow one; it was not a broad one:
it extended only to the width of a skirt,
Bt 30–31 for its one path was under water
and its other path under thin barley.

Bt 24–27 *šzp nb mnḫ* — R omits the adjective. *šzp* is the term for an image that can receive (*šzp*) the spirit of a god. Nemtinakht here wishes for one that would enable him to incapacitate the peasant.

Bt 27–29 *jst r.f* — B1 24 adds a superfluous *jr* "as for."

zmꜣ-tꜣ n r n wꜣt — Nemtinakht's house itself does not figure in the account, but rather his fields; *pr* therefore probably has the broader sense of "estate" (house and land) here. The phrase *zmꜣ-tꜣ* refers to a place where boats can land (literally, "join land"). Since the peasant has been following a path along the river (Bt 19–20), at this point the path abuts the landing stage (*r n wꜣt* "mouth of the path"). See further below.

ḥns pw nj wsḫ js pw — since these are A *pw* nominal sentences, *ḥns* and *wsḫ* are masculine singular participles rather than unmarked adjectives (§ 7.15). As such, they refer to *r n wꜣt* "mouth of the path."

qn.n.f r sḫw n dꜣjw — despite the spelling in Bt 29 and R 7,5 B1 25 indicates that the verb form is the *sḏm.n.f* rather than a geminated *sḏm.f.* The verb is probably *qnj* "embrace" and the clause is emphatic, with the prepositional phrase as the rheme: literally, "it embraced (only) to the width of a skirt." The term *dꜣjw*, written ideographically in Bt and B1, denotes a rectangular piece of cloth that can be as wide as three feet (90 cm) but is often narrower, since it is also the everyday garment worn between the legs and secured by a belt (Janssen 2008, 52–53; Parkinson 2012b, 42). The path at this point was therefore at most three feet wide, with one side abutting the grain field and the other, the water of the landing, as indicated by the next couplet.

Bt 30–31 *šmꜥ* — the term denotes barley with two rows of seeds rather than six (called *jtj-mḥ* "full barley": Müller-Wollerman 1987). R routinely substitutes *jtj* "barley, grain."

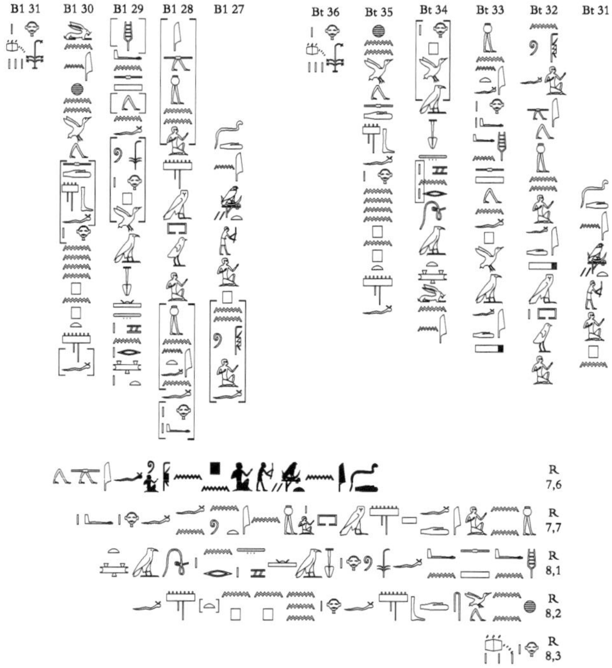

Bt 31–33 *ḏd.jn nmtj-nḫt.(w) pn n šmsw.f* 3
j.zj jn n.j jfd m prw.j 4
jn.jn.t(w).f ḥr ʿ 2
Bt 33–36 *ʿḥʿ.n zn.n.f pꜣ jfd [ḥr p]ꜣ zmꜣ-tꜣ n r wꜣt* 5
wn.jn ḥn.n sdb.f ḥr mw 4
npnpt.f ḥr šmʿ 2

Bt 31–33 So, that Nemtinakht said to his follower,
"Go, get me a sheet from my household stores,"
and it was fetched immediately.
Bt 33–36 Then he opened the sheet on the landing of the path's mouth,
so that its fringe landed on the water
and its hem on the thin barley.

Bt 31–33 *jfd* — the term denotes a square or rectangular piece of cloth (from *jfdw* "four": i.e., four-sided: Janssen 2008, 21).

m prw.j — Coptic **πωρ** (in **ϫενεπωρ** "roof," from *ḏꜣḏꜣ n pr* "head of the house") indicates that the word *pr* "house" ended in a vowel (*páru), but this ending is never shown in writing. The *w* in Bt 32 and B1 28 must therefore reflect a different ending, probably of a derived noun.

jn.jn.t(w).f ḥr ʿ — R 7,7 and perhaps also B1 28 add *n.f* "to him."

Bt 33–36 *sdb.f … npnpt.f* — sheets were typically hemmed on one end of the warp and left unhemmed on the other, with the lengthwise threads untrimmed.

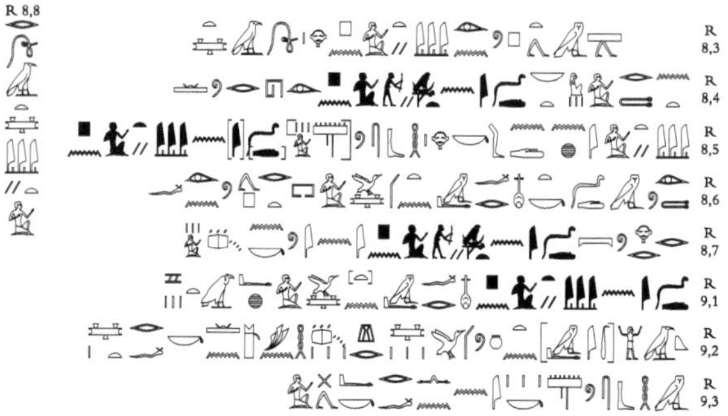

B1 31–32 *jw.jn [r.f sḫtj pn]* 2
ḥr wꜣt nt rmṯ nbt 2
B1 32–33 *ḏd.jn nmtj-nḫt.(w) pn* 2
jr h[rw sḫtj 3
nj ḫnd.k ḥr ḥbsw.j 2
B1 33–35 *ḏd.jn sḫtj pn* 2
jry.j ḥzt.k nfr mjṯn.j 4
prt pw jr.n.f r ḥrw 3
B1 35–36 *ḏd.jn nmtj-nḫt.(w) pn* 2
j[n] j[w] n.k šmʿ.j r wꜣt 2
B1 36–37 *ḏd.jn sḫtj pn* 2
nfr [mj]ṯn.j 2
B1 37–40 *jḫmt qꜣ.ṯ mjṯn ḫr šmʿ* 4
ḥn.k r.f wꜣt.ṯn m ḥbsw.k 3
jn nn r.f dj.k swꜣ.n ḥr wꜣt 3

B1 31–32 So, the peasant came
on the path of everyone
B1 32–33 and Nemtinakht said,
"Be careful, peasant!
Would you step on my clothes?"
B1 33–35 So, the peasant said,
"I will do what you would bless. My route is good."
What the peasant did was go up.
B1 35–36 But Nemtinakht said,
"Is my thin barley to be a path for you?"
B1 36–37 So, the peasant said,
"My route is good.

B1 37–40 The bank is high and the route is under thin barley,
but you furnish our path with your clothes.
So, won't you let us pass on the path?"

B1 31–32 R 8,3 has *šmt pw jr.n sḫtj pn* "what the peasant did was come."

B1 32–33 *jr hrw* — literally, "make calm."

jn ḫnd.k — B1 uses ⟨hieroglyph⟩ as a spelling of the particle.

B1 33–35 *jry.j ḥzt.k* — Bt 40 probably had the more usual construction *jry.j r ḥzt.k* "I will act according to what you would bless." R has *jr.ṯw m ḏdt.k* "it will be done as what you say." The remainder of Bt is lost after this point.

B1 35–36 R has put the final words of the second line *r wꜣt sḫtj* "to (be) a path, peasant" in a column at the left of the page (8,8).

B1 37–40 *wꜣt.ṯn* — the ⟨hieroglyph⟩ represents the pronounced final *t* of *wꜣt* before the suffix pronoun *n*: see the note to ShS. 7 *jzwt.ṯn*. R 9,2 has simply *wꜣt*.

dj.k swꜣ.n — R 9,3 has *dj.k swꜣ.j* "you let me pass."

B1 40–41 *ꜥḥꜥ.n mḥ.n wꜥ m nꜣ n ꜥꜣ* 4
r.f m bꜣt nt šmꜥ 3
B1 41–42 *ḏd.jn nmtj-nḫt.(w) pn* 2
mj.k wj r nḥm ꜥꜣ.k sḫtj 3
B1 42–43 *ḥr wnm.f šmꜥ.j* 2
mj.k sw r hbt ḥr qn.f 2

B1 40–41 Then one of the donkeys filled his mouth
with a sprig of thin barley.

B1 41–42 So, Nemtinakht said,
  “Look, I have to confiscate your donkey, peasant,
B1 42–43 because of his eating my thin barley.
  He will have to thresh because of his audacity.”

B1 40–41 For the rather abrupt segue in B1, R has a more measured transition:

> *pḥ.n.f r.f ḏd mdt [tn]*
> *jw mḥ.n wꜥ [m] nꜣ n ꜥꜣ r.f m bꜣt nt jtj*
> But no sooner had he finished saying this
> than one of the donkeys filled his mouth with a sprig of barley —

literally, “At that (*r.f*), he reached saying this speech and one of the donkeys filled his mouth,” an emphatic construction (§ 25.8.3).

B1 42–43 *mj.k sw r hbt ḥr qn.f* — donkeys were used to trample (*hbj*) grain on a threshing floor to separate the husks from the seeds. *qn* is probably a verbal noun from *qnj* “persevere, be diligent,” with the extended meaning “bravery, audacity.”

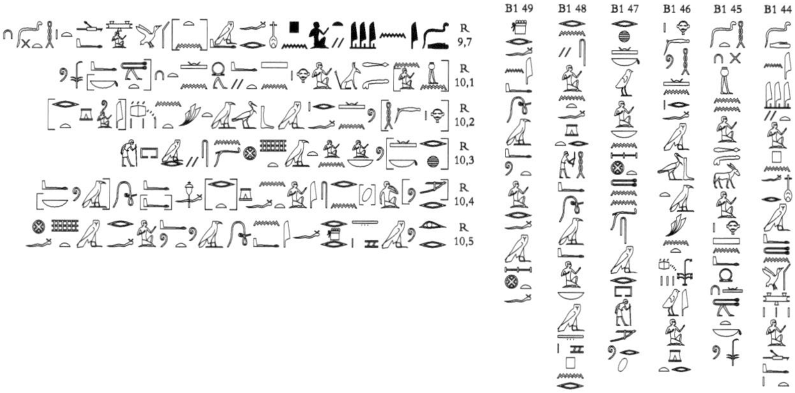

B1 44	*ḏd.jn sḫtj pn*	2
	nfr mjṯn.j	2
B1 44–45	*wꜥt ḥḏt 10*	3
	jn.n.j ꜥꜣ.j ḥr šnꜥ 10	3
B1 45–46	*jt.k sw ḥr mḥw n r.f*	3
	m bꜣt nt šmꜥ	2
B1 46–48	*jw.j grt rḫ.kw nb n spꜣt ṯn*	3
	n-s(j) (j)m(j)-r pr wr zꜣ-mrw rnsj	3
B1 48–49	*ntf grt ḥw ꜥwꜣ nb m tꜣ r ḏr.f*	5
	jn ꜥwꜣ.tw.j r.f m spꜣt.f	2

B1 44 So, the peasant said,
"My route is good.
B1 44–45 One that damages ten?
I got my donkey for ten units of value
B1 45–46 and you will take it for a mouthful
of a sprig of thin barley?
B1 46–48 Moreover, I know the owner of this estate:
it belongs to chief steward Meru's son Rensi,
B1 48–49 and he is the one who beats every robber in the whole land.
So, shall I be robbed in his estate?"

B1 44–45 *wꜥt ḥḏt 10* — the feminine refers to B1 41 *bꜣt* "sprig." The peasant's virtual question compares the value of the donkey (see next) to that of the sprig of barley, and is overly generous, since the latter is much less than a tenth of the donkey's value.

B1 45–46 *jn.n.j ꜥꜣ.j ḥr šnꜥ 10* — since the composition dates to the first half of Dyn. XII, the *šnꜥ* (R *šnꜥtj*) is probably not the 1/12 deben measure noted in § 9.7.3. Instead, it refers to a commonly accepted standard that was used to evaluate commodities being exchanged in the barter economy of ancient Egypt (Allen 2002, 155).

ḥr mḥw n r.f m bꜣt nt šmꜥ — literally, "because of the filling of its mouth with a sprig of thin barley."

B1 48–49 *ntf grt ḥw ꜥwꜣ nb* — R 10,4–5 has *ntf g[rt] ḫsf [ꜥ]wꜣ[w nb] jrrw* "and he is the one who punishes any robbery that is done."

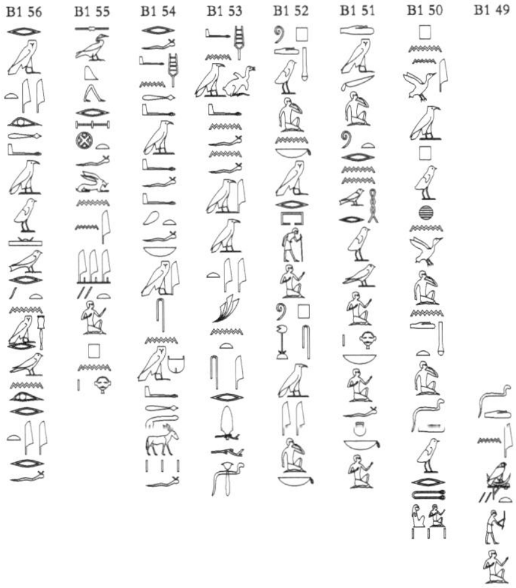

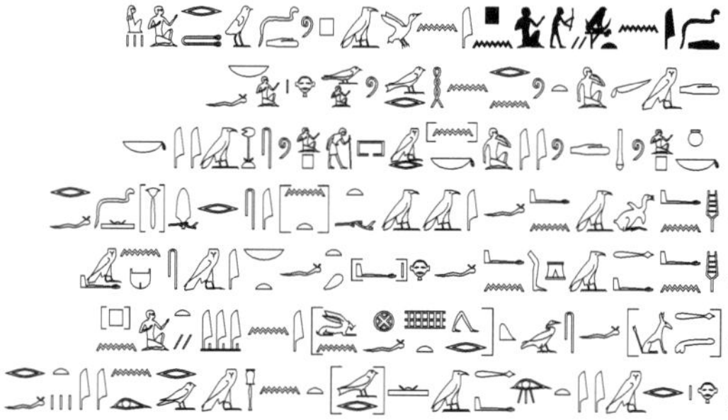

R 10,6
R 10,7
R 11,1
R 11,2
R 11,3
R 11,4
R 11,5

B1 49–51 *ḏd.jn nmtj-nḫt.(w) pn* 2
jn pꜣ pw ḫn n mdt ḏdw rmṯ 5
dm.tw rn n ḥwrw ḥr nb.f 4
B1 51–52 *jnk pw mdw n.k* 2
(j)m(j)-r pr wr pw sḫꜣy.k 2
B1 53–55 *ꜥḥꜥ.n ṯꜣ.n.f n.f jꜣꜣt nt jsr wꜣḏ r.f* 5
ꜥḥꜥ.n ꜥꜣ(g.n).f ꜥt.f nb jm.s 4
nḥm ꜥꜣw.f sꜥq.(w) r spꜣt.f 4
B1 55–56 *wn.jn sḫtj pn ḥr rmyt ꜥꜣw wrt* 5
n mr n jryt r.f 3

B1 49–51 So, Nemtinakht said,
"In fact, *this* is the phrase people say:
'A poor man's name is uttered only because of his lord.'
B1 51–52 The one who speaks to you is I,
but the one you mention is the chief steward."
B1 53–55 Then he took himself a branch of green tamarisk to him,
then he pummeled his every limb with it;
his donkeys were confiscated and taken into his estate.
B1 55–56 So, the peasant was weeping very greatly
because of the pain of what was done to him.

B1 49–51 *jn pꜣ pw ḫn n mdt ḏdw rmṯ* — R 10,6 omits *ḫn n mdt* (literally, "phrase of speech"). This is an A *pw* B sentence. The particle *jn* here probably does not signal a question but instead serves to emphasize the demonstrative pronoun *pꜣ*, as it does for the initial element in the participial statement and the *jn* A *sḏm.f* construction (§§ 23.10–11, 25.3).

dm.tw rn n ḥwrw ḥr nb.f — an emphatic sentence, with the prepositional phrase *ḥr nb.f* as the rheme (§ 25.6). Nemtinakht's citation of this proverb is meant to identify the peasant as the "poor man" and himself as the "lord," so that the peasant's mention of Nemtinakht's superior is pointless—as indicated in the next couplet.

B1 51–52 *jnk pw mdw n.k* — see § 23.11.

B1 53–55 *ꜥḥꜥ.n ṯꜣ.n.f n.f jꜣꜣt nt jsr wꜣḏ r.f* — R 11,2 omits the reflexive dative *n.f.*

ꜥꜣ(g.n).f — R 11,3 has the correct form *ꜥꜣg.n.f,* as well as the prepositional phrase *ḥr [ꜥ]t.f nbt* "on his every limb" rather than B1's direct object. The verb is used to describe the actions of a bull's pawing the ground and of crushing dates and denotes a violent beating.

nḥm ꜥꜣw.f sꜥq.(w) r spꜣt.f — B1 clearly indicates that all the peasant's donkeys were seized. The second verb is the 3pl stative (§ 19.3): literally, "they were caused to enter." The last clause indicates that the peasant's donkeys and goods were meant to become Nemtinakht's permanent possessions.

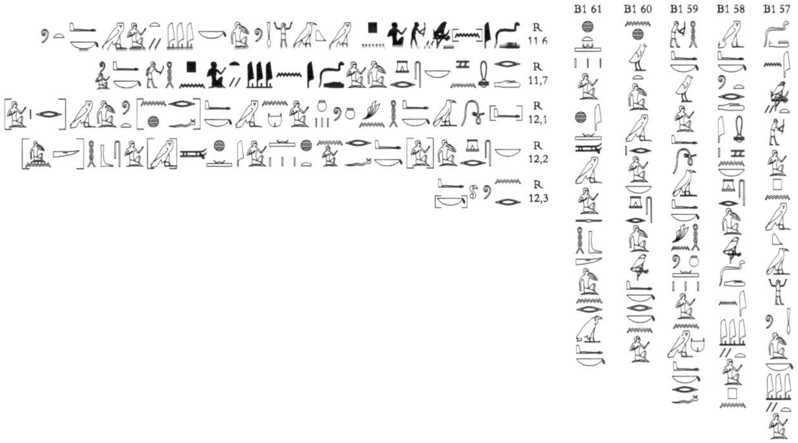

B1 57–58 *ḏd.jn nmtj-nḫt.(w) pn* 2
m qꜣ ḫrw.k sḫtj 3
mj.k tw r dmj n nb-sgr 2
B1 58–60 *ḏd.jn sḫtj pn* 2
ḥw.k wj ꜥwꜣ.k ḫnw.j 3
nḥm.k r.f nḫwt m r.j 3
B1 60–61 *nb-sgr dj.k r.k n.j ḫwt.j* 3
jḫ tm.j sbḥ (n) nr.k 3

B1 57–58 So, Nemtinakht said,
"Don't raise your voice, peasant!
Look, you are headed for the harbor of the Lord of Silencing."
B1 58–60 So, the peasant said,
"You beat me, you rob my property;
and now you would take the complaint from my mouth?

B1 60–61 Lord of Silencing, you should give me my things;
then I will stop crying for fear of you."

B1 57–58 *m qꜣ ḫrw.k* — literally, "don't (let) your voice become high" (§ 15.4).

mj.k tw r dmj n nb-sgr — literally, "look, you are toward the harbor of the Lord of Silencing" (§ 10.8). The sentence means that the peasant is in danger of death: i.e., "if you don't quiet down, you'll be silenced permanently." In the New Kingdom and later, the Lord of Silencing is associated with the realm of the dead.

B1 60–61 *nb-sgr* — the peasant's use of the vocative, addressed to Nemtinakht, is ironic. Nemtinakht is "Lord of Silencing" because he has ordered the peasant to be silent.

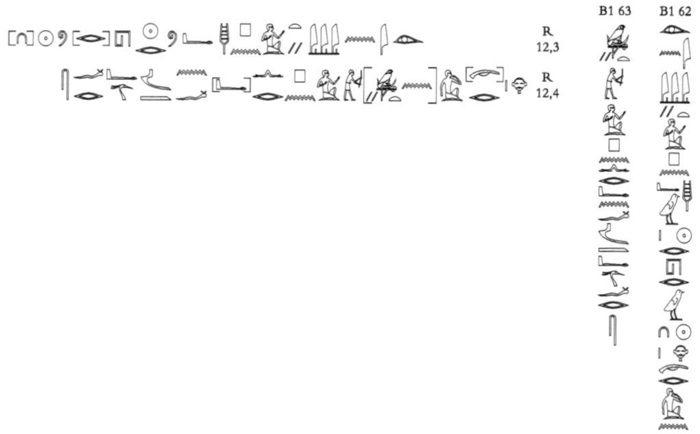

B1 62–63 *jr.jn sḫtj pn ꜥḥꜥw r hrw 10* 4
ḥr spr n nmtj-nḫt.(w) pn 2
nj rdj.n.f mꜣꜥ.f r.s 3

B1 62–63 So, the peasant spent a period of up to ten days
petitioning to that Nemtinakht,
but he wouldn't give heed to it.

B1 62–63 *ꜥḥꜥw r hrw 10* — literally, "a span of time to ten days," the length of an Egyptian week (§ 9.8).

nj rdj.n.f mꜣꜥ.f r.s — literally, "he wouldn't give his temple to it." The phrasing uses a deliberate word-play on the adjective *mꜣꜥ* "just" (Parkinson 2012b, 58).

Episode 4 — Appealing to the Chief Steward (B1 63–82; R 12,5–13,10)

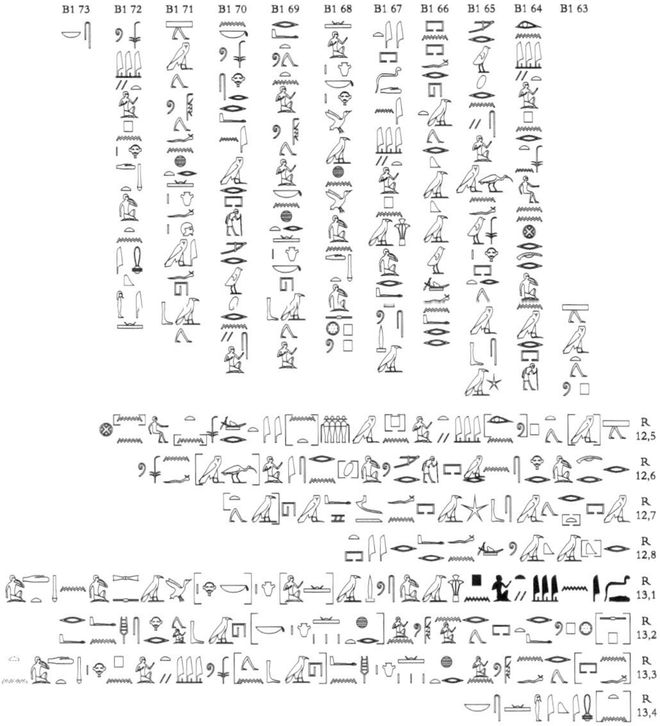

B1 63–65	*šmt pw jr.n sḫtj pn r nn-nswt*	4
	r spr n (j)m(j)-r pr wr zꜣ-mrw rnsj	4
B1 65–67	*gm.n.f sw ḥr prt m sbꜣ n pr.f*	4
	r hꜣt r qꜣqꜣw.f n ˁrryt	3
B1 67–68	*ḏd.jn sḫtj pn ḥꜣ rdj.t(w) swḏꜣ.j jb.k*	5
	ḥr pꜣ ḫn n mdt	2
B1 68–70	*zp pw rdjt jwt n.j šmsw.k n ḫrt jb.k*	5
	hꜣb.j n.k sw ḥr.s	2
B1 70–73	*rdj.jn (j)m(j)-r pr wr zꜣ-mrw rnsj*	4
	šm šmsw.f n ḫrt jb.f dp jm.f	4
	hꜣb sw sḫtj pn ḥr mdt tn mj qj.s nb	4

B1 63–65 What the peasant did was to go to Herakleopolis
to appeal to chief steward Meru's son Rensi.

B1 65–67 He found him emerging from the gate of his house
to go down to his barge of office.
B1 67–68 So, the peasant said, "Would that I could inform you
of the substance of a matter.
B1 68–70 The case is only having a follower of your choosing come to me
so that I might send him to you about it."
B1 70–73 So, chief steward Meru's son Rensi had
a follower of his choosing go to him
so that the peasant might send him about that matter in its entirety.

B1 63–65 R 12,5 adds *m ḫntyt* "upstream" in the first line.

B1 65–67 *ḥr prt m sbꜣ n pr.f r hꜣt* — the *sbꜣ* is the front gate of the wall surrounding the house rather than the door of the house itself; the peasant would not have been allowed inside the chief steward's compound. R 12,7 has *m prt m sbꜣ.f n mꜣꜥm hꜣt* "emerging from his gate of the riverbank and going down," implying that the house lay on the shore of the river.

qꜣqꜣw.f n ꜥrryt — literally, "his barge of the portal"; *ꜥrryt* refers to the entrance of the chief steward's office.

B1 67–68 *swḏꜣ.j jb.k* — literally, "I could make sound your mind": see Essay 25.

pꜣ ḫn n mdt —this phrase, and the synonym *pꜣ ṯꜣz n mdt* in R 13,1, is normally a compound expression meaning "phrase of speech." Here, however, *mdt* is separate, as indicated by the suffix pronoun of *ḥr.s* in B1 70 / R 13,2 and the use of *mdt* alone in B1 72 / R 13,3.

B1 68–70 *zp pw rdjt* — since neither B1 nor R have genitival *n* before *rdjt*, this is not an A *pw* sentence ("it is a case of having") but an A *pw* B sentence: literally, "having … is the case."

rdjt jwt n.j — R 13,2 has *rdjt pr n.j* "having … come out to me."

n ḫrt jb.k — literally, "of what (might be) in your mind": see the note to ShS. 20 *jr r.k* (or *jrr.k*) *m ḫrt jb.k*.

B1 70–73 R 13,2–3 has a couplet in place of B1's tercet:

ꜥḥꜥ.n rdj.[n.f p]r n.f šmsw n ḫrt jb
ꜥḥꜥ.n [hꜣb.n] sw sḫtj pn ḥr mdt [tn] mj qj.s nb
Then he had a follower of choice go out to him.
Then the peasant sent him about that matter in its entirety.

The scribe of R originally wrote *tn* at the end of 13,2 and repeated it at the beginning of 13,3, then noticed the repetition and erased the first *tn*. For *mj qj.s nb*, literally "like all its character," see § 6.7.

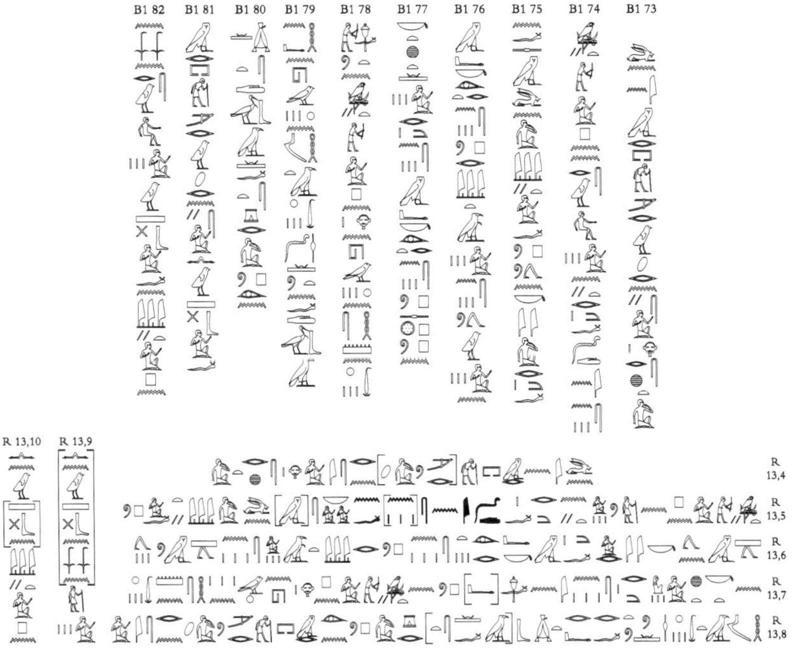

B1 73–74 *wn.jn (j)m(j)-r pr wr zꜣ-mrw rnsj* 4
ḥr srḫt nmtj-nḫt.(w) pn n sr(j)w ntj r gs.f 4
B1 74–75 *ḏd.jn.sn n.f smwn sḫtj.f pw* 4
jw n ky r gs.f 2
B1 76–77 *mj.k jrrt.sn pw r sḫtjw.sn* 2
jww n ktḫt r gs.sn 3
mj.k jrrt.sn pw 1
B1 77–80 *zp pw n ḥsf.tw n nmtj-nḫt.(w) pn* 3
ḥr nh n ḥsmn ḥnꜥ nh n ḥmꜣt 4
wḏ.tw n.f dbꜣ st dbꜣ.f st 3
B1 80–82 *gr pw jr.n (j)m(j)-r pr wr zꜣ-mrw rnsj* 5
nj wšb.f n nn n sr(j)w 3
wšb.f n sḫtj pn 2

B1 73–74 As a result, chief steward Meru's son Rensi
was denouncing that Nemtinakht to the officials who were beside him.
B1 74–75 So, they said to him, "Perhaps he is a peasant of his
who came to another besides him.

B1 76–77 Look, that is what they do to their peasants
who come to others besides them;
look, that is what they do.

B1 77–80 It is a case of that Nemtinakht being punished
for some natron and some salt.
Let him be ordered to replace it and he will replace it."

B1 80–82 What chief steward Meru's son Rensi did was to be quiet;
he did not respond to those officials
or respond to the peasant.

B1 73–74 *srḫt* — literally, "making known": see the note to Kagemni 1,10.

B1 74–75 *jw n ky* — R 13,6 has *šm n ky* "who went to another."

B1 76–77 *sḫtjw.sn jww* — R 13,6 has *sḫtjw.sn šmw* "their peasants who go." R also omits the third line of the tercet, making this a couplet.

B1 77–80 *zp pw n ḥsf.tw* — R 13,7 has *jn ḥsf pw* "Is it (a matter of) punishing?"

wḏ.tw n.f dbꜣ st dbꜣ.f st — R 13,8 has *wḏ.tw r.f rdjt ḏb[ꜣ.f st]* "So, let him be ordered to have him replace it"—literally, "let having him replace it be ordered"; *rdjt* is an infinitive.

B1 81–82 *nj wšb.f ... wšb.f* — this is an unusual construction in which the negative *nj* governs both verbs. R 13,9–10 has two adverb clauses: *[nn wšb n nn n] srjw nn w[šb n] sḫtj pn* "without responding to those officials, without responding to the peasant." The chief steward's "quiet" is an unwillingness to render a verdict (see Parkinson 2012b, 65–66), perhaps only because he intended to deliberate further.

Episode 5 — The First Discourse (B1 83–102; R 14,1–16,8)

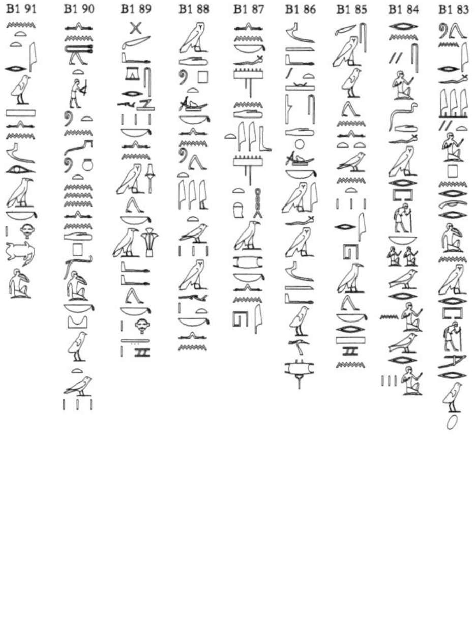

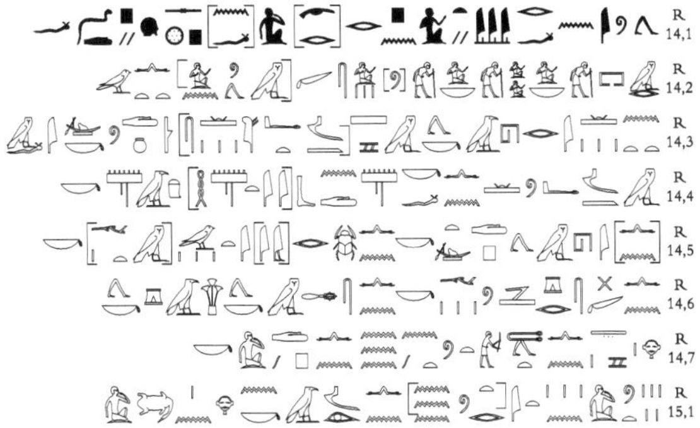

B1 83–84	*jw.jn r.f sḫtj pn r spr*	3
	n (j)m(j)-r pr wr z3-mrw rnsj	3
B1 84–85	*ḏd.f (j)m(j)-r pr wr nb.j*	3
	wr n wrw sšmw n jwtt nt(t)	4
B1 85–86	*jr h3.k r šj n m3ʿt*	3
	sqd.k jm.f m m3ʿw	3
B1 87–88	*nn kf ndbyt ḥt3.k*	2
	nn jhm dpwt.k	2
B1 88–89	*nn jwt jyt m ḫt.k*	3
	nn zw3 sgrgw.k	2
B1 89–90	*nn sḫm.k ḥ3ʿʿ.k ḥr t3*	3
	nn jt tw nwt	2
B1 90–91	*nn dp.k ḏwt nt jtrw*	3
	nn m3.k ḥr snḏ	2

B1 83–84 So, the peasant came to petition
 to chief steward Meru's son Rensi,
B1 84–85 saying, "Chief steward, my lord,
 greatest of the great, leader of everything!
B1 85–86 If you go down to the lake of Maat
 and sail in it with the right wind,
B1 87–88 no full sail of yours will rip open,
 nor will your boat stall;
B1 88–89 no mishap will come in your mast,
 nor will your yards be cut away;
B1 89–90 nor will you go headlong and run up on land,
 nor will a swell take you;
B1 90–91 nor will you taste the evil of the river,
 nor will you see fear's face.

B1 83–84 For the second line, R 14,1 has *r [spr n.f] zp dpj* "to petition to him the first time."

B1 84–85 R 14,2 has *wr nb wrw* "great one, lord of the great."

jwtt nt(t) — "literally, what is not and what is" (§ 22.8) The scribe of B1 has omitted the second *t* of *ntt*.

B1 85–86 *mꜣꜥw* — the determinative in B1 indicates a noun from the adjective *mꜣꜥ* "correct." In R 14,4 the scribe has understood "in correctness."

B1 87–88 *nn kf ndbyt ḥtꜣ.k* — this and the next seven lines all begin with the *nn sḏm.f* construction (§ 18.14). Sails were stitched together from several pieces of cloth; the metaphor here means that a *mꜣꜥw* "right wind" will not cause the seams to rip apart. The second line refers to a lack of wind; the couplet therefore means that the wind will be neither too strong nor too light.

B1 88–89 This couplet moves from the sail to the *sgrgw* "yards" (the two horizontal wood beams to which the sail was lashed) and the mast, to which the yards were tied.

B1 89–90 *sẖm.k ḥꜣꜥꜥ.k* — R 14,6 has *sẖm.k ḥꜣg.k*. The first verb refers to precipitous flight—in this case, a boat out of control. The meaning of the second verb is deduced from the prepositional phrase *ḥr tꜣ* "on land"; R's *ḥꜣg* is also used of a bull pawing the ground with his hoof.

B1 90–91 Both lines probably refer to crocodiles (Parkinson 2012b, 74). For *ḏwt* "evil," R 15,1 has *djwt* "cry" (the spelling is from *djw* "five"), probably from a misunderstanding of *ḏwt* > *dwt* (§ 2.8.4). For R's *mꜣn.k*, see § 18.2.

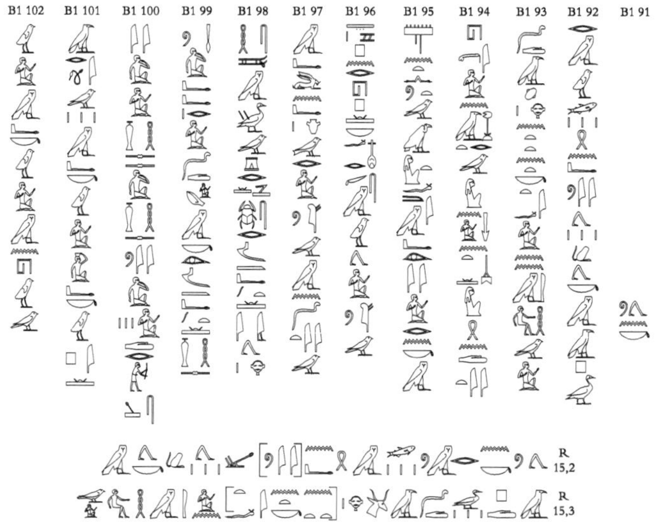

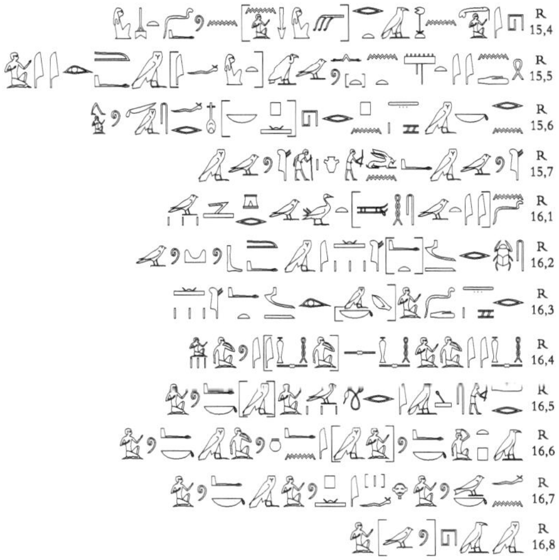

B1 91–93 *jw n.k rmw šnʿy.w* 3
pḥ.k m ꜣp(dw) ḏdꜣ 3
B1 93–94 *ḥr ntt ntk jt n nmḥ* 3
hj n ḫꜣrt 2
B1 94–95 *sn n wḏʿt* 2
šndyt nt jwt(j) mjwt.f 2
B1 95–96 *jmj jry.j rn.k m tꜣ pn* 4
r hp nb nfr 2
B1 96–97 *sšmw šw m ʿwn jb* 3
wr šw m nḏyt 3
B1 98–99 *sḥtm grg sḫpr mꜣʿt* 4
jj ḥr ḫrw dd-r 2
B1 99–100 *ḏd.j sḏm.k jr mꜣʿt* 4
ḥzy ḥzz ḥzyw 3
B1 100–102 *dr sꜣjr mj.k wj ꜣtp.kw* 3
jp wj mj.k wj m nhw 3

B1 91–93 Fish will come to you restrained,
and you will end up with fatted fowl —
B1 93–94 because you are father to the orphan,
husband to the widow,
B1 94–95 brother to the divorced,
and kilt to the motherless.

B1 95–96 Let me make your name in this land
to every good custom:
B1 96–97 a leader free of greed,
a great one free of anything evil,
B1 98–99 a destroyer of falsehood and creator of Maat,
who has come at the voice of the pleader.
B1 99–100 When I speak, may you hear: do Maat,
O blessed one whom the blessed bless!
B1 100–102 Repel need: look, I am loaded.
Take account of me: look, I am in loss."

B1 91–93 *šnꜥy.w* — 3pl stative from *šnꜥj* "restrain"; R 15,2 has *m šnꜥ[yw]* "as restrained" (passive participle). The line means that fish will not dart away from nets.

B1 95–96 This couplet means that the peasant intends to hold up the chief steward as a model by which conduct could be judged. Egypt had no written law code; each case was tried on its own merits and by reference to similar cases in the past (*hp* "custom").

B1 96–97 *nḏyt* — this word, usually translated "baseness," may be an abstract derived from *n(j)-ḏwt* "belonging to evil."

B1 98–99 *dd-r* — literally, "one who gives mouth." R 16,2–3 has replaced this line with *jmj bw-ḏw r tꜣ* "put evil down," probably understanding the preceding line as two imperatives: "annihilate lying, bring about Maat."

B1 99–100 *ḏd.j sḏm.k* — a balanced sentence (§ 25.9).

ḥzy ḥzz ḥzyw — the first and third words are passive participles; the second is a relative *sḏm.f*. The author has deliberately used the same verb for all three forms, a literary device used more than once in this composition.

B1 100–102 R has expanded this couplet to a tercet:

R 16,5–8	*dr sꜣjr.j [m]j.k wj ꜣtp.kw [m] jꜥnw*	Repel my need: look, I am loaded with woe;
	mj.k wj fn.kw ḥr.f	look, I am afflicted with it.
	jp wj mj.k wj m ꜣhw	Take account of me: look, I am in distress.

Episode 6 — Informing the King (B1 102–118; R 16,8–19,7)

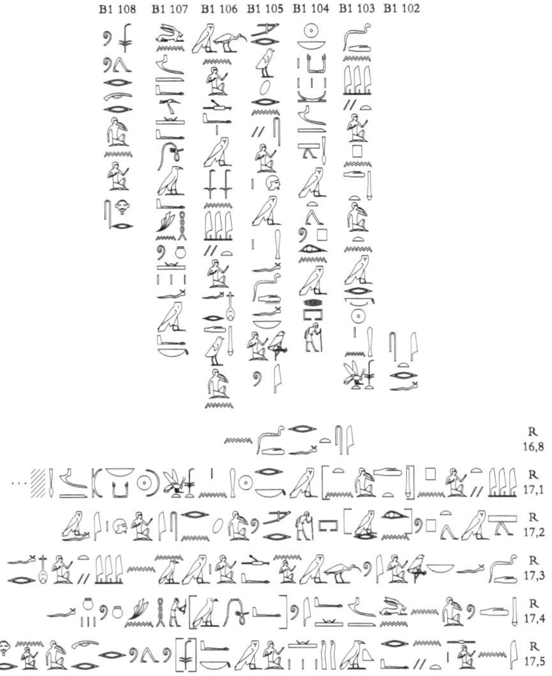

B1 102–104 *jst r.f ḏd.n sḫtj pn mdt tn* 3
m rk ḥm n nswt-bjt NB-KꜢW-Rꜥ *mꜣꜥ ḫrw* 4
B1 104–105 *šmt pw jr.n (j)m(j)-r pr wr zꜣ-mrw rnsj* 5
dp m ḥm.f ḏd.f 2
B1 105–107 *nb.j jw gm.n.j wꜥ m nn n sḫtj* 4
nfr mdw n wn mꜣꜥ 2
B1 107–108 *ꜥwꜣ ḥnw.f* 2
mj.k sw jw r spr n.j ḥr.s 3

B1 102–104 Now, the peasant said this speech
in the time of the Incarnation of Dual King Nebkaure, justified.
B1 104–105 What chief steward Meru's son Rensi did was to go
before His Incarnation, saying,
B1 105–107 "My lord, I have found one of those peasants
who is truly fine of speaking.

B1 107–108 His property was stolen:
look, he has come to petition to me about it."

B1 and R have different versions of this episode.

B1 102–104 *NB-KꜢW-Rꜥ* — a king of Dyn. X, ca. 2040 BC. R 17,1 has *NB-KꜢ-Rꜥ*.

B1 105–107 *nn n sḫtj* — i.e., the peasantry as a social group (Parkinson 2012b, 87).

B1 107–108 For the first line, R 17,4–5 has *jw [ꜥwꜢ] ḥnw.f jn z(j) ntj r ꜥqꜢ.j* "his property has been stolen by a man who affects my (reputation for) straightness"; *ntj r ꜥqꜢ.j* means literally, "who pertains to my straightness." Note the difference between passive *ꜥwꜢ* in B1, stating a simple past event, and *jw [ꜥwꜢ]* in R, reporting the event from the standpoint of the moment of speaking (see § 10.3).

mj.k sw jw — the verb is the 3ms stative of the stem *jj*, often written *jw* (for *j.w*).

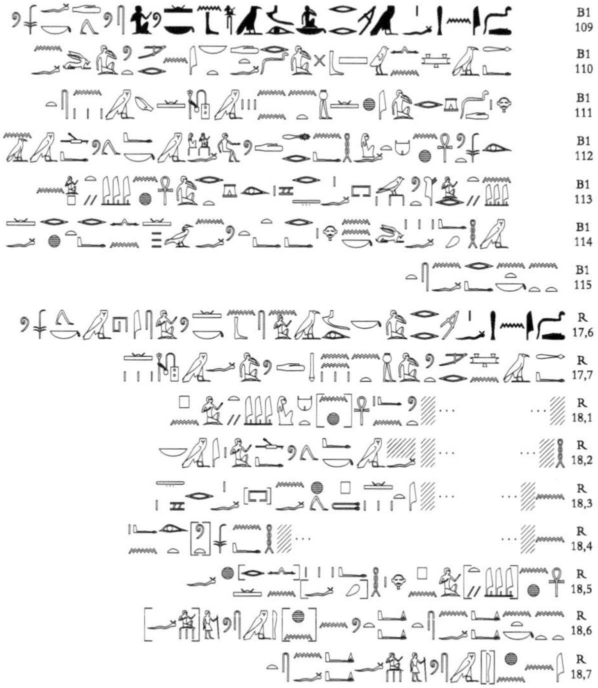

B1 109 ***ḏd.jn ḥm.f*** 2
m mrr.k mꜢ.j snb.kw 3
B1 109–10 *swdf.k sw ꜥꜢ* 2
nn wšb r ḏdt.f nbt 3

B1 110–11 *jn mwrt wn.f ḥr ḏd gr* 4
jḫ jn.t(w) n.n m zḫꜣ sḏm.n st 3
B1 112–13 *jr swt ꜥnḫ ḥjmt.f ḥnꜥ ẖrdw.f* 3
mj.k jw wꜥ m nꜣ n sḫtj 3
r šwt pr.f r tꜣ 3
B1 113–15 *jr grt ꜥnḫ sḫtj pn m ḥꜥw.f* 3
wnn.k ḥr rdjt dj.tw n.f ꜥqw 4
nn rdjt rḫ.f ntt ntk rdj n.f st 4

B1 109 **So, His Incarnation said,**
"As you love to see me healthy,
B1 109–10 you should delay him here
without answering anything he says,
B1 110–11 so that he will keep speaking further;
then it should be brought to us in writing so that we may hear it.
B1 112–13 But see to the life of his woman and children.
Look, one of those peasants comes
only about the total emptiness of his house.
B1 113–15 Also, see to the life of that peasant himself:
you shall be having rations given to him
without letting him know that you are the one who gave them to him."

B1 109–11 The indentation of lines 109–14 is occupied by the short column B1 108.

m mrr.k mꜣ.j — see § 21.9. R 17,6 has *mrr.k mꜣn.j*: see §§ 25.8, 13.3.2c.

swdf.k sw — R 17,6 has *sjhm.k sw* "you should detain him."

jn mrwt wn.f ḥr ḏd gr — literally, "for the sake of him being speaking more"; *jn* is a spelling of the preposition *n* at the beginning of a clause. R 17,6–18,1 collapses the two couplets of B1 into one:

sjhm.k sw ꜥꜣ
n mrwt jn.t(w) n.n mdw.f m zḫꜣ [sḏm.n st]
you should detain him here
so that his speaking is brought to us in writing and we might hear it.

B1 112–13 *jr swt ꜥnḫ ḥjmt.f* — literally, "act so that his woman might live." R 18,1–2 has *[jr s]wt ꜥ n ꜥnḫ ḥjmt sḫtj pn ḥ[nꜥ ẖrdw].f* "But make a document for the life of that peasant's wife and his children."

mj.k jw — the first clause of an emphatic sentence; the rheme is the last line of the tercet.

r šwt pr.f r tꜣ — literally, "with respect to the emptiness of his house to the ground." The king means that peasants of the Wadi Natrun typically come to the Nile Valley to trade for grain when their own stores of grain are exhausted.

R 18,2–4 has a slightly different version of the last two lines of the tercet:

mj.k jw wꜥ jm nb n [sḫtjw]
ptḫ.n.f [pr].f r tꜣ
Look, every one of the peasants comes
only when he has let his house fall to the ground.

B1 113–15 *m ḥꜥw.f* — literally, "in his limbs."

wnn.k ḥr rdjt — the verb *wnn* here allows a SUBJECT–*ḥr-sḏm* construction to serve as the first clause of an emphatic sentence (§ 25.12); the rheme is the *nn rdjt* clause.

R's version (18,4–7) expands this final tercet of the king's speech into two couplets with lines taken from the next section of this episode in B1 (B1 113–17):

ḥnꜥ s[wt] jrt ꜥ n ꜥnḫ n [sḫtj] pn ḥr ḥꜥw.[f]
[n]n [r]ḫ.f ntt ntk dd n.f st
dd.tw n [ḫ]nmsw.[f]
jn ḫnmsw.f dd n.f st
But also making a document for this peasant's life himself
without his knowing that you are the one who gives it to him:
one should give to his friends,
and his friends are the ones who should give it to him.

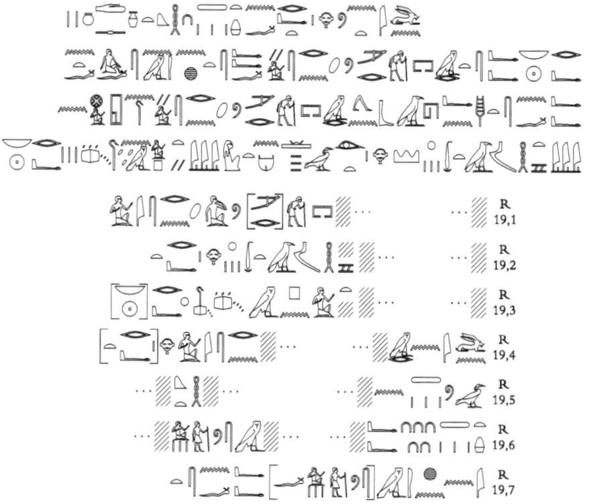

B1 115
B1 116
B1 117
B1 118
R 19,1
R 19,2
R 19,3
R 19,4
R 19,5
R 19,6
R 19,7

B1 115–16 *wn.jn.tw ḥr rdjt n.f t 10* 3
ḥnqt ds 2 rꜥ nb 2
B1 116–17 *dd st (j)m(j)-r pr wr zꜣ-mrw rnsj* 4
dd.f st n ḫnms.f 2
ntf dd n.f st 2

B1 117–18 *ꜥḥꜥ.n hꜣb.n (j)m(j)-r pr wr zꜣ-mrw rnsj* 5
n ḥqꜣ-ḥwt n sḫt-ḥmꜣt 2
B1 118 *ḥr jrt ꜥqw n ḥjmt sḫtj pn* 2
m jtj ḥqꜣt 3 rꜥ nb 2

B1 115–16 So, he was being given ten (loaves of) bread
and two jars of beer each day.
B1 116–17 Whenever chief steward Meru's son Rensi gave it,
he would give it to his friend,
and he was the one who would give it to him.
B1 117–18 Then chief steward Meru's son Rensi sent word
to the mayor of Salt Field
B1 118 about making rations for the wife of the peasant
of three heqat of barley every day.

B1 115–17 This couplet and tercet are omitted in R.

dd st … dd.f st — a balanced sentence (§ 25.9).

ḥnꜥ swt jrt is literally, "But together with making"; *rḫ.f* is an infinitive. The first line of the second couplet is emphatic, with the prepositional phrase as the rheme.

B1 117–18 *ḥqꜣ-ḥwt* — literally, "enclosure ruler," the man in charge of a walled compound (including a walled town).

jtj ḥqꜣt 3 rꜥ nb — B1 uses the older notation, in which strokes represent individual heqat (§ 9.7.4). This is an extremely generous allotment, amounting to ninety heqat a month. The amount is intended to demonstrate that the king was not entirely heartless in detaining the peasant. In R 19,3, which uses the later convention described in § 9.7.4, the amount is a more realistic, but still generous, one heqat a day.

R 19,4–7 This version adds a tercet and couplet:

wn.jn (j)m(j)-r [pr wr zꜣ-mrw] rnsj
ḥr [rdjt] ꜥqw n [sḫtj pn
m] ḥnqt [ds 10] t 50
dd.[f st n ḫn]msw.[f]
jn ḫnm[sw.f] dd n.f st
So, chief steward Meru's son Rensi
was giving rations to the peasant
of ten jars of beer and fifty bread.
He would give it to his friends,
and his friends were the ones who would give it to him.

This reflects the king's orders in R 18,4–7 and corresponds to the two couplets of B1 115–17. Note that the ration here is five times that in B1 (Parkinson 2012b, 96).

Episode 7 — The Second Discourse (B1 119–170; R 20,1–28,8)

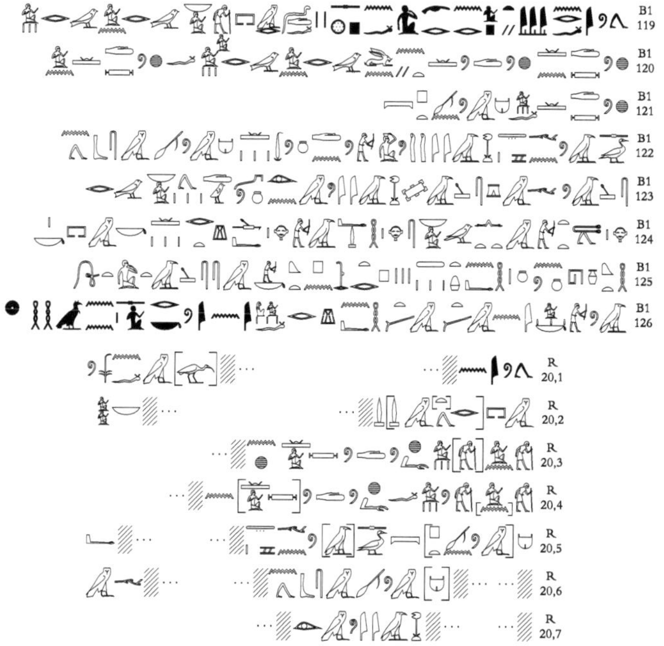

B1 119 ***jw.jn r.f sḫtj pn r spr n.f zp 2*** 4
ḏd.f (j)m(j)-r pr wr nb.j 3
B1 119–20 *wr n wrw* 2
ḫwd n ḫwdw 2
B1 120–21 *ntj wn wr n wrw.f* 4
ḫwd n ḫwdw.f 2
B1 121–22 *ḥmw n pt* 2
zꜣw n tꜣ 2
ḫꜣy fꜣ wdnw 3
B1 122–23 *ḥmw m sbn* 2
sꜣw m gsꜣ 2
ḫꜣy m jr nwdw 3
B1 123–24 *nb wr.(w) ḥr jtt m jwtt nb.s* 4
ḥr ḥꜥḏꜣ ḥr wꜥ 2

B1 124–26 *ẖrwt.k m pr.k* 2
ḥnqt hnw 1 ḥnʿ t 3 2
ptr pnqt.k m ssꜣt twꜣw.k 3
B1 126 *jn m(w)t m(w)t ḥnʿ ẖrw.f* 3
jn jw.k r z(j) n nḥḥ 2

B1 119 **So, the peasant came to appeal to him twice,**
saying, "Chief steward, my lord!
B1 119–20 Greatest of the great,
richest of the rich,
B1 120–21 for whose great there is one greater;
for whose rich, one richer!
B1 121–22 Rudder of the sky,
beam of the earth,
measuring-line that carries the weight!
B1 122–23 Rudder, don't drift!
Beam, don't tilt!
Measuring-line, don't make deviation!
B1 123–24 Lord great from taking what has no owner,
from plundering on his own!
B1 124–26 Your needs are in your house.
One hin of beer and three bread:
what is that as your dole in sating your dependants?
B1 126 It is a mortal who dies as well as his underlings—
are you to be eternal?

In his second discourse, the peasant moves from the plane of the general to more specific comments aimed at the chief steward, initially laudatory, then increasingly critical. After its opening, the discourse is interrupted by the chief steward before concluding.

B1 119 *zp 2* — literally, "time two": the number is cardinal rather than ordinal.

R 20,1–2 has a tercet, with the second line added: *[g]m.n.f sw m pr[t m ḏꜣ]ḏꜣ[t]* "and he found him emerging from the council."

B1 119–20 *wr n wrw* — see § 6.8.

B1 120–21 *ntj wn wr n wrw.f* — literally, "who there is a great one for his great ones."

B1 121–23 The chief steward is equated with the rudder of the Sun's boat, which guides (*mꜣʿ*) the boat, with a beam standing upright on earth, and with the line that holds a plumb-bob, used to measure vertical straightness. R is lost after this point until the end of the discourse.

B1 123–24 This couplet is best understood as a vocative, addressed to the chief steward, rather than a statement ("a great lord is taking"). As such, *wr* is a 3ms stative, used as an unmarked relative after the vocative *nb* (compare the use of the *sḏm.f* in this function, § 22.16). This couplet is anticipatory to the stinginess implied by the tercet that follows.

B1 124–26 *ḫrwt.k* — a plural nisbe. The term is used to refer to necessary supplies (ancestor of Coptic **ϩⲣⲉ** "food"). The line means "your house contains whatever you might need."

ḥnqt hnw 1 ḥnꜥ t 3 — the liquid measure is equivalent to half a quart (§ 9.7.4). This is meant to be understood as the chief steward's daily dole to each of his dependants, and as quite miserly: compare the amount given to the peasant in B1 115–16.

ptr pnqt.k — literally, "what is that which you bail out." The image is of tossing out the dole like water bailed from a boat.

B1 126 This couplet means "you are just as mortal as your underlings, and therefore deserving of no better or worse": *jn m(w)t m(w)t* is literally, "it is a dier who dies." The second line is rhetorical, since the chief steward is not going to live forever. The reason for the use of red ink is unclear; perhaps it marks where the scribe resumed writing after a hiatus.

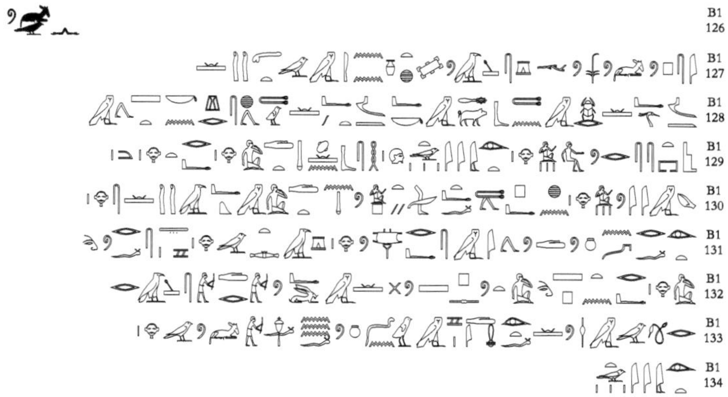

B1 126–28	***nj jw*** *js pw jwsw gsꜣ.(w)*	3
	tḫ nnm.(w)	2
	mt mꜣꜥ ḫpr.(w) m ṯnbḫ	4
B1 128–29	*mj.k mꜣꜥt wṯḫ.s ḫr.k*	3
	nš.t(j) m jst.s	2
B1 129	*sr(j)w ḥr jrt jyt*	3
	dp-ḥsb n mdt ḥr rdjt hr gs	4
B1 130–31	*sḏmyw ḥr ḫnp jtt.f*	3
	sjꜣtj pw n mdt m ꜥqꜣ.s	3
	ḥr jrt r.f nwdw jm.s	3

B1 131–32 *rdj ṯꜣw ḥr gꜣt ḥr tꜣ* 4
srfw ḥr rdjt nšp.tw 3
B1 132–33 *pzšw m ꜥwnw* 2
dr sꜣjr m wḏ jr.t(w).f 4
B1 133–34 *dmj m wḏnw.f* 2
ẖsf jw ḥr jrt jyt 3

B1 126–28 "**For it is wrong**, a crossbar that has tilted,
a plumb-bob that has gone off,
one truly precise that has become a stray.
B1 128–29 Look, Maat flees under you,
alienated from its place.
B1 129 Officials are doing a wrong,
the standard of speech is being put aside.
B1 130–31 The judge{s} is snatching what he would take:
he is one who cuts short a speech from its accuracy,
deviating from it.
B1 131–32 The air-giver is causing need on earth,
the warmer is making one pant;
B1 132–33 the apportioner is an appropriator,
the dispeller of need is one who orders it made;
B1 133–34 the harbor is in its torrent:
he who should bar wrong is doing a wrong."

B1 126–28 *nj jw js pw jwsw gsꜣ.(w)* — as written, this line is an A *pw* B sentence meaning, "a crossbar that tilts is not a wrong." Since this is at variance with Maat, the initial negative must be a spelling of the particle *jn*, used here to emphasize the following *jw*; *js* then marks the sentence as subordinate to the preceding statement(s). *jwsw* is the term for the crossbar of the scale (), which should be completely level to ensure parity between the two things being weighed. The term *jw* generally means "wrong" as an abstract concept, as opposed to *jyt* (e.g., B1 129/134), which denotes a specific instance of "wrong."

gsꜣ.(w) ... *nnm.(w)* ... *ḫpr.(w)* — 3ms statives used as unmarked relative clauses after undefined antecedents (§ 22.11).

tḫ — the plumb-bob serves to ensure that the crossbar is precisely at right angles to the upright, and that the two pans are level when empty.

mt mꜣꜥ — a *mtr* (> *mtj*) is a "witness," here probably referring not to a person but to a standard by which something can be measured.

B1 129 *dp-ḥsb n mdt* — see the note to Ptahhotep 42–50. The phrase here means a standard by which truth can be distinguished from falsehood.

ḥr rdjt ḥr gs — the infinitive here probably has passive sense (i.e., literally, "is upon the putting on the side"), since the subject is not an active agent: it is not the "standard" that "puts aside," but those who misuse it.

B1 130–31 *sḏmyw ḥr ḫnp jtt.f* — the plural is probably an error, since the 3ms suffix pronoun can only refer to a singular antecedent. Despite its spelling with only one *t*,  is probably the feminine relative *sḏm.f*; a *sḏm.f* ("when he takes") makes less sense, since judges should not "take" at all.

sjꜣtj pw n mdt m ꜥqꜣ.s — literally, "he is a shortener of speech from its accuracy." *sjꜣtj* is a nisbe from the verb *sjꜣṯ* "shorten"; the determinative shows that a person is meant. The verb is used of "shorting" an amount of grain, so that the measurer can take some for himself (see B1 135–36). The line here means that the judge cuts short the plaintiff's speech, so that he is not able to represent himself accurately.

B1 130–31 *rdj ṯꜣw ... srfw* — the king and officials were thought of as "giving air" to supplicants. *srf* means "to warm"; the image here is one of excess, causing one to pant from heat.

B1 133–34 *dmj m wḏnw.f* — the suffix pronoun may refer to the wrongdoer in the previous lines but more likely refers to *dmj*. *wḏnw* is a strong, destructive current; the image here is of a harbor, which should be a place of refuge, subjected to it.

 B1 134
B1 135

B1 134–35 ***ḏd.jn (j)m(j)-r pr wr zꜣ-mrw rnsj*** 4
jn ꜥꜣt pw n.k jmy ḥr jb.k r jt tw šmsw.j 5

B1 134–35 **So, chief steward Meru's son Rensi said,**
"Are your things more important to you than my follower robbing you?"

Prompted perhaps by the critical reference to his own riches, the chief steward interrupts to ask whether the peasant is more concerned with his property or with justice against Nemtinakht. The interruption also serves to relieve the flow of the second discourse, which is the longest of the nine.

B1 134–35 The second line is an A *pw* B sentence marked as a question by initial *jn*. For *n.k jmy* "yours," used here as a noun, see § 8.10. The statement following *r* is an unmarked noun clause with the *sḏm.f* (§ 21.9); the verb *jṯj* can mean "rob" when used with the object of a person (*tw* "you"); *ḥr jb.k* is more literally "in your mind." The scribe has written only one seated man after *šmsw*, which is either the determinative or the 1s suffix pronoun.

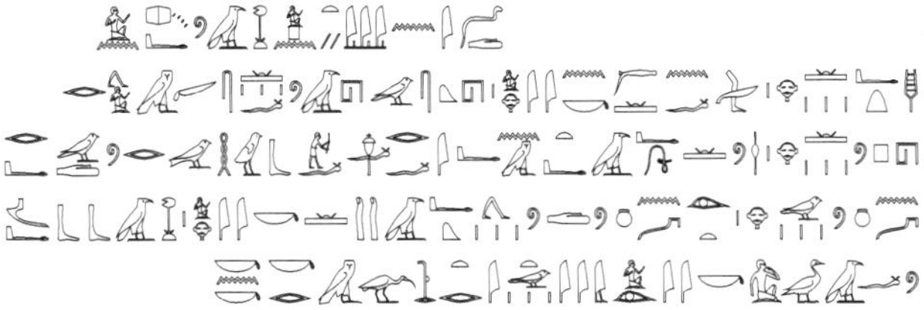

B1 135
B1 136
B1 137
B1 138
B1 139

B1 135–36 *ḏd.jn sḫtj pn* 2
ḫꜣw n ꜥḥꜥw ḥr sjꜣt n.f 4
mḥ.n ky ḥr hqs ḥꜣw.f 4
B1 136–37 *sšm r hpw ḥr wḏ ꜥwꜣt* 3
nmj jr.f ḫsf.f bw ḥwrw 3
B1 137–38 *dr nw ḥr jrt nwdw* 3
ꜥqꜣ ky ḥr ḫꜣbb 3
B1 138–39 *wfꜣ ky jr jyt* 4
j(n) tr gm.k r.k n.k 2

B1 135–36 So, the peasant said,
"The weigher of piles is shorting for himself,
another has become full by cheating his neighbors.
B1 136–37 The leader according to custom is ordering robbery:
who then will bar poverty?
B1 137–38 The dispeller of deviance is deviating,
another is accurate by being crooked,
B1 138–39 another connives with the wrongdoer:
so, do you find anything of yourself in this?

Instead of answering the chief steward's question, the peasant continues with his tirade, elaborating on the theme set in the last three stanzas of his speech, the perversion of responsibilities.

B1 138–39 *j(n) tr gm.k r.k n.k* — literally, "with respect to yourself (*r.k*), do you find for yourself?," meaning "do you recognize anything of yourself in these descriptions?" The scribe has omitted the *n* of the initial particle *jn*; while *jtr* can be a spelling of *tr*, that particle is enclitic and cannot stand at the beginning of a clause.

B1 139
B1 140
B1 141
B1 142

B1 139–40	***ḥ(w)ꜥ ḫsf ȝw*** *jyt*	4
	jw bj(ȝ) r jst.f nt sf	4
B1 140–41	*wḏ r.f pw jr n jrr r rdjt jr.f*	5
	dwȝ n.f nṯr pw ḥr jrrt.f	2
B1 141–42	*njt ḫt pw dp ꜥ st.t(w)*	2
	wḏ ḫt pw n nb ḥnt	2
B1 142–43	*ḥȝ ȝ ȝt sḥtm*	1
	spnꜥ m rwj.k	2
B1 143–44	*ꜥnd m ȝpdw.k*	2
	ḫbȝ m qbḥw.k	2
B1 144–45	*pr mȝw šp.w{t} sḏmw sḫ.w*	5
	sšmw ḫpr.(w) m stnmw	3

B1 139–40 “**Brief is punishment and long** a wrong:
  character should return to its place of yesterday.
B1 140–41 So, ‘Do for the doer to make him do’ is the command:
  it means thanking him for what he does;
B1 141–42 it means parrying something before one shoots;
  it means ordering for the master of assignment.
B1 142–43 Oh, for a moment of destruction! —
  overturning in your clap-net,
B1 143–44 decrease in your bird-catch,
  carnage in your waterfowl-catch!
B1 144–45 The seer comes out blind and the hearer deaf,
  for the leader has become a misleader.”

B1 139–40 The red ink may reflect a change of subject. The couplet means that there is too little prevention and too much wrongdoing, and the last line expresses a wish for a return to traditional values.

B1 140–42 The scribe originally wrote *jrt* after *wḏ r.f pw*, then changed it to *jr* by erasing the *t*. The original sentence would mean, “So, doing … is the command.” This and the next couplet are an Egyptian version of the Golden Rule, “Do unto others as you would have them do unto you.”

njt — the initial 𓈖 is a biliteral *nj* here, followed by two phonetic complements. The verb comes from the negative particle *nj* and means basically "reject": the sense here is of preventing an action before it happens.

wḏ ḫt pw — literally, "it is commanding something": the sense is reciprocation.

B1 142–44 In these two couplets, the peasant wishes for the chief steward to experience loss, so that he will better understand the peasant's plight. Wildfowl were caught in a *rwj*, a net spread open on the ground and pulled shut when birds landed on it; the line wishes for a *spnʿ* "causing to capsize" of the net, so that the birds escape.

B1 144–45 *šp.w{t}* — the scribe has added a superfluous *t* below the determinative, perhaps from a misreading of the hieratic version of the determinative 𓁹.

sšmw … stnmw — the verbs from which these nouns are derived mean basically "cause to go" and "cause to get lost."

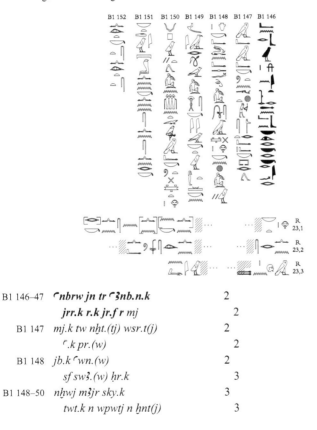

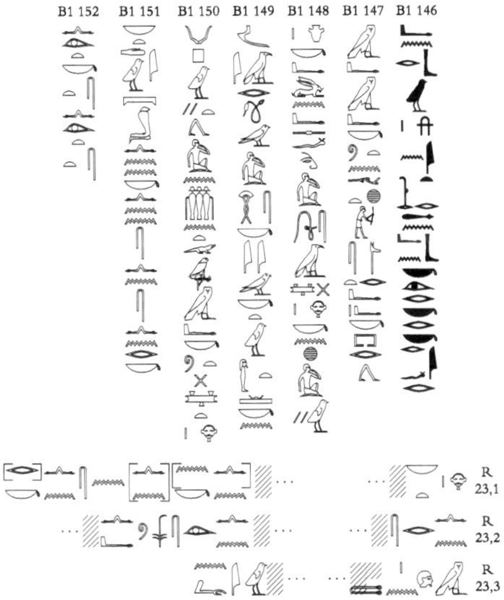

B1 146–47 ***ʿnbrw jn tr ʿꜣnb.n.k*** 2
***jrr.k r.k jr.f r** mj* 2
B1 147 *mj.k tw nḫt.(tj) wsr.t(j)* 2
ʿ.k pr.(w) 2
B1 148 *jb.k ʿwn.(w)* 2
sf swꜣ.(w) ḥr.k 3
B1 148–50 *nḫwj mꜣjr sky.k* 3
twt.k n wpwtj n ḫnt(j) 3

B1 150–52 *mj.k tw sw3.t(j) ḥr nbt-jdw* 2
nn n.k nn n.s nn (r).s nn r.k 4
nj jrt.k st nj jrt.(s) st 2

B1 146–47 **"Basket, have you closed shut?**
What **then are you good for**?
B1 147 Look, you are forceful and powerful,
your arm active,
B1 148 but your mind has become greedy
and kindness has passed you by.
B1 148–50 How pitiful is the needy one you wipe out!
You resemble the messenger of Khenti.
B1 150–52 Look, you have surpassed the Lady of Pestilence:
not for you, not for her; not against you, not against her;
you have not yet done it, she has not yet done it.

The peasant now begins berating the chief steward for his apparent lack of concern for his plight.

B1 146–47 *ꜥnbrw ... ꜥ3nb.n.k* — the verb is probably a spelling of the later verb *ꜥnb* "close shut," chosen here because of its alliteration with the noun — note that in the Middle Kingdom, *3* is a kind of *l* or *r* (§ 2.4): thus, *ꜥnbr* ~ *ꜥlnb* / *ꜥrnb*. Compare the similar sound-play in B1 162–63.

jrr.k r.k jr.f r mj — another alliterative line, literally "so (*jr.f*), as far as you're concerned (*r.k*), to what (end) do you act?" (emphatic sentence: § 25.5).

B1 147 *ꜥ.k pr.(w)* — literally, "your arm has emerged": see the note to Sin. B 52.

B1 148–50 *ḫnt(j)* — a god associated with crocodiles, and therefore a manifestation of rapacity.

B1 150–52 *nbt-jdw* is an epithet of Sekhmet, goddess of violence. The second and third lines of the tercet equate the chief steward with her; they mean, "whatever can be said for or against her can also be said of you, and you haven't done anything she hasn't done" (for the last line, see § 19.14). In R 23,2–3, the last line is reconfigured as the first of a couplet, possibly to be restored as *[nn jr.k sf] nn jr.s sw* "You will not do kindness, she will not do it"; the second line may have been *nj dj.[t(w) k js] m dp n [rm]ṯ [r] wjn* "you have not been placed at the head of people in order to reject" (cf. Parkinson 2012b, 129).

B1 152

B1 152–53	*sf nb-t*	2
	nẖt n ẖnr	2
B1 153–54	*twt ṯꜣwt n jwt(j) ẖwt.f*	3
	ẖnp ẖwt jn ẖnj	2
B1 154–55	*zp bjn.(w) (n) jwt(j) šwjw*	3
	nn r.f ṯs.tw jm.f	2
	ḥ(j)ḥ(j) n.f pw	1

B1 152–53 “A bread-owner should be kind:
force is for the deprived.

B1 153–54 Stealing is fit for the one with no things,
and snatching things by the deprived.

B1 154–55 The lot of the have-not and empty is bad.
So, he should not be blamed:
he is one who seeks for himself.”

B1 154–55 *zp bjn.(w) (n) jwt(j) šwjw* — for *jwt(j)* see § 22.8; the scribe has omitted the indirect genitive before it. R 23,6 has *zp bgs.(w) n jwt(j) šwtyw* “the case of the have-not and empty has become injured”; *šwtyw* is probably a noun formed from *šwt* “emptiness.”

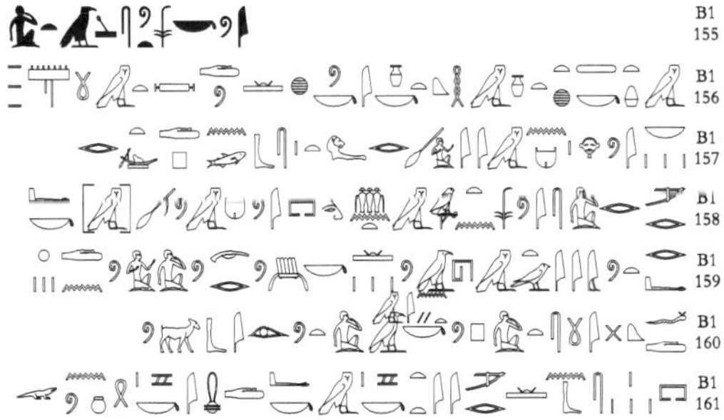

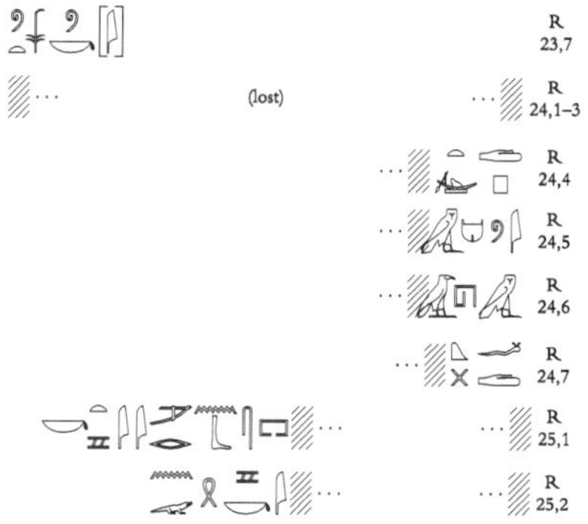

B1 155–57 ***jw.k swt sꜣ.t(j)*** *m t.k* 2
tḫ.t(j) m ḥnqt.k 2
jw.k ḫwd.t(j) m šsrw nbw 3
B1 157–58 *jw ḥr n ḥmy r ḥꜣt* 2
sbn dpt r mrr.s 3
B1 158–59 *jw nswt m ḫnt* 2
jw ḥmw m ʿ.k 2
rdj.tw jyt m hꜣw.k 3
B1 159–60 *ꜣw sprw wdn fdq.(w)* 4
jšst pw ntj jm kꜣ.tw 3
B1 160–61 *jr jbw snb mryt.k* 4
mj.k dmj.k šn.w 2

B1 155–57 **But you are sated** with your bread
and drunk with your beer;
you are rich in all kinds of fine linen.
B1 157–58 The helmsman's face is to the front,
but the boat glides as it likes.
B1 158–59 The king is forward,
the rudder is in your hand,
but a wrong is put in your vicinity.
B1 159–60 Arrival is long and the anchor has parted;
'What is that which is there?,' one will say,
B1 160–61 'Make shelter, your shore is healthy':
but look, your harbor is crocodile-infested."

Continuing to berate the chief steward, the peasant now turns to nautical metaphors, beginning with a couplet that contrasts with the preceding tercet.

B1 155–57 *ḥwd.t(j)* — the scribe has miscopied this word: the bookroll is an error for 𓎛, and the hieratic determinative is misshapen.

B1 158–59 This tercet identifies the chief steward as responsible for the king's well-being: he steers the "ship of state" while the king sits forward. The last line means that the placid voyage is threatened by "a wrong"—namely, the one perpetrated on the peasant and as yet not redressed.

B1 159–60 *sprw* — despite its spelling as the word meaning "petitioner," the nautical metaphors that precede and follow, as well as the adjective *ꜣw* "long," indicate that this word should be *spr* "arrival"; the scribe was evidently influenced by the frequent use of *spr* "petition" in this text. The clause means that the voyage has been long.

wdn fdq.(w) — the first word is written as a noun rather than an adjective, indicating that *fdq* is the stative rather than an infinitival subject. The clause may mean that the rope holding the ship's anchor, a stone weight (*wdn*), has come loose, requiring the ship to be beached.

jšst pw ntj jm — the scribe originally omitted the last two words, then added them above the line. The question is probably voiced by one of the sailors, looking at the shore, and anticipates the second line of the next couplet.

B1 160–61 The first line is probably a comment by another sailor. The couplet means that, while everything looks to be well, hidden dangers lurk (the peasant's unredressed plight). The word *mryt* has a superfluous second *t*. The last word, *šn.w*, means "ringed"; the determinative adds the additional notion "by crocodiles."

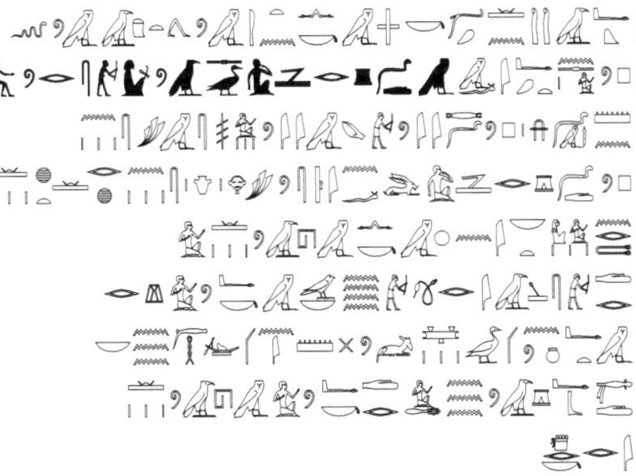

B1 162
B1 163
B1 164
B1 165
B1 166
B1 167
B1 168
B1 169
B1 170

R 25,3
R 25,4
R 25,5

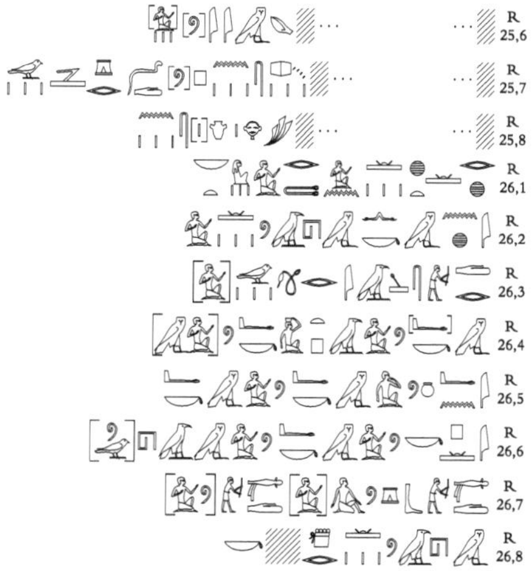

B1 162–63	*ꜥqꜣ ns.k jm.k tnmw*	4
	tꜣmw pw n z(j) ꜥt jm.f	4
	m ḏd grg zꜣw sr(j)w	4
B1 164–65	*mnḏm pw ꜥḏyw sḏmyw*	3
	sm.sn pw ḏd grg	2
	wn.f js.w ḥr jb.sn	3
B1 165–66	*rḫ ḫt n rmṯ nbt*	2
	jn ḫm.k m hꜣw.j	2
B1 167–68	*dr sꜣjr-n-mw nb*	2
	mj.k wj ẖr mjtnw jw	2
B1 168–70	*mjn mḥ nb šd bgꜣw*	2
	ẖdr.kw m hꜣw jr ḏr.k	3

B1 162–63 “Let your tongue be straight, so that you don’t get lost:
that part of a man is his bane.
Don’t tell lies; beware of officials.
B1 164–65 Judges are a winnowing basket,
telling lies is their chaff:
it will be light in their mind.
B1 165–66 Most knowledgeable of all people,
are you unaware of my circumstance?
B1 167–68 Dispeller of all water-need,
look, I am on the route of stranding.
B1 168–70 Moorer of all on water, rescue the shipwrecked,
for I am anguished in circumstance at your side.”

The peasant ends his second discourse with a "teaching" on lying and a plea to the chief steward for help.

B1 162–63 The motivation for the use of red ink in one line is not clear.

tꜣmw — this word is otherwise unknown; the translation is a guess (Parkinson 2012b, 139) based on the determinative and context. The word was clearly chosen for its similarity to *tnmw* in the first line; R 25,3 has *tꜣrmw*, suggesting an alternation between *n* (*tnmw*) and *l* (*tlmw*). In the second line, *ꜥt jm.f* "part of him" undoubtedly refers to the tongue. Note the reversal of the two key words in both lines: *ns* ... *tnmw* and *tlmw* ... *ꜥt jm.f.*

B1 164–65 This tercet is based on the agricultural image of winnowing, in which threshed grain is separated from its husks (*sm* "chaff") by tossing it in the air from a basket (*mnḏm*): the lighter chaff blows away, while the seeds fall back into the basket. In the metaphor, officials who serve as judges are the basket and lying is the chaff, which they can easily distinguish by its lightness (*js.w ḥr jb.sn* "light in their mind").

B1 167–70 The last two couplets revert to a nautical metaphor. *sꜣjr-n-mw* is apparently a compound phrase, determined as a unit by the "bad bird" (Parkinson 2012b, 142); *ẖr mjtnw jw* means literally, "under the route of stranding," probably as an expression of possession (§ 8.2.15). For the first couplet, R 26,3–6 substitutes two repeated from the end of the first discourse.

Episode 8 — The Third Discourse (B1 170–215; R 27,1–31,8)

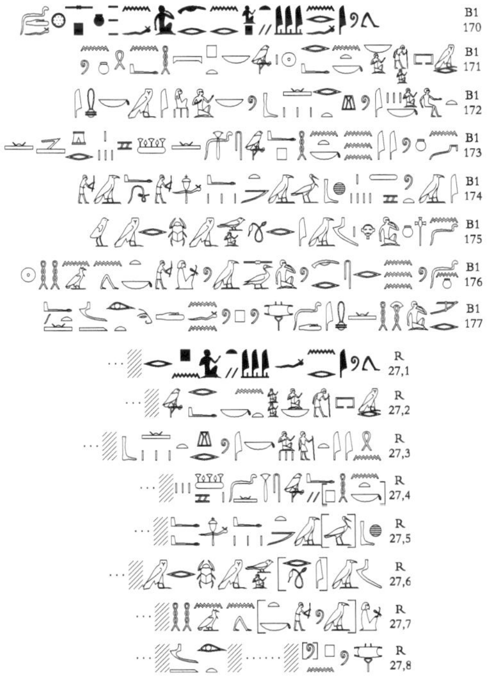

B1 170–71 ***jw.jn r.f sẖtj pn r spr n.f 3nw zp*** 4
ḏd.f (j)m(j)-r pr wr nb.j 3
B1 171–73 *ntk rꜥ nb pt ḥnꜥ šnwt.k* 3
jw ẖrwt bw-nb jm.k mj nwy 3
B1 173–74 *ntk ḥꜥp(j) swꜣḏ šꜣw* 3
grg jꜣwt ḫbꜣt 3
B1 174–76 *ḫsfꜥwꜣ nḏ ḥr mꜣjr* 4
m ḫpr m wḏnw r sprw 3
B1 176–77 *zꜣw tkn nḥḥ mr wꜣḥ* 4
mj ḏd ṯꜣw pw n fnd jrt mꜣꜥt 4

B1 170–71 **So, the peasant came to appeal to him a third time,**
saying, "Chief steward, my lord!
B1 171–73 You are the Sun, lord of the sky, with your entourage,
what everyone has is from you, like the waters.
B1 173–74 You are the Inundation, who makes green the fields
and furnishes the hacked mounds.
B1 174–76 Bar robbery, be concerned with the needy,
don't become a torrent against the petitioner.
B1 176–77 Beware of continuity's nearness; desire to last,
as is said, 'Doing Maat is air for the nose.'

In the first part of his third discourse, the peasant compares the chief steward's attributes to those of gods.

B1 171–73 *mj nwy* — see the note to ShS. 35–36 *nwyt jm.f nt mḥ 8*. This is a reference to the limitlessness of the chief steward's potential benevolence.

B1 173–74 *ḥꜥp(j)* — this continues the imagery of the last couplet's *nwy*.

grg jꜣwt ḫbꜣt — the basic sense of *grg* is "set up and make operational." The verb *ḫbꜣ* "hack up" usually has destructive connotations, but it can also refer to tilling, which may be the sense here: the inundation supplies needed nutrients to tilled soil.

B1 174–76 *nḏ ḥr* usually has the connotation "ask about" and is often used with reference to inquiring about someone's condition (see the note to Sin. B 166 *nḏ.j ḫrt*). Here, "asking about" implies concern for the needy.

m ḫpr m wḏnw — this reprises the theme of the previous two couplets. The peasant asks that the chief steward's "waters" be beneficial rather than destructive.

B1 176–77 This couplet reminds the chief steward to consider his afterlife and posthumous reputation. Two pages of R (28–29) are lost after this couplet.

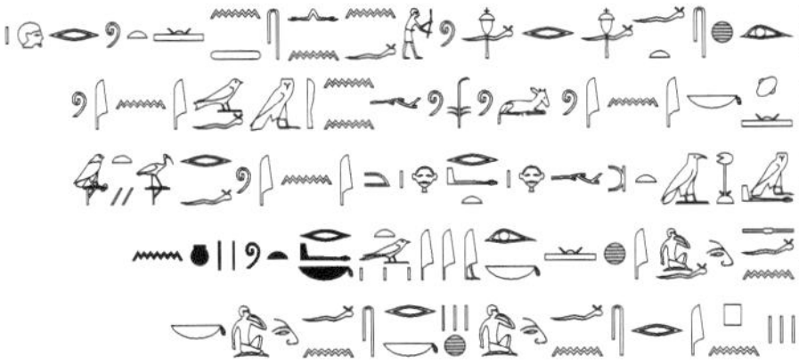

B1 178
B1 179
B1 180
B1 181
B1 182

B1 178–79	*jr ḫsft r ḫsfw n.f*	2
	nn sn tw r dp-ḥsb.k	2
B1 179–80	*jn jw jwsw nnm.f*	2
	jn jw mjḫꜣt ḥr rdjt ḥr gs	3
B1 180–81	*jn jw r.f ḏḥwtj zfn.f*	2
	jḫ jr.k jyt	2
B1 181–82	***rdj.k tw (r) 2nw n** 3 pn*	3
	jr sfn 3 ḫr.k sfn.k	3

B1 178–79 "Do punishment to the one who ought to be punished:
there is no one who comes up to your standard.
B1 179–80 Does the crossbar go off?
Is the scale being partial?
B1 180–81 Is Thoth lenient in that respect?
Then you may do wrong.
B1 181–82 **You make yourself the equal of these three:**
If the three are lenient, you may be lenient."

B1 178–79 *jr ḫsft r ḫsfw n.f* — literally, "do punishment against the one punished to him"; *ḫsfw* is a passive participle.

nn sn tw r dp-ḥsb.k — a negated statement of existence (§ 11.4), literally, "one who imitates you with respect to your standard is not."

B1 179–82 These three couplets use the imagery of the scale. The point is that the scale is an impartial witness to truth; as the scale, in the person of Thoth, god of measurement, does not "do wrong," then neither should the chief steward. The last couplet equates the chief steward with the scale and Thoth: as they cannot be "lenient" to something they measure, neither can the chief steward show leniency to Nemtinakht.

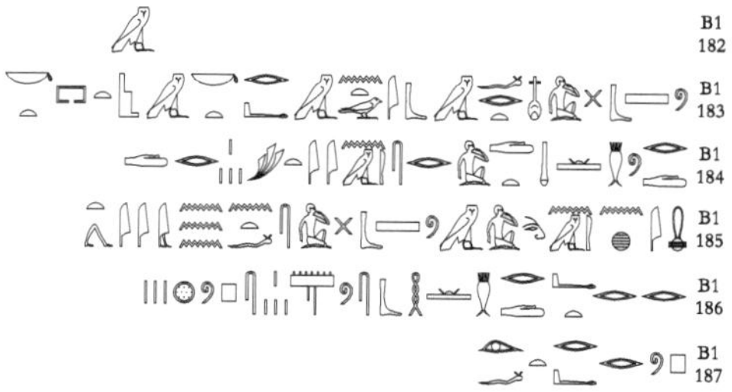

B1 182–83 *m wšb nfrt m bjnt* 3
m rdj kt m jst kt 3
B1 184–85 *rdw(j) mdt r snmyt* 3
r dmj n ẖnm m wšb.s 3
B1 185–87 *ntf jyt r rdjt rd ḥbsw.s pw* 4
zp 3 pw r rdjt jr.f 3

B1 182–83 "Don't answer something good with something bad,
don't put the one in the other's place.
B1 184–85 How much more than fodder does speech grow,
more than touching the smell by its answer!
B1 185–87 Watering what comes, to cause growth, is its cover;
this is three occasions to make it happen."

B1 184–87 The peasant now changes to an agricultural metaphor to imply that his speaking will continue unabated until it is answered.

rdw(j) mdt r snmyt — this is probably an adjectival sentence, with the active participle of *rd* "grow" as predicate: literally, "how growthful is speaking." *snmyt* is a noun from *snm* "feed" (causative of *wnm* "eat") and therefore refers to fodder. The actual plant is uncertain but is probably alfalfa—specifically, the variety known as *barsim* in Egypt—which has a very fast rate of growth.

r dmj n ẖnm m wšb.s — alfalfa has a rich, pungent smell. The line means that the "smell" of speaking grows faster than the reply to it.

ntf jyt ... ḥbsw.s pw — literally, "watering what comes … it is its clothing." The suffix pronoun probably refers to *mdt* in the preceding couplet. The use of *ḥbsw* "clothing" here may derive from the idiom *ḥbs ḥr r* "cover the face to," which occurs later in this discourse (B1 198), meaning "ignore." In other words, ignoring speaking is like watering plants: both cause growth.

zp 3 pw r rdjt jr.f — literally, "it is three occasions (§ 9.4) to make it do (so)"; the suffix pronoun refers to the infinitive *ntf* in the preceding line (§ 13.8). The line refers to the fact that this speech is the peasant's third petition and means, "this is the third time you've encouraged speaking by not answering."

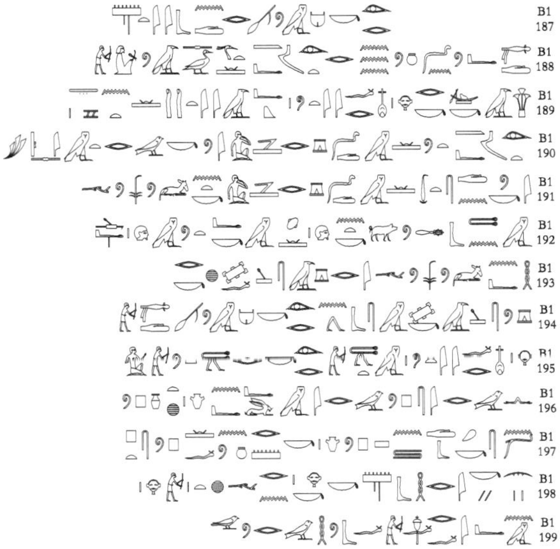

B1 187–89	*jr r.k ḥmw r ndbyt*	3
	šd wḏnw r jrt mȝꜥt	3
	zȝw ḥȝ.k r.k ḥr nfryt	3
B1 189–91	*ꜥqȝyt nt tȝ jrt mȝꜥt*	4
	m ḏd grg jw.k wr.t(j)	3
	m jz jw.k dns.t(j)	2
B1 191–92	*m ḏd grg ntk jwsw*	4
	m ṯnbḫ ntk dp-ḥsb	3
B1 192–94	*mj.k tw m dp wꜥ ḥnꜥ jwsw*	3
	jr gȝsȝ.f ḫr.k gwsȝ.k	2
B1 194–95	*m sbn jr r.k ḥmw*	3
	šd ḥr nfryt	2
B1 195–96	*m jt jr r.k r jtw*	3
	nj wr js pw wr jm ꜥwn jb	4
B1 196–98	*tḫ pw ns.k dbn pw jb.k*	4
	rmnw(j).f pw sptj.kj	2
B1 198–99	*jr ḥb(s).k ḥr.k r nḫt ḥr*	3
	nmj jr.f ḫsf.f bw ḥwrw	3

B1 187–89 “So, make rudder to full sail,
take the torrent to make direction,
beware of sailing backward at the tiller.

B1 189–91 Accuracy of the land, that makes Maat,
don't tell lies, for you are important;
don't become light, for you are weighty.
B1 191–92 Don't tell lies: you are the crossbar.
Don't stray: you are the standard.
B1 192–94 Look, you are one head with the crossbar:
if it tilts, you may tilt.
B1 194–95 Don't drift, but work the rudder,
pull on the tiller.
B1 195–96 Don't take, but act against the taker:
one great from it, and greedy, is not a great one.
B1 196–98 Your tongue is the plumb-bob, your mind is the weight,
your lips are its arms.
B1 198–99 If you cover your face to rapacity,
who then will bar poverty?"

B1 187–89 *r ndbyt* — the idiom means "so that the wind fills the sail completely."

šd wḏnw — the image is of sailing on the Nile, against the current. Sailing upstream was (and is) possible because the prevailing wind is from the north.

ḥꜣ.k ... ḥr nfryt — the verb comes from the preposition *ḥꜣ* "behind," and refers here to being pushed downstream by the current. The *nfryt* was the rope by which the rudder was controlled.

B1 189–94 A tercet anticipates the "scale" metaphor of the next two couplets, equating the chief steward with the model (*ꜥqꜣyt* "accuracy"), scale, and standard by which Maat is measured.

gꜣsꜣ.f ... gwsꜣ.k — both words are a spelling of *gsꜣ* "tilt."

B1 195–96 In this couplet, the peasant returns to the nautical metaphor with which this section opened, before finishing the section with another reference to the scale.

wr jm — the prepositional adverb refers to the action of referred to in the first line ("take"): i.e., one who has become great by stealing is not great.

B1 196–98 *dbn* — this refers to an item of known weight, which is put in one pan of the scale for an item to be weighed against in the other pan.

rmnw(j).f — the suffix pronoun refers to *jwsw* rather than to an unmentioned *mḫṯꜣt* "scale," which is feminine. The arms are those of the crossbar on either side of the central fulcrum.

B1 198–99 *ḥb(s).k* — the scribe has omitted the 𓋴 with which the verb *ḥbs* is regularly written.

nḫt ḥr — literally, "force of face," with *ḥr* in the sense of "attention, intent." The idiom was probably chosen to play against the preceding *ḥbs ḥr*.

B1 199–201	*mj.k tw m ḥwrw n rḫtj*	2	
	ꜥwn jb ḥr ḥḏt ḫnms		2
B1 201–202	*bṯn mjḥnk.f n twꜣ.f*	3	
	sn.f pw jy jn.n.f		3
B1 202–204	*mj.k tw (m) mjḫntj ḏꜣ nb hmt*	3	
	ꜥqꜣy ꜥqꜣ.f fdq.w		3
B1 204–205	*mj.k tw m ḥrj šnꜥw*	1	
	nj rdj.n.f swꜣ šw ḥr ꜥ		4
B1 205–207	*mj.k tw (m) ṯnḥr n rḫyt*	2	
	ꜥnḫ m ḥwrw nw ꜣpdw		3

B1 207–208	*mj.k tw (m) wdpw rš.f pw rḫs*	3
	nn jꜣtjw jrj r.f	3
B1 208–209	*mj.k tw m zꜣw*	1
	nj ḏw.s js r.j nj jp.n.k	3

B1 199–201 Look, you are a poor washerman,
greedy in damaging friendship,
B1 201–202 one who spurns his patron for his dependant,
whose brother is the one who comes bringing.
B1 202–204 Look, you are a ferryman who ferries the one with a fare,
an accurate one whose accuracy is shattered.
B1 204–205 Look, you are a warehouse chief
who does not let pass the empty-handed.
B1 205–207 Look, you are a raptor of the subjects,
who lives on the poor of birds.
B1 207–208 Look, you are an attendant whose joy is slaughter,
for whom there is no cutting it short.
B1 208–209 Look, you are the guardian;
its evil is not because of me: you do not take account.

The peasant ends his second discourse with a litany comparing the chief steward with despicable elements of society and nature.

B1 199–202 *ḥwrw n rḫtj* — literally, "poor one of a washerman." Doing laundry was considered a particularly unpleasant means of earning a living.

bṯn mjḥnk.f n twꜣ.f — the verb *bṯn* "resist" is sometimes written in hieratic with a  sign because of a misreading of . *mḥnk* is a noun of agent from the verb *ḥnk* "endow"; the suffix pronoun of *twꜣ.f* refers to this noun. The meaning is that the chief steward is spurning the king in favor of Nemtinakht.

sn.f pw jy jn.n.f — literally, "the one who comes having fetched is his brother," an A *pw* B nominal sentence used as an unmarked relative clause. The line means that he associates only with people who bring him gifts.

B1 202–204 The scribe omits the "*m* of predication" (§ 10.6) several times in this section. The first line has the same theme as the last line of the preceding couplet: it refers to a ferryman who accepts only a paying customer (*nb hmt* "owner of a fare"). This contrasts with the ideal altruism sometimes expressed in tomb biographies, where the deceased reports having "ferried the stranded."

B1 204–205 A third couplet on the same theme: *nj rdj.n.f swꜣ šw ḥr ꜥ*, literally "he does not let pass one empty on arm," is an unmarked relative clause meaning that he only admits someone bringing a gift. R 31,3–4 has *m[j].k [tw m] šnꜥyw [... šn]ꜥy[w]* "Look, you are a policeman (literally, "restrainer") who [...] the restrained."

B1 205–207 *mj.k tw (m) ṯnḥr n rḫyt* — a *ṯnḥr* is a bird that catches and eats other birds. This line means that the chief steward preys on the common people; it is particularly evocative in Egyptian, since the word *rḫyt* "subjects" is written with the sign of a hoopoe (G 22) in hieroglyphic and the subjects are often depicted symbolically by this sign. R 31,4–6 has *[jw.k] mj ṯjnḥr [n rḫyt] ḏʿr ḥwrw n ȝpd[w]* "You are like a raptor of the subjects, who seeks out the poor of birds."

B1 207–208 *wdpw* — the term denotes a servant who carries food from the kitchen to the table or, in this case, from the slaughterhouse to the kitchen.

nn jȝṯjw jrj r.f — literally, "there is no cutting short with respect to it with respect to him," an unmarked relative clause meaning, apparently, he cannot get enough of it.

B1 208–209 *nj ḏw.s js jr.j* — an adverbial sentence (*ḏw.s jr.j* "its evil is with respect to me"), negated as an emphatic sentence (§ 25.11); the rheme is the prepositional phrase *r.j*. The antecedent of the first suffix pronoun is not clear; it probably refers to all the misbehavior cited in the preceding couplets. The line means, "I am not to blame for your bad conduct: it is because you don't take heed of what I am saying." R 31,7–8 has *mj.k [tw m zȝw] n ḏw.s r.j* "Look, you are the guardian of its evil against me."

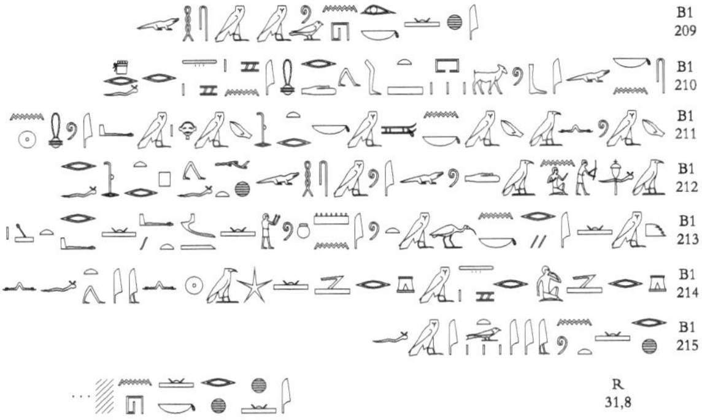

B1 209–10 *jḫ jr.k nhw m msḥ skn* 4
jbw tš.(w) r dmj n tȝ r ḏr.f 5
B1 211 *sḏmw nj ȝ sḏm.n.k* 2
tm.k tr sḏm ḥr mj 2
B1 211–13 *jw mjn ȝ ḫsf n.j ȝdw* 3
jw msḥ ḫt.f 2
ptr r.f km jrj n.k 3
B1 213–14 *gm.tw jmnw mȝʿt* 2
rdj.t(w) sȝ grg r tȝ 3
B1 214–15 *m grg dwȝ nj jjt.f* 3
nj rḫ.n.tw jyt jm.f 3

B1 209–10 "Thus you make loss as a ravenous crocodile,
and shelter is gone from the harbor of the whole land.
B1 211 Hearer, you just don't hear:
why do you fail to hear?
B1 211–13 For right now a raging crocodile punishes me.
But a crocodile retreats.
So, what is the profit in that for you?
B1 213–14 Maat's hiddenness will be found
and lying's back put on the ground.
B1 214–15 Don't set up the morning before it comes:
a wrong in it cannot be known."

B1 209–210 R 31, 8 has *jḫ rḫ.k [...]* "thus you know [...]." The rest of the papyrus is lost.

B1 211 *sḏmw* means both "hearer" and "judge." For the rest of this couplet, see §§ 15.7.1 and 25.11.

B1 211–13 This tercet probably refers to Nemtinakht. Following on the last line of the penultimate couplet, it means, "Since there is no shelter, I am beset by another crocodile besides you; once it has finished with me, there will be nothing left for you."

B1 213–15 The last two couplets serve as a caution to the chief steward. In the first, the peasant warns that justice will ultimately win out; the two passives *gm.tw* and *rdj.t(w)* imply that this is beyond the control of the chief steward. The second therefore warns him not to anticipate a trouble-free future; its two lines contain a word play between *jjt* "comes" and *jyt* "a wrong."

Episode 9 — The Chief Steward's Reaction (B1 215–224)

B1 215
B1 216
B1 217

B1 215–16	*jst r.f ḏd.n sḫtj pn mdt tn*	3
	n (j)m(j)-r pr wr zꜣ-mrw rnsj	3
	m pgꜣ n ꜥrryt	2
B1 217–18	*ꜥḥꜥ.n rdj.n.f*	2
	ꜥḥꜥ jmj-zꜣ 2 r.f ḫr smjw	4
	ꜥḥꜥ.n ꜥꜣg.sn ꜥt.f nbt jm	4
B1 218–20	*ḏd.jn sḫtj pn zꜣ mrw tnm.ḥr.f*	4
	ḥr.f šp.(w) r mꜣꜣt.f zḫ.(w) r sḏmt.f	5
	th jb ḥr sḫꜣyt n.f	3
B1 220–21	*mj.k tw m njwt nn ḥqꜣ-ḥwt.s*	2
	mj ḫt nn wr.s	2
B1 221–23	*mj dpt nn sḫry jm.s*	3
	zmꜣyt nn sšmw.s	2
B1 223	*mj.k tw m šnt(j) j⸢ṯ⸣ꜣ*	3
	ḥqꜣ-ḥwt šzpw	2
B1 224	*(j)m(j)-r w ḫsf ḥꜥḏꜣ*	3
	ḫpr.(w) m jmj-ḥꜣt n jrr	3

B1 215–16 Now, the peasant said this speech
to chief steward Meru's son Rensi
at the opening of the portal.

B1 217–18 Then he had
two bodyguards attend to him with whips.
Then they pummeled his every limb with them.
B1 218–20 So, the peasant said, "Meru's son has to have gone astray,
his face blind to what he sees and deaf to what he hears,
absent-minded to what has been mentioned to him.
B1 220–21 Look, you are a town without its mayor,
like a body of people without its chief,
B1 221–23 like a boat without a pilot in it,
a confederation without its leader.
B1 223 Look, you are a sheriff who steals,
a mayor who receives,
B1 224 a district-overseer who should bar plunder
but has become the paragon of the one who does it."

The chief steward, probably angered by the descriptions of him in the third discourse, has the peasant beaten.

B1 215–16 *m pgꜣ n ꜥrryt* — that is, in the gateway to his office compound. This public venue is probably the reason for the chief steward's stern reaction to the peasant's tirade.

B1 218–20 *th jb* — literally, "overlooking of mind."

B1 220–23 Two couplets (or a quatrain) in which the peasant uses metaphors to describe the chief steward as being out of control.

sẖry — a nisbe from *sẖr* "system," thus, the one who makes the boat's system.

B1 223–24 Two couplets (or a quatrain) in which the peasant returns to his criticism of the chief steward's honesty.

šnt(j) j⸢ṯ⸣ꜣ — the noun is a nisbe from *šnṯ* "dispute." In the participle, the scribe has forgotten to add the horizontal line to the first sign (), which distinguishes it in hieratic from .

jmj-ḥꜣt — literally, "the one in the front."

Episode 10 — The Fourth Discourse (B1 225–256)

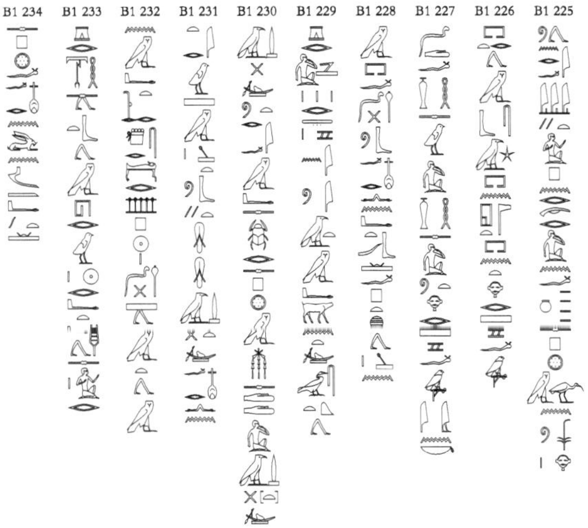

B1 225	*jw.jn r.f sẖtj pn*	2
	r spr n.f 4nw zp	2
B1 225–26	*gm.n sw ḥr prt*	2
	m sbꜣ n ḥwt-nṯr nt ḥr(j)-šj.f	3
B1 227–28	*ḏd.f ḥzw ḥz tw ḥr(j)-šj.f*	4
	jj.n.k m pr.f	2
B1 228–29	*ḥḏ bw nfr nn ꜥb.t(w).f*	3
	ptẖ sꜣ n grgw r tꜣ	4
B1 229–30	*jn jw tꜣ mjẖnt sꜥq.t(j)*	2
	ḏꜣ.tw jr.f mj	2
	sẖpr zp m msdd	3
B1 230–31	*ḏꜣt jtrw m sꜣ ṯbwtj*	2
	ḏꜣt nfr nn	3
B1 232–33	*nmj tr sḏr r šzp*	3
	ḥḏ šmt m grḥ zbt m hrw	5
B1 233–34	*rdjt ꜥḥꜥ zj*	3
	r zp.f nfr n wn mꜣꜥt	3

B1 225 So, the peasant came
to appeal to him a fourth time
B1 225–26 and found him emerging
from the gate of the temple of Harsaphes,

B1 227–28 saying, "Blessed one! May Harsaphes bless you,
from whose house you have come.
B1 228–29 Once goodness is damaged it will not be reassembled
when the back of lying is thrown to the ground.
B1 229–30 Is that ferry docked?
Then who can be ferried,
with the one who can bring it about unwilling?
B1 230–31 Crossing the river by sandals:
a good crossing or not?
B1 232–33 Who can sleep until dawn?
Damaged are going by night and sending by day,
B1 233–34 and letting a man attend
to his truly good affairs.

The fourth discourse is more of an "instruction" than the first three, although parts of it are directed as an accusation against the chief steward.

B1 225–26 *gm.n sw* — as written, this is an unusual example of the omission of the subject in a compound verb phrase ("the peasant came … and found"), but the scribe may also have omitted the suffix pronoun unintentionally.

ḥr(j)-šj.f — "He Who Is on His Lake," the chief god of Herakleopolis.

B1 228–29 This couplet uses the passive *sḏm.f* in the initial clause of an emphatic sentence (see § 25.8.3) and adverbially in the third clause (§ 20.14). The couplet means that damage to goodness is permanent, even after the misdeed that caused the damage has been redressed.

B1 229–30 The fourth discourse uses tercets, of which this is the first, to break the overall pattern of couplets that characterized the first three discourses. This tercet reframes the theme of the preceding couplet, with the demonstrative *tꜣ* marking the connection: "that ferry" refers to the "damaging of goodness." The extended metaphor means that it is difficult to persuade a ferryman to take his boat back across the river once he has docked, just as damage to goodness cannot be repaired. *sꜥq.t(j)* is a 3fs stative, literally "caused to enter." *sḫpr zp m msdd* is an adverbial sentence used as an unmarked adverb clause (§ 20.7), literally "the one who brings about the deed is one who hates (to do it)."

B1 230–31 This couplet's question is ironic: it is clearly impossible to "cross the river on the back of sandals"; for the final *nn*, see § 15.6.8.

B1 232–34 These two couplets sound a theme common in wisdom texts, which is the generally dismal state of affairs at the time the discourse is made (see Text 6). Here the peasant extends beyond his own plight to that of society as a whole. The use of the passive *sḏm.f ḥḏ* "has been damaged" in the first couplet and the adjective *nfr* "is good" in the second hark back to *ḥḏ bw nfr* "goodness has been damaged" in the opening couplet. The second couplet here refers both to society as a whole and to the peasant himself, who only wants to "attend to his affairs" (literally, "stand to his case").

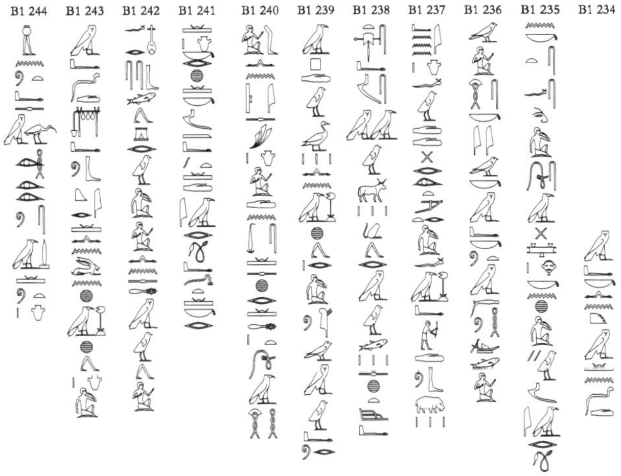

B1 234–36 *mj.k nn km n ḏd n.k st* 2
sf swꜣ.(w) ḥr.k 3
nḫwj mꜣjr sky.k 3
B1 236–37 *mj.k tw m mḥw jʿ jb.f* 3
wdd r jrt mrt.f 3
B1 237–39 *ḫꜣʿ dbw st smꜣmw* 4
pḥ rmw sḫt ꜣpdw 4
B1 239–40 *nn ḫꜣḫ-r šw m wʿrw* 3
nn jz-jb dns sḫr ẖt 2
B1 240–42 *wꜣḥ jb.k rḫ.k mꜣʿt* 4
dꜣjr stpt.k r nfr bss grw 5
B1 242–44 *nn sẖmw mjḏd bw jqr* 3
nn wn ḫꜣḫ-jb jn.tw ʿ 4
sgmḥ jrtj swḏꜣ.tw jb 4

B1 234–36 "Look, there is no profit for the one who tells it to you:
kindness has passed you by.
How lamentable is the needy one you wipe out!
B1 236–37 Look, you are a marsh-hunter who washes his mind,
who pushes to do what he wants:
B1 237–39 who spears hippopotami and shoots wild bulls,
who attacks fish and nets birds.
B1 239–40 There is no hasty-mouth who is free of flight,
no lighthearted who is weighty of the belly's advice.

B1 240–42 Set your mind and learn Maat,
suppress your choice in favor of the quiet man's entry.

B1 242–44 There is no one rash who penetrates accomplishment;
but there is none impulsive when the arm is used,
when the eyes have been made to see and one is informed.

B1 234–36 The opening line of this tercet means, "telling you this is useless." The second and third lines repeat B1 148–49 of the second discourse.

B1 236–39 This pair of couplets expands on the theme of the chief steward's predatory behavior (from the peasant's point of view).

mḥw — the word is probably a nisbe *mḥwj* from *mḥw*, itself derived from *mḥj* "be in water." The determinatives give the sense of the word.

jꜥ jb.f — the expression is similar to the English idiom "let off steam."

B1 239–40 This couplet and the next thirteen lines are cast in the mode of an "instruction," such as that of Ptahhotep. This is a deliberate conceit on the part of the author, reflecting his overall theme of the perversion of Maat: here the instruction is offered by a subordinate to a superior, the reverse of the typical pattern in wisdom literature (for its effect on Egyptian audiences, think of a son giving his father a talk on the birds and the bees).

wꜥrw — the noun is different from the feminine *wꜥrt* used to describe Sinuhe's flight. It may mean "running on," with reference to speech.

dns sḫr ḫt — a *nfr ḥr* construction (§ 6.5) with a direct genitive as the second element. The "belly's advice" refers to unthinking action: see Ptahhotep 243–44.

B1 240–42 *wꜣḥ jb.k* — the suffix pronoun was added secondarily.

r nfr bss grw — literally, "with respect to the good of the quiet man entering." The line apparently means "give preference to the quiet man over your personal choice."

B1 242–44 The second and third lines of this tercet contain three unmarked adverb clauses. *jn.tw ꜥ*, literally "the arm is fetched," modifies *ḫꜣḫ-jb*, literally "hasty of mind," meaning "none impulsive in acting," the two clauses of the last line describe the circumstances that keep one from implusive acting, namely observation ("the eyes have been caused to see") and information ("the mind is made sound": see Essay 25).

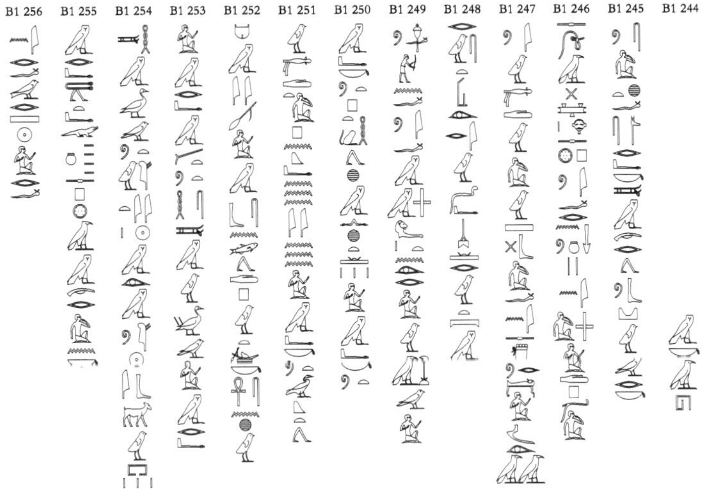

B1 244–45 *m kꜣhsw ḫft wsr.k* 2
tm spr bw ḏw r.k 4
B1 246 *swꜣ ḥr zp jw.f r snw(j)* 3
jn wnm dp 2
B1 247–48 *jw wšdw wšb.f* 2
jn sḏr mꜣꜣ rswt 3
B1 248–49 *jr wḏʿ rwt m ḥsfw n.f* 2
jw.f m jm(j) ḥꜣt n jrr 2
B1 249–51 *wḫꜣ mj.k tw pḥ.t(j)* 2
ḥm-ḫt mj.k tw wšd.t(j) 2
B1 251–52 *pnqy-mw mj.k tw ʿq.t(j)* 2
ḥmy m sbn dpwt.k 3
B1 252–54 *sʿnḫw m rdj m(w)t.tw* 3
sḥmtw m rdj ḥtm.tw 3
B1 254–55 *šwyt m jr m šw* 3
⌜jb⌝w m rdj jt mzḥ 4
B1 255–56 *4nw zp ꜣ m spr n.k* 2
jn r.f wrš.j r.f 2

B1 244–45 "Don't be harsh when you are powerful,
so that evil does not reach you.
B1 246 When a case is passed over, it will become two:
it is the eater who tastes.

B1 247–48 "For the one questioned replies,
and it is the sleeper who sees a dream.
B1 248–49 As for a court judge who ought to be punished,
he is the paragon of a doer.
B1 249–51 Fool, look, you are reached;
know-nothing, look, you are questioned.
B1 251–52 Water-bailer, look, you are taking on water;
helmsman, don't let your boat drift.
B1 252–54 Life-giver, don't make one die;
destroyer, don't make one be destroyed.
B1 254–55 Shade, don't act as sunlight;
shelter, don't let the crocodile take.
B1 255–56 The *fourth time* of appealing to you!
Shall I spend the day at it?"

B1 244–45 For this couplet, see § 20.16.

B1 246–48 The first line clearly refers to the case that the peasant is bringing to the chief steward. The next four are various metaphors for the central message that a solution is possible only by engagement with the problem, not by ignoring it.

B1 248–49 The peasant ends his "instruction" with a maxim that is both general in its validity and specific to the chief steward himself. A *wḏꜥ rwt* is a "separater of the portal," meaning one who judges at the gateway of a temple, where public hearings were normally held. *ẖsfw n.f* is a passive participle with referential dative: literally, "one punished to him." *jmj-ḥꜣt n jrr* is repeated from the end of the third discourse (B1 224).

B1 249–55 The peasant now addresses four couplets directly to the chief steward, urging him to take notice and act as he should.

mj.k tw pḥ.t(j) — the sense of the verb here is "found out for what you are."

ẖm-ḫt — literally, "one who does not know something."

mj.k tw wšd.t(j) — i.e., like a student who has not studied for an exam, you have to respond, even though you know nothing.

mj.k tw ꜥq.t(j) — literally, "look, you are entered."

Episode 11 — The Fifth Discourse (B1 256–270, B2 Af)

B1 270 B1 269 B1 268 B1 267 B1 266 B1 265 B1 264 B1 263 B1 262 B1 261 B1 260 B1 259 B1 258 B1 257 B1 256

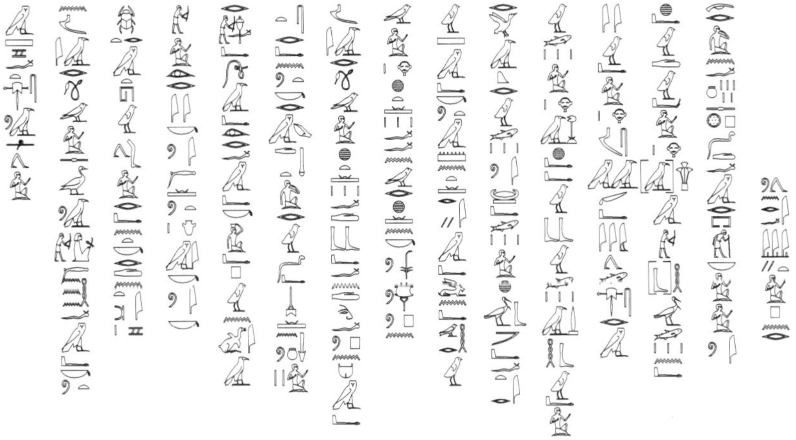

B2 Af2 B2 Af1

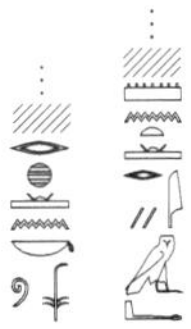

B1 256–57 *jw.jn r.f sḫtj pn r spr n.f 5nw zp* 4
ḏd.f (j)m(j)-r pr wr nb.j 3
B1 257–59 *jw ḫwdw ḥr ḥ3m ḥb3w* 2
nyw ḥr sm3m jy 2
B1 259–61 *st-rmw ḥr ḫ3{ḫ}ʿ(r) wbbw* 3
ḏ3bḥw r p3qrw 2
B1 261–62 *jw wḥʿ ḫb3.f jtrw* 3
mj.k tw m mnt jrj 3

B1 262–63 *m ꜥwn ḥwrw ḥr ḫwt.f* 3
fn rḫ.n.k sw 2
B1 263–65 *ṯꜣw pw n mꜣjr ḫwt.f* 3
dbb fnd.f pw nḥm st 2
B1 265–66 *rdj.n.tw.k r sḏm mdt* 2
r wḏꜥ snwj r ḫsf ꜥwꜣ 2
B1 266–67 *jr r.f* 2
mj.k fꜣ pw n jṯꜣ jrry.k 3
B1 267–68 *jw mḥ.tw jb jm.k* 3
jw.k ḫpr.t(j) m thw 2
B1 268–70 *rdj.n.t(w).k r dnjt n mꜣjr* 3
zꜣw mḥ.f 2
mj.k tw m šj.f-stꜣw 2

B1 256–57 So, the peasant came to appeal to him a fifth time,
saying, "Chief steward, my lord!
B1 257–59 The hand-netter is catching *ḥbꜣ*-fish,
the spearer killing the come-fish,
B1 259–61 the fish-shooter throwing at *wbbw*-fish,
and the trawler at *pꜣqrw*-fish.
B1 261–62 For the fisherman hacks the river:
look, you are the same kind.
B1 262–63 Don't rob a poor man of his things,
a helpless one you know.
B1 263–65 His things are air to a needy man;
to take them away is to stop up his nose.
B1 265–66 You were appointed to hear,
to judge, and to bar robbery.
B1 266–67 Act against it!
Look, it is the stealer's support that you make.
B1 267–68 One trusts in you,
but you have become a transgressor.
B1 268–70 You were appointed to be a dam for the needy man
lest he become flooded,
but you are his dragging lake."

This discourse uses the metaphor of fishing, in which the peasant likens the chief steward to various kinds of fishermen and himself, by analogy, to the fish they catch.

B1 257–59 *ḫwdw* — the term refers to fishing with a hand-net. The first  is for , taken from the verb *ḫwj* "defend."

jy — probably a participle denoting a fish that "comes" and is caught rather than a term for a specific species.

B1 259–61 *ḫ3{ḫ}ʿ(r)* — the  is superfluous. The verb refers to harpooning. The preposition *r* has probably been omitted in error, since "throwing" a fish makes no sense.

B1 261–62 *ḫb3* — the verb refers to the act of hoeing, likening the fisherman's relationship with the water to that of a farmer to the land.

mj.k tw m mnt jrj — literally, "look, you are the kind thereunto."

B1 262–63 *fn rḫ.n.k sw* — an unmarked relative clause after an undefined antecedent. This is a direct reference to the peasant himself.

B1 265–66 *r sḏm mdt r wḏʿ snwj* — literally, "to hear a matter and to separate two (opponents)."

B1 266–67 *jr r.f* — the suffix pronoun refers to the infinitive *ʿw3* in the preceding couplet. The signs following can be read *m ʿ.k* "with your arm," but the lack of a stroke suggests the interjection *mj.k* instead.

f3 — a noun rather than the infinitive ("carrying"), which should be *f3t*. This is an A *pw* sentence in which A is *f3 n jṯ3 jrry.k* "the support of the stealer that you make."

B1 267–68 *jw mḥ.tw jb jm.k* — literally, "the mind is filled with you"; *mḥ jb m* "filling the mind with" is an idiom for "trust in."

B1 268–70 *z3w mḥ.f* — literally, "beware (that) he is in water": the sense of *z3w* as an imperative can often be conveyed best by the English conjunction "lest."

šj.f st3w — the  sign is a mistake for ; the seated man at the end indicates that the scribe was thinking of the metaphor as applying to the chief steward. The verb *sṯ3* "drag" can refer to a treacherous current. The metaphor means that instead of saving the peasant from trouble, the chief steward is dragging him into it.

Episode 12 — The Sixth Discourse (B1 270–296, B2 Ag–20)

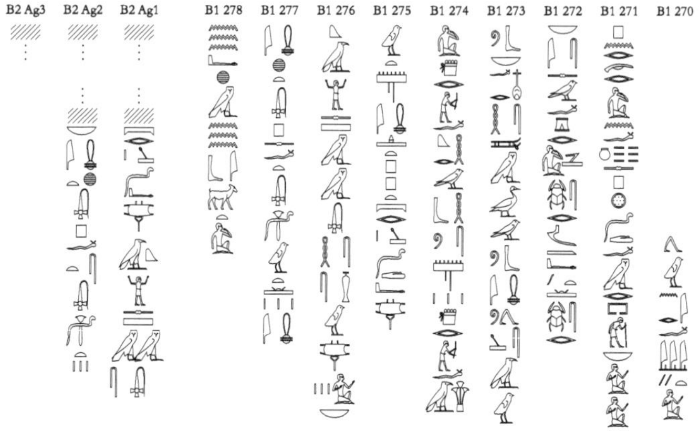

B1 270–71	*jw.jn r.f sḫtj pn r spr n.f 6nw zp*	4
	ḏd.f (j)m(j)-r pr wr nb.j	3
B1 272	*nb sjz.f grg*	3
	sḫpr mꜣꜥt	2
B1 272–73	*sḫpr bw nb nfr*	3
	sḥtm bw (ḏw)	2
B1 273–75	*mj jw sꜣw ḏr.f ḥqr*	4
	ḥbsw ḏr.f ḥꜣwt	3
B1 275–76	*mj ḥtp pt r sꜣ ḏ{d}ꜥ qꜣ*	4
	sšmm.s ḥsw nb	2
B1 277–78	*mj ḫt p⸢fs⸣t wꜣḏwt*	3
	mj mw ꜥḫm jbt	3

B1 270–71 So, the peasant came to appeal to him a sixth time.
saying, "Chief steward, my lord!
B1 272 Lord who makes lying easy,
bring about Maat!
B1 272–73 Bring about all goodness,
destroy evil,
B1 273–75 like satiety comes and ends hunger,
clothing, and ends nakedness;
B1 275–76 like the sky becomes calm after a high gale
and warms all who were cold;
B1 277–78 like fire that cooks raw things,
like water that quenches thirst.

Unlike his previous speeches, the peasant's sixth discourse is less concerned with generalities than with directly pleading to the chief steward.

B1 272 *nb sjz.f grg* — a *sḏm.f* used as an unmarked relative clause after a vocative (§ 22.16).

B1 272–73 *sḥtm bw (ḏw)* — the scribe has omitted the word, antithesis of *nfr*.

B1 275–76 *ḏ{d}ꜥ* — the scribe has written instead of. B2 Ag1 has the correct spelling.

B1 277–78 *p⌜fs⌝t* — the spelling is meant to show the initial affrication of $p > p^f$ (see the note to Sin. B 26–27) but has metathesized the *s* and *f*. B2 Ag2 has the correct spelling.

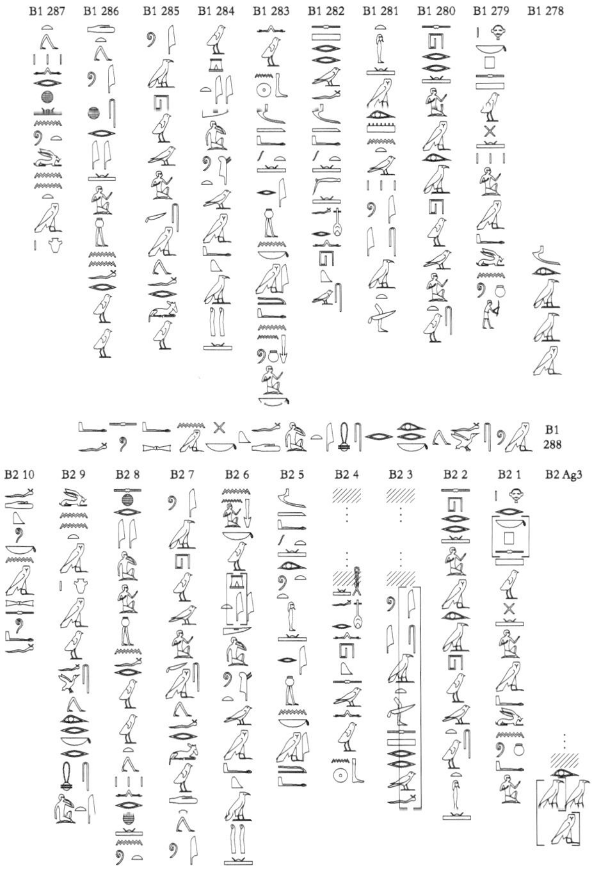

B1 278–81 *mꜣꜣ m ḥr.k pzšw m ꜥwnw* 4
shrr m jr ꜣhw 3
stwt m jr mnt 3

B1 281–83	*jw sjꜣt sšrr.f mꜣꜥt*	3
	mḥ nfr	2
	nj hqs nj wbn mꜣꜥt	3
B1 283–84	*jr jn.k jmj n snnw.k*	3
	wgyt šw.t(j) m ꜥqꜣ	3
B1 285–87	*jw ꜣhw sšm.f r jwdt*	3
	jw sẖry jnn.f rwwt	3
	nj rẖ.n.tw wnnt m jb	3
B1 288	*m wsf jr r.k r smjt*	3
	fdq.k nmj ṯꜣz.f	3

B1 278–81 "See for yourself the divider a grasper,
the pacifier a distress-maker,
the evener a pain-maker.

B1 281–83 For shorting lessens Maat.
Fill well:
Maat neither cheats nor overflows.

B1 283–84 If you get, give to your fellow:
what has been chewed is devoid of correctness.

B1 285–87 For the one in distress leads to alienation,
the accuser brings departure:
what exists in the mind cannot be known.

B1 288 Don't delay, but act according to the report:
you part and who will tie together?

B1 278–81 This tercet describes the peasant's situation, in which Maat is reversed: the one who should divide things equally taking for himself, the peacemaker a troublemaker, and the one who should set an example causing pain.

mꜣꜣ m ḥr.k — literally, "see with your face."

B1 281–83 This tercet is based on the metaphor of doling out grain: "fill well" means to fill the sack of the receiver properly, without shorting. The third line means that Maat implies proper measurement, neither too little nor too much.

jw sjꜣt sšrr.f — literally, "shorting belittles." *sjꜣt* (<*sjꜣṯ*) is a masculine infinitive.

nj hqs nj wbn mꜣꜥt — a rare example of two verb-phrases with a single subject. *wbn* means "swell up"; when used of the sunrise (whence the determinative) it refers to the sun "swelling up" over the horizon.

B1 283–84 *snnw.k* — literally, "your second." B2 6 has *sn.k* "your brother."

wgyt — a passive participle from *wgj* "chew." The line means that it is improper to hand down something that has been used up.

B1 285–87 *jwdt* — literally, "separation."

jw sḫry jnn.f rwwt — *sḫry* is metathesized from *srḫy*, a noun from *srḫ* "cause to know," a term for accusing someone (causing them to be known to officials). B1's *jnn.f* is either a rare geminated 3ae-inf. *sḏm.f* in the SUBJECT–*sḏm.f* construction (another possible example in B1 292: see below) or an error for B2 8 *jn.f*; a *sḏm.n.f* is unlikely in this context. *rwwt* is a noun from the geminated stem of *rwj* "leave," here a synonym of *jwdt* in the first line.

B1 288 *jr r.k r smjt* — the verb can also be read *jrr.k* "you should act" as the predicate of an emphatic sentence with *r smjt* as the rheme; however, the preceding *m wsf* "don't delay" indicates that an action is commanded here, rather than an action directed toward a specific goal. The *smjt* is the "report" that the peasant has made of the crime committed against him.

fdq.k is a *sḏm.f* used as an initial condition (§ 25.8.1). For *nmj ṯ3z.f*, see § 23.10.

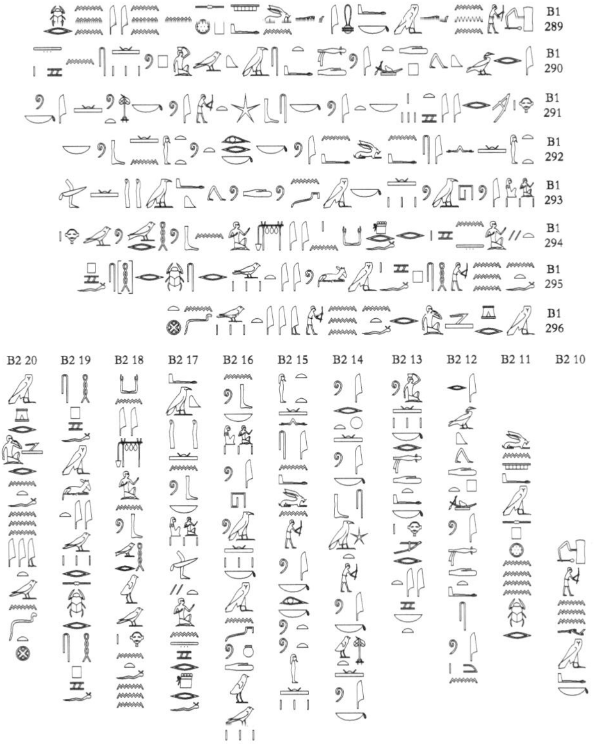

B1 289 *ꜥḥ3-mw m ꜥ.k mj ḫt wn* 4
zp n mwy ḫpr.(w) 3
B1 290–91 *jr ꜥq dpt jw šd.t(w).s* 3
3q 3tpw.s n t3 ḥr mryt nbt 4

B1 291–92 *jw.k sbꜣ.t(j) jw.k ḥmw.t(j)* 2
jw.k t(w)t.(tj) nj js n ꜥwn 2
B1 292–94 *jw.k jr.k tw t(w)t.(tj) n bw-nb* 3
jw hꜣw.k m nwdw 2
ꜥqꜣ sjꜣtj n tꜣ r ḏr.f 4
B1 294–96 *kꜣny n bw ḥwrw ḥr ntf ḥsp.f m jwyt* 4
r sḫpr [ḥ]sp.f m grg 2
r ntf jyt n ḏt 2

B1 289 "The water-fighter is in your hand like an open stick,
and the time of the water-battle has come.
B1 290–91 If the boat enters it will be taken,
and its load will be utterly ruined on each shore.
B1 291–92 You are educated, you are skilled,
you are exemplified, but not for grasping.
B1 292–94 You make yourself exemplified to everyone,
but your circumstances are in disarray,
and the shorter sets the standard for the whole land.
B1 294–96 The gardener of poverty is watering his plot with wrong,
to make his plot grow lying,
to water a wrong for the estate."

B1 289–91 These two couplets may be based on a game depicted in some Middle Kingdom tombs, in which the occupants of two or more boats battle each other with poles, trying to capsize their opponents' boat. The phrase *ꜥḥꜣ-mw*, with the wood determinative, probably refers to the pole; the meaning of *mj ẖt wn* "like an open stick" is unclear. *mwy*, a noun from *mw* "water," may refer to the contest. The second couplet may mean that if the boat enters the battle, it will be capsized and its contents (and crew) strewn along each side of the river; *ꜣq n tꜣ* means "become ruined to land." The entire metaphor makes the chief steward responsible for guarding the ship of Maat from inimical forces. In B2 12–13, the last line reads *jw gs n ꜣtpw.k r šdt.k ḥr mryt nbt* "half of your cargo will be what you save on any shore."

B1 291–92 In B2 14, the first line has an additional initial clause *jw.(k) rḫ.t(j)* "you are knowledgeable," with the first suffix pronoun erroneously omitted. For *nj js n ꜥwn*, see § 11.7.

B1 292–94 *jw.k jr.k* — B2 15 has the usual writing of the verb. The form in B1 probably has an irregular complementary 𓂋, although the apparently geminated form in the same construction in B1 286 suggests the possibility of geminated *jrr.k*. B1 *t(w)t.(tj)* and B2 15 *tw(t.tj)* are the same 2s stative as in B1 292 and B2 15 (top).

ꜥqꜣ sjꜣtj — literally, "the shorter is accurate"—an ironic statement. B2 17 adds an unnecessary *n bw-nb* "for everyone" after the adjectival predicate.

B1 294–96 *r sḫpr [h]sp.f m grg* — literally, “to make his plot evolve with lying”: i.e., “lying” is the crop he intends to grow.

Episode 13 — The Seventh Discourse (B1 297–320, B2 21–50)

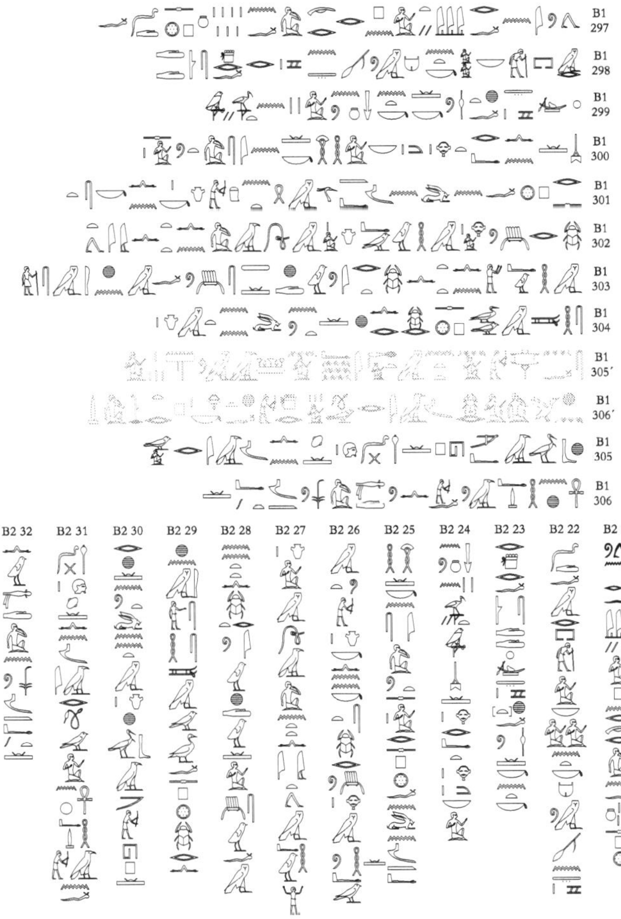

B1 297–98 *jw.jn r.f sḫtj pn r spr n.f 7nw zp* 4
ḏd.f (j)m(j)-r pr wr nb.j 3
B1 298–99 *ntk ḥmw n tꜣ r ḏr.f* 3
sqdd tꜣ ḫft wḏ.k 3

B1 299–300	*ntk snnw n ḏḥwtj*	2
	wḏꜥ nn rdjt ḥr gs	3
B1 300–301	*nb wꜣḥ.k*	2
	njs tw zj r zp.f n wn mꜣꜥ	4
B1 301–302	*m šnt jb.k n(n) n.k st*	3
	ḫpr ꜣw-ḥr m ḥwꜥ-jb	3
B1 302–303	*m wꜣ nj ntt nj jjt*	3
	m ḥꜥw nj ntt nj ḫprt	3
B1 303–304	*jw wḫd sꜣw.f m ẖnms*	3
	sḥtm.(f) zp ḫpr.(w)	3
	nj rḫ.n.tw wnnt m jb	3
B1 305–306	*ḫbꜣ hp ḥḏ dp-ḥsb*	4
	nn mꜣjr ꜥnḫ ḥꜥḏꜣw.f	3
	nj wšd sw mꜣꜥt	2

B1 297–98 So, the peasant came to appeal to him a seventh time,
saying, "Chief steward, my lord!
B1 298–99 You are the rudder of the entire land:
the land sails according as you command.
B1 299–300 You are a second Thoth,
who decides without being partial.
B1 300–301 Lord, may you last,
so that a man may call you to his truly just cause.
B1 301–302 Don't let your mind get contentious—it is not for you—
or the well-disposed will become short-tempered.
B1 302–303 Don't start on what has not yet come,
don't get excited at what has not yet happened.
B1 303–304 For forbearance extends in friendship,
and destroys a misdeed that has happened:
what exists in the mind cannot be known.
B1 305–306 Custom has been mutilated and the standard damaged.
None needy can live when he has been plundered:
Maat does not address him.

In his seventh discourse, the peasant becomes less circumspect and more direct in describing his situation.

B1 298–99 *ntk ḥmw* — probably a statement of identity and therefore with one stress (*intakḥímu) rather than one of specification with two (*inták ḥímu "*you* are the rudder").

sqdd tꜣ ḫft wḏ.k — an emphatic sentence, with the prepositional phrase as the rheme (§ 25.6).

B1 299–300 *ntk snnw n ḏḥwtj* — the first two words are probably a statement of identity, with one stress: literally, "you are the second of Thoth."

nn rdjt ḥr gs — literally, "without putting on the side." B2 24 has a pejorative *ḥr rdjt ḥr gs* "being partial."

B1 300–301 *mꜣꜥ* — in B2 25, the determinative is written to the side at the bottom of the papyrus.

B1 301–302 *n(n) n.k st* — the *n* of *nn* is omitted because it is in contact with the *n* of *n.k* (see § 2.8.2): *nˇnník. B2 26 has the full spelling.

ꜣw-ḥr ... *ḥwꜥ-jb* — literally, "long of face ... short of mind." The first phrase is similar to *ꜣw-jb* "long of mind," meaning "happy."

B1 302–303 The first 𓂋 in each clause is for the preposition *n* (§ 8.2.6); B2 27–28 has omitted the preposition in the first clause and has the regular spelling 𓈖 in the second. The relative clauses contain a *nj sḏmt.f* construction with omitted subject (§ 19.16).

B1 303–304 The first two lines means that friendship extends forbearance and overlooks a misdeed (for this nuance of *zp*, see Ptahhotep 422). The third line is repeated from B1 287 / B2 8–9.

B1 305–306 The scribe originally overlooked this tercet and the next three couplets and wrote two lines corresponding to the couplet of B1 310 and most of the next tercet (B1 311–12) before realizing his error. He then erased the two lines and continued his copy on the next page of the papyrus.

nn mꜣjr ꜥnḫ ḥꜥḏꜣw.f — the first line of the tercet describes the peasant's plight in general terms. With this second line, the peasant begins a more personal narrative. The statement is one of negative existence (§ 11.4), literally "There is none needy who lives when he has been plundered." The final verb is a passive *sḏm.f* in an unmarked adverb clause (§ 20.14). B2 31 has recast this in more general terms as an active participle with following dative (*ḥꜥḏꜣ n.f*): "There is none needy who lives and plunders for himself."

nj wšd sw mꜣꜥt — the sense of this line depends on the verb *wšd*, which can have the connotation of questioning in a criminal proceeding. The implication is that it is typically the powerful who commit plunder, not the weak. For B1's gnomic *nj wšd* (§ 18.13), B2 32 has the more common *nj sḏm.n.f* construction.

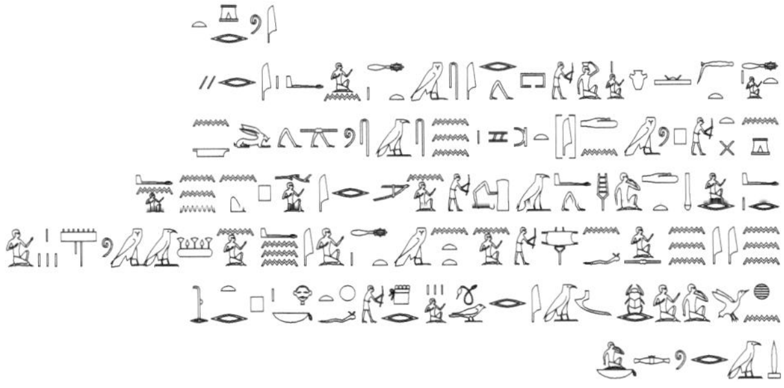

B1 306
B1 307
B1 308
B1 309
B1 310
B1 311
B1 312

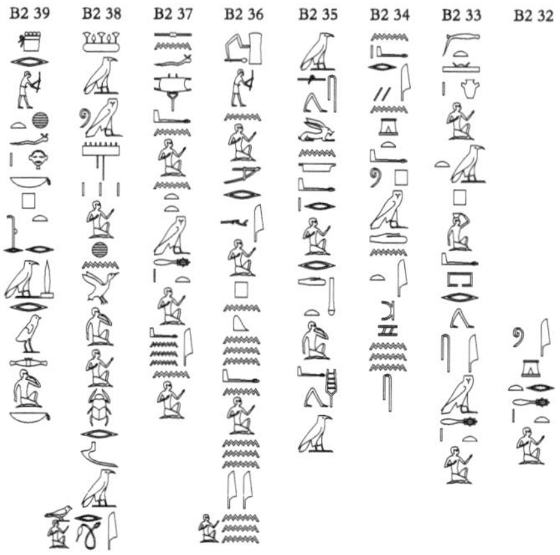

B1 306–307 *jw grt ẖt.j mḥ.t(j) jb.j ꜣtp.(w)* 4
pr js m ẖt.j n ꜥ jrj 4
B1 308–309 *ngt pw m dn[j]t mw.s ꜣs.w* 4
wn r.j r mdt 3
B1 309–10 *ꜥḥꜥ ꜣ ꜥḥꜣ n.j mrj* 3
pnq n.j mwy 2
B1 310 *snf.n.j ntt m ẖt.j* 3
jꜥ.n.j šꜣmw.j 2
B1 311–12 *ẖn.j ḫpr.(w)* 2
mꜣjrw.j ḏr.(w) ḫft ḥr.k 3
ptr ḏꜣrw.k 2

B1 306–307 “Now, my belly is full and my mind laden,
and for that reason it comes from my belly.
B1 308–309 It is a breach in the dam: its water rushed out
when my mouth was opened to speak.
B1 309–10 Just stand up and fight for me, you brace!
Bail for me, water-man!
B1 310 Now that I have vented what was in my belly,
and washed my soiled linen,
B1 311–12 my statement is over,
my needs are ended before you:
what else do you require?

B1 306–307 The second line is an emphatic sentence subordinated by means of *js* (§ 25.10); the prepositional phrase *n ꜥ jrj* is the rheme. The subject of the verb is omitted. The line means literally, "and (*js*) something comes from my belly for the situation (ꜥ) thereunto." The notions of the belly being "full" and disgorging its contents are those of emotional rather than physical states.

B1 309–310 *ꜥḥꜥ ꜣ ꜥḥꜣ n.j* — two imperatives, the first strengthened by means of the particle *ꜣ* (§ 15.7.1). The combination clearly plays on the sounds of the first three words.

mrj — the word refers to an object of wood, but the exact meaning is otherwise unknown. The context of the preceding couplet suggests a wood beam used to shore up the weak point in a dam. This couplet as a whole uses the metaphor of the peasant as a breached dam and the chief steward as the one who can repair it. The seated man after *mrj* can be a determinative, as interpreted here, or the 1s suffix pronoun: *mrj.j* "my brace."

pnq n.j mwy — the metaphor continues with the peasant imploring the chief steward to clear away the "water" that has gushed forth from him. The word *mwy* can be a nisbe of *mw* "water," with the seated man as determinative, as interpreted here, or the noun *mw* "water," with the seated man representing the 1s suffix pronoun (*máwi > *máyi): "bail for me my waters."

B1 310–12 The couplet and the first two lines of the tercet are not a statement that the peasant has given up his petition, but a prelude to the last line of the tercet.

ḫn.j ḫpr.(w) — literally, "my phrase has evolved."

ptr ḏꜣrw.k — literally, "What is your requirement?": after seven petitions, an exasperated comment on the part of the peasant.

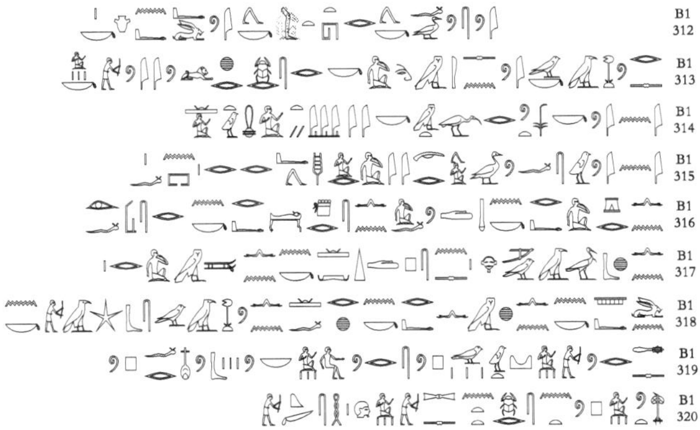

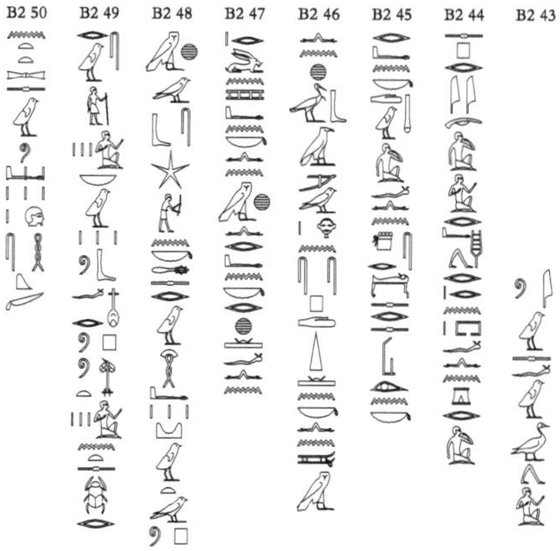

B1 312–13 *jw ⸢ws⸣f.k r tht.k* 3
jw ꜥwn jb.k r swḫꜣ.k 2
jw snm.k r sḫpr ḫrwyw.k 3
B1 314–15 *jn jw.k swt r gmt ky sḫtj mjtw.j* 2
jn jw wsfw spry r ꜥḥꜥ r r n pr.f 5
B1 316 *nn gr rdj.n.k mdw.f* 3
nn sḏr rdj.n.k rs.f 3
B1 317–18 *nn ḫbꜣ ḥr n sspd.n.k* 3
nn tm r wn.n.k 3
B1 318 *nn ḫm rdj.n.k rḫ.f* 3
nn wḫꜣ sbꜣ.n.k 2
B1 319 *ẖsrw ḏwt pw sr(j)w* 2
nbw bw-nfr pw 1
B1 320 *ḥmwt pw nt sḫpr ntt* 3
ṯꜣzw dpj ḥsq.(w) 3

B1 312–13 “Your neglect will mislead you,
your greed will fool you,
your rapacity will create your enemies.
B1 314–15 But will you find another peasant like me?
Will a neglected petitioner stand at the door of his house?
B1 316 There is none quiet whom you have made speak,
none sleeping whom you have made awaken;
B1 317–18 no face of one you have made sharp will diminish,
no mouth you have opened will close;

B1 318 there is none ignorant whom you have made learn,
none foolish whom you have instructed.
B1 319 Officials are dispellers of evil;
they are masters of goodness;
B1 320 they are craftsmen of creating what is,
who can tie on a severed head."

B1 312–13 *jw ⸢ws⸣f.k r tht.k* — the scribe has metathesized the first two consonants. The determinative of *tht* was originally , erased and overwritten with .

snm.k — literally, "your feeding."

B1 314–15 The first question echoes the chief steward's words in B1 105–107 "My lord, I have found one of those peasants who is truly fine of speaking." This may be self-aggrandizement on the peasant's part, but more likely, in view of the second line, it implies "What will you do when someone else comes to appeal to you?"

wsfw spry — literally, "one neglected who petitions": two participles, the first passive, the second active. The line means, "Can you expect a petitioner whom you ignore to stay home and not keep coming to you?"

B1 316–18 These three couplets are statements of the chief steward's power and effectiveness.

nn ḫbꜣ ḥr n sspd.n.k — the statement means that one whom the chief steward has made aware ("sharp") cannot become unaware. *ḫbꜣ* is a spelling of the verb  *ḫbj* "diminish."

wḫꜣ — B2 48 substitutes *ḫm* "ignorant," as in the first line.

B1 319–20 These two couplets are meant to remind the chief steward of his duty. The first is the more realistic; the second, the more hyperbolical.

ḥmwt — a collective, hence the feminine genitival adjective *nt*.

ṯꜣzw dpj ḥsq — this phrase means "they can do the impossible"; the reference is to a magician's feat. In B2 50, the scribe initially wrote plural strokes after the first determinative of *ṯꜣzw*, then overwrote them with the arm determinative without erasing.

Episode 14 — The Eighth Discourse (B1 320–357, B2 50–90)

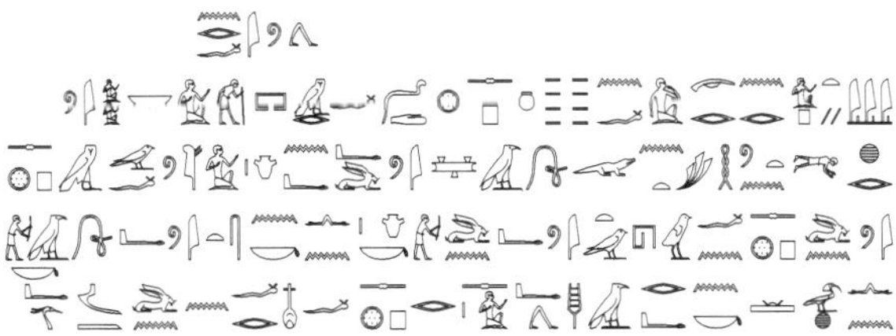

B1 320
B1 321
B1 322
B1 323
B1 324

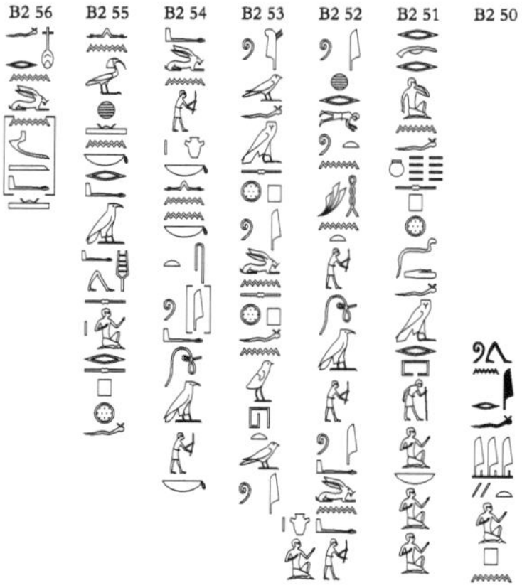

B1 320–21 *jw.jn r.f sḫtj pn r spr n.f 8nw zp* 4
ḏd.f (j)m(j)-r pr wr nb.j 3
B1 321–23 *jw ḫr.tw n ḥnt wꜣ.(w)* 3
jw ꜥwn-jb šw.f m zp 3
jw wn zp.f n wht 3
B1 323–24 *jw ꜥwn jb.k nn n.k st* 3
jw ꜥwꜣ.k nn ꜣḫ n.k 2
B1 324 *rdj ꜣ ꜥḥꜥ zj* 3
r zp.f nfr n wn mꜣꜥ 3

B1 320–21 So, the peasant came to appeal to him an eighth time,
saying, "Chief steward, my lord!
B1 321–23 Now one falls far because of rapacity;
now the greedy man becomes devoid of a cause:
now his cause exists for failure.
B1 323–24 Now you are greedy: it is not for you;
now you rob: it is not useful for you.
B1 324 A man should just be allowed to attend
to his truly good cause.

In his eighth discourse, the peasant returns to accusations against the chief steward for the disorder that prevails through his neglect.

B1 321–24 The three lines of the opening tercet and the two of the following couplet all have statements introduced by *jw*, indicating their relevance to the time of the peasant's speaking (reflected in this translation by "now"). The tercet speaks in general terms of the "greedy man," and the couplet narrows the accusation to the chief steward himself.

wꜣ.(w) — 3ms stative used as an unmarked adverb clause (§ 20.8), literally, “he being far.”

ꜥwn-jb — in B2 52, the second word of this phrase is written to the left of the column at the bottom of the page.

ꜥwꜣ.k — the suffix pronoun is written below the line so as not to extend the line more to the left.

B1 324 The first line uses the passive *sḏm.f* of *rdj* in the *rdj sḏm.f* construction (§ 21.8), emphasized by means of the enclitic particle *ꜣ* (§ 15.7.1).

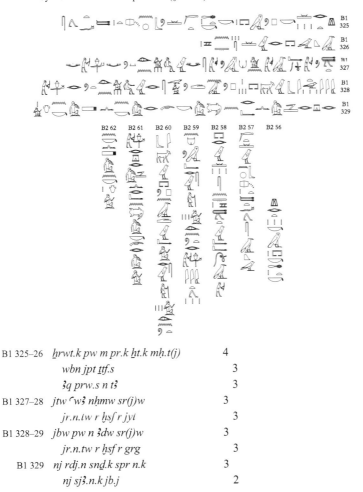

B1 325–26 *ẖrwt.k pw m pr.k ẖt.k mḥ.t(j)* 4

wbn jpt ṯṯf.s 3

ꜣq prw.s n tꜣ 3

B1 327–28 *jtw ꜥwꜣ nḥmw sr(j)w* 3

jr.n.tw r ḫsf r jyt 3

B1 328–29 *jbw pw n ꜣdw sr(j)w* 3

jr.n.tw r ḫsf r grg 3

B1 329 *nj rdj.n snḏ.k spr n.k* 3

nj sjꜣ.n.k jb.j 2

B1 325–26 It means your needs are in your house, your belly full;
the oipe swells and overflows,
so that its excess goes to ruin on the ground.

B1 327–28 Let the robber be arrested whom the officials have saved,
appointed for a bar against wrongs.

B1 328–29 A shelter for the aggressor are officials,
appointed for a bar against lying.

B1 329 Your fear does not allow appealing to you:
you do not perceive my mind.

B1 325–26 *ḫrwt.k pw m pr.k* — an adverbial sentence serving as the predicate of an A *pw* sentence (§ 21.12). The line refers to the couplet of B1 323–24.

jpt — see § 9.7.4.

ꜣq prw.s n tꜣ — *prw* refers to the grain that "emerges" (*prj*) from the overflow mentioned in the preceding line. Together, the two lines mean that the chief steward has so much that he is not concerned with waste.

B1 327–29 These two couplets have the same last line, a *sḏm.n.f* with the passive suffix *tw*, used to modify *sr(j)w* in the first line. The first line in the first couplet has a passive *sḏm.f* (*jtw*), and a relative *sḏm.f* (*nḥmw*) modifying *ꜥwꜣ*; in the second line, B2 59 has *r ḥsf jyt* "to bar wrongs." In the second line of the second couplet, the scribe of B2 60–61 has omitted the preposition *r* before *ḥsf* in changing columns. The two couplets as a whole refer to Nemtinakht (*ꜥwꜣ* "the robber" and *ꜣdw* "the aggressor").

B1 329 *snḏ.k* — the suffix pronoun can be subjective ("your fear") or objective ("fear of you"). Since the peasant is in fact appealing, the first seems likelier here, and the sense, as indicated by the second line, is that of successful appealing.

spr — as written, this is an infinitive. B2 61 has *spr.j*, probably the *sḏm.f* of the *rdj sḏm.f* construction: "does not let me appeal."

nj sjꜣ.n.k jb.j — this line follows as a consequence of the preceding one. The sense is that the chief steward does not understand what the peasant is saying.

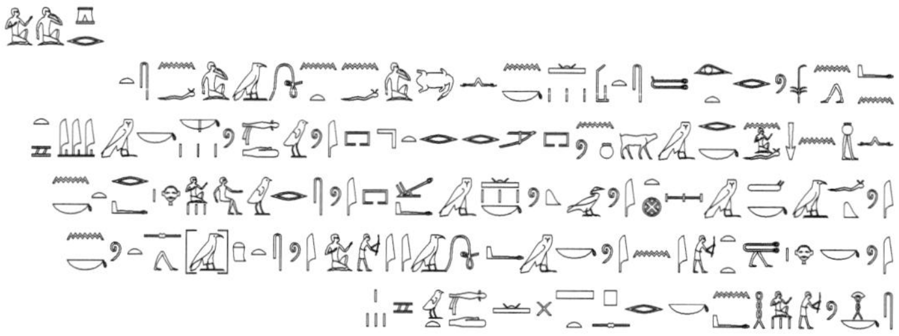

B1 329
B1 330
B1 331
B1 332
B1 333
B1 334

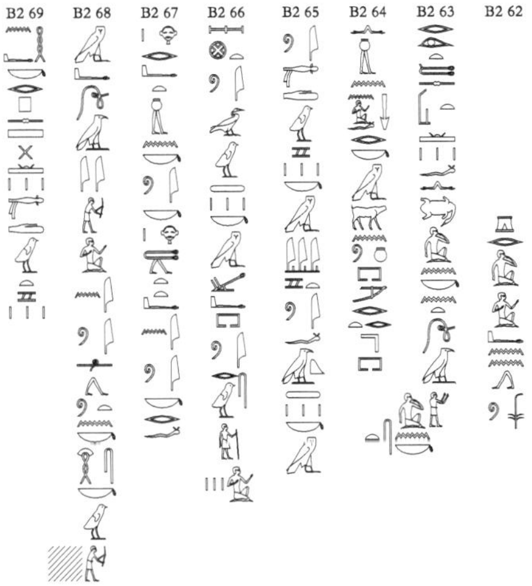

B1 329–31 *gr ꜥnn sw r jrt ṯzwt n.k* 4
nj snḏ.n.f n twꜣ n.f st 2
nj jn sn.f r.k m ẖnw mrrt 4
B1 331–32 *jw {w}šdw.k m sḫt jw fqꜣ.k m spꜣt* 4
jw ꜥqw.k m šnꜥ 2
B1 332–34 *jw sr(j)w ḥr rdjt n.k* 2
jw.k ḥr jtt jn jw.k m ꜥwꜣy 2
jw stꜣ.tw n.k skw ḥnꜥ.k r pzšt šdwt 4

B1 329–31 The quiet man who turns to make accusation of you,
he is not afraid of raising it for himself,
his brother not being fetched against you in the street.
B1 331–32 Your plots are in the field, your reward is in the cultivation,
your income is in the storehouse.
B1 332–34 Officials are giving to you
and you are taking: are you a robber?
One is dragged to you, troops with you, for the division of plots of land."

B1 329–31 *ꜥnn sw* — the verb *ꜥnn* is transitive: "who turns himself."

r jrt ṯzwt n.k — the position of the prepositional phrase shows that it belongs with *ṯzwt* rather than *jrt*: thus, "make accusation because of you" rather than "make to you accusation." B2 63 has *r jrt ṯzwt.f* "to make his accusation," without the prepositional phrase.

nj snḏ.n.f n twꜣ n.f st — *twꜣ* is an infinitive (§ 13.5.2). B2 63 has *nj snḏ.n.k n twꜣ n.k st* "you are not afraid of it being raised to you" (for the passive translation, see § 13.7). In B1, the first two lines mean that the reasonable (*gr* "quiet") man does not fear making accusation against the chief steward; in B2, they mean that the chief steward does not fear having accusations against others made to him. B2's text is probably conditioned by the first line of the preceding couplet. B1's version contrasts the accuser's (i.e., the peasant's) lack of fear with that of the chief steward, and is better suited to the context and to the third line of the tercet.

nj jn sn.f r.k m ẖnw mrrt — this line elaborates on the prepositional phrase *n.f* in the preceding line: it means that the accuser is not afraid to make an accusation by himself, without any supporter (as is the peasant's case). *m ẖnw mrrt*, literally "inside the street," denotes a public accusation, rather than one brought before officials.

B1 331–32 This couplet returns to the theme of the tercet in B1 325–26 and sets up the accusation in the following couplet.

{w}šdw.k — the scribe has added an erroneous *w* at the beginning of the word, probably thinking of *wšd* "address." At the end, the scribe originally wrote the suffix pronoun before the plural strokes; he later corrected the mistake by drawing a stroke over the *k*, to cancel it, and squeezing in another *k* before the following preposition.

B1 332–33 This tercet accuses the chief steward of taking bribes. For the first line, B2 66–67 has *jw sr(j)w ḥr rdjt jn.k* "officials are letting you get." The last line rebukes the chief steward for using force (*skw ḥnꜥ.k* "troops are with you") to compel land divisions; B2 68 frames this as a question, with introductory *jn*: "Is one is dragged to you, troops with you, for the division of plots of land?" In B2 68 the determinatives of a seated man and plural strokes were probably written to the left of the striking-man determinative at the bottom of the page, now lost.

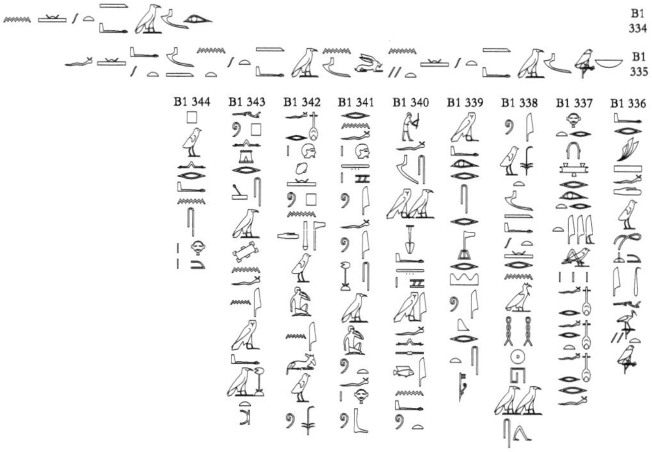

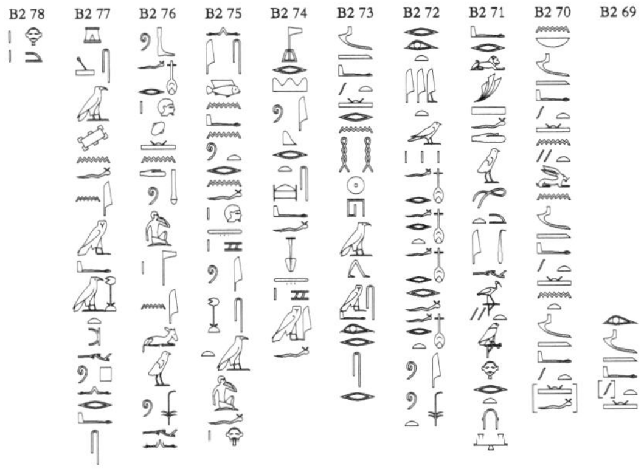

B1 334–35 *jr mꜣʿt n nb mꜣʿt* 3
ntj wn mꜣʿt nt mꜣʿt.f 3
B1 336–37 *ʿr šfdw gstj ḏḥwtj* 3
ḥr.t(j) r jrt jyt 2
B1 337–39 *nfr nfrt nfr r.f* 3
jw swt mꜣʿt r nḥḥ 2
hꜣꜣ.s m ʿ jrr s(j) r ẖr(j)-nṯr 3
B1 339–41 *jw qrs.t(w).f zmꜣ tꜣ jm.f* 4
nj zjn.tw rn.f dp tꜣ 3
B1 341–42 *{jw.f} jw sẖꜣ.tw.f ḥr bw nfr* 2
dp-ḥsb pw n mdw-nṯr 2
B1 342–44 *jn jwsw pw nj g{r}sꜣ.n.f* 2
jn mjḫꜣt pw nj rdj.n.s ḥr gs 3

B1 334–35 "Do Maat for the Lord of Maat,
the Maat of whose Maat exists.
B1 336–37 Pen, scroll, palette of Thoth,
keep away from doing wrong.
B1 337–39 The good man's good is better than him,
for Maat is continual;
it goes down with the one who does it to the necropolis.
B1 339–41 He is entombed, being buried,
and his name is not erased on earth,
B1 341–42 for it is remembered because of goodness:
it is the standard of hieroglyphic writing,
B1 342–44 for it is a crossbar that does not tilt,
for it is a scale that does not lean to one side.

The end of the peasant's eighth petition is an extended discourse on Maat, replete with plays on words.

B1 334–35 The term *nb mꜣꜥt* can refer to the Sun, creator of Maat, but here more likely to the king, responsible for Maat on earth. The construction of the second line is the same as in B1 120–21; the line means that the king's Maat is identical with the cosmic Maat.

B1 336–37 The first line identifies the chief steward as the instrument of Thoth, who is also called "Lord of Maat," in the form of the scroll on which Thoth records the final judgment (Essay 8, Fig. 8), the reed brush with which he writes, and the scribal palette that holds the red and black ink. In the word *gstj* "palette," the scribe originally wrote , as in B2 71, then drew a stroke through the .

B1 337–39 The theme of this tercet and the next three couplets is Maat's eternal nature and its value for the one who adheres to it. The first line is an adjectival sentence in which *nfr* is used both as an adjectival predicate and as a noun; the subject is *nfrt nfr* "the good man's good." The sentence means that goodness is greater than the man who exemplifies it. B2 72 adds a second  at the end of the line, which is probably a 3fs stative *nfr.t(j)* referring to *nfrt*: "it having become good," which stresses the temporal nature of *nfrt nfr* as an instance of Maat, as described in the second line. The third line anticipates the next three couplets and means that a man's reputation for Maat persists after his death. B2 73 has the regular form of the verb; in B1, the geminated stem probably stresses the continual relevance of the statement: i.e., "it always goes down."

B1 339–44 *zmꜣ tꜣ jm.f* — an adverbial sentence serving as an unmarked adverb clause, literally "there being burial with him"—*zmꜣ tꜣ* "joining the earth" is a term for burial.

nj zjn.tw rn.f — the negated *sḏm.f* with gnomic sense (§ 18.13). B2 75 has *nj sjn.n.tw rn.f* "his name cannot be erased."

{jw.f} jw sḫꜣ.t(w).f — the final suffix pronoun probably refers to the man, in view of the next tercet. The scribe wrote *jw.f*, perhaps thinking of *jw.f sḫꜣ.w*, with the stative, then continued with the proper construction, as in B2 75, without correcting *jw.f*.

mdw-nṯr "god's speech" is the term for hieroglyphic writing (§ 1.4). This term indicates that the *pw* of the three A *pw* sentences refers to the name rather than to the name's owner. B2 76 omits the first two *pw*'s, probably by accident but possibly as a long topicalization to which the third *pw* refers: "The standard of hieroglyphic writing, a crossbar that does not tilt, it is a scale."

jn jwsw pw ... jn mjḫꜣt pw — these can be understood as questions (§ 11.11.2), to which the two following *nj sḏm.n.f* clauses supply an answer, but *jn* is actually a specifying particle; at the head of a sentence it means something like "it is the fact that" (or in questions, "is it the fact that"). These two sentences are better understood as explanations of the first line. The *nj sḏm.n.f* clauses are therefore unmarked relative clauses. In B1 343 *gsꜣ.n.f*, the scribe wrote a ligatured  instead of a simple .

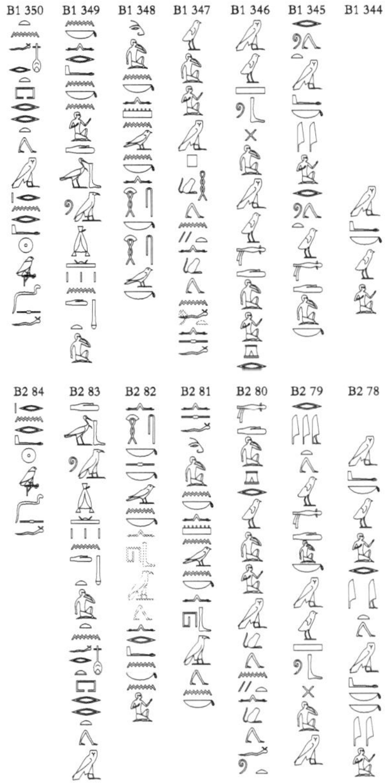

B1 344–46 *mj.k wj r jwt mj.(k) ky r jwt* 2
wšd.k m wšbw 2

B1 346–47 *m wšd grw* 2
m pḥ ntj nj pḥ.n.f 3

B1 347–49 *nj sf.n.k nj mn.n.k* 2
nj sksk.n.k 1

B1 349–50 *nj rdj.n.k n.j db3w n mdt tn nfrt* 4
prrt m r n rʿ ḏs.f 4

B1 344–46 "Whether I will come or another will come,
you should respond with an answer.

B1 346–47 Don't grill the quiet man,
don't attack one who does not attack.

B1 347–49 You do not show mercy, you do not feel pain,
you do not wipe out anything.

B1 349–50 You do not give me a return for this good speech
that comes from the mouth of the Sun himself.

B1 344–46 The peasant now returns to his appeal to the chief steward. The *mj.k ... mj.(k)* clauses in the first line serve as a "whether ... or" construction (cf. § 15.6.7; the scribe has omitted the second *k* probably because it is in contact with the *k* of *ky*: § 2.8.2). For *jwt ... jwt*, with the geminated stem (§ 12.6.2), B2 78–79 has the base form *jjt ... jyt*.

B1 346–47 *ntj nj pḥ.n.f* — the scribe originally wrote *nj pḥ.n tw*, then erased the *tw* and overwrote it with the suffix pronoun. B2 80 has *nj pḥ.f tw* "who has not attacked you."

B1 347–49 In the second line, B2 adds *nj hꜣb.n.k* "you do not send word" at the beginning; the fact that *nj sksk.n.k* has only a single stress suggests that the scribe of B1 may have inadvertently omitted this clause. After *nj sksk.n.k*, the scribe of B2 repeated *nj hꜣb* before continuing with the next couplet; at some later point, he noticed the error and erased it. The meaning of *nj sksk.n.k* is apparently that the chief steward does not "wipe out" any of the misdeeds that the peasant reports to him.

B1 349–50 The second line means that the peasant's words conform with Maat, created by the Sun.

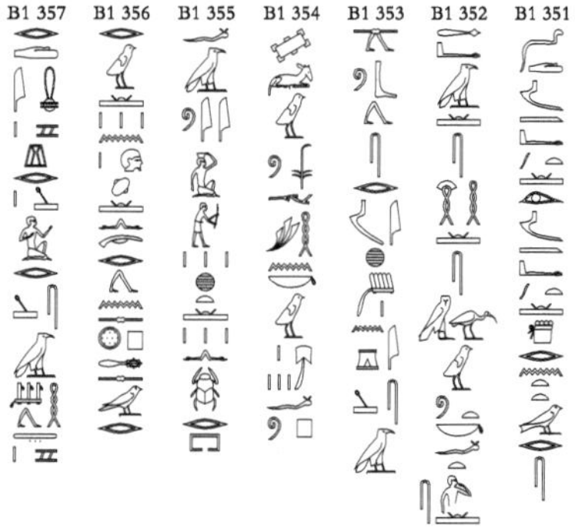

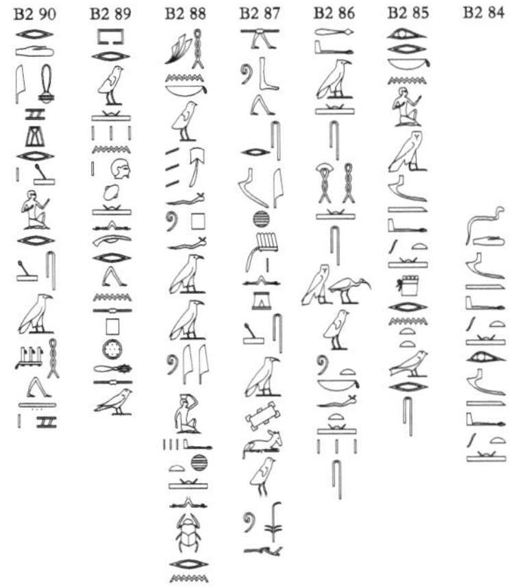

B1 351–53 *ḏd mꜣꜥt jr mꜣꜥt* 4
ḏr ntt wr s(j) ꜥꜣ s(j) wꜣḥ s(j) 3
gmw.tw kft.s zbw.s r jmꜣḫ 4

B1 353–55 *jn gsꜣ jwsw* 2
ḥnkw.f pw fꜣyw ḫwt 3

B1 355–57 *nj ḫpr prw n dp ḥsb* 3
nj spr.n zp ḫz r {r} dmj 3
ḫr(j)-sꜣ r sꜣḥ tꜣ 2

B1 351–53 "Speak Maat, do Maat,
since it is great, it is important, it is lasting.
When its revelation is found, it sends to honor.

B1 353–55 Does the crossbar tilt?
Those that carry things are its pans.

B1 355–57 No excess happens to the standard;
no unworthy cause can arrive at harbor
or the bearer to landfall."

B1 351–53 The grammar of the third line is uncertain; the first clause could also read *gmw tw kft.s* "when its revelation finds you," though this is less likely. The *w* ending of both verbs has been interpreted as that of the "prospective *sḏm.f*" (Parkinson 2012b, 285–86; see Essay 26), but they more likely represent the stressed vowel of both forms (*gimátu … *sibás: see § 18.2). For *jmꜣḫ* "honor, worth," see Essay 21).

B1 353–55 The sense of this couplet is that everything is weighed in the scale of Maat. The *ḥnkw* are the "pans" at either end of the crossbar (); the determinative indicates that they were made of leather rather than metal. In the last line, B2 88 has *fȝȝyw ḫt* "that carry a thing," with the geminated stem.

B1 355–57 *nj ḫpr* — for this gnomic negation, B2 88 has *nj ḫpr.n* "cannot happen." The term *prw* "excess," also found in B1 326, refers here to an erroneous over-weight.

r {r} dmj — the scribe has repeated the preposition at the top of the column.

ẖr(j)-sȝ — the determinative in both copies shows that this is a compound noun. It is a nisbe phrase, literally "the one under the back," meaning "the one who has the back" (that carries the "vile cause"). The third line is a second subject of *nj spr.n* in the second line.

B1 ends at this point, where the scribe reached the end of the verso. The scribe may have intended to complete the text on a second papyrus.

Episode 15 — The Ninth Discourse (B2 91–115)

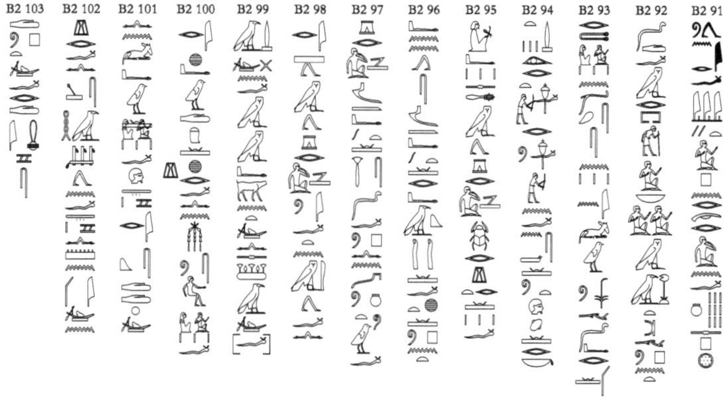

B2 91–92 ***jw.jn r.f*** *sḫtj pn r spr n.f 9nw zp* 4
ḏd.f (j)m(j)-r pr wr nb.j 3

B2 92–94 *mḫȝt pw nt rmṯ ns.sn* 3
jn jwsw ḏʿr ḏȝt 3
jrr ḫsft r ḫsfw n.f 3

B2 94–95 *sn.tw dp-ḥsb r.k* 3
zȝw sḫm grg 3

B2 95–96 *ḫpr ẖrwt.f* 2
ʿnn s(j) mȝʿt r ʿqȝ.f 3

B2 96–97 *ḫt pw nt grg mȝʿt* 3
swȝḏ.f pw nj nw.tw.f 2

B2 98–99 *jr šm grg jw.f tnm.f* 3
nj ḏȝ.n.f m mḫnt nj sšȝ.[f] 3

B2 100–101 *jr ḫwd ẖr.f nn msw.f* 3
nn jwꜥw.f dp tꜣ 2
B2 101–103 *jr sqdd ẖr.f nj sꜣḥ.n.f tꜣ* 3
nj mjn.n dpwt.f r dmj.s 3

B2 91–92 **So**, the peasant **came** to appeal to him a ninth time,
saying, "Chief steward, my lord!
B2 92–94 The scale of people is their tongues;
the crossbar is what seeks out imbalance,
and does punishment to the one who should be punished.
B2 94–95 Let the standard be likened to you,
lest lying rush headlong
B2 95–96 When its needs come about,
Maat turns to correct it.
B2 96–97 Maat is the property of lying:
It means that, though made to flourish, it cannot be harvested.
B2 98–99 If lying walks, it gets lost;
it cannot cross in the ferry nor be landed.
B2 100–101 As for the one who gets rich from it, he has no children,
he has no heirs on earth.
B2 101–103 As for the one who sails with it, he cannot touch land,
his boat cannot moor at its harbor.

The ninth, and last, petition of the peasant begins with a discourse on the antithesis of Maat and falsehood and ends with a final plea for justice.

B2 92–94 The sense of the tercet's first line is explained by the two following lines: people pass judgment by their speech, and public opinion will serve as punishment—a veiled threat to the chief steward for his inaction.

B2 94–95 *zꜣw sḫm grg* — literally, "beware that lying rushes headlong": see the note to B1 268–70.

B2 95–96 *ꜥnn s(j) mꜣꜥt r ꜥqꜣ.f* — literally, "Maat turns itself toward its correctness." The last suffix pronoun refers to *grg* "lying."

B2 96–97 The first line means that lying presupposes Maat. Compare the English expression "The exception proves the rule," meaning that the existence of the rule is established by the fact of an exception to it.

swꜣḏ.f pw nj nw.tw.f — literally, "It is that it is made to flourish (but) it cannot be gathered in," a sentence serving as the predicate of an A *pw* sentence (§ 21.12).

B2 98–99 *nj sšꜣ.[f]* — the verb is a passive *sḏm.f*, a form of transitive *sḫꜣꜣ/sšꜣꜣ* "land (a boat)."

B2 100–101 *ḫwd ḫr.f* — the sign is an error for the determinative ; for the spelling, see the note to B1 257–59. For the prepositional phrase, the scribe originally wrote *ḫr.f*, with , then later added the correct sign to the left of it.

jwꜥw.f — the scribe originally wrote a bookroll as determinative, then overwrote it with the determinatives .

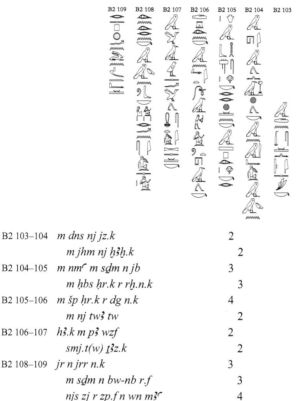

B2 103–104 *m dns nj jz.k* 2
m jhm nj ḫꜣḫ.k 2
B2 104–105 *m nmꜥ m sḏm n jb* 3
m ḥbs ḥr.k r rḫ.n.k 3
B2 105–106 *m šp ḥr.k r dg n.k* 4
m nj twꜣ tw 2
B2 106–107 *hꜣ.k m pꜣ wzf* 2
smj.t(w) ṯꜣz.k 2
B2 108–109 *jr n jrr n.k* 3
m sḏm n bw-nb r.f 3
njs zj r zp.f n wn mꜣꜥ 4

B2 103–104 "Don't become heavy: you have not become light;
don't stall: you have not hurried.
B2 104–105 Don't be biased in listening to the mind,
don't cover your face to one you know.
B2 105–106 Don't be blind to one who looks to you,
don't reject one who depends on you.

B2 106–107 You should descend from this neglect:
let your sentence be reported.
B2 108–109 Do for the one who does for you,
don't listen to everyone against him.
Summon a man for his just cause.

B2 103–104 This couplet urges moderation. It can be paraphrased as "You are not light, but don't be heavy; you do not hasten, but don't stall."

B2 106–107 The second line means, "Let your decision be announced."

B2 108–109 The sense of the prepositional phrase *r.f* in the second line is "in preference to him."

zp.f n wn mꜣꜥ — literally, "his cause of true existence."

B2 109–11 *nn sf n wzfw* 2
nn ḫnms n zḫ mꜣꜥt 3
nn hrw nfr n ꜥwn-jb 2
B2 111-13 *ḫpr wṯzw m mꜣjry* 3
mꜣjry r sprw 2
ḫpr ḫft(j) m smꜣmw 3
B2 113–15 *mj.k wj ḥr spr n.k nj sḏm.n.k st* 3
jw.j r šmt r spr ḥr.k n jnpw 4

B2 109–11 "There is no yesterday for the negligent,
no friend for the one deaf to Maat,
no good time for the greedy.

B2 111–13 When an accuser becomes one who is needy,
the needy one will be an appealer,
and the opponent becomes the slain.
B2 113–15 Look, I am appealing to you and you don't hear it.
I will go to appeal about you to Anubis."

B2 111–13 This tercet refers to the peasant's own situation. In the last line, the *ḫft(j)* "opponent" is the peasant himself, and its reference to *smꜣmw* "one who is slain" (passive participle of *smꜣ* "kill") foreshadows the final couplet.

B2 113–15 The peasant now abandons all hope of redress. Since Anubis is the god of the cemetery, the second line apparently means that, without hope, he will go off to die. The reference to Anubis is ironic, in view of the peasant's name (see the note to R 1,1), bringing the composition full circle and creating "a sense of great finality" (Parkinson 2012b, 303).

Episode 16 — Conclusion (B2 115–129)

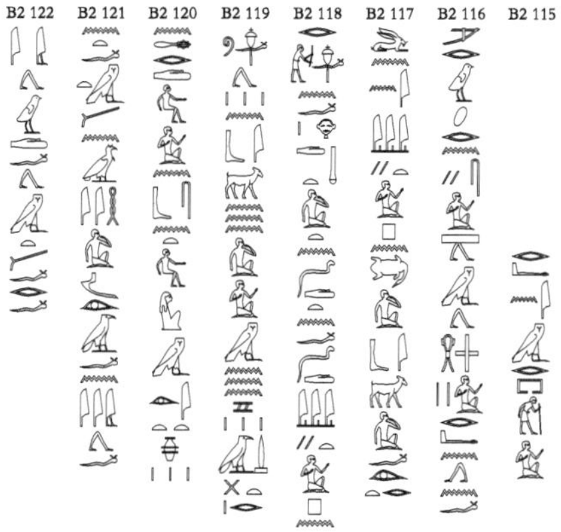

B2 115–16 *rdj.jn (j)m(j)-r pr wr zꜣ-mrw rnsj* 4
šm jmj-zꜣ 2 r ꜥnn.f 3
B2 117–18 *wn.jn sḫtj pn snḏ.(w)* 3
jb.f jrr.t(w) r ḫsf n.f 3
ḥr mdt tn ḏdt.n.f 2
B2 118–20 *ḏd.jn sḫtj pn* 2
ḫsfw n jb m mw 3
ḏꜣt r n ḫrd n sbnt m jrtt 4
B2 121–22 *ntf m(w)t n nḥy mꜣ.f n jy.f* 5
jj wdf m(w)t.f r.f 4

B2 115–16 So, chief steward Meru's son Rensi had
two bodyguards go to turn him back.
B2 117–18 So, the peasant was afraid,
thinking it was done to punish him
for the speech he had said.
B2 118–20 So, the peasant said,
"The meeting of the thirsty man with water,
the mouth of the nursing child coming across milk,
B2 121–22 that is death for one who prays and looks to its coming
when his death's delay comes against him."

The chief steward prevents the peasant from leaving and reveals that he has had the entirety of the nine discourses recorded.

B2 117–18 For this tercet, see § 25.10. The geminated stem of *jrr.t(w)* may indicate an ongoing process ("it was being done"). Alternatively, the form may be *jr.t(w)*, since the scribe commonly uses a complementary 𓂋 before *t* with this verb.

B2 118–20 *mw* — the spelling with the determinative and plural strokes is unusual and may indicate a body of water ("waters") rather than the substance, although the latter fits the context better.

ẖrd n sbnt — literally, "child of a nursemaid."

B2 121–22 *nḥy mꜣ.f n jy.f* — literally, "a prayer who looks to its coming": the words following *nḥy* are an unmarked relative clause; the first suffix pronoun refers to (undefined) *nḥy*; the second, to the infinitive *m(w)t*.

wdf m(w)t.f is a direct genitive with two infinitives, serving as subject of *jj*.

B2 122–24	*ḏd.jn (j)m(j)-r pr wr zꜣ-mrw rnsj*	4	
	m snḏ sḫtj		2
	mj.k jrr.k r jrt ḥnꜥ.j		3
B2 124–26	*rdj.jn sḫtj pn ꜥnḫ*	3	
	ḥr wnm.j ꜣ m t.k		2
	swrj.j ꜣ [m ḥnqt].k r nḥḥ		3
B2 126–28	*ḏd.(j)n (j)m(j)-r pr wr zꜣ-mrw rnsj*	4	
	zꜣ grt ꜥꜣ		2
	sḏm.k nꜣy.k n sprwt		3
B2 128–29	*rdj.jn.f šd.t(w).s ḥr ꜥrt mꜣt*	4	
	sprt nbt r ḫr[t.s]		3

B2 122–24 So, chief steward Meru's son Rensi said,
"Don't fear, peasant.
Look, you should act to act with me."
B2 124–26 So, the peasant made an oath, saying,
"Shall I just eat of your bread
and just drink of your beer continually?"
B2 126–28 So, chief steward Meru's son Rensi said,
"Now, wait here,
and you will hear those appeals of yours."
B2 128–29 So, he had them read out from a new scroll,
each appeal according to its content.

B2 122–24 *jrr.k r jrt ḥnꜥ.j* — an emphatic sentence with *r jrt ḥnꜥ.j* the rheme: "it is to act with me that you should act." The chief steward is advising the peasant to deal with him rather than to seek recourse with Anubis.

B2 124–26 *ḥr* — *ḏd* is understood: see § 14.7.

The second and third lines are best understood as a "virtual" question (§ 11.11.1), with verbal predicates. The peasant means, "Am I going to have to depend on you for eternity?"

B2 128–29 *ḥr ꜥrt mꜣt* — the preposition is used here in the sense of origin, "from on" (§ 8.2.10). The phrase "new scroll" means that the peasant's discourses were recorded on a fresh, unused roll of papyrus, a practice common for official or archival documents.

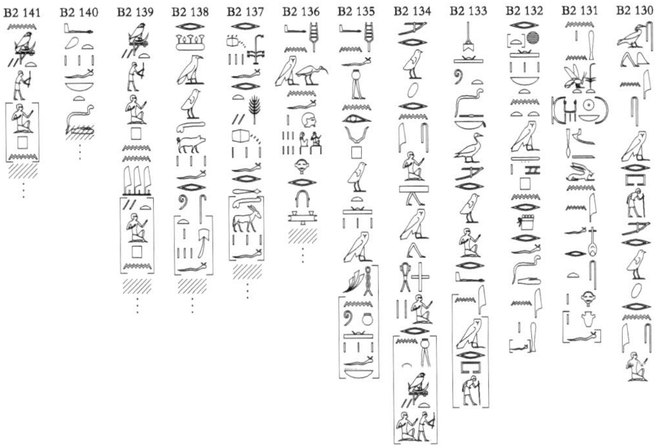

B2 130–31 *sꜥq.jn s(j) (j)m(j)-r pr wr zꜣ-mrw rnsj* 4
r ḥm n nswt-bjt NB-KꜢW-Rꜥ mꜣꜥ ḫrw 4
B2 131–32 *wn.jn nfr st ḥr jb.[f]* 3
r ḫ[t] nbt ntt m tꜣ pn r ḏr.f 4
B2 132–33 *ḏd.jn ḥm.[f]* 2
wḏꜥ tw ḏs.k zꜣ mrw 3
B2 133–34 *rdj.j[n (j)m(j)-r pr wr] zꜣ-mrw rnsj* 4
šm jmj-zꜣ 2 r [jnt nmtj-nḫt.(w)] 4
B2 135–36 *ꜥḥꜥ.n jn wpwt m ḥn[w.f nb]* 4
ꜥḥꜥ.n gm n.f dp 6 3
B2 136–38 *ḥr [r mrw.f] r šmꜥ.f r btj.f* 4
r ꜥꜣ[w.f r mnmnt.f] r šꜣw.f r ꜥw[t.f nbt 4
B2 138–40 *ꜥḥꜥ.n rdj ḥnw] nmtj-nḫt pn n sḫt[j pn* 4
ꜥꜣg] ꜥwt.f nbt 3
B2 140–41 *ḏ[d.jn (j)m(j)-r pr wr zꜣ-mrw rnsj]* 4
n nmtj-nḫt.(w) [pn ... 2+x
...] x

B2 130–31 So, chief steward Meru's son Rensi brought it in
to the Incarnation of Dual King Nebkaure, justified,
B2 131–32 and it was better in his mind
than anything that is in this entire land.
B2 132–33 So, His Incarnation said,
"You judge yourself, Meru's son."

B2 133–34 So, chief steward Meru's son Rensi had
two bodyguards go to get Nemtinakht.
B2 135–36 Then an inventory was fetched of all his property.
Then he was found to have six servants
B2 136–38 apart from his tenants, from his thin barley, his emmer,
his donkeys, his cattle, his pigs, and all his animals.
B2 138–40 Then Nemtinakht's property was given to the peasant,
and he was pummeled on all his limbs.
B2 140–41 So, chief steward Meru's son Rensi said
to Nemtinakt, " …
… ."

At the end of the narrative, the peasant's discourses are presented to the king, who orders the chief steward to pass judgment. Nemtinakht is arrested, and all his property is given to the peasant.

B2 130–31 *sʿq.jn s(j)* — literally, "caused it to enter."

B2 132–33 *wḏʿ tw* — an imperative with dependent pronoun (§ 15.3).

B2 135–37 *ʿḥʿ.n gm n.f dp 6* — literally, "then six head were found for him." This is a use of the preposition *n* to express possession (§ 11.9.2). For *dp* "head," see the note to ShS. 177–79. The number could be *60* but *6* is probably more realistic.

B2 140–41 The length of the lacuna after *ḏ[d]* best suits the title and name of the chief steward as speaker, if in fact the verb is *ḏd*. The content of the speech can only have occupied the third line of a tercet.

The Colophon (B2 142)

B2 142

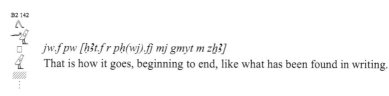

jw.f pw [ḥꜣt.f r pḥ(wj).fj mj gmyt m zẖꜣ]
That is how it goes, beginning to end, like what has been found in writing.

The column has enough space for the same colophon as in Sin. B 311, written by the same scribe.

BIBLIOGRAPHY

Allen, James P. *The Heqanakht Papyri.* Publications of the Metropolitan Museum of Art Egyptian Expedition 27. New York, 2002.

Griffith, Francis Ll. "Fragments of Old Egyptian Stories from the British Museum and Amherst Collections." *Proceedings of the Society of Biblical Archaeology* 14 (1892), 451–72.

Harris, John R. *Lexicographical Studies in Ancient Egyptian Minerals*. Berlin, 1961.

Janssen, Jac. J. *Daily Dress at Deir el-Medîna: Words for Clothing*. GHP Egyptology 8. London, 2008.

Müller-Wollerman, Renate. "Die sogenannte ober- und unterägyptische Gerste." *Varia Aegyptiaca* 3 (1987), 39–41.

Parkinson, Richard B. *The Tale of the Eloquent Peasant*. Oxford, 1991.

———. *Reading Ancient Egyptian Poetry, Among Other Histories*. Oxford, 2009.

———. *Four 12th Dynasty Literary Papyri (Pap. Berlin P. 3022–5): a Photographic Record*. London and Berlin, 2012.

———. *The Tale of the Eloquent Peasant: a Reader's Commentary*. Lingua Aegyptia Studia Monographica 10. Hamburg, 2012.

Vernus, Pascal. "La date du *Paysan Eloquent*." In Sarah Israelit-Groll, ed., *Studies in Egyptology Presented to Miriam Lichtheim* (Jerusalem, 1990), II, 1033–47.

Vogelsang, Friedrich, and Alan H. Gardiner. *Die Klagen des Bauern*. Literarische Texte des Mittleren Reiches 1. Leipzig, 1908.

TEXT 6
THE DEBATE BETWEEN A MAN AND HIS SOUL

THIS TEXT SURVIVES in a single copy, a papyrus now in Berlin (pBerlin 3024) and the Morgan Library and Museum, New York (pAmherst III) (Parkinson 2012, CD folder "Pap. Berlin P. 3024"). The beginning of the text, an estimated eight columns (*1–*8), is lost, and the following twenty-two (*9–1) are fragmentary.[1] The papyrus is contemporary with Sinuhe B, but the text probably dates to early Dyn. XII (Vernus 1990, 185).

Like the story of Sinuhe, the text is put in the mouth of a first-person narrator. It becomes clear in the course of the composition that the narrator is facing a personal crisis, brought on by his own circumstances and by the times he is living in; the reason may have been given in the beginning of the text, now lost. The crisis prompts an internal debate about which is better: life, with its anguish, or death, with its uncertainties. The two sides of the debate are framed as a dialogue between the narrator and his ba, or soul (Essay 7).

When the text on the Berlin papyrus begins, the narrator's soul is speaking. The Amherst fragments indicate two previous speeches, one by the soul (ending in col. *12) and one by the man (from col. *12 to somewhere between cols. *14 and *25). Initially, the soul is arguing for death and the man is resisting. The man gives a long reply to the soul (cols. 3–55), after which the two characters reverse positions. In a speech and three parables (cols. 55–85), the soul argues for life, and the man counters by espousing death in four litanies (cols. 85–147). The soul is given the last word (cols. 147–54), in which he urges a compromise: make the best of life, and wait for death until it comes. Ultimately, the text is an affirmation of life, even in the most difficult of circumstances. Despite the arguments of both characters in favor of death, there is no indication that the man is contemplating suicide; rather, he is debating the merits of a difficult life on earth versus life after death.

The text is unique not only because of its theme but also because of its dialogue between the narrator and his soul (*bꜣ*). Elsewhere, an internal conversation is with the mind (*jb*) or heart (*ḥꜣtj*), and the soul's realm of activity is the afterlife. The text is also one of the most consciously poetic Middle Egyptian compositions, with language and imagery that are at the pinnacle of Middle Kingdom literature.

1 See Parkinson 2009, 88; Allen 2011, 9–10. Column numbers with asterisks are those of the estimated 28 columns lost or preserved only in the fragments of pAmherst III. Columns of the Berlin papyrus begin with 1. The text occupies most of the papyrus, an estimated original 284 of 392 cm.

Part 1 — Introduction and First Exchanges (*1–3)

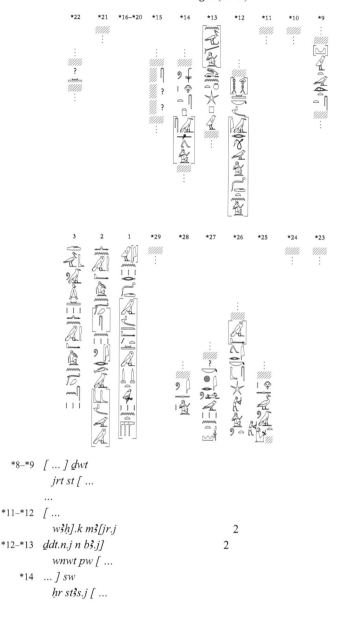

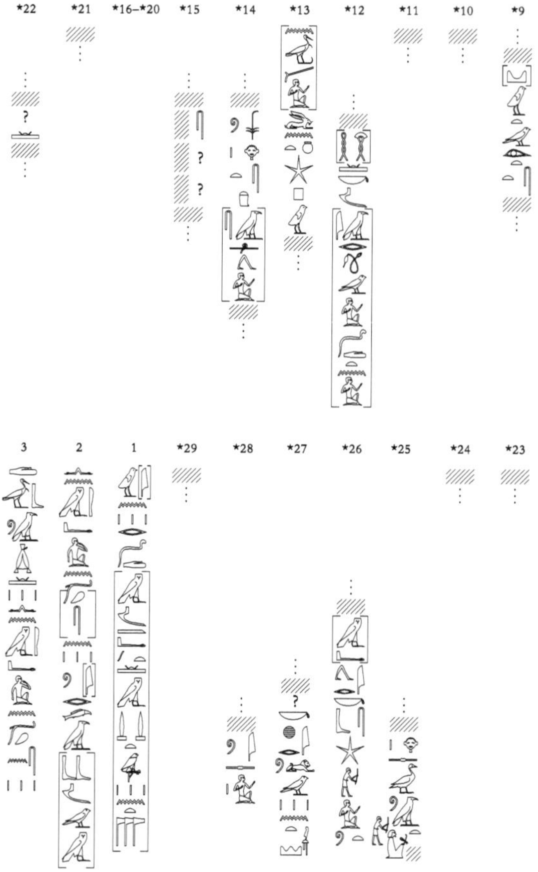

*8–*9 *[…] ḏwt*
jrt st […
…
*11–*12 *[…*
wꜣḥ].k mꜣ[jr.j 2
*12–*13 *ḏdt.n.j n bꜣ.j]* 2
wnwt pw […
*14 *…] sw*
ḥr stꜣs.j […

...

*25–*26 *...] ḥr*
zꜣw t[w ...

*26–*27 *[m]j r.k sbꜣ.j tw [...* 2+x
...].k jẖrw n jmnt 2+x

*28–*29 *[...*
jw zj [...]

1–2 *[j]w.n r ḏd [m mꜣʿt m ḏꜣḏt nt nṯrw]* 4
nj nmʿ.n ns.[s]n 2

2–3 *[j]w r ẖꜣ[bb m] dbꜣw* 2
nj nmʿ.n ns.sn 2

*8–*9 [...] evil.
Doing it [...

...

*11–*12 [...
that you might lay down my need."

*12–*13 What I said to my ba:
"It is the hour [...

*14 ...] him,
because of dragging me [...

...

*25–*26 ...] the face.
Beware of [...

*26–*27 So, come, that I may instruct you [...
...] you the hostile nature of the West.

*28–*29 [...
For a man [...].

1–2 We are to speak truly in the tribunal of the gods:
their tongue cannot be biased.

2–3 It would be crooked in return:
their tongue cannot be biased."

1–3 This is the end of the ba's second speech. It apparently refers to the final judgment before the tribunal of forty-two gods who monitored the trial (see Fig. 8 in Essay 8).

ḏd [m mꜣʿt] — literally, "to speak by means of Maat."

[j]w r ẖꜣ[bb m] dbꜣw — the unexpressed subject of this pseudo-verbal sentence is probably the "bias" denied in the repeated line "their tongue cannot be biased." In other words, if the gods were biased, it would be a "crooked" response to "speaking by means of Maat."

Part 2 — The Man's Second Speech (3–55)

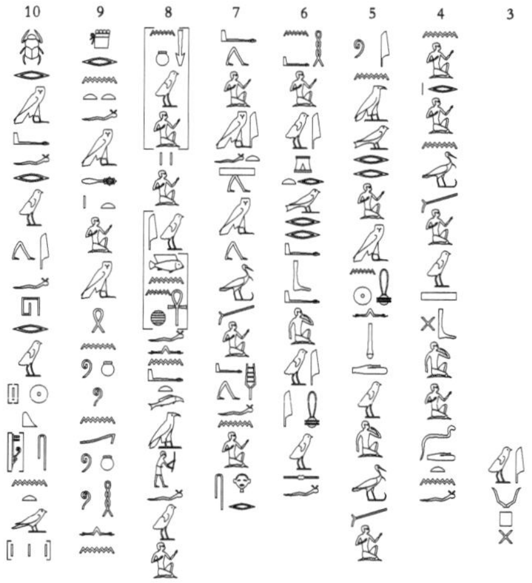

3–4 *jw wp.n.j r.j n bꜣ.j* 3
wšb.j ḏdt.n.f 2
5–6 *jw nꜣ wr.(w) r.j m mjn* 4
nj mdw bꜣ.j ḥnꜥ.j 3
6–7 *jw grt wr r ꜥbꜥ* 2
jw mj wzf jmt.f šm bꜣ.j 4
7–8 *ꜥḥꜥ.f n.j ḥr.s* 2
[snnw].j w[jn ꜥnḫ].f 3
8–10 *nn dj.t(w) ẖꜣ.f wj* 2
ḏr ntt.f m ẖt.j m šnw nwḥ 3
nn ḫpr m ꜥ.f rwj.f hrw qsn[w]t 4

3–4 I opened my mouth to my ba,
that I might answer what he had said.
5–6 "This has become too much for me now:
my ba does not agree with me.
6–7 It is also too much to exaggerate:
my ba going is like one who ignores what he is in.
7–8 He should attend to it for me,
my second, who rejects his life.
8–10 He will not be allowed to resist me,
since he is in my belly in a rope mesh.
Escaping a day of difficulties will not happen to him.

After an introductory couplet, the man's second response to his soul consists of two equal parts, each with thirty-six lines (3–29 and 29–55). In the first half, the man speaks of his soul in the third person.

5–6 *nj mdw bꜣ.j ḥnꜥ.j* — literally, "my ba does not speak with me," with the sense of "in accord with me." This sense of *ḥnꜥ* appears elsewhere in the text (cols. 40, 114, 126).

6–7 *jw mj wzf jmt.f šm bꜣ.j* — an adverbial sentence in which the noun clause *šm bꜣ.j* "(that) my ba goes" is the subject and *mj wzf jmt.f* "like one who ignores what he is in" the predicate. The unusual word order (cf. § 10.2) is perhaps because the normal order *jw šm bꜣ.j mj wzf jmt.f* could be interpreted as "my ba goes like one who ignores what he is in." The nisbe *jmt* has the "reverse" sense discussed in § 8.9. The line as a whole means that the soul's arguing for death ("going") is a way of ignoring the problems he is facing.

7–8 *ꜥḥꜥ.f n.j ḥr.s* — the 3fs suffix pronoun refers to the nisbe *jmt* in col. 7.

8–10 *ḏr ntt.f m ẖt.j m šnw nwḥ* for *ḏr ntt* see § 21.4. The clause refers to the union of body and soul during life. The phrase *m šnw nwḥ* "in a mesh of rope" reflects the inescapable nature of the union as well as the notion of the ba as a bird () caught in a woven net of the sort used to trap wild birds.

nn ḫpr m ꜥ.f rwj.f hrw qsn[w]t — literally, "(that) he escapes a day of difficulties will not happen with him," with *rwj.f hrw qsn[w]t* an unmarked noun clause serving as subject of *ḫpr* (§ 21.11). For *m ꜥ.f* see the note to ShS. 21–23.

11–12 *mj.tn bꜣ.j ḥr tht.j* 3
nj sḏm.n.j n.f 1
12–13 *ḥr stꜣs.j r m(w)t nj jjt.(j) n.f* 4
ḥr hꜣꜥ.(j) ḥr ḫt r smꜣmt.j 3
14–15 *ptr mnt.f […]* 2+x
ḥr [rdjt] sꜣ.f r [sn].f 3

15–17 *tk(n).f jm.j hrw qsnwt* 3
ʿḥʿ.f m pf gs mj jr-nḥnw 3
pꜣ js pw prr jn.f sw r.f 4

11–12 "But look, my ba is misleading me.
I cannot listen to him,
12–13 because of dragging me to death before I have come to it,
because of throwing me on the fire to incinerate me.
14–15 What is his suffering […],
giving his back to his brother?
15–17 He should be near me on a day of difficulties,
and stand on yonder side like a jubilation-maker,
for that is who goes out and brings himself to it.

11–12 *mj.ṯn* — it is unclear who is being addressed; perhaps only the audience of the composition.

12–13 *smꜣmt.j* — the verb is caus. 2-lit. *sꜣm* "make burn," which has an infinitive in *–t* (§ 13.3).

14–15 The lacuna in the first line probably contained a *sḏm.f* such as *šm.f*, to which the second line is a circumstantial clause: i.e., "What is his suffering, that he would go, turning his back on his brother?"

15–17 In the first line, the scribe has omitted the third radical of the verb *tkn* "be near." In the second line, *pf gs* refers to the West, which is "yonder side" (§ 5.9) from the viewpoint of the land of the living; the line means that the soul should regard the West as a place of happy afterlife and not as an escape from life.

pꜣ js pw prr jn.f sw r.f — an A *pw* sentence subordinated by *js* (§ 20.5). This line describes the normal kind of soul, who "goes out" after death and "brings himself" to the West.

17–19 *bꜣ.j wḫꜣ.(w) r sdḥ ꜣh ḥr ꜥnḫ* 4
jhm wj r m(w)t nj jjt.j n.f 4
19–20 *snḏm n.j jmnt* 2
jn jw qsnt pw 1
20–21 *pẖrt pw ꜥnḫ* 2
jw ḫtw ẖr.sn 2
21–22 *ḫn{t}d.k r.k ḥr jsft* 2
wꜣḥ mꜣjr.j 2

17–19 "My ba is too foolish to suppress pain while living,
one who prods me to death before I have come to it,
19–20 who sweetens the West for me:
'Is it something difficult?
20–21 Life is a cycle;
trees fall.
21–22 So, you should tread on disorder:
lay down my need.

17–19 The SUBJECT–stative construction in the first line implies that the soul "has become foolish."

jhm — this verb, also written *hjm* in col. 49–50, is the same as the later verb *hmw* "prod."

19–21 "Sweetens the West for me" means "makes the West attractive to me." In the second line of the first couplet, and the seven couplets that follow, the man quotes the soul's attempt to persuade him that death is preferable to life—here and in the second couplet, by arguing that it is an easy and natural transition in the cycle of life.

21–22 The verb in the first line is *ḫnd* "tread." The scribe has made a ligatured hieratic  instead of a simple .

23–24	*wḏꜥ wj ḏḥwtj*	2
	ḥtp nṯrw	2
24–25	*ḫsf ḫnsw ḥr.j*	3
	zẖꜣ m mꜣꜥt	2
25–26	*sḏm rꜥ mdw.j*	3
	sg(r) wjꜣ	2
26–27	*ḫsf jsds ḥr.j*	3
	m ꜥt ḏsr[t]	2
28–29	*[ḏr] ntt sꜣr.j wdn.(w)*	3
	nj [wnt] fꜣ n.f n.j	3

23–24 ‘Let Thoth judge me
and the gods become content;
24–25 let Khonsu intervene for me,
he who writes truly;
25–26 let the Sun hear my speech,
he who quiets the sun-bark;
26–27 let Isdes intervene for me
in the sacred room—
28–29 since my misery has become heavy
and there is no one to lift it to himself for me.’

23–27 These four couplets refer to the final judgment. Thoth is the recorder of the proceedings (Essay 8, Fig. 8). Khonsu and Isdes are both forms of the same god, the former in his role as the moon; the latter, as the plumb-bob of the scale. The trial in this case takes place before the Sun (Re) rather than Osiris as in the later Book of the Dead. The “sacred room” is the judgment hall.

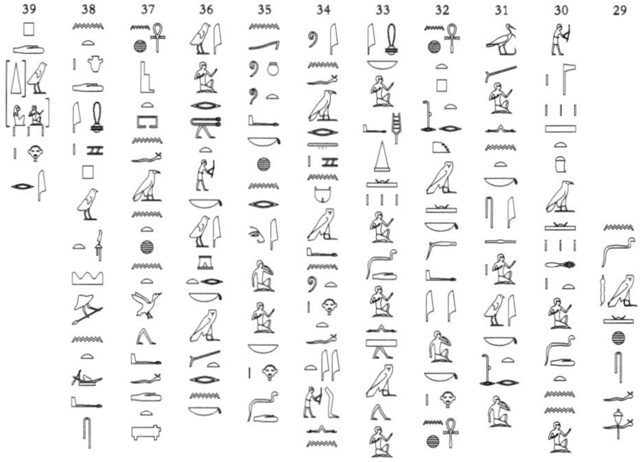

29–32 *nḏm ḫsf nṯrw šṯȝw ẖt.j* 4
ḏdt.n n,j bȝ.j 2
nj ntk js zj 2
32–34 *jw.k tr ʿnḫ.t(j) ptr km.k* 3
mḥy.k ḥr ʿnḫ mj nb ʿḥʿw 3
ḏd nj šm.j jw nȝ r tȝ 4
34–36 *nḥmn tw ḥr tfyt nn nwt.k* 3
ẖnrj nb ḥr ḏd jw.j r jṯt.k 4
36–37 *jw grt.k m(w)t.(tj)* 2
rn.k ʿnḫ.(w) 2
37–38 *jst nfȝ nt ḫnt* 3
ʿfdt nt jb 2
38–39 *dmj pw jmnt* 2
ẖn.t(w) spdw ḥr jr(j) 3

29–32 "It would be sweet for the gods to bar my belly's secrets,
what my ba said to me:
'You are not a man.
32–34 Are you even alive? What do you gain,
caring about life like an owner of riches
who says, "I won't go," even when they're lost?
34–36 In fact, you are being uprooted without caring,
and everyone deprived is saying, "I will rob you."
36–37 And you are dead,
with your name alive.
37–38 Yonder is a place of alighting,
storage-chest of the mind.
38–39 The West is a harbor
to which the perceptive are rowed.'

The second half of the man's second speech continues quoting the soul's arguments for death. At the end, the man urges the soul to wait until his son can arrange for a proper afterlife in the normal manner.

29–32 *ḫsf nṯrw štȝw ẖt.j* — an unmarked noun clause used as the subject of the adjectival predicate *nḏm* (§ 21.11). The phrase *štȝw ẖt.j* refers to the man's innermost thoughts, which the next line reveals are the arguments of his soul for death.

ḏdt.n n.j bȝ.j — this phrase stands in apposition to *štȝw ẖt.j* and introduces the second direct quotation of the soul's words.

32–34 *jw.k tr ʿnḫ.t(j)* — the particle *tr* identifies this as a "virtual" question (§§ 15.7.11, 11.11.1).

nj šm.j — this most likely refers to "going" from life to death. It therefore does not have the usual meanings of the negation, gnomic or past/perfect (§ 18.13); nor is it likely to be future, since that connotation is normally expressed by *nn sḏm.f*. It can be understood as "present for future," like the affirmative pseudo-verbal SUBJECT–*m-sḏm* (§ 14.2).

jw nꜣ r tꜣ — the demonstrative refers to *ꜥḥꜥw* "riches." The prepositional phrase, literally "to the ground," is used like the English adverbs "down" and "away." The couplet refers to a man who clings to life when he has lost all that mattered to him.

34–36 *nn nwt.k* —infinitive with pronominal object (§ 13.5), literally "not taking care of yourself."

37–38 *ꜥfdt nt jb* — the metaphor means a place in which the *jb* "mind, heart" is permanently stored, probably a reference to the coffin.

38–39 *spdw ḥr* — literally, "sharp of face." With this final line, the soul is trying to convince the man that anyone who can see the reality of his situation would prefer death to life.

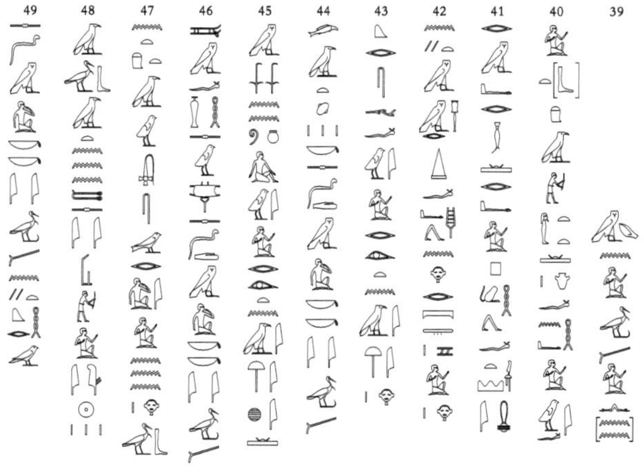

39–40	*sḏm n.j bꜣ.j*	2	
	n[n n].j [b]tꜣ		2
40–41	*t(w)t jb.f ḥnꜥ.j*	3	
	jw.f r mꜥr		1
41–43	*rdj.j pḥ.f jmnt*	3	
	mj ntj m mr.f		2
	ꜥḥꜥ.n ḥr(j)-tꜣ ḥr qrs.f		3
43–45	*jw.j r jrt njꜣj ḥr ẖꜣt.k*	2	
	sḏdm.k ky bꜣ m nnw		4
45–47	*jw.j r jrt njꜣj jḫ tm.f ḥsw*	3	
	sḏdm.k ky bꜣ nt(j) tꜣ.w		4

47–49 *swrj.j mw ḥr bꜣbꜣt* 3
ṯzy.j šwj 2
sḏ(d)m.k ky bꜣ ntj ḥqr.(w) 4

39–40 "My ba should listen to me
without making me guilty.
40–41 If his mind is in accord with me,
he will be fortunate.
41–43 I will make him reach the West
like one in his pyramid,
to whose entombment a survivor has attended.
43–45 I am to make an awning over your corpse,
and you will make jealous another ba in inertness.
45–47 I am to make an awning and it won't get cold,
and you will make jealous another ba who is hot.
47–49 I will drink water at the flood
and lift away dryness,
and you will make jealous another ba who is hungry.

39–40 *n[n n].j [b]tꜣ* — literally, "without guilt for me."

41–43 *ḥr(j)-tꜣ* — the term means literally, "one on earth," and refers to those left behind when someone has died.

43–49 These two couplets and tercet elaborate on the man's promise in the preceding couplet, to provide for a proper burial for his soul (and himself). They are also the first (preserved) lines in which the man addresses his soul directly.

njꜣj — the exact meaning of the term is unknown; the translation is conjectured from the "sunshade" determinative. The term evidently refers, pars pro toto, to a proper tomb.

m nnw — the verb from this root is used as a participle in cols. 63–64, referring to victims of drowning, who have no proper burial. A *bꜣ m nnw* therefore means one who has no tomb.

jḫ tm.f ḥsw — see §§ 18.11 and 18.15. The suffix pronoun cannot refer to the soul, which is addressed in the second person here, nor to the *ẖꜣt* "corpse," which is feminine, and must therefore refer to *njꜣj* "awning." The contrast between "cold" and "hot" apparently means that the tomb will keep the soul from both extremes of temperature.

bꜣbꜣt — this refers to the waters of the inundation, viewed as a means of renewal. The contrast between drinking and hunger, analogous to the contrast in the preceding couplet, means that the tomb will provide for the soul's sustenance.

49–51 *jr hjm.k wj r m(w)t m pꜣ qj* 3
nn gm.k ḫnt.k ḥr.s m jmnt 4
51–53 *wꜣḥ jb.k bꜣ.j sn.j* 3
r ḫprt jwꜥw drpt(j).fj 3
53–55 *ꜥḥꜥt(j).fj ḥr ḥꜣt hrw qrs* 3
sḏꜣy.f ḥnkyt n ẖr(j)-nṯr 3

49–51 If you prod me toward death in that manner,
you will not find a place to land on in the West.
51–53 Set your mind, my ba, my brother,
until the heir has grown up who will make offerings,
53–55 who will attend to the tomb on entombment-day,
transporting the bier to the necropolis."

49–51 *pꜣ qj* — the demonstrative refers to the soul's previous arguments.

ḫnt.k ḥr.s — a relative *sḏm.f*, "that which you can land on."

53–55 *sḏꜣy.f ḥnkyt n ẖr(j)-nṯr* — *ḥnkyt* means "bed" but probably refers here to the bier: cf. Sin. B 193–94. The preposition *n* could mean "for the necropolis," but the verb suggests "to the necropolis." The usual preposition with places is *r* (§ 8.2.7); the use of *n* here may connote "into" rather than *r* "toward."

Part 3 — The Soul's Third Speech (55–68)

55–56	*jw wp.n n.j bꜣ.j r.f*	3	
	wšb.f ḏdt.n.j		2
56–58	*jr sḫꜣ.k qrs nḥꜣt jb pw*	3	
	jnt rmyt pw m sjnd zj		2
58–59	*šdt zj pw m pr.f*	2	
	ḫꜣꜥ.(w) ḥr qꜣꜣ		2
59–60	*nn pr.n.k r ḥrw*	2	
	mꜣ.k rꜥw		2
60–62	*qdw m jnr n mꜣt*	3	
	ḫws qn.(w)		2
	mrw nfrw m kꜣt nfrt		4
62–63	*ḫpr sqdw m nṯrw*	3	
	ꜥbꜣw jrj wš.w		3
63–65	*mj nnw m(w)tw ḥr mryt*	3	
	n gꜣw ḥr(j)-tꜣ		1
65–67	*jt.n nwy pḥ(wj).fj*	3	
	jꜣḫw m mjtt jrj		3
	mdw n.sn rmw spt n mw		4
67–68	*sḏm r.k n.j*	2	
	mj.k nfr sḏm n rmṯ		3
	šms hrw nfr smḫ mḥ		4

55–56 My ba opened his mouth to me
  that he might answer what I had said.
56–58 "As for you bringing to mind entombment, it is heartache;
  it is bringing tears by saddening a man;
58–59 it is taking a man from his house
  so that he is left on the hill.
59–60 You won't be able to go up
  and see suns.
60–62 Those who built in stone of granite,
  with construction finished,
  fine pyramids in fine work,
62–63 once those who commissioned building become gods,
  what was dedicated to them has been razed,
63–65 like the inert who have died on the riverbank,
  for want of a survivor—
65–67 the water having taken its end,
  and Sunlight likewise—
  they whom the fish and lip of the water claim.
67–68 So, listen to me;
  look, it is good for people to listen:
  follow a good time, forget care.

The roles now reverse and the soul begins arguing for life, first by pointing out the ultimate futility of the man's promise of a proper burial and then with an exhortation to enjoy life.

55–56 The scribe originally omitted the suffix pronoun of *wšb.f*, then erased the first three signs of col. 56 and wrote them higher to make room for the suffix pronoun.

58–59 *ḫꜣꜥ.(w)* — in this case, the stative represents an unmarked adverb clause of result, expressing a state that results from the action of the governing clause rather than one that pertains at the time of that action. English can do the same thing with some of its past participles: for example, *The hunters shot the lion dead* (resultant state) versus *The hunters found the lion dead* (concomitant state).

59–60 This couplet is an explicit denial of the hope of every Egyptian, to *prt m hrw* "come forth in the daytime" (see Essay 8). The plural *rꜥw* "suns" evidently reflects the desire to do this every day.

60–67 This is an inordinately complex sentence, spanning a tercet, two couplets, and a final tercet. The opening tercet is an extended example of topicalization, anticipatory to *sqdw* in the first line of the next couplet. That couplet is the central part of the sentence, which is an emphatic construction with an initial adverb clause (*ḫpr* ...: § 25.8.3), and the second couplet is an extended prepositional phrase. The final tercet is an adverb clause; its final line is a relative clause serving as an appositive to *nnw* in the first line of the second couplet, thus mirroring the beginning of the sentence.

ḫpr sqdw m nṯrw — i.e., once the tomb owners have died. *sqdw* is an active participle from the causative of *qd*: literally, "those who caused building."

ꜥbꜣw jrj — passive participle with prepositional adverb: literally, "(the tombs) dedicated with respect thereunto."

mj nnw — this couplet is meant to equate the ultimate fate of the owners of fine tombs with that of people who die with no tomb.

jt.n nwy pḥ(wj).fj — the suffix pronoun can only refer to *nwy*. The sense is probably that of the water getting the corpse in the end.

jꜣḫw m mjtt jrj — literally, "sunlight in the likeness thereunto." The first word is written with an ideogram. The reference to sunlight in addition to water evidently reflects the image of a body lying partly submerged on the riverbank.

mdw n.sn rmw spt n mw — a relative clause whose antecedent is *nnw* in the preceding couplet. *mdwj n* can mean "speak for," in the sense of claiming something, as well as "speak to." The phrase *spt n mw* has double meaning, referring both to the shore ("lip" of the river) and to the mouth that is "speaking for" the corpse.

67–68 The scribe wrote a reed-leaf after *nfr*, then wrote *sḏm* over it without erasing it.

Part 4 — The Soul's First Parable (68–80)

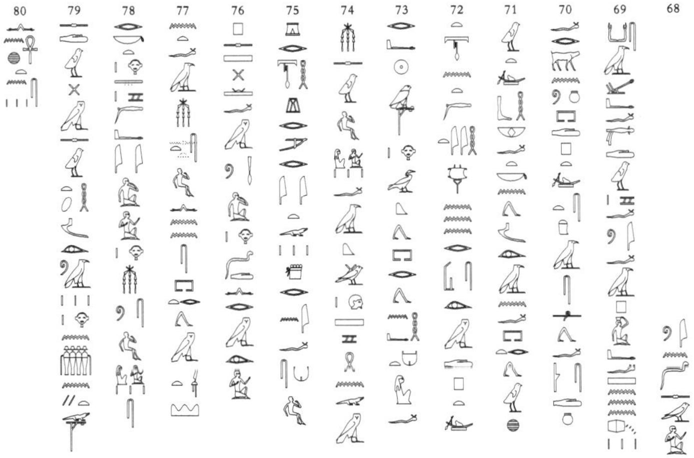

68–70 *jw nḏs skꜣ.f šdw.f* 3
jw.f ꜣ(t)p.f šmw.f r ḫnw dpt 3

70–71 *stȝs.f sqdwt* 2
ḥ(ȝ)b.f tkn.(w) 2
71–73 *mȝ.n.f prt wḫt nt mḥyt* 3
rs.(w) m dpt rꜥ ḥr ꜥq 4
73–75 *pr.(w) ḥnꜥ ḥjmt.f msw.f* 3
ȝq.(w) dp šj 2
šn.(w) m grḥ ẖr mryt 3
75–77 *ḏr.jn.f ḥms.(w) pzš.f m ḫrw* 4
ḥr ḏd nj rm.j n tfȝ mst 3
77–78 *nn n.s prt m jmnt* 2
r kt ḥr tȝ 2
78–80 *mḥy.j ḥr msw.s* 2
sd.w m swḥt 2
mȝw ḥr n ḫntj nj ꜥnḫ.sn 4

68–70 "A man plowed his plot
and he loaded his harvest inside a boat,
70–71 that he might sail with the current,
his festival near.
71–73 When he saw the darkness of a norther's emergence,
he watched in the boat as the Sun was setting.
73–75 He disembarked with his wife and his children,
and they perished atop a depression
ringed by night with riverbankers.
75–77 So, he ended up seated and crying out loud,
saying, 'I do not weep for that one who was born,
77–78 though there is for her no emerging from the West
to another birth on earth.
78–80 I care about her children,
broken in the egg,
who saw the face of Khenti before they had lived.'

To reinforce his exhortation to "forget care" and enjoy life, the soul now relates two parables on the uncertainty of life. This one is about a man struck by tragedy in the midst of happiness.

68–70 The SUBJECT–*sḏm.f* construction elsewhere in this text has the gnomic sense usual in Middle Egyptian (§ 18.6). Neither that nor the older progressive meaning suits this context, which calls for a past tense, as in the third couplet and following tercet. In this case, the *sḏm.f* describes a single past action (§ 18.4) and the subject in each line is topicalized (§ 17.4). For *nḏs*, literally "little man," see the note to ShS. 69–70. In the second line, the scribe has omitted the second radical of *ȝtp*.

70–71 *stꜣs.f sqdwt* — literally, "that he might flow by sailing." For the meaning of *stꜣs*, see the notes to Sin. B 228–30 and Peas. B1 268–70. *sqdwt* is a verbal noun from *sqdj* "sail," here used adverbially.

ḥ(ꜣ)b.f tkn.(w) — the reference is probably to a personal celebration after a successful harvest.

71–73 *mꜣ.n.f prt wḫt nt mḥyt* — literally, "he saw the emerging of the darkness of a norther(ly wind)." As the next line indicates, this refers to the time of sunset, when the wind, predominantly from the north in Egypt, picks up as the land cools. The "water" determinative reflects the action of the wind on the river.

rs.(w) — this line and the next two use the stative of intransitive verbs as a past tense (§ 16.5).

rꜥ ḥr ꜥq — literally, "the Sun entering," referring to its entering the Duat below the western horizon at sunset (see Essay 2).

73–75 *ꜣq.(w) dp šj* — since the boat is moored at the riverbank, *šj* here probably refers not to a "lake" but to one of the natural "basins" near the river: see the note to Sin. B 295–96.

šn.(w) — 3ms stative serving as an unmarked relative clause (§ 22.11): the determinative reflects what the depression was "ringed" by.

mryt(jw) — a plural nisbe from *mryt* "riverbank," in this case referring to crocodiles that live along the shore.

75–77 *pzš.f m ḫrw* — literally, "spreading out by voice." The verb is a spelling of 2ae-gem. *pšš* "spread out."

tfꜣ mst — this refers to the wife and is meant to contrast her full life with that of her children, who (though technically also "born") did not live beyond childhood. In the passive participle *mst*, the scribe originally wrote , then altered it to .

77–78 This couplet reflects the fact that the Egyptians did not believe in physical reincarnation. The feminine *kt* "another" refers to an unexpressed *mswt* "birth."

78–80 The moral of the children's untimely death reinforces the soul's injunction to enjoy life. For Khenti, see the note to Peas. B1 148–50.

Part 5 — The Soul's Second Parable (80–85)

80–81 *jw nḏs dbḥ.f mjšrwt* 3
jw ḥjmt.f ḏd.s n.f jw r msyt 3
82–83 *jw.f pr.f r ḫntw r.s sṯ r ꜣt* 4
ꜥn.n.f sw r pr.f jw.f mj ky 3
83–85 *ḥjmt.f ḥr šsꜣ n.f* 3
nj sḏm.n.f n.s 2
sṯ.(w) n.f wš.(w) jb n wpwtjw 3

80–81 "A man requested an evening meal,
and his wife told him, 'Supper is coming.'
82–83 He went outside at that, only for a moment.
When he turned back to his house, he was like another man.
83–85 His wife was pleading with him,
but he wouldn't listen to her,
being offended and unreceptive to those of the household."

This section, the shortest of the composition, is also the most obscure. It evidently is meant to underscore the unpredictability of life.

80–81 For the SUBJECT–*sḏm.f* constructions, see the note to cols. 68–70, above. The wife's words mean literally, "It will be supper." In *msyt*, the scribe originally wrote  below , then erased it, wrote next to  and  below.

82–83 *sṯ r ꜣt* — the initial word is the subordinating particle normally spelled *sk* or *jst* (§ 15.6.5), here used to subordinate a prepositional phrase as an adverb clause.

ʿn.n.f — despite the position of the determinative, the context indicates that this is a *sḏm.n.f* rather than a geminated *sḏm.f*, which would have imperfective sense (§ 12.4.2). The construction is emphatic (§ 25.8.3).

83–85 *sṯ.(w) n.f* — stative of the verb later spelled *sꜣt*, with the dative expressing the reflexive nature of the verb: literally, "having become offended for himself" (presumably by the wife's initial refusal to serve him a meal).

wš.(w) jb — a second stative, literally "stripped of mind," meaning "barren" and therefore unreceptive to entreaties.

wpwtjw — a plural nisbe from *wpwt* "inventory"; the term comes from accounts that list the "inventory" of a household. The line means that he was unreceptive to the attempts of other members of the family to mollify him.

Part 6 — The Man's First Litany (85–103)

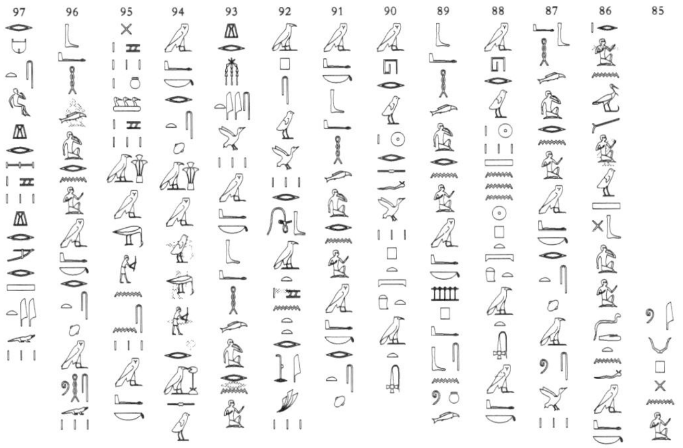

The man now responds with a series of four poems in litany form. The first three of these are written in tercets, with a common initial line and different second and third lines; the fourth is in couplets, with each first line beginning with the same words.

85–86 *jw wp.n.j r.j n bꜣ.j* 3
wšb.j ḏdt.n.f 2
86–88 *mj.k bʿḥ rn.j* 2
mj.k r st ꜣsw 1
m hrww šmw pt tꜣ.t(j) 3
88–90 *mj.k bʿḥ rn.j* 2
mj.k (r) šzp sbnw 1
m hrw rzf pt tꜣ.t(j) 3

91–93 *mj.k bꜥḥ rn.j* 2
mj.k r st ꜣp⸢d⸣w 1
r bwꜣt nt trjw ẖr msyt 3
93–95 *mj.k bꜥḥ rn.j* 2
mj.k r st ḥꜣmw 1
r ẖꜣzw nw zšw ḥꜣm n.sn 3
95–97 *mj.k bꜥḥ rn.j* 2
mj.k r st msḥw 1
r ḥmst ẖr ꜥḏw ẖr mryt 3

85–86 I opened my mouth to my ba,
that I might answer what he had said.
86–88 "Look, my name reeks:
look, more than carrion's smell
on harvest days, when the sky is hot.
88–90 Look, my name reeks:
look, more than an eel-trap
on catch day, when the sky is hot.
91–93 Look, my name reeks:
look, more than ducks' smell,
than a rise of reeds with a brood.
93–95 Look, my name reeks:
look, more than the smell of fowled birds,
than the channels of nests fowled for them.
95–97 Look, my name reeks:
look, more than crocodiles' smell,
than a site of slaughter with riverbankers.

After the usual introductory couplet, this first litany describes the man's personal situation as one of opprobrium.

85–86 The scribe wrote 𓈖 after 𓏤𓂋, then erased it and wrote the 1s suffix pronoun.

86–88 *bꜥḥ* — the verb *bꜥḥj* means "flood, teem." The meaning is that of an overwhelming smell.

ꜣsw — this is a form of the word *ꜣjs* "offal," usually written with the 𓄹 determinative. The bird and plural determinatives here indicate the meaning "carrion." *šmw* "harvest" took place between mid-February and mid-May.

88–90 *šzp sbnw* — the scribe has omitted the preposition *r* before this phrase. The first word is written like the verb *šzp* "receive," but the first five stanzas of the poem otherwise make comparisons to things or animals, not actions. Despite the determinative, what is meant here is the wicker-work trap in which eels are traditionally caught, reflected in the "fence" hieroglyph . The word *sbnw* means "gliders," an apt reference to eels.

91–93 *ꜣp⌈d⌉w* — the scribe has written instead of , perhaps influenced by *ꜣsw* in col. 87.

bwꜣt nt trjw — this refers to a rise of ground in the midst of marshy reeds, where a duck's nest would be located. The scribe originally omitted the determinatives of *bwꜣt* and wrote the of *nt* before noticing his mistake and correcting it.

93–95 The scribe wrote the of *rn.j* too low at the end of the column and erased it before writing *rn.j* higher up. In col. 94, he wrote *ḥꜣm* and part of the first sign of the next word before erasing the determinatives and the partial sign and correcting *ḥꜣm* to *ḥꜣmw*. The corrected word is probably a masculine plural passive participle with plural strokes omitted rather than a verbal noun "fowling" (see the note to cols. 88–90, above). The last line refers to channels within a marsh, along which wild birds' nests would be situated; the suffix pronoun refers to the preceding line's *ḥꜣmw*. *ḥꜣm* is a passive participle modifying *zšw*; the suffix pronoun of *n sn* refers to *ḥꜣmw* of the second line.

95–97 In col. 96, the scribe wrote the second determinative of *bꜥḥ* before realizing that he had omitted the first one.

r ḥmst ḫr ꜥḏw ḫr mryt — despite its spelling, is neither *ꜥḏ* "desert edge" nor *spꜣt* "cultivation," since neither of these are frequented by crocodile. Instead, it is a verbal noun of the verb *ꜥḏ* "slaughter," written as a "false plural" (§ 4.6). *ḥmst* is therefore the noun meaning "site" rather than the infinitive of *ḥmsj* "sit down." For *mryt*, see the note to cols. 73–75, above.

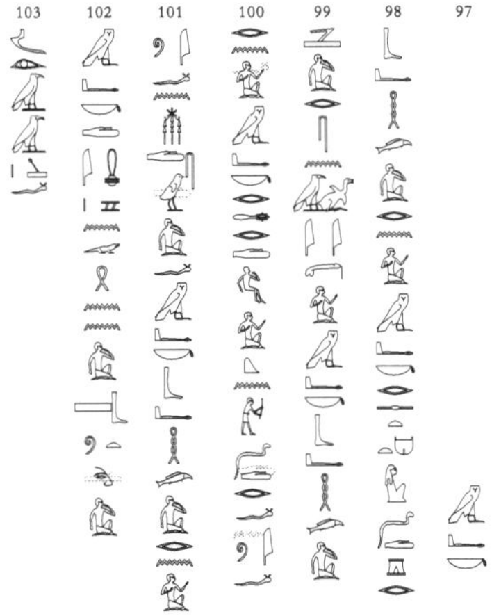

97–99 *mj.k bꜥḥ rn.j* 2
mj.k r zt-ḥjmt 1
ḏd grg r.s n ṯꜣy 4

99–101 *mj.k bꜥḥ rn.j* 2
mj.k r ḫrd qn 2
ḏd r.f jw.f {jw.f} n msdw.f 3

101–103 *mj.k bꜥḥ rn.j* 2
mj.k (r) dmj n jt(y) 2
šnn bštw mꜣꜣ sꜣ.f 4

97–99 Look, my name reeks:
look, more than a married woman
about whom the lie of a lover is told.
99–101 Look, my name reeks:
look, more than a brave boy
about whom is said, 'He is for one he should hate.'
101–103 Look, my name reeks:
look, more than the harbor of the sire
that plots sedition whenever his back is seen.

97–99 *zt-ḥjmt* — this compound term, rather than simply *ḥjmt*, indicates a woman who is either married or of an age when sexual intercourse was considered acceptable.

ḏd grg r.s n ṯꜣy — an unmarked relative clause with the passive *sḏm.f* (§ 22.13). The noun *ṯꜣy* can mean "husband" as well as "male," but the lack of a suffix pronoun (*ṯꜣy.s*) indicates the latter: thus, "of a male" rather than "to her husband." The line means that the woman is accused of adultery; *ṯꜣy* has a sexual connotation here.

99–101 This stanza is the male counterpart to the preceding one, referring to a young man accused of homosexual behavior: *msdw.f* "one he should hate" (corrected from *msdd.f* "one he hates") is the senior lover (cf. Ptahhotep's Maxim 31).

rn.j — corrected from *rn.f.*

ḏd r.f jw.f {jw.f} n — the scribe originally wrote *ḏd n* at the bottom of col. 100, then erased the 𓂋 and 𓈖, wrote the 𓂋 higher up, and added *jw.f.* He then repeated *jw.f* erroneously at the top of the next column.

101–103 *(r) dmj n jt(y)* — the scribe has omitted the preposition, the second 𓆊, and probably also the determinative 𓅆, of the usual spelling 𓆊𓆊𓅆. It is possible to read 𓆊 as *mzḥ* "crocodile," but the word *bštw* in the third line indicates a reference to the king; note that the poem moves from the natural world in the first five stanzas to that of human society in the last three.

bštw — the scribe originally wrote a bookroll determinative before replacing it with 𓀏.

mꜣꜣ sꜣ.f — an unmarked adverb clause with the passive *sḏm.f* (§ 20.14) is likelier than either an active participle ("which sees his back") or a passive one ("whose back is seen"); the geminated stem indicates multiple actions: i.e., "whenever the king's back is turned."

Part 7 — The Man's Second Litany (103–130)

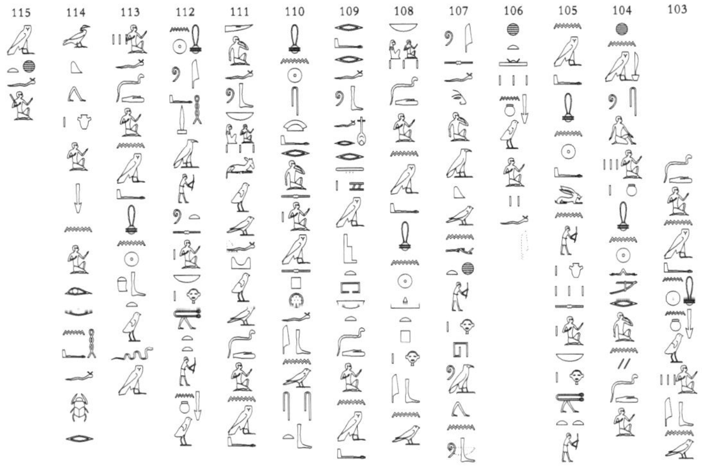

103–104	*ḏd.j n mj mjn*	3
	snw bjn.(w)	2
	ḫnmsw nw mjn nj mr.nj	3
104–106	*ḏd.j n mj mjn*	3
	ꜥwn jbw	2
	zj nb ḥr jtt ḫwt snnw.f	3
106–108	*(ḏd.j n mj mjn)*	3
	jw zf ꜣq.(w)	2
	nḫt ḥr hꜣ.w n bw-nb	3
108–109	*ḏd.j n mj mjn*	3
	ḥtp ḥr bjn	2
	rdj r.f bw nfr r tꜣ m jst nbt	4
109–11	*ḏd.j n mj mjn*	3
	sḫꜥr zj m zp.f bjn	4
	ssbt.f bw-nb jw.f ḏw.(w)	4
111–13	*ḏd.j n mj mjn*	3
	jw ḥꜥḏꜣ.tw	1
	zj nb ḥr jtt snw.f	3
113–15	*ḏd.j n mj mjn*	3
	btw m ꜥq-jb	2
	sn jrr ḥnꜥ.f ḫpr.(w) m ḫftj	5

103–104 "To whom can I speak now?
Brothers have become bad;
friends nowadays, they do not love.
104–106 To whom can I speak now?
Minds are greedy,
every man taking his fellow's things.
106–108 To whom can I speak now?
Kindness has perished,
sternness has descended on everyone.
108–109 To whom can I speak now?
There is contentment with bad,
so that goodness has been put down in every place.
109–11 To whom can I speak now?
When a man causes anger by his bad deed,
he makes everyone laugh, though his misdeed is evil.
111–13 To whom can I speak now?
One plunders,
every man robbing his brothers.
113–15 To whom can I speak now?
the one who should be avoided is an intimate,
the brother once acted with has become an enemy.

The second litany, twice as long as the first, moves from the man's personal situation to that of society in general, bemoaning its currently miserable state. Like the first litany, it is in tercets, with the exception of two couplets at the end.

103–104 *mjn* — this means both "now" and "today" in the general sense ("nowadays"), as opposed to *hrw pn* ("this day") for specific reference.

nj mr.nj — see § 17.5.

106–108 The scribe wrote the reed-leaf of *jw* that begins the second line of the tercet, then realized that he had forgotten the first line, and erased it. Perhaps while waiting for the erasure to dry, he wrote the second line in col. 107, but never returned to add the missing first line at the end of col. 106.

nḫt ḥr — literally, "force of face."

bw-nb — the scribe wrote *nb* at the bottom of col. 107, then erased it and wrote *bw*.

108–109 *ḥtp ḥr bjn* — an adjectival sentence with omitted subject (§ 8.5).

109–11 *sḫꜥr zj ... ssbt.f* — an emphatic or balanced sentence (§ 25.8.3, 25.9).

jw.f ḏw.(w) — perhaps for *m jw.f ḏw* “by his evil deed,” with the preposition omitted in error. After *jw*, the scribe began to write the first sign of *ḏw* before realizing that he had forgotten the suffix pronoun.

111–13 For *jṯj* “take posession” meaning “rob,” see the note to Peas. 134–35.

113–15 *btw* — a passive participle from *bṯ* “shun”; the  sign is an error for , and the determinative is from the word *btw*, referring to a serpent that “should be avoided.”

ꜥq-jb — literally, “one who enters the mind.”

sn jrr ḥnꜥ.f — see § 24.6.

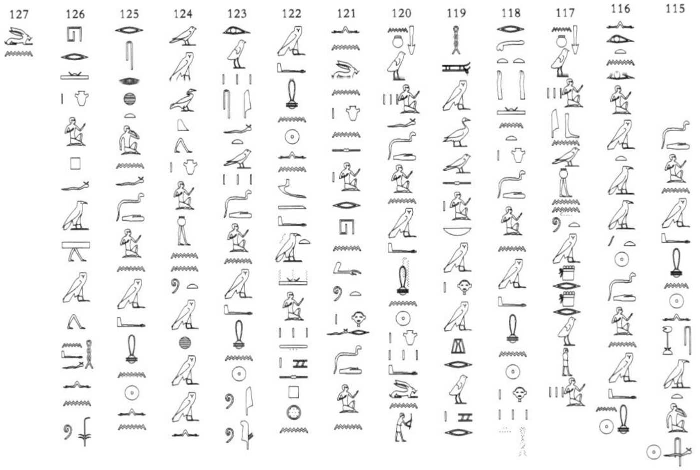

115–16 *ḏd.j n mj mjn* 3
nj sḫꜣ.t(w) sf 2
nj jr.t(w) n jr m tꜣ ꜣt 3
116–18 *ḏd.j n mj mjn* 3
snw bjn.(w) 2
jnn.tw m ḏrḏrw r mtt nt jb 4
118–20 *ḏd.j n mj mjn* 3
ḥrw ḥtm(w) 2
zj nb m ḥr m ẖrw r snw.f 4
120–21 *ḏd.j n mj mjn* 3
jbw ꜥwn.(w) 2
nn wn jb n zj rhn.tw ḥr.f 5
121–23 *ḏd.j n mj mjn* 3
nn mꜣꜥtjw 1
tꜣ zp.(w) n jrw jsft 4

123–25 *ḏd.j n mj mjn* 3
jw šw m ꜥq-jb 2
jnn.tw m ḫmm r srḫt n.f 4
125–27 *ḏd.j n mj mjn* 3
nn hr-jb 1
pfꜣ šm ḥnꜥ.f nn sw wn.(w) 4

115–16 "To whom can I speak now?
Yesterday is not remembered,
no one does for the doer in this time.
116–18 To whom can I speak now?
Brothers have become bad;
one resorts to strangers for innermost thoughts.
118–20 To whom can I speak now?
Faces are obliterated,
every man with face down toward his brothers.
120–21 To whom can I speak now?
Minds have become greedy;
there is no man's mind to depend on.
121–23 To whom can I speak now?
There are no righteous,
the land left over to those who make disorder.
123–25 To whom can I speak now?
There is lack of an intimate;
one resorts to an unknown to reveal to.
125–27 To whom can I speak now?
There is no calm-minded;
the one once walked with, he is no more.

116–18 *jnn.tw m ḏrḏrw* — the verb *jnj* used with the preposition *m* has the sense of "resort to" (literally, "get from"). The scribe originally wrote *jn.t* before erasing the *t* and writing a second *n*.

r mrr nt jb — literally, "to the middle of the mind."

118–20 At the bottom of col. 118, the scribe began to write *ḥtm*, then changed his mind, erased it, and wrote the word at the top of the next column. The sense of *ḥrw ḥtm.(w)* is the eradication of face-to-face encounters, as indicated by the final line of the tercet.

120–21 After *n mj* the scribe wrote , then erased it.

121–23 *mꜣꜥtjw* — the scribe first wrote , then erased and overwrote .

123–25 The last line contains a contrast between *ẖmm* "unknown" and *srḫt* "make known."

125–27 *pfȝ šm ḥnꜥ.f* — this is the same construction as col. 114 *sn jrr ḥnꜥ.f*. The demonstrative *pfȝ* refers to *hr-jb* and indicates that such a person is distant (in the past).

127–29 *ḏd.j n mj mjn* 3
jw.j ȝtp.kw ẖr mȝjr n gȝw ꜥq-jb 3
129–30 *ḏd.j n mj mjn* 3
nf ḥw tȝ nn wn pḥw(j).fj 5

127–29 "To whom can I speak now?
I am loaded with need for lack of an intimate.
129–30 To whom can I speak now?
The injustice that has hit the land has no end.

127–29 *mȝjr* — the scribe initially wrote the bookroll determinative, then erased it and substituted the "bad bird."

129–30 *ḥw tȝ* — the scribe omitted the initial 𓎛 of the verb and wrote as far as the 𓇾 of *tȝ* before realizing his error and correcting it.

pḥw(j).fj — for unknown reasons, the scribe has erased the dual strokes after the noun, although the suffix pronoun reflects them (§ 5.7). Note that this litany ends appropriately with the word meaning "end," which also serves as a segue to the subject of the third litany.

Part 8 — The Man's Third Litany (130–142)

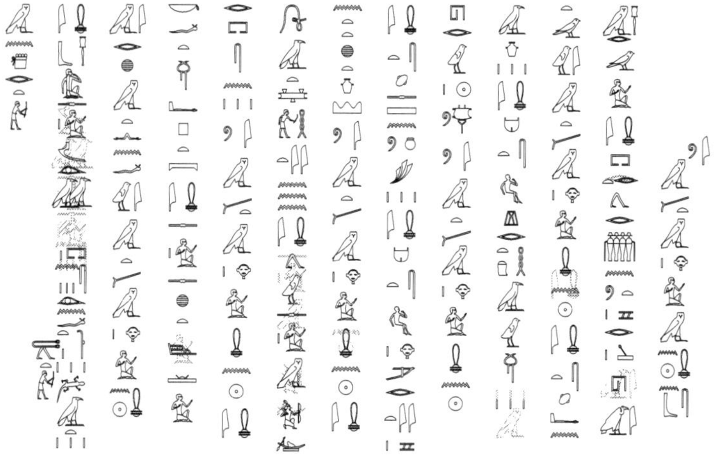

130–32 *jw m(w)t m ḥr.j m mjn* 3
(mj) snb mr 2
mj prt r ḫntw r sꜣ hjmwt 3
132–34 *jw m(w)t m ḥr.j mjn* 3
mj st ʿntjw 1
mj ḥmst ẖr ḥtꜣw hrw ṯꜣw 3
134–36 *jw m(w)t m ḥr.j mjn* 3
mj st zšnw 1
mj ḥmst ḥr mryt-nt-tḫt 3
136–38 *jw m(w)t m ḥr.j mjn* 3
mj wꜣt ḥwyt 1
mj jw zj m mšʿ r pr.sn 4
138–40 *jw m(w)t m ḥr.j mjn* 3
mj kft pt 1
mj zj sḫt jm r ḫmt.n.f 4
140–42 *jw m(w)t m ḥr.j mjn* 3
mj ꜣb zj mꜣꜣ pr.sn 4
jr.n.f rnpwt ʿšꜣt jt.(w) m nḏrt 5

130–32 "Death is in my sight now,
like a sick man getting well,
like going outside after mourning.

132–34 Death is in my sight now,
like myrrh's smell,
like sitting under sails on a windy day.
134–36 Death is in my sight now,
like lotuses' smell,
like sitting on the Bank of Inebriation.
136–38 Death is in my sight now,
like the flood's ebbing,
like a man coming home from an expedition.
138–40 Death is in my sight now,
like the sky's clearing,
like a man enmeshed thereby to what he did not know.
140–42 Death is in my sight now,
like a man longs to see home,
when he has spent many years taken in captivity.

After bemoaning his own state of affairs and the character of society in general, the man turns in his third litany to the only solution that can be envisioned, death.

130–32 The scribe made a number of corrections in this tercet: *jw* was omitted, then added to the right of the column; *pr* was altered to *prt* by erasing and overwriting the ; the initial sign of *hjmwt* was omitted. This is also the only tercet that has *m mjn* instead of just *mjn*.

hjmwt — this is a verbal noun from the verb *jhm* "mourn," with metathesis of the first two radicals.

132–34 This tercet also has a number of scribal corrections:  erased and changed to *mjn*; plural strokes and  erased at the bottom of col. 133 and replaced by plural strokes.

hrw ṯꜣw — literally, "a day of wind," a noun phrase used adverbially.

134–36 *mryt-nt-tḫt* — the "mountain range" determinative shows that this phrase is a unit, and that it refers to a place outside the Nile Valley. Intoxication was viewed as an altered state of consciousness that made it possible to commune with the gods. The line therefore refers to passing from the world of the living to that of the West.

136–38 The scribe initially omitted the  of *mjn*.

mj wꜣt ḥwyt — literally, "like the flood's going away." This is a stylistic antonym to the third line's "coming home." It refers to the receding of the annual Inundation; since the Inundation was viewed as a source of new life, the imagery reflects the ebbing of life forces.

In the third line, the scribe initially forgot the verb *jw* and wrote as far as the determinative of *msꜥ* before realizing his error and correcting it.

pr.sn — literally, "their house" (Gunn 1950).

138–40 *mj zj sḫt jm* — the verb form is a passive participle of *sḫt* "weave, trap." The line's imagery is that of a man entranced by the clearing of the sky, which reveals things he could not see before. The bookroll determinative reflects the metaphorical use of the verb. This scribe sometimes adds a seated man after participles referring to men; here originally as the first determinative and subsequently erased.

140–42 The second line has a threefold correction. After *mj ꜣb*, the scribe first wrote *mꜣꜣ zj [pr].sn*, which he then corrected to *zj mꜣꜣ zj pr.sn*, and finally to *zj mꜣꜣ pr.sn* by erasing the second *zj*.

jt.(w) — this word was initially omitted and later inserted to the left of the column.

Part 9 — The Man's Fourth Litany (142–147)

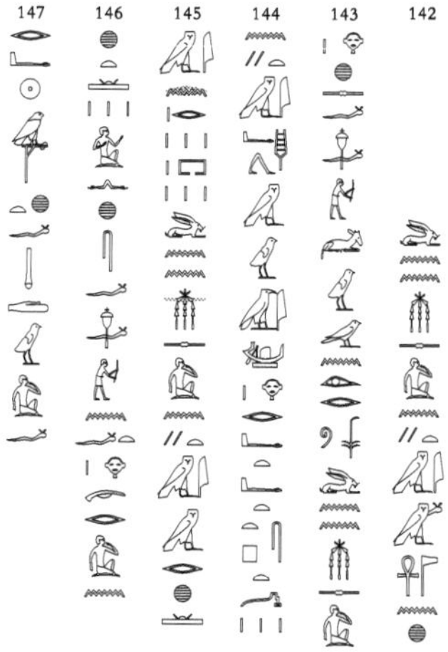

142–43 *wnn ms ntj jm m nṯr ꜥnḫ* 5
ḥr ḫsf jw n jrr sw 2
143–45 *wnn ms ntj jm ꜥḥꜥ.(w) m wjꜣ* 5
ḥr rdjt dj.t(w) stpwt jm n rw-prw 5
145–47 *wnn ms ntj jm m rḫ-ḫwt* 4
nj ḫsf.n.t(w).f ḥr spr n rꜥ ḫft mdw.f 4

142–43 Surely, he who is there will be a living god,
punishing for his misdeed the one who does it.
143–45 Surely, he who is there will be standing in the bark,
having choice cuts given from it to the temples.
145–47 Surely, he who is there will be a knower of things,
not barred from appealing to the Sun when he speaks."

From the prospective view of death in the third litany, the man moves to praise of the afterlife (*jm* "there") in the last and shortest of the litanies.

142–43 The scribe began to write the suffix pronoun *f* after *jm* but corrected it to the preposition *m* before completing the sign.

ḥr ḫsf jw n jrr sw — Egyptian "punishes" the crime "to" the miscreant: literally, "punishing the misdeed to the one who does it."

143–45 *wjꜣ* — the bark in which the Sun sails across the sky.

n rw-prw — literally, "to the mouths of houses"; the phrase refers to the entryways to chapels of the gods within a temple, where offerings were placed. The preposition was corrected from *r*.

145–47 *ms* — the scribe initially forgot the first sign.

nj ḫsf.n.t(w).f — a negated passive *sḏm.n.f* used as an unmarked relative clause after undefined *rḫ-ḫwt*.

ḫft mdw.f — the suffix pronoun refers to the deceased, not the Sun.

Part 10 — The Soul's Final Speech (147–154)

147–48	*ḏdt.n n.j bꜣ*	(heading)
148–49	*jmj r.k nḫwt ḥr ẖꜣꜣ*	3
	nsw.j pn sn.j	2
149–51	*wdn.k ḥr ꜥḫ*	2
	mj ꜥḥꜣ.k ḥr ꜥnḫ	2
	mj ḏd.k mr wj ꜥꜣ	3

151–52 *wjn n.k jmnt* 2
mr ḥmj pḥ.k jmnt 3
sꜣḥ ḥꜥw.k tꜣ 3
153–54 *ḫny.j r sꜣ wrd.k* 2
jḫ jr.n dmj n zp 3

147–48 What the ba said to me:
148–49 "So, put complaint on the stake,
you to whom I belong, my brother.
149–51 You should make offering on the brazier,
inasmuch as you fought for life,
inasmuch as you said, 'Desire me here.'
151–52 Reject the West for yourself,
but desire that you reach the West
when your body touches the earth.
153–54 I will alight after your weariness:
then we will make harbor at the occasion."

After the man and the soul have each argued for both death and life, the soul offers the final solution, a true synthesis of both sides: reject death, but look forward to the afterlife when it comes.

147–48 The scribe originally wrote *ḏd.n*, then corrected it to *ḏdt.n*.

148–49 *ḫꜣꜣ* — this refers to a method of execution by impaling. The soul is urging the man to stop thinking about death by putting his complaints to death.

nsw.j pn — literally, "this my belonger," a unique use of the adjectival phrase *n(j)-sw* "he belongs" (§ 7.8) as a noun.

149–51 The first line urges the man to make a burnt offering to the gods, and is an ironic reminder of the man's complaint in his second speech that the soul was "throwing me on the fire to incinerate me." The scribe initially omitted the *n* of *wdn*.

mr wj ꜥꜣ — the soul is paraphrasing the man's second speech: i.e., "you (soul) should desire that I stay here (in the land of the living)."

151–52 *sꜣḥ ḥꜥw.k tꜣ* — i.e., when you are buried. The scribe originally wrote *sꜣḥ.k*.

153–54 The first line is corrected from *ḫny.f r sꜣ wrd.j* "He will alight after my weariness." *wrd* "weariness" is a euphemism for death, as is *zp* "occasion." The last line is a promise to spend eternity together, and reflects the standard Egyptian concept of the afterlife, in which the ba re-enters the body in the tomb each evening (Essay 8).

The Colophon (154–155)

155 154

jw.f pw ḥꜣt.f r pḥ(wj).fj mj gmyt m zẖꜣ
That is how it goes, beginning to end, like what has been found in writing.

BIBLIOGRAPHY

Allen, James P. *The Debate between a Man and His Soul, a Masterpiece of Ancient Egyptian Literature.* Culture and History of the Ancient Near East 44. Leiden, Brill.

Gunn, Battiscombe. "An Egyptian Expression for 'Home'." *Journal of Egyptian Archaeology* 36 (1950), 111–12.

Parkinson, Richard B. *Reading Ancient Egyptian Poetry, Among Other Histories.* Oxford, 2009.

————. *Four 12th Dynasty Literary Papyri (Pap. Berlin P. 3022–5): a Photographic Record.* London and Berlin, 2012.

Vernus, Pascal. *Future at Issue. Tense, Mood and Aspect in Middle Egyptian: Studies in Syntax and Semantics.* Yale Egyptological Studies 4. New Haven, 1990.

TEXT 7
THE HERDSMAN'S TALE

WHAT IS LEFT OF THIS STORY survives on a papyrus that was glued by the scribe of Text 6 to the end of the papyrus on which that text is written (Parkinson 2012, CD folder "Pap. Berlin P. 3024"). The attached piece contained 33 columns of text; the scribe erased the first and last four but left the middle 25 untouched. The surviving text probably came from near the beginning of the composition; it is unknown how much is lost at the end. The papyrus is older than the one to which it was glued, and the text was probably composed in the early XIIth Dynasty (Vernus 1990, 185).

In the first section of the tale, the herdsman is speaking to his fellow cattle-herders, describing an unsettling encounter with a divine temptress. He urges his companions to take the herd across the river to another pasture. To protect them, he cites a "water-song," some lines of which form part of a contemporary spell from the Coffin Texts. The last lines of the text describe a second encounter with the goddess.

In its theme, the Herdsman's Tale is more like the story of the Shipwrecked Sailor than those of Sinuhe or the Eloquent Peasant, describing an encounter with supernatural beings rather than the world of human society.

Episode 1 — First Encounter with the Temptress (1–7)

1–2 *mj.ṯn wj hꜣ.kw (r) zš* 2
jw.f tkn.(w) m mjẖr pn 2
3–4 *jw mꜣ.n.j zt ḥjmt jm.f* 3
nn s(j) m ḥmw rmṯ 1

4–6 *šnwy.j ḏdf.(w) mꜣꜣ.j srw.s* 3
n nʿʿ n jwn.s 2
6–7 *nn zp jry.j ḏdt.n.s* 3
šfšft.s ẖt ḥʿw.j 2

1–2 "Look, I went down to a marsh
that is nearby this lowland.
3–4 I saw a woman in it
who was not a human being.
4–6 My hair crawled when I saw her head-pelt,
because of the smoothness of her skin.
6–7 I would never do what she said,
for respect for her is throughout my limbs.

1–2 The story takes place along the shore of the river, in a low-lying area (*mjẖr*) that borders the marshy area with wild fowl (*zš*) at the edge of the water.

3–4 *zt ḥjmt* — see the note to Debate 97–99.

m ḥmw rmṯ — literally, "from the incarnations of people": the woman was immediately recognizable as other than human.

4–6 *srw.s* — the noun refer to the pelt of a donkey used as part of a magic spell to cure a female complaint (pBM 10059, 40: Grapow 1958, 482) and as a head-covering for women representing Isis and Nephthys in a religious ceremony (pBM 10188, 1, 3–4: Faulkner 1932–33, 1). This evidence indicates that the temptress is either Isis or Nephthys.

6–7 *nn zp jry.j ḏdt.n.s* — see § 18.14. This probably refers to sexual advances.

šfšft.s ẖt ḥʿw.j — *šfšft* connotes both respect and awe. The line evidently means that the herdsman both respects and fears the goddess too much to "do what she said."

Episode 2 — The Herdsman's Advice (8–13)

8–9 ***ḏd.j n.ṯn** jḫ kꜣw ḥꜣ.n* 3
jḫ ḏꜣ bḥzw 2
9–11 *sḏr ꜥwt r r n mꜣḥ* 4
mnjww m sꜣ jrj 3
11–13 *smḥ.n n ḥꜣ kꜣw* 3
m ꜥ qbw rdj.(w) r pḥ(wj).fj 3
rḫw-ḫwt nw mnjww ḥr šdt ḥsw mw 3

8–9 "**I tell you**, therefore, bulls, let's sail back,
so the calves will cross
9–11 and the herd spend the night at the mouth of the pasture,
with the herdsmen in charge of them.
11–13 Our skiff for sailing back, bulls!,
with the cattle put at its stern,
and the knowledgeable of the herdsmen reciting the boat-song of water,

8–9 *jḫ kꜣw ḥꜣ.n jḫ ḏꜣ bḥzw* — see § 18.11. For *ḥꜣ.n*, see the note to Peas. 187–89. The herdsman addresses his fellow herders here and in the third couplet as "bulls."

8–9 *mꜣḥ* — the word is otherwise unattested. It may be related to *ꜣḥt* "field."

11–12 *smḥ.n n ḥꜣ* — an adverbial sentence used as a command (§ 10.2).

m ꜥ qbw rdj.(w) —the signs before the stative may represent either a noun *mjqbw* or the compound preposition *m ꜥ* followed by a noun *qbw*; neither of the nouns is known elsewhere. In the reading adopted here, *m ꜥ* governs an unmarked noun clause with SUBJECT–stative (§ 21.9).

ḥsw mw — the determinative identifies this as a water-song sung in the boat.

Episode 3 — The Water-Song (14–22)

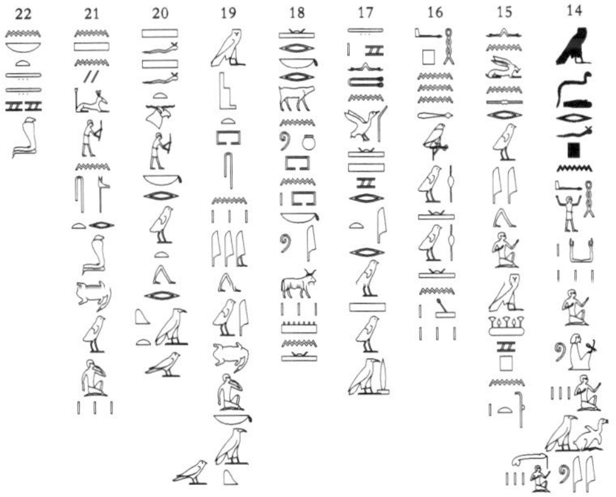

14 ***m ḏd r.f pn** ḥꜥ kꜣw.j* 3
mnjww ṯꜣyw 2
15–17 *nn wn srwy m šꜣ pn rnpt ḥꜥp-ꜥꜣ* 4
wḏ wḏ n sꜣw tꜣ 3
nj ṯn šj r jtrw 3
17–19 *wḏꜣ r.k r ẖnw n pr.k* 3
jw qbw mn.(w) m jst.sn 3
19–20 *jy jw snḏ.k ꜣq.(w)* 3
šfšft.k rw.t(j) 2
20–22 *r ꜣqt nšnj n wsrt* 3
snḏw n nbt-tꜣwj 2

14 "**with these words**: 'My kas are aroused,
herdsmen and males.
15–17 There is no repeller in this swamp, in a year of big Inundation,
when command is commanded to the land's backs
and basin cannot be distinguished from river.
17–19 So, be sound to the inside of your house,
for the cattle are set in their place.
19–20 Welcome, for fear of you has perished
and awe of you has left,
20–22 until the storm of the Powerful One has perished,
and the fear of the Two Lands' lady.'"

14 *m ḏd r.f pn* — this is most likely an infinitive modified by *pn*, with referential *r.f* (§ 15.7.2): literally, "in this saying with respect to it." The unusual position of *r.f* is perhaps conditioned by the fact that *m ḏd pn r.f* could be understood as "in this saying about/against it."

kꜣw.j mnjww ṯꜣyw — the last two nouns are in apposition to the first: in other words, the "herdsmen and males" are recipients of the speaker's life force (see Essay 7). The word *ṯꜣy* "male" can have the connotation of "man's man, he-man." The couplet means that "macho herdsmen" have been "aroused" to action.

15–17 *srwy* — a participle from the verb *srwj* "cause to leave."

rnpt ḥꜥp-ꜥꜣ — the noun phrase is used adverbially (§ 8.14).

wḏ wḏ n sꜣw tꜣ — the line refers to the fact that the inundation "commands" the land by its presence. The first word can also be an active participle, "who commands command." The "backs" of the land are the mounds in which seeds are planted.

nj ṯn šj r jtrw — For *šj* "basin," see the note to Sin. B 295–96. The line refers to a flood so high that the surface of water over the basins is at the same level as that of the river.

17–19 This couplet and the next two also appear, in a slightly different form, as part of Coffin Texts Spell 836 (CT VII, 36i-s), attested in only one source. The spell begins with the title:

gstj ʿn n sm jp
jn n.f srw pw wḏꜣ r
jr.f n.n ḥsw-mw
Beautiful palette of this sem-priest,
which the official sound of mouth got for him
so that he might make for us a water-song.

In the first column,  is probably an error for and *jp* is for *jpn* "this." In the third column,  is probably an error for the determinative . The spell continues:

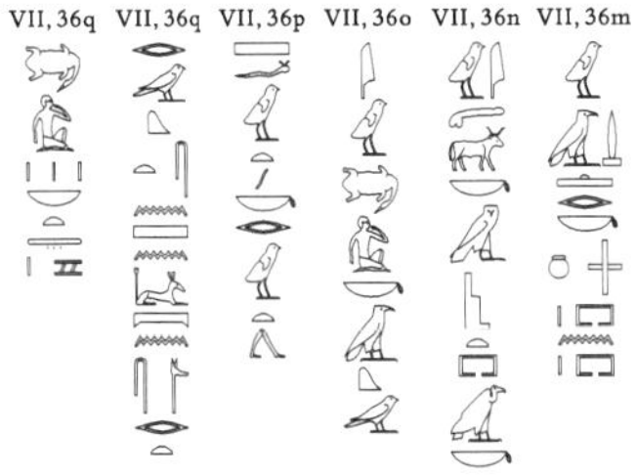

wḏꜣ r.k m ẖnw n pr
jw kꜣ.k m jst mjwt.k
jw snḏ.k ꜣq.(w)
šfwt.k rw.t(j)
r ꜣqt nšn n wsrt
snḏw nbt tꜣ
So, be sound inside of the house,
for your bull is in your mother's place.
Fear of you has perished
and awe of you has left,
until the Powerful One's storm has perished,
and the fear of the land's lady.

In the first column,  is a writing of *m ẖnw* "inside." In the second-last column, the scribe has garbled the word *ꜣqt*.

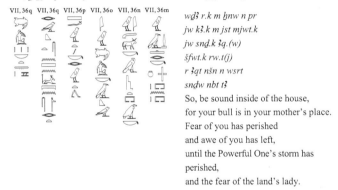

wḏꜣ r.k — the bookroll determinative here and in CT VII, 36m, rules out the verb *wḏꜣ* "proceed," which would make more sense in the context. The person addressed is probably the Inundation.

19–20 *jy* — this is probably a form of  *jjwj* (§ 23.8). The couplet tells the Inundation that he can come, because no one is afraid of him.

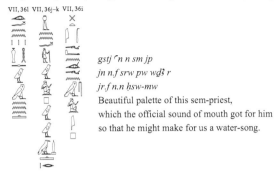

20–22 The "Powerful One" and the "lands' lady" are the king's uraeus. Since the uraeus's "storm" and the fear of it will not perish, the couplet means that no one will ever be afraid of the Inundation.

Episode 4 — Second Encounter with the Temptress (22–25)

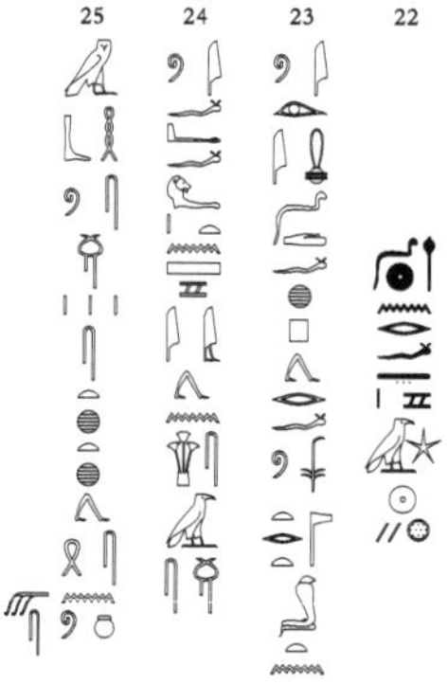

22–23 ***ḥḏ.n r.f tꜣ*** *dwꜣ zp 2* 4
jw jr mj ḏd.f 2
23–24 *ḫp r.f sw nṯrt tn* 2
jw.f dj.f ḥꜣt n šj 3
24–25 *jj.n.s ḫꜣ.s m ḥbsw.s* 3
tḫtḫ.s šnw.s 2

22–23 **So, by the time of dawn**, first thing in the morning,
it had been done as he said.
23–24 But this goddess accosted him
as he was heading to the basin.
24–25 She came shedding her clothes
and messing up her hair.

22–23 *ḥḏ.n r.f tꜣ* — an emphatic sentence (§ 25.8.3).

dwꜣ zp 2 — for *dwꜣ dwꜣ* "early, early."

jw jr — passive *sḏm.f* with omitted subject. The line means that that cattle had been taken to the other side of the river.

23–24 *jw.f dj.f ḥꜣt n šj* — literally, "he was giving front to the basin." The use of SUBJECT–*sḏm.f* as a progressive is an indication of the early date of this composition (§ 18.6).

24–25 *ḫꜣ.s m ḥbsw.s* — literally, "getting naked from her clothes."

tḫtḫ.s šnw.s — compare the English idiom *letting her hair down*. The action means that she was shedding all sense of propriety, in order to seduce the herdsman.

BIBLIOGRAPHY

Faulkner, Raymond O. *The Papyrus Bremner-Rhind (British Museum No. 10188)*. Bibliotheca Aegyptiaca 3; Brussels, 1932–33.

Grapow, Hermann. *Grundriss der Medizin der Alten Ägypter*, V. *Die medizinische Texte in hieroglyphischer Umschreibung autographiert*. Berlin, 1958.

Parkinson, Richard B. *Four 12th Dynasty Literary Papyri (Pap. Berlin P. 3022–5): a Photographic Record*. London and Berlin, 2012.

Vernus, Pascal. *Future at Issue. Tense, Mood and Aspect in Middle Egyptian: Studies in Syntax and Semantics*. Yale Egyptological Studies 4. New Haven, 1990.

TEXT 8
HYMNS TO SENWOSRET III

UNLIKE THE PREVIOUS SEVEN TEXTS, hymns are literature composed for a purpose outside that of their own existence. In this case, the purpose is to honor the pharaoh Senwosret III of Dyn. XII (ca. 1878–1840 BC). Because the hymns refer to his "taking possession of the Two Lands" and do not mention the Nubian policy for which he became famous (including the string of forts in the Sudan), it is likely that the occasion was his accession to the throne.

The six hymns of this text are inscribed on a single papyrus now in the museum of University College, London (pUC 32157: Griffith 1898, pls. 1–3; Collier and Quirke 2004, 16–19, pls. 1–2), part of an archive found in the workers' village at Illahun. While other literary compositions are written as continuous text, all but the first of these hymns are laid out on the papyrus in discrete lines, similar to the arrangement of modern poetry. This feature indicates that the papyrus was the libretto for an actual ceremony, and is therefore contemporary with the reign of Senwosret III, probably the beginning of his first regnal year (ca. 1878 BC), rather than an archival copy.

The papyrus preserves six hymns, inscribed on three pages. The first of these contains what is probably an overall title (1, 1) followed by Hymn 1, which praises the king for the safety he brings to Egypt. Page 2 contains a song of rejoicing addressed to the king (Hymn 2: 2, 1–10) and another song of praise (Hymn 3: 2, 11–20). On Page 3 is a song celebrating the king's arrival (Hymn 4: 3, 1–10), and two short hymns that are only partially preserved (Hymn 5: 3, 11–4; Hymn 6: 3, 15–20), the first of which is addressed to the gods.

The verso of the papyrus contains the end of a story in a different hand, indicating that the papyrus was reused sometime after being inscribed with the hymns. Since the beginning of the story was to the right of the preserved part of the verso, the recto may have continued more hymns to the left, now lost.

Hymn 1 — Title and Encomium (1, 1–11)

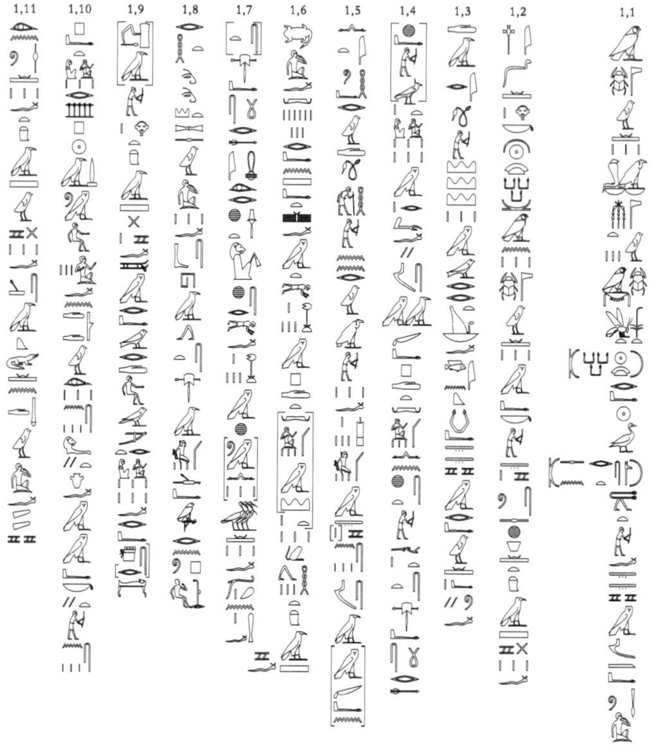

1,1 *ḥrw nṯr(j) ḫprw* (title)
nbtj nṯr(j) mswt
bjk-nbw ḫpr
nswt-bjt Ḫʿ-K3W-Rʿ
z3-rʿ Z-N-WSRT
jṯ.f t3wj m m3ʿ ḫrw

1,1 Horus Divine of Evolution,
Two Ladies Divine of Birth,
Gold Falcon Who Has Evolved,
Dual King Khakaure,
Sun's Son Senwosret,
as he takes possession of the Two Lands in justification.

1,2 *j.nḏ ḥr.k Ḫꜥ-Kꜣw-Rꜥ* 3
ḥrw.n nṯr(j) ḫprw 2
1,2–3 *mjk tꜣ swsḫ tꜣšw.f* 4
dꜣjr ḫꜣswt m wrrt.f 3
1,3–4 *jnq tꜣwj m (j)r(j)-ꜥw ꜥwj.f* 3
[ḫw] rḫwt m r ꜥwj.fj 3
1,4–5 *smꜣm pdwt nn sḫt ḫt* 3
st sšr nj jtḥ rwd 4
1,5–6 *ḥw.n nrw.f jwntjw m tꜣ.sn* 4
smꜣ[m.n] snḏ.f pdt 9 3
1,6 *rdj.n šꜥt.f m(w)t ḫꜣw m pḏ[w]t* 5
[m ḫꜣs]w[t] pḥw tꜣš.f 2
1,7 *st šsr mj jrr sḫmt* 4
sḫr.f ḫꜣw m ḫ[mw] bꜣw.f 4
1,7–8 *ns n ḥm.f rtḥ ḫnt* 4
ṯꜣzw.f sbhꜣ sttjw 3
1,8–9 *wꜥ rnpw [ꜥḥꜣ] ḥr tꜣš.f* 4
tm rdj wrd mrwt.f 4
1,9–10 *rdj [s]ḏr pꜥt r ššp* 4
ḏꜣmw.f nqdd.sn ḥꜣtj.f m mjktj.sn 4
1,11 *jr.n wḏw.f tꜣšw.f* 3
sꜣq.n mdw.f jdbwj 3

1,2 Greetings, Khakaure,
our Horus, divine of evolution;
1,2–3 who protects the land, who broadens its borders,
who suppresses countries with his crown;
1,3–4 who encompasses the Two Lands with his arms' embrace,
who defends the subjects with his action;
1,4–5 who kills archers without a blow of the stick,
who shoots the arrow with the bowstring undrawn;
1,5–6 dread of whom has hit the pillar-bowmen in their land,
fear of whom has killed the Nine Bows;
1,6 whose butchery has made thousands of archers die
in the countries of those who attack his border;
1,7 who shoots the arrow like Sekhmet does,
felling thousands of those who ignore his impressiveness.
1,7–8 The tongue of His Incarnation is what restrains the Foreland,
his phrases, what make the Asiatics flee.

1,8–9 Young Unique One, who fights for his border,
who does not let his dependants grow weary;
1,9–10 who lets the elite lie abed until daylight,
while his cohort sleep with his heart as their protector;
1,11 whose decrees have made his borders,
whose speech has gathered in the Two Banks.

1,1 *ẖprw ... mswt* — these are verbal nouns written as "false plurals" (§ 4.6).

1,3–4 The two lines of this couplet play on the phrases *(j)r(j)-ꜥw ꜥwj.f* and *r ꜥwj.fj*. The first of these is a nisbe phrase "what pertains to the arm" made into an abstract noun, which is used as the first noun of a direct genitive, meaning something like "his arms' arming." The second is the common compound noun meaning "action."

1,4–5 *nj jtḥ rwd* — this is a negated passive *sḏm.f* used as an unmarked adverb clause: literally, "the bowstring not having been drawn."

1,5–6 *jwntjw* — a plural nisbe from *jwnt* "bow shaped like a pillar." These were nomads from the Sinai.

pdt 9 — as in the term *psḏt* "Ennead" (Essay 12), the number is understood figuratively, in this case referring to the totality of Egypt's enemies.

1,7–8 These are two A B nominal sentences that do not conform to the usual pattern for such sentences (§ 7.7). They are used here instead of the normal A *pw* B sentence as a stylistic device. Since B in both cases is an active participle, they can also be understood as examples of the participial statement (§ 23.10) with *jn* omitted, also for stylistic reasons.

ẖnt — this term refers to Nubia, the land "in front of" Egypt from the Egyptian point of view (see Essay 2).

1,9–10 *ḏꜣmw.f nqdd.sn* — a SUBJECT–*sḏm.f* construction with gnomic sense (§ 18.6). For *ḏꜣmw*, see the note to Kagemni 1,12–2,2.

Hymn 2 — Rejoicing (2,1–10)

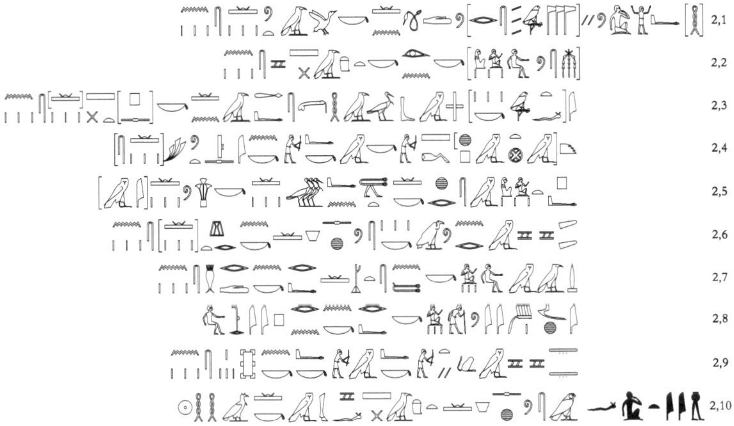

2,1	*[ḥ]ʿwj [nṯrw*	2
	sr]wd.n.k pꜣwt.sn	2
2,2	*(ḥʿwj) [msw].k*	2
	jr.n.k tꜣš.sn	2
2,3	*(ḥʿwj) j[tw.k] jm(j) bꜣḥ*	3
	sʿꜣ.n.k [pz]št.sn	2
2,4	*(ḥʿwj) km[t m ḫ]pš.k*	3
	mjk.n.k jzwt.[s]	2
2,5	*(ḥʿwj) pʿt m sḫr.k*	3
	jt.n bꜣw.k ḥꜣw [jm]	4
2,6	*(ḥʿwj) jdbwj m nrw.k*	3
	swsḫ.n.k ḫr[w]t.sn	2
2,7	*(ḥʿwj) ḏꜣmw.k n ṯst*	3
	rdj.n.k rd.sn	2
2,8	*(ḥʿwj) jmꜣḫyw.k*	2
	rdj.n.k rnpy.(sn)	2
2,9	*(ḥʿwj) tꜣwj m pḥtj.k*	3
	mjk.n.k jnbw.sn	2
2,10	***jnyt.f***	(heading)
	ḥrw swsḫ tꜣš.f	3
	wḥm.k nḥḥ	2

2,1 How excited are the gods,
for you have made firm their offerings.
2,2 How excited are your children,
for you have made their border.
2,3 How excited are your fathers of before,
for you have enlarged their portion.
2,4 How excited is Egypt with your strong arm,
for you have protected its traditions.
2,5 How excited are the elite with your counsel,
for your impressiveness has brought excess thereby.
2,6 How excited are the Two Banks with the dread of you,
for you have broadened what they have.
2,7 How excited are your cohort for promotion,
for you have made them grow.
2,8 How excited are your honored ones,
for you have made them grow young.
2,9 How excited are the Two Lands with your strength,
for you have protected their walls.
2,10 **Its refrain**:
Horus who broadens his border,
may you repeat continuity!

2,1 *[ḥ]ꜥwj* — the adjectival predicate is meant to be repeated at the beginning of each couplet.

2,3 *jm(j) bꜣḥ* — nisbe of *m bꜣḥ* "in the presence," here used temporally: i.e., "(the time) that was before."

2,4 *jzwt.[s]* — literally, "its old things."

2,8 *rdj.n.k rnpy.(sn)* — the scribe has probably forgotten the last suffix pronoun. For the concept, see the note to ShS. 168–69.

2,10 The couplet is meant to be repeated as a chorus after each couplet of the hymn.

Hymn 3 — Praise (2, 11–20)

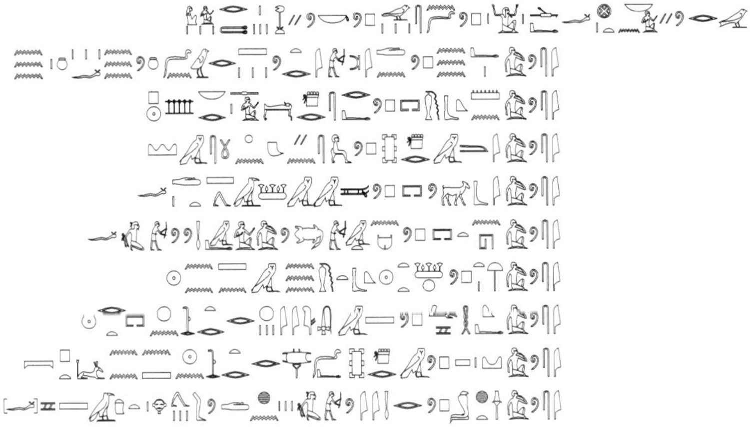

2,11
2,12
2,13
2,14
2,15
2,16
2,17
2,18
2,19
2,20

2,11	*wrwj nb n njwt.f*	3
	wꜥ ḥḥ pw	1
	nḏsw pw kwj ḫꜣw rmṯ	2
2,12	*(wrwj nb n njwt.f)*	3
	jsw ꜥ pw	1
	dnj jtrw r wḏnw.f nw mw	4
2,13	*(wrwj nb n njwt.f)*	3
	jsw mnqb pw	1
	rdj sḏr zj nb r šzp	4
2,14	*(wrwj nb n njwt.f)*	3
	jsw jmḏr pw špsj	2
	n bjꜣ n šsm	2
2,15	*(wrwj nb n njwt.f)*	3
	jsw jbw pw	1
	tmm šꜣš ḏrt.f	3
2,16	*(wrwj nb n njwt.f)*	3
	jsw nht pw	1
	nḥmt snḏw m ꜥ ḫrww.f	3
2,17	*(wrwj nb n njwt.f)*	3
	jsw šwt pw ꜣḫtt	2
	qbt m šmw	2
2,18	*(wrwj nb n njwt.f)*	3
	jsw qꜥḥ pw šm.(w)	2
	šwy r tr n prt	3

2,19 *(wrwj nb n njwt.f)* 3
jsw ḏw pw 1
mḏr ḏꜥ r tr n nšnn pt 4
2,20 *(wrwj nb n njwt.f)* 3
jsw sḫmt pw 1
r ḫrwyw ḫndw ḥr tꜣš.[f] 3

2,11 How great is the lord for his town!
He is one in a million;
other thousands of people are lesser beings.
2,12 How great is the lord for his town!
Indeed, he is the dike
that dams the river against its torrent of water.
2,13 How great is the lord for his town!
Indeed, he is the cool room
that lets every man sleep until daylight.
2,14 How great is the lord for his town!
Indeed, he is a fine bulwark
of metal of the Sinai.
2,15 How great is the lord for his town!
Indeed, he is the refuge
whose hand is not avoided.
2,16 How great is the lord for his town!
Indeed, he is the shelter
that saves the fearful from his enemy.
2,17 How great is the lord for his town!
Indeed, he is an Inundation shade,
a cool place in Harvest.
2,18 How great is the lord for his town!
Indeed, he is a warm corner,
dry at the season of Growing.
2,19 How great is the lord for his town!
Indeed, he is the mountain
that blocks the gale at the time of the sky's storm.
2,20 How great is the lord for his town!
Indeed, he is Sekhmet
against the enemies who tread on his border.

2,11 The first line is meant to be repeated before each succeeding couplet. The first couplet contrasts numbers: *wʿ ḥḥ* "one of a million" versus *ḫꜣw rmṯ* "thousands of people." The last line is an A *pw* B sentence, literally "other thousands of people are small ones."

2,14 *špsj* — the reading is not certain; the signs are damaged in the original.

2,15 The last line is an example of a negated passive participle (§ 24.8) used in the construction discussed in §§ 24.6–7.

2,17–18 These two couplets refer to the seasons of the agricultural year (§ 9.8). Inundation (July to November) and Harvest (March to July) are the hottest period of the year; Growing (November to March), the coolest and wettest. The verb forms *šm.(w)* and *šwy* (from *šwj.w*) are statives, used as unmarked relative clauses after undefined antecedents (§ 22.11).

Hymn 4 — The King's Accession (3,1–10)

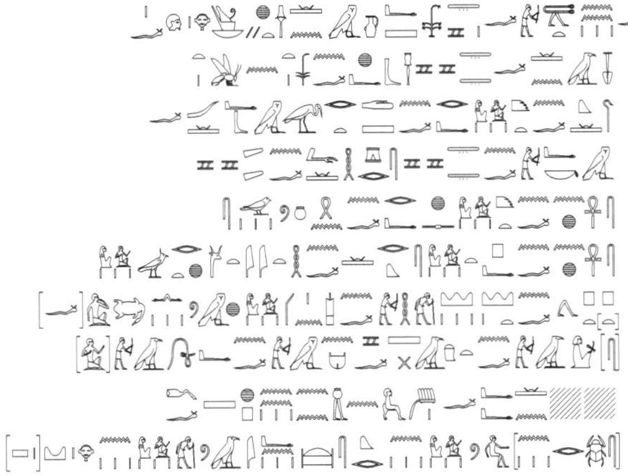
3,1
3,2
3,3
3,4
3,5
3,6
3,7
3,8
3,9
3,10

3,1	*[j]j.n.f n.n*	2
	jt.f tꜣ šmʿ	2
	ẖnm.n sḫmtj ḥr dp.f	3
3,2	*(jj.n.f n.n)*	2
	zmꜣ.n.f tꜣwj	2
	ꜣbḫ.n.f swt n bjt	3
3,3	*(jj.n.f n.n)*	2
	ḥqꜣ.n.f kmt	2
	rdj.n.f dšrt m ʿb.f	3
3,4	*(jj.n.f n.n)*	2
	mjk.n.f tꜣwj	2
	sgrḥ.n.f jdbwj	2

3,5 *(jj.n.f n.n)* 2
sꜥnḫ.n.f kmt 2
ḫsr.n.f šnw.s 2
3,6 *(jj.n.f n.n)* 2
sꜥnḫ.n.f pꜥt 3
srq.n.f ḥtyt rḫwt 2
3,7 *(jj.n.f n.n)* 2
p[t]pt.n.f ḫꜣswt 2
ḥw.n.f jwn(tj)w ḫmw snḏ.[f] 4
3,8 *(jj.n.f n.n)* 2
[s]zꜣ.n.f tꜣš.f 2
nḥm.n.f ꜥwꜣ 2
3,9 *(jj.n.f n.n)* 2
[…].n ꜥwj.f jmꜣḫ 3
n jnn n.n ḫpš.f 2
3,10 *(jj.n.f n.n)* 2
[sḫpr.n] ẖrdw.n 2
qrs.n jꜣww.n ḥr ḏw 3

3,1 He has come to us,
taking possession of the Nile-Valley's land,
the Double Crown having united on his head;
3,2 He has come to us,
having joined the Two Lands,
having mingled the sedge with the bee;
3,3 He has come to us,
having begun to rule the Blackland,
having put the Redland in his collection;
3,4 He has come to us,
having protected the Two Lands,
having calmed the Two Banks;
3,5 He has come to us,
having given life to Egypt,
having dispelled its troubles;
3,6 He has come to us,
having given life to the elite,
having made breathe the subjects' throat;
3,7 He has come to us,
having trampled the countries,
having hit the pillar-bowmen who knew not fear of him;

3,8 He has come to us,
having made his border guarded,
having saved the robbed;
3,9 He has come to us,
his arms having […] the state of honor
that his strong-arm gets for us;
3,10 He has come to us,
so that we might raise our children
and entomb our elders on the hill.

3,1 The first line is meant to be repeated before each succeeding couplet. Despite the alignment, this probably includes *n.n* as well as *jj.n.f.*

jt.f — since most of the remaining couplets have a *sḏm.n.f* in each line, it is possible that the scribe has omitted the *n* here.

3,2 The second line refers to the king's title *n(j)-swt-bjt* "he to whom the sedge and the bee belong": see Essay 6.

3,3 *ḥqꜣ.n.f* — see the note to Sin. B 70–71.

3,8 *[s]zꜣ.n.f* — a causative of the verb *zꜣw* "guard." The reading is not quite certain: the second sign is preserved only as a trace.

nḥm.n.f ꜥwꜣ — cf. Sin. B 96–97.

3,9 The lost verb is probably something like  *swꜣḥ* "make last"; the lacuna is too large for  "make fixed."

n jnn n.n ḫpš.f — for this construction, see § 21.10.

Hymn 5 — Beseeching the Gods (3,11–15)

3,11 *[…*
…]
3,12 *mr.ṯn Ḫꜥ-Kꜣw-Rꜥ ꜥnḫ ḏt r nḥḥ* 4
[…]

3,13 *wdd jr.f kꜣw.ṯn* 3
nḥm.[f ...

3,14 *zꜣw.n rḫ snfj ḏb [fnḏw* 5
...]

3,15 *ḏb(ꜣ).ṯn n.f m ꜥnḫ wꜣs* 3
ḥḥ n [...]

3,11 [...
...].

3,12 May you love Khakaure, alive forever continually,
[...],

3,13 who is commanded to make your sustenance,
and rescue [...];

3,14 our guard, who knows how to aerate when noses are blocked,
...].

3,15 May you repay him with life and authority,
a million [...].

3,11 The lost first line most likely invoked the plural beings addressed in the rest of the hymn, probably the gods but perhaps the king's deceased ancestors.

Hymn 6 — Invoking Blessings (3,16–20)

3,16 *ḥz.t(j) Ḫꜥ-Kꜣw-Rꜥ ꜥnḫ ḏt r n[ḥḥ* 4
[...]

3,17 *fꜣ.t(j) ṯꜣw m wj[ꜣ ...* 3+x
...]

3,18 *ẖkry m ḏꜥm r[...* 2+x
...]

3,19 *[...] n jdbwy*
r sḥns [...]

3,20 *[...] n.sn mjt n [...*

...].

3,16 May Khakaure, alive forever continually, be blessed
[...].

3,17 May the wind be raised in the bark [...
...],

3,18 adorned with electrum [...
...].

3,19 [...] for the Two Banks
to narrow [...],

3,20 [...] for them the path of [...
...].

This hymn is largely fragmentary, but it seems to be about traveling, perhaps in the barge of state after the king's coronation.

3,17 *fꜣ.t(j) ṯꜣw* — the seated man appears to be an error.

3,18 *ẖkry* — probably a 3ms stative.

3,20 *mjt* — a form of *mṯn* "path," showing loss of the final *n* that also appears in the Coptic descendant of this word, ⲙⲟⲉⲓⲧ.

BIBLIOGRAPHY

Collier, Mark, and Stephen Quirke. *The UCL Lahun Papyri: Religious, Literary, Legal, Mathematical and Medical.* BAR International Series 1209. London, 2004.

Goedicke, Hans. "Remarks on the Hymns to Sesostris III." *Journal of the American Research Center in Egypt* 7 (1968), 23–26.

Griffith, Francis Ll. *The Petrie Papyri: Hieratic Papyri from Kahun and Gurob (principally of the Middle Kingdom)*, 2 vols. London, 1898.

Osing, Jürgen. "Zu zwei literarischen Werken des Mittleren Reiches," In J. Osing and E.K. Nielsen, ed., *The Heritage of Ancient Egypt: Studies in Honour of Erik Iversen* (CNI Publications 13; Copenhagen, 1992), 101–19.

Consecutive Translations

The Story of the Shipwrecked Sailor

Recitation by an able **follower**.
Be informed, high official:
look, we have reached home.
The mallet has been taken, the mooring-post has been hit,
and the prow-rope is set on land.
Praise has been given, and thanks,
and every man is embracing the other.
Our crew has returned safe,
with no loss of our expedition.
We have reached Wawat's wake,
we have gone by Bigga.
So, look, we have returned in peace;
our land, we have reached it.

So, listen to me, high official:
I am free of excess.
Wash yourself, put water on your fingers:
then you can answer when you are addressed.
You can speak to the king with your wits about you;
you can answer without stuttering.
For the mouth of a man saves him;
for his speech makes leniency for him.
But you act as you have in mind;
speaking to you is wearisome.

Nonetheless, let me relate to you something similar
that happened to me myself,
when I went to the mining country for the sire.
I went down to the sea in a boat
of a hundred twenty cubits in length
and forty cubits in width,
a hundred twenty sailors in it
of the choice of Egypt.
Whether they saw sky or saw land,
their mind was more observant than lions.
They could predict a gale before it came,
a thunderstorm before it happened.

A gale came up while we were at sea,
  before we could touch land,
the wind lifted repeatedly,
  with a swell of eight cubits from it.
  The mast was what broke it for me.
Then the boat died,
  and of those who were in it, not one survived.
Then I was put on an island
  by a wave of the sea.
I spent three days alone,
  my mind as my only companion,
lying inside a thicket,
  having embraced the shade.
Then I stretched my legs
  to learn what I might put in my mouth.

I found figs and grapes there,
  and all (kinds of) fine vegetables.
Green and ripe sycamore figs were there,
  and melons as if cultivated.
Fish were there, and birds:
  there was nothing that was not inside it.
Then I sated myself,
  and put some down because of how much was on my arms.
I took a fire-stick, created a fire,
  and made a burnt offering to the gods.

Then I heard a sound of thunder;
  I thought it was a wave of the sea.
Trees were cracking,
  the ground was quaking.
When I uncovered my face,
  I found it was a snake who was coming.
He was thirty cubits long,
  and his beard, it was greater than two cubits.
His body was plated with gold,
  his eyebrows were real lapis-lazuli,
  and he was bent forward.

He opened his mouth at me,
  as I was on my belly in his presence,
saying to me, "Who fetched you?
  Who fetched you, mister? Who fetched you?

If you delay telling me who fetched you to this island,
  I will make you find yourself as ash,
  having become one who has not been seen."
But he spoke to me without my hearing it,
  though I was in his presence, because I had fainted.
Then he put me in his mouth,
  took me away to his place of residence,
and set me down without my being touched,
  sound, with nothing taken from me.

He opened his mouth at me,
  as I was on my belly in his presence.
Then he said to me, "Who fetched you?
  Who fetched you, mister?
Who fetched you to this island,
  whose two sides are in the waters?"
Then I answered him,
  my arms bent in his presence,
  saying to him, "It was I.
I went down to the mining country on the sire's mission
  in a boat of a hundred twenty cubits in length
  and forty cubits in width,
a hundred twenty sailors in it
  of the choice of Egypt.
Whether they saw sky or saw land,
  their mind was more observant than lions.
They could predict a gale before it came,
  a thunderstorm before it happened.
Each one of them, his mind was more observant
  and his arm more forceful than his companion;
  there was no fool in their midst.
A gale came up while we were at sea,
  before we could touch land,
the wind lifted repeatedly,
  with a swell of eight cubits from it.
  The mast was what broke it for me.
Then the boat died,
  and of those who were in it, not one survived except me,
  and here I am beside you.
Then I was fetched to this island
  by a wave of the sea."

So, he said to me, "Don't fear, don't fear, mister.
    Don't blanch because you have reached me.
Look, the god, he has let you live
    by fetching you to this island of ka.
There is nothing that is not inside it,
    for it is full of all good things.
Look, you are to spend month upon month,
    until you have completed four months inside this island.
A boat is to come from home,
    with sailors you know in it.
You will go home with them,
    and die in your town.

How happy is he who relates what he has tasted
    when something painful passes.
So, let me relate to you something similar
    that happened in this island.
I was in it with my siblings
    and children amid them.
We totaled seventy-five snakes,
    consisting of my offspring and my siblings,
    without me mentioning to you, from experience, the little daughter I got.

Then a star came down,
    and those went up in fire from it.
But it happened while I was not along:
    they burned up when I was not in their midst.
Then I died for them,
    after I found them as one pile of corpses.
If you have persevered, with your mind firm,
    you will fill your embrace with your children;
you will kiss your wife and see your home:
    it is better than anything;
you will reach home and be in it
    amid your siblings."

At that, I wound up prostrate on my belly,
    having touched the ground in his presence,
and saying to him, "I will relate your impressiveness to the sire
    and make him aware of your greatness.
I will have fetched to you *jbj*-oil and *ḥknw*-oil,
    jwdnb-resin and *ẖzꜣyt*-resin, the incense of temple stores,
    with which every god is contented.

And when I relate what happened to me,
 what I have seen of your impressiveness,
you will be thanked in the town
 in front of the council and the whole land.
I will slaughter for you bulls as a burnt offering,
 having wrung the necks of birds for you.
I will have fetched to you ships
 loaded with every specialty of Egypt,
like that which is done for a god people love,
 in a far-off land that people don't know."

Then he laughed at me, at what I said to him,
 in error in his opinion,
saying to me, "Do you have so much myrrh,
 and have you become owner of incense?
For I am lord of Punt
 and myrrh, it is mine.
That *ḥknw*-oil you said would be fetched,
 it is the chief thing of this island.
And when you come to separate yourself from this place,
 you will never see this island,
 once it has become waters."

Then that boat came
 as he had predicted before.
Then I went
 and put myself on a high tree,
 and I recognized those who were in it.
Then I went to report it
 and I found him aware of it.
Then he said to me, "Farewell,
 farewell, mister, to your house.
 You will see your children.
Put my good name in your town.
 Look, that is what I need from you."

Then I put myself on my belly,
 my arms bent in his presence.
Then he gave me a shipment of myrrh and *ḥknw*-oil,
 jwdnb-resin, *ẖzꜣyt*-resin, *tj-šps* wood,
 šꜣꜥzẖ plants, galena, tails of giraffe,
 big lumps of incense, teeth of elephant,

hounds, monkeys, apes:
every good specialty.
Then I loaded it onto that boat.

Once I had put myself on my belly
to thank him,
then he said to me,
"Look, you are to arrive home in two months.
You will fill your embrace with your children
and be rejuvenated inside your entombment."
Then I went down to the shore
in that boat's vicinity.
Then I was calling to the expedition
that was in that boat.
I gave praise on the shore
to the lord of that island,
and those who were in it did likewise.

What we did was to sail downstream
to home and the sire.
We arrived home in month two,
like all that he had said.
Then I entered to the sire
and presented him with the cargo
that I had gotten inside that island.
Then he thanked me
in front of the council and the whole land.
Then I was appointed follower
and endowed with two hundred servants.

See me, after my touching land,
after my seeing what I have tasted.
So, listen, high official:
look, it is good for people to listen.
Then he said to me,
"Don't act so accomplished, friend.
What is the point of giving water to a bird
at the dawn of its slaughter in the morning?"

**That is how it goes, beginning to end, like what has been found in writing,
in the writing of the scribe of accomplished fingers,
Ameny's son Amenaa, lph.**

The Story of Sinuhe

Member of the elite, high official, dignitary,
administrator of the sire's estates in the Asiatics' land,
true king's acquaintance, whom he desired, follower Sinuhe, who says:
I am a follower who follows his lord,
king's-apartment servant of the member of the elite, great of blessing,
king's wife of Senwosret in United of Places,
king's daughter of Amenemhat in High of Perfection,
Neferu, possessor of honor.

Regnal year 30, 3 Inundation 7.
The god's ascent to his Akhet, Dual King Sehetepibre,
going off to the sky, united with the sun-disk,
the god's body mingled with the one who made it.
The residence was in stillness,
minds in grief,
the great double gate shut,
the circle with head on lap,
the elite in mourning.

Now, His Incarnation had sent an expedition to the land of the Tamahu,
his eldest son in charge of it,
the young god Senwosret,
he having been sent to hit the deserts
and to smash those in Tjehenu.
And as he was returning,
having gotten captives of the Tjehenu
and all kinds of herds without limit,
the courtiers of the escort were sending word to the western side
to let the king's son know
events had happened in the audience-hall.
The messengers found him on the way;
they reached him at the time of nightfall.
He did not dally at all:
the falcon flew off with his followers,
without letting his expeditionary force know it.

But word was sent to the king's children
who were in his following in this expedition,
and one of them was summoned while I was in attendance.
I heard his voice as he was speaking,
while I was on a rise some distance away,

and my mind became confused, my arms spread out,
    with trembling fallen on my every limb,
and I took myself off by leaps and bounds
    to look for a place to hide
until I put myself between two bushes,
    until the path made its going.

My making off upstream.
I did not intend to arrive at that residence,
    having anticipated that unrest would develop,
    and I did not think to live after him.
I traversed Two-Maats Canal in the area of Sycamore,
    landed at Snefru's Island,
    and spent the day on the edge of the cultivation.

I set out when it was daytime
    and met a man standing in the mouth of my path.
    He avoided me, being afraid for himself.
When the time of supper came,
    I set foot at Steer Harbor.
I crossed in a barge with no rudder,
    by means of a gust of the west wind.
I passed by the eastern side of the quarry
    on the upland of Red Mountain's Lady.

My giving a path to my feet downstream.
I touched the Ruler's Walls,
    made to bar the Asiatics.
I took up my crouch in a bush,
    in fear that the watchmen on duty on the enclosure might see.

My making off at the time of dusk.
At dawn I reached Peten,
    and landed at an island of the Great Black.
Thirst fell and surprised me,
    so that I was seared, my throat dusty.
    I said, "This is the taste of death."

My lifting up my mind and collecting my limbs.
I heard the sound of a herd's lowing,
    and spotted Asiatics.
Their pathfinder recognized me,
    who had once been in Blackland,

Then he gave me water
and cooked milk for me.
I went with him to his tribesmen.
What they did was good.

Country gave me to country.
I left Byblos and went on to Qatna.
When I had spent half a year there,
Ammunanši fetched me —
he was a ruler of Upper Retjenu —
saying to me, "It is good you are with me.
You will hear the speech of Blackland."
He said this because he knew of my character
and had heard of my experience,
Egyptians who were there with him having witnessed to me.

Then he said to me,
"On account of what have you reached here? What is it?
Is there something that happened at home?"
Then I said to him,
"Dual King Sehetepibre has proceeded to the Akhet,
and what will happen because of it is unknown."
I also said, by way of persuasion,
"When I came back from an expedition to Tamahu-land,
it was recounted to me and my mind became feeble.
My heart—that's not what was in my body,
and it brought me away on the ways of flight.
I was not reproached, no one spat at my face,
I did not hear a wretched phrase,
my name was not heard in the herald's mouth.
I do not know who brought me to this country:
it is like a god's plan."

Then he said in response to me,
"What will that land be like without him,
that effective god, terror of whom used to be throughout the countries
like Sekhmet in a year of plague?"
So, I said, answering him,
"Surely his son has entered the palace
and taken the inheritance of his father."

Moreover, he is a god without equal,
with none in existence preceding him.

He is a master of wisdom, accomplished of plans, effective of governance:
going up and going down are in accordance with his command.
He is the one who suppressed countries when his father was in his palace,
reporting what he had decided should happen.
He is also a forceful one who acts with his forearm,
an active one with none like him
when he is seen descending on archery
and charging opposition.
He is a horn-deflecter who softens hands:
his enemies cannot muster troops.
He is one who takes vengeance, who splits open foreheads:
none can stand in his vicinity.
He is stretched of strides when he wipes out the fugitive:
there is no recourse for the one who shows him the back.
He is steady-minded in the moment of backing,
he is a returner who does not show his back.
He is stout-minded when he sees a multitude:
he allows no inactivity in his mind.
He is aggressive when he sees a halt:
his descending on archery is his joy.
When he takes up the shield, he pounds;
he does not have to repeat an act of his killing.
There is none who can escape his arrow,
none who can draw his bow.
Archers flee his arms
like the impressiveness of the Great Goddess.
He fights having anticipated the outcome,
he takes no heed of the aftermath.
He is a master of kindness, great of sweetness:
he has taken possession through love.
His town loves him more than itself,
they are more excited about him than their god.
Men and women surpass
exultation in him, now that he is king.
He took possession in the egg;
his face was toward it from before he was born.
Those born with him are multiple,
but he is a unique one of the god's giving.

How joyful the land he has begun to rule!
He is one who broadens borders.

He is to take possession of the southern lands,
    he will not consider the northern countries.
He was made to hit the Asiatics,
    to trample the sand-trekkers.
Send word to him, let him know your identity
    as one who inquires about His Incarnation from afar.
He will not fail to do good
    to the country that will be loyal to him."
So, he said in response to me, "And so, Blackland must be happy,
    because it knows he will be firm.
But you are here and will stay with me;
    what I will do for you is good."

He put me as leader of his children
    and married me to his eldest daughter.
He had me choose from his country,
    from the choice of what he had,
    on his border with another country.
It was a good land,
    called Rush.
There were figs in it, and grapes:
    it had more wine than water.
Much was its honey and many its olive-trees,
    with every kind of fruit on its trees.
There was barley there, and emmer,
    with no limit of all kinds of herds.
Great indeed was what accrued to me as an adoptee:
    his putting me as a tribe's ruler
    in the choice of his country.
Rations were made for me in daily amounts,
    and wine as daily fare,
meat cooked and fowl in roasts,
    apart from the country's flocks:
for game would be hunted for me and presented to me,
    apart from the catch of my hounds,
and many sweets would be made for me,
    and milk into everything cooked.
When I had spent many years,
    my boys grew into strongmen,
    each man his tribe's suppresser.

The messenger who would come north or go south to home
    used to stop by me, for I made every person stop.
I used to give water to the thirsty,
    I put the lost on the path, I rescued the robbed.

Asiatics started to defy
    and cause opposition to the hand of the countries' rulers,
    and I discussed their movement,
for that ruler of Retjenu had me spend many years
    as marshaler of his army.
Every country I went away from,
    once I had made my attack in it,
    was driven from pasture and its wells.
I plundered its herds and got its underlings,
    their food having been taken away.
I killed some of its people by my strongarm,
    by my bow, by my strides, by my accomplished plans.
It became useful in his mind and he desired me,
    when he learned how I had persevered.
He put me as leader of his children,
    when he saw my arms being firm.

Coming of a strongman of Retjenu,
    challenging me in my tent.
He was a champion without peer,
    for he had subdued it entirely.
He said he would fight with me,
    he anticipated that he would rob me:
he intended to plunder my herds
    with the counsel of his tribe.
That ruler, he consulted with me.
    I said, "I do not know him.
Am I his ally,
    striding about in his camp?
Is it a fact that I have opened his tent-flap
    or scaled his walls?
It is contrary-mindedness,
    because he sees me doing his job.
I am surely like a bull of the wild in the midst of another herd,
    whom the alpha-bull attacks
    while the steer fastens on to him.
Is there a dependant loved to the same degree as the chief servant?

No bowman is allied with a reed-man.
Who can fasten papyrus to a mountain?
Does a bull want to fight
and a champion bull want to back off
in terror of one whom he matches?
If his mind is set on fighting,
let him say what he has in mind.
Is the god unaware of what he has fated
or aware what the situation is like?"

During the night, I strung my bow
and shot my arrows,
gave play to my dagger
and embellished my weapons.
At dawn, Retjenu came,
having incited its tribes
and collected the countries around it,
having intended this fight.
Every heart smoldered for me,
women and men were keening.
Every mind was sick for me, saying,
"Is there another strongman who can fight against him,
who can stand up to his shield, his axe, his clutch of spears?"
Afterward, I made his weapons come out.
I made his arrows pass by me
to no avail, one chasing the other.
He charged me and I shot him,
and my arrow stuck in his neck.
He cried out and fell on his nose,
and I felled him with his axe.
I emitted my cry of victory over his back,
while every Asian was moaning;
I gave praise to Montu,
while his dependants mourned for him.
That ruler, Ammunanši,
put me in his embrace.
I got his things and plundered his herds:
what he intended to do to me, I did it to him;
I took possession of what was in his tent,
and stripped his camp.

Since enlargement has come from it, broadening in my riches,
    and increase in my herds,
the god has to have acted in contentment
    to one whom he reproached and led astray to another country:
    now his mind is washed.
Though a fugitive flees for his circumstances,
    my core is at home.
Though a crawler crawls for hunger,
    I give bread to my neighbor.
Though a man leaves his land for nakedness,
    mine are white clothes and fine linen.
Though a man runs for lack of one he can send,
    I have many dependants.
My house is good, my place is broad,
    but my thought is in the palace.

Whichever god fated this flight,
    may you become content and put me home.
Perhaps you are to let me see the place
    my mind spends the day in.
What is more important than interring my corpse
    in the land you gave me birth in?
It means, come after, so that a good deed may happen
    and the god give me contentment.
May he act in such a way as to improve the end
    for one he has afflicted, whose mind is pained;
    for one he has pressed into life on the desert.
So, if now it is that he has become content,
    may he hear the prayer of one far away,
and turn the arm from where he has landed
    to the place he got him from.
May the king of Blackland be gracious to me,
    for I live by his grace.
May I greet the land's mistress who is in his palace
    and hear the messages of her children;
    then my body will rejuvenate.
For old age has descended,
    and fatigue, it has come suddenly upon me.
My eyes have become heavy,
    my arms inert.

My legs, they have lost how to follow the mind;
 one close to the funeral procession is weary:
they send me to the towns of continuity,
 and I will follow the Lady to the Limit.
Then she will speak well for me to her children,
 and send continuity over me.

Now, the Incarnation of Dual King Kheperkaure, justified, was told
 about the situation that I was in.
As a result, His Incarnation sent word to me,
 with gifts of the king's own,
delighting a humble servant
 like a ruler of any country,
and the king's children who were in his palace
 were letting me hear their messages.

Copy of the decree brought to your servant, about fetching him to Egypt.
Horus Living One of Birth, Two Ladies Living One of Birth,
 Dual King Kheperkare,
 Sun's Son Amenemhat, alive forever continually:
 king's decree to follower Sinuhe.
Look, this decree of the king is brought to you
 to let you know that although you have gone around countries,
 having gone up from Qatna to Retjenu,
country gave you to country
 only under the counsel of your mind for you.
What did you do,
 that one should act against you?
You did not blaspheme, that your speech should be barred;
 you did not argue with the counsel of officials,
 that your phrases should be contradicted.
That plan that got your mind,
 not that was in mind for you.
That sky of yours who is in the palace,
 she is set, she is firm now,
her headgear from the kingship of the land,
 her children in the audience-hall.
You shall keep the finery of their giving to you,
 and live on their generosity.

Make a return to Egypt,
that you may see the home you gew up in,
kiss the earth at the great double gate,
and join with the courtiers.
For since it is now that you have started to age
and have lost potency,
think of the day of entombment,
when you are sent to the state of honor.
The evening is separated for you with cedar oil
and bandaging in Tayet's arms.
The procession's following is made for you on the day of interment,
the mummy-case of gold, with head of lapis-lazuli,
the sky above as you lie on the bier,
oxen drawing you, chanters in front of you.
Funerary dances are done for you at your tomb's mouth,
the offering-list is recited for you,
and slaughter is done at the mouth of your offering-slabs,
your columns constructed of limestone
amid the king's children.
Your death will not be on the desert,
Asians will not bury you,
you will not be put in the skin of a ram
when your grave is made.
This has become too long now to wander:
be concerned about illness, and come back.

This decree reached me
as I was standing in the midst of my tribe.
When it was read to me, I put myself on my belly
and touched the ground.
I put it opened on my breast
and went around my camp, yelling,
"How was this done for a servant
whose mind went astray to strange countries?
And the determination that saved me from death has to be good,
for your ka is to let me make my body's end at home."

Copy of the response to this decree.
Palace-servant Sinuhe, who says:
In very good peace!

The flight your servant did, in his ignorance, has been learned
by your ka, young god, lord of the Two Lands,
whom the Sun desires and Montu, lord of Thebes, blesses.
Amun, lord of the Two Lands' throne, Sobek and the Sun,
Horus, Hathor, Atum and his Ennead,
Sopdu, Young of Impressiveness, Semseru, Eastern Horus;
Lady of the Cavern, uniting with your head;
the first conclave of Nu,
Min, Horus in the midst of the countries;
the Uraeus, Lady of Punt, Nut,
Horus the Elder and Sun,
and all the gods of Canal-land and the islands of the sea—
may they give life and dominion to your nose
and unite you with their generosity;
may they give you continuity without limits
and eternity without end;
may fear of you be repeated in the flatlands and deserts,
may what the sun disk encircles be subdued to you.
This is the prayer of your servant for his lord,
now that he has been saved from the West.
The lord of perception, who perceives the subjects
perceives in the incarnation of the escort
what your servant has been afraid to say,
for it is like a big thing to repeat it:
the great god, the Sun's likeness, himself informing one who works for him.
For your servant is in the hand of one who consults about him
and just should be put under his counsel.
For Your Incarnation is Horus who takes possession:
your arms are forceful against all lands.
Moreover, Your Incarnation should command to have fetched to him
the *mēki* from Qatna, the *khantuadiš* from the south of Kizzu,
or the *munines* from the two lands of the woodworks:
they are rulers renowned of names,
who grew up in love of you,
without thinking of Retjenu:
it is yours, as something like your hounds.
The flight that your servant did, it was not anticipated,
it was not in my mind, I did not contrive it.
I do not know how I was separated to the place:
it is like the guidance of a dream,

like **a Deltan** seeing himself **in Elephantine**,
    a man of the marshland in Bowland.
I did not fear, no one ran after me,
    I did not hear a wretched phrase,
    my name was not heard in the herald's mouth —
nothing but my goosebumps,
    my feet scurrying, my mind managing me,
    the god who fated that flight pulling me.
For I am not haughty, prominent, feared,
    a man his land knows,
whereas the Sun has put fear of you throughout the land,
    terror of you in every country.
It does not matter if I am at home or I am in this place,
    for you are one who covers this Akhet.
The sun disk rises for love of you;
    water in the river, it is drunk when you like;
    air in the sky, it is breathed when you say.
Your servant is to hand over
    to **my brood your servant made in this place**,
    now that what has been done is to come for your servant.
Let Your Incarnation do as he likes:
    one lives from the air of your giving.
May the Sun, Horus, and Hathor desire that fine nose of yours
    that Montu, lord of Thebes, desires to live forever.

My being allowed to spend a day in Rush
    handing over my things to my children:
my eldest son in charge of my tribe,
    my tribe and all my things in his hand,
my personnel, my every herd,
    my fruit trees, and my every date tree.
What your servant did was to come upstream.
    When I set down on Horus's Ways,
the marshaler there who was in charge of the patrol
    sent a message to the interior
    to let it be known.
So, His Incarnation had come an overseer of field-workers,
    an efficient one of the king's house,
with masted ships in his wake
    loaded with the generosity of the king's own

for the Asiatics who had come in charge of me,
sending me to Horus's Ways.
I called each one of them by name,
while every attendant was at his duty.
I set off after the wind was raised for me,
with kneading and brewing beside me
until I reached the harbor of Lisht.

So, it was dawn, very early,
when a summons came for me,
ten men coming, ten men going,
conducting me to the palace.
I touched forehead to ground between the sphinxes,
while the king's children stood in the thickness making my reception,
and the courtiers who conduct to the Marsh
were putting me on the way to the audience hall.
I found His Incarnation on the great seat
in a thickness of electrum.
At that I wound up stretched out on my belly,
and I lost consciousness in his presence.
That god was addressing me in delight,
but I was like a man possessed by darkness,
my ba gone,
my limbs feeble.
My heart — not *it* was in my body,
that I might know life from death.

So, His Incarnation said to one of those courtiers,
"Lift him up; have him speak to me."
So, His Incarnation said, "Look, you have returned
after roaming countries.
The flight has taken a toll on you, old man:
you have reached old age.
Not insignificant is your corpse's interment:
nor will you be buried by bowmen.
Don't act against yourself any more.
You did not answer when your name was pronounced:
be not afraid of punishment."
I answered with the answer of one afraid,
"What will my lord say to me about it?
I should answer with no haste on my part,
for he is a god:

it is that terror exists in my belly,
  like the cause of the fated flight.
Look, I am in your presence, and life is yours:
  let Your Incarnation do as he likes."

So, one had the king's children conducted in,
  and His Incarnation said to the king's wife,
"Look, Sinuhe has returned
  as an Asian that the Asiatics have created."
She emitted a very great cry,
  with the king's children in one shriek,
and they said in response to His Incarnation,
  "Is it really he, sire my lord?"
  and His Incarnation said, "It is really he."
Now, they had brought their menits and their scepters,
  and their sistra were in their hand.
So, they presented them to His Incarnation
  and they said to His Incarnation,
"May your hands be toward something good, lasting king,
  the ornaments of the sky-lady.
May the Gold give life to your nose
  and the stars' lady unite with you.
Let the Nile-Valley crown go downstream and the Delta Crown upstream,
  joined and reconciled through the mouth of Your Incarnation.
Now that the Green has been put on your brow,
  distance for yourself dependants from evil,
so that the Sun, the Two Lands' lord, will be content for you,
  and acclaim will be yours like the Lady to the Limit.
Lower your horn, loosen your arrow,
  give air to the one who is in suffocation.
Give us our good outlay
  in this pathfinder, the Northwind's son,
  a bowman born in Canal-land.
He made a flight for fear of you,
  he left the land for terror of you.
No face of one who sees your face should blanch,
  no eye that looks at you should fear."
So, His Incarnation said, "He should not fear
  or babble for terror.
He is to be a courtier among the officials
  and will be put amid the circle.

You proceed to the morning audience-hall
    to make his attendance."

At that, my emergence from inside the audience hall,
    the king's children giving me their arms
    as we went thereafter to the great double gate.
I was taken to a king's son's house with finery in it,
    a bathroom in it, and icons of the Akhet,
sealed things from the treasury in it,
    clothes of king's linen,
    myrrh and first-class king's oil of officials:
whatever he might want in every room,
    every attendant at his duty.
Years were made to pass from my limbs;
    I was depilated and my hair was combed,
while a cargo was given to the desert
    and clothes to the sand-trekkers.
I was dressed in fine linen and anointed with first-class oil,
    as I lay on a bed.
I gave over the sand to those in it,
    and oil of a tree to the one anointed with it.

I have been given the house of a basin-owner,
    the kind that a courtier should have.
Many craftsmen are building it,
    its every tree has been planted anew.
Food is fetched for me from the palace
    three and four times a day,
apart from what the king's children give,
    without a moment of stopping.
A pyramid has been built for me
    of stone amid the pyramids,
the overseer of stone-masons receiving its ground,
    the overseer of seal-bearers writing,
    the sculptors carving,
the overseer of works on the plateau
    crossing the land for it;
every kind of artifact put in a strong-room,
    its possessions have been made therefrom;
I have been given ka-servants, and a plateau plot has been made for me,
    with fields in it, in front of the harbor,
    like what is done for a top courtier.

My statue has been plated with gold,
    its kilt with electrum:
the king is the one who had it made;
    there is none lowly for whom the like has been done.
I have the blessings of the king's presence
    until the day of mooring has come.

That is how it goes, beginning to end, like what has been found in writing.

THE LOYALIST INSTRUCTION

Beginning of the teaching that he made to his children.
I will say something important and have you hear;
  I will let you know the method of continuity,
  the system of living correctly, of conducting a lifetime in peace.
Worship the king—Nimaatre, alive forever—
  in your innermost beings,
  associate his incarnation with your minds.
He is Perception, which is in hearts,
  for his eyes probe every torso.
He is the Sun, by whose rays one sees;
  how much more illuminating of the Two Lands is he than the sundisk!
How much more freshening is he than a high inundation,
  for he has filled the Two Lands with the force of life.
Noses are refreshed when he is distant from storming,
  his contentment is necessary for inhaling air.
He gives sustenance only to those in his following,
  he feeds the one who adheres to his path.
The king is ka, his mouth is excess;
  the one who will exist is the one he fosters.
He is Khnum for every body,
  the begetter who creates the subjects.
He is Bastet, who defends the Two Lands,
  for the one who worships him will be one whom his arm shelters.
He is Sekhmet against the one who transgresses his command,
  for the one he detests will be one who has rejection.
Fight for his name, be respectful of his oath,
  and be free of any laxity.
For the one the king has loved will be worthy:
  there is no tomb for the one who rebels against His Incarnation,
  and his body is something thrown into the water.
If you do this, your body will be sound,
  and you will find it so for eternity.

The Instruction of Kagemni's Father

Maxim x+1 — Moderation in Behavior

Sound is the cautious, blessed is the moderate,
open is the tent to the quiet man.
Broad is the place of the one calm in speech,
sharp are knives against him who oversteps the path.
There should be no haste except at its proper time.

Maxim x+2 — Advice against Overeating

If you sit down with a multitude,
hate the bread you love.
Suppressing the appetite is a little moment;
gluttony is a taboo, for it is pointed at.
For a cup of water quenches thirst,
a mouthful of herbs settles the appetite.
For a good thing substitutes for goodness,
for a little bit substitutes for much.
He who is untimely voracious for his belly is a wretch:
those forget one whose belly made free in their house.

Maxim x+3 — How to Behave When Others Overindulge

If you sit down with a glutton,
you should eat only when his lust has passed.
If you drink with a drunkard,
you should accept once his appetite is satisfied.
Don't rage for meat beside one who is ravenous:
you should accept only when he gives to you.
Don't reject it, then it will be something soothing.
As for him who is free of an accusation of bread,
no word can take control of him.
He whose face is averted from feeding the appetite,
the harsh man has to be kinder to him than his mother,
and everyone is his dependant.

Maxim x+4 — Advice against Hubris

Let your name emerge,
but be quiet with your mouth when you are summoned.
Don't get big-headed about power in the midst of your cohort,
lest you create opposition.
One cannot know what might happen,
or what the god might do when he punishes.

CONCLUSION

So, the vizier had his boys summoned
after he came to understand the manner of people,
their nature being what had come upon him.
In the end, he said to them,
"As for everything in writing on this scroll,
hear it as I say it; don't exceed what is decided."
So, they were putting it on their bellies,
and they were reading it like what is in writing.
So, it was better in their mind
than anything that is in this entire land,
so they conducted themselves accordingly.

Then the Incarnation of Dual King Huni moored for him.
Then the Incarnation of Dual King Snefru was installed as effective king in this entire land.
Then Kagemni was made city-overseer and vizier.

That is how it goes.

THE INSTRUCTION OF PTAHHOTEP

INTRODUCTION

Teaching of city-overseer and vizier Ptahhotep
during the Incarnation of Dual King Izezi, alive forever continually.
City-overseer and vizier Ptahhotep says:

"Sire, my lord,
distinction has happened, old age has descended.
Distress has come, helplessness is renewing,
one lies from it anguished every day.
The eyes have shrunk, the ears have grown deaf,
strength is collapsing for the weary-minded.
The mouth has grown quiet and cannot speak,
the mind is closed and cannot remember yesterday,
the bone is in pain at length.
Goodness has become badness,
every sense is gone.
What old age does to people is bad in every respect;
the nose is stopped up and cannot breathe
for the effort of standing and sitting.
Let your servant be ordered to make a staff of old age,
and I will tell him the speech of listeners,
the ways of forebears who once listened to the gods.
Then the same will be done for you,
troubles will be driven from the subjects,
and the Two Banks will work for you."
So, the Incarnation of that god said,
"So, teach him to speak from the start,
and he will be a model for officials' children.
Let hearing enter him,
and exactness of every thought said to him.
There is none born experienced."

PROLOGUE

Beginning of the phrases of good speech
said by member of the elite, high official,
god's father, god's beloved,
king's son, eldest of his body,
city-overseer and vizier Ptahhotep,
in teaching the ignorant to learn
according to the standard of good speech,

as what is useful for him who will listen,
    as what is distressful for him who will overstep it.
So, he said to his son:
Don't get big-headed over your knowledge,
    but consult with the ignorant like the knowledgeable.
The limit of craft is not attained:
    there is no craftsman complete in his mastery.
Good speech is more hidden than malachite,
    yet it is found with maidservants at the millstones.

MAXIM 1 — AN ARGUMENTATIVE SUPERIOR

If you find a conversant in his moment
    and determined, one more accomplished than you,
bend your arms,
    bow your back,
challenge your mind with respect to him
    and he won't be able to match you.
You belittle one who speaks badly
    by not opposing him in his moment.
He will be called, "He is an ignoramus,"
    when the suppression of your mind has matched his resources.

MAXIM 2 — AN ARGUMENTATIVE EQUAL

If you find a conversant in his moment,
    your equal, who is on your level,
you make your accomplishment become more than his
    by being quiet while he is speaking badly.
Great will be the reproach by the hearers,
    while your name is good in the knowledge of officials.

MAXIM 3 — AN ARGUMENTATIVE SUBORDINATE

If you find a conversant in his **moment**
    who is an inferior and not your equal,
don't let your mind rage at him because he is wretched:
    put him aside and he will punish himself by himself.
Don't address him to ease your mind,
    don't wash the mind to one who is opposed to you:
    he is one in difficulty, damaged, inferior.
One will have a mind to do what you have in mind
    when you oppose him by the opposition of officials.

MAXIM 4 — MAAT

If you are a leader,
    giving commands for the conduct of many,

seek out for yourself every kind of effective deed,
 until your conduct is without error in it.
Maat is great, its sharpness lasting:
 it has not been able to be disturbed since Osiris's time.
Bypassing customs is punished;
 it is what is bypassed in the intent of the greedy man.
Arrogance is what takes away riches;
 transgression has not once moored its case.
For he says, "As for me, I net by myself";
 he does not say, "I net by my service."
In the end, Maat lasts:
 a man should not say, "It is my father's area."

MAXIM 5 — TRUST IN GOD

You should not make plans by people:
 the god makes opposition in like fashion.
For a man thinks to live thereby,
 and he is devoid of the bread of the mouth.
For a man thinks to become powerful,
 and he says, "I ensnare my own cleverness."
For a man thinks to rob another,
 and he ends up giving to one he did not know.
No plans of people have ever come about:
 what happens is what the god decrees.
Therefore, live inside calmness,
 and what they give will come of its own accord.

MAXIM 6 — TABLE MANNERS

If you are a guest at the table of one greater than you,
 you should accept what is given when it is given to you.
You should stare at what is in your presence;
 don't shoot him with much staring:
 pestering him is the ka's abomination.
Don't talk to him until he calls:
 one cannot know what might be bad in the mind.
If you speak when he addresses you,
 what you say will be good in the mind.
As for a great man who is at bread,
 his custom is according as his ka dictates:
he will give to the one he favors,
 and the outcome is a matter of obscurity.
The ka is what stretches out his arms;
 the great man gives, and a man cannot attain it.

For the eating of bread is under the god's system:
only the ignorant will complain about it.

MAXIM 7 — SLANDER

If you are a man of entrée,
whom one great man sends to another,
be completely exact when he sends you;
do for him the mission as he says.
Be mindful of denigrating
by speech that will debase one official to another;
hold Maat in its true form.
Washing of the heart should not be repeated
in the speech of any people, whether of great or small:
it is the ka's abomination.

MAXIM 8 — BEHAVIOR WHEN SUCCESSFUL

If you farm and there is growth in the field,
and the god puts it greatly in your hand,
don't let your mouth get sated beside your neighborhood:
quiet makes for great respect.
As for the man of character who owns things,
he gains like a crocodile in the council.
Don't brag to one who is childless,
don't become inferior by boasting of it.
For there is many a father in distress,
and the mother who has given birth, another is more content than she.
The single man is the one whom the god fosters,
while the one with a tribe, it asks for his service.

MAXIM 9 — BEHAVIOR TOWARD SOMEONE SUCCESSFUL

If you are lowly, serve an accomplished man.
Let all your conduct be good before the god
with regard to one you know who was little before.
Don't get big-headed regarding him
because of what you know about him before:
respect him for what has happened to him.
Things do not come of themselves:
it is their custom for one they love;
as for overflow, it collects for him itself.
The god is the one who made his accomplishment,
intervening on his behalf while he was asleep.

MAXIM 10 — PERSEVERANCE TOWARD GOALS

Follow your mind as long as you exist.
Don't add to what is said.
Don't lessen the time of following the mind:
wasting its moment is the ka's abomination.
Don't divert the task of daily requirements
in excess of founding your house.
The things of one who follows the mind come about;
things will not be able to accumulate when he is sluggish.

MAXIM 11 — TREATMENT OF A SON

If you are an accomplished man,
you should make a son, the god willing.
If he is exact, serves your character,
and tends your things properly,
do for him all goodness:
he is your son; he belongs to your ka's ejaculation.
You should not separate your mind from him.
But seed can make strife.
If he errs and violates your way,
having disobeyed all that is said,
his mouth going with wretched speech,
you should task him completely according to his mouth,
pushed from you as hateful to them:
he is one decreed obstructive in the womb.
Their guidance cannot err;
the one they strand cannot find a way across.

MAXIM 12 — BEHAVIOR IN COURT

Whenever you are in court, stand and sit
according to your steps decreed for you the first day:
don't bypass, or you will turn out to be banned.
Sharp is the face of the one who enters reported,
wide the place of the one summoned.
Court operates to a standard;
every procedure is according to measure.
The god is the one who advances a place;
those who give the shoulder are not appointed.

MAXIM 13 — CONCERN FOR NEIGHBORS

If you are with people,
make a dependant a confidant for yourself.

A confidant who does not circulate the saying in his belly
becomes a commander of himself,
a property-owner whose way is "What can I give?,"
your name good without your speaking,
your body nourished.
Pay attention to your neighbors,
and one will gather for you as what you have not known.
The mind of one who listens to his belly is such
that it puts disdain of him place of love of him,
his mind bare, his limbs unanointed.
For the mind of those the god gives is great,
but he who listens to his belly belongs to an enemy.

MAXIM 14 — CONDUCT AS A MESSENGER

Report your assignment without negligence,
for your manner is put in the counsel of your lord.
As for him who is fluent when he speaks,
it will not go hard for the report's messenger;
no one will reply, "Just what am I supposed to learn?"
He who is more important than his charge is the one who errs:
if he thinks of opposition to him because of it,
he is quiet, saying, "I have spoken."

MAXIM 15 — LEADERSHIP

If you are a leader,
wide-ranging of methods in what you have decreed,
do things of distinction:
those will be remembered in days that come after.
Contention does not come amid blessings;
the concealed crocodile gets in when disregard happens.

MAXIM 16 — DEALING WITH A PETITIONER

If you are a leader,
let your hearing a petitioner's speaking be calm.
Don't rebuff him from wiping his belly
of what he had planned to say to you.
One who has a wrong loves washing his mind
more than the doing of what he has come about.
As for one who makes rebuffing of petitions,
it is said, "To what end is he contravening them?"
Not all that he has petitioned about is what will come about,
so a good hearing means smoothing the mind.

MAXIM 17 — LUST

If you want to make friendship last
    in a home to which you enter,
as lord, as brother, or as friend
    to any place in which you have entrée,
be mindful of getting near the women:
    no place in which it is done can be good.
No face can be sharp while splitting it open,
    for a thousand men are diverted from what is best for them:
a short moment, the likeness of a dream;
    one attains death by experiencing it.
It is a wretched liaison, an inimical shooting,
    one emerges from doing it with the mind rejecting it.
As for him who fails by lusting for it,
    no plan can succeed with him.

MAXIM 18 — GREED

If you want your conduct to be good,
    take yourself away from everything evil.
Be mindful about an instance of greed:
    it is a painful disease of the shunned serpent.
    no entrée can develop from it.
For it entangles fathers and mothers
    and maternal siblings
    and it alienates wife and husband.
It is robbery, everything bad;
    it is a sack of everything despised.
A man lasts who is truly straight
    and has walked according to his steps,
He makes a will thereby,
    but greed has no tomb.

MAXIM 19 — GREED

Don't become greedy about a division;
    don't become covetous except for what you have.
Don't become greedy about your neighbors:
    respect is greater for kindness than force.
He who undercuts his neighbors is small
    and devoid of what contention might get.
A little of what one is grasping about
    is what creates strife out of placidity.

MAXIM 20 — TREATMENT OF A WIFE

When you are accomplished and establish your house,
you should love your wife with ardor.
Fill her belly, clothe her back;
ointment is the prescription for her limbs.
Make her happy as long as you exist:
she is a useful field for her lord,
and you should not adjudicate her.
Keep her away from control of her foot:
her eye when it looks is her gale;
your restricting her is the way to keep her in your house.
The vulva she gives at her disposal is water:
since it is requested, make for it a basin.

MAXIM 21 — CLOSE FRIENDS

Content your intimates with what has come to you,
for it has come to one whom the god blesses.
As for him who fails to content his intimates,
one says, "He is a stingy ka."
What might happen cannot be known:
he should think of tomorrow.
The proper ka is the ka
that one can become content by.
When occasions of blessings happen,
intimates are the ones who say, "Welcome!"
Contentment is not fetched to harbor,
but intimates are fetched when there is ruin.

MAXIM 22 — GOSSIP

You should not repeat gossip
about a speech you have not heard:
it is the mark of belly-heat.
Repeat a speech that is seen, not heard,
when the one it belongs to is entirely out of the discussion.
Look, your interlocutor knows all too well,
for robbery is decreed when it is done.
The instigator will customarily do it out of hate:
look, it is a nightmare that ought to be covered over.

MAXIM 23 — SPEAKING

If you are an accomplished **man**
who sits in consultation with his lord,

collect your mind with respect to accomplishment:
your quiet, it is more effective than valerian.
You should speak only when you know your solution:
it is the craftsman who speaks in counsel.
Speaking is harder than any work:
the one who solves it is the one who subordinates it.

MAXIM 24 — EMOTIONS AND TIME

If you are powerful, you should make respect of you
through knowledge and calmness of speaking.
Don't give commands except for guidance,
for defiance leads to error.
Don't let your mind get big, and it won't be humbled;
don't be inactive, but beware when you tread.
When you answer a speech in its flaming,
prepare yourself, control yourself,
for flames and hotheadedness dissipate,
but the seemly of tread, his path has been built.
The one who worries for the whole day,
he will not be able to spend a good moment;
the one who is frivolous for the whole day,
he will not be able to establish a house—
the one fully shot,
like one who plies the rudder after docking;
the other preoccupied,
for his mind has listened to "If only ..."

MAXIM 25 — AN ANGRY SUPERIOR

Don't insert yourself in the moment of a great one,
don't vex the mind of one who is burdened.
His obstruction happens against one who contradicts him,
and the ka is released from the one who loves him.
He is one who gives sustenance along with the god;
what he loves is what is done for him.
So, turn the face back after a storm,
for peace is with his ka, and obstruction is with the enemy.
He is sustenance, which makes love grow.

MAXIM 26 — PATRONAGE

Teach a great man what is useful for him,
create his acceptance in people's midst.

When you make his wisdom come to his lord's attention,
your nourishment will be from his ka;
for the belly of love is focused on contenting
and your back will be clothed from it:
when his acceptance exists, your face will live.
Your house is with your titulary whom you love:
it is alive because of that,
and makes a good support of you as well.
It also means setting love in the belly of those who love you;
look, he is a ka who loves hearing.

MAXIM 27 — LEGAL SITUATIONS

If you act as advocate for a court,
a representative of the peace of many,
remove the yokes of an action.
When you contest with someone who is biased,
keep him from stating his opinion to officials
and making the matter biased to them:
turn your case over to judgment.

MAXIM 28 — PAST OFFENSES

If you are lenient about a matter that has happened,
and incline toward a man because of his rectitude,
pass over it, do not think of it,
since he will be quiet for you from the first day.

MAXIM 29 — RICHES

If you become big after your smallness,
acquiring property after lack in the past,
in a town you know, through experience of what happened to you before,
don't rely on your riches:
they happened to you from the god's giving.
You are no better than another like you
to whom the same has happened.

MAXIM 30 — OPPOSITION

Bow your back to your boss,
your overseer from the king's house,
and your house will be set from his property,
and your recompense as it should be.
An opponent as boss is a difficulty:
one lives only while he is lenient;
the shoulder cannot bend because of its stripping.

Don't seize neighbors' houses;
    don't appropriate the property of one near you,
    lest he complain about you until you are tried.
Resentment is grief for the mind:
    if he experiences it, he will be a litigant;
    it is a difficulty of opposition in a nearby place.

MAXIM 31 — HOMOSEXUAL BEHAVIOR

You should not have sex with a woman-boy,
    though you know what is barred would be water on his heart,
    for there is no cooling for what is in his belly.
He should not spend the night to do what is barred:
    he will cool down only after he breaks his desire.

MAXIM 32 — AN OFFENSE FROM A FRIEND

If you investigate the character of a friend,
    one who has been cursing about you,
approach him,
    make a case with him alone,
    until you are no longer troubled by his condition.
Discuss with him after a time,
    test his mind with a case of dispute.
When what he has seen comes out of him,
    he will make a case that you can get angry about,
    or he is friendly.
Don't grimace in explaining the dispute to him;
    don't respond with a case of denigration;
    don't sever yourself from him; don't trample him.
His case has not once failed to come up;
    no one can escape from the one who has fated him.

MAXIM 33 — GENEROSITY

Let your face be bright in the time of your existing;
    if something goes out of the storehouse, it does not reenter.
The bread of sharing is what is coveted;
    the one empty in his belly is an accuser.
Opposition becomes sorrow-causing:
    don't make it something near you.
Kindness is a man's memorial
    for the years after the staff of authority.

MAXIM 34 — GENEROSITY

Be aware of your juniors while your things exist;
don't let your nature be wretched to your friends.
It is a shore that fills,
which is greater than its finery,
for one man's things are for another.
The nature of a man of standing is useful for him,
for a good character will be a memorial.

MAXIM 35 — DISCIPLINE

Punish in kind, teach in measure,
for the treatment of misdeeds sets a kind of example.
As for a case other than about wrongdoing,
it is one that makes a complainer become an opponent.

MAXIM 36 — A FAT WIFE

If you marry a wife who is fat
and frivolous, whom her townsfolk know,
who is twice the norm and to whom spending time is precious,
don't divorce her; let her eat,
for her frivolity assesses the proper dose.

CONCLUSION

If you hear these things I have said to you,
your every method will be to the fore;
as for any pertinent instance of Maat, that is their worth.
Their memory will dance in the mouth of people
because of the perfection of their phrases.
When any maxim is used,
it cannot perish in this land forever,
the doing of it expressed to perfection,
and officials speak in accord with it.
It is teaching a man to speak to the future:
he hears it and becomes a craftsman.
It is good to speak to the future:
that is what will hear it.
When a good thing comes from one who is boss,
it is continually valid,
and all his wisdom will be eternal.
It is the knowledgeable who helps his ba,
by setting his goodness on earth through it.

The knowledgeable is sated, because of what he knows,
    by an official, because of his good deed
    through the action of his mind and his tongue.
His lips are accurate when he is speaking,
    his eyes when seeing,
    and both his ears hearing what is useful for his son;
one who acts in accord with Maat,
    being free of lying.

Hearing is useful
    for a son who has heard.
When hearing enters in a hearer,
    the hearer becomes the heard,
good of hearing, good of speaking:
    a hearer, master of what is useful.
Hearing is useful for the hearer:
    hearing is better than anything that is,
    for love of what is good ensues.
How good it is for a son to receive when his father speaks,
    old age happens to him from it.
One who hears is one whom the god loves;
    one whom the god hates cannot hear.
The mind is what makes its owner
    into one who hears or one who does not hear;
    a man's mind is lph for him.
The hearer is the one who hears speaking,
    but he who does what is said is the one who loves hearing.
How good it is when a son listens to his father;
    how joyful is he to whom this is said,
    a son who is pleasing for having hearing.
The hearer to whom it is said becomes effective in the womb
    and worthy with his father,
for his memory is in the mouth of the living
    who are on earth or who will exist.

When a man of standing accepts his father's speaking,
    no plan of his can err.
You will make of your son a hearer,
    who will be accomplished in the opinion of officials,
who guides his mouth according to what has been said to him,
    who is seen as a hearer.
A son who is accomplished, his steps are distinguished,
    while the interference of him who does not hear errs.

The knowledgeable rises early to establish himself,
  while the fool struggles.

As for the fool who does not hear,
  he will not be able to do anything.
He sees knowledge as ignorance,
  what is useful as what is painful.
He does everything hateful
  to the point that he is reprimanded every day.
He lives on that which one dies from,
  condemnation is his income.
His character from it is in the knowledge of officials,
  because of dying alive every day.
His deeds are passed over
  from the multitude of wrongs on him every day.

A son who has heard, who follows Horus,
  it goes well for him after he hears.
He grows old and reaches honor,
  and relates likewise to his children,
in renewing his father's teaching,
  each man taught as he did.
When hc relates to his offspring,
  then they will tell their children.
Set an example in giving your observation:
  make Maat firm and your offspring will live.
As for a standard that has come under disorder,
  then people who will see the like say, "Look, that's it";
  and those who will hear the like also say, "Look, that's it."
See to all of them; soothe the multitude:
  no finery will be able to be complete without them.
Don't take away a word, don't add it;
  don't put one in place of another.
Be careful about opening the restraints on you,
  guard against speaking like a pundit: listen to yourself.
If you want to fix yourself in the mouth of hearers,
  speak only when you have mastered the craft.
When you speak from a state of completeness,
  all your advice will be as it should.

Submerge your mind, order your mouth,
  then your advice will be among the officials.

Be completely exact with your master,
    act so that he is told, "He is that one's son,"
and so that those who will hear it are told,
    "Moreover, blessed is he to whom he was born."
Set your mind during the time of your speaking
    and say things of distinction:
then the officials who hear will say,
    "How good is the issue of his mouth."

Act until your master says about you,
    "How good is he whom his father has taught!
When he emerged from him, foremost of his body,
    he had told him completely while he was in the womb;
    what he has done is greater than what was said to him.
Look, a good son of the god's giving,
    who has added to what he was told.
His master has to have been doing Maat,
    for his mind has acted similarly according to his steps."
You will reach me with your limbs sound,
    the king content with all that happens,
    and you will achieve years of life.
What I have done on earth is not small:
    I have achieved one hundred and ten years of life
    of the king's giving to me blessings beyond those before,
    from doing Maat for the king to the state of honor.

That is how it goes, beginning to end, like what has been found in writing.

THE DISCOURSES OF THE ELOQUENT PEASANT

There once was a man named Khueninpu.
He was a peasant of Salt Field,
and he had a wife named Meret.
So, that peasant said to that wife of his,
"Look, I am going down to Blackland
to get provisions there for my children.
Now, go measure for me the barley
that is in the storehouse as the balance as of yesterday."
Then he measured for her six heqat of barley.
So, that peasant said to that wife of his,
"Look, I will give you twenty heqat of barley
for income with your children.
And you make me those six heqat of barley
into bread and beer for every day,
and I will live on it."

What that peasant did was to go down to Blackland,
having loaded his donkeys with
reeds
palm fronds
natron
salt
sticks of *jrwjw*-wood
staves of Farafra
leopard skins
wolf pelts
pebbles
ochre
ꜥbꜣw stones
jnbj plants
tbw plants
wbn plants
with every good product of Salt Field.

What the peasant did was to go
upstream to Herakleopolis.
What he did was to arrive
at the district of Fefi's House, on the north of Madaniat,
and he found a man standing there on the riverbank
whose name was Nemtinakht;

he was a man of standing, son of a man named Isery,
    they were personnel of the chief steward Meru's son Rensi.
So, that Nemtinakht said, when he saw the donkeys of the peasant,
    which were pleasing in his mind,
saying, "Would that I had any effective amulet,
    so that I could steal the property of that peasant from him!"
Now, that Nemtinakht's house was on the landing
    of the mouth of the path.
It was a narrow one; it was not a broad one:
    it extended only to the width of a skirt,
for its one path was under water
    and its other path under thin barley.
So, that Nemtinakht said to his follower,
    "Go, get me a sheet from my household stores,"
    and it was fetched immediately.
Then he opened the sheet on the landing of the path's mouth,
    so that its fringe landed on the water
    and its hem on the thin barley.

So, the peasant came
    on the path of everyone
and Nemtinakht said,
    "Be careful, peasant!
    Would you step on my clothes?"
So, the peasant said,
    "I will do what you would bless. My route is good."
    What the peasant did was go up.
But Nemtinakht said,
    "Is my thin barley to be a path for you?"
So, the peasant said,
    "My route is good.
The bank is high and the route is under thin barley,
    but you furnish our path with your clothes.
    So, won't you let us pass on the path?"

Then one of the donkeys filled his mouth
    with a sprig of thin barley.
So, Nemtinakht said,
    "Look, I have to confiscate your donkey, peasant,
because of its eating my thin barley.
    It will have to thresh because of his audacity."

So, the peasant said,
    "My route is good.
One that damages ten?
    I got my donkey for ten units of value
and you will take it for a mouthful
    of a sprig of thin barley?
Moreover, I know the owner of this estate:
    it belongs to chief steward Meru's son Rensi,
and he is the one who beats every robber in the whole land.
    So, am I to be robbed in his estate?"
So, Nemtinakht said,
    "In fact, this is the phrase people say:
    'A poor man's name is uttered only because of his lord.'
The one who speaks to you is I,
    but the one you mention is the chief steward."
Then he took himself a branch of green tamarisk,
    then he pummeled his every limb with it;
    his donkeys were confiscated and taken into his estate.
So, the peasant was weeping very greatly
    because of the pain of what was done to him.
So, Nemtinakht said,
    "Don't raise your voice, peasant!
    Look, you are headed for the harbor of the Lord of Silencing."
So, the peasant said,
    "You beat me, you rob my property;
    and now you would take the complaint from my mouth?
Lord of Silencing, you should give me my things;
    then I will stop crying for fear of you."
So, the peasant spent a period of up to ten days
    petitioning to that Nemtinakht,
    but he wouldn't give heed to it.

What the peasant did was to go to Herakleopolis
    to appeal to chief steward Meru's son Rensi.
He found him emerging from the gate of his house
    to go down to his barge of office.
So, the peasant said, "Would that I could inform you
    of the substance of a matter.
The case is only having a follower of your choosing come to me
    so that I might send him to you about it."

So, chief steward Meru's son Rensi had
    a follower of his choosing go to him
    so that the peasant might send him about that matter in its entirety.
As a result, chief steward Meru's son Rensi
    was denouncing that Nemtinakht to the officials who were beside him.
So, they said to him, "Perhaps he is a peasant of his
    who came to another besides him.
Look, that is what they do to their peasants
    who come to others besides them;
    look, that is what they do.
It is a case of that Nemtinakht being punished
    for some natron and some salt.
    Let him be ordered to replace it and he will replace it."
What chief steward Meru's son Rensi did was to be quiet;
    he did not respond to those officials
    or respond to the peasant.

So, the peasant came to petition
    to chief steward Meru's son Rensi,
saying, "Chief steward, my lord,
    greatest of the great, leader of everything!
If you go down to the lake of Maat
    and sail in it with the right wind,
no full sail of yours will rip open,
    nor will your boat stall;
no mishap will come in your mast,
    nor will your yards be cut away;
nor will you go headlong and run up on land,
    nor will a swell take you;
nor will you taste the evil of the river,
    nor will you see fear's face.
Fish will come to you restrained,
    and you will end up with fatted fowl —
because you are father to the orphan,
    husband to the widow,
brother to the divorced,
    and kilt to the motherless.
Let me make your name in this land
    to every good custom:
a leader free of greed,
    a great one free of anything evil,

a destroyer of falsehood and creator of Maat,
  who has come at the voice of the pleader.
When I speak, may you hear: do Maat,
  O blessed one whom the blessed bless!
Repel need: look, I am loaded.
  Take account of me: look, I am in loss."

Now, the peasant said this speech
  in the time of the Incarnation of Dual King Nebkaure, justified.
What chief steward Meru's son Rensi did was to go
  before His Incarnation, saying,
"My lord, I have found one of those peasants
  who is truly fine of speaking.
His property was stolen:
  look, he has come to petition to me about it."
So, His Incarnation said,
  "As you love to see me healthy,
you should delay him here
  without answering anything he says,
so that he will keep speaking further;
  then it should be brought to us in writing so that we may hear it.
But see to the life of his woman and children.
  Look, one of those peasants comes
  only about the total emptiness of his house.
Also, see to the life of that peasant himself:
  you shall be having rations given to him
  without letting him know that you are the one who gave them to him."
So, he was being given ten bread
  and two jars of beer each day.
Whenever chief steward Meru's son Rensi gave it,
  he would give it to his friend,
  and he was the one who would give it to him.
Then chief steward Meru's son Rensi sent word
  to the mayor of Salt Field
about making rations for the wife of the peasant
  of three heqat of barley every day.

So, the peasant came to appeal to him twice,
  saying, "Chief steward, my lord!
Greatest of the great,
  richest of the rich,

for whose great there is one greater;
    for whose rich, one richer!
Rudder of the sky,
    beam of the earth,
    measuring-line that carries the weight!
Rudder, don't drift!
    Beam, don't tilt!
    Measuring-line, don't make deviation!
Lord great from taking what has no owner,
    from plundering on his own!
Your needs are in your house.
    One hin of beer and three bread:
    what is that as your dole in sating your dependants?
It is a mortal who dies as well as his underlings—
    are you to be eternal?
For it is wrong, a crossbar that has tilted,
    a plumb-bob that has gone off,
    one truly precise that has become a stray.
Look, Maat flees under you,
    alienated from its place.
Officials are doing a wrong,
    the standard of speech is being put aside.
The judge{s} is snatching what he would take:
    he is one who cuts short a speech from its accuracy,
    deviating from it.
The air-giver is causing need on earth,
    the warmer is making one pant;
the apportioner is an appropriator,
    the dispeller of need is one who orders it made;
the harbor is in its torrent:
    he who should bar wrong is doing a wrong."
So, chief steward Meru's son Rensi said,
    "Are your things more important than my follower robbing you?"
So, the peasant said,
    "The weigher of piles is shorting for himself,
    another has become full by cheating his neighbors.
The leader according to custom is ordering robbery:
    who then will bar poverty?

The dispeller of deviance is deviating,
  another is accurate by being crooked,
another connives with the wrongdoer:
  so, do you find anything of yourself in this?
Brief is punishment and long a wrong:
  character should return to its place of yesterday.
So, 'Do for the doer to make him do' is the command:
  it means thanking him for what he does;
it means parrying something before one shoots;
  it means ordering for the master of assignment.
Oh, for a moment of destruction! —
  overturning in your clap-net,
decrease in your bird-catch,
  carnage in your waterfowl-catch!
The seer comes out blind and the hearer deaf,
  for the leader has become a misleader.
Basket, have you closed shut?
  What **then are you good for**?
Look, you are forceful and powerful,
  your arm active,
but your mind has become greedy
  and kindness has passed you by.
How lamentable is the needy one you wipe out!
  You resemble the messenger of Khenti.
Look, you have surpassed the Lady of Pestilence:
  not for you, not for her; not against you, not against her;
  you have not yet done it, she has not yet done it.
A bread-owner should be kind:
  force is for the deprived.
Stealing is fit for the one with no things,
  and snatching things by the deprived.
The lot of the have-not and empty is bad.
  So, he should not be blamed:
  he is one who seeks for himself.
But you are sated with your bread
  and drunk with your beer;
  you are rich in all kinds of fine linen.
The helmsman's face is to the front,
  but the boat glides as it likes.
The king is forward,
  the rudder is in your hand,
  but a wrong is put in your vicinity.

Arrival is long and the anchor has parted;
 'What is that which is there?,' one will say,
'Make shelter, your shore is healthy':
 but look, your harbor is crocodile-infested.
Let your tongue be straight, so that you don't get lost:
 that part of a man is his bane.
 Don't tell lies; beware of officials.
Judges are a winnowing basket,
 telling lies is their chaff:
 it will be light in their mind.
Most knowledgeable of all people,
 are you unaware of my circumstance?
Dispeller of all water-need,
 look, I am on the route of stranding.
Moorer of all on water, rescue the shipwrecked,
 for I am anguished in circumstance at your side."

So, the peasant came to appeal to him a third time,
 saying, "Chief steward, my lord!
You are the Sun, lord of the sky, with your entourage,
 what everyone has is from you, like the waters.
You are the Inundation, who makes green the fields
 and furnishes the hacked mounds.
Bar robbery, be concerned with the needy,
 don't become a torrent against the petitioner.
Beware of continuity's nearness; desire to last,
 as is said, 'Doing Maat is the breath of the nose.'
Punish the one who deserves to be punished:
 there is no one who comes up to your standard.
Does the crossbar go off?
 Is the scale being partial?
Is Thoth lenient in that respect?
 Then you may do wrong.
You make yourself the equal of these three:
 If the three are lenient, you may be lenient.
Don't answer something good with something bad,
 don't put the one in the other's place.
How much more than fodder does speech grow,
 more than touching the smell by its answer!
Watering what comes, to cause growth, is its cover;
 this is three occasions to make it happen.

So, make rudder to full sail,
    take the torrent to make direction,
    beware of sailing backward at the tiller.
Accuracy of the land, that makes Maat,
    don't tell lies, for you are important;
    don't become light, for you are weighty.
Don't tell lies: you are the crossbar.
    Don't stray: you are the standard.
Look, you are one head with the crossbar:
    if it tilts, you may tilt.
Don't drift, but make rudder,
    pull on the tiller.
Don't take, but act against the taker:
    one great from it, and greedy, is not a great one.
Your tongue is the plumb-bob, your mind is the weight,
    your lips are its arms.
If you cover your face to rapacity,
    who then will bar poverty?
Look, you are a poor washerman,
    greedy in damaging friendship,
one who spurns his patron for his dependant,
    whose brother is the one who comes bringing.
Look, you are a ferryman who ferries the one with a fare,
    an accurate one whose accuracy is shattered.
Look, you are a warehouse chief
    who does not let pass the empty-handed.
Look, you are a raptor of the subjects,
    who lives on the poor of birds.
Look, you are an attendant whose joy is slaughter,
    for whom there is no cutting it short.
Look, you are the guardian;
    its evil is not because of me: you do not take account.
Thus you make loss as a ravenous crocodile,
    and shelter is gone from the harbor of the whole land.
Hearer, you just don't hear:
    why do you fail to hear?
For right now a raging crocodile punishes me.
    But a crocodile retreats.
    So, what is the profit in that for you?
Maat's hiddenness will be found
    and lying's back put on the ground.

Don't set up the morning before it comes:
  a wrong in it cannot be known."

Now, the peasant said this speech
  to chief steward Meru's son Rensi
  at the opening of the portal.
Then he had
  two bodyguards attend to him with whips.
  Then they pummeled his every limb with them.
So, the peasant said, "Meru's son has to have gone astray,
  his face blind to what he sees and deaf to what he hears,
  absent-minded to what has been mentioned to him.
Look, you are a town without its mayor,
  like a body of people without its chief,
like a boat without a pilot in it,
  a confederation without its leader.
Look, you are a sheriff who steals,
  a mayor who receives,
a district-overseer who should bar plunder
  but has become the paragon of the one who does it."

So, the peasant came
  to appeal to him a fourth time
and found him emerging
  from the gate of the temple of Harsaphes,
saying, "Blessed one! May Harsaphes bless you,
  from whose house you have come.
Once goodness is damaged it will not be reassembled
  when the back of lying is thrown to the ground.
Is that ferry docked?
  Then who can be ferried,
  with the one who can bring it about unwilling?
Crossing the river by sandals:
  a good crossing or not?
Who can sleep until dawn?
  Damaged are going by night and sending by day,
and letting a man attend
  to his truly good affairs.
Look, there is no profit for the one who tells it to you:
  kindness has passed you by.
  How lamentable is the needy one you wipe out!

Look, you are a marsh-hunter who washes his mind,
who pushes to do what he wants:
who spears hippopotami and shoots wild bulls,
who attacks fish and nets birds.
There is no hasty-mouth who is free of flight,
no lighthearted who is weighty of the belly's advice.
Set your mind and learn Maat,
suppress your choice in favor of the quiet man's entry.
There is no one rash who penetrates accomplishment;
but there is none impulsive when the arm is used,
when the eyes have been made to see and one is informed.
Don't be harsh when you are powerful,
so that evil does not reach you.
When a case is passed over, it will become two:
it is the eater who tastes.
For the one questioned replies,
and it is the sleeper who sees a dream.
As for a court judge who ought to be punished,
he is the paragon of a doer.
Fool, look, you are reached;
know-nothing, look, you are questioned.
Water-bailer, look, you are taking on water;
helmsman, don't let your boat drift.
Life-giver, don't make one die;
destroyer, don't make one be destroyed.
Shade, don't act as sunlight;
shelter, don't let the crocodile take.
The *fourth time* of appealing to you!
Shall I spend the day at it?"

So, the peasant came to appeal to him a fifth time,
saying, "Chief steward, my lord!
The hand-netter is catching *ḥbꜣ*-fish,
the spearer killing the come-fish,
the fish-shooter throwing at *wbbw*-fish,
and the trawler at *pꜣqrw*-fish.
For the fisherman hacks the river:
look, you are the same kind.
Don't rob a poor man of his things,
a helpless one you know.

His things are air to a needy man;
to take them away is to stop up his nose.
You were appointed to hear,
to judge, and to bar robbery.
Act against it!
Look, it is the stealer's support that you make.
One trusts in you,
but you have become a transgressor.
You were appointed to be a dam for the needy man
lest he become flooded,
but you are his dragging lake."

So, the peasant came to appeal to him a sixth time.
saying, "Chief steward, my lord!Lord who makes lying easy,
bring about Maat!
Bring about all goodness,
destroy evil,
like satiety comes and ends hunger,
clothing, and ends nakedness;
like the sky becomes calm after a high windstorm
and warms all who were cold;
like fire that cooks raw things,
like water that quenches thirst.
See for yourself the divider a grasper,
the pacifier a distress-maker,
the evener a pain-maker.
For shorting lessens Maat.
Fill well:
Maat neither cheats nor overflows.
If you get, give to your fellow:
what has been chewed is devoid of correctness.
For the one in distress leads to alienation,
the accuser brings departure:
what exists in the mind cannot be known.
Don't delay, but act according to the report:
you part and who will tie together?
The water-fighter is in your hand like an open stick,
and the time of the water-battle has come.
If the boat enters it will be taken,
and its load will be utterly ruined on each shore.
You are educated, you are skilled,
you are exemplified, but not for grasping.

You make yourself exemplified to everyone,
    but your circumstances are in disarray,
    and the shorter sets the standard for the whole land.
The gardener of poverty is watering his plot with wrong,
    to make his plot grow lying,
    to water a wrong for the estate."

So, the peasant came to appeal to him a seventh time,
    saying, "Chief steward, my lord!
You are the rudder of the entire land:
    the land sails according as you command.
You are a second Thoth,
    who decides without being partial.
Lord, may you last,
    so that a man may call you to his truly just cause.
Don't let your mind get contentious—it is not for you—
    or the well-disposed will become short-tempered.
Don't start on what has not yet come,
    don't get excited at what has not yet happened.
For forbearance extends in friendship,
    and destroys a misdeed that has happened:
    what exists in the mind cannot be known.
Custom has been mutilated and the standard damaged.
    None needy can live when he has been plundered:
    Maat does not address him.
Now, my belly is full and my mind laden,
    and for that reason it comes from my belly.
It is a breach in the dam: its water rushed out
    when my mouth was opened to speak.
Just stand up and fight for me, you brace!
    Bail for me, water-man!
Now that I have vented what was in my belly,
    and washed my soiled linen,
my statement is over,
    my needs are ended before you:
    what else do you require?
Your neglect will mislead you,
    your greed will fool you,
    your rapacity will create your enemies.
But will you find another peasant like me?
    Will a neglected petitioner stand at the door of his house?

There is none quiet whom you have made speak,
    none sleeping whom you have made awaken;
no face of one you have made sharp will diminish,
    no mouth you have opened will close;
there is none ignorant whom you have made learn,
    none foolish whom you have instructed.
Officials are dispellers of evil;
    they are masters of goodness;
they are craftsmen of creating what is,
    who can tie on a severed head."

So, the peasant came to appeal to him an eighth time,
    saying, "Chief steward, my lord!
Now one falls far because of rapacity;
    now the greedy man becomes devoid of a cause:
    now his cause exists for failure.
Now you are greedy: it is not for you;
    now you rob: it is not useful for you.
A man should just be allowed to attend
    to his truly good cause.
It means your needs are in your house, your belly full;
    the oipe swells and overflows,
    so that its excess goes to ruin on the ground.
Let the robber be arrested whom the officials have saved,
    appointed for a bar against wrongs.
A shelter for the aggressor are officials,
    appointed for a bar against lying.
Your fear does not allow appealing to you:
    you do not perceive my mind.
The quiet man who turns to make accusation of you,
    he is not afraid of raising it for himself,
    his brother not being fetched against you in the street.
Your plots are in the field, your reward is in the cultivation,
    your income is in the storehouse.
Officials are giving to you
    and you are taking: are you a robber?
    One is dragged to you, troops with you, for the division of plots of land.
Do Maat for the Lord of Maat,
    the Maat of whose Maat exists.
Pen, scroll, palette of Thoth,
    be far from doing wrongs.

The good man's good is better than him,
    for Maat is continual;
    it goes down with the one who does it to the necropolis.
He is entombed, being buried,
    and his name is not erased on earth,
for it is remembered because of goodness:
    it is the standard of hieroglyphic writing,
for it is a crossbar that does not tilt,
    for it is a scale that does not lean to one side.
Whether I will come or another will come,
    you should respond with an answer.
Don't grill the quiet man,
    don't attack one who does not attack.
You do not show mercy, you do not feel pain,
    you do not wipe out anything.
You do not give me a return for this good speech
    that comes from the mouth of the Sun himself.
Speak Maat, do Maat,
    since it is great, it is important, it is lasting.
    When its revelation is found, it sends to honor.
Does the crossbar tilt?
    Those that carry things are its pans.
No excess happens to the standard;
    no vile cause can arrive at harbor
    or the bearer to landfall."

So, the peasant **came** to appeal to him a ninth time,
    saying, "Chief steward, my lord!
Their tongues are the scale of people;
    the crossbar is what seeks out imbalance,
    and does punishment to the one who should be punished.
Let the standard be likened to you,
    lest lying rush headlong.
When its needs come about,
    Maat turns to correct it.
Maat is the property of lying:
    It means that, though made to flourish, it cannot be harvested.
If lying walks, it gets lost;
    it cannot cross in the ferry nor be landed.

As for the one who gets rich from it, he has no children,
    he has no heirs on earth.
As for the one who sails with it, he cannot touch land,
    his boat cannot moor at its harbor.
Don't become heavy: you have not become light;
    don't stall: you have not hurried.
Don't be biased in listening to the mind,
    don't cover your face to one you know.
Don't be blind to one who looks to you,
    don't reject one who depends on you.
You should descend from this neglect:
    let your sentence be reported.
Act for the one who acts for you,
    don't listen to everyone against him.
    Summon a man for his just cause.
There is no yesterday for the negligent,
    no friend for the one deaf to Maat,
    no good time for the greedy.
When an accuser becomes one who is needy,
    the needy one will be an appealer,
    and the opponent becomes the slain.
Look, I am appealing to you and you don't hear it.
    I will go to appeal about you to Anubis."

So, chief steward Meru's son Rensi had
    two bodyguards go to turn him back.
So, the peasant was afraid,
    thinking it was done to punish him
    for the speech he had said.
So, the peasant said,
    "The meeting of the thirsty man with water,
    the mouth of the nursing child coming across milk,
that is death for one who prays and looks to its coming
    when his death's delay comes against him."
So, chief steward Meru's son Rensi said,
    "Don't fear, peasant.
    Look, you should act to act with me."
So, the peasant made an oath, saying,
    "Shall I just eat of your bread
    and just drink of your beer continually?"

So, chief steward Meru's son Rensi said,
    "Now, wait here,
    and you will hear those appeals of yours."
So, he had them read out from a new scroll,
    each appeal according to its content.
So, chief steward Meru's son Rensi brought it in
    to the Incarnation of Dual King Nebkaure, justified,
and it was better in his mind
    than anything that is in this entire land.
So, His Incarnation said,
    "You judge yourself, Meru's son."
So, chief steward Meru's son Rensi had
    two bodyguards go to get Nemtinakht.
Then an inventory was fetched of all his property.
    Then he was found to have six servants
apart from his tenants, from his thin barley, his emmer,
    his donkeys, his cattle, his pigs, and all his animals.
Then Nemtinakht's property was given to the peasant,
    and he was pummeled on all his limbs.
So, chief steward Meru's son Rensi said
    to Nemtinakt, " …
    … ."

That is how it goes, beginning to end, like what has been found in writing.

THE DEBATE BETWEEN A MAN AND HIS SOUL

[…] evil.
    Doing it […
…
[…
    that you might lay down my need."

What I said to my ba:
    "It is the hour […
…] him,
    because of dragging me […
…
…] the face.
    Beware of […
So, come, that I may instruct you […
    …] you the hostile nature of the West.
[…
    For a man […].
We are to speak truly in the tribunal of the gods:
    their tongue cannot be biased.
It would be crooked in return:
    their tongue cannot be biased."

I opened my mouth to my ba,
    that I might answer what he had said."
This has become too much for me now:
    my ba does not agree with me.
It is also too much to exaggerate:
    my ba going is like one who ignores what he is in.
He should attend to it for me,
    my second, who rejects his life.
He will not be allowed to resist me,
    since he is in my belly in a rope mesh.
    Escaping a day of difficulties will not happen to him.
But look, my ba is misleading me.
    I cannot listen to him,
because of dragging me to death before I have come to it,
    because of throwing me on the fire to incinerate me.
What is his suffering […],
    giving his back to his brother?

He should be near me on a day of difficulties,
    and stand on yonder side like a jubilation-maker,
    for that is who goes out and brings himself to it.
My ba is too foolish to suppress pain while living,
    one who prods me to death before I have come to it,
who sweetens the West for me:
    'Is it something difficult?
Life is a cycle;
    trees fall.
So, you should tread on disorder:
    lay down my need.
Let Thoth judge me
    and the gods become content;
let Khonsu intervene for me,
    he who writes truly;
let the Sun hear my speech,
    he who quiets the sun-bark;
let Isdes intervene for me
    in the sacred room—
since my misery has become heavy
    and there is no one to lift it to himself for me.'
It would be sweet for the gods to bar my belly's secrets,
    what my ba said to me:
    'You are not a man.
Are you even alive? What do you gain,
    caring about life like an owner of riches
    who says, "I won't go," even when they're lost?
In fact, you are being uprooted without caring,
    and everyone deprived is saying, "I will rob you."
And you are dead,
    with your name alive.
Yonder is a place of alighting,
    storage-chest of the mind.
The West is a harbor
    to which the perceptive are rowed.'
My ba should listen to me
    without making me guilty.
If his mind is in accord with me,
    he will be fortunate.

I will make him reach the West
    like one in his pyramid,
    to whose entombment a survivor has attended.
I am to make an awning over your corpse,
    and you will make jealous another ba in inertness.
I am to make an awning and it won't get cold,
    and you will make jealous another ba who is hot.
I will drink water at the flood
    and lift away dryness,
    and you will make jealous another ba who is hungry.
If you prod me toward death in that manner,
    you will not find a place to land on in the West.
Set your mind, my ba, my brother,
    until the heir has grown up who will make offerings,
who will attend to the tomb on entombment-day,
    transporting the bier to the necropolis."

My ba opened his mouth to me
    that he might answer what I had said.
"As for you bringing to mind entombment, it is heartache;
    it is bringing tears by saddening a man;
it is taking a man from his house
    so that he is left on the hill.
You won't be able to go up
    and see suns.
Those who built in stone of granite,
    with construction finished,
    fine pyramids in fine work,
once those who commissioned building become gods,
    what was dedicated to them has been razed,
like the inert who have died on the riverbank,
    for want of a survivor—
the water having taken its end,
    and Sunlight likewise—
    they whom the fish and lip of the water claim.
So, listen to me;
    look, it is good for people to listen:
    follow a good time, forget care.

A man plowed his plot
    and he loaded his harvest inside a boat,

that he might sail with the current,
    his festival near.
When he saw the darkness of a norther's emergence,
    he watched in the boat as the Sun was setting.
He disembarked with his wife and his children,
    and they perished atop a depression
    ringed by night with riverbankers.
So, he ended up seated and crying out loud,
    saying, 'I do not weep for that one who was born,
though there is for her no emerging from the West
    to another birth on earth.
I care about her children,
    broken in the egg,
    who saw the face of Khenti before they had lived.'

A man requested an evening meal,
    and his wife told him, 'Supper is coming.'
He went outside at that, only for a moment.
    When he turned back to his house, he was like another man.
His wife was pleading with him,
    but he wouldn't listen to her,
    being offended and unreceptive to those of the household."

I opened my mouth to my ba,
    that I might answer what he had said.
"Look, my name reeks:
    look, more than carrion's smell
    on harvest days, when the sky is hot.
Look, my name reeks:
    look, more than an eel-trap
    on catch day, when the sky is hot.
Look, my name reeks:
    look, more than ducks' smell,
    than a rise of reeds with a brood.
Look, my name reeks:
    look, more than the smell of fowled birds,
    than the channels of nests fowled for them.
Look, my name reeks:
    look, more than crocodiles' smell,
    than a site of slaughter with riverbankers.
Look, my name reeks:
    look, more than a married woman
    about whom the lie of a lover is told.

Look, my name reeks:
  look, more than a brave boy
  about whom is said, 'He is for one he should hate.'
Look, my name reeks:
  look, more than the harbor of the sire
  that plots sedition whenever his back is seen.

To whom can I speak now?
  Brothers have become bad;
  friends nowadays, they do not love.
To whom can I speak now?
  Minds are greedy,
  every man taking his fellow's things.
To whom can I speak now?
  Kindness has perished,
  sternness has descended on everyone.
To whom can I speak now?
  There is contentment with bad,
  so that goodness has been put down in every place.
To whom can I speak now?
  When a man causes anger by his bad deed,
  he makes everyone laugh, though his misdeed is evil.
To whom can I speak now?
  One plunders,
  every man robbing his brothers.
To whom can I speak now?
  the one who should be avoided is an intimate,
  the brother once acted with has become an enemy.
To whom can I speak now?
  Yesterday is not remembered,
  no one does for the doer in this time.
To whom can I speak now?
  Brothers have become bad;
  one resorts to strangers for innermost thoughts.
To whom can I speak now?
  Faces are obliterated,
  every man with face down toward his brothers.
To whom can I speak now?
  Minds have become greedy;
  there is no man's mind to depend on.

To whom can I speak now?
    There are no righteous,
    the land left over to those who make disorder.
To whom can I speak now?
    There is lack of an intimate;
    one resorts to an unknown to reveal to.
To whom can I speak now?
    There is no calm-minded;
    the one once walked with, he is no more.
To whom can I speak now?
    I am loaded with need for lack of an intimate.
To whom can I speak now?
    The injustice that has hit the land has no end.

Death is in my sight now,
    like a sick man getting well,
    like going outside after mourning.
Death is in my sight now,
    like myrrh's smell,
    like sitting under sails on a windy day.
Death is in my sight now,
    like lotuses' smell,
    like sitting on the Bank of Inebriation.
Death is in my sight now,
    like the flood's ebbing,
    like a man coming home from an expedition.
Death is in my sight now,
    like the sky's clearing,
    like a man enmeshed thereby to what he did not know.
Death is in my sight now,
    like a man longs to see home,
    when he has spent many years taken in captivity.

Surely, he who is there will be a living god,
    punishing for his misdeed the one who does it.
Surely, he who is there will be standing in the bark,
    having choice cuts given from it to the temples.
Surely, he who is there will be a knower of things,
    not barred from appealing to the Sun when he speaks.

What the ba said to me:
"So, put complaint on the stake,
    you to whom I belong, my brother.

You should make offering on the brazier,
    inasmuch as you fought for life,
    inasmuch as you said, 'Desire me here.'
Reject the West for yourself,
    but desire that you reach the West
    when your body touches the earth.
I will alight after your weariness:
    then we will make harbor at the occasion."

That is how it goes, beginning to end, like what has been found in writing.

THE HERDSMAN'S TALE

. . .

"Look, I went down to a marsh
that is nearby this lowland.
I saw a woman in it
who was not a human being.
My hair crawled when I saw her head-pelt,
because of the smoothness of her skin.
I would never do what she said,
for respect for her is throughout my limbs.

"**I tell you**, therefore, bulls, let's sail back,
so the calves will cross
and the herd spend the night at the mouth of the pasture,
with the herdsmen in charge of them.
Our skiff for sailing back, bulls!,
with the cattle put at its stern,
and the knowledgeable of the herdsmen reciting the boat-song of water,

"**with these words**: 'My kas are aroused,
herdsmen and males.
There is no repeller in this swamp, in a year of big Inundation,
when command is commanded to the land's backs
and basin cannot be distinguished from river.
So, be sound to the inside of your house,
for the cattle are set in their place.
Welcome, for fear of you has perished
and awe of you has left,
until the storm of the Powerful One has perished,
and the fear of the Two Lands' lady.'"

So, by the time of dawn, first thing in the morning,
it had been done as he said.
But this goddess accosted him
as he was heading to the basin.
She came shedding her clothes
and messing up her hair.

. . .

HYMNS TO SENWOSRET III

TITLE

Horus Divine of Evolution,
    Two Ladies Divine of Birth,
    Gold Falcon Who Has Evolved,
Dual King Khakaure,
    Sun's Son Senwosret,
    as he takes possession of the Two Lands in justification.

HYMN 1

Greetings, Khakaure,
    our Horus, divine of evolution;
who protects the land, who broadens its borders,
    who suppresses countries with his crown;
who encompasses the Two Lands with his arms' embrace,
    who defends the subjects with his action;
who kills archers without a blow of the stick,
    who shoots the arrow with the bowstring undrawn;
dread of whom has hit the pillar-bowmen in their land,
    fear of whom has killed the Nine Bows;
whose butchery has made thousands of archers die
    in the countries of those who attack his border;
who shoots the arrow like Sekhmet does,
    felling thousands of those who ignore his impressiveness.
The tongue of His Incarnation is what restrains the Foreland,
    his phrases, what make the Asiatics flee.
Young Unique One, who fights for his border,
    who does not let his dependants grow weary;
who lets the elite lie abed until daylight,
    while his cohort sleep with his heart as their protector;
whose decrees have made his borders,
    whose speech has gathered in the Two Banks.

HYMN 2

How excited are the gods,
    for you have made firm their offerings.
How excited are your children,
    for you have made their border.
How excited are your fathers of before,
    for you have enlarged their portion.

How excited is Egypt with your strong arm,
for you have protected its traditions.
How excited are the elite with your counsel,
for your impressiveness has brought excess thereby.
How excited are the Two Banks with the dread of you,
for you have broadened what they have.
How excited are your cohort for promotion,
for you have made them grow.
How excited are your honored ones,
for you have made them grow young.
How excited are the Two Lands with your strength,
for you have protected their walls.
Its refrain:
Horus who broadens his border,
may you repeat continuity!

HYMN 3
How great is the lord for his town!
He is one in a million;
other thousands of people are lesser beings.
How great is the lord for his town!
Indeed, he is the dike
that dams the river against its torrent of water.
How great is the lord for his town!
Indeed, he is the cool room
that lets every man sleep until daylight.
How great is the lord for his town!
Indeed, he is a fine bulwark
of metal of the Sinai.
How great is the lord for his town!
Indeed, he is the refuge
whose hand is not avoided.
How great is the lord for his town!
Indeed, he is the shelter
that saves the fearful from his enemy.
How great is the lord for his town!
Indeed, he is a shade at Inundation,
cool in Harvest.
How great is the lord for his town!
Indeed, he is a warm corner,
dry at the season of Growing.

How great is the lord for his town!
    Indeed, he is the mountain
    that blocks the gale at the time of the sky's storm.
How great is the lord for his town!
    Indeed, he is Sekhmet
    against the enemies who tread on his border.

HYMN 4

He has come to us,
    taking possession of the Nile-Valley's land,
    the Double Crown having united on his head;
He has come to us,
    having joined the Two Lands,
    having mingled the sedge with the bee;
He has come to us,
    having begun to rule the Blackland,
    having put the Redland in his collection;
He has come to us,
    having protected the Two Lands,
    having calmed the Two Banks;
He has come to us,
    having given life to Egypt,
    having dispelled its troubles;
He has come to us,
    having given life to the elite,
    having made breathe the subjects' throat;
He has come to us,
    having trampled the countries,
    having hit the pillar-bowmen who knew not fear of him;
He has come to us,
    having made his border guarded,
    having saved the robbed;
He has come to us,
    his arms having […] the state of honor
    that his strong-arm gets for us;
He has come to us,
    so that we might raise our children
    and entomb our elders on the hill.

HYMN 5

[…
    …].

May you love Khakaure, alive forever continually,
[…],
who is commanded to make your sustenance,
and rescue […];
our guard, who knows how to aerate when noses are blocked,
…].
May you repay him with life and authority,
a million […].

HYMN 6

May Khakaure, alive forever continually, be blessed
[…].
May the wind be raised in the bark […
…],
adorned with electrum […
…].
[…] for the Two Banks
to narrow […],
[…] for them the path of […
…].

Printed in Great Britain
by Amazon

70014429R00272

Middle Egyptian Literature

A companion volume to the third edition of the author's popular *Middle Egyptian: an Introduction to the Language and Culture of Hieroglyphs*, this book contains eight literary works from the Middle Kingdom, the golden age of Middle Egyptian literature. Included are the compositions widely regarded as the pinnacle of Egyptian literary arts, by the Egyptians themselves as well as by modern readers.

The works are presented in hieroglyphic transcription, transliteration, and translation, accompanied by notes cross-referenced to the third edition of *Middle Egyptian*. These are designed to give students of Middle Egyptian access to original texts and the tools to practice and perfect their knowledge of the language. The principles of ancient Egyptian verse, in which all the works are written, are discussed in the Introduction, and the transliterations and translations are versified, to give students practice in this aspect of Egyptian literature as well. Consecutive translations are also included both for reference and for readers more concerned with Middle Egyptian literature than language.

James P. Allen is the Wilbour Professor of Egyptology at Brown University. He is a former curator of Egyptian art at the Metropolitan Museum of Art in New York and president of the International Association of Egyptologists. His previous publications include *Genesis in Egypt: the Philosophy of Ancient Egyptian Creation Accounts* (1989), *The Heqanakht Papyri* (2002), *The Ancient Egyptian Pyramid Texts* (2005), *The Debate between a Man and His Soul* (2010), *The Ancient Egyptian Language, an Historical Study* (2013), and three editions of *Middle Egyptian: An Introduction to the Language and Culture of Hieroglyphs* (2000, 2011, 2014).